Understanding
Negotiable Instruments
and Payment Systems

William H. Lawrence
Professor of Law
University of San Diego, School of Law

ISBN: 978-1-4224-7538-6

Library of Congress Cataloging-in-Publication Data

Lawrence, William H.
Understanding negotiable instruments and payments systems/ by
  William H. Lawrence.
    p. cm. -- (Understanding series)
  Includes bibliographical references and index.
  ISBN 0-8205-4671-2 (softbound)
    1. Negotiable instruments--United States. 2. Payment--United States. I. Title. II.
Understanding series(New York,N.Y)
    KF957.L394
    346.73'096--dc21

2002034135

This publication is designed to provide accurate and authoritative information in regard to the subject matter covered. It is sold with the understanding that the publisher is not engaged in rendering legal, accounting, or other professional services. If legal advice or other expert assistance is required, the services of a competent professional should be sought.

LexisNexis, the knowledge burst logo, and Michie are trademarks of Reed Elsevier Properties Inc, used under license. Matthew Bender is a registered trademark of Matthew Bender Properties Inc.

Copyright © 2002 Matthew Bender & Company, Inc., a member of the LexisNexis Group.
All Rights Reserved. Published 2002.

No copyright is claimed in the text of statutes, regulations, and excerpts from court opinions quoted within this work. Permission to copy material exceeding fair use, 17 U.S.C. § 107, may be licensed for a fee of 10¢ per page per copy from the Copyright Clearance Center, 222 Rosewood Drive, Danvers, Mass. 01923, telephone (978) 750-8400.

Editorial Offices
744 Broad Street, Newark, NJ 07102 (973) 820-2000
201 Mission St., San Francisco, CA 94105-1831 (415) 908-3200
701 East Water Street, Charlottesville, VA 22902-7587 (804) 972-7600
www.lexis.com

DEDICATION

For my wife, Yvonne, with all my love.
W.H.L.

ACKNOWLEDGMENTS

I gratefully acknowledge the financial support provided by a summer research grant from the University of San Diego. I also wish to recognize publicly the valuable comments provided on an early draft by Professor William H. Henning, School of Law, University of Missouri-Columbia.

September 2002

William H. Lawrence

TABLE OF CONTENTS

Page

CHAPTER 1
INTRODUCTION TO INSTRUMENTS

§ 1.01	Distinguishing Instruments from Other Personal Property	1
§ 1.02	Scope — § 3-102	3
§ 1.03	Historical Context	5

CHAPTER 2
NEGOTIABILITY

§ 2.01	Relevance of Negotiability			10
	[A]	Introduction		10
	[B]	The Rule of Derivative Title		10
	[C]	Negotiability		11
		[1]	Goods	11
		[2]	Indispensable Paper	13
	[D]	The Shelter Principle		16
§ 2.02	Requisites of Negotiability — § 3-104(a)			17
	[A]	Introduction		17
	[B]	Unconditional Promise or Order — § 3-106		18
		[1]	Promise — § 3-103(a)(9)	18
		[2]	Order — § 3-103(a)(6)	18
		[3]	Unconditional — § 3-106	19
			[a] Express and Implied Conditions	20
			[b] Reference to Other Writings	21
			[c] Reference to Account or Fund	22
			[d] Countersignatures	22
	[C]	Writing Signed by the Maker or Drawer — § 3-103(a)(6), (9)		23
		[1]	Writing	23
		[2]	Signed	24
	[D]	Fixed Amount of Money — §§ 3-107, 3-112		25

			Page
		[1] Fixed Amount	25
		[2] Money	26
	[E]	Payable to Order or Bearer — § 3-109	27
		[1] Words of Negotiability	27
		[2] Payable to Bearer	28
		[3] Payable to Order	28
	[F]	Payable on Demand or at a Definite Time — § 3-108	31
		[1] In General	31
		[2] On Demand	31
		[3] Definite Time	32
	[G]	No Other Undertaking or Instruction	34
		[1] General Principle	35
		[2] The Exceptions	35
§ 2.03	Types of Negotiable Instruments — § 3-104		36
	[A]	The Basic Categories	36
		[1] Notes	37
		[2] Drafts	37
	[B]	Variations	38
		[1] Cashier's Checks	38
		[2] Certified Checks	39
		[3] Teller's Checks	40
		[4] Traveler's Checks	40
		[5] Money Orders	41

CHAPTER 3
TRANSFER AND NEGOTIATION

§ 3.01	Overview	43
§ 3.02	Transfer by Assignment	44
	[A] Common Law	44
	[B] Uniform Commercial Code (U.C.C.)	47
§ 3.03	Transfer of an Instrument — § 3-203	48
§ 3.04	Negotiation of an Instrument — § 3-201	51
	[A] Holder Status — § 1-201(20)	52
	[B] Indorsement — § 3-204	53

				Page
	[1]	Indorsements: Special and Blank — § 3-205		55
		[a]	Special	56
		[b]	Blank	58
		[c]	Right to Require a Special Indorsement	59
		[d]	Must Convey Entire Instrument	60
	[2]	Indorsements: Restrictive and Nonrestrictive — § 3-206		61
		[a]	Prohibiting Further Transfer	61
		[b]	Conditional Indorsements	62
		[c]	Collection and Deposit Indorsements	62
		[d]	Trust Indorsements	65
§ 3.05	Person Entitled to Enforce Instrument — § 3-301			65
§ 3.06	Issue — § 3-105			67
	[A]	Delivery — § 1-201(14)		67
	[B]	Relationship of the Original Parties — § 3-117		70

CHAPTER 4
CONTRACT OBLIGATIONS

§ 4.01	Liability on the Instrument — Fundamentals — § 3-401		73
§ 4.02	The Contracts		75
	[A]	Maker — § 3-412	75
	[B]	Acceptor — § 3-413	78
	[C]	Drawer — § 3-414	80
	[D]	Indorser — § 3-415	81
§ 4.03	Disclaimer of Contract Liability — §§ 3-415(b), 3-414(e)		83
§ 4.04	Surety Liability on the Instrument — § 3-419		85
	[A]	Signing for Accommodation	85
	[B]	Liability	86
	[C]	Rights	86
	[D]	Establishing Accommodation Status	88
	[E]	Defenses	89

			Page
	[F]	Words Guaranteeing Collection	91
§ 4.05	Authority to Sign		91
	[A]	Signature by Authorized Representative — § 3-402	91
	[B]	Unauthorized Signatures — § 3-403	94
§ 4.06	Enforcement of Lost, Destroyed, or Stolen Instruments — § 3-309		96
	[A]	Introduction	96
	[B]	Enforcing the Instrument	97
	[C]	Adequate Protection Against Loss	98
	[D]	Special Rules on Cashier's Checks, Teller's Checks, and Certified Checks — § 3-312	100

CHAPTER 5
SATISFYING THE CONDITIONS OF CONTRACTUAL LIABILITY

§ 5.01	Introduction		103
§ 5.02	The Conditions		103
	[A]	Presentment — § 3-501	104
	[B]	Dishonor — § 3-502	106
	[C]	Notice of Dishonor — § 3-503	107
§ 5.03	Time Requirements		108
	[A]	Presentment — §§ 3-414(f), 3-415(e)	108
	[B]	Dishonor — § 3-502	108
		[1] Payment Context	108
		[2] Acceptance Context	110
	[C]	Notice of Dishonor — § 3-503(c)	111
§ 5.04	Consequences of Failure to Satisfy the Conditions		112
	[A]	Indorsers — § 3-415(c)	112
	[B]	Drawers — § 3-414(f)	112
§ 5.05	Excused Presentment and Notice of Dishonor — § 3-504		114
	[A]	Delay	114
	[B]	Complete Excuse	114

CHAPTER 6
HOLDER IN DUE COURSE

§ 6.01	Requirements To Qualify — § 3-302(a)	118

				Page
[A]	Introduction			118
[B]	Value			119
	[1]	The Article 3 Definition — § 3-303		120
		[a]	Consideration Performed	120
		[b]	The Executory Promise Exceptions	122
		[c]	Security Interest or Lien on Instrument	123
		[d]	Payment or Security for Antecedent Debt	124
	[2]	The Article 4 Definition — §§ 4-210, 4-211		124
[C]	Good Faith			128
[D]	Notice			132
	[1]	The General Definition — § 1-205(25), (26)		132
		[a]	Actual Knowledge	132
		[b]	Imputed Knowledge	132
		[c]	Constructive Notice	134
	[2]	Specifics of Article 3 — § 3-302(a)(2)		134
		[a]	Notice That Instrument is Overdue — § 3-304	134
		[b]	Notice That Instrument Has Been Dishonored	135
		[c]	Notice of a Claim	136
		[d]	Notice That Any Party Has a Defense or Claim in Recoupment	138
		[e]	Notice of Unauthorized Signature or Alteration	141
[E]	Questionable Authenticity — § 3-302(a)(1)			142
[F]	Exclusions — § 3-302(c)			143
[G]	Payee as Holder in Due Course			144

§ 6.02 Rights of Holder In Due Course 145

[A]	Free From Claims — § 3-306			145
[B]	Free From Defenses — § 3-305(b)			146
	[1]	Defenses Against the Holder		146
	[2]	Real Defenses — § 3-305(a)(1)		147
		[a]	Infancy	147

			Page
		[b] Other Incapacity, Duress or Illegality	148
		[c] Fraud	149
		[d] Discharge in Insolvency Proceedings	151
	[C]	Rights Passed Through Shelter — § 3-203(b)	151
§ 6.03	Absence of Any Holder-in-Due-Course Rights		154
	[A]	Claims and Defenses — § 3-306	154
	[B]	*Jus Tertii*: Assertion of the Rights of Third Parties — § 3-305(c)	154
§ 6.04	Negotiation That May be Rescinded — § 3-202		157
	[A]	Effectiveness of Negotiation	157
	[B]	The Remedy of Rescission	157
§ 6.05	Procedural Aspects — § 3-308		159
	[A]	Effectiveness of Signatures	159
	[B]	Production of the Instrument	161
	[C]	Burden to Prove Holder-in-Due-Course Rights	161
§ 6.06	Holders in Due Course and Consumers		163
	[A]	The Problem	163
	[B]	The Federal Trade Commission Rule	166

CHAPTER 7
DISCHARGE

§ 7.01	Introduction		169
§ 7.02	Liability on the Instrument		171
	[A]	Payment — § 3-602	171
		[1] General Rule	171
		[2] The Exceptions	173
		[a] Indemnity or Injunction	174
		[b] Stolen Instruments	175
	[B]	Tender of Payment — § 3-603	177
	[C]	Cancellation or Renunciation — § 3-604	178
	[D]	Reacquisition — § 3-207	179
	[E]	Discharge of Indorsers and Accommodation Parties — § 3-605	181

				Page
		[1]	Rights of Recourse	181
		[2]	Rights in Collateral	183
	[F]	Material Alteration — § 3-407		188
		[1]	Requirements	188
		[2]	Effect	190
	[G]	Acceptance of Draft by Bank — §§ 3-414(c), 3-415(d)		192
	[H]	Acceptance Varying Draft — § 3-410		192
§ 7.03	Liability on the Underlying Transaction			193
	[A]	Effect of Taking an Instrument — § 3-310		193
	[B]	Accord and Satisfaction — § 3-311		196

CHAPTER 8
WARRANTY LIABILITY

§ 8.01	Overview			198
	[A]	Correlations with Other Warranty Law		198
		[1]	Sales of Goods	198
		[2]	Assignments	199
	[B]	Distinct from Liability on the Instrument		199
§ 8.02	Organization of Warranty Provisions			200
	[A]	Determining the Applicable Category of Warranty		200
	[B]	Determining the Applicable Article		202
§ 8.03	Transfer Warranties — §§ 3-416, 4-207			204
	[A]	Who Gives the Warranties		204
		[1]	Transfer	204
		[2]	Consideration	204
	[B]	To Whom the Warranties Run		205
	[C]	The Warranties		207
		[1]	In General	207
		[2]	Entitled to Enforce the Instrument	207
		[3]	Signatures Authentic and Authorized	209
		[4]	No Alterations	210
		[5]	No Defense or Claim in Recoupment	212
		[6]	No Knowledge of Insolvency Proceedings	213
§ 8.04	Presentment Warranties — §§ 3-417, 4-208			214

			Page
	[A]	Who Gives the Warranties	214
	[B]	To Whom the Warranties Run	214
	[C]	The Warranties	215
		[1] When Unaccepted Drafts are Paid or Accepted	215
		[a] Entitled to Enforce the Instrument	215
		[b] No Knowledge Signature of Drawer is Unauthorized	216
		[c] No Alterations	217
		[2] When Instruments Other Than Unaccepted Drafts are Paid	218
§ 8.05	Breach of Warranties — §§ 3-416(b), 3-417(b)		219
	[A]	Accrual and Termination of Cause of Action	219
	[B]	Damages	220

CHAPTER 9
PREVENTION OF UNJUST ENRICHMENT

§ 9.01	Restitution: Recovery of Payment Made by Mistake		223
	[A]	Introduction	223
	[B]	Pre-Code Law	224
		[1] *Restatement of Restitution*	224
		[2] The Dominant Case Law	226
	[C]	U.C.C. — § 3-418	228
		[1] Warranties and Finality	229
		[2] Problems With Customers' Accounts	231
		[3] Beneficiaries of Finality	233
		[4] The Double-Forgery Problem	236
	[D]	Rationales for Finality	237
§ 9.02	Subrogation: Recovery by Assertion of Rights of Others		241
	[A]	The Subrogation Concept — § 4-407	241
	[B]	Stop-Payment Orders	242
	[C]	Other Grounds for Objection by Buyers	245
	[D]	Burden of Proof — § 4-403(c)	247

CHAPTER 10
TORT CONCEPTS

§ 10.01 Introduction 250

§ 10.02 Negligence 250

    [A] Negligence Contributing to Forgeries or Alterations — § 3-406 250

        [1] The Doctrine of *Young v. Grote* 250

        [2] Preclusion 251

            [a] Rationale 251

            [b] Applying the Preclusion 251

        [3] Negligence 255

            [a] Tort Standard 255

            [b] Substantially Contributes 258

        [4] Comparative Negligence 258

    [B] Customer Negligence With Respect to Statement of Account — § 4-406 260

        [1] The Customer's Duty 260

        [2] Consequences of Customer Noncompliance 264

        [3] Comparative Negligence of the Bank 265

        [4] Time Limits on Customer's Rights 266

§ 10.03 Strict Liability 269

    [A] Introduction 269

    [B] Imposters and Nominal or Fictitious Payees — § 3-404 271

        [1] Applicable Rules 271

            [a] The Impostor Rule 271

            [b] The Nominal or Fictitious Payee Rule 273

        [2] The Indorsement 277

        [3] Comparative Negligence 278

    [C] Fraudulent Indorsements by Employees — § 3-405 279

§ 10.04 Conversion — § 3-420 282

    [A] The Proper Defendant 282

        [1] Thieves, Finders and Their Transferees . . . 282

			Page
	[2]	Collection, Payment, and Indorsements	284
	[3]	Representatives: Depositary and Collecting Banks	285
[B]	The Proper Plaintiff		286
	[1]	Payees and Indorsees: Delivery	287
	[2]	Issuers and Acceptors Excluded	288
[C]	Damages		289
[D]	The Case of Restrictive Indorsements — § 3-206(c)		289

CHAPTER 11
CHECK COLLECTION AND PAYMENT

§ 11.01 Overview		292
[A] Article 4		292
[B] Regulation CC		293
[C] Amendments to Article 4		294
§ 11.02 Forward Collection		295
[A] Agency Status of Collecting Banks		295
	[1] Rights as Special Agents — § 4-201(a)	295
	[2] Collecting Bank as Holder — § 4-205(1)	296
[B] Ways that Checks are Collected		296
	[1] Collection Through the Federal Reserve	297
	[2] Direct Presentment by Collecting Banks	299
	[3] Collection Through Clearinghouses	300
	[4] Collection Through Transmission of Information: Truncation	300
	[5] Presentment by the Customer	301
[C] Duties of Collecting Banks in Forwarding Checks — §§ 4-202, 4-204		301
§ 11.03 Payor Banks		302
[A] Deferred Posting — § 4-301		302
	[1] Statutory Authorization	302
	[2] Noncompliance With Time Limits	304
[B] Over-the-Counter Presentment for Cash		305
[C] Final Payment — § 4-215(a)		306
	[1] Introduction	306

Page

      [2] The Definition 307
  [D] Competing Claims to a Drawer's Account
      Balance — § 4-303 308
      [1] The Priorities Approach 308
      [2] When Payment Attains Priority 310

§ 11.04 The Return Process 311
  [A] The Reasons for Regulation CC 311
      [1] Inefficient Check-Return Procedures 311
      [2] Check-Hold Practices 312
  [B] Funds Availability 314
  [C] Revised Check Return 317
      [1] Expeditious Return 317
      [2] Notice of Nonpayment 320
      [3] Indorsements 320
      [4] Warranties 322

CHAPTER 12
RELATIONSHIP BETWEEN A PAYOR BANK AND ITS CUSTOMER

§ 12.01 Introduction 323
§ 12.02 Contractual Basis of the Relationship 324
  [A] The Deposit Contract 324
  [B] The Implicit Contract — § 4-401 325
      [1] Items Creating an Overdraft 326
          [a] Joint Accounts 327
          [b] Dishonor Following Pattern of Honoring
              327
          [c] Service Charges 328
      [2] Unauthorized or Missing Signatures 329
      [3] Alterations 331
      [4] Stop-Payment Orders; Postdated Checks ... 332
§ 12.03 Wrongful Dishonor — § 4-402 333
  [A] Liability 333
      [1] Payor Bank 333
      [2] Customer 333
      [3] Dishonor That is Wrongful 334

		Page
	[B] Damages	335
§ 12.04	Customer's Right to Stop Payment — § 4-403	337
	[A] The Right	337
	[B] Reasonable Opportunity to Act	338
	[1] Timeliness	339
	[2] Manner	340
	[C] Oral or Written	341
	[D] The Bank as Acceptor or Drawer	342
§ 12.05	Stale Checks — § 4-404	344
§ 12.06	Customer Death or Incompetence — § 4-405	345

CHAPTER 13
PAYMENT BY CASH

§ 13.01	Development of the Concept of Cash	349
§ 13.02	Legal Tender	351
§ 13.03	Free Transferability of Cash	351
§ 13.04	Allocation of Loss	352

CHAPTER 14
PAYMENT BY CREDIT CARD

§ 14.01	Relationship of the Participants	355
§ 14.02	Federal Legislation	358
	[A] Background	358
	[B] Scope	360
	[C] Disclosure	364
	[1] Solicitation and Application Disclosures	365
	[2] Initial Disclosure Statement	367
	[3] Periodic Statements	368
	[D] Sanctions	369
	[E] Card Issuance	370
	[F] Unauthorized Use	371
	[G] Criminal Liability for Fraud	374
	[H] Treatment of Credits	375
	[I] Error-Resolution Procedures	376
	[J] Claims and Defenses of Cardholders	378

		Page
[K]	Anti-Setoff Provision	379

CHAPTER 15
ELECTRONIC FUND TRANSFERS

			Page
§ 15.01	The Systems		382
	[A]	Introduction	382
	[B]	Automated Clearing Houses (ACHs)	382
	[C]	Bill Payment by Telephone	384
	[D]	Automated Teller Machines (ATMs)	384
	[E]	Point-of-Sale Systems (POS)	385
	[F]	Check Guarantee	385
	[G]	Wire Transfers	386
	[H]	Smart Cards	387
§ 15.02	The Electronic Fund Transfer Act and Regulation E		388
	[A]	Background	388
	[B]	Scope	389
	[C]	Card Issuance	391
	[D]	Disclosure	392
	[E]	Liability for Unauthorized Transfers	393
	[F]	Documentation	396
	[G]	Error Resolution	397
	[H]	Stop Payment	399
	[I]	Financial Institution Liability	399
	[J]	Enforcement	400
§ 15.03	Operating Rules and Regulation J		401
	[A]	Automated Clearing Houses (ACHs)	402
	[B]	Debit Cards	403
	[C]	Wire Transfers	404
§ 15.04	Article 4A of the U.C.C.		407
	[A]	Scope	407
	[B]	Transfer Relationships	410
		[1] Acceptance	410
		[a] By a Receiving Bank Other Than the Beneficiary's Bank	411
		[b] By the Beneficiary's Bank	412

			Page
	[2]	Rejection	414
	[3]	Payment	415
[C]	Allocation of Loss		418
	[1]	Erroneous Execution	418
	[2]	Erroneous Payment Orders	419
	[3]	Unauthorized Transfers	421
	[4]	Insolvency	422

TABLE OF CASES TC-1
TABLE OF STATUTES TS-1
INDEX I-1

Chapter 1

INTRODUCTION TO INSTRUMENTS

SYNOPSIS

§ 1.01 Distinguishing Instruments from Other Personal Property

§ 1.02 Scope — § 3-102

§ 1.03 Historical Context

§ 1.01 Distinguishing Instruments from Other Personal Property

Although this treatise deals primarily with negotiable instruments, a wider perspective is taken here at the outset. A brief examination of the entire range of personal property for purposes of the Uniform Commercial Code (U.C.C. or Code) demonstrates where instruments fit within the array. Although the law governing negotiable instruments is derived from multiple sources, most of it is codified in the U.C.C. The various subjects governed by the articles of the Code are neither a comprehensive nor a random selection of concepts relevant to commercial transactions; and certain fundamental principles flow through them and serve as unifying themes that bind the articles together.[1] Placing negotiable instruments within the context of the other forms of personal property shows that these instruments are a discrete subject within a broad and integrated code.

Personal property can be divided into three overarching categories: goods, indispensable paper, and intangibles. Goods and intangibles essentially cover opposite ends of the spectrum that runs from tangible to intangible personal property. Goods are moveable, tangible property whose value depends upon its physical characteristics; the definitions of goods exclude any of the property that comprises the intangible and indispensable paper categories.[2] Intangibles are comprised of choses in action, like accounts and other contract rights, and certain miscellaneous rights, such as informational rights and rights protected by patent, trademark, and copyright law.[3]

---

[1] Concepts like the rule of derivative rights, negotiability, agency, priority, loss allocation, and the hierarchy of buyer, bona fide purchaser, and buyer in the ordinary course of business permeate most of the U.C.C. articles. The general provisions of Article 1, which apply to all transactions under each article, further demonstrate that the U.C.C. is a unified code.

[2] U.C.C. §§ 2-105(1); 9-102(a)(44).

[3] U.C.C. § 9-102(a)(42).

Neither the legal nor the business community recognizes any single physical embodiment as representative of the property rights associated with pure intangibles. Even when there is a writing that shows the existence of the right, its value is purely evidentiary; that is, that paper need not be delivered for a transfer of the right to be effective. Pure intangibles are transferred using the common-law assignment mechanism, and the assignee need not receive any physical totem in order to enforce its rights.

The category of indispensable paper occupies a middle ground between goods and intangibles. The right itself, such as an obligation to pay money, is intangible; but with these types of property the right is reified, meaning that it is embodied in a writing. The writing itself is tangible, of course, but its value does not lie in its physical characteristics. Rather, its value is in the rights embodied in the paper. Because the writing is recognized as the single embodiment of those rights, the mechanism used to transfer the rights is physical delivery to the transferee of the paper itself. Because the transferee needs the paper to enforce the rights, the paper is referred to as "indispensable."

Another characteristic that joins the various types of indispensable paper is that they are the only property on which our legal system will confer full-fledged attributes of negotiability. This concept, which is covered in detail in the next chapter,[4] essentially enables a qualifying transferee to attain greater rights in the transferred property than were possessed by the transferor. This attribute of negotiability operates as a significant exception to the doctrine of derivative rights, a general rule governing property transfers which limits the rights of a transferee to precisely those possessed by the transferor.

Indispensable paper consists of three major categories: negotiable documents of title, negotiable instruments, and chattel paper. The most common forms of negotiable documents of title are bills of lading issued by a carrier upon shipment of goods and warehouse receipts issued by a warehouseman upon storage of goods.[5] All documents of title, whether negotiable or nonnegotiable, represent the right to possession of the covered goods. The issuer of a negotiable document will not release the goods to anyone without surrender of the document, so a person wanting to take delivery of the goods will need to be in possession of the document. Negotiable documents of title are sometimes referred to as "goods paper" because they represent title to the goods that have been shipped or stored. This means that the owner of these goods can sell them and transfer title by transferring the document.

Two basic types of instruments[6] are governed by the Code. The first type, certificated securities, can be called "investment paper." They are an interest in property commonly dealt in as a medium for investment.[7] Paper

---

[4] *See* § 2.02 *infra.*

[5] U.C.C. §§ 1-201(15); 7-201(2).

[6] Article 9 also identifies a third type of instrument — one that is nonnegotiable — for certain transactions that are beyond the scope of this work. *See* U.C.C. § 9-102(a)(47).

[7] U.C.C. § 8-102(a)(4).

constituting stock or a bond is valuable because of the investment share that it represents, which can be traded or redeemed. The owner of 100 shares of stock represented by a certificated security can effectuate a sale by delivery of the security to the buyer. Similarly, the owner of a bond can sell the right to enforce the bond by delivery.

The other type of instrument is the primary subject matter of this text. Negotiable instruments, also known as commercial paper, can be readily identified as "money paper," because this form of indispensable paper derives its value from obligations to pay money that are indicated on the paper.[8] The basic forms of negotiable instruments are notes and drafts.[9]

Chattel paper is a form of personal property created when a debtor signs a writing (or writings) that evidences an obligation to pay money coupled with a security interest in or lease of specific goods.[10] The monetary obligation is sometimes represented by a negotiable instrument. Chattel paper functions like indispensable paper in certain respects and like a pure intangible in others. Specialized provisions of Article 9 govern this form of property and a detailed analysis is beyond the scope of this book.

§ 1.02 Scope — § 3-102

Article 3 "applies to negotiable instruments."[11] The term "instrument" is used extensively throughout Article 3 and for purposes of this Article means "negotiable instrument."[12] The requisites for a negotiable instrument under Article 3, discussed in detail in the next chapter,[13] are codified in section 3-104(a). They essentially describe a writing creating the unconditional right to the payment of a fixed amount of money. Writings that meet the requisites for a negotiable instrument, and that are not otherwise excluded, are within the scope of Article 3. Writings for the payment of money that do not fall within its scope generally are governed under ordinary contract law.

Article 3 includes a specific provision that limits its scope. The provision excludes money, payment orders that are part of an Article 4A funds transfer (as opposed to payment orders that are drafts within the scope of Article 3), and investment securities.[14] Even though money[15] may technically meet the requirements of section 3-104(a) on negotiability, it is excluded from Article 3 because of inherent differences. Money is negotiable

---

[8] U.C.C. § 3-104(a).

[9] U.C.C. § 3-104(e). Notes include certificates of deposit and drafts include checks. *See* § 2.03 *infra*.

[10] U.C.C. § 9-102(a)(11).

[11] U.C.C. § 3-102(a).

[12] U.C.C. § 3-104(b).

[13] *See* § 2.02 *infra*.

[14] U.C.C. § 3-102(a).

[15] " 'Money' means a medium of exchange authorized or adopted by a domestic or foreign government and includes a monetary unit of account established by an intergovernmental organization or by agreement between two or more nations" U.C.C. § 1-201(24).

at common law or under different statutes, but Article 3 does not apply to it. The mutual exclusivity of Articles 3 and 4A is made apparent by Article 3's exclusion of payment orders that are part of an Article 4A funds transfer and Article 4A's definition of "payment order" specifically excluding drafts governed by Article 3.[16]

Investment securities also are excluded from Article 3. The original uniform codification on the law of negotiable instruments, the Negotiable Instruments Law (N.I.L.), did not distinguish between instruments intended for investment and instruments that created money paper. The distinction was unnecessary at the time of the codification because the securities market was not active then. The N.I.L., however, proved to be a burden on the subsequent development of the bond market. Marketability depended upon the bonds being negotiable, but negotiability required that the payment obligation of the corporate issuer not be subject to conditions. Bond obligations had to be subject to conditions in other writings, however, so an impasse was created. The problem was resolved by the Uniform Commercial Code, which separated the treatment of investment securities and commercial paper. Any instrument that qualifies under section 8-102(1)(a) is governed exclusively by that Article, even if it also technically satisfies the section 3-104(a) definition of a negotiable instrument.

Section 3-102(b) provides that the provisions of Article 9 control the provisions of Article 3 in the event of conflict. Negotiable instruments often play an important role in secured transactions, and the two Articles are relatively well coordinated (more so with the 1998 revision of Article 9 than its predecessor). Nevertheless, conflicts do occur, and a mechanism for resolving them is a necessity.

Section 3-102(b) also provides that the provisions of Article 4 control the provisions of Article 3.[17] Article 4 becomes applicable whenever an instrument is introduced into the bank-collection process.[18] Instruments often fulfill their intended purposes without entering bank collection. Many promissory notes and drafts are transferred and paid outside of bank collection, so none of the transactions affecting them ever invoke Article 4. Because checks are by definition orders to pay drawn upon a bank, checks inevitably enter the bank-collection process, and as soon as they do, Article 4 applies. In addition, ordinary drafts that are payable through a bank and notes that are payable at a bank[19] come within the scope of Article 4 once they enter the bank-collection process. Many similar transactions are governed by Articles 3 and 4, making conflict between the two articles likely. If Article 4 is silent on a point covered in Article 3, the latter Article

---

[16] U.C.C. § 4A-103(a)(1)(iii). For an explanation of payment orders that are part of an Article 4A funds transfer, see § 15.04[B] *infra*.

[17] The same hierarchy is recognized in section 4-102(a).

[18] The bank collection process is used for the collection of instruments in addition to negotiable instruments covered by Article 3. Article 4 thus is written in terms of items. " 'Item' means an instrument or a promise or order to pay money handled by a bank for collection or payment." Article 4A payment orders, as well as credit and debit card slips, are excluded. U.C.C. § 4-104(a)(9).

[19] U.C.C. § 4-106(a),(b).

governs.[20] In the event of conflicting provisions, however, Article 4 controls.[21]

As a study on payment systems, many of which center around the use of negotiable instruments, this text focuses extensively on the provisions of Article 3 and on Article 4 to the extent that it governs bank collection of negotiable instruments. Article 3, however, is not a comprehensive codification of the law of negotiable instruments. Consequently, provisions within the Article must be examined for their intended scope, and when a particular problem falls outside that scope, reference must be made to common law.[22] Furthermore, the Code in general is far from comprehensive in its treatment of payment systems. Payments by means of negotiable instruments are governed by Articles 3 and 4. Article 4A on wholesale fund transfers was promulgated in 1989 and has been adopted by most states. Other payment systems, including cash, credit card, and electronic funds transfers, are not governed by the Code at all. An explanation of the law governing these payment methods requires an examination of both common law and other statutory sources.[23]

§ 1.03 Historical Context

Fourteenth-century merchants developed the use of the draft, or bill of exchange, as a means to conduct their transactions while avoiding the risk associated with the transport of large sums of money. A merchant in Italy desiring to place funds into the hands of someone in London could accomplish the objective by means of a draft. Having made prior arrangements with a party in London, the Italian merchant would issue a written order to that party to pay the person designated in the draft to receive payment. The party in London upon whom the order was drawn would make the payment when the designated person presented the paper. The party in London might have agreed to make the payment because doing so discharged a debt that the party owed to the Italian merchant for goods sold or for money lent. Alternatively, the party in London might have agreed because the Italian merchant also agreed to honor the party's drafts drawn on him.

Another mechanism could be used to achieve the same result. Rather than drawing a draft upon someone in London, the Italian merchant might have used a local money changer. The merchant would pay the money changer, who in turn would draw a draft on another money changer in London with whom an account was maintained. The designated payee on the draft would receive payment from the London money changer upon presenting the draft.

---

[20] U.C.C. § 4-102(a).

[21] *See, e.g.*, Available Iron & Metal Co. v. First Nat'l Bank, 56 Ill. App. 3d 516, 371 N.E.2d 1032, 23 U.C.C. Rep. Serv. 694 (1977) (even though notice of dishonor may be oral under Article 3, it is not sufficient for a bank under Article 4).

[22] *See* U.C.C. § 1-103.

[23] For discussion of the alternative payment systems, see Chapters 13-15 *infra*.

The modern banking role in England did not develop until the seventeenth century. Before that time, London merchants typically deposited their valuables for safekeeping with the King's mint in the Tower of London. After Charles I, in 1640, unilaterally borrowed 200,000 pounds from their deposits, merchants increasingly took their business to goldsmiths who offered the service of safekeeping valuables in addition to trading in gold and silver plate. The goldsmiths began to make arrangements with their depositors to make loans with the money on deposit, thereby converting the relationship from bailor-bailee to that of creditor-debtor. That is, rather than holding the bailed property *in specie*, the goldsmith became a debtor of the merchant. The goldsmiths also began to honor orders drawn on them by their depositors ordering them to pay designated persons. Checks, patterned on the form of drafts, evolved as the instrument by which a depositor ordered payment.

In addition to instruments that served as a safe and convenient means to transmit funds, commercial practice in the seventeenth century also developed instruments of credit. The time draft was the initial development. This type of draft allowed a stated period of time before payment was due. A seller of goods could draw such a draft on the buyer, who would then sign it. By signing the draft, the buyer engaged to pay it when it became due.[24] If the seller did not want to finance the sale by holding the draft until the due date, the seller could transfer it to a lender for less than its face value (*i.e.*, at a discount). The lender would then be paid the face amount of the draft by presenting it to the buyer for payment on the maturity date. The time draft thus served both as a credit instrument and an instrument to transmit funds.

When the credit function alone was desired, the promissory note became the instrument of choice. The debtor signed a writing promising to make payment to a lender (or to the bearer of the note) on a specified date in the future. The lender could hold the note and await payment at maturity, or, as with the time draft, the lender could discount the note to someone else. The note provided written evidence of the borrower's obligation to pay money.

The law merchant was the original source of the law of negotiable instruments. It was not law *per se*, but rather a body of commercial custom that evolved as merchants in England entered into more commerce with merchants on the continent. Drafts, checks and notes were governed originally by the custom of merchants that developed concerning the transmission of funds and evidence of credit. Rather than recourse through the courts, special tribunals of merchants were used to enforce these customs.

Eventually, the law merchant was absorbed into the English common law, but the process was quite difficult. The common-law courts understandably were resistant to the acceptance of principles that evolved outside their purview and often from foreign sources. The common-law doctrine on the nonassignability of choses in action also posed a formidable barrier. By

---

[24] The signing of a draft by the drawee is called an "acceptance," a concept that is described in detail in § 4.02[B] *infra*.

the early eighteenth century, however, drafts had come to be seen as freely transferable, but the same attribute was denied to promissory notes.[25] Parliament stepped in at this point, however, and with the passage of the Statute of Anne,[26] made promissory notes freely transferable as well.

Throughout all of the eighteenth century, England did not have any official paper currency, and several denominations of gold and silver coins were in short supply.[27] Increasing mercantile activities forced merchants to adopt money substitutes. Consequently, drafts and notes came to be circulated widely though several hands before ultimately being presented for payment or acceptance. Lord Mansfield decided two major cases that helped assure the acceptability of instruments as money substitutes.[28] His rulings that a holder of a negotiable instrument who acquires it in good faith and for value takes free of the claim of a prior owner of the instrument state the fundamental principle of negotiability.[29]

Since 1882, negotiable-instrument transactions in England have been governed by the Bills of Exchange Act. It served as a model for the National Conference of Commissioners on Uniform State Laws (NCCUSL), which promulgated the Uniform Negotiable Instruments Law (N.I.L.) in 1896. All of the states adopted the law by 1924. The American Bankers Association drafted the Bank Collection Code, which was adopted in about twenty states. The law of negotiable instruments and bank collections was revised and modernized through Articles 3 and 4 of the Uniform Commercial Code. The Code was promulgated in 1952 through the joint efforts of NCCUSL and the American Law Institute.

By the 1980s, changing commercial practices and technological innovations in the handling of negotiable instruments again created an impetus for change in the codification scheme. Draft revisions on Articles 3 and 4 were completed by 1990, and the revisions have now been widely enacted. A new Article 4A on wholesale fund transfers was also promulgated and has been enacted by most states.[30] Congress also passed legislation that preempted certain aspects of Article 4 check collections and empowered the Board of Governors of the Federal Reserve System to enact regulations that preempt substantial portions of Articles 3 and 4.[31] The initial incursion by the Board is Regulation CC, which implements the preemption required by this legislation and also exercises some of the discretion authorized by it.[32] All of this modernized law of negotiable instruments and alternative payment systems is explained in this text.

---

[25] Buller v. Crips, 6 Mod Rep. 29, 87 Eng. Rep. 793 (1704).

[26] 3 & 4 Anne, ch. 9, § 1 (1704).

[27] Bank of England notes did not become legal tender until 1833.

[28] Miller v. Race, 97 Eng. Rep. 398 (K.B. 1758); Peacock v. Rhodes, 99 Eng. Rep. 402 (K.B. 1781).

[29] For discussion of these cases, see § 2.01[C][2] *infra*.

[30] For discussion of Article 4A, see § 15.04 *infra*.

[31] Expedited Funds Availability Act, Pub. L. No. 100-86, 101 Stat. 552, 12 U.S.C. §§ 4001–4010.

[32] 12 C.F.R. Part 229. For discussion of the legislation and Regulation CC, see §§ 11.01[B], 11.04 *infra*.

Chapter 2
NEGOTIABILITY

SYNOPSIS

§ 2.01   **Relevance of Negotiability**
       [A]   Introduction
       [B]   The Rule of Derivative Title
       [C]   Negotiability
            [1]   Goods
            [2]   Indispensable Paper
       [D]   The Shelter Principle

§ 2.02   **Requisites of Negotiability — § 3-104(a)**
       [A]   Introduction
       [B]   Unconditional Promise or Order — § 3-106
            [1]   Promise — § 3-103(a)(9)
            [2]   Order — § 3-103(a)(6)
            [3]   Unconditional — § 3-106
                 [a]   Express and Implied Conditions
                 [b]   Reference to Other Agreements
                 [c]   Reference to Account or Fund
                 [d]   Countersignatures
       [C]   Writing Signed by the Maker or Drawer — § 3-103(a)(6),(9)
            [1]   Writing
            [2]   Signed
       [D]   Fixed Amount of Money — §§ 3-107, 3-112
            [1]   Fixed Amount
            [2]   Money
       [E]   Payable to Order or Bearer — § 3-109
            [1]   Words of Negotiability
            [2]   Payable to Bearer
            [3]   Payable to Order
       [F]   Payable on Demand or at a Definite Time — § 3-108
            [1]   In General
            [2]   On Demand
            [3]   Definite Time
       [G]   No Other Undertaking or Instruction
            [1]   General Principle
            [2]   The Exceptions

§ 2.03   **Types of Negotiable Instruments — § 3-104**
       [A]   The Basic Categories
            [1]   Notes
            [2]   Drafts
       [B]   Variations

[1] **Cashier's Checks**
[2] **Certified Checks**
[3] **Teller's Checks**
[4] **Traveler's Checks**
[5] **Money Orders**

§ 2.01 Relevance of Negotiability

[A] Introduction

Most forms of personal property can be transferred.[1] Physical possession of personal property, however, is not sufficient to establish an unassailable right to the property. A transferee might receive property that is subject to claims of ownership or security interests of prior parties. When the property consists of an enforceable right, such as the right to receive payment of money on a promissory note, the transferee may encounter defenses asserted in resistance to an attempt to enforce the right. The concept of negotiability is relevant in these disputes because it determines the circumstances in which transferees can acquire rights in personal property that are greater than the rights of their transferors. Because negotiability is the exception, the discussion below begins with the general rule.

[B] The Rule of Derivative Title

A pervasive principle of Anglo-Saxon property-law jurisprudence is that title is derived. A transferee of property receives the rights that the transferor has in the property,[2] and the general rule is that the transferor can convey nothing more. The familiar maxim of assignment law reflects the rule of derivative title: the assignee stands in the shoes of the assignor.[3] The U.C.C. recognizes the derivative title principle in most of the articles that address transfers of ownership of personal property.[4]

Although a transferee's qualification for bona fide purchaser (BFP) status sometimes can improve the rights acquired in a transfer, the circumstances are exceptional and by no means universal. BFP trappings are not always an adequate guarantee against susceptibility to claims and defenses passed

---

[1] An exception would be a license issued by a governmental agency, which is nonassignable by statute.

[2] Cundy v. Lindsay, 3 App. Cas. 459 (H.L. 1878). "Title, like a stream, cannot rise higher than its source." Barthelmess v. Cavalier, 2 Cal. App. 2d 477, 487, 28 P.2d 484, 490 (1934).

[3] "The right of an assignee is subject to any defense or claim of the obligor which accrues before the obligor receives notification of the assignment. . . ." Restatement (Second) of Contracts § 336(2)(1981). *See also* U.C.C. § 9-318(1).

[4] U.C.C. §§ 2-403(1), 2A-304(1), 2A-305(1), 7-504(1), 8-301(1), 9-315(a)(1). Derivative rights under Article 3 are covered in section 3-203(a),(b). For discussion of these rights, see § 3.03 *infra*.

on by a transferor. The starting point is the rule of derivative title, and parties who seek to deviate from it must make their case under established exceptions.

Several categories of BFPs simply cannot make that case. A good-faith purchaser, for example, cannot acquire title to goods from a thief.[5] The rightful owner of the goods, therefore, can replevy them or recover damages for conversion from the thief's transferee, irrespective of the transferee's bona fides. Similarly, a lessee of goods can transfer at most the interest in the goods remaining under the terms of the lease. A transferee cannot assert BFP status to defeat the ownership interest of the lessor.[6] A bona fide purchaser for value can also be subordinate to the rights of a competing secured party who perfects the security interest.[7] Purchasers of intangibles also do not enhance their rights with respect to the purchased property simply because they act in good faith and without notice of competing claims and defenses.[8]

The supremacy of the rule of derivative title reflects the initial common-law approach to ownership of property. Ownership was protected and could not be defeated even by subsequent parties who paid value for the property while unaware of the prior owner's claim. Initially-acquired property rights prevailed over subsequent acquisition as a method of allocating the loss between innocent parties.

[C] Negotiability

The growth of expanding marketplaces gave rise to mercantile interests that required alterations in the sacrosanct treatment of vested property interests. The distribution system for goods became more and more dependent on selling agents, and the fraud of dishonest agents raised recurring problems of how to allocate the resulting losses. The law began to evolve in response to this new mercantile age to provide select protection of the exchange even over established property interests. Significantly, the protection remains as an exceptional concept even today and is supported by strong policy considerations.

[1] Goods

One of the rationales used to justify favoring a transferee over the true owner of goods is the culpability of the owner. Owners who do not take adequate steps to protect their interests in the property they introduce into

---

[5] "One who purchases stolen property from a thief, no matter how innocently, acquires no title in the property; title remains in the owner." Olin Corp. v. Cargo Carriers, Inc., 673 S.W.2d 211, 216 (Tex. Ct. App. 1984).

[6] McDonald's Chevrolet, Inc. v. Johnson, 176 Ind. App. 399, 376 N.E.2d 106 (1978) (lessee who absconded with motor home had no title to pass to truck dealer, who in turn could not convey good title to BFP who purchased from the dealer). See U.C.C. § 2A-305(1).

[7] U.C.C. § 9-317(b), (d).

[8] U.C.C. § 9-317(d). "[T]he assignment of a non-negotiable contract right ordinarily transfers what the assignor has but only what he has." Restatement (Second) of Contracts § 336, Comment b. See also U.C.C. § 9-404(a).

the stream of commerce have less-compelling equities when confronted by a party who has innocently purchased the property. The owner's culpability provided courts with a theoretical basis for shifting the loss in the commercial setting of the distribution of goods.

The concept of voidable title served well in this context. It represented a middle ground between the extreme cases where a transferee receives the owner's title through a sale of the property by the owner but receives nothing through a sale by a thief who has stolen the owner's property. Through the voidable-title doctrine, a person who acquires possession of an owner's goods by defrauding the owner cannot keep them against a claim by the owner. However, because the owner's entrustment of the goods to the fraudulent party facilitates the opportunity to deceive subsequent transferees, the voidable-title doctrine protects subsequent transferees of the goods if they qualify as bona fide purchasers.[9] The defrauding party acquires title that is voidable at the owner's option, but the defrauding party also attains the power to pass good title to subsequent BFPs.[10] The doctrine of voidable title is thus an exception to the rule of derivative title because it recognizes circumstances under which a transferee can acquire rights that are greater than the rights of the transferor.

In addition, entrustment of goods to persons in the business of selling that type of goods empowers such persons to transfer all of the entrustor's interest in the goods to a subsequent buyer in the ordinary course of business.[11] Hence, an owner who leaves a television set for repair by a merchant who also sells televisions loses the property claim to the set if the merchant wrongfully adds the repaired set to the store's inventory and sells it to an innocent customer. This exceptional circumstance, in which the buyer acquires greater rights than the seller has in the property, is justified by the entrustor's action. Entrusting the goods to these sellers voluntarily places possessions in the hands of the only entity that can pass them on to a buyer in ordinary course of business. These buyers are BFPs who purchase in ordinary course from a person engaged in selling goods of that kind,[12] which typically is a purchase from the inventory of a merchant. The entrustor thereby creates indicia of apparent authority in the seller that the buyer is justified in relying upon.

This reliance gives rise to an additional policy that supports the protection afforded to buyers in the ordinary course of business. Buyers can attain this status and its accompanying protection only by purchasing in the regular commercial marketplace. This exception to the rule of derivative title thereby is limited to typical commercial transactions in which the expectations of regularly observed business practices should be the highest. The expectation provides some limited protection favoring the transfer over

---

[9] Mowrey v. Walsh, 8 Cowen 238 (N.Y. Sup. Ct. 1828).

[10] "A person with voidable title has the power to transfer a good title to a good faith purchaser for value." U.C.C. § 2-403(1).

[11] U.C.C. § 2-403(2). A buyer in the ordinary course is best understood as a limited type of BFP. *See also* U.C.C. § 9-320(a).

[12] U.C.C. § 1-201(9).

prior property interests. The protection is based on the policy of facilitating the free flow of commerce.

Note, however, that the protection does not rise to the level of the concept of market overt, in which a buyer from an established marketplace can be assured of acquiring goods free from all prior claimants.[13] Only claimants who incur a necessary degree of responsibility by entrusting the goods can be deprived of their property interest.[14] Furthermore, all persons who entrust their goods to a bailee do not lose to BFPs who receive the goods from the bailee. The entrustment must be to a person engaged in the business of selling goods of the type entrusted or it must be sufficient to invoke the doctrine of voidable title.

[2] Indispensable Paper

The reification of certain intangible rights, meaning that the rights are embodied in a writing, gave rise to new forms of commercial property. Documents and instruments can constitute forms of indispensable paper because the rights they represent are tied to the writing.[15] The business and legal communities recognize the writing as the single physical embodiment of the right it represents. The other distinguishing characteristic of commercial property that comprises the indispensable paper category is that these property forms can be fully negotiable.

When markets for these new types of commercial property opened during the nineteenth century, the common-law courts conferred only "quasi-negotiable" status on the paper. The courts adhered to the concept of entrusting, so that owners did not lose their property interest in the paper to BFPs unless they voluntarily entrusted it to someone who in turn transferred it. Elimination of the entrusting requirement and the accession to full negotiability followed.

The relevance of negotiability is that it allows transferees who qualify to take rights in indispensable paper that are greater than their transferors' rights. It is precisely the same principle involved in the BFP doctrine on goods, and the concept of negotiability is appropriately applied to goods in this context. Goods never attained the legal status of fully negotiable, however, as entrusting remains a critical element for BFP success. Consequently, the terminology of negotiability is much more commonly used in conjunction with indispensable paper — the forms of personal property that are fully negotiable — than it is with goods. Nevertheless, despite the differences between these major categories of personal property, the fundamental principle that certain BFPs enjoy exceptions to the rule of derivative

---

[13] Market overt was a unique English approach. Pursuant to trade usage, certain places at specified times were designated markets where a good-faith purchaser was assured of attaining good title to the items purchased, even if the goods had been stolen from their original owner.

[14] For example, a buyer in ordinary course cannot deprive an owner of title by innocently purchasing from a merchant goods that were stolen from the owner. Brown & Root, Inc. v. Ring Power Corp., 450 So. 2d 1245 (Fla. Ct. App. 1984).

[15] See § 1.01 *supra* for a description of these forms of paper.

title is similar. Article 3 uses the term "holder in due course" of negotiable instruments.[16] Compared with transferees of other forms of personal property, a holder in due course is simply a specialized form of bona fide purchaser.

A transferee's position with respect to prior parties is more complicated when the property is indispensable paper rather than goods. The transferee of the paper should be concerned not only about the prospect of claims by prior owners, but also with the enforceability of the transferred property right. The paper transferred is valuable property to the transferee only to the extent that the rights it reifies are enforceable. The transferee thus should be concerned with whether the parties whose obligations are indicated on the indispensable paper can successfully assert defenses to avoid performing. A transferee of indispensable paper may be vulnerable both to assertions of superior claims to the paper and of defenses against enforceability of the rights embodied in the paper.

The rules of negotiability allow qualifying transferees to take indispensable paper free from all claims and most defenses. Complexities involved with each form of paper have led to variations in substance and terminology, but the fundamental principle prevails. Thus, a holder in due course takes free from all claims to the negotiable instrument and from most defenses of any party to the instrument.[17] Through these rules of negotiability, transferees can acquire rights in the property transferred that exceed the rights held by their transferors.

It remains to explain why commercial paper is clothed with the attributes of full negotiability. Because commercial paper is "money paper," the logical starting place is with money itself. Money is not goods; rather it represents an obligation on the part of the issuer. It also is specifically excluded from the scope of Article 3.[18] The common-law rule on money is stated by Lord Mansfield in *Miller v. Race*: "So, in case of money stolen, the true owner cannot recover it, after it has been paid away fairly and honestly upon a valuable and bona fide consideration: but before money has passed in currency, an action may be brought for the money itself."[19] Lord Mansfield applied the same principle to the stolen bank note at issue in the case.[20] The rationale advanced was the need to protect commerce: "A bank-note is constantly and universally, both at home and abroad, treated as money, as cash; and paid and received, as cash; and it is necessary, for the purposes of commerce, that their currency should be established and secured."[21] Lord

---

[16] U.C.C. § 3-302.

[17] U.C.C. §§ 3-305, 3-306.

[18] U.C.C. § 3-102(a).

[19] 97 Eng. Rep. 398, 401 (K.B. 1758).

[20] These private notes issued by banks were a written promise to pay money upon demand. Because the only official currency was gold and silver coins that were both heavy and in short supply, customers deposited coins with banks in exchange for these notes. The acceptability of the notes in the marketplace led to their free transferability as a substitute for official money. Bank of England notes did not become legal tender until 1833.

[21] Miller v. Race, 97 Eng. Rep. 398, 402 (1758). This proposition is still a valid statement of the common-law approach to money. "It is absolutely necessary for commerce and business to continue that one who receives money . . . is not put on inquiry as to the source from which the funds have been derived." Transamerica Ins. Co. v. Long, 318 F. Supp. 156 (W.D. Pa. 1970).

Mansfield subsequently recognized the principle of negotiability of money as applicable on the same grounds to instruments that served as a money substitute: "If this rule [of derivative title] applied to bills and promissory note, it would stop their currency."[22]

This justification is not as directly relevant in our modern economy. The serious shortage of official currency was the original impetus that forced merchants to turn to substitutes for money. Having moved from a simple barter-exchange system to a money-based system, the shortage of money required protection of acceptable substitutes. Times have changed and negotiable instruments no longer are transferred through as many hands as they were in the late eighteenth century. The role of money itself also has diminished. Our economy has evolved into a modern banking system in which negotiable instruments have replaced direct transfers of money to a large extent.[23] In addition to its use as a payment system, negotiable instruments serve as a system for credit. In both contexts, negotiability continues to serve modern objectives.[24]

Checks are popular payment instruments in our modern economy. In this capacity they still serve as a substitute for money, although rather than passing the check along to someone else as payment, payees today are more likely to deposit a check with their bank to be collected.[25] Once checks reach the banking system, they are transferred from bank to bank for collection, and the depositor is likely, in turn, to issue his or her own checks against the increased balance. Negotiability serves to enhance the efficiency of this paper-based payment system. Negotiability serves to approximate the legal positions of a holder of money and a holder of a check, which in turn promotes the acceptability of checks in the marketplace and their transfer through the bank-collection system.

The role of negotiability regarding promissory notes is different because notes are used as instruments for the extension of credit rather than for payment.[26] Many initial payees of promissory notes seek to discount them to a bank or other financing agency. Sellers of goods who receive promissory notes from their customers in particular often must sell the paper in order to replenish their inventories. Negotiability of the note facilitates these transfers by reducing the risks associated with the note. When financing

---

[22] Peacock v. Rhodes, 99 Eng. Rep. 402, 403 (K.B. 1781).

[23] *See* Chapter 15 for a description of the next stage of evolution, in which electronic transmissions eliminate the physical transfer of paper.

[24] A growing body of literature questions the current appropriateness of at least some aspects of negotiability in the commercial paper context. The drafters of the revision to Article 3 considered the issue carefully, and elected to retain the negotiability concept.

[25] Although payees commonly deposit checks they receive into their checking accounts, the transfer of checks in the marketplace is far from atypical. Check-cashing services provide the service for a fee and some retail establishments take two-party checks. The higher fees currently charged for checking accounts means some recipients of checks must turn to these sources because they do not maintain a personal checking account.

[26] Some instruments are used both as a medium of payment and a medium of credit. For example, a buyer of goods who accepts a draft issued by the seller becomes obligated to pay it. The seller can then discount the draft to a purchaser or use it as collateral to secure a loan.

agencies can take the note free of claims and most defenses, they are more willing to finance the seller's transactions and extend more favorable credit terms. As a result, the seller has a more favorable and expansive market in which to discount the notes. The seller, in turn, can offer buyers greater credit on more favorable terms. The legal benefit provided to the financing agency thus also benefits the buyer and the seller in the form of a more expansive credit marketplace. The availability of relatively inexpensive credit, which our society depends on, is in large part the result of the principle of negotiability.[27]

Negotiability operates in additional contexts to help assure adequate levels of affordable credit. Short-term instruments in the form of promissory notes, certificates of deposit, and bankers' acceptances are sold to institutional investors by banks and businesses seeking to borrow unsecured operating funds. Qualifying commercial paper also can be used as collateral by borrowing banks to secure loans from the Federal Reserve System.[28] Negotiability enhances the acceptability of commercial paper in these contexts.

[D] The Shelter Principle

Good-faith purchasers who qualify for an exception to the rule of derivative title still would face residual susceptibility to prior claims and defenses if they could not transfer their own interest in the property to subsequent parties. In addition to the right to use and enjoy the property personally, full ownership includes the right to convey one's own rights in the property. The free alienability of property would be impeded if the superior rights attained by qualifying transferees were personal to them only.

The exceptions favoring BFPs operate in conjunction with the rule of derivative title to preclude this result. A transferee derives the rights that the transferor has in the property. Consequently, even when transferees do not fall within any exceptions, they still receive the rights of a qualifying BFP who transfers the property. The transfer of the benefit of an exception to the rule of derivative title is known as the "shelter principle." For example, even a transferee of a promissory note who does not qualify as a holder in due course can enjoy the rights of a transferor who does qualify.[29] Thus, one who has the "rights" of a holder in due course, acquired derivatively, has the same ownership and enforcement rights as the transferor who has the "status" of holder in due course.

---

[27] Growing concerns about consumer protection led to a variety of responses in the 1960s and 1970s. Many of the advantages of negotiability are no longer available in the context of paper created in consumer sales transactions. *See* § 6.06[B] *infra*.

[28] *See* 12 U.S.C.A. § 341 *et seq.*; 12 C.F.R. Part 201.

[29] The application of the shelter principle to transfers of negotiable instruments is explained in detail in Chapter 6. *See* § 6.02[C] *infra*.

§ 2.02 Requisites of Negotiability — § 3-104(a)

[A] Introduction

Negotiability is a matter of form. The requisites of negotiability describe the attributes that an instrument must have and cannot have in order to be considered a negotiable instrument. An instrument that meets all of the requisites of section 3-104(a) is negotiable. If even a single one of these requisites is missing, the instrument generally cannot qualify.[30]

The requisites of negotiability serve three basic objectives: the creation of money paper, the enhancement of certainty of payment, and the indication of an intent to create paper that is negotiable. The first objective is met by requiring that the maker or drawer sign a writing that contains a promise or order to pay a fixed amount of money.[31] The certainty of payment of that money is advanced by requiring that the instrument be payable on demand or at a definite time, and by precluding conditions to the promise or order to pay as well as additional undertakings or instructions by the maker or drawer. Some compromises with the ideal of certainty proved to be necessary in drafting the provisions on negotiability in Article 3. Generally, however, the exceptions are limited and serve commercial purposes. Finally, to be negotiable, an instrument must include "magic words of negotiability."[32] These words manifest the intention of the maker or drawer to issue an instrument that is negotiable and thus subject to the unique legal rules that govern these obligations.

If instruments are to be freely acceptable and move quickly through the stream of commerce, they must be clearly recognizable and understandable. The requisites of negotiability satisfy these needs through formal statutory requirements that keep negotiable instruments simple and focused on the obligation to pay money. A prospective transferee should evaluate the credit worthiness of parties obligated on an instrument, but if the instrument is negotiable, the transferee does not have to investigate the satisfaction of conditions limiting the obligations to pay or speculate when the payment becomes due. The need to evaluate and understand the writing quickly is further advanced by the requirement that negotiability is determined only and always by what appears on the face of the instrument. Separate agreements, understandings, and writings do not have any effect on the negotiability of an instrument.

Although the requisites of negotiability are stated in section 3-104(a), most of Part 1 of Article 3 deals with them. Section 3-103 provides some critical definitions. Sections 3-105 through 3-110 expand upon the concepts

---

[30] For a narrow possible exception with respect to checks, see U.C.C. § 3-104(c) and § 2.02[E] *infra*.

[31] With a note, the maker promises to pay. With a draft, the drawer orders another (the drawee) to pay. See § 2.03[A] *infra*.

[32] The "magic words" will show that the maker or drawer understands from the outset that he or she may be called upon to pay someone other than the payee. Thus, the instrument must ordinarily be payable to whomever is bearing it or to the order of a named person.

for purposes of Article 3. These additional provisions must be consulted in order to understand the elements necessary to create a negotiable instrument.

[B] Unconditional Promise or Order — § 3-106

"'[N]egotiable instrument' means an *unconditional promise or order*...."[33]

[1] Promise — § 3-103(a)(9)

Promise is defined as "a written undertaking to pay money signed by the person undertaking to pay."[34] A mere I.O.U. does not qualify.[35] The Code rejects prior cases that held acknowledgments of debts to be promises: "An acknowledgment of an obligation by the obligor is not a promise unless the obligor also undertakes to pay the obligation."[36] Although the maker does not have to use the word "promise," the use of language not specifically approved in Article 3 is ill-advised. It raises an issue that might lead to litigation on whether the other language is an equivalent. The doubt raised can also undercut the marketability of the paper.

Language of promise is a requirement for a note.[37] Notes generally include an express promise in the form of "I promise to pay." The person who undertakes this obligation is the maker.[38] A certificate of deposit is simply a type of note.[39] It is defined as "an instrument containing an acknowledgment by a bank that a sum of money has been received by the bank and a promise by the bank to repay the sum of money."[40]

[2] Order — § 3-103(a)(6)

Order is defined as "a written instruction to pay money signed by the person giving the instruction."[41] The instrument must communicate a clear command to pay it. An authorization for payment is not an order "unless the person authorized to pay is also instructed to pay."[42] The verb used ought to be in an imperative form, such as "direct" or "order," and not words like "beseech" or "ask." The most common form of the order is the simple command "pay." Words of courtesy, such as "Please Pay" or "Kindly Pay," will not convert an order into a request.

---

[33] U.C.C. § 3-104(a) (emphasis added).
[34] U.C.C. § 3-103(a)(9).
[35] U.C.C. § 3-103, Comment 3.
[36] U.C.C. § 3-103(a)(9).
[37] "An instrument is a 'note' if it is a promise . . . ." U.C.C. § 3-104(e).
[38] "'Maker' means a person who signs or is identified in a note as a person undertaking to pay." U.C.C. § 3-103(a)(5).
[39] "A certificate of deposit is a note of the bank." U.C.C. § 3-104(j).
[40] U.C.C. § 3-104(j).
[41] U.C.C. § 3-103(a)(6).
[42] U.C.C. § 3-103(a)(6).

Persons who issue negotiable instruments with orders do not expressly promise that they will pay. Rather, they order someone else to make payment. Any negotiable instrument that is written as an order is a draft.[43] If the draft is payable on demand[44] and the entity ordered to pay it is a bank, it fits into the special category of drafts called checks.[45] The person who orders payment on a draft (including a check) signs as the drawer.[46] Chapter 4 explains how drawers engage to pay the instrument if the party ordered to pay does not do so, despite the absence of such an express statement of obligation on the face of the instrument.[47] The normal expectations, however, are that the person ordered to pay actually will pay the instrument.

The person ordered to pay a draft is the drawee.[48] The drawee bank's name ordinarily is printed on the face of checks. On other drafts, the name of the drawee generally is inserted following the word "To" on the face of the draft.

The order to pay may be directed to more than one person, provided that a correct form is used. The order may be addressed jointly (such as "To S. Holmes and D. Watson") or in the alternative (such as "To L. Lane or C. Kent"). Allowing alternative drawees recognizes the corporate practice of listing numerous drawees on dividend checks for commercial convenience.[49] Drawees may not be named in succession (such as "To E. Scrooge, and if Scrooge fails to pay, then to T. Tim"). Unlike the joint and alternative forms, drawees named in succession would impose an additional burden on the holder. The holder of an instrument needs to present it for payment to only one of the drawees,[50] so an order to either joint or alternative drawees does not inconvenience the holder. By its express terms, an order addressed to successive drawees could require more than one presentment, and therefore, is not permitted.[51]

[3] Unconditional — § 3-106

The promise or order of an instrument must be unconditional to be negotiable. The requirement is included to remove the uncertainties associated with contingencies that might affect payment of the instrument. An enhanced risk of nonpayment and the necessity to investigate satisfaction of attached conditions would impair the widespread acceptance of negotiable instruments as a medium of payment and credit. The Code, therefore,

---

[43] "An instrument . . . is a 'draft' if it is an order." U.C.C. § 3-104(e).

[44] *See* § 2.02[F][2] *infra*.

[45] " 'Check' means (i) a draft, other than a documentary draft, payable on demand and drawn on a bank or (ii) a cashier's check or teller's check." U.C.C. § 3-103(f). For an explanation of cashier's checks and teller's checks, see § 2.03[B][1], [3] *infra*.

[46] " 'Drawer' means a person who signs or is identified in a draft as a person ordering payment." U.C.C. § 3-103(a)(3).

[47] *See* § 4.02[C] *infra*.

[48] " 'Drawee' means a person ordered in a draft to make payment." U.C.C. § 3-103(a)(2).

[49] U.C.C. § 3-103, Comment 2.

[50] *See* § 5.02[A] *infra*.

[51] U.C.C. § 3-103, Comment 2.

continues the early common-law requirement that a negotiable instrument must be a "courier without luggage."[52]

In order to affect negotiability adversely, a condition must be expressed in the instrument itself. For this purpose a promise or an order cannot be made conditional by statements expressed by the party issuing the instrument or by a separate underlying agreement between the immediate parties to the instrument. The rights of the parties to the instrument may be affected by conditions included in other writings,[53] but the nature and extent of their rights is a question that is separate from the determination of whether the instrument is negotiable. Negotiability is determined exclusively by the terms on the face of an instrument. Therefore, only the instrument itself has to be examined.[54] If the promise or order as written in the instrument is not expressly conditional, that element of negotiability is satisfied.

Several issues are readily foreseeable on whether a specific promise or order is conditional. Section 3-106 amplifies on the concept by indicating that certain facts do make a promise or order unconditional and designating other statements whose inclusion will have the opposite legal effect. These directives are discussed below.

[a] Express and Implied Conditions

Section 3-106(a) makes a promise or order unconditional unless it falls under one of two stated tests. The first of these tests is that the instrument states an express condition to payment.[55] Both conditions precedent and subsequent destroy negotiability if they are stated expressly in the instrument. If payment is expressly conditioned on the occurrence of an event, such as "I promise to pay if I get a grade of 'A' on my commercial law exam," the instrument is nonnegotiable. The instrument does not later become negotiable if the event occurs, as it could require a holder of the instrument to ascertain the facts concerning the event. Negotiability is determined as of the time the instrument is issued.

By implication, and consistent with prior law, implied and constructive conditions do not affect the negotiability of an instrument. Most instruments are issued as part of a broader agreement between the parties and implied conditions might affect the agreement, particularly concerning the time when payment is due. The resulting constructive condition of

---

[52] Overton v. Tyler, 3 Pa. 346, 347 (1846).

[53] See U.C.C. § 3-117; § 3.06[B] infra.

[54] "The rationale is that the holder of a negotiable instrument should not be required to examine another document to determine rights with respect to payment." U.C.C. § 3-106, Comment 1.

[55] Illinois State Bank v. Yates, 678 S.W.2d 819, 39 U.C.C. Rep. Serv. 204 (Mo. Ct. App. 1984) (reservation of right to divert payment to a person other than the payee made the promise conditional); First State Bank v. Clark, 91 N.M. 117, 570 P.2d 1144, 22 U.C.C. Rep. Serv. 1186 (1977) (inclusion of notation on the instrument that "note may not be transferred . . . without written consent . . ." defeated negotiability).

performance of the other party's performance before the obligation to pay becomes due does not destroy negotiability.[56]

[b] Reference to Other Writings

A maker or drawer who prepares an instrument often includes a reference in the instrument to other writings associated with it. Section 3-106 provides some guidance on interpreting these recitations. Some references normally are used to maintain a record, as when the drawer of a check makes a notation of the purpose of the check on the space commonly provided in the lower left-hand corner. On the other hand, the reference to another writing also might be to incorporate additional terms or to control the payment obligations on the instrument.

The second test for making an instrument conditional for purposes of precluding negotiability under Article 3 addresses references to another writing that might be included in an instrument. The instrument is conditional if it states "(ii) that the promise or order is subject to or governed by another writing, or (iii) that rights or obligations with respect to the promise or order are stated in another writing."[57] Such a reference shows an intent to control the payment obligation by terms in the other writing.[58] On the other hand, "[a] reference to another writing does not of itself make the promise or order conditional."[59] Thus, an indication of the consideration for the instrument or the transaction giving rise to the instrument does not affect negotiability.[60]

The absence of any terms in the referenced writing that would condition the payment obligation shown on the instrument is irrelevant. If the instrument indicates that the holder must refer to the other writing, the promise or order is considered conditional on that basis alone. Thus, the Virginia Supreme Court correctly refused to examine the referenced agreement because the promissory notes that stated "payable as set forth in that certain agreement . . ." were nonnegotiable on their face.[61]

Section 3-106 includes one exception to the general rule that promises and orders governed by another agreement are not unconditional. The

---

[56] In Home Center Supply, Inc. v. Certainteed Corp., 59 Md. App. 495, 476 A.2d 724, 38 U.C.C. Rep. Serv. 1300 (Md. Ct. Spec. App. 1984), the court held that a promissory note that stated "For value received I promise to pay . . ." was unconditional. The underlying agreement for the payee to extend a line of credit to the maker gave rise only to a constructive condition to the obligation to pay evidenced by the note.

[57] U.C.C. § 3-106(a).

[58] Holly Hill Acres, Ltd. v. Charter Bank, 314 So. 2d 209, 17 U.C.C. Rep. Serv. 144 (Fla. Dist. Ct. App. 1975) (promissory note stated that it was secured by a real estate mortgage and "[t]he terms of said mortgage are by this reference made a part hereof"); Booker v. Everhart, 294 N.C. 146, 240 S.E.2d 360, 24 U.C.C. Rep. Serv. 165 (1978) (promissory note stated, "in lieu of a property settlement supplementing that certain *Deed of Separation and Property Settlement* . . .the terms of which are incorporated herein by reference").

[59] U.C.C. § 3-106(a).

[60] Strickland v. Kafko Mfg., Inc., 512 So. 2d 714, 4 U.C.C. Rep. Serv. 2d 1502 (Ala. 1987) (check including notation "for pool to be delivered" not conditional).

[61] Salomonsky v. Kelly, 232 Va. 261, 349 S.E.2d 358, 2 U.C.C. Rep. Serv. 2d 939 (1986).

negotiability of an instrument is not impaired by a clause that makes "a reference to another writing for a statement of rights with respect to collateral, prepayment, or acceleration."[62] The provision obviously requires a holder to examine the separate writing to ascertain these applicable rights. The exception is carved out in recognition of the convenience that has evolved in stating these types of terms in an accompanying loan agreement, security agreement, or mortgage.[63]

[c] Reference to Account or Fund

Another exception to the dual tests of when promises and orders are conditional changes the approach of prior law. It provides that a condition precluding negotiability is not created "because payment is limited to resort to a particular fund or source."[64] Thus, for example, a court holding that a note was nonnegotiable because payment was limited to foreclosure on the collateral[65] would be changed by this provision. In removing this former restriction to negotiability, the drafters of the revision rejected the reasoning that the general credit of the drawer or maker must support enforceability of the instrument. They reasoned instead that market forces based on the willingness of potential buyers to take instruments payable only from particular funds will determine the marketability of such instruments, but that Article 3 nevertheless should apply.[66]

[d] Countersignatures

Section 3-106 also precludes the requirement of a countersignature by a person whose specimen signature appears on an instrument from making the instrument nonnegotiable.[67] The primary instrument to which this provision applies is a traveler's check. The countersignature requirement is a condition to payment, which gives rise to a defense when the proper signature is not made.[68] It nevertheless is excluded as a condition for purposes of determining negotiability.[69] The rationale is that the commercial world treats traveler's checks like money substitutes, so they should be governed by the provisions of Article 3.[70]

---

[62] U.C.C. § 3-106(b)(i).

[63] U.C.C. § 3-106, Comment 1.

[64] U.C.C. § 3-106(b)(ii).

[65] See United Nat'l Bank v. Airport Plaza Ltd. Partnership, 6 U.C.C. Rep. Serv. 2d 1161 (Fla. Ct. App. 1987).

[66] U.C.C. § 3-106, Comment 1.

[67] U.C.C. § 3-106(c).

[68] See U.C.C. § 3-106, Comment 2; § 2.03[B][4] infra.

[69] U.C.C. § 3-106, Comment 2. For discussion of this exception, see § 2.03[B][4] infra.

[70] A final exception to the tests of unconditional promise or order is provided in section 3-106(d). For discussion of this exception, see § 6.06[A] infra.

[C] Writing Signed by the Maker or Drawer — § 3-103(a)(6), (9)

Section 3-104(a) does not specifically mention any requirement of a writing signed by a maker or drawer. The requirements nevertheless are incorporated as requisites of negotiability through the definitions of "promise" and "order." A promise "means a *written* undertaking to pay money *signed* by the person undertaking to pay,"[71] and an order "means a *written* instruction to pay money *signed* by the person giving the instruction."[72] Because section 3-104(a) requires that an instrument must include a promise or an order to be negotiable, the requirements of a signed writing are also mandated. Consistent with prior law, "the term 'negotiable instrument' is limited to a signed writing that orders or promises payment of money."[73]

[1] Writing

Consistent with the concept that negotiable instruments are a type of indispensable paper,[74] they must be in written form. The Code defines "written" or "writing" to include "printing, typewriting or any other intentional reduction to tangible form."[75] Clearly the definition covers any process that produces words in readable form, including engraving, stamping, and mimeographing, as well as writing in long-hand or printing. The definition also affirms pre-Code cases that held instruments written in pencil to be valid.[76]

The definition of "writing" is so broad that it might lead to assertions that recordings or computerized tapes can qualify as an "other intentional reduction to tangible form." Courts have held that parties who taped their oral contract reduced the contract "to tangible form."[77] For purposes of section 3-104, however, the preamble proviso to the general definitions of Article 1 should apply to the requirement of a writing. The general definitions of Article 1 are prefaced with the caveat "unless the context otherwise requires."[78] The traditional treatment of negotiable instruments as a type of indispensable paper and several of the requirements for dealing with them suggest that verbal and electronic forms cannot constitute negotiable instruments. Although the Code permits the expansion of

---

[71] U.C.C. § 3-103(a)(9) (emphasis added).

[72] U.C.C. § 3-103(a)(6) (emphasis added).

[73] U.C.C. § 3-104, Comment 1.

[74] See discussion in § 1.01 *infra* on distinguishing instruments from other forms of personal property.

[75] U.C.C. § 1-201(46).

[76] Reed v. Roark, 14 Tex. 329 (1855). Preparing an instrument in a manner that is easily erasable, however, might lead to a finding of negligence contributing to a subsequent material alteration. *See* § 10.02[A] *infra*.

[77] Ellis Canning Co. v. Bernstein, 348 F. Supp. 1212, 11 U.C.C. Rep. Serv. 443 (D. Colo. 1972) (tape recording held to satisfy the writing requirement of the section 8-319 statute of frauds).

[78] U.C.C. § 1-201.

commercial law through custom and usage,[79] commercial practice does not recognize these forms as written instruments.

Some commentators contend that negotiability also should exclude any writings prepared on unusual surfaces.[80] Their reasoning that such writings do not serve any legitimate commercial purpose is correct, but their conclusion that these writings are not negotiable is both erroneous and unnecessary. The Code does not specify that an instrument must appear only on paper of certain dimensions. Nevertheless, instruments prepared on unusual surfaces often lose the advantage of ready acceptance that is associated with negotiability because prospective recipients refuse to take them. Furthermore, a checking-account contract with a bank is likely to require the bank to honor only checks that are drawn on pre-encoded forms prepared by the bank.

[2] Signed

A signature is required to authenticate the information contained in a negotiable instrument. Although most people sign by writing their full name, it is not the use of their name that indicates they have signed for purposes of commercial law. The Code defines the term "signed" to include "any symbol executed or adopted by a party with present intention to authenticate a writing."[81] "The question always is whether the symbol was executed or adopted by the party with present intention to authenticate the writing.[82]

The means of authentication are somewhat narrower for purposes of Article 3 than for some other signature requirements under the Code. For example, the comments to the Code definition of "signed" indicate that authentication is not determined by the type of symbol used, how it is applied, or where it appears on the writing.[83] The manner of application and the location on an instrument nevertheless can constitute significant evidence concerning requisite intent. The name preprinted on customized checks does not constitute a drawer's signature.[84] The drawer wants the information printed for convenience, but not to authenticate the writing. A full signature in the lower right-hand corner of an instrument is recognized as evidence of an intent to sign as a drawer or maker because it is

---

[79] U.C.C. § 1-102(2)(b).

[80] The I.R.S. has been the payee of more than one negotiable shirt. For a humorous account, see Herbert, *The Negotiable Cow*, Uncommon Law 201 (7th ed. 1957).

[81] U.C.C. § 1-201(39). First Sec. Bank v. Fastwich, Inc., 612 S.W.2d 799, 30 U.C.C. Rep. Serv. 1609 (Mo. Ct. App. 1981) (typed name of corporation on a promissory note constituted signature); Planters' Chem. & Oil Co. v. Morris, 19 Ala. App. 670, 100 So. 200 (1924) (pre-Code case, holding that a signature by mark "X" was sufficient to sign a promissory note, would be decided the same under the Code).

[82] U.C.C. § 1-201, Comment 39.

[83] "Authentication may be printed, stamped or written; it may be by initials or by thumbprint. It may be on any part of the document and in appropriate cases may be found in a billhead or letterhead." U.C.C. § 1-201, Comment 39.

[84] Littky & Mallon v. Michigan Nat'l Bank, 94 Mich. App. 29, 287 N.W.2d 359, 28 U.C.C. Rep. Serv. 715 (1979).

the standard practice. Although that location is not mandated as exclusive, the signature at least must appear on the face of the instrument.[85] The signature may appear solely in the body of an instrument, as follows: "I, Honest John, promise to pay." Additional features of the form of the instrument, however, might undercut the necessary indication of intent to authenticate. If a signature line is included at the bottom of the instrument and it remains unsubscribed, the maker has not manifested a sufficient present intent simply through the use of his or her name in the body of the instrument.

[D] Fixed Amount of Money — §§ 3-107, 3-112

" '[N]egotiable instrument' means an unconditional promise or order *to pay a fixed amount of money, with or without interest or other charges described in the promise or order . . . .*"[86]

[1] Fixed Amount

Uncertainty about the amount that is payable under an instrument can have an adverse impact on its alienability because a prospective purchaser would have difficulty determining an acceptable price to pay for the instrument. The promise or order to pay money, therefore, must indicate a fixed amount in order for the instrument to be negotiable.

The "fixed amount" requirement does *not* mean that a purchaser on the date of purchase must be able to determine the amount that ultimately will be paid on the instrument. "[T]he requirement of a 'fixed amount' applies only to principal."[87] The amount of principal that is to be paid must be determinable from the terms of the instrument. References to interest or other charges tied to the promise or order to pay the principal amount of money are irrelevant with respect to the negotiability of the instrument.

The exclusion of concern with interest is a new approach to negotiability that was heralded with the revision of Article 3. Previously, the guiding principle had been that the total amount payable should be determinable from information on the instrument with any necessary computation and without having to refer to outside sources.[88] Thus, for example, notes payable with interest "at bank rates" were not negotiable because the bank rates could not be determined from the instrument.[89] The primary motivation for the change appears to have been the desire to extend negotiability

---

[85] *See* North Valley Bank v. National Bank, 437 F. Supp. 70, 23 U.C.C. Rep. Serv. 93 (N.D. Ill. 1977) (signatures on an enclosed letter and legend stamped on back of an envelope held not valid to authenticate an enclosed instrument intended to be a draft).

[86] U.C.C. § 3-104(a) (emphasis added).

[87] U.C.C. § 3-112, Comment 1.

[88] The revision changes this requirement: "The amount or rate of interest may be stated or described in the instrument in any manner and may require reference to information not contained in the instrument." U.C.C.§ 3-112(b).

[89] A. Alport & Sons, Inc. v. Hotel Evans, Inc., 65 Misc. 2d 374, 317 N.Y.S.2d 937, 8 U.C.C. Rep. Serv. 1040 (N.Y. Sup. Ct. 1970).

to notes with variable interest rates.[90] Revised Article 3 provides that "[i]nterest may be stated in an instrument as a fixed or variable amount of money or it may be expressed as a fixed or variable rate or rates."[91] Variable-interest-rate instruments have become too widespread and important in our economy to continue excluding them from the scope of Article 3.

As originally drafted, Article 3 also had to include exceptions to the general rule on "fixed amount" in order to accommodate a variety of charges. For example, the drafters allowed the inclusion of a provision to add or deduct exchange at the current rate, even though the determination of that rate required consultation of outside sources in the marketplace.[92] The drafters relaxed the general principle against references to such sources in light of the commercial need to provide for exchange rates in international-trade transactions. A similar deference to commercial necessity explains the allowance of attorney fees and collection costs upon default. Because purchasers of negotiable instruments often would not deal with an instrument unless it both protected them against the incurrence of such costs and was negotiable, denying negotiability would not be realistic. By limiting application of the fixed-amount requirement to the principal only, the drafters of the revision have eliminated any need for including exceptions for specific charges, as all additional charges are now permitted.

The certainty of the sum that is payable on an instrument can be cast into doubt when the terms used are contradictory. For example, the numbers on a check might be different from the amount written in words. Article 3 includes some rules of construction by which to resolve these contradictions: "If an instrument contains contradictory terms, typewritten terms prevail over printed terms, handwritten terms prevail over both, and words prevail over numbers."[93]

[2] Money

An instrument must be payable in money if it is to be negotiable. The restriction of instruments to money paper promotes their acceptance and free transferability. Written promises to pay in commodities, such as gold dust or beaver pelts, are not negotiable under the Code because the uncertain and fluctuating value of such commodities impairs their acceptance in modern commerce.[94]

---

[90] *See* Taylor v. Roeder, 234 Va. 99, 360 S.E.2d 191, 4 U.C.C. Rep. Serv. 2d 652 (1987) (sixty-day note that provided for interest at "[t]hree percent (3.00%) over Chase Manhattan Prime to be adjusted monthly" held to be nonnegotiable).

[91] U.C.C. § 3-112(b).

[92] Exchange is the value of the currency of one country in terms of the currency of another country.

[93] U.C.C. § 3-114; Western Union Telegraph Co. v. People's Nat'l Bank, 169 N.J. Super. 272, 404 A.2d 1178, 26 U.C.C. Rep. Serv. 1235 (1979) (the words "One Hundred — 00/100 Dollars" on a money order controlled over the numerals "$1,200.00").

[94] Means v. Clardy, 735 S.W.2d 6, 5 U.C.C. Rep. Serv. 2d 119 (Mo. Ct. App. 1987) (note "to be paid out of cabinets" at a shop not negotiable).

Money is defined in the Code as a "medium of exchange authorized or adopted by a domestic or foreign government as a part of its currency."[95] The key requirement is that a government recognizes the circulating medium as part of its official currency. A promise or order to pay in a medium of exchange sanctioned by a government provides the greater certainty in value that negotiability depends on for free circulation.

The Code rejects the view adopted in some earlier cases that "money" is limited to legal tender. Legal tender is currency that the law requires to be accepted in discharge of an obligation. It can be only a part of the official currency that a government adopts.[96] Currently in the United States all official currency is also legal tender.

A medium of exchange authorized or adopted by a foreign government is acceptable as money. Thus, an instrument payable in Swiss francs or Japanese yen is for a fixed amount of money even though it is negotiated in the United States. The instrument does not have to be payable in the country that authorized or adopted the currency.

Unless otherwise specified, the instrument may be paid in either the designated foreign currency or in United States dollars.[97] The parties may require the instrument to be paid in a particular foreign currency, but the requirement must be specified expressly on the instrument. The exchange rate for an instrument that states the amount payable in a foreign currency is to be determined by using "the current bank-offered spot rate at the place of payment for the purchase of dollars on the day on which the instrument is paid."[98]

[E] Payable to Order or Bearer — § 3-109

" '[N]egotiable instrument' means an unconditional promise or order to pay a fixed amount of money . . . if it:

(1) *is payable to bearer or to order at the time it is issued or first comes into possession of a holder . . . .*"[99]

[1] Words of Negotiability

A negotiable instrument must include language indicating that the instrument is either payable to order or payable to bearer.[100] Words of

---

[95] U.C.C. § 1-201(24).

[96] Federal Reserve notes, silver certificates, and national bank notes did not constitute legal tender prior to passage of the Legal Tender Act of 1933. 31 U.S.C. § 392.

[97] U.C.C. § 3-107.

[98] U.C.C. § 3-107.

[99] U.C.C. § 3-104(a)(2) (emphasis added).

[100] Article 3 includes one narrow exception. If this requisite of negotiablity is the only one that is missing, and the writing qualifies as a check, the writing is a negotiable instrument. U.C.C. § 3-104(c). With most banks requiring the use of pre-printed checks, the only likely circumstance that would invoke this provision is when a drawer strikes out the words "to the order of" before issuing the check. The drafters felt that the absence of the words could be easily overlooked and should not affect the rights of holders who give value for such a check. U.C.C. § 3-104, Comment 2.

negotiability are a formal requirement that manifests the intention of the maker or drawer to issue a negotiable instrument. They readily enable a prospective purchaser to determine that a negotiable instrument is intended. Section 3-109 establishes when an instrument is payable either to bearer or to order.

[2] Payable to Bearer

An instrument payable to "cash" or to "the order of cash" undoubtedly is the most common form of bearer paper.[101] In addition to these designations, Article 3 also recognizes any language that "otherwise indicates that it is not payable to an identified person."[102] Thus, instruments payable to "a Happy Birthday" or "petty cash" qualify as bearer paper. The use of such unusual forms, however, can defeat the advantages of negotiability, as prospective transferees may not want to deal with such an instrument.

As one would clearly expect, an instrument payable to bearer also creates a bearer instrument.[103] An instrument payable to the order of bearer also creates bearer paper.[104] For example, checks have the words "pay to the order of" printed on the line for naming the payee. Adding the term "bearer" on the payee line makes the check a bearer instrument. Section 3-109 also provides that a promise or order is payable to bearer if it "otherwise indicates that the person in possession of the promise or order is entitled to payment."[105] This provision goes to the essence of the concept of a bearer instrument, which is that the right to payment is intended to run to whomever is in possession of the instrument (the bearer of the instrument), rather than a specific payee. Consider an instrument made payable to a specified person or bearer, such as "George Washington or bearer." Because payment would be appropriate if made to any person in possession of the instrument, the promise or order is payable to bearer.[106]

In a break with prior law, Article 3 makes an instrument that does not state a payee an instrument payable to bearer.[107] Although such an instrument is still classified as an incomplete instrument,[108] the check is nevertheless enforceable in such an incomplete form and, because it does not state a payee, it is payable to bearer.[109]

[3] Payable to Order

An instrument is payable to order "if it is payable (i) to the order of an identified person or (ii) to an identified person or order."[110] "Pay to the order

---

[101] U.C.C. § 3-109(a)(3).
[102] Id.
[103] U.C.C. § 3-109(a)(1).
[104] Id.
[105] Id.
[106] U.C.C. § 3-109(a)(1) and Comment 2.
[107] U.C.C. § 3-109(a)(2).
[108] See U.C.C. § 3-115. For a discussion of incomplete instruments see § 7.02[F][1] infra.
[109] U.C.C. § 3-115, Comment 2.
[110] U.C.C. § 3-109(b).

of Miss Marple" and "pay Miss Marple or her order" illustrate this drafting. It empowers the payee to receive payment of the instrument or to use an indorsement to order that payment be made to a designated third party or to the bearer.[111]

The use of the term "order" arose in response to frustrations that merchants experienced with early English common-law courts. These courts would not permit a subsequent holder of a contract to sue one of the original parties to it because there was not any privity between the plaintiff and the defendant. This approach obviously limited the free transferability of commercial paper. Merchants therefore devised two methods to create the necessary privity. By making the original promise or order payable to bearer or the holder of the instrument, privity passed with the physical delivery of the instrument. This solution was often unsatisfactory, however, because paper in bearer form lacks necessary safety.[112] The ultimate solution was to make the instrument payable to a specified person or to whomever that person further ordered the paper to be paid. An instrument made payable to "Uriah Heep or order" or to "Uriah Heep or his assigns" meant that the person to whom Heep ordered payment acquired privity because the original promise ran directly to him or her.

Section 3-109 also provides that an instrument cannot be payable to order if it is payable to bearer.[113] It changes the approach of prior law that provided that an instrument payable both to order and to bearer was payable to order unless the bearer words were handwritten or typewritten. The drafters felt that the bearer and order terms are simply contradictory, so that a transferee of the instrument ought to be able to rely on the bearer terms.[114]

The intent of the person signing an instrument as the issuer[115] is controlling for identification of the person to whom the instrument is initially payable.[116] This rule is provided in recognition of the fact that several persons might have the same name as the designated payee and the fact that sometimes a payee may be designated incorrectly. An instrument is payable to the person intended by the drawer or maker, even if the designation of the payee's name is completely erroneous.[117]

---

[111] "A promise or order that is payable to order is payable to the identified person." U.C.C. § 3-109(b).

[112] See § 3.04[B][1] *infra* and accompanying text for discussion of the consequences of theft of a bearer instrument compared with theft of an order instrument.

[113] U.C.C. § 3-109(b).

[114] U.C.C. § 3-109, Comment 2.

[115] "'Issue' means the first delivery of an instrument by the maker or drawer, whether to a holder or nonholder, for the purpose of giving rights on the instrument to any person." U.C.C. 3-105. For an explanation of the concept of issue, see § 3.06 *infra*.

[116] U.C.C. § 3-110(a). If the signature of the issuer of an instrument is accomplished through automated means like a check-writing machine, the intent of the party who supplied the name or identification of the payee controls in determining the proper payee. U.C.C. § 3-110(b).

[117] "The instrument is payable to the person intended by the signer even if that person is identified in the instrument by a name or other identification that is not that of the intended

The designation used on an order instrument does not have to be the name of a person. Section 3-110 recognizes a broad principle that "[a] person to whom an instrument is payable may be identified in any way, including by name, identifying number, office, or account number."[118] It provides several rules indicating to whom an instrument is payable in a variety of categories of payees.

The first rules deal with instruments payable to an account.[119] If only the account number is identified as the payee, the instrument is payable to the person to whom the account is payable. On the other hand, if the name of a person is added to an account number as the stated payee, the instrument is payable to the named person. This latter rule applies even if the named person is not the owner of the stated account. The remaining rules cover a number of different entities that are likely to deal with negotiable instruments.[120] Instruments payable to a trust, an estate, or a described trustee or representative are payable to the trustee, the representative, or the successor of either. Some pre-Code cases held that an instrument payable to a decedent's estate was bearer paper because it did not name a person as the payee. Since bearer paper clearly is not intended in these cases, Article 3 treats instruments payable to the order of an estate or trust as payable to the order of the appropriate representative of the designated payee.[121]

An instrument might name a specific individual together with words describing the payee as an officer or agent of a specified entity. For example, an instrument could be payable to the order of "Sergeant Pepper, Secretary of the Lonely Hearts Club," "Lucy Sky, President of Diamonds Co." or "E. Rigby, agent of I. Walrus." If the represented party is a person or a legal entity, the instrument is payable to the represented person, the representative, or the successor of the representative. If the represented party does not have a legal identity, the instrument is payable to a representative of the members, but not to the entity itself.

An instrument payable to "an office or to a person described as holding an office . . . is payable to the named person, the incumbent of the office, or a successor to the incumbent."[122] The intention of the maker or drawer of such instruments generally is to pay the office and not the individual officer, but the officer must be a holder in order to enforce payment or negotiate the instruments.

---

person." U.C.C. § 3-110(a). Electrical Distributors, Inc. v. SFR, Inc., 166 F.3d 1074, 37 U.C.C. Rep. Serv. 2d 485 (10th Cir. 1999) (lower court did not err in applying its finding that the intent of the signer of the check was that three shareholders were the payees, even though the check named a corporation as the payee).

[118] U.C.C. § 3-110(c).

[119] U.C.C. § 3-110(c)(1).

[120] U.C.C. § 3-110(c)(2).

[121] Joffe v. United Cal. Bank, 141 Cal. App.3d 541, 190 Cal. Rptr. 443, 36 U.C.C. Rep. Serv. 191 (1983) (check payable to "Continental Financial Systems-Wells Fargo Escrow Trust Account" held payable to representative of the escrow account).

[122] U.C.C. § 3-110(c)(2)(iv).

All of these rules are provided for the purpose of determining who can deal with an instrument as a holder.[123] Holder status enables the holder to enforce payment of the instrument or to further negotiate the instrument by providing any needed indorsement. Holder status does not establish ownership of the instrument or of its proceeds since a holder may be an agent of the owner.[124]

Section 3-110(d) addresses instruments that are payable to multiple payees. An instrument payable to "A and B" is payable to both of them acting jointly. Neither person, acting alone, can enforce payment or negotiate the instrument. An instrument payable to "A or B" is payable to them alternatively, meaning that it is payable to either one of them individually. If the intent is ambiguous, the instrument is payable to the multiple persons alternatively.[125] Thus, an instrument payable to "A and/or B" is payable alternatively.[126]

[F] Payable on Demand or at a Definite Time — § 3-108

" '[N]egotiable instrument' means an unconditional promise or order to pay a fixed amount of money . . . if it:

> (2) *is payable on demand or at a definite time. . . .*"[127]

[1] In General

Uncertainty about the time for payment impairs the commercial acceptance of money paper. Negotiability requires that holders and prospective purchasers of an instrument be able to ascertain from its face when the instrument is payable. Article 3 provides two alternative methods to satisfy this requirement. The instrument can be payable at the discretion of the holder to demand payment or it can be payable at a certain time. Section 3-108 amplifies on the concepts and is explained below.[128]

[2] On Demand

Instruments that expressly state they are payable "on demand" or "at sight" or otherwise indicate that they are payable at the will of the holder are payable on demand.[129] These express terms clearly indicate that the

---

[123] U.C.C. § 3-110(c). For an explanation of the holder concept, see U.C.C. § 1-201(20) and § 3.04[A] *infra*.

[124] U.C.C. § 3-110, Comment 3.

[125] City First Mortgage Corp. v. Florida Residential Prop. & Cas. Joint Underwriting Ass'n, 37 U.C.C. Rep. Serv. 2d 126 (Fla. Cty. Ct. 1998) (check that simply listed four separate persons as payees held to be ambiguous and thus payable alternatively); J.R. Simplot, Inc. v. Knight, 139 Wash. 2d 534, 988 P.2d 955, 40 U.C.C. Rep. Serv. 2d 57 (Wash. 1999) (hyphen between check payees is ambiguous because it can be used to divide or compound words).

[126] U.C.C. § 3-110, Comment 4.

[127] U.C.C. § 3-104(a)(2) (emphasis added).

[128] The determination of when an instrument is payable also affects a number of issues other than negotiability, such as the time that a cause of action accrues, the applicable statute of limitations, when interest runs on the instrument, and when the instrument is overdue.

[129] U.C.C. § 3-108(a).

instrument is to be paid when the holder demands payment from the payor indicated on the instrument. The term "at sight" simply indicates the time when the instrument is presented to the payor for payment.

Instruments that do not state any time for payment are also payable on demand.[130] Article 3 simply recognizes the general intention of the parties to create demand instruments when they do not state a payment date. In other words, the demand nature of the instrument is implicit in the absence of express language creating an inference to the contrary.[131]

An instrument that limits a holder's discretion to demand payment is not payable on demand. For example, a court held that a note in which the maker promised to pay "[a]t the earliest possible time after date" was comparable to phrases like "as soon as circumstances will permit me," "when he was able," and "as soon as he could."[132] These phrases are not equivalent to no time for payment being stated in the instrument, but instead create a condition to the promise to pay.[133] The court held that the note was not payable either on demand or at a definite time.[134]

A demand instrument does not have to be dated to be negotiable. The fact that an instrument is undated, antedated, or postdated does not affect negotiability.[135] When an instrument payable on demand is antedated or postdated, the stated date determines when it is payable.[136]

[3] Definite Time

An instrument is payable at a definite time if it is payable "at a fixed date or dates."[137] An instrument is also payable at a definite time if it is payable "at a time or times readily ascertainable at the time the promise or order is issued."[138] This latter provision provides certainty that an

---

[130] Kawac, Inc. v. Cohen, 1996 U.S. Dist. LEXIS 16250, 39 U.C.C. Rep. Serv. 2d 466 (E.D. Pa. 1996) (note with caption "Demand Promissory Note" stated that payment was payable to holder "on demand" and did not state a specified due date).

[131] Estate of Shanteau v. Shanteau, 510 N.E.2d 701, 4 U.C.C. Rep. Serv. 2d 781 (Ind. Ct. App. 1987) (provision for annual interest did not affect the character as a demand note when the due date was left blank).

[132] Williams v. Cooper, 504 S.W.2d 564, 14 U.C.C. Rep. Serv. 426, 428 (Tex. Civ. App. 1973).

[133] It does not matter that the condition becomes fully satisfied because the uncertainty concerning its fulfillment is present when the instrument is executed. Krajcir v. Egidi, 712 N.E.2d 917, 38 U.C.C. Rep. Serv. 2d 1213 (Ill. Ct. App. 1999) (note was made nonnegotiable by the inclusion of a provision that the note was payable "on the date of final endorsement by the United States Department of Housing and Urban Development Loan on Project No. 071-35488 PM/L8 known as Spaulding Re-Hab").

[134] See also Barton v. Scott Hudgens Realty & Mortgage, Inc., 136 Ga. App. 565, 222 S.E.2d 126, 18 U.C.C. Rep. Serv. 982 (1975) (promise to pay upon "evidence of an acceptable permanent loan" and "acceptance of the commitment" was not a negotiable instrument).

[135] U.C.C. § 3-113. See Smith v. Gentilotti, 371 Mass. 839, 359 N.E.2d 953, 20 U.C.C. Rep. Serv. 1222 (1977) (instrument payable on demand still negotiable despite being postdated 15 years).

[136] Section 3-113(a). But see U.C.C. § 4-401(c); § 12.02[B][4] infra.

[137] U.C.C. § 3-108(b).

[138] U.C.C. § 3-108(b).

instrument payable "on the second Tuesday of October 1997" or one payable "on Thanksgiving Day 1999" is negotiable.

A draft payable "on elapse of a definite period of time after sight or acceptance" also is considered to be payable at a definite time.[139] Such an instrument is payable following its acceptance and the passage of the stated time period after acceptance.[140] The holder can establish the payable date by presenting it for acceptance.

This last category of instruments is the most liberal application of the definite-time concept. Until the instrument is accepted by the dated signature of the drawee on the instrument itself, the time of payment cannot be determined from the face of the instrument. Prior to acceptance, the time for payment is in fact indefinite because it depends initially upon presentment by the holder. In this respect the instrument is like a demand instrument that can be presented at any time. Since the holder initially can demand only acceptance and not payment, the instrument cannot be payable on demand. Despite the conceptual strains that this category induces, its inclusion is sensible. The time when payment is due is just as calculable for an instrument payable "30 days after sight" as it is for one payable "at sight."

If an instrument states a definite time at which it is payable, it can include an acceleration clause and still be considered payable at a definite time. Any type of acceleration clause is acceptable. It can be at the maker's option, enabling the maker to prepay a note, or at the holder's option, enabling the holder to call the instrument early. Acceleration can be unrestricted or limited to specified circumstances. It can occur automatically upon the occurrence of a designated event, such as an increase in the lender's prime rate to a specified level. Acceleration can depend on events uncertain to occur, as well as events that are certain as to the time of their occurrence.

Even though an acceleration clause creates some uncertainty as to the time of payment, the drafters believed that the uncertainty was not as great as it is in the case of demand notes. An instrument payable at a definite time but subject to an acceleration clause at least states a date on which the instrument matures. It is equally clear that the drafters were interested in advancing the interests of lending institutions, which almost always include an acceleration clause in a negotiable instrument.

Historically courts have been hostile to the enforceability of acceleration clauses, particularly when they could be invoked "at will" or "when the holder deems himself insecure." The drafters of the Code, however, perceived the objections to be based on abuses of such powers, and not related to uncertainties in the time for payment. The drafters also recognized that denying negotiability to instruments with these clauses would not resolve abuses because they would still be enforceable under general contract law principles. Therefore, to protect against abusive creditors, the Code permits

---

[139] U.C.C. § 3-108(b).
[140] For discussion of the concept of acceptance, see § 4.02[B] *infra*.

holders to exercise "at will" or "deemed insecure" acceleration clauses only when they believe in good faith that the prospect of payment has been impaired.[141]

Sometimes instruments are drafted with both time and demand provisions. For example, a note might expressly state that it is payable on demand but also provide for a maturity date or for monthly installments.[142] When the terms of an instrument indicate that it is payable at a fixed date, but also payable upon demand made before the fixed date, the instrument is payable on demand until the fixed date.[143] On the fixed date the instrument becomes payable at a definite time if a previous demand for payment has not been made. These instruments thus are treated as instruments payable at a definite time subject to acceleration at will by the holder.

An instrument stating that it is payable at a definite time subject to an extension at the option of the holder does not impair negotiability. The clause providing for the right of extension merely states an already implicit right.[144] Despite the inclusion of the extension clause, other provisions of Article 3 might limit the holder's right. For example, a holder may not exercise this option over the objection of a maker who tenders full payment when the instrument is due. The holder cannot choose to refuse payment under these circumstances in order to keep a favorable rate of interest running on a note.

An instrument stating that it is payable at a definite time subject to an extension at the option of the maker or acceptor, or automatically upon the occurrence of a specified event, also is negotiable, provided that a definite time limit is stated for the extension. Without a definite time limit for extensions outside the control of the holder, the holder cannot ascertain when the instrument is payable and, therefore, the instrument is not negotiable. When the time of extension is stated in the instrument, it is functionally equivalent to an instrument payable at the ultimate date with the possibility of acceleration.[145] For example, a note payable on January 1, 1999, which gives the maker the right to extend payment until October 1, 1999, is comparable to a note payable on the October date subject to acceleration.

[G] No Other Undertaking or Instruction

" '[N]egotiable instrument' means an unconditional promise or order to pay a fixed amount of money . . . if it:

> (3) *does not state any other undertaking or instruction by the person promising or ordering payment to do any act in addition to the*

---

[141] U.C.C. § 1-208.

[142] *See* C & Z, Inc. v. Oklahoma Tax Comm'n, 6 U.C.C. Rep. Serv. 1080 (Okla. 1969) (note payable "on demand" or "in 240 monthly payments").

[143] U.C.C. § 3-108(c).

[144] U.C.C. § 3-108, Comment.

[145] U.C.C. § 3-108, Comment.

payment of money, but the promise or order may contain [specified provisions]."[146]

[1] General Principle

If a maker or drawer includes undertakings or instructions other than terms directed toward the payment of a fixed amount of money, the payment obligation could become entangled in those other terms. The payment obligation might even be only a relatively minor part of the overall responsibilities undertaken in the writing. The resulting lack of certainty concerning payment could defeat the free transferability of drafts and notes. Consequently, with a few specified exceptions, negotiability is precluded for instruments that include such undertakings or instructions. Thus, an instrument is not negotiable if it obligates the maker or drawer to obtain and pay for insurance[147] or if it obligates the maker or drawer to pay taxes or other assessments.[148] Section 3-104(a) indicates that a negotiable instrument can be "with or without interest *or other charges*" (emphasis added), which might appear to authorize these types of charges. The only charges that are authorized, however, are charges that are described as part of the promise or order to pay a fixed amount of money.

The prohibition against making promises other than a promise to pay applies only to drawers and makers. Obligations incurred by other persons, such as payees, will not adversely impact negotiability. Thus, the Massachusetts Supreme Court held that a provision in a promissory note that required the holder to obtain group credit life insurance on the maker's life, without any additional charge to the maker, did not adversely affect negotiability of the instrument.[149]

[2] The Exceptions

Most of the exceptions included in section 3-104(a)(3) were included to benefit creditors.[150] Creditors are the initial payees on a major portion of the negotiable instruments passed in commerce, and they felt they required more protection than simply the promise to pay. They desired to include promises and powers that would enhance their leverage to ensure payment of instruments. Clauses that increase the rights of holders or decrease the rights of makers or drawers are likely to improve the chances for free transferability of instruments among holders. The exceptions of section 3-104(a)(3) were included to accommodate the credit industry.

---

[146] U.C.C. § 3-104(a)(3) (emphasis added).

[147] U.C.C. § 3-104(a)(3). *See* Chrysler Credit Corp. v. Friendly Ford, Inc., 535 S.W.2d 110, 19 U.C.C. Rep. Serv. 849 (Mo. Ct. App. 1976).

[148] Insurance Agency Managers v. Gonzales, 578 S.W.2d 803, 25 U.C.C. Rep. Serv. 754 (Tex. Ct. App. 1979).

[149] Universal C.I.T. Credit Corp. v. Ingel, 347 Mass. 119, 196 N.E.2d 847, 2 U.C.C. Rep. Serv. 82, 3 U.C.C. Rep. Serv. 303 (1964).

[150] 2 State of New York, Report of the Law Revision Commission: Study of the Uniform Commercial Code 820 (1955).

Initial drafts of Article 3 precluded negotiability for writings that created security interests. The drafters clearly desired to simplify negotiable instruments and deny negotiability for any form of security agreement, including conditional sales contracts. Creditors, however, often are particularly desirous of obtaining collateral to secure a note, as it is an exceptionally good means of leverage against the maker. Following extensive debate on appropriate terms on collateral, the drafters abdicated and allowed major provisions on collateral.

An instrument may contain a statement that the obligor has given collateral to secure obligations.[151] The obligation can be the one undertaken on the instrument or any other obligation of the obligor, thus permitting the use of cross-collateral provisions without destroying negotiability. An instrument can also contain an undertaking or power to maintain or protect collateral. A promise by the maker of a note to insure collateral does not render the note nonnegotiable, but a promise to obtain insurance on the maker's life has the opposite effect.

The negotiability of an instrument also is not affected by a provision in the instrument that empowers a holder to proceed against the collateral. The provision need not be limited, as it was in the Negotiable Instrument Law, to default at maturity. The power can extend to a failure to pay an installment of principal or interest.

A term that authorizes a holder to confess judgment will not destroy negotiability. Confession of judgment clauses are unenforceable in nearly all jurisdictions, but the inclusion of the clause does not affect negotiability of the instrument.

Article 3 also authorizes a term that creates "a waiver of the benefit of any law intended for the advantage or protection of an obligor."[152] The exception applies to the waiver of benefits provided in Article 3, such as presentment and notice of dishonor, as well as the waiver of rights in other laws, such as a homestead exemption. The provision refers to waivers for the advantage or protection of "any obligor," which means the waivers can affect the rights of makers, drawers, acceptors, or indorsers. The determination that these waiver clauses do not adversely affect negotiability does not validate them if they otherwise are unenforceable under local law.

§ 2.03 Types of Negotiable Instruments — § 3-104

[A] The Basic Categories

Negotiable instruments are divided into two general categories: notes and drafts. "An instrument is a 'note' if it is a promise and is a 'draft' if it is an order."[153] Notes include certificates of deposit and drafts include checks.

---

[151] Hughes v. Tyler, 485 So. 2d 1026, 42 U.C.C. Rep. Serv. 1699 (Miss. 1986) (statement that promissory note was secured by a mortgage).

[152] U.C.C. § 3-104(a)(3).

[153] U.C.C. § 3-104(e).

[1] Notes

A note is a two-party instrument issued by a maker to a payee. Rather than ordering a third person to pay the instrument, the maker promises to pay it in accordance with the terms on its face. Notes are used primarily for credit functions. They facilitate the purchase of goods and services on credit, as well as serve to evidence a debt for borrowed money. They are not commonly utilized for a payment function.[154] Notes can be either a time note payable at a definite time or a demand note payable upon demand of the payee.

A negotiable instrument is a certificate of deposit if it contains "an acknowledgment by a bank that a sum of money has been received by the bank and a promise by the bank to repay the sum of money."[155] The party that makes the promise must always be a bank and is referred to as the maker.[156] "A certificate of deposit is a note of the bank."[157] Like all notes, it is a two-party instrument. The party to whom the promise is made is known as the payee. Certificates of deposit serve a credit function rather than a means of payment. Banks generally pay a higher rate of interest on certificates than on passbook accounts in exchange for the depositor agreeing to leave the funds on deposit for a specified time period.

[2] Drafts

An instrument that is an order to pay money is a draft. "Bill of exchange" is a synonymous term,[158] but its use is restricted primarily to international transactions. The most common form of draft is a check, used widely as a convenient means of payment without having to deal with currency. Checks and other drafts are three-party instruments. The person who orders the payment on a draft is the drawer,[159] and the person against whom it is drawn is the drawee. The drawee is thus the person ordered to pay.[160] The person to whom the draft is payable is known as the payee. By delivering a completed check or other draft to the payee, the drawer has given the payee a written order that directs the drawee to pay money to the payee or to whomever the payee designates through an appropriate indorsement. The payee (or the person properly designated) must collect the money from the drawee by physically presenting the draft or check and demanding payment.

---

[154] The promissory note, even when payable on demand and fully secured, is still, as its name implies, only a promise to pay, and does not represent the paying out or reduction of assets. Don E. Williams Co. v. Commission of Internal Revenue, 429 U.S. 569, 21 U.C.C. Rep. Serv. 152 (1962).

[155] U.C.C. § 3-104(j); Ames v. Great S. Bank, 672 S.W.2d 447, 38 U.C.C. Rep. Serv. 897 (Tex. 1984).

[156] "'Maker' means a person who signs or is identified in a note as a person undertaking to pay." U.C.C. § 3-103(a)(5).

[157] U.C.C. § 3-104(j).

[158] U.C.C. § 3-104, Comment 4.

[159] "'Drawer' means a person who signs or is identified in a draft as a person ordering payment." U.C.C. § 3-103(a)(3).

[160] "'Drawee' means a person ordered in a draft to make payment." U.C.C. § 3-103(a)(2).

A check is distinguished from other drafts by two essential attributes: it is a draft "drawn on a bank" and "payable on demand."[161] A writing drawn in the same form as a check, except that it is directed to a drawee other than a bank,[162] is a sight draft.[163] It is collected like a check by making presentment for payment upon the drawee. Obviously, the drawee is unlikely to pay a draft without a prior agreement with the drawer to honor the drawer's drafts. The same observation is true for checks drawn on a bank with which the drawer does not have an account or adequate deposited funds.

Unlike checks, a draft can also be a time instrument. Time drafts are commonly used to finance the sale of goods. Rather than paying the draft when it is presented, the drawee simply accepts the draft by signing it, thereby becoming contractually bound to pay the draft on the due date.[164] Under the terms of the sales contract, the buyer may be required to accept the draft in order to obtain possession of the negotiable bill of lading under which the goods were shipped. The bill of lading must be surrendered before the carrier will release possession of the goods. The signed draft, known as a trade acceptance, can be held by the seller pending payment on the due date, or the seller can realize cash for it currently by discounting it with a lender. The banker's acceptance operates similarly, except that the buyer's bank signs the acceptance on the draft rather than the buyer. This draft often is more valuable because a bank, rather than the buyer, is obligated to make the payment when it becomes due. A distant seller might be uncertain as to the buyer's credit because the parties have not conducted prior business, whereas the buyer's credit relationship with its bank is very good. By entering into a satisfactory arrangement with the bank to satisfy the obligation, the buyer provides the incentive for the bank to sign an acceptance on the time draft.

[B] Variations

[1] Cashier's Checks

A cashier's check is a draft drawn by a bank on itself.[165] An authorized officer of the bank signs a check that is an order to the bank itself to pay.[166] It is distinguishable from a teller's check, which is an instrument drawn

---

[161] U.C.C. § 3-104(f); Leaderbrand v. Central State Bank, 202 Kan. 450, 450 P.2d 1, 6 U.C.C. Rep. Serv. 172 (1969).

[162] "'Bank' means a person engaged in the business of banking including a savings bank, savings and loan association, credit union, or trust company." U.C.C. § 4-105(1).

[163] A sight draft that is drawn on a bank is a check. Bank of Am., N.T.S.A. v. Security Pac. Nat'l Bank, 23 Cal. App. 3d 638, 100 Cal. Rptr. 438, 10 U.C.C. Rep. Serv. 434 (1972).

[164] *See* U.C.C. § 3-413; § 4.02[B] *infra*; National Bank of N. Am. v. Beinhorn, 10 U.C.C. Rep. Serv. 847 (N.Y. Sup. Ct. 1972).

[165] "'Cashier's check' means a draft with respect to which the drawer and drawee are the same bank or branches of the same bank." U.C.C. § 3-104(g).

[166] Kaufman v. Chase Manhattan Bank, N.A., 370 F. Supp. 276, 13 U.C.C. Rep. Serv. 477 (S.D. N.Y 1973).

by one bank on another bank rather than on itself. Because both the drawer and the drawee are the same banking entity, a cashier's check is essentially a two-party instrument between the drawer-drawee bank and the payee. Consequently, the Code recognizes that the obligation of the issuer of a cashier's check incurs the same obligation to the pay the instrument as a maker of a promissory note.[167] The obligation on the instrument rests entirely on the bank. Therefore, even though the bank signed in the capacity of a drawer, it is treated as a maker.[168]

Generally, cashier's checks are purchased from the bank. A seller may be unwilling to accept a personal check from a buyer because of concerns that the buyer may not have sufficient funds on deposit to cover the check or that the buyer might stop payment on the check following the purchase. The buyer usually can overcome these concerns by procuring a cashier's check. The buyer's bank prepares the check and gives it to the buyer, while immediately debiting the buyer's account for the amount of the check plus a fee for the service. The check names the seller as the payee. The buyer's name does not appear on the check and, unless the buyer indorses it before negotiating it to the seller, the buyer is not a party to the instrument. The buyer, referred to as a remitter of the check,[169] can now give the seller a check for which the buyer's account has already been debited and on which a bank is the liable party.[170]

[2] Certified Checks

A certified check is a personal check that is certified for its genuineness and sufficiency of funds for payment by the bank upon which it is drawn. Certification of a check constitutes acceptance.[171] Either the drawer or the holder can request the drawee bank to certify the check. If the bank chooses to certify, an authorized officer of the bank signs the check, thereby making the bank liable to pay it.[172] To protect itself against subsequent withdrawals from the drawer's account that might leave an insufficient balance to cover the certified check, the drawee will place a hold or debit the drawer's account for the amount of the check at the time that it is certified.

A certified check is like a cashier's check in that a bank has signed it and thereby incurred liability. A bank signs a cashier's check in the capacity of a drawer, although it incurs liability as a maker,[173] whereas a bank signs

---

[167] U.C.C. § 3-412. For discussion of this section, see § 4.02[A] *infra*.

[168] Sochaczewski v. Wilmington Sav. Fund Soc'y, 508 A.2d 895, 2 U.C.C. Rep. Serv. 2d 181 (Del. Super. 1986).

[169] "'Remitter' means a person who purchases an instrument from its issuer if the instrument is payable to an identified person other than the purchaser. U.C.C. § 3-103(a)(11).

[170] Significant controversy has arisen over recognition of rights of the bank or its customer to assert defenses that arise in transactions involving cashier's checks. For discussion of these issues, see § 12.04[D] *infra*.

[171] "'Certified check' means a check accepted by the bank on which it is drawn." U.C.C. § 3-409(d).

[172] For an explanation of the contractual undertaking associated with acceptance, see U.C.C. § 3-413; § 4.02[B] *infra*.

[173] See § 2.03[B][1] *supra*.

a certified check as an acceptor.[174] Because of the difficulties of processing certified checks through the automated bank-processing system, modern banks prefer to issue a cashier's check rather than to certify their customers' personal checks.

[3] Teller's Checks

A "'teller's check' means a draft drawn by a bank (i) on another bank, or (ii) payable at or through a bank".[175] In the first of these variations, one bank is the drawer of a check that is an order on another bank as the drawee to pay. The issuing bank can use such a check to order payment from funds that it has on account with another bank.

Some drafts are drawn on a drawee other than a bank but state that they are "payable through" a designated bank. The payable through bank is a collecting bank to make presentment for payment on the drawee, but it is not authorized to pay the instrument.[176] Claims agents of insurance companies commonly use payable-through drafts drawn on a home office to settle claims because it enables the home office to be sure the insured party has signed required forms. Although payable-through drafts generally are not checks because they are not drawn on a bank, a draft payable at or through a bank is a teller's check if it is drawn by a bank.

[4] Traveler's Checks

"'Traveler's check' means an instrument that (i) is payable on demand, (ii) is drawn on or payable at or through a bank, (iii) is designated by the term 'traveler's check' or by a substantially similar term, and (iv) requires, as a condition to payment, a countersignature by a person whose specimen signature appears on the instrument".[177] Traveler's checks can be in the form of a note or a draft, and can be issued both by banks and nonbanks.[178] The requirement that the instrument be "drawn on or payable at or through a bank" does not require an identification of the bank through words on the instrument; the inclusion of an appropriate routing number that identifies the bank is sufficient.[179]

---

[174] The nature of the liability incurred by signing in each of these capacities is explained in Chapter 4. See Imports, Etc., Ltd. v. ABF Freight System, Inc., 162 F.3d 528, 37 U.C.C. Rep. Serv. 2d 344 (8th Cir. 1998) (shipper entitled to recover losses from freight company for accepting a certified check when the contract specified a cashier's check because the court found a certified check is much easier to forge).

[175] U.C.C. § 3-104(h).

[176] U.C.C. § 4-106(a). "An item identifying a 'payable through' bank can be presented for payment to the drawee only by the 'payable through' bank. The item cannot be presented to the drawee over the counter for immediate payment or by a collecting bank other than the 'payable through' bank." U.C.C. § 4-106, Comment 1.

[177] U.C.C. § 3-104(i).

[178] U.C.C. § 3-104, Comment 4.

[179] U.C.C. § 3-104, Comment 4.

Traveler's checks were devised to provide the cash equivalent of currency with greater safety.[180] They enjoy widespread acceptance around the world because they are drawn by major financial companies with sound reputations.

Even though the requirement of a countersignature on a traveler's check is a condition to the obligation to pay, the drafters nevertheless wanted them to be governed by Article 3 because of the universal treatment of such instruments as money substitutes. They accomplished their objective by specifically excluding the countersignature requirement as a condition for purposes of determining negotiability.[181] The countersignature requirement is a condition to payment, which gives rise to a defense when the proper signature is not made.[182]

[5] Money Orders

A money order is a draft sold by the issuer that enables the purchaser to transmit funds on the credit of the issuer.[183] Money orders are generally purchased by persons who do not have checking accounts but need the safety or convenience of such an instrument to complete a transaction. When buying a money order, the purchaser pays the amount of the money order and a fee to the issuer in exchange for the instrument.

A personal money order is a draft sold by the drawee to the drawer. At the time of the sale, only the amount of the money order is filled in, usually with a check imprinter. The purchaser will add the date and the payee and sign it as the drawer. Personal money orders thus resemble ordinary checks.[184] The drawee does not sign the instrument and therefore does not incur liability to the payee. A personal money order sold by a bank is a check, whereas a sale by any other entity creates a draft.

Bank money orders and postal money orders are distinct. Bank money orders are sold by and drawn only on banks. A bank money order is like a personal check if it is signed by the purchaser as a drawer or a teller's check if it is signed by the bank as the drawer. A postal money order is a draft drawn on the post office.[185] Postal money orders generally are not

---

[180] "A traveler's check is an instrument for payment that combines the marketability of cash with the safety of a bank draft." Xanthopoulos v. Thomas Cook, Inc., 629 F. Supp. 164, 170, 42 U.C.C. Rep. Serv. 883, 892 (S.D. N.Y. 1985).

[181] U.C.C. § 3-106(c). See § 2.02[B][3][d] supra.

[182] "If the person whose specimen signature appears on an instrument fails to countersign the instrument, the failure to countersign is a defense to the obligation of the issuer, but the failure does not prevent a transferee of the instrument from becoming a holder of the instrument." U.C.C. § 3-106(c). A transferee can become a holder because the countersignature is not provided for purposes of indorsement, but rather of identification. U.C.C. § 3-106, Comment 2. A forged countersignature creates a defense, but that defense is not valid against a subsequent party who takes the traveler's check as a holder in due course.

[183] People v. Norwood, 26 Cal. App. 3d 148, 103 Cal. Rptr. 7, 11 U.C.C. Rep. Serv. 118 (1972).

[184] "The distinction between a check and a money order . . .is that the latter is frequently issued, as here, with the amount printed on the face by the drawee." Burke v. First Peoples Bank, 412 A.2d 1089, 1093, 29 U.C.C. Rep. Serv. 176, 181 (1980).

[185] "Postal money orders are subject to federal law." U.C.C. § 3-104, Comment 4.

negotiable because they usually limit transferability to the first transferee and they often are not payable to order or to bearer.[186]

---

[186] United States v. First Nat'l Bank, 263 F. Supp. 298, 4 U.C.C. Rep. Serv. 89 (D. Mass. 1967) (postal money order stated, "More than one endorsement is prohibited by law").

Chapter 3
TRANSFER AND NEGOTIATION

SYNOPSIS

§ 3.01 Overview
§ 3.02 Transfer by Assignment
    [A] Common Law
    [B] Uniform Commercial Code (U.C.C.)
§ 3.03 Transfer of an Instrument — § 3-203
§ 3.04 Negotiation of an Instrument — § 3-201
    [A] Holder Status — § 1-201(20)
    [B] Indorsement — § 3-204
        [1] Indorsements: Special and Blank — § 3-205
            [a] Special
            [b] Blank
            [c] Right to Require a Special Indorsement
            [d] Must Convey Entire Instrument
        [2] Indorsements: Restrictive and Nonrestrictive — § 3-206
            [a] Prohibiting Further Transfer
            [b] Conditional Indorsements
            [c] Collection and Deposit Indorsements
            [d] Trust Indorsements
§ 3.05 Person Entitled to Enforce Instrument — § 3-301
§ 3.06 Issue — § 3-105
    [A] Delivery — § 1-201(14)
    [B] Relationship of the Original Parties — § 3-117

§ 3.01 Overview

A person may want to pass his or her ownership interests and enforcement rights[1] in a negotiable instrument to another person. An ownership interest in the instrument can be passed through the familiar process of assignment, in which case the assignee's interest is governed by the principle of derivative title, applicable through the law of property independent of Article 3. The assignee will receive whatever interest the assignor

---

[1] While other interests and rights also apply to negotiable instruments, this chapter focuses on ownership interests and enforcement rights.

had in the instrument. If the assignor owned the instrument free from any colorable claim by a third party, that will also be the state of the assignee's title. If, on the other hand, the assignor acquired the instrument by theft, the assignee will take subject to the claim of the true owner. In other words, to the extent that the assignor's interest is susceptible to other claims, the assignee is subject to the same deficiencies. The discussion in this chapter commences with a brief review of principles of assignment law as it applies to negotiable instruments.

A person may also be interested in passing the right to enforce an instrument.[2] The approach here is to "transfer the instrument," a process governed by Article 3. Comparable to the rule of derivative title, the transferee, as a baseline of rights, receives any right of the transferor to enforce the instrument. Hence, both title and enforcement rights are, at a minimum, derivative.

Because an instrument is property that is fully negotiable, the interests and rights of transferees dealing with instruments may extend beyond those which are derived. The concept of "negotiation" plays a major role in this respect. Care must be exercised by anyone unfamiliar with the terminology to avoid confusing "negotiability" and "negotiation." Negotiability refers to the form of the paper, whereas negotiation is a method of transfer of possession. Thus, a negotiable instrument may be negotiated, but a particular transfer of interests or rights may not qualify as a negotiation. The previous chapter covered the requisites of negotiability and stressed that negotiability is desirable to promote free transferability. This chapter focuses on the process of negotiation. As the discussion below explains, the factor that distinguishes negotiation from assignment is the status conferred upon the transferee. Negotiation is any change of possession to a person who acquires the status of a holder.[3] Most significantly, the attainment of holder status as a transferee opens the prospect of qualifying as a holder in due course. The rights of a holder in due course are the highest level of rights attainable. Under appropriate circumstances, they can enable a transferee to have greater rights and interests in the instrument than the transferor had. Therefore, most of the discussion in this chapter is devoted to explaining negotiation.

§ 3.02 Transfer by Assignment

[A] Common Law

Although early common law did not recognize "choses in action" as being transferable, most rights today can be assigned. A few limiting factors do restrict the effectiveness of some purported assignments. Some assignments are ineffective because lawmakers have determined that they would violate public policy.[4] In addition, rights that are considered to be personal are

---

[2] Enforcement entails the right to receive payment from a party obligated to pay it.
[3] U.C.C. § 3-201(a).
[4] In re Nance, 556 F.2d 602 (1st Cir. 1977) (no assignment of wages earned by employees).

not assignable. Assignments that might materially alter the nature of the duty undertaken or subject the obligor to some new risk are not assignable.[5] In relation to negotiable instruments, it is significant to note that courts have universally held that the right to receive money under a contract is never personal.[6] A primary reason for this rule is that the law does not consider the debtor's contract to have been materially changed by having to pay a different party than the one with whom the debtor contracted. Thus, the obligation to pay a fixed amount of money that is represented by negotiable instruments is never barred from assignability.

An assignment is simply the voluntary transfer of a right from one party to another.[7] Most often the right transferred is the right to the payment of money. An assignment requires a present transfer, so that a statement of entitlement or a promise to transfer in the future does not qualify. In other words, a party who fails to fulfill a promise to make an assignment in the future may be liable for breach of contract, but the rights at issue will remain with the promisor and cannot be enforced by the promisee. The assignor does not have to use the term "assign" or any other term of art in order to assign a right. An effective assignment of a contract right requires only that the owner of the right manifest a present intention to transfer it to the designated party. When the assignment is accomplished, the transferor of the right is designated as the assignor and the transferee is the assignee. Although an effective assignment need not be in writing, the statute of frauds provision of Article 1 precludes the enforceability of any assignment of a contract right to the extent that it exceeds $5,000 unless a signed writing evidences the transaction.[8]

The most general principle governing assignments is that the assignee "stands in the shoes of the assignor." This colorful phrase simply recognizes that assignments follow the rule of derivative title. Assignors cannot transfer any greater property interest than they have. A thief who steals goods from their owner and sells them to a bona fide purchaser cannot convey good title, and the BFP must relinquish the goods to the true owner. In a similar vein, a thief who steals a written assignment of a right to the payment of money cannot successfully transfer ownership of the writing to a subsequent transferee.

The rights that an assignee receives are also subject to any defenses or claims that the obligor could have asserted against the assignor in the absence of the assignment. If the assignor does not actually have a right against the purported obligor, the assignee does not acquire any rights against the supposed obligor either. The obligor thus can resist payment based on any contract defense that arises under the transaction creating the assigned contract right, such as lack of consideration, breach of warranty, or duress. Counterclaims or setoffs that could have been made against the assignor at the time of the assignment are also valid against

---

[5] Restatement (Second) of Contracts § 317(2)(a) (1979).

[6] Northwest Cooperage & Lumber Co. v. Byers, 133 Mich. 534, 95 N.W. 529 (1903).

[7] Restatement (Second) of Contracts § 317(1).

[8] U.C.C. § 1-206(1).

the assignee. An assignee is susceptible to the same deficiencies that could have been used to assail the assignor's position in the absence of an assignment.

Transactions can be structured to eliminate some of these risks to an assignee. The assignor can contract with the original obligor through a term under which the obligor agrees to waive all defenses and counterclaims against an assignee. The use of such waiver clauses in consumer sales transactions came under judicial attack, until finally, in 1976, a rule promulgated by the Federal Trade Commission defeated their effectiveness.[9] Courts routinely enforce such clauses in agreements between commercial entities,[10] but they are not utilized that often in this context. When an effective clause is utilized, it confers upon a qualifying assignee of a contract right[11] many of the same legal advantages that would be realized if the assignee had become a holder in due course of a negotiable instrument.

One burden imposed on an assignee is the requirement to notify the obligor of the assignment. If not notified that the right to performance has been assigned, the obligor is likely to pay or otherwise perform directly to the assignor. This performance will discharge the obligor from further liability. The assignee should promptly notify the obligor that the right has been assigned so that any continued performance given to the assignor will not constitute a defense that can be successfully asserted against the assignee.

If the assignor continues to receive the performance of the obligor after an effective assignment, the assignee may be able to proceed against the assignor for a breach of warranty. One of the implied warranties given by an assignor to an assignee is that the assignor "will do nothing to defeat or impair the value of the assignment and has no knowledge of any fact which would do so."[12] If the assignor does not have any further right to receive the benefits of performance by the obligor,[13] the assignor would breach the warranty by wrongfully continuing to receive such performance.

The assignor may extend additional warranties to the assignee. Absent a disclaimer, the assignor impliedly warrants that the right being assigned actually exists, that it is free of all defenses and counterclaims, and that any writing evidencing the right assigned which induced the assignee to accept the assignment is genuine and is what it purports to be. The assignor, however, does not impliedly warrant that the obligor will actually perform. Any warranty of the obligor's performance would have to be made expressly by the assignor.

---

[9] 16 C.F.R. § 433. The rule is discussed extensively in Chapter 6. *See* § 6.06[B] *infra*.

[10] Chase Manhattan Bank v. Lake Tire Co., 496 N.E.2d 129, 2 U.C.C. Rep. Serv. 2d 300 (Ind. Ct. App. 1986).

[11] *Cf.* U.C.C. §§ 9-403, 9-404(a). The assignee must have BFP-type attributes to obtain these advantages.

[12] Restatement (Second) of Contracts § 333(1)(a).

[13] Under non-notification secured financing, the debtor who assigns accounts as collateral to secure a loan continues, by agreement with the assignee-secured party, to collect payments from the account debtor.

[B] Uniform Commercial Code (U.C.C.)

The Uniform Commercial Code codifies several provisions that govern the assignment of personal property interests. The most relevant provisions for purposes of comparison with the law of negotiable instruments are found in Article 9.[14] A contract right for the payment of money, whether or not it has yet been earned by performance, is an account under section 9-102(a)(2).[15] This category of personal property is particularly significant because transactions within the scope of Article 9 include the outright sale of accounts, in addition to assignments of accounts as collateral to secure a loan.[16] Sales of accounts are so related to commercial financing that the drafters elected to make them subject to the rules of Article 9, primarily for the purpose of subjecting the buyer to a public-notice requirement in order to defeat the claims of later assignees. Security interest is defined to include the interest of a buyer of accounts.[17] Some transfers of accounts are excluded because they are irrelevant to commercial financing transactions,[18] but the transfer of commercially significant accounts is covered by Article 9.

The applicability of Article 9 imposes additional requirements on the assignee of a security interest in an account. The security interest must be created in compliance with section 9-203, meaning essentially that a security agreement describing the accounts must be in writing and signed by the assignor, the assignee must give value, and the assignor must have rights in the accounts. The statute of frauds incorporated in section 9-203 supersedes the general statute of frauds in section 1-206(1) and its $5,000 limitation. If any of these elements of section 9-203 are not satisfied, the security interest is not enforceable against the obligor or the assignor. Steps to perfect the security interest are generally necessary to achieve the highest possible priority over other claimants in the same account.[19] A prior filing of a financing statement adequately describing the accounts[20] generally will give the secured party an interest that is superior to subsequent buyers or lenders claiming the same accounts.[21]

Even with compliance with these additional requirements of Article 9, a secured party with an interest in accounts remains susceptible to the rule of derivative title. Section 9-404 codifies basic common-law principles of the law of assignments. Thus the assignee is subject to all terms on the underlying contract giving rise to the account and "any defense or claim in

---

[14] *See also* U.C.C. § 2-210 (assignment of rights arising from a contract for sale of goods).

[15] To qualify as an account, the right to payment of money cannot be evidenced by an instrument or chattel paper.

[16] U.C.C. § 9-109(a)(3). The transfer of a limited interest in accounts as collateral for a loan is a conditional assignment, while a sale of accounts is an outright assignment. Both types of transactions are subject to the common-law rules governing assignment, as augmented by certain provisions of Article 9.

[17] U.C.C. § 1-201(37).

[18] U.C.C. § 9-109, Comment 12.

[19] U.C.C. §§ 9-308(a), 9-310(a), (b).

[20] U.C.C. §§ 9-501, 9-502.

[21] U.C.C. § 9-322(a)(1).

recoupment arising from the transaction that gave rise to the contract" and "any other defense or claim of the account debtor [the obligor] against the assignor which accrues before the account debtor receives a notification of the assignment."[22]

When a right to payment of money is evidenced by a negotiable instrument, Article 3 applies. Article 9 will also apply to an instrument when a debtor uses it as collateral to secure a loan. The sale of a promissory note is also within the scope of Articles 3 and 9. The sale of any other type of instrument is governed by the common law of property and Article 3.

Even though an instrument qualifies as negotiable, its transfer may still be governed by the law of assignments. This observation simply recognizes that the starting point for establishing the rights of parties with respect to negotiable instruments is the principle of derivative title. The base principle is that the transferee will receive the same rights as the transferor.

Because it is fully negotiable property, however, the most extensive exceptions to principles of derivative title are possible with negotiable instruments. As a consequence, a transferee may receive greater rights than those of its transferor, including freedom from prior claims to the instrument and freedom from most defenses. The next several chapters establish the legal framework of these relationships. The remainder of this chapter addresses the transfer and negotiation aspects.

§ 3.03 Transfer of an Instrument — § 3-203

An understanding of negotiable instruments law requires a solid conceptualization of what a negotiable instrument is. A negotiable instrument is a form of *personal property* consisting of a *written obligation* to pay money. Sometimes the personal property considerations might be in issue. For example, the transferee of a negotiable instrument may face a claim of conversion brought by a party claiming to be the rightful owner of the instrument, or a party may bring a replevin action claiming that he or she was induced to part with the instrument through fraud. On other occasions the payment obligations may be in dispute. For example, the transferee might seek payment from someone based on the information on the instrument, but be rebuffed because that person contends that he or she did not incur the liability or because he or she asserts an affirmative contract defense, like discharge or duress. A person who takes a negotiable instrument thus should be concerned with both the personal property interests in the instrument and the enforceability of the payment obligations.

These two aspects of negotiable instruments are bifurcated in the Article 3 approach to transfer of an instrument. Section 3-203(a) provides that "[A]n instrument is transferred when it is delivered by a person other than its issuer for the purpose of giving to the person receiving delivery the right

---

[22] U.C.C. § 9-404(a).

to enforce the instrument." Transfer is thus defined to address only the enforceability of the payment obligations. Article 3 does not specifically address the transfer of ownership of an instrument.

The Comments stress that "[t]he right to enforce an instrument and ownership of the instrument are two different concepts."[23] Most people are aware that having a check in bearer form is risky because a thief or finder might receive payment. The technical reason is that, even though neither the thief nor the finder qualifies as the owner of the instrument, either of these entities may enforce the check.[24] For an additional illustration of the difference between ownership and enforcement rights, assume that I purchase a promissory note from you, but for whatever reason you do not give me immediate possession. I clearly may qualify as the new owner of the note, but I cannot yet enforce it.[25] Ownership of the instrument and the right to enforce it are distinct concepts.

Although the transfer of an instrument often will pass title to the transferee, the conveyance of ownership to instruments is not governed by Article 3. The transfer of title to an instrument is determined under the law of personal property,[26] and the touchstone principle is the rule of derivative title. As will be explained in Chapter 6, the concept of negotiability and Article 3 ultimately also have an impact in this area: even though Article 3 does not govern the transfer of title to negotiable instruments, it does include a provision under which some parties attain priority over a prior party with good title or other property claims to the instrument.[27] For now, simply recognize that the transfer of title is not covered directly by Article 3. As a rule, whether title is transferred turns on the intent of the parties to the transaction.

As the definition of transfer makes clear, it is concerned with "giving to the person receiving delivery the right to enforce the instrument."[28] An Article 3 transfer of the instrument thus has to do with conveyance of the transferor's rights to enforce the payment obligations on an instrument. Section 3-203(b) states the legal consequence of the transfer of an instrument. Although the section appears at first glance to state the rule of derivative title, it is not directed toward title. Section 3-203(b) provides that "[t]ransfer of an instrument . . . vests in the transferee any right of the transferor to enforce the instrument . . . ." By limiting the codified rights that vest from transfer to passage of the tranferor's right to enforce an

---

[23] U.C.C. § 3-203, Comment 1.

[24] Either can enforce the instrument because a thief or finder of bearer paper will qualify as a holder. U.C.C. §§ 1-201(20), 3-301. See §§ 3.04[A], 3.05 infra. "A person may be a person entitled to enforce the instrument even though the person is not the owner of the instrument or is in wrongful possession of the instrument." U.C.C. § 3-301. The purpose here is to facilitate the discharge of the maker or drawer, who expects to pay anyone who is bearing the instrument, not to facilitate the designs of the thief.

[25] See U.C.C. § 3-301 (definition of "person entitled to enforce an instrument" generally requires the person to be in possession of the instrument or at least to have been in possession).

[26] U.C.C. § 3-203, Comment 1.

[27] See U.C.C. § 3-306; § 6.02[A] infra.

[28] U.C.C. § 3-203(a).

instrument, the provision basically states a "rule of derivative enforcement rights." This legal effect is reinforced by section 3-301, which includes among the persons with the right to enforce an instrument "a nonholder in possession of the instrument who has the rights of a holder."

Thus, in summary, a transferee's basic rights in a negotiable instrument are derivative of the transferor's rights: the enforcement rights based on section 3-203(b) and the ownership rights based on common law.

This bifurcation of the sources of the derivative rights is critical because of the different requirements for the rights to pass under these different legal sources. Section 3-203(a), which deals with transfer of enforcement rights, establishes two essential requirements for transfer of an instrument— delivery and a specific intent on the part of the transferor that the transferee have the right of enforcement.[29] Delivery is a term of art under the Code meaning "*voluntary* transfer of possession."[30] The theft or loss of an instrument may result in a change of possession, but it is not a delivery, and thus not a transfer of the instrument. For the derivative right to enforce the instrument to pass to the transferee, the transferor must deliver the instrument to the transferee. By way of contrast, the instrument itself generally does not have to be delivered in order to assign one's property rights in the instrument.[31]

The other requirement for transfer of an instrument is that the person delivering it do so in order to give the person receiving delivery the right to enforce the instrument. Transferring an instrument for any other purpose is excluded. This provision is aimed primarily at excluding delivery to a drawee for the purpose of receiving payment of the instrument.[32]

The following diagram can help illustrate the concept of transfer under Article 3.

D'er ---- ▶P ——— ▶X ——— ▶Y ·········▶ Bank
                                                  (pays)

Diagram 3.1

Drawer (D'er) issues a check to Payee (P). P then transfers the check to X and X, in turn, transfers the check to Y. Y then presents the check to the bank upon which it is drawn (Bank) for payment, and Bank pays Y. The transfers in the diagram are designated by the solid lines in the downstream flow of the check toward ultimate payment. In order to obtain payment of the check from Bank, Y will be required to give Bank possession of the check, but, because this delivery is not for the purpose of giving Bank

---

[29] Springfield Oil Services, Inc. v. Mermelstein, 914 F. Supp. 258, 30 U.C.C. Rep. Serv. 2d 217 (N.D. Ill. 1996) (transfer of the notes was made because these requirements were satisfied, irrespective of whether the notes had been indorsed).

[30] U.C.C. § 1-201(14) (emphasis added).

[31] Scheid v. Shields, 269 Or. 236, 524 P.2d 1209 (1974).

[32] U.C.C. § 3-203, Comment 1.

the right to enforce the check, it is not a transfer of the check. The change of possession to Bank is best referred to as surrender of the instrument for payment.[33] In order to distinguish this relinquishment of the instrument from transfer of the instrument, the diagram shows the movement of the check from Y to Bank by a dotted line. In addition, for reasons that are explained later in this chapter,[34] the definition of transfer in section 3-203(a) requires a delivery "by a person other than its issuer." The issue of the check in the diagram was from Drawer to Payee, and is distinguished by use of the broken line. The downstream flow of this check thus was issue, followed by two transfers, and concluded by surrender as part of the presentment for payment.

§ 3.04 Negotiation of an Instrument — § 3-201

Negotiation is very closely related to the concept of transfer of an instrument, but it is broader in its scope. "Negotiation" is defined in Article 3 as "a transfer of possession, whether voluntary or involuntary, of an instrument by a person other than the issuer to a person who thereby becomes its holder."[35] Any transfer of an instrument that results in conferring holder status on the transferee is a transfer by negotiation. In fact, this is the most common method by which instruments are negotiated.[36] However, a party who acquires an instrument without the voluntary participation of the prior possessor, such as a thief or a finder of the instrument, will also attain holder status if the instrument is in bearer form. In such cases the thief or finder will also take the instrument by negotiation. As we shall see, this rule is not designed to protect the thief or finder. It protects the obligor since payment to a holder discharges the instrument,[37] and with bearer paper the obligor is expected to pay whoever is "bearing" (has possession of) it.

Article 3 makes a crucial distinction between transfer of the instrument and transfer of possession. *Transfer of an instrument* is defined in section 3-203(a), and it requires two elements: (1) delivery (a voluntary transfer of possession), plus (2) the transferor's intent to give the transferee the right to enforce the instrument. *Transfer of possession* is an essential component of the definition of negotiation in section 3-201(a). The transfer of possession, however, can be either voluntary or involuntary. The other essential aspect for negotiation is that the person who acquires possession must qualify as a holder. Thus, negotiation by transfer will result when someone becomes a holder through delivery of the instrument with the intent that the holder be able to enforce the instrument. Sometimes, however, holder status is conferred through an involuntary transfer of possession, and that

---

[33] *See* U.C.C. § 3-501(b)(2)(iii); § 5.02[A] *infra*.

[34] *See* § 3.06[A] *infra*.

[35] U.C.C. § 3-201(a).

[36] "Normally, negotiation occurs as the result of a voluntary transfer of possession of an instrument by a holder to another person who becomes the holder as a result of the transfer." U.C.C. § 3-201, Comment 1.

[37] U.C.C. § 3-602(a). *See* 7.02[A] *infra*.

transfer of possession is also negotiation. The crux of negotiation is the acquisition of possession of an instrument by anyone who qualifies as a holder. Negotiation thus refers to a change of possession,[38] whether voluntary or involuntary, and thus irrespective of whether the transfer of possession is by means of a transfer of the instrument.

When negotiation occurs through an involuntary change of possession, as when a thief steals a check in bearer form, the party from whom the check was stolen obviously does not actively participate. Thus the language in the definition that refers to "a transfer of possession . . . of an instrument *by* a person other than the issuer" is problematic. The intent of the drafters, however, is readily ascertainable. To paraphrase the definition, negotiation essentially is a change of possession, whether voluntary or involuntary, of an instrument from a person other than the issuer to a person who thereby becomes its holder.

Consider the following diagram on negotiation.

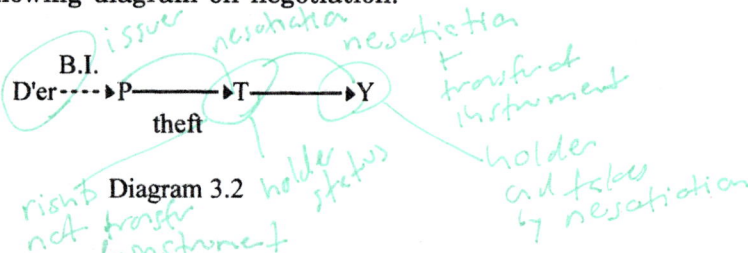

Diagram 3.2

Drawer (D'er) issues a bearer instrument to Payee (P). Thief (T) steals the instrument from P. Because the instrument is in bearer form, T qualifies as a holder upon acquiring possession, and the transfer of possession from P to T constitutes negotiation. The transfer of possession was not voluntary on the part of P, however, and thus does not constitute transfer of the instrument because delivery is missing. T voluntarily delivers the instrument to Y, and thereby transfers the instrument. Because the instrument is still in bearer form, Y is a holder and Y takes by negotiation through transfer of the instrument.

[A] Holder Status — § 1-201(20)

The pivotal concept for negotiation is the creation of holder status. In a transfer of an instrument the transferee can qualify as a holder only if the transfer is by negotiation. A finder or thief can qualify as a holder only by taking the instrument through negotiation (which, as will be seen shortly, will occur only by stealing or finding an instrument in bearer form). Other than the issue of an instrument (which is covered later),[39] negotiation is the exclusive means by which someone can become a holder of a negotiable instrument.

---

[38] "Negotiation always requires a change in possession of the instrument because nobody can be a holder without possessing the instrument, either directly or through an agent." U.C.C. § 3-201, Comment 1.

[39] *See* § 3.06 *infra*. In short, issue refers to the first delivery by the maker or drawer. Transfer and negotiation refer to subsequent changes of possession.

Although it is difficult to appreciate at this early stage of the analysis, the holder concept has enormous significance in the law of negotiable instruments. Suffice it for now to conclude merely that holder status plays a major role with respect to the subsequent transferability of an instrument. Additionally, holder status is a necessary prerequisite for attainment of the highest level of rights and protections — holder in due course status.

For purposes of negotiable instruments, "holder" means "the person in possession if the instrument is payable to bearer or, in the case of an instrument payable to an identified person, if the identified person is in possession."[40] The definition includes dual requirements: To be a holder a person must be in possession of an instrument and the instrument essentially must run to that person. The determination of whether an instrument runs to a particular person depends on whether the instrument is characterized as order paper or bearer paper. This characterization depends on the form of the instrument as it was originally prepared or according to the effect following any appropriate indorsements.

Order paper runs only to the order of the designated person. An instrument that is drawn to the order of a named payee is order paper and (assuming no indorsements) runs only to the person named.[41] The only possible person who can qualify as a holder on such an instrument is the named payee, and that person can qualify only so long as possession of the instrument is retained. When the person to whom order paper runs does not have possession of it, no one is a holder of the instrument. Bearer paper, on the other hand, runs to whoever bears it. In other words, bearer paper always runs to the person who possesses it. An instrument drawn in bearer form is bearer paper (assuming no indorsements), so that anyone who acquires possession of the instrument becomes a holder.

[B] Indorsement — § 3-204

Indorsements can change the nature of the paper and the person to whom it runs. The last indorsement by a holder controls whether the instrument continues as order paper or bearer paper, as well as the specific person, if any, to whom the instrument runs.[42] An appropriate indorsement on an instrument that indicates a specific indorsee is called a "special indorsement" and causes the instrument to run only to that person.[43] The designated payee then becomes the only person who, upon attaining possession, can qualify as the holder of the instrument, at least until the instrument is properly indorsed again.[44] An appropriate indorsement on

---

[40] U.C.C. § 1-201(20).

[41] United Overseas Bank v. Veneers, Inc., 375 F. Supp. 596, 14 U.C.C. Rep. Serv. 1349 (D. Md. 1973) (bank not a holder upon receipt of possession because instrument was drawn to the order of the payee-customer and had not been indorsed).

[42] Northside Bldg. & Inv. Co., Inc. v. Finance Co. of Am., 119 Ga. App. 131, 166 S.E.2d 608, 6 U.C.C. Rep. Serv. 345 (1969) (finance company not a holder despite possession of promissory note because the last indorsement was not to the finance company but rather to its transferor).

[43] U.C.C. § 3-205(a).

[44] Wright v. Bank of Cal., N.A., 81 Cal. Rptr. 11, 6 U.C.C. Rep. Serv. 1165 (Ct. App. 1969) (indorsement generally required on all instruments except bearer paper).

an instrument that does not designate a specific indorsee is a "blank indorsement" and makes the instrument bearer paper that runs to anyone who attains possession.[45] As long as it is in bearer form, anyone who possesses it is a holder. The use of indorsements can convert order paper to bearer paper, and vice-versa. In addition, an indorsement can be used on an order instrument to change the person to whom it runs.

Consider the following illustration. If a check is issued to John Doe as the named payee, Doe becomes the holder upon attaining possession of the check, because it is drawn to his order. If Doe indorses the check "Pay Richard Roe, /s/ John Doe," the check then runs to Roe and Roe becomes the holder if he gets possession, because the check is indorsed to him. If Roe subsequently indorses the check without designating a specific indorsee, anyone who acquires possession will qualify as a holder because the check is indorsed in blank. A subsequent holder could reconvert the check from bearer paper by indorsing it to name a specific payee, such as Kelly Coe. The check would then run only to Coe, and only she could qualify as a holder from the time of the latest indorsement. She would not actually become a holder, however, until she receives the check. If Coe later gives the check to Paula Poe, but does not indorse it, Poe would not qualify as a holder of the check. Poe would have the necessary possession, but the check would not run to her, because the last indorsement leaves it running to Coe. There would be a transfer to Poe, and Poe would have the right to enforce the instrument as a result of that transfer, but Poe would lack holder status and therefore be ineligible for holder-in-due-course status.[46]

The requirements for negotiation depend on whether the instrument is in bearer or order form at the time a person acquires possession. If the instrument is in bearer form — either because it was issued as bearer paper and has not been indorsed or because the last indorsement by a holder does not designate a specific indorsee — "it may be negotiated by transfer of possession alone."[47] A bearer instrument runs to whoever is in possession, so once anyone acquires possession, the dual elements for holder status are satisfied. A transfer of possession of an instrument in order form would place the transferee in possession, but it would not confer holder status if the instrument ran to someone else. In addition to the change in possession, negotiation of an order instrument requires "its indorsement by the holder."[48]

All indorsements must be written on the instrument itself.[49] Subsequent transferees must be able to determine by examining the instrument

---

[45] U.C.C. § 3-205(b); Lamson v. Commercial Credit Corp., 187 Colo. 382, 531 P.2d 966, 16 U.C.C. Rep. Serv. 756 (1975) (indorsement by payee in only its name before deposit in its bank account made the checks bearer paper).

[46] Poe would also have a specifically-enforceable right to Coe's signature. U.C.C. § 3-203(c).

[47] U.C.C. § 3-201(b).

[48] U.C.C. § 3-201(b); Town of Freeport v. Ring, 727 A.2d 901, 38 U.C.C. Rep. Serv. 2d 1225 (Me. Sup. Jud. Ct. 1999) (signature of the payee was required to negotiate a check made out to his order).

[49] U.C.C. § 3-204(a); Shepherd Mall State Bank v. Johnson, 603 P.2d 1115, 27 U.C.C. Rep. Serv. 1019 (Okla. 1979) (writing on separate sheet of paper does not have the effect of an indorsement).

whether indorsements have been made. The adverse impact on free alienability of commercial paper would be intolerable if transferees were required to rely on indorsements on separate writings to establish their holder status. Although they are generally placed at the top of the reverse side of the instrument, the Code does not require any specific location for indorsements.[50] However, the promulgation of Regulation CC by the Governing Board of the Federal Reserve System has added a requirement of zones on checks for indorsement by specified parties.[51] In the unusual event that so many indorsements have been written that no more space is available on the instrument, a separate piece of paper (called an allonge) can be affixed to the instrument to become part of it.[52]

All indorsements fit into three mutually exclusive classifications under Article 3. Any indorsement is blank or special, restrictive or nonrestrictive, and qualified or unqualified. Each of these classifications serves a distinct function.[53] The category of qualified or unqualified relates to the question of the contractual undertaking that results from an indorser signing a negotiable instrument. It is covered in the next chapter in the discussion of those undertakings.[54] The other two classifications of indorsements are explained below.

[1] Indorsements: Special and Blank — § 3-205

The classification of an indorsement as special or blank determines whether the instrument is order or bearer paper and whether a subsequent indorsement is necessary for further negotiation. The distinguishing requirements and the legal consequences for these indorsements are codified in section 3-205. The last indorsement by a holder affects the subsequent characterization of the instrument as order or bearer paper.

---

[50] United States v. Tufi, 536 F.2d 855, 19 U.C.C. Rep. Serv. 543 (9th Cir. 1976) (indorsement on front of instrument valid). In the event of ambiguity concerning the capacity in which a signature is made, the Code treats it as an indorsement. U.C.C. § 3-204(a).

[51] 12 C.F.R. § 35. For discussion of the indorsement standard of Regulation CC, see § 11.04[C][3] *infra*.

[52] U.C.C. § 3-204(a). "An indorsement on an allonge is valid even though there is sufficient space on the instrument for an indorsement." U.C.C. § 3-204, Comment 1. The court in Estrada v. River Oaks Bank & Trust Co., 550 S.W.2d 719, 22 U.C.C. Rep. Serv. 83 (Tex. Ct. App. 1977), appropriately did not recognize a single collateral assignment that was stapled to four unindorsed promissory notes as an allonge or an indorsement. A single signature could not serve as an indorsement of all four notes because it could not be so attached to each note as to become a part of each different note. The court also would not allow it as an indorsement of only one of the notes because the circumstances were ambiguous as to which note would have been intended to be indorsed.

[53] " 'Indorsement' means a signature, other than that of a signer as maker, drawer, or acceptor, that alone or accompanied by other words is made on an instrument for the purpose of (i) negotiating the instrument, (ii) restricting payment of the instrument, or (iii) incurring indorser's liability on the instrument. . . ." U.C.C. § 3-204(a).

[54] *See* § 4.03 *infra*.

[a] Special

A special indorsement contains the signature of the indorser and "identifies a person to whom it makes the instrument payable."[55] An indorsement providing either "Pay Ebenezer Scrooge" or "Pay to the order of Ebenezer Scrooge" qualifies. The absence of the words "to the order of" does not destroy negotiability of the instrument because indorsements have nothing to do with negotiability. Negotiability is determined exclusively by the terms of the instrument itself. An instrument issued payable to order or to bearer contains the requisite words of negotiability,[56] and the negotiability is completely unaffected by any subsequent indorsements.

A special indorsement by the holder of an instrument makes the instrument payable to the person identified.[57] Irrespective of the characterization of the paper prior to the indorsement, following a special indorsement by the holder, the instrument is order paper.[58]

From the time of the indorsement, the instrument runs to the specified indorsee. Thereafter, only that person can qualify as its holder. Furthermore, because the instrument runs to the specified payee, no further negotiation to any other person will be possible without the indorsement of the specified payee.[59]

An indorsement made by an inappropriate party will have legal consequences that will be covered later,[60] but for present purposes, such an indorsement is ineffective to negotiate order paper.[61] Therefore, if an indorsement is made by someone other than the holder personally, the effectiveness of the indorsement turns initially upon the authority of that person to sign on behalf of the holder.[62] An unauthorized signature[63] is not made on behalf of the holder, and thus cannot serve as the necessary indorsement required for negotiation. As a result, the delivery of an instrument with an indorsement forged in the name of the person to whom an order instrument runs is not negotiation and cannot confer holder status on the transferee.[64] Furthermore, because the instrument will continue to

---

[55] U.C.C. § 3-205(a).

[56] U.C.C. § 3-104(a) ("payable to bearer or to order *at the time it is issued or first comes into possession of a holder*")(emphasis added). See § 2.02[E] *supra*.

[57] U.C.C. § 3-205(a).

[58] Coltharp v. Calcasieu-Marine Nat'l Bank, 199 So. 2d 568 (La. Ct. App. 1967) (check indorsed in blank and then specially indorsed).

[59] U.C.C. § 3-205(a).

[60] See § 4.05[B] *infra*.

[61] Behring Int'l, Inc. v. Greater Houston Bank, 662 S.W.2d 642, 38 U.C.C. Rep. Serv. 544 (Tex. Ct. App. 1983).

[62] When the indorsement is authorized, its effectiveness also depends upon its form. U.C.C. § 3-402. See § 4.05[A] *infra*. It is sufficient for present purposes to recognize that an authorized signature in the name of the person to whom the instrument runs will be an effective indorsement.

[63] "'Unauthorized' signature or indorsement means one made without actual, implied or apparent authority and includes a forgery." U.C.C. § 1-201(43).

[64] Summerlin v. National Serv. Indus., Inc., 72 N.C. App. 476, 325 S.E.2d 12, 40 U.C.C. Rep. Serv. 1762 (1985) (wife deposited husband's check without authority).

run to the person whose name was forged on the indorsement, <u>no further transferees of the instrument will be able to qualify as holders</u>.

The diagram below should help visualize the relationship of the parties to these legal concepts. The words included in quotation marks above each transfer of possession indicate what the transferor wrote on the instrument.

```
                    "Pay X"
         O.I.       "P"  ─signed
     D'er ----▶ P ─────────▶ X
                 │           │
                 │       "Pay Y"   signed
                 ▼       "X" ─          "Y"
                 T ──────────▶ Y ──────────▶ Z
```

Diagram 3.3

Drawer (D'er) issues <u>an order instrument to Payee (P)</u>, which makes P the holder of the instrument. <u>P later specially indorses the instrument to X and delivers it to X</u>, whereby <u>X became the new holder</u> of the instrument through negotiation. Thief (T) steals the instrument from X, which gives T only wrongful possession. T did not acquire the check through negotiation because, in addition to the change in possession, negotiation requires X's indorsement. X also did not assign or transfer her ownership interest in the instrument or the right to enforce it to T. Possession changed hands, but it was simply a wrongful taking through which T acquired neither an interest in the instrument nor any right to enforce it. The downward direction of the arrow symbolizes a change in possession that did not involve either negotiation or a transfer by the prior party. T then specially indorses the instrument to Y with a forgery of X's name. Because the prior indorsement shows that the instrument runs to X, T had to forge X's signature in order to deceive Y into believing that the instrument would run to her upon delivery. T transferred the check to Y, but not by negotiation, and Y does not become a holder.[65] Consequently Y receives only T's right to enforce the instrument, and T does not have any.[66] The chain of title to the instrument was broken with the forged indorsement, and therefore, all subsequent transferees will trace their title through the thief. Irrespective of anything that Y does, short of acquiring X's indorsement on the instrument, the subsequent transfer to Z cannot confer holder status on Z and thus cannot qualify as negotiation. The check is still properly payable only to X.

Occasionally a check will be payable to a specific person but the name on the instrument will be stated incorrectly or misspelled. Article 3 recognizes an indorsement by the intended person to be effective whether it is provided in the mistaken or misspelled name or it is written in the

---

[65] At this point, no one is a holder of the instrument because it continues to run to X.
[66] *See* U.C.C. § 3-301; § 3.05 *infra*.

person's correct name.[67] Because an indorsement in either form is an effective indorsement by the holder, it will transfer the indorser's interest and is a negotiation. Either indorsement is likely to be commercially unacceptable to the transferee, however. An indorsement in a name or spelling that differs from the indorser's correct name poses potential problems if the identity of the indorser must be proven. If an indorsement solely in the correct name of the indorser differs from the name on the instrument, it may raise doubts of prospective parties to the instrument whether the holder's indorsement was provided. The Code, therefore, recognizes that the indorser in these circumstances can indorse the instrument in both the incorrect form that appears on the instrument and the correct form. Because the dual-form indorsement is desirable to protect the interests of the person receiving the instrument from the indorser, a person who is paying the instrument or purchasing it can require an indorsement in both names.[68]

[b] Blank

A blank indorsement does not designate any specific indorsee.[69] All that is required is a signature.[70] If the instrument that is indorsed was order paper, the indorsement in blank by the holder converts it to bearer paper.[71] Because bearer paper runs to anyone who possesses it, a change in possession is all that is required for further negotiation until the instrument is specially indorsed.[72]

Bearer paper is risky because anyone who acquires possession, even a thief, becomes a holder and can negotiate the paper to someone else who might qualify as a holder in due course. To address this risk, the Code allows a holder to convert a blank indorsement that consists only of a signature into a special indorsement. The holder can make the conversion simply "by writing, above the signature of the indorser, words identifying the person to whom the instrument is made payable."[73] Holders can make these instruments payable to their own order by inserting their own name together with the payment instruction above the indorser's signature. Alternatively, they can include the name of some other person to whom they wish the instrument to run.

---

[67] U.C.C. § 3-204(d); Agaliotis v. Agaliotis, 38 N.C. App. 42, 247 S.E.2d 28, 25 U.C.C. Rep. Serv. 179 (1978) (father's indorsement of check erroneously naming his son as payee did not violate any rights of the son because the father was the proper payee).

[68] U.C.C. § 3-204(d).

[69] "If an indorsement is made by the holder of an instrument and it is not a special indorsement, it is a 'blank indorsement.'" U.C.C. § 3-205(b).

[70] All indorsements require a signature. U.C.C. § 3-204(a).

[71] U.C.C. § 3-205(b).

[72] U.C.C. §§ 3-205(b), 3-201(a).

[73] U.C.C. § 3-205(c).

Compare the results on the facts diagrammed below with the outcome of the related facts in the previous diagram.

```
            O.I.    "P"
     D'er----▶P──────▶X──────▶T──────▶Y──────▶Z
                      theft
```

Diagram 3.4

Drawer (D'er) again issues an order instrument to Payee (P), which makes P the holder of the instrument, but this time P makes a blank indorsement, rather than a special indorsement, before delivering the instrument to X. X still qualifies as a holder, because the instrument runs to her while she is in possession, and the transfer of the instrument to X was by negotiation. Thief (T), however, also acquires the instrument by negotiation, and T is a holder of the instrument in the form of bearer paper. T is empowered to negotiate the instrument, which is accomplished simply by delivering it to Y. Y is a holder, and if she meets the additional bona fide purchaser requisites to qualify as a holder in due course,[74] Y takes the instrument free from X's claim of ownership.[75] As will be explained subsequently, Z will be similarly protected, either by qualifying as a holder in due course in her own right or by relying on derivative rights to take any holder in due course rights available to Y.[76] X could have protected herself against the risk of the loss of her ownership interest in the instrument by inserting the words "Pay X" or "Pay to the order of X" above the blank indorsement of P.

[c] Right to Require a Special Indorsement

A transferee who takes order paper cannot qualify as a holder without the indorsement of the person to whom the instrument runs. Even a purchaser who pays value and fully expects to take the instrument by negotiation cannot achieve holder status without the indorsement. To protect these transferees when the indorsement is omitted fraudulently or by oversight, Article 3 creates a right that is enforceable by an action in specific performance against a transferor who refuses to indorse: "Unless otherwise agreed, if an instrument is transferred for value and the transferee does not become a holder because of lack of indorsement by the transferor, the transferee has a specifically enforceable right to the unqualified indorsement of the transferor. . . ."[77] Negotiation will not occur until

---

[74] U.C.C. § 3-302(a). *See* § 6.01 *infra*.

[75] U.C.C. § 3-306. *See* § 6.02[A] *infra*. If T enforced payment of the instrument, X would still suffer harm. Because T is a holder, payment to T effects a discharge of D's obligation to pay. With a special indorsement, payment to T would not have this effect. For discussion of the discharge concepts, see § 7.02[A] *infra*.

[76] *See* § 6.02[C] *infra*.

[77] U.C.C. § 3-203(c).

the indorsement is made, but codification of the right facilitates the process of getting the indorsement.[78]

A transferee for value is not entitled to the unqualified indorsement of the transferor when the parties have agreed otherwise. For example, a holder might pledge promissory notes to secure a loan by delivering the notes to the secured party and assigning them as collateral. Pursuant to the security agreement, the secured party might not be entitled to the indorsement of the transferor until default on the secured transaction, or the secured party might be empowered in the security agreement to indorse on behalf of the transferor-debtor in the event of default.

[d] Must Convey Entire Instrument

An instrument can be negotiated only if it conveys the entire instrument.[79] Consequently, an indorsement in the form "Pay 1/2 to A" is not effective for negotiation because it does not convey the entire instrument.[80] Actually, the requirement is even more stringent because "[a]ny indorsement which purports to convey to any party less than the entire amount of the instrument is not effective for negotiation."[81] Thus, an indorsement in the form "Pay 1/2 to A and 1/2 to B" also would be ineffective for negotiation, and neither A nor B would qualify as a holder. The indorsement would burden the obligor with having to pay more than one person, and it would split the cause of action on the instrument. The instrument itself cannot be split, so further negotiation of the instrument or of the split interests would adversely affect free alienability of negotiable instruments. Any indorsement that purports to convey less than the entire instrument operates only as a partial assignment,[82] and its legal effect is left to local law.[83] The appropriate form in which to negotiate an instrument to two parties is to have the instrument run to them both without apportioning it, such as "Pay A and B." This indorsement is effective for negotiation because "it transfers the entire cause of action to A and B as tenants in common."[84] If the maker or drawer pays the instrument to either A or B

---

[78] The transferee nevertheless incurs risk in delaying before acquiring the indorsement. A transferee cannot qualify as a holder in due course until all of the elements of section 3-302(a) are satisfied. Delay in getting the indorsement delays attainment of holder status and leaves the transferee vulnerable to intervening notice of a defense or claim to the instrument that will preclude holder in due course status. In Northside Bldg. & Inv. Co. v. Finance Co. of Am., 119 Ga. App. 131, 166 S.E.2d 608, 6 U.C.C. Rep. Serv. 345 (1969), the transferee was not able to have the note indorsed until after it had notice that an installment on the note was overdue. Thus, it could not qualify as a holder in due course.

[79] U.C.C. § 3-203(d).

[80] Hewett v. Marine Midland Bank, 86 A.D.2d 263, 449 N.Y.S.2d 745, 33 U.C.C. Rep. Serv. 1696 (1982) (indorsee had only rights of a partial assignee of $600,000 note indorsed to the extent of the first $300,000).

[81] U.C.C. § 3-203, Comment 5.

[82] U.C.C. § 3-203(d).

[83] U.C.C. § 3-203, Comment 5.

[84] U.C.C. § 3-203, Comment 5. Further negotiation of the instrument will require the indorsement of both of the joint tenants. U.C.C. § 3-110(d). Foremost Ins. Co. v. First City Sav. & Loan Ass'n, 374 So. 2d 840, 27 U.C.C. Rep. Serv. 713 (Miss. 1979) (transferee of check

without obtaining the indorsement of the other, the payment will not discharge the maker's or drawer's obligation to the other.[85]

[2] Indorsements: Restrictive and Nonrestrictive — § 3-206

Indorsements are also classified as restrictive or nonrestrictive. This classification determines whether subsequent transferees must apply the purchase price that they give for the instrument, and whether the payor of the instrument must pay the proceeds, consistent with a restriction in the indorsement. Generally, restrictive indorsements impose limitations on how value given should be applied or paid. Applying value properly can be important to a transferee because noncompliance will preclude attainment of holder in due course status[86] and make the transferee liable for conversion.[87] Certain parties, however, are not affected by restrictive indorsements.[88]

Prior law recognized four categories of restrictive indorsements: (1) prohibitions of further transfer, (2) conditional indorsements, (3) indorsements for collection or deposit, and (4) trust indorsements. Revised Article 3 includes provisions in section 3-206 on all four categories. With respect to the first two categories, however, it both precludes any legal effectiveness for the restrictions and ends their characterization as restrictive indorsements.

[a] Prohibiting Further Transfer

Certainly an indorsement that flatly prohibits any further transfer of the instrument might appropriately be designated as a restrictive indorsement.[89] If this type of restriction were recognized to be effective, however, it would undercut the policy of free alienability of commercial paper to an intolerable extent. Article 3 therefore precludes the effectiveness of the restriction: "An indorsement limiting payment to a particular person or otherwise prohibiting further transfer or negotiation of the instrument is not effective to prevent further transfer or negotiation of the instrument."[90] Because the indorsement is not effective as a restrictive indorsement, it is not even described as restrictive.[91]

---

issued to joint payees that was not indorsed by one of the payees held not a holder); Pamar Enterprises, Inc. v. Huntington Banks of Michigan, 228 Mich. App. 727, 35 U.C.C. Rep. Serv. 2d 1298 (1998) (instrument payable jointly may be negotiated, discharged, or enforced only by all of them). Order paper that has been indorsed "Pay A or B" can be negotiated by either person acting alone. U.C.C. § 3-110(d).

[85] This statement is subject to some limitations based on estoppel or ratification.

[86] U.C.C. § 3-206(e).

[87] U.C.C. § 3-206(c)(1), (2).

[88] See § 3.04[B][2][c] infra.

[89] See U.C.C. § 3-206, Comment 2 (e.g., "Pay A only").

[90] U.C.C. § 3-206(a).

[91] U.C.C. § 3-206, Comment 2.

[b] Conditional Indorsements

Conditional indorsements are treated precisely the same way. An indorser might condition negotiation on the occurrence of a specified event. For example, the payee on a note might include with her signature the following language: "Pay Midas after he delivers to me the title to his gold mine." If they were effective, conditional indorsements would also affect the free alienability of instruments because satisfaction of the condition would not be apparent on the face of the instrument and would thus require independent investigation. Conditional indorsements, therefore, are also denied any effectiveness,[92] and the indorsements consequently are also not considered to be restrictive.

[c] Collection and Deposit Indorsements

Collection and deposit indorsements are the most common forms of restrictive indorsements. They are created by the inclusion of the words "for collection," "for deposit," "pay any bank" or any other terms that signify a purpose of collection by a bank for the indorser or for a particular account.[93] The indorsements are used when the indorser wishes to restrict the way in which the value given by any subsequent taker or payor will be applied or paid.[94] Section 3-206(c) states specific rules that dictate the consequences of failing to comply with these restrictive indorsements.

A check will not be paid until it is presented for payment to the bank upon which it is drawn and the bank decides to honor it. The payee of a check drawn on a bank in a distant city thus faces an initial problem of how to accomplish the required presentment. The payee could travel to the distant bank and make personal presentment, but the cost and inconvenience of the travel might well exceed the value of the check. Alternatively, the payee might utilize the services of an agent, particularly if the agent is already located in the distant city. The bank will insist upon paying only a holder in order to achieve discharge on the check for the drawer,[95] so the payee's blank or special indorsement to the agent will be required before forwarding the check to the agent. Negotiation to the agent is only for purposes of collection, however, so the payee should add the words "for collection only" to make the indorsement restrictive. The payor bank then will have to pay the amount of the check to the agent, and the agent should remit those proceeds to the payee. If the bank does not comply with the restriction but instead pays in an inconsistent manner, such as applying the check to a debt that the agent owes to the bank or crediting the check

---

[92] "A person paying the instrument or taking it for value or collection may disregard the condition, and the rights and liabilities of that person are not affected by whether the condition has been fulfilled." U.C.C. § 3-206(b).

[93] U.C.C. § 3-206(c).

[94] La Junta State Bank v. Travis, 727 P.2d 48, 2 U.C.C. Rep. Serv. 2d 805 (Colo. 1986) (indorsement "for deposit" requires depositary bank or other taker to apply funds in accordance with that direction).

[95] Technically, discharge occurs when payment is made to any party with a right to enforce the instrument, but as precaution the payor bank will insist that the presenter be a holder.

to agent's personal account, the bank will be liable to the payee for conversion.[96]

Rather than presenting the check for payment to the bank, the agent might exercise the right of a holder and negotiate the check to another party. The transferee must apply the value given for the check consistently with the payee's restrictive indorsement. This requirement will be satisfied by paying the agent the amount of the check, because it is precisely this form of payment that the indorsement envisions. On the other hand, if the transferee takes the check in exchange for cancelling a debt of the agent or extending credit or some other exchange to the agent, the value given for the check would not be applied consistently with the restrictive indorsement and the transferee would be liable for conversion.[97] The collection indorsement thus protects the payee against improper applications of value for the instrument by either subsequent transferees or the payor, although the payee still bears the risk that the chosen agent may abscond with the money received.

An even more efficient method can be used to collect the check. The payee can use the bank-collection system, in which the collecting banks will act as agent and subagents of the payee.[98] The payee simply has to deposit the check in his or her account with a local bank to initiate the collection process.[99] The check is then passed through banking channels to the city in which the payor bank is located, whereupon the collecting bank makes the necessary presentment for payment.[100] Under traditional bank-collection procedures, once a check was deposited for collection, banks often indorsed it "pay any bank." This restrictive indorsement locked the check into the bank-collection system because it allowed only a bank to acquire the rights of a holder until a bank specially indorsed the check to a person who is not a bank.[101] If the check were lost or stolen during collection, the finder or thief could not qualify as a holder and thus would lack the power to negotiate the check. Regulation CC now affects the use of this particular restrictive indorsement.[102] Chapter 11 describes the check-collection system in detail and explains this application of Regulation CC.[103]

A deposit indorsement can provide comparable protection for the indorser. A payee who indorses a check "for deposit only" provides notice to

---

[96] U.C.C. § 3-206(c)(3) (direct presentment for payment over the counter by the indorser's agent).

[97] U.C.C. § 3-206(c)(1) (person, other than a bank, who purchases the check from the indorser's agent).

[98] U.C.C. § 4-201(a). See § 11.02[A][1] *infra*.

[99] This bank is known as the depositary bank, as it is the first bank to take the check for collection. U.C.C. § 4-105(2).

[100] The bank by which the check is payable as drawn is the payor bank. U.C.C. § 4-105(3). The payor bank is also commonly referred to as the drawee bank. All banks that handle the check for collection, with the exception of the payor bank, are known collectively as collecting banks. U.C.C. § 4-105(5).

[101] U.C.C. § 4-201(b).

[102] 12 C.F.R. § 229.35(c).

[103] See § 11.04[C][3] *infra*.

the depositary bank that the check is to be credited to the payee's account.[104] The payee then can safely mail the check to the bank or give it to his or her agent to take to the bank. The only way that a depositary bank can apply value consistently with the indorsement is to credit the payee's account. If the bank gives money over the counter for the check, either to a thief or to the agent, it will have converted the check and incur liability to the payee.[105] Similarly, the bank cannot credit the check to any account other than the payee's or apply the check to an outstanding indebtedness.[106]

Article 3 exempts some banks from having to observe a restrictive indorsement. Section 3-206(c)(4) identifies them as follows:

> [A] payor bank [which is not also the depositary bank] or an intermediary bank may disregard the indorsement and is not liable if the proceeds of the instrument are not received by the indorser or applied consistently with the indorsement.

The practical effect of this provision is that the only bank that will be affected by a restrictive indorsement made by someone outside of the bank-collection chain will be the first bank to deal with the instrument.[107] When a customer deposits a check for collection with a depositary bank, the bank teller should examine the check for restrictive indorsements. When someone presents the check directly to the payor bank and demands payment, the teller again should look for restrictive indorsements before paying it. When a depositary bank forwards a check for collection, and it passes through additional intermediary banks prior to presentment for payment, these intermediary banks will not have a practical opportunity to examine the check. These banks typically handle checks in bulk with sorting machines that read encoded information to route them properly to the payor bank. These machines cannot read indorsements on the checks. Similarly, checks presented to the payor bank through the bank-collection system are often sorted and paid through automated systems, so that again it is

---

[104] Mid-Atlantic Tennis Courts, Inc. v. Citizens Bank & Trust Co., 658 F. Supp. 140, 4 U.C.C. Rep. Serv. 2d 137 (D. Md. 1987).

[105] U.C.C. § 3-206(c)(2); Cairo Cooperative Exchange v. First Nat'l Bank, 228 Kan. 613, 620 P.2d 805, 30 U.C.C. Rep. Serv. 1025 (1980).

[106] Brite Lite Lamps Corp. v. Manufacturers Hanover Trust Co., 34 U.C.C. Rep. Serv. 1221 (N.Y. Sup. Ct. 1982) (bank deposited checks restrictively indorsed by corporate payee into the personal account of an employee of the payee); Salsman v. National Community Bank, 102 N.J. Super. 482, 246 A.2d 162, 5 U.C.C. Rep. Serv. 779, *aff'd on opinion below*, 105 N.J. Super. 164, 251 A.2d 460 (1969) (bank allowed check restrictively indorsed to an estate to be deposited into personal account of an attorney). The court in Spenser v. Sterling Bank, 35 U.C.C. Rep. Serv. 2d 398 (Ca. Ct. App. 1998), erroneously concluded that the deposit into a third-party's account of a check, which had been indorsed in the name of the payee "For Deposit Only," was not inconsistent with the restrictive indorsement. The court reasoned that the indorsement did not use "words indicating a purpose of having the instrument collected by a bank for the indorser or for a particular account." To the contrary, the quoted language from section 3-206(c) clearly establishes that the words "for deposit" do establish such an indication.

[107] La Sara Grain Co. v. First Nat'l Bank, 673 S.W.2d 558, 38 U.C.C. Rep. Serv. 963 (Tex. 1984); Underpinning & Foundation Constructors, Inc. v. Chase Manhattan Bank, 46 N.Y.2d 459, 386 N.Y.S.2d 1319, 414 N.E.2d 298, 25 U.C.C. Rep. Serv. 1104 (1979).

impractical for bank personnel to examine each individual check. Section 3-206(c)(4) is simply a concession to these banks in recognition of the volume of checks and the automated procedures that they have had to implement to cope with it. The rights of a restrictive indorser thus can apply only against parties outside of the bank-collection process or against the first bank in the collection process.

[d] Trust Indorsements

A final category of restrictive indorsements is trust indorsements. These indorsements indicate that the indorsee holds the instrument for the benefit of a third person, and are designated by language such as "Pay A in trust for B," "Pay A for B," or "Pay A as agent for B." Trustees often legitimately sell trust assets, so a holder under a trust indorsement is empowered to negotiate the instrument, and bona fide purchasers have the opportunity to attain holder-in-due-course status. The possibility also exists, however, that the trustee may wrongly transfer an instrument for his or her own benefit rather than for the beneficiary.

A trust indorsement does not in itself constitute any notice of breach of fiduciary duty by the trustee. A subsequent transferee and the person who pays the instrument are unaffected by the restriction in the indorsement, so long as they do not have notice of the trustee's breach.[108] In the absence of notice of breach of fiduciary duty,[109] the instrument can be purchased from the indorsee or it can be paid without concerns over whether the indorsee violated a fiduciary duty to the indorser.

§ 3.05 Person Entitled to Enforce Instrument — § 3-301

The revision to Article 3 includes a new defined term: a "person entitled to enforce" an instrument, who is "(i) the holder of the instrument, (ii) a nonholder in possession of the instrument who has the rights of a holder, or (iii) a person not in possession of the instrument who is entitled to enforce the instrument pursuant to Section 3-309 or 3-418(d)."[110] Although discussion of the last category in this definition must be deferred,[111] the categories based on holder status and nonholder in possession are directly relevant to the discussion in this chapter.

By far the most common means of attaining the right to enforce an instrument is to become the holder of the instrument. By taking an instrument that runs to him or her, a person can acquire the right to enforce the instrument and, alternatively, the right to negotiate it to someone else. Because these rights apply to any holder of an instrument, even finders

---

[108] U.C.C. § 3-206(d)(2).

[109] For elaboration on the standard of notice of breach of fiduciary duty *see* U.C.C. § 3-307 and § 6.01[D][2][c] *infra*.

[110] U.C.C. § 3-301.

[111] *See* §§ 4.06, 9.01[C][1] *infra*.

and thieves of instruments that qualify (*i.e.*, those in bearer form) can enforce them.[112]

Another person who is entitled to enforce an instrument is "a nonholder in possession of the instrument who has the rights of a holder."[113] This category is a direct result of the concept of transfer. Any transfer of an instrument vests in the transferee the right of the transferor to enforce the instrument.[114] If the transfer is by negotiation, the transferee receives possession of the instrument and qualifies as a holder. If a prior indorsement that is required for the instrument to run to the transferee is missing, however, the transferee cannot qualify as a holder. When such an instrument is transferred, the transferee is a nonholder in possession of the instrument. Through the derivative rights principle, the transferee will receive any rights to enforce the instrument that were vested in its transferor.[115]

For an illustration of this concept, consider the facts diagramed below.

```
                  "Pay X"
                    "P"
    D'er----▶P────────▶X────────▶Y
```

Diagram 3.5

Drawer (D'er) issues a draft to Payee (P), who indorses the draft through a special indorsement to X. X becomes a holder upon receiving possession of the draft with the special indorsement. X then transfers the draft to Y, but for whatever reason fails to indorse it. Y cannot qualify as a holder of the draft despite having possession because it still runs to X. Y qualifies as a nonholder in possession of the instrument. Y also has X's rights as a holder because the draft was transferred by X to Y. Y thus is a person entitled to enforce the draft. If Y had stolen the draft from X, Y could not enforce it.[116] The draft was order paper running to X, so Y could not qualify

---

[112] The purpose of allowing the rights of a holder to apply to anyone who qualifies for the status is not to protect scoundrels like finders and thieves who wrongfully deal with the paper as though it is their own. Rather, the desired free transferability of negotiable instruments depends upon bona fide purchasers being able to take instruments free of claims and defenses of prior parties without having to investigate beyond what appears on the instrument itself.

[113] U.C.C. § 3-301; Ninth RMA Partners, L.P. v. Krass, 57 Conn. App. 1, 746 A.2d 826, 41 U.C.C. Rep. Serv. 2d 585 (Conn. Ct. App. 2000) (FDIC succeeded to the rights of the holder by federal law when the holder bank became insolvent, and subsequent transferees acquired the rights of a holder to enforce the instrument).

[114] U.C.C. § 3-203(b).

[115] The court in Copple v. Boatman's First Nat'l Bank of Oklahoma, 958 P.2d 820, 37 U.C.C. Rep. Serv. 2d 702 (Okla. Ct. Civ. App. 1998), could not ascertain whether the transferee was a person entitled to enforce a check and thus had to remand the case. The payee on the check was "CCSI," but the nature of the payee's business association was not shown on the record and the authority of the individual making the transfer to act on behalf of the payee was unknown.

[116] Furthermore, if D paid Y, D would not be discharged.

as a holder. Y would be a nonholder in possession of the draft but, because the draft had not been transferred to him, Y did not acquire the rights of a holder.

Even though a nonholder in possession of an instrument who has the rights of a holder can enforce an instrument just like a holder, a holder will enjoy significant procedural advantages in attaining payment. Holders are entitled to presumptions of entitlement to payment upon producing the instrument, whereas the transferee who is not a holder must prove the derivative rights.[117] Subsequent discussion will explain these procedural differences and demonstrate the importance of the concept of persons who are entitled to enforce an instrument.[118] For now, an identification of the first two categories of parties that fit the definition is sufficient.

§ 3.06 Issue — § 3-105

[A] Delivery — § 1-201(14)

"Issue" is the "first delivery of an instrument by the maker or drawer, whether to a holder or nonholder, for the purpose of giving rights on the instrument to any person."[119] It generally occurs when a maker or drawer prepares a negotiable instrument and delivers it directly to the payee. As will be seen in the next chapter,[120] a drawer or maker incurs contract liability by signing a negotiable instrument. Issue is the process whereby the maker or drawer extends rights on the instrument representing that payment obligation to another person, usually the payee.[121]

Issue requires delivery, and delivery refers to "voluntary transfer of possession."[122] The issuance of an instrument, however, even to a payee that qualifies as a holder of the instrument, does not constitute either transfer of the instrument or negotiation of the instrument. Section 3-203(a) requires delivery for the transfer of an instrument, but it specifically excludes delivery by an issuer, just as section 3-201(a) excludes delivery by an issuer in defining negotiation. Issue nevertheless involves a transfer (issue requires delivery, which is a voluntary transfer of possession), so it is important to understand why the drafters have distinguished transfers that are issue.[123]

The distinction is based on the conceptualization of what a transferee receives through each form of transfer. The legal consequence of the

---

[117] U.C.C. § 3-203, Comment 2.

[118] *See* § 6.05 *infra*.

[119] U.C.C. § 3-105(a).

[120] *See* § 4.02[A], [C] *infra*.

[121] Issue is thus analogous to the requirement of delivery to confer a gift under personal property law.

[122] U.C.C. § 1-201(14).

[123] Another type of transfer that also must be distinguished is a transfer for purposes of payment of an instrument. For discussion of this type of transfer, see § 3.03 *supra* and § 5.02[A] *infra*.

transfer of an instrument is that the transferee receives the transferor's right to enforce the instrument.[124] This legal effect would not benefit a designated payee of an instrument because neither a maker nor a drawer has any right to enforce order paper that it signs. Makers and drawers incur contractual payment obligations on the negotiable instruments that they issue. Consequently, issue of an instrument is the voluntary transfer of an instrument "for the purpose of giving rights on the instrument to any person."[125] Essentially, issue is the process whereby the maker or drawer both confers a property interest in the instrument on the payee and satisfies a formalistic requirement for the enforceability of its contract obligation.[126] The diagram below uses the broken line to distinguish the transfer through issue by the drawer to the payee from the transfer of the instrument by the payee to X.

D'er ---- ▶P ——— ▶X

Diagram 3.6

The drawer (D'er) issued the instrument to give the payee (P) rights on the instrument, whereas P transferred the instrument to give X P's rights to enforce the instrument.

Even though a maker or a drawer does not issue an instrument that it signs, the instrument is nevertheless "binding on the maker or drawer, but nonissuance is a defense."[127] Thus, a drawer of a check who prepares and signs it but retains possession by placing it into a desk drawer does not deliver it, and the payee would not have a cause of action based on the check against the drawer,[128] even if the drawer stated that the check belongs to the payee.[129] As subsequent discussion will show, however, the defense of nonissuance will be available only against a party who does not have the rights of a holder in due course.[130] Consequently a drawer or maker who prepares and signs an instrument in bearer form but does not issue it nevertheless runs the risk that a finder or thief may introduce it into the stream of commerce by transferring it to another person. The same risk

---

[124] U.C.C. § 3-203(b). See § 3.03 *supra*.

[125] U.C.C. § 3-105(a).

[126] Note that the significance of issue does not lie in the rule of derivative title. The first delivery to a holder (issue) establishes initial title to the instrument in the payee and enforcement rights against the drawer or maker of the instrument. Subsequent deliveries differ because they are the means by which a transferor passes his or her title and rights to enforce the instrument to someone else.

[127] U.C.C. § 3-105(b).

[128] McCain v. P.A. Partners, Ltd., 445 So. 2d 271 (Ala. 1984) (discharged employee could not sue employer for conversion based on employer withholding payroll check).

[129] Jones v. Phillips, 237 Ga. App. 24, 513 S.E.2d 241, 38 U.C.C. Rep. Serv. 2d 1222 (1999) (because the note was not delivered, it was unenforceable, even though the maker admitted executing it).

[130] See U.C.C. 3-105, Comment 2; §§ 6.01[D][2][d], 6.03[A] *infra*.

applies if the named payee on an order instrument were to steal the instrument from the drawer or maker. In the hands of a holder in due course, the instrument would be enforceable against the drawer or maker.

Comparable treatment is provided for instruments that are conditionally issued or that are issued for a special purpose. The delivery of an instrument can be conditioned upon the occurrence of a stated event, such as additional signatures of other parties on the instrument.[131] Sometimes an instrument is delivered to a transferee to be used only for a special purpose. The delivery might be for security[132] or to enable the payee to acquire a specific automobile.[133] A defense of misuse arises when the transferee uses the instrument for some other purpose. Instruments that are conditionally issued or that are issued for a special purpose are binding on the maker or drawer, but "failure of the condition or special purpose to be fulfilled is a defense."[134] The defense, however, will be valid only against a person who does not have the rights of a holder in due course.[135]

Delivery of an instrument to a remitter also constitutes issue. A remitter is "a person who purchases an instrument from its issuer if the instrument is payable to an identified person other than the purchaser."[136] If a buyer is going to make a purchase of a large-ticket item, such as an automobile, the seller may be unwilling to accept the buyer's personal check. The seller would incur the risks that the buyer might not have sufficient funds to cover the check or that the buyer would stop payment on the check after issuing it. The seller is more likely to prefer a cashier's check because a bank incurs an obligation to the payee by signing the check, the buyer's account is already debited for the amount of the check, and the buyer cannot stop payment on the check. The cashier's check purchased from the bank will show the bank as the drawer and the seller as the payee, and it will be given to the buyer as the remitter. The remitter becomes the owner of the check by purchasing it. The remitter is not a holder because it is drawn to the order of the seller. The bank's voluntary transfer of possession to the remitter, however, is delivery, and it qualifies as issue.[137] Further

---

[131] Kelley v. Carson, 120 Ga. App. 450, 171 S.E.2d 150, 7 U.C.C. Rep. Serv. 47 (1969) (agreement that note to raise money for a corporation was not to be used unless four other persons signed notes of the same amount). *See also* Merchants Nat'l Bank v. Professional Men's Assoc., 409 F.2d 600, 6 U.C.C. Rep. Serv. 37 (5th Cir. 1969), *cert. denied*, 396 U.S. 1009 (1970) (note to be repaid only from maker's profits).

[132] Ventures, Inc. v. Jones, 101 Idaho 837, 623 P.2d 145, 30 U.C.C. Rep. Serv. 1601 (1981) (notes were interim security only, given until adequate security was provided).

[133] American Underwriting Corp. v. Rhode Island Hosp. Trust Co., 111 R.I. 415, 303 A.2d 121, 12 U.C.C. Rep. Serv. 698 (1973) (draft to enable debtor to obtain her repossessed car).

[134] U.C.C. § 3-105(b).

[135] Mandel v. Sedrish, 3 U.C.C. Rep. Serv. 524 (N.Y. Sup. Ct. 1966).

[136] U.C.C. § 3-103(a)(11).

[137] Issue includes the first delivery of an instrument by the drawer to a nonholder for the purpose of giving rights on the instrument to any person. U.C.C. § 3-105(a). In the hypothetical, the bank voluntarily transferred possession of the check that it drew to the remitter (the automobile purchaser) for the purpose of giving rights on the check to the automobile seller.

delivery of the check to the seller will constitute negotiation and will confer holder status.[138]

[B] Relationship of the Original Parties — § 3-117

Between the immediate parties, a negotiable instrument is merely a contract. Consequently, the general contract principle that all of the writings executed by the parties as part of the contract are to be considered in determining the rights and duties of the parties applies to negotiable instruments.[139] Many instruments are issued pursuant to an underlying agreement that is reduced to writing.[140] In addition, written security agreements are commonly executed as part of the total transaction.[141] Under section 3-117, any agreement that is executed as part of the same transaction can affect or modify the obligations on an instrument.[142] A contemporaneous written agreement thus is as legitimate a source of terms of the contract between the original parties to an issued instrument as the instrument itself.

Reading contemporaneous writings together to determine the rights and duties of the parties does not extend so far as to destroy negotiability of the instrument when a term in a writing affects a term in the instrument. The negotiability of an instrument is always to be determined by what appears on the face of the instrument alone. An instrument that states, however, that it is subject to or governed by the terms of another agreement is not unconditional,[143] and therefore cannot be negotiable.[144] An instrument that simply refers to or states that it arises out of a separate agreement is nevertheless unconditional,[145] and, assuming satisfaction of the remaining required elements, is negotiable, even though the rights of the original parties are indeed affected by the separate agreement.

---

[138] If the drawer who prepares and signs a check does not deliver it to the remitter or payee, the drawer does not issue the check, the payee cannot become a holder, and the payee has no rights in the completed check. Rex Smith Propane, Inc. v. National Bank of Commerce, 372 F. Supp. 499, 14 U.C.C. Rep. Serv. 978 (N.D. Tex. 1974) (bank cancelled completed cashier's check before issuing it).

[139] Perry v. Cain, 581 P.2d 891, 24 U.C.C. Rep. Serv. 912 (Okla. 1978) (indemnity agreement executed together with promissory note).

[140] Knut Co. v. Knutson Const. Co., 433 N.W.2d 149, 7 U.C.C. Rep. Serv. 2d 1124 (Minn. Ct. App. 1988) (purchase agreement compelling arbitration).

[141] U.C.C. § 3-117, Comment 1; Merchants Nat'l Bank & Trust Co. v. Professional Men's Ass'n, Inc., 409 F.2d 600, 6 U.C.C. Rep. Serv. 337 (5th Cir. 1969).

[142] Sanden v. Hanson, 201 N.W.2d 404, 11 U.C.C. Rep. Serv. 1002 (N.D. 1972) (restrictions of standby agreement applied to note); Merchants Nat'l Bank & Trust Co. v. Professional Men's Ass'n, Inc., 409 F.2d 600, 6 U.C.C. Rep. Serv. 337 (5th Cir. 1969) (note, security agreement, and cover letter all considered together); West v. Turchioe, 761 A.2d 382, 40 U.C.C. Rep. Serv. 2d 249 (N.H. 1999) (court determined that the terms on a separate handwritten agreement did not modify or otherwise nullify the promissor's obligation on the promissory note).

[143] U.C.C. § 3-106(a)(ii); Holly Hill Acres, Ltd. v. Charter Bank, 314 So. 2d 209, 17 U.C.C. Rep. Serv. 144 (Fla. Ct. App. 1975) (note provided that terms of mortgage securing it "are by this reference made a part hereof").

[144] U.C.C. § 3-104(a). See § 2.02[B][3][b] supra.

[145] U.C.C. § 3-106(a).

A separate agreement executed as part of the same transaction may also have an effect upon subsequent transferees, as well as the immediate obligee. An agreement that modifies, supplements, or nullifies the obligation on an instrument creates a defense to the obligation.[146] That defense, however, would not be valid against a subsequent holder in due course that took the instrument without notice of the agreement.

---

[146] U.C.C. § 3-117; General Inv. Corp. v. Angelini, 58 N.J. 396, 278 A.2d 193, 9 U.C.C. Rep. Serv. 1 (1971) (finance company took note subject to limitation that maker's liability was not to begin until sixty days after the work was properly completed).

Chapter 4
CONTRACT OBLIGATIONS

SYNOPSIS

§ 4.01 Liability on the Instrument — Fundamentals — § 3-401

§ 4.02 The Contracts
    [A] Maker — § 3-412
    [B] Acceptor — § 3-413
    [C] Drawer — § 3-414
    [D] Indorser — § 3-415

§ 4.03 Disclaimer of Contract Liability — §§ 3-415(b), 3-414(e)

§ 4.04 Surety Liability on the Instrument — § 3-419
    [A] Signing for Accommodation
    [B] Liability
    [C] Rights
    [D] Establishing Accommodation Status
    [E] Defenses
    [F] Words Guaranteeing Collection

§ 4.05 Authority to Sign
    [A] Signature by Authorized Representative — § 3-402
    [B] Unauthorized Signatures — § 3-403

§ 4.06 Enforcement of Lost, Destroyed, or Stolen Instrument — § 3-309
    [A] Introduction
    [B] Enforcing the Instrument
    [C] Adequate Protection Against Loss
    [D] Special Rules on Cashier's Checks, Teller's Checks, and Certified Checks — § 3-312

§ 4.01 Liability on the Instrument — Fundamentals — § 3-401

"Obligation on an instrument depends on a signature that is binding on the obligor."[1] This statement from the Comments establishes the fundamental principle that underlies liability on the instrument. A binding signature on the instrument is necessary to incur the liability associated

---

[1] U.C.C. § 3-401, Comment 1.

with the promises embodied in any negotiable instrument.[2] In the absence of a binding signature, a person is not liable on an instrument.[3]

Conversely, persons who do sign instruments become liable in the capacity in which they sign. Article 3 establishes specific statutory contracts for each signer in his or her capacity as maker, acceptor, drawer, or indorser.[4] Contracts incurred by signing an instrument are referred to as liability "on the instrument." A lawsuit brought on the instrument is premised on contract liability arising from the defendant's signature.

Liability on the instrument is by no means the only type of liability that persons can incur when dealing with negotiable instruments. A number of different legal theories provide a variety of means for incurring liability in these transactions. Everyone who transfers an instrument, for example, gives warranties, irrespective of whether they also sign the instrument.[5] These additional theories are developed in subsequent chapters of this text. The concern here is the liability incurred by reason of signing a negotiable instrument.

To be liable on the instrument, a person's signature must appear on the instrument itself. It is the only way that Article 3 contracts become applicable. A signature on a separate writing is not sufficient, even if it indicates a willingness to be bound on the instrument.[6]

The Code does not require strict formalities with respect to the signature requirement. It can be made "(i) manually or by means of a device or machine, and (ii) by the use of any name, including a trade or assumed name, or by a word, mark, or symbol executed or adopted by a person with present intention to authenticate a writing."[7] Evidence is always admissible to identify the party who signed the instrument and thereby became liable on it.[8] The signer's present intent to authenticate the writing is crucial in the context of section 3-401 because the absence of this element would eliminate the intent necessary to support a contract theory of liability.[9] Furthermore, a person who signs an instrument and includes

---

[2] A signature does not have to be made by the person to be bound. A signature by an authorized agent or representative can also provide a signature that is binding on the principal. U.C.C. § 3-401(a). For discussion of signatures by representatives, see § 4.05 [A] *infra*.

[3] U.C.C. § 3-401(a).

[4] U.C.C. §§ 3-412–3-415. See § 4.02 *infra*.

[5] U.C.C. §§ 3-416, 3-417, 4-207, 4-208.

[6] Fewox v. Tallahassee Bank & Trust Co., 249 So. 2d 55, 9 U.C.C. Rep. Serv. 476 (Fla. Dist. Ct. App. 1971), *cert. denied*, 252 So. 2d 799 (Fla. 1971) (signature on separate letter of guaranty did not result in liability on the instrument).

[7] U.C.C. § 3-401(b); First Sec. Bank v. Fastwich, Inc., 612 S.W.2d 799, 30 U.C.C. Rep. Serv. 1609 (Mo. Ct. App. 1981) (typed name of corporation constituted its signature on note); Nichols v. Seale, 493 S.W.2d 589, 12 U.C.C. Rep. Serv. 711 (Tex. Civ. App. 1973), *rev'd on other grounds*, 505 S.W.2d 251, 14 U.C.C. Rep. Serv. 457 (Tex. 1974) (assertion by signer of note that "The Fashion Beauty Salon" was an assumed name for "Mr. Carl's Fashion, Inc.").

[8] U.C.C. § 3-401, Comment 2.

[9] Simpson v. Milne, 677 P.2d 356, 36 U.C.C. Rep. Serv. 1262 (Colo. Ct. App. 1983) (payee not entitled to recover on an offsetting note executed as a fiction to ease the mind of the payee's dying wife and not intended to represent an actual promise to pay).

language showing the lack of any contractual intent, such as the term "witness," is not liable on the instrument.[10]

§ 4.02 The Contracts

In the absence of an explicit disclaimer,[11] everyone who signs a negotiable instrument promises to pay it. This promise is a significant part of the conceptual basis for recognizing liability on the instrument as contractual liability. An additional reason for characterizing the liability as contractual is that the liability is voluntarily assumed by signing an instrument. No one is otherwise contractually liable.[12] The signature constitutes the outward manifestation of an intent to be bound that subsequent parties are reasonably entitled to rely upon. Many people undoubtedly do not realize that they enter a contract upon signing an instrument because they are unaware of these aspects of negotiable instruments law. However, even these individuals should anticipate that in the event a check they write bounces, they generally will have to pay the merchant to whom they issued the check, or that, in the event that a check they indorse and cash at their bank is returned unpaid by the payor bank, they will have to reimburse their bank. These consequences have their legal support in the Article 3 contracts.[13]

Persons who sign instruments incur obligations in one of four capacities: maker, acceptor, drawer, or indorser. Makers and drawers are the parties who execute and issue negotiable instruments. The terms for these parties often are used interchangeably by courts, but doing so is erroneous because the contracts of the two parties differ considerably. Drawers execute drafts (including checks), whereas makers execute notes (including certificates of deposit). An acceptor is a drawee who signs a check or other draft and thereby engages to honor it. An indorser is essentially any other person who signs any type of negotiable instrument. Indorsers most commonly sign as a requirement to negotiate instruments or because subsequent transferees insist on their signatures in order to secure a right of recourse on the instrument in the event that the party who is expected to pay does not comply.

[A] Maker — § 3-412

A maker "is obliged to pay the instrument (i) according to its terms at the time it was issued or, if not issued, at the time it first came into

---

[10] *See* U.C.C. § 3-204(a); Chidakel v. Blonder, 431 A.2d 594, 31 U.C.C. Rep. Serv. 1642 (D.C. Ct. App. 1981) (initials "H.B." under the printed term "Attest:" on a note clearly showed signature in capacity of a witness). *See also* Norton v. Knapp, 64 Iowa 112, 19 N.W. 867 (1884) (drawee's signature together with the words "Kiss my foot" not an acceptance); U.C.C. § 3-410, Comment 2.

[11] *See* § 4.03 *infra*.

[12] U.C.C. § 3-401(a).

[13] Laurel Bank & Trust Co. v. Sahadi, 32 Conn. Supp. 172, 345 A.2d 53, 17 U.C.C. Rep. Serv. 1259 (1975) (indorser-depositor of check liable to depository bank upon receipt of timely notice of dishonor of the check by the drawee bank).

possession of a holder, or (ii) if the issuer signed an incomplete instrument, according to its terms when completed, to the extent stated in Section 3-115 and 3-407."[14] This undertaking to pay the instrument is absolute.[15] The maker of a note or certificate of deposit is the party expected to pay, and this contract creates that obligation.[16]

The reference to the terms of the instrument at the time of issuance or the possession by a holder reflects the reality that instruments are sometimes altered.[17] The maker's contract to pay a stated sum of money on specified terms is fixed at the time the maker issues the instrument and is not changed if someone subsequently alters a term, such as the amount or the due date.[18] A maker who prepares an incomplete instrument always incurs contract liability in accordance with the completion terms authorized,[19] and sometimes even incurs liability for an unauthorized completion.[20]

The maker of an instrument is obligated to pay it when the instrument becomes due.[21] Even though a demand for payment is not a condition to a maker's liability, holders generally will pursue that course before initiating a lawsuit. If the maker pays, the lawsuit is not necessary. Furthermore, dishonor is a condition of indorser liability. Dishonor of a note payable at a definite time occurs automatically on the day after the note is due, and no demand for payment (presentment) is necessary.[22] With a demand note, presentment is necessary for dishonor, and is therefore required to enforce the obligation of an indorser.[23]

When parties sign an instrument as co-makers, they are jointly and severally liable, unless the instrument clearly specifies otherwise.[24] The

---

[14] U.C.C. § 3-412. The same contractual liability applies to the issuer of a cashier's check or other draft drawn on the drawer. The form of these latter instruments is clearly in the order form of a draft. Because the order is drawn on the drawer, however, the liability on such an instrument is stated as being the same as that of a maker of a note. U.C.C. § 3-412, Comment 1. The contract provisions applicable to drawers are made inapplicable to the issuer of these instruments. U.C.C. § 3-414(a).

[15] As used here, absolute means unconditional. Even though the maker's obligation is absolute, he or she may be able to assert a defense against the party seeking to enforce the note.

[16] Grand Island Prod. Credit Ass'n v. Humphrey, 223 Neb. 135, 388 N.W.2d 807, 2 U.C.C. Rep. Serv. 2d 193 (1986) (wife who signed note jointly and severally liable despite separation from her husband and co-maker).

[17] The effect of alterations on negotiable instruments is discussed in Chapter 7. *See* § 7.02[F] *infra*; U.C.C. § 3-407.

[18] Through the application of the tort principle of negligence, a maker can become liable for a subsequent alteration if the maker's negligence substantially contributes to it. U.C.C. § 3-406. *See* § 10.02 [A] *infra*.

[19] U.C.C. §§ 3-412, 3-115(b).

[20] The maker will be liable for an unauthorized completion when a drawee pays an instrument or a holder in due course seeks to enforce it. U.C.C. § 3-407(3). This result shows the risk placed on a maker who prepares incomplete instruments. *See* U.C.C. § 3-407, Comment 2. For development of these rules concerning incomplete instruments *see* § 7.02[F][2] *infra*.

[21] Whiteside v. Douglas County Bank, 145 Ga. App. 775, 245 S.E.2d 2, 24 U.C.C. Rep. Serv. 171 (1978) (obligation is unconditional).

[22] U.C.C. § 3-502(a)(3). *See* § 5.03[b][1] *infra*.

[23] *See* §§ 3-415(a), 3-502(a)(1).

[24] U.C.C. § 3-116(a).

Code applies this rule of joint and several liability to all parties who sign in the same capacity as part of the same transaction in order to preclude any ambiguity concerning the apportionment of liability among them. The holder of the instrument has the option to proceed against the co-makers together or any one of them individually.[25] The rule is not overcome by language in the instrument like "I promise to pay" or "we promise to pay." Greater specificity, through language like "we jointly promise" or "we promise severally," is required.[26]

Because several parties can deal with a note once it has been signed and issued by a maker, the Code needs to identify the party or parties to whom the maker's contract obligation runs. It does this by indicating that "[t]he obligation is owed to a person entitled to enforce the instrument or to an indorser who paid the instrument under Section 3-415."[27] A person entitled to enforce an instrument includes a holder and a nonholder who has the rights of a holder through the shelter principle.[28] A person that fits into either of these categories is the person that the maker should pay in order to discharge the contract obligation. If the maker refuses to pay a person entitled to enforce the instrument, that person might then turn to the liability incurred by a person who signed the instrument as an indorser.[29] The maker's obligation will then extend to any indorser who pays the instrument.

Consider the following fact pattern:

```
            "P"
M----▶P─────────▶H·········▶M
                      (dishonors)
```

Diagram 4.1

Maker (M) issues a note to Payee (P), who indorses and negotiates it to Holder (H). Rather than paying the note to Holder when it is due, Maker dishonors the note. Maker should have paid the note to Holder because Holder is a person entitled to enforce the note. Rather than continuing to pursue Maker's obligation, however, Holder may now demand payment

---

[25] A party that pays the instrument "is entitled to receive from any party having the same joint and several liability contribution in accordance with applicable law." U.C.C. § 3-116(b); Grimes v. Grimes, 47 N.C. App. 353, 267 S.E.2d 372, 29 U.C.C. Rep. Serv. 1332 (1980) (co-maker entitled to common-law right of contribution from other co-maker).

[26] Ghitter v. Edge, 118 Ga. App. 750, 165 S.E.2d 598, 5 U.C.C. Rep. Serv. 1254 (1968).

[27] U.C.C. § 3-412.

[28] U.C.C. § 3-301. Such a person also includes persons entitled to enforce an instrument under section 3-309 (lost or stolen instruments) or section 3-418(d) (recovered payment of an instrument paid by mistake). These latter provisions are covered later in this text. *See* §§ 4.06, 9.01[C][1] *infra*.

[29] For discussion of the contract liability of indorsers *see* § 4.02[D] *infra*.

from Payee on her liability as an indorser. If Payee pays Holder, Maker's payment obligation will then extend to Payee.

[B] Acceptor — § 3-413

The acceptor is obliged to pay the draft "according to its terms at the time it was accepted."[30] The terms of a draft at the time of an acceptor's signature may not be the same as the terms executed by the drawer. Someone subsequent to the drawer might have altered a term on the draft before it is presented to the drawee for an acceptance signature. Because the acceptor promises to pay the draft "according to its terms at the time it was accepted," the acceptor is liable for any alterations that precede acceptance.[31]

Consider the facts diagramed below:

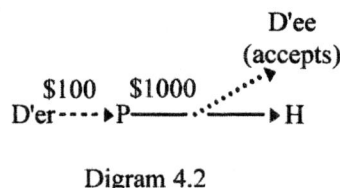

Digram 4.2

Drawer (D'er) issues a draft for $100 to Payee (P). Payee fraudulently raises the amount to $1,000 before presenting the draft for acceptance to Drawee (D'ee), and Drawee accepts. Payee subsequently negotiates the instrument to Holder (H). Upon acceptance, Drawee incurred an obligation on the instrument for $1,000, even though the draft was issued for $100. Drawee's intent was to agree to honor the draft as it appeared when Drawee signed.

A unique set of rules applies with respect to alterations to the amount of a draft that are made after the acceptor has signed.[32] The acceptor can include the amount that is accepted with the acceptance signature, and thereby fix the obligation to that amount.[33] If the acceptor does not include the amount of the acceptance, a subsequent holder in due course can enforce the draft for the amount of the instrument at the time it was taken by the holder in due course.[34] Thus, if the drawee in the facts diagrammed above

---

[30] U.C.C. § 3-413(a)(i). This obligation is imposed "even though the acceptance states that the draft is payable 'as originally drawn' or equivalent terms." *Id.* The acceptor's liability will be on drafts that order the acceptor as the drawee to pay and that the drawee accepts by signing the draft.

[31] Brower v. Franklin Nat'l Bank, 311 F. Supp. 675, 7 U.C.C. Rep. Serv. 1021 (S.D. N.Y. 1970).

[32] The liability with respect to the acceptance of a draft that is an incomplete instrument parallels the liability incurred by a maker. *See* § 4.02 [A] *supra*.

[33] U.C.C. § 3-413(b). The effect of an acceptance that varies the terms of a draft are covered at § 7.02[H] *infra*. *See* U.C.C. §§ 3-410, 3-413(a)(ii).

[34] U.C.C. § 3-413(b).

accepted the draft as drawn for $100 but failed to write that amount with the acceptance, the drawee would leave open the possibility of greater liability. If the payee, for example, raised the draft to $1,000 after the acceptance and then negotiated it to H as a holder in due course, the drawee's obligation would be for $1,000.

The parties to whom the contract obligation of an acceptor extends [35] include the same parties covered by the contract obligation of a maker. Thus, the acceptor's obligation is owed to a person entitled to enforce the instrument. If the acceptor does not pay this person and the person then receives payment from an indorser, the acceptor's obligation is then owed to the indorser who pays the draft. Additionally, however, the obligation will extend to the drawer if the drawer pays the draft.

A draft is simply an order directed to the drawee to pay according to the terms of the draft. [36] The drawee has not signed the instrument upon issuance and consequently is not liable on it. [37] The payee or other holder of the draft can ascertain whether the drawee will comply by demanding payment when it is due or by demanding assurances of future payment through incurrence of liability on the instrument. The drawee incurs an obligation for future payment by accepting the draft. [38] Acceptance is customarily accomplished by writing the word "accepted" and signing vertically across the face of the draft. [39] However, the signature of the drawee alone is sufficient, [40] and it can appear anywhere on the instrument and still be effective. [41] By signing the draft, the drawee incurs liability on the instrument. When the drawee refuses to pay or to accept upon proper demand, the payee can pursue rights of recourse against the drawer of the draft. [42]

The signature of the drawee must appear on the instrument to constitute an acceptance. [43] This requirement eliminates the effectiveness of virtual and collateral acceptances recognized under prior law. A written agreement to accept drafts written in the future constitutes a virtual acceptance. A collateral acceptance is an acceptance provided in a separate writing rather

---

[35] U.C.C. § 3-413(a).

[36] U.C.C. § 3-104(e); In re Fasano/Harriss Pie Co., 43 B.R. 871, 40 U.C.C. Rep. Serv. 538 (Bankr. W.D. Mich. 1984).

[37] U.C.C. §§ 3-401(a), 3-408 ("the drawee is not liable on the instrument until the drawee accepts it").

[38] " 'Certified check' means a check accepted by the bank on which it is drawn." U.C.C. § 3-409(d). A bank is not obligated to certify a check. *Id.* A check is a demand instrument that calls for payment rather than acceptance. U.C.C. § 3-409, Comment 4.

[39] " 'Acceptance' means the drawee's signed agreement to pay a draft as presented." U.C.C. § 3-409(a).

[40] U.C.C. § 3-409(a).

[41] The location of the signature is irrelevant because the drawee has no other reason to sign than to accept. U.C.C. § 3-409, Comment 2.

[42] General Motors Acceptance Corp. v. General Accident Fire & Life Assurance Corp., 67 A.D.2d 316, 415 N.Y.S.2d 536, 26 U.C.C. Rep. Serv. 97 (1979) (liability of drawee is independent from the liability of drawer).

[43] U.C.C. § 3-409(a); Galaxy Boat Mfg. Co. v. East End State Bank, 641 S.W.2d 584, 35 U.C.C. Rep. Serv. 180 (Tex. Ct. App. 1982) (acceptance of a draft cannot be oral).

than on the instrument. These acceptances were recognized as effective as a concession to slow communication facilities that created long periods of doubt about whether a draft would be accepted. Modern improvements in communications eliminate the need for an exception to the basic premise that in order to incur liability on an instrument, a person's signature must appear on it.

The Code does continue another distinction that applies only to the effectiveness of an acceptor's contract obligation. The general rule is that an obligation on an instrument is not effective until the instrument is delivered. An acceptance, however, "becomes effective when notification pursuant to instructions is given or the accepted draft is delivered for the purpose of giving rights on the acceptance to any person."[44] When the presenter and drawee are a distance apart, notification of an acceptance can eliminate uncertainty about the drawee's response to the demand for acceptance during the time the draft is in return transit.

Payees and other holders cannot do anything to force a drawee to incur liability on the instrument. Until the drawee accepts the draft by signing it, the drawee is not liable on the instrument.[45] Furthermore, "[A] check or other draft does not of itself operate as an assignment of funds in the hands of the drawee available for its payment."[46] Payees take checks in the belief that the drawee bank will pay them, but the provision cited above prevents a payee from holding the bank liable for nonpayment.[47] A drawee bank that arbitrarily refuses to pay over the proper order of a drawer may incur liability for wrongful dishonor to its drawer-customer based on the underlying deposit contract,[48] but the disappointed holder of the check will have to rely on its rights of recourse against parties obligated on the instrument.[49]

[C] Drawer — § 3-414

A drawer of an unaccepted draft that is dishonored "is obliged to pay the draft (i) according to its terms at the time it was issued or, if not issued, at the time it first came into possession of a holder, or (ii) if the drawer signed an incomplete instrument, according to its terms when completed,

---

[44] U.C.C. § 3-409(a).

[45] U.C.C. §§ 3-401(a), 3-409(a).

[46] U.C.C. § 3-408; United States v. Four Million, Two Hundred Fifty-Five Thousand, 762 F.2d 895, 41 U.C.C. Rep. Serv. 859 (11th Cir. 1985), *cert. denied*, 474 U.S. 1056, 106 S. Ct. 795, 88 L.Ed2d 772 (1986) (holders of checks drawn against an account that had been forfeited for violations of federal laws lacked standing to contest the forfeiture as they did not have an ownership interest in the funds); Sabin Meyer Regional Sales Corp. v. Citizens Bank, 502 F. Supp. 557, 30 U.C.C. Rep. Serv. 595 (N.D. Ga. 1980) (oral representation that account would contain enough funds to cover checks did not raise the check to status of an assignment).

[47] Seattle-First Nat'l Bank v. Kim, 38 Wash. App. 101, 684 P.2d 773, 39 U.C.C. Rep. Serv. 537 (1984); Atlantic Cement Co., Inc. v. South Shore Bank, 36 U.C.C. Rep. Serv. 809 (D. Mass. 1983), *aff'd*, 730 F.2d 831 (1st Cir. 1984).

[48] *See* § 12.03 *infra*.

[49] U.C.C. §§ 3-414 (obligation of drawer), 3-415 (obligation of indorser).

to the extent stated in Sections 3-115 and 3-407."[50] This obligation extends to a person entitled to enforce the draft or to an indorser who paid it.[51] Thus, the obligation of the drawer is exactly like the obligation of a maker, with one significant difference. The drawer's obligation on an unaccepted draft does not arise until the draft is dishonored.[52]

This condition that the draft be dishonored goes to the difference between these two parties, who are otherwise quite similar. A drawer is similar to a maker in the sense that both parties execute instruments and issue them. Whereas the maker of a note promises to pay, a drawer of a draft orders the drawee to pay. All parties dealing with a draft generally expect the drawee to comply with this order. The drawee of an unaccepted draft is not liable on the instrument, however, which leaves the drawer as the party with primary liability.[53] In the event that the drawee refuses to pay as ordered, the drawer is liable for payment.

The nature of a drawer's liability changes when the drawee accepts a draft. The expectation that the drawee will pay is even greater because of acceptance. By signing the draft, the drawee accepts and becomes the party primarily liable on the instrument, and the drawer's liability becomes secondary as a type of guarantor of payment.[54] When the acceptor is not a bank, the liability of the drawer becomes like the liability of an indorser, which is how the liability is stated in section 3-414(d). In addition to dishonor of the draft, the drawer's liability is also conditioned upon receipt of notice of dishonor.[55] The drawer who pays the draft also has a right of recourse against the acceptor.[56] When a draft is accepted by a bank, the drawer is discharged from any further contract liability.[57]

[D] Indorser — § 3-415

Although an indorser can sign any form of negotiable instrument, parties dealing with instruments do not look primarily to the indorser for payment. As was just explained in the discussion of the drawer's contract, the person expected to pay a draft is the drawee. The maker unconditionally promises to pay a note and, consequently, people expect the maker to make payment on that type of instrument. Acceptors also commit themselves unconditionally to pay the drafts that they sign. Hence, indorsers incur backup liability

---

[50] U.C.C. § 3-414(b). This provision does not apply "to cashier's checks or other drafts drawn on the drawer." U.C.C. § 3-414(a). The contract obligation of drawers of these instruments is covered in section 3-412 as the equivalent of the liability of a maker of a note. *See* § 4.02 [A] *supra*.

[51] U.C.C. § 3-414(b).

[52] The requirement of dishonor is covered in detail in the next chapter, but its basic application can be easily summarized. Generally, a drawee dishonors a draft by refusing the demand for payment by a person entitled to enforce the draft. U.C.C. §§ 3-501, 3-502.

[53] U.C.C. § 3-414, Comment 2.

[54] U.C.C. § 3-414, Comment 4.

[55] For discussion of the concept of notice of dishonor, see §§ 5.02[C], 5.03[C] *infra*.

[56] U.C.C. § 3-413(a).

[57] U.C.C. § 3-414(c). This provision is discussed in the chapter on discharge. *See* § 7.02[G] *infra*.

based on an undertaking to pay in the event that the persons expected to pay fail to do so.

The basic contract of an indorser provides as follows:

> [I]f an instrument is dishonored, an indorser is obliged to pay the amount due on the instrument (i) according to the terms of the instrument at the time it was indorsed, or (ii) if the indorser indorsed an incomplete instrument, according to its terms when completed, to the extent stated in Sections 3-115 and 3-407.[58]

In addition to the condition of dishonor, the liability of an indorser is also conditioned on notice of dishonor.[59] Once the conditions are satisfied, an indorser's liability is based on the terms of the instrument at the time he or she indorsed it. This aspect of the contract of indorsers parallels the liability incurred by acceptors. An indorser incurs liability based on the terms of the instrument at the time of signing it. Consequently, an indorser's contract covers alterations that occur after the instrument is issued and prior to indorsing, but not alterations that are made subsequently.

Like the contract obligations of other parties to an instrument, the indorser's contract runs to a person entitled to enforce the instrument or to an indorser who pays it. Unlike other parties, however, several different indorsers can sign an instrument in independent transactions.[60] Therefore, section 3-415(a) limits the obligation of an indorser to "a subsequent indorser who paid the instrument." An indorser's contract runs downstream to subsequent indorsers and any person entitled to enforce the instrument, but not to prior indorsers. Upon satisfaction of the conditions, an indorser becomes liable to pay a person entitled to enforce the instrument and any other downstream indorser who pays the instrument. Following payment to any of these parties, the indorser then can look upstream to enforce the contract obligation of prior indorsers or, depending upon the type of instrument involved, the drawer, the maker, or the acceptor.

---

[58] U.C.C. § 3-415(a).

[59] U.C.C. §§ 3-415(c), 3-503(a). The requirement of notice of dishonor is covered in detail in the next chapter, but its basic application can be easily summarized. Notice of dishonor requires reasonable identification of the instrument and an indication that it has been dishonored or has not been paid. U.C.C. § 3-503(b).

[60] Only one party, the drawee, can be an acceptor. A draft has either one drawer or drawers that are jointly and severally liable on the same transaction, and the same relationship applies to the maker or makers of a note.

Assuming that the conditions to liability are satisfied for all of the parties, consider the facts diagrammed below:

$$D'er \cdots \blacktriangleright P \xrightarrow{"P"} X \xrightarrow{"X"} Y \xrightarrow{"Y"} H \cdots\cdots \blacktriangleright D'ee$$
$$(\text{dishonors})$$

Diagram 4.3

Drawer (D'er) issues a draft to Payee (P). With blank indorsements by each of the successive transferors, the instrument is negotiated to X, Y, and Holder (H). H presents the draft for payment to Drawee (D'ee), but D'ee instead dishonors it. H has the option of pursuing the contract liability of any of the three indorsers (P, X, or Y) or of D'er. If she pursues Y and Y pays, Y has rights of recourse against both P and X on their indorser contracts and against D'er on his contract. If she pursues X, however, X can only turn upstream against P or D'er. Even though Y also indorsed the instrument, his indorsement came after X's indorsement, and because indorsers are liable to one another in the order they indorsed, Y did not incur liability on the instrument to X. Contract liability runs downstream to subsequent parties. Therefore, in enforcing that liability, each indorser must look upstream for prospective defendants. If H pursues P on P's indorsement contract and P pays, P will have recourse only against D'er. Recovery against D'er, either directly by H or by one of the indorsers who pays the instrument, will leave ultimate liability on D'er because D'er does not have rights of recourse against any other party. Having issued an order to pay to the D'ee that was dishonored, D'er is now required to stand behind the draft by paying it.

The order of liability among indorsers can be critical. Even though D'er should pay the instrument in the illustration provided above, he may be unable to pay. The indorser with no further right of recourse (P in the illustration above) will then face the prospect of ultimate liability.

§ 4.03 Disclaimer of Contract Liability — §§ 3-415(b), 3-414(e)

Indorsers and some drawers who would otherwise incur liability on the instrument can disclaim that liability.[61] The most common method of disclaimer is to include the words "without recourse" with the drawer's or indorser's signature. These words make it clear that even in the event the draft is dishonored, the person entitled to enforce the instrument will not have recourse on the instrument against the signer. Other words that unambiguously communicate the same intent also can be used for a disclaimer.

---

[61] U.C.C. §§ 3-415(b), 3-414(e).

The disclaimer changes the contract of the drawer or indorser, so irrespective of the language used, it must appear on the instrument itself and cannot be proven by parol evidence.[62]

Disclaimers by drawers are rare. Payees generally are unwilling to take an unaccepted draft with the drawer's disclaimer because neither the drawer nor the drawee is liable on it. Because "[t]here is no legitimate purpose served by issuing a check on which nobody is liable,"[63] a drawer's disclaimer of liability is not effective if the draft is a check.[64] Drawers can disclaim their liability on drafts that are not checks because some commercially reasonable transactions can be facilitated with such instruments. For example, if the drawer's order is required because the drawer controls funds in the hands of the drawee, but the parties intend for an indorser to be the obligor, the drawer might draw without recourse in order to avoid liability on the instrument.[65]

A transferor who wishes to negotiate an instrument that runs to his or her order without incurring liability on it can do so by indorsing without recourse. Again, however, the disclaimer may affect the prospective transferee's willingness to take the instrument with the disclaimer included. When instruments are not paid and parties look upstream on their rights of recourse, they generally turn to the transferor with whom they dealt. For this reason, transferees often require their transferors to indorse bearer paper even though the indorsement is not necessary to negotiate the instrument. Consequently, the prospective transferee may be unwilling to allow the disclaimer.

An indorsement "without recourse" is classified as a qualified indorsement.[66] The previous chapter explained how all indorsements are classified as either blank or special and as either restrictive or nonrestrictive.[67] The third classification is that indorsements are either qualified or unqualified. An unqualified indorser assumes all of the contract obligations of section 3-415. A qualified indorser is simply one who disclaims the contract applicable to an indorsement.

---

[62] P.J. Panzeca, Inc. v. Llobell, 19 U.C.C. Rep. Serv. 564 (N.Y. Sup. Ct. 1976) (disclaimer of indorser's contract liability based on alleged oral agreement of payee not to sue held ineffective).

[63] U.C.C. § 3-414, Comment 5.

[64] U.C.C. § 3-414(e).

[65] The Comments provide another illustration based on a documentary sale. *See* U.C.C. § 3-414, Comment 5.

[66] Hartford Life Ins. Co. v. Title Guarantee Co., 520 F.2d 1170, 17 U.C.C. Rep. Serv. 1252 (D.C. App. 1975).

[67] *See* § 3.04[B] *supra*.

§ 4.04 Surety Liability on the Instrument — § 3-419

[A] Signing for Accommodation

The liability incurred by signing an instrument may not be sufficient inducement to convince a prospective creditor to proceed with the transaction. The creditor still runs the risk that the signer may not be able or willing to pay the instrument. The creditor can enhance its position by taking a mortgage or security interest in real or personal property of the debtor. Alternatively, the creditor can increase its assurances of payment if someone with more solid financial standing assumes liability for the payment. Laypersons thus refer to needing someone to co-sign their instrument. Principles of the law of suretyship govern the rights and liabilities of the parties in these transactions.

A surety relationship involves three parties. The debtor for whom the debt is incurred is the principal. The person to whom the debt obligation runs is the creditor. The person who agrees to answer for the debt of the principal is the surety.[68]

When a surety and a principal evidence their obligation by signing the same negotiable instrument, the surety is known as an accommodation party.[69] An instrument is signed "for accommodation" when a party to the instrument, referred to as an accommodation party, "signs the instrument for the purpose of incurring liability on the instrument without being a direct beneficiary of the value given for the instrument."[70] The value for the instrument must not flow to the accommodation party, but must be "given for the benefit of a party to the instrument"[71] (the accommodated party), meaning that the principal must also sign the instrument.

A surety who signs a separate agreement to support the obligation of a party to a negotiable instrument is not an accommodation party. Such a party's obligations are not governed by the Code. A surety who signs a note as evidence of a promise to pay the principal's debt when the principal does not sign the note is likewise not an accommodation party.[72] Such a party's liability on the instrument is governed by Article 3, but he or she is also a common law surety and may have defenses based on that status. If the note is signed to borrow money for another person who does not promise the creditor repayment, the signer is not even a surety.

---

[68] More precisely, "[s]uretyship is the relation which exists where one person has undertaken an obligation and another person is also under an obligation or other duty to the obligee, who is entitled to but one performance, and as between the two who are bound, one rather than the other should perform." Restatement of Security § 82 (1941).

[69] U.C.C. § 3-419(a).

[70] U.C.C. § 3-419(a).

[71] U.C.C. § 3-419(a).

[72] Bank of Am. v. Superior Court of San Diego County, 4 Cal. App. 3d 435, 84 Cal. Rptr. 421, 7 U.C.C. Rep. Serv. 713 (1970).

[B] Liability

The liability of accommodation parties is determined by the capacity in which they sign.[73] An accommodation party's signature on an instrument can be as a maker, acceptor, drawer, or indorser. By signing in one of these capacities, the accommodation party incurs the applicable statutory liability on the instrument.[74] If the signature is as a maker or an acceptor, the accommodation party is obligated to pay the instrument when it becomes due. The relevant conditions must be satisfied before payment can be required from an accommodation drawer or indorser.[75] In this respect, an accommodation party is indistinguishable from any other party on an instrument.

As between the accommodation party (surety) and the accommodated party (principal), accommodation status can result in significant modification of the general rules of liability on the instrument. Section 3-419(e) provides that an accommodated party who pays does not have any right of recourse against the accommodation party. Assume that the maker signs a note as an accommodation party for accommodation of the indorser. If the maker dishonors the note and the holder recovers against the indorser, the indorser's right of recourse against the maker is cut off by section 3-419(e). The same subsection also terminates any claim for contribution if the parties had signed as co-makers of the note and the accommodated party paid the entire amount when it became due.

[C] Rights

Section 3-419(e) grants a specific right of recourse on the instrument in favor of an accommodation party against the party accommodated. Sometimes a right of recourse is available based on the respective capacities in which the two parties sign. For example, an accommodation indorser who pays an instrument has a right of recourse against an accommodated maker or drawer because indorsers generally have such a right. When the accommodation party signs as a maker or drawer, however, the general rules of liability on the instrument do not provide a right of recourse. In this situation, section 3-419(e) gives the accommodation party, upon paying the instrument, a right of recourse against the accommodated party, even if it means suing a party downstream on the instrument. Consider the following diagram:

---

[73] U.C.C. § 3-419(b); Bank of Ripley v. Sadler, 671 S.W.2d 454, 39 U.C.C. Rep. Serv. 544 (Tenn. 1984).

[74] Madill Bank & Trust Co. v. Herrmann, 738 P.2d 567, 3 U.C.C. Rep. Serv. 2d 1436 (Okla. Ct. App. 1987) (maker); Oak Park Currency Exchange, Inc. v. Maropoulos, 48 Ill. App. 3d 437, 363 N.W.2d 54, 21 U.C.C. Rep. Serv. 1380 (1977) (indorser).

[75] Home Center Supply of Md., Inc. v. Certainteed Corp., 59 Md. App. 495, 476 A.2d 724, 38 U.C.C. Rep. Serv. 1300 (1984).

```
         "X"
      M----▶C.........▶M
              (pays)
```

Diagram 4.4

Maker (M) signs a promissory note as an accommodation party for the accommodated party (X), who indorses the note before it is issued to Creditor (C). M pays the note when it becomes due. As an accommodated party, X's liability on the instrument runs to M once M has paid.

This special right of recourse in favor of accommodation parties is based on the principle of subrogation.[76] An accommodation party signs only as a surety for a debt that benefits the principal. Therefore, in order to prevent unjust enrichment of the principal, a surety, through subrogation, is entitled to assert the rights of the creditor against the principal debtor.[77]

In addition to rights of recourse on the instrument, the accommodation party also has rights available under general principles of suretyship law.[78] A surety's right of reimbursement from the principal entitles an accommodation party to recover the amount paid based on an implied promise of indemnification by the accommodated party.[79] Unlike subrogation, reimbursement is not tied to the creditor's rights against the principal. A surety's equitable right of exoneration enables an accommodation party to compel the principal debtor to pay the instrument when it becomes due, even if the accommodation party is primarily liable and the principal is an indorser.[80] This right does not prejudice the creditor's right to proceed on the accommodation party's liability.[81] When two or more persons sign in the same capacity as accommodation parties, they generally are jointly and severally liable.[82] The party who pays is entitled to contribution from the other sureties for their proportionate share of the debt.[83]

---

[76] Lindsey v. Zeller, 10 Kan. App. 2d 4, 690 P.2d 394, 39 U.C.C. Rep. Serv. 1367 (1984).

[77] Restatement of Security § 141(a); Simpson v. Bilderbeck, Inc., 76 N.M. 667, 417 P.2d 803, 3 U.C.C. Rep. Serv. 737 (1966) (accommodation party who signed as co-maker subrogated to rights of holder bank).

[78] O'Hara v. First Nat'l Bank, 613 S.W.2d 306, 31 U.C.C. Rep. Serv. 743 (Tex. Civ. App. 1980) (accommodation co-maker entitled to ordinary rights of suretyship).

[79] U.C.C. § 3-419(e); Restatement of Security §§ 104, 108; Payne v. Payne, 219 Va. 12, 245 S.E.2d 133, 24 U.C.C. Rep. Serv. 387 (1978).

[80] Restatement of Security § 112. Some states have statutes on the right of exoneration. Minn. Stat. Ann. § 540.11 (1986).

[81] Murphy v. Bank of Dahlonega, 151 Ga. App. 264, 259 S.E.2d 670, 27 U.C.C. Rep. Serv. 1046 (1979) (accommodation maker liable without resort to the principal).

[82] U.C.C. § 3-116(a).

[83] U.C.C. § 3-116(b); Restatement of Security § 149; Fleck v. Ragan, 514 N.E.2d 1287, 5 U.C.C. Rep. Serv. 2d 644 (Ind. Ct. App. 1987).

[D] Establishing Accommodation Status

As described above, accommodation parties are in the first instance liable in the capacities in which they sign the instruments. Occasionally it becomes important to establish accommodation status. As the discussion above explained, accommodation status affects the rights and obligations of the accommodation party and the accommodated party with respect to each other. Accommodation parties sometimes have special defenses to liability based on the law of suretyship (some of which are codified in Article 3). Notice of accommodation status of a party, therefore, can also be relevant in determining whether such defenses are effective against a party seeking to enforce the instrument.[84] The discussion of this legal effect is reserved for the chapter on discharge.[85]

Proof of accommodation status can be found in a number of different sources. The person signing the instrument might add words that help prove the status.[86] Accommodation status sometimes can be inferred from the way a surety signs an instrument.[87] An anomalous indorsement provides notice that an instrument is signed for accommodation.[88] The sole effect of an anomalous indorsement is to make the signer liable on the instrument as an indorser.[89] Because it is not needed to negotiate the instrument and because it is a common method for becoming a surety, an anomalous indorsement creates a presumption that it is for accommodation purposes.[90] Before delivery of the instrument to the creditor, the accommodation party simply indorses a note prepared by the accommodated party as the maker. Anyone examining the note can clearly see that the indorsement is anomalous because the note runs on its face to the payee-creditor, who ordinarily would be the first party to indorse the note.

Even though sufficient evidence establishes a presumption of accommodation status, the presumption can be rebutted by evidence that the signer in fact was a direct beneficiary of the value given for the instrument.[91] In one case, for example, the court held that the signer was not an

---

[84] *See* U.C.C. § 3-605(h).

[85] *See* § 7.02[E] *infra*.

[86] U.C.C. § 3-419(c); Holcomb State Bank v. Adamson, 107 Ill. App. 3d 908, 63 Ill. Dec. 704, 438 N.E.2d 635, 34 U.C.C. Rep. Serv. 940 (1982) (attached memo indicated accommodation status).

[87] The converse is true as well. The notes in Nester v. O'Donnell, 301 N.J. Super. 198, 693 A.2d 1214, 35 U.C.C. Rep. Serv. 2d 533 (1997), were signed "MDN, INC., herein singly referred to as the 'Borrower,' HARRY NESTER and MARY NESTER, all of which are herein collectively referred to as the 'Undersigned,' jointly and severally promise to pay" the amounts involved. The appellate court affirmed the trial court's holding that the joint and several liability made all of the parties responsible together and individually, so that the individuals were not accommodation parties.

[88] U.C.C. § 3-419(c). "'Anomalous indorsement' means an indorsement made by a person who is not the holder of the instrument." U.C.C. § 3-205(d).

[89] U.C.C. § 3-205, Comment 3.

[90] U.C.C. § 3-419(c); Bizzocco v. Chinitz, 193 Conn. 304, 476 A.2d 572, 39 U.C.C. Rep. Serv. 540 (1984).

[91] U.C.C. § 3-419, Comment 3.

accommodation party because he was benefitted by being released from a prior note.[92] In other cases, wives have been held not to be accommodation parties on their husbands' notes because of benefits they received from the notes.[93] In the absence of a showing that she received any benefit from the note, however, a wife was held to be an accommodation party on her husband's note.[94] Similarly, a father co-signing for a loan to his son was an accommodation party to the transaction because all of the benefit of the loan went to the son.[95]

[E] Defenses

Just as accommodation parties are liable in the capacity in which they sign, they retain the defenses available to a party who signs in the same capacity. Thus, for example, an accommodation indorser who is not given timely notice of dishonor will be discharged to the same extent as an ordinary indorser. In addition, some traditional suretyship defenses are codified and others are available through general principles of law and equity. The rules of discharge and suretyship defenses are covered in Chapter 7.[96]

Certain other issues concerning possible defenses for accommodation parties remain. An accommodation signer might argue, for example, that the creditor did not provide any consideration to the accommodation party. The argument fails under fundamental principles of suretyship law.[97] The consideration that the creditor provides to the principal also supports the obligation of the surety.[98] When the loan has already been made and the instrument issued to the creditor before the accommodation party's signature is added, the accommodation party is still liable even though the creditor does not provide any new consideration in the form of additional credit or an extension in the time to pay.[99] An accommodation party also cannot successfully assert a defense of the lack of consideration from the party accommodated.[100]

Consumers often have co-signed notes in complete ignorance of the lack of defenses against the creditor. Because they sign simply to facilitate credit

---

[92] Mooney v. GR & Associates, 746 P.2d 1174, 5 U.C.C. Rep. Serv. 2d 1419 (Utah Ct. App. 1987).

[93] Willis v. Willis, 30 U.C.C. Rep. Serv. 1332 (D. D.C. 1980), *aff'd on this point*, 655 F.2d 1333, 32 U.C.C. Rep. Serv. 202 (D.C. Cir. 1981); Riegler v. Riegler, 244 Ark. 483, 426 S.W.2d 789, 5 U.C.C. Rep. Serv. 150 (1968).

[94] Burke v. Burke, 89 Ill. App. 3d 826, 412 N.E.2d 204, 30 U.C.C. Rep. Serv. 590 (1980).

[95] American Oil Co. v. Valenti, 179 Conn. 349, 426 A.2d 305, 28 U.C.C. Rep. Serv. 118 (1979).

[96] *See* § 7.02[E] *infra*.

[97] U.C.C. § 3-419(b).

[98] U.C.C. § 3-419, Comment 2; Cissna Park State Bank v. Johnson, 21 Ill. App. 3d 445, 315 N.E.2d 675, 15 U.C.C. Rep. Serv. 667 (1974).

[99] U.C.C. § 3-419, Comment 2; State Bank v. Omega Electronics, Inc., 634 S.W.2d 234, 34 U.C.C. Rep. Serv. 934 (Mo. Ct. App. 1982).

[100] Gill v. Commonwealth Nat'l Bank, 504 S.W.2d 521, 14 U.C.C. Rep. Serv. 428 (Tex. Civ. App. 1973).

for someone else without receiving any direct benefit from the proceeds, they may not adequately contemplate the consequences that can befall them. Therefore, the Federal Trade Commission promulgated a trade regulation designed to apprise sureties in consumer-credit transactions. A creditor is guilty of a deceptive act under the Federal Trade Commission Act if it incurs the obligation of a surety in an extension of consumer credit without giving the surety the following notice before the surety becomes obligated.[101]

NOTICE TO CO-SIGNOR

You are being asked to guarantee this debt. Think carefully before you do. If the borrower doesn't pay the debt, you will have to. Be sure you can afford to pay it if you have to, and that you want to accept this responsibility.

You may have to pay the full amount of the debt if the borrower does not pay. You may also have to pay late fees or collection costs, which increase this amount.

The creditor can collect this debt from you without first trying to collect from the borrower. The creditor can use the same collection methods against you that can be used against the borrower, such as suing you, garnishing your wages, etc. If this debt is ever in default, that fact may become part of *your* credit record.

This notice is not the contract that makes you liable for the debt.[102]

For the most part, an accommodation party can assert any claims or defenses that would be available to the accommodated party against the person entitled to enforce the instrument.[103] Basic contract defenses that affect the accommodated party's obligation thus are generally available to the accommodation party as well.[104] On the other hand, principal debtors are required to provide accommodation signers on their instruments in order to protect creditors against certain specific risks. These risks generally relate to the principal's solvency and contractual capacity. For example, a lender who is concerned with the financial stability of a corporate entity will want its officers or principal stockholders to sign the corporate notes.[105] Similarly, an automobile dealer who sells a car on an installment-payment plan to a minor will want the minor's parent to sign the note as well.[106] To the extent that the accommodated party's defense stems from discharge in insolvency proceedings, infancy, or lack of legal capacity, the defense is

---

[101] As the regulatory agencies with jurisdiction over banks, the Federal Reserve Board and the Federal Home Loan Bank Board have adopted similar rules. 12 C.F.R. §§ 227.14, 535.3.

[102] 16 C.F.R. § 444.3 (emphasis in original).

[103] U.C.C. § 3-305(d).

[104] Worthen Bank & Trust Co., N.A. v. Utley, 748 F.2d 1269, 39 U.C.C. Rep. Serv. 1378 (8th Cir. 1984) (material alteration); Household Fin. Co. v. Watson, 552 S.W.2d 111, 17 U.C.C. Rep. Serv. 152 (Mo. Ct. App. 1975) (instrument paid).

[105] State Bank v. Owens, 31 Colo. App. 351, 502 P.2d 965, 11 U.C.C. Rep. Serv. 1024 (1972).

[106] Murphy v. Bank of Dahlonega, 151 Ga. App. 264, 259 S.E.2d 670, 27 U.C.C. Rep. Serv. 1046 (1979).

not available to the accommodation party because these risks passed to the accommodation party by reason of the accommodation signature.[107]

[F] Words Guaranteeing Collection

An accommodation party can alter the nature of his or her contract by including with the signature words that unambiguously indicate that the signer is guaranteeing collection rather than payment of the obligation of another party to the instrument.[108] With the inclusion of such words with the signature, the signer is obliged to pay the amount due on the instrument, provided that the person entitled to enforce the instrument first proceeds against the accommodated party by execution on a judgment, unless such a proceeding would be useless.[109] In other words, the Code imposes a unique set of conditions to the liability of a party guaranteeing collection. The person entitled to enforce the instrument must have reduced the claim against the accommodation party to a judgment, with the execution returned unsatisfied. The requirement is excused only if the accommodated party is insolvent or in insolvency proceedings or cannot be served with process, or if it is otherwise apparent that payment cannot be recovered from the party.[110] A guarantee of collection restricts the signer's obligation considerably.

§ 4.05 Authority to Sign

[A] Signature by Authorized Representative — § 3-402

Article 3 recognizes fundamental principles of agency law by allowing an agent or other authorized representative[111] to sign an instrument on behalf of another person. Business reasons or simple convenience lead individuals to authorize another person to sign their instruments. Organizations like corporations or partnerships can act only through their authorized agents. Thus, the ability to bind a principal through the signature of an authorized agent is an important tenet of the law of negotiable instruments.

Article 3 defers to agency law to determine when the agency relationship is established. An agent's authority to sign a negotiable instrument is created just as it is in any other case of representation.[112] The

---

[107] U.C.C. § 3-305(d).

[108] U.C.C. § 3-419(d).

[109] U.C.C. § 3-419(d).

[110] Floor v. Melvin, 5 Ill. App. 3d 463, 283 N.E.2d 303, 11 U.C.C. Rep. Serv. 109 (1972) (dismissal for failure to state a cause of action affirmed because complaint against guarantor did not allege prosecution of claim to judgment against principal obligor on the note and did not allege insolvency of the obligor).

[111] "'Representative' includes an agent, an officer of a corporation or association, and a trustee, executor or administrator of an estate, or any other person empowered to act for another." U.C.C. § 1-201(35).

[112] U.C.C. § 3-402(a) ("the represented person is bound by the signature to the same extent the represented person would be bound if the signature were on a simple contract").

authorization to sign for another person can be based on express authority, authority implied in law or in fact, or merely apparent authority.[113] If the represented person is bound under the principles of agency law, the signature of the representative is the "authorized signature of the represented person."[114] The represented person is then just as liable on the instrument as if his or her signature had been made in person.[115]

When the signature of the represented person is authorized, the represented person will be liable on the instrument whether or not that person is identified in the instrument.[116] The authorized agent's signature of the principal's name or the agent's name on an instrument constitutes an authorized signature and binds the principal on the instrument in the capacity in which the agent signed it. An agent's signature of only the principal's name, such as "Paula Principal," will be effective. A signature only in the name of an agent, such as "Alex Agent," will also bind the principal on the instrument. If the agent acted only with apparent authority, non-Code principles might give the principal rights against the agent.

Agents must exercise caution in order to avoid incurring their own personal liability on the instrument. Authorized representatives often will be required by their transferees to sign their names to the instrument, as well as the names of their principals. The agent's signature shows the person who signed on behalf of the principal. Agents signing instruments in their own name can become liable in the capacity in which they sign.[117]

Section 3-402(b)(1) states a general rule under which an agent who signs his or her own name as part of an authorized signature of a represented person will escape personal liability. The signature must show that it is made on behalf of a represented person who is identified in the instrument.[118] The agent thus should do two things: (1) name the principal, and (2) indicate representative capacity. A signature in the form "Queen Elizabeth, by James Bond, agent" fully satisfies the requirement. Anyone who reads such a signature should understand that the agent is signing to bind the principal and only identifies himself or herself as the person signing for the principal.

---

[113] Restatement (Second) of Agency §§ 7-8 (1957). *See* H. REUSCHLIEN & W. GREGORY, THE LAW OF AGENCY AND PARTNERSHIP 34-38, 41-44, 57-64 (2nd ed. 1990); Senate Motors, Inc. v. Industrial Bank, 9 U.C.C. Rep. Serv. 387 (D.C. Sup. Ct. 1971) (actual, implied, or apparent authority may be the basis of representation).

[114] U.C.C. § 3-402(a).

[115] U.C.C. §§ 3-401(a)(ii), 3-402(a).

[116] This approach is a change in the revision of Article 3 that corrects an anomaly under the prior law and brings Article 3 into conformity with agency-law principles. *See* U.C.C. § 3-402, Comment 1.

[117] Authorized representatives who are required to pay instruments should be entitled to indemnification from their principals. Restatement (Second) of Agency §§ 438, 439 (1958).

[118] In Mundaca Investment Corp. v. Febba, 727 A.2d 990, 38 U.C.C. Rep. Serv. 2d 464 (N.H. 1999), the defendants wrote the word "trustee" after their signatures. Section 3-402(b)(1) requires, however, that in addition the represented person be "identified in the instrument." This requirement was not met by reading the notes together with the mortgages executed as part of the same transaction, even though the mortgages identified the trust as the borrower.

The agent might comply with less than all of the requirements. In the illustration, the agent might indicate representative capacity but not name the principal, as in "James Bond, agent." Alternatively, he might name the principal but omit the reference to representative capacity by signing "Queen Elizabeth, James Bond." The principal would be bound on both signatures because the signatures are authorized. The agent would be "liable on the instrument to a holder in due course that took the instrument without notice that the representative was not intended to be liable on the instrument."[119] The representative can escape personal liability with respect to any other person by proving that the original parties did not intend the representative to be personally liable on the instrument. This understanding is common when an agent acts for a disclosed principal. Under these rules governing ambiguous signatures by authorized representatives, the mutual intent that the representative not be bound is treated as a contract defense that is cut off only by subsequent holders in due course of the instrument.[120]

A final provision can preclude liability on the instrument for an authorized representative who does not indicate representative status. When the representative signs as the drawer of a check and the check is payable from an account of a represented person who is identified on the check (which is nearly inevitable in this age of personalized check forms), the signer is not liable on the check.[121] As an exception to the rules of section 3-402(b), it is limited to checks only because of valid policy grounds. The legitimate commercial expectations of the holder of a corporate payroll check certainly do not include the belief that the individual signing the check is personally liable on the instrument. On the other hand, corporate notes are commonly signed by officers or shareholders in their individual capacities because a lender or supplier might not extend credit to the business without these individuals also incurring liability on the instrument.[122] Authorized representatives who desire to sign a note on behalf of an organization without binding themselves can sign their name and office, together with the name of the organization they represent.[123] An authorized officer's signature in the form "Her Majesty's Secret Service, Ltd., James Bond, President" is sufficient.

---

[119] U.C.C. § 3-402(b)(2).

[120] Mundaca Investment Corp. v. Febba, 727 A.2d 990, 38 U.C.C. Rep. Serv. 2d 464 (N.H. 1999) (genuine issues of material fact concerning the intent of the original parties and whether the subsequent transferee of the notes was a holder in due course who took without notice that the defendants did not intend to be personally liable on the notes).

[121] U.C.C. § 3-402(c); Peterson v. Holtrachem, Inc., 239 Ga. App. 838, 521 S.E.2d 648, 40 U.C.C. Rep. Serv. 2d 527 (Ga. Ct. App. 1999) (part-time employee not personally liable on company check imprinted with company's name after the check was returned for insufficient funds).

[122] Rotuba Extruders, Inc. v. Ceppos, 46 N.Y.2d 223, 413 N.Y.S.2d 141, 385 N.E.2d 1068, 25 U.C.C. Rep. Serv. 765 (1978).

[123] U.C.C. § 3-402, Comment 2.

[B] Unauthorized Signatures — § 3-403

Article 3 also codifies fundamental principles of agency law in relation to unauthorized signatures. "[A]n unauthorized signature is ineffective except as the signature of the unauthorized signer in favor of a person who in good faith pays the instrument or takes it for value."[124] An unauthorized signature means "one made without actual, implied, or apparent authority and includes a forgery."[125] The Code does not draw the criminal law distinction between a forgery and the signature of an agent who exceeds the scope of authority.

Generally, an unauthorized signature is not an effective signature of the person that it names. Consequently, the person who is named on the instrument has not signed it and thus does not incur liability on it.[126] If the instrument runs to the order of that person, the unauthorized signature will not be effective to negotiate the instrument. Subsequent transferees of the instrument will not qualify as holders, nor will they derivatively receive the right to enforce the instrument.

The unauthorized signer, on the other hand, incurs liability on the instrument in favor of anyone who in good faith pays the instrument or takes it for value.[127] This approach is entirely consistent with the definition of "signed," which recognizes any symbol executed with the intent to authenticate the writing.[128] A forger uses the name of the person signed in order to perpetrate a fraud, but because using the name was not authorized to bind the person named, the name used is simply the symbol executed as the forger's signature. The signature is just as effectively the forger's as if the forger had signed his or her own actual name. The signer is fully liable on the instrument in whatever capacity the signature is made.

These basic rules of nonliability of the person named and liability of the unauthorized signer are subject to some exceptions. One of these exceptions is ratification of the unauthorized signature by the person named.[129] Ratification reverses the effect of both rules: the person named becomes liable and the unauthorized signer is relieved from liability on the instrument.[130] Ratification is the retroactive adoption of the signature as though it had been originally authorized.

Ratification does not excuse the unauthorized signer from liability to the person whose name is signed or from criminal liability.[131] The signer has

---

[124] U.C.C. § 3-403(a).

[125] U.C.C. § 1-201(43).

[126] U.C.C. § 3-401(a); Nat'l Credit Union Admin. v. Michigan Nat'l Bank, 771 F.2d 154, 41 U.C.C. Rep. Serv. 1573 (6th Cir. 1985).

[127] U.C.C. § 3-403(a); European Am. Bank & Trust Co. v. Starcrete Int'l Indus., Inc., 613 F.2d 564, 28 U.C.C. Rep. Serv. 722 (5th Cir. 1980).

[128] U.C.C. § 1-201(39); Aetna Cas. & Sur. Co. v. Hepler State Bank, 6 Kan App. 2d 543, 630 P.2d 721, 32 U.C.C. Rep. Serv. 187 (1981) (unauthorized use of stamp).

[129] U.C.C. § 3-403(a) ("An unauthorized signature may be ratified for all purposes of this Article.").

[130] U.C.C. § 3-403, Comment 3; Richards v. Arthaloney, 216 Neb. 11, 342 N.W.2d 642, 38 U.C.C. Rep. Serv. 234 (1983).

[131] U.C.C. § 3-403(c).

acted wrongly with respect to the person whose name is signed and is liable for any losses caused to that person from the signature.[132] A forgery is also a violation of criminal law, and a ratification will not relieve the forger from this liability. Criminal laws advance the interests of society, and rights of the state cannot be altered by a private ratification. Some pre-Code cases did not allow ratification of a forgery because the forgery is a criminal act. The Code drafters allow it because the person ratifying simply assumes liability to others on the instrument without altering the criminal liability of the forger.[133]

Ratification is determined by the principles of agency law applied in the relevant jurisdiction.[134] It can be expressed by a statement of the named party manifesting an intention to adopt the writing. It also can be implied through actions by the named party that lead to the same conclusion. The most common circumstance occurs when the named party obtains a benefit from the proceeds of the instrument and retains it upon becoming fully informed of the facts. For example, a husband forged his wife's signature to obtain a loan to build a supermarket. Upon learning of the forgery, the wife did not disavow it, but rather assisted in the operation of the supermarket and benefitted financially from it.[135]

In addition to liability assumed through ratification of an unauthorized signature, a person whose name is improperly signed sometimes can be precluded from denying the signature. A representation by the person whose name is signed that the signature is genuine could lead to an estoppel in favor of a purchaser who detrimentally relies upon the representation. Negligence of the person whose name is signed can also result in preclusion to deny the signature by that person. Several separate Code sections address the relevance of negligence. Section 3-406 is a general section dictating when a person's negligence preludes the assertion of an unauthorized signature. Sections 3-404 and 3-405 address specific circumstances when an unauthorized indorsement is considered to be effective. Section 4-406 governs the effect of a bank customer's negligence in failing to report unauthorized signatures. All four of these sections are covered in a subsequent chapter of this text.[136]

---

[132] Atlas Bldg. Supply Co., Inc. v. First Independent Bank, 15 Wash. App. 367, 550 P.2d 26, 19 U.C.C. Rep. Serv. 572 (1976).

[133] Funds For Business Growth, Inc. v. Woodland Marble & Tile Co., 433 Pa. 281, 278 A.2d 922, 9 U.C.C. Rep. Serv. 255 (1971) (Pennsylvania law disallowing ratification of forgeries modified by Article 3).

[134] U.C.C. § 4-403, Comment 3.

[135] Rakestraw v. Rodrigues, 8 Cal. 3d 67, 104 Cal. Rptr. 57, 500 P.2d 1401, 11 U.C.C. Rep. Serv. 780 (1972).

[136] *See* Chapter 10 *infra*.

§ 4.06 Enforcement of Lost, Destroyed, or Stolen Instruments — § 3-309

[A] Introduction

Even though negotiable instruments are a form of indispensable paper, with the right to the payment of money tied to the paper itself, the law must deal with the inevitable circumstances where production of the paper by the party entitled to enforce it is impossible. The party could lose the instrument through careless handling; fire or some other calamity could destroy the writing; or a thief could steal it. The law could respond by treating negotiable instruments like money, and thus impose a high risk on loss of possession. In several respects, however, including cases of lost instruments, the law utilizes measures that make instruments safer than money.

This favorable protection of enforcement rights is easily justified. If the law were to deny any enforceability of a lost instrument simply because the party entitled to enforce it cannot produce the writing, it would foster unjust enrichment in many cases. For example, assume that an individual buys goods and issues a check or a promissory note to the seller, but a fire destroys the instrument while it is in the seller's possession. The Article 2 payment obligation of the buyer[137] is suspended upon issuance of the instrument.[138] If the seller were not allowed a form of recovery for the destroyed instrument, the buyer would receive the windfall of not having to pay for the goods purchased.

To avoid such an inequitable result, Article 3 recognizes a cause of action in favor of the person entitled to enforce a lost, destroyed, or stolen instrument.[139] Even though not in possession of the instrument, a person who is entitled to enforce the instrument is still allowed to do so if requirements specified in Article 3 are satisfied.[140] Such enforcement of these instruments is simply enforcement of the contract liability of the parties that signed the instrument. Because of the impossibility of presentment under these circumstances, any required presentment for payment is excused.[141]

---

[137] U.C.C. § 2-301.

[138] U.C.C. § 3-310(b). *See* § 7.03 *infra*.

[139] U.C.C. § 3-309.

[140] *See* § 4.06[B] *infra*.

[141] *See* U.C.C. § 3-504(a); § 5.05[B] *infra*. Dishonor occurs automatically when the check is not duly paid. U.C.C. § 3-502(e).

The obligor on the instrument who is required to pay will have a legitimate concern about potential double liability. If the instrument resurfaces in the hands of a holder in due course, which is a very real possibility with bearer paper (including paper that was originally payable to order but has been indorsed in blank by the holder), the obligor will face a second demand for payment on the obligation and will not be able to resist paying it. To protect the obligor against this eventuality, a court cannot enter judgment to pay unless it finds that the person required to pay is adequately protected against such loss.[142] The court can thus provide a means of ensuring that the owner of an instrument does not unjustly pass his or her loss to a prior obligor on the instrument.

[B] Enforcing the Instrument

A lost, destroyed, or stolen instrument can be enforced only by a person entitled to enforce it.[143] The Article 3 definition of "person entitled to enforce" an instrument includes, in addition to the holder of the instrument and a nonholder in possession of the instrument who has the rights of a holder, "a person not in possession of the instrument who is entitled to enforce the instrument pursuant to Section 3-309."[144] Section 3-309 includes several requirements that must be satisfied in order to enforce a lost, destroyed, or stolen instrument.[145]

The person seeking to enforce the instrument must have been in possession of the instrument and entitled to enforce it when the loss of possession occurred.[146] In other words, the person seeking to enforce the instrument had to have been a holder of the instrument or a person in possession of the instrument who had the rights of a holder at the time possession was lost.[147] The objective is to continue, after the loss of possession, a preexisting right to enforce the instrument, not to create an enforcement right in another entity.[148]

---

[142] U.C.C. § 3-309(b). *See* § 4.06[C] *infra*.

[143] U.C.C. § 3-309(a).

[144] U.C.C. § 3-301.

[145] U.C.C. § 3-309(a).

[146] Weaver Landfill, Inc. v. Eastman Envtl. Transp. Services, 37 U.C.C. Rep. Serv. 2d 342 (Va. Jud. Cir. Ct. 1998) (plaintiff could not enforce note as its affidavit showed it never possessed the original note); Western Nat'l Bank v. Rives, 927 S.W.2d 681, 33 U.C.C. Rep. Serv. 2d 500 (Tex. Ct. App. 1996) (provision cannot be used by a plaintiff that cannot establish that it had prior possession).

[147] Hathorn v. Loftus, 726 A.2d 1278, 37 U.C.C. Rep. Serv. 2d 676 (N.H. 1999) (because note was indorsed to transferee before its delivery and subsequent loss, transferee had qualified as a holder and could use section 3-309).

[148] Courts have held that a party that has enforcement rights under section 3-309 can assign those rights through the shelter principle to a subsequent transferee. Beal Bank, S.S.B. v. Caddo Parish-Villas South, Ltd., 218 B.R. 851, 34 U.C.C. Rep. Serv. 2d 1103 (N.D. Tex. 1998); NAB Asset Venture II, L.P. v. Lenertz, Inc., 36 U.C.C. Rep. Serv. 2d 474 (Minn. Ct. App. 1998) (unpublished opinion); YYY Corp. v. Gazda, 761 A.2d 395, 41 U.C.C. Rep. Serv. 2d 222 (N.H. 2000). For an explanation of the shelter principle, see § 6.02[C] *infra*.

The loss of possession of the instrument cannot be the result of a transfer by the person entitled to enforce the instrument or of a lawful seizure. A transfer of the instrument requires delivery for the purpose of giving the person receiving delivery the right to enforce the instrument.[149] Having voluntarily relinquished the instrument and the right to enforce it, the transferor does not retain any residual enforcement right.[150] Although loss of possession through lawful seizure is not voluntarily incurred by the possessor, the legal basis for the seizure preempts the prior enforcement right.

Finally, the person entitled to enforcement who has been deprived of possession can continue to enforce the instrument only if he or she "cannot reasonably obtain possession of the instrument because the instrument was destroyed, its whereabouts cannot be determined, or it is in the wrongful possession of an unknown person or a person that cannot be found or is not amenable to service of process."[151] If the instrument can be traced to a person whose possession is wrongful against the party who lost it or from whom it was stolen, the remedy would be replevin.[152]

In addition to proving entitlement to enforce a lost, destroyed, or stolen instrument, a person not in possession also must prove the terms of the instrument. Banks often satisfy this requirement by introducing a photostatic copy of the missing instrument as evidence of its contents.[153] Valid proof of the debt or other transaction that induced the issuance of the instrument can also help satisfy this requirement.[154]

[C] Adequate Protection Against Loss

If an instrument is lost or stolen while in bearer form, the need for protection of the party required to pay it is obvious. Anyone who finds or who steals the instrument is a holder and might negotiate it to someone else who qualifies as a holder in due course. Even the defense of theft is not valid against a holder in due course seeking to enforce the contract liability of prior parties. Thus, the party entitled to enforce the instrument should be required to provide protection for the person required to pay in the event that the instrument surfaces and can be further enforced against the payor.[155]

---

[149] U.C.C. §§ 3-203(a), 1-201(14).

[150] If the instrument were lost after it had been delivered to an agent for the purpose of depositing it into the principal's account, the instrument would not have been transferred and section 3-309 would still be available.

[151] U.C.C. § 3-309(a)(iii).

[152] See U.C.C. § 3-202, Comment 2.

[153] Laurel Bank & Trust Co. v. Sahadi, 32 Conn. Supp. 172, 345 A.2d 53, 17 U.C.C. Rep. Serv. 1259 (1975). See also Crawford v. 733 San Mateo Co., 854 F.2d 1220, 8 U.C.C. Rep. Serv. 2d 75 (10th Cir. 1988) (copy of note).

[154] United States v. Jenkins, 860 F.2d 1083, 6 U.C.C. Rep. Serv. 2d 1198 (8th Cir. 1988); Chase Manhattan Bank v. Concord Utilities Corp., 7 U.C.C. Rep. Serv. 52 (N.Y. Civ. Ct. 1969).

[155] "The court may not enter judgment in favor of the person seeking enforcement unless it finds that the person required to pay the instrument is adequately protected against loss that might occur by reason of a claim by another person to enforce the instrument." U.C.C. § 3-309(b).

If the instrument is in order form when it is lost or stolen, the payor is protected against double liability. Subsequent possessors cannot qualify as holders of the instrument,[156] so none of them could become holders in due course. Without the indorsement of the person to whom the instrument runs, the instrument is not properly payable to subsequent possessors. Parties to the instrument can resist any demands for payment,[157] and if a drawee pays, the drawer can insist that the drawee recredit the deposit account.[158]

Although an admission by a section 3-309 claimant that the instrument was in bearer form when lost or stolen easily suggests the need for adequate protection, the claimant's assertion that the instrument was in order form does not necessarily preclude the need for protection. The legal consequences that protect the person required to pay against double liability depend on the instrument being in order form, and risks concerning the form of the instrument abound. The claimant might be mistaken about the form of the paper, having forgotten that the instrument had been indorsed in blank. The assertion that the paper was in order form could be an outright lie. A lost instrument in order form could be found at a later date and indorsed by the claimant. In fact, the instrument might never have been lost or stolen; it could still be in the claimant's possession or already have been purposefully negotiated. The person required to pay bears the risk of these events because success in resisting further payment on the instrument depends on it not coming into the hands of a holder in due course. Even when the instrument was in order form when lost or stolen, the defendant can incur expenses in defending against demands to pay the instrument.

Ultimately, the determination of whether to require protection, as well as the type of protection, is within the discretion of the court. Although prior law specified requiring security to indemnify the defendant against loss, the revisions to Article 3 do not designate any specific type of protection.[159]

---

[156] The instrument would not run to the possessor as it would be either drawn or indorsed to another person. U.C.C. § 1-201(20).

[157] The contract obligations of all parties run to a person entitled to enforce the instrument or to subsequent indorsers who pay the instrument. U.C.C. §§ 3-412–3-415. Payment discharges the payor's obligation only if it is made to a person entitled to enforce the instrument. U.C.C. § 3-602(a). See § 7.02 [A] *infra*. Furthermore, obligors on an instrument are not obliged to pay an instrument that has been lost or stolen if the person seeking enforcement does not have the rights of a holder in due course. U.C.C. § 3-305(c). See § 6.03[B] *infra*.

[158] U.C.C. § 4-401(a). See § 12.01[B][2] *infra*.

[159] Bobby D. Assoc. v. DiMarcantonio, 751 A.2d 673, 41 U.C.C. Rep. Serv. 2d 878 (Pa. Super. Ct. 2000) (trial court assured adequate protection by requiring plaintiffs to execute an indemnification agreement in favor of defendants).

Courts are likely to consider several factors in exercising their discretion. The requirement for protection might be dispensed with when much time has elapsed [160] or the facts might leave little doubt that the instrument was destroyed or that the instrument was in order form when lost or stolen. [161] Banks sometimes have benefitted from their established financial status in the community by being relieved of posting any security. [162]

[D] Special Rules on Cashier's Checks, Teller's Checks, and Certified Checks — § 3-312

The revision to Article 3 includes some special rules with respect to recovery for lost, destroyed, or stolen cashier's checks, teller's checks, and certified checks. [163] The objective of the rules is to provide an effective means for the person who loses such a check to get a refund without incurring the expense of posting a bond, while also protecting the bank that incurred liability on the check. [164] Note that the provisions of section 3-309 apply only to a person entitled to enforce the check, and thus do not apply to the remitter of a cashier's check or teller's check or to the drawer of a certified check.

The special rules are premised on the empirical observation that virtually all of the applicable types of checks are presented for payment within 90 days of the date or certification of the check. [165] The claimant is required to provide the bank with a declaration of loss. [166] The claim then is not enforceable, however, until at least 90 days from the date or certification of the check. [167] During the 90-day period, and thereafter until the claim is asserted, the bank can pay the check in accordance with its obligation and attain a discharge. [168] If the claim becomes effective before the check is presented for payment, the bank must pay the claimant and thereby attains discharge from liability with respect to the check. [169] Under the

---

[160] *But see* Santos v. First Nat'l State Bank, 186 N.J. Super. 52, 451 A.2d 401, 35 U.C.C. Rep. Serv. 518 (1982) (held four years from issuance of a cashier's check not sufficient to preclude requirement of security because presentment would be proper any time during statute of limitations).

[161] U.C.C. § 3-309, Comment. NAB Asset Venture II, L.P. v. Lenertz, Inc., 36 U.C.C. Rep. Serv. 2d 474 (Minn. Ct. App. 1998) (unpublished opinion) (upheld district court finding that a claim on the same instrument was highly unlikely because of the absence of indorsements in blank, the passage of four years, and the fact that the makers were no longer in business).

[162] Laurel Bank & Trust Co. v. Sahadi, 32 Conn. Super. 172, 345 A.2d 53, 17 U.C.C. Rep. Serv. 1259 (1975) (no security required of bank because it maintained considerable attachable assets within the state); National Shawmut Bank v. International Yarn Corp., 322 F. Supp. 166, 8 U.C.C. Rep. Serv. 1278 (S.D. N.Y. 1970) (letter of indemnity sufficient because plaintiff was a banking institution).

[163] U.C.C. § 3-312.

[164] U.C.C. § 3-312, Comment 1.

[165] U.C.C. § 3-312, Comment 3.

[166] U.C.C. § 3-312(b),(a)(3).

[167] U.C.C. § 3-312(b)(1).

[168] U.C.C. § 3-312(b)(2).

[169] U.C.C. § 3-312(b)(4).

latter situation, the claimant that received payment from the bank is responsible for the amount of the check if a person with the rights of a holder in due course subsequently presents the check for payment.[170]

---

[170] U.C.C. § 3-312(c).

Chapter 5
SATISFYING THE CONDITIONS OF CONTRACTUAL LIABILITY

SYNOPSIS

§ 5.01　Introduction

§ 5.02　The Conditions
　　　　[A]　Presentment — § 3-501
　　　　[B]　Dishonor — § 3-502
　　　　[C]　Notice of Dishonor — § 3-503

§ 5.03　Time Requirements
　　　　[A]　Presentment — §§ 3-414(f), 3-415(e)
　　　　[B]　Dishonor — § 3-502
　　　　　　　[1]　Payment Context
　　　　　　　[2]　Acceptance Context
　　　　[C]　Notice of Dishonor — § 3-503(c)

§ 5.04　Consequences of Failure to Satisfy the Conditions
　　　　[A]　Indorsers — § 3-415(c)
　　　　[B]　Drawers — § 3-414(f)

§ 5.05　Excused Presentment and Notice of Dishonor — § 3-504
　　　　[A]　Delay
　　　　[B]　Complete Excuse

§ 5.01 Introduction

The contracts of drawers and indorsers require that certain conditions be satisfied to enforce contract liability. The provisions of Article 3, Part 5 and some provisions in sections 3-414 and 3-415 cover these conditions. They dictate what the conditions are, when they must be met, the consequences of failure to satisfy them, and when the conditions are excused or waived. These provisions are explained in this chapter.

§ 5.02 The Conditions

The obligations of drawers and indorsers are enforceable only after the instrument is dishonored. Dishonor is thus one of the conditions to the contract liability of these parties. Dishonor is the refusal by the party who was expected to pay or to accept to do so. As the discussion below will demonstrate, dishonor generally cannot occur unless the instrument is properly presented. Presentment is the method by which payment or acceptance is requested of the expected payor. Enforceability of an indorser's contract liability also requires notice of dishonor.[1] Notice of dishonor is the method by which an indorser is apprised that the instrument was dishonored.

[A] Presentment — § 3-501

Presentment is "a demand made by or on behalf of a person entitled to enforce an instrument (i) to pay the instrument made to the drawee or a party obliged to pay the instrument or, in the case of a note or accepted draft payable at a bank, to the bank, or (ii) to accept a draft made to the drawee."[2] No technical requirements or special form of demand are required.[3] The demand, however, must be made by a person entitled to enforce an instrument or by someone acting on that person's behalf.[4] This requirement is consistent with the provision providing that a party making payment will be discharged only to the extent that the payment is made to a person entitled to enforce the instrument.[5]

Although mere demand is initially sufficient to constitute presentment, the party upon whom presentment is made has a right to insist on certain additional requirements that must be met to continue the validity of the presentment.[6] These requirements are for the protection of the person asked to pay or accept an instrument.[7] Thus, exhibition of the instrument by the presenter can be required.[8] Acceptance of an instrument would be physically impossible without exhibiting the instrument because the acceptance signature must be written on the instrument. Any prudent person will also require exhibition of the instrument before paying it in order to verify its existence and its terms. On the other hand, a person who intends to

---

[1] Notice of dishonor to a drawer is also required when a draft is accepted and the acceptor is not a bank. U.C.C. §§ 3-414(d), 3-503(a). In such cases, the drawer's liability is similar to that of an indorser, hence the equal treatment.

[2] U.C.C. § 3-501(a); Wolverton Farmers Elevator v. First Am. Bank, 851 F.2d 223, 6 U.C.C. Rep. Serv. 2d 1203 (8th Cir. 1988) (instruction to hold a check until sufficient funds are deposited to cover it was not a present demand for immediate payment and thus not presentment); Rose v. United States Nat'l Bank, 218 Neb. 97, 352 N.W.2d 594, 39 U.C.C. Rep. Serv. 561 (1984) (telephone call by holder of check to drawee bank to ascertain adequacy of funds in the account was not presentment).

[3] Presentment does not require indorsement by the presenter. A drawee does not take by negotiation, so an indorsement is not necessary. Merriman v. Sandeen, 267 N.W.2d 714, 24 U.C.C. Rep. Serv. 718 (Minn. 1978).

[4] Brown v. Fifth Third Bank, 10 Ohio App. 3d 97, 10 Ohio B.R. 120, 460 N.E.2d 739, 38 U.C.C. Rep. Serv. 177 (1983) (presentment by authorized agent).

[5] U.C.C. § 3-602(a). See § 7.02[A][1] *infra*.

[6] U.C.C. § 3-501(b)(2).

[7] Wright v. Bank of Cal., N.A., 276 Cal. App. 2d 485, 81 Cal. Rptr. 11, 6 U.C.C. Rep. Serv. 1165 (1969)(section indicates precautions available to drawee and does not create a duty to require them).

[8] The right to require exhibition of the instrument is waived when the parties agree otherwise, as in an electronic-presentment agreement. U.C.C. § 3-501, Comment.

dishonor an instrument may not care to see it. In such a case, the mere demand for payment would be sufficient to satisfy the condition of presentment.

A person upon whom presentment for payment or acceptance is made can also require "reasonable identification [of the presenter] and, if presentment is made on behalf of another person, reasonable evidence of authority to do so."[9] A person paying or accepting wants to be certain to deal with the proper party because subsequent rights and liabilities will be significantly affected.[10] In the event that payors or acceptors incur losses on the instrument, they have certain rights against their presenters that they might wish to pursue.[11] Identification of the presenter is, therefore, important to persons asked to pay or accept and they are entitled to demand identification that is reasonable under the circumstances.

Finally, the person upon whom presentment is made can require surrender of the instrument upon full payment or a signed receipt on the instrument itself for any partial or full payment.[12] This requirement is very important as it provides a payor with evidence that payments were made. Surrender of the instrument enables the payor to cancel it and precludes any further opportunities for negotiation or presentment of the instrument. Signed receipts on the instrument itself provide notice of payment to any subsequent transferees and prevent them from qualifying as holders in due course as to those payments.[13]

If the presenting party fails to comply with any of these requirements following a request by the party upon whom presentment is made, the initially effective presentment is invalidated.[14] As a result, the condition of presentment will not be satisfied and the party to whom presentment is made will not dishonor the instrument by refusing to pay or to accept it.

Presentment can be made by any commercially reasonable means.[15] The presentment is not effective, however, until it actually reaches the

---

[9] U.C.C. § 3-501(b)(2).

[10] *See* U.C.C. § 3-602(a) (party who pays is discharged only to extent of payment to a person entitled to enforce the instrument); U.C.C. § 4-401(a) (drawee bank can charge customer's account only for items that are properly payable).

[11] *See* U.C.C. §§ 3-417, 4-208 (presentment warranties); U.C.C. § 4-407 (subrogation rights).

[12] Although the surrender of the instrument through presentment results in a change of possession of the instrument from the presenter to the payor, the instrument is not transferred because the delivery is not for the purpose of giving the payor the right to enforce the instrument. U.C.C. § 3-203(a). *See* § 3.03 *supra*.

[13] U.C.C. § 3-601(b); Bank of Miami v. Florida City Express, Inc., 367 So. 2d 683, 25 U.C.C. Rep. Serv. 1102 (Fla. Ct. App. 1979) (maker who required neither surrender of notes nor signed receipt on the instruments held required to pay holder in due course to whom the original holder had negotiated the notes).

[14] U.C.C. § 3-501(b)(3); Florida Nat'l Bank v. Citizens Bank, 474 So. 2d 852, 41 U.C.C. Rep. Serv. 1348 (1985) (collecting bank, in failing to comply with reasonable requests imposed by payor bank, did not make valid presentment).

[15] U.C.C. § 3-501(b)(1).

obligor.[16] When there is more than one maker, acceptor, drawer, or other payor, presentment to any one of them is sufficient.[17] If that person refuses to pay or accept, the presenter can treat the instrument as dishonored rather than incurring the trouble and expense of making additional presentments. In the event of an acceptance, only the person who signs becomes liable on the instrument. If the liability of the other drawee is desired, an additional presentment for that person's signature is necessary.

[B] Dishonor — § 3-502

Dishonor is simply the nonpayment of an instrument or nonacceptance of an instrument within the time parameters provided in section 3-502. Dishonor can result because the person to whom presentment is made expressly refuses to pay or accept, because due payment or acceptance cannot be obtained within the prescribed time, or because presentment is excused and the instrument is not duly accepted or paid.[18]

A party seeking to impose liability on a drawer or indorser bears the burden of proof to establish satisfaction of the relevant conditions. The person who presents an instrument or knows of events that create an excuse for presentment can testify about the relevant facts. The testimony of the person denying acceptance or payment is also relevant. These approaches are both time consuming and expensive. Accordingly, the Code recognizes three additional sources of proof that are not only admissible as evidence, but also create a presumption that dishonor has occurred and of any notice of dishonor that is therein shown.[19] The presumption means that "the trier of fact must find the existence of the fact presumed unless and until evidence is introduced which would support a finding of its nonexistence."[20]

Production of a document, regular in form, that purports to be a protest is one of the relevant sources of evidence. "A protest is a certificate of dishonor made by a United States consul or vice consul, or a notary public or other person authorized to administer oaths by the law of the place where dishonor occurs."[21] Protest is generally used only in international transactions.

A purported stamp on the instrument or an accompanying writing of the drawee, payor bank, or presenting bank that states reasons for refusing

---

[16] U.C.C. § 3-501(b)(1); Catalina Yachts v. Old Colony Bank & Trust Co., 497 F. Supp. 1277, 32 U.C.C. Rep. Serv. 241 (D. Mass. 1980) (presentment of check at Bank A for computer processing did not constitute receipt of check by Bank B).

[17] U.C.C. § 3-501(b)(1); First Arlington Nat'l Bank v. Stathis, 90 Ill. App. 3d 802, 46 Ill. Dec. 175, 413 N.E.2d 1288, 32 U.C.C. Rep. Serv. 260 (1980), later app., 115 Ill. App. 3d 403, 71 Ill. Dec. 145, 450 N.E.2d 833, 36 U.C.C. Rep. Serv. 1284 (1983) (demand letters sent to business addresses of husbands were sufficient without additional individual letters to the wives who also signed the notes).

[18] U.C.C. § 3-502(e). The basis for excuse of presentment is covered below. See § 5.05 infra.

[19] U.C.C. § 3-505.

[20] U.C.C. § 1-201(31).

[21] U.C.C. § 3-505(b).

acceptance or payment consistent with dishonor is also satisfactory evidence. A payor bank often will stamp an instrument or accompanying ticket before returning a check. Several reasons for a justifiable refusal to pay or accept would not be consistent with dishonor, including missing indorsement, missing signature, illegible signature, forgery, altered payee, altered date, post-dated, and not drawn on the payor bank. Stated reasons within the provision that invoke the presumption are insufficient funds, garnished account, no account, and payment stopped.

Finally, any book or record of the drawee, payor bank, or any collecting bank that is kept in the regular course of business and shows dishonor is also admissible evidence sufficient to create a presumption of dishonor. Evidence as to who made the entry is not required. The improbability of falsification of books maintained in the ordinary course of business justifies the presumption.

[C] Notice of Dishonor — § 3-503

The obligation of an indorser cannot be enforced unless the indorser receives notice of dishonor of the instrument or the notice of dishonor is excused.[22] Notice of dishonor is thus a condition to the liability of indorsers.[23] The notice requirement is not technical. It can be given in any reasonable manner if it identifies the instrument and indicates that it has been dishonored or has not been paid or accepted.[24] It can be by oral, written, or electronic communication. The return of an instrument placed into the check-collection system is sufficient notice of dishonor.[25]

Because notice of dishonor can be given by any person, notice to a party from a single source satisfies the condition of notice of dishonor for all parties who have a right of recourse against the party notified.[26] Thus, if the holder notifies a particular indorser, that notification will operate for the benefit of all parties with rights of recourse against that indorser. The payee will not be able to avoid liability by asserting that a particular party did not personally provide notice of dishonor. Repetitious notices would not further protect the payee, and thus are not required.

---

[22] U.C.C. § 3-503(a). Notice of dishonor is also required for the drawer of a draft accepted by an acceptor other than a bank. *Id.*; U.C.C. § 3-414(d).

[23] Brannons No. Seven, Inc. v. Phelps, 665 P.2d 860, 36 U.C.C. Rep. Serv. 225 (Okla. Ct. App. 1983) (summary judgment not available when issue of fact existed as to whether indorser received notice of dishonor).

[24] U.C.C. § 3-503(b).

[25] Serve v. First Nat'l Bank, 143 Ga. App. 239, 237 S.E.2d 719, 22 U.C.C. Rep. Serv. 1001 (1977) (return of check stamped "account closed").

[26] U.C.C. § 3-503(b).

§ 5.03 Time Requirements

[A] Presentment — §§ 3-414(f), 3-415(e)

Article 3 includes time periods for proper presentment for payment to invoke the contract liability of drawers and indorsers. The time period with respect to both parties applies only to checks. With respect to drawers, a check must be either presented for payment or given to a depositary bank for collection within 30 days after its date.[27] The time period for indorsers is also 30 days, but it runs from the date the indorsement was made.[28]

Consider the facts in the following diagram as an explanation of the times for presentment:

```
              "P"    "X"   "Y"   "Z"
D'er ----▶P——▶X——▶Y——▶Z——▶H·········▶Bank
 4/1    4/3   4/8  4/10  5/1      5/10
```

Diagram 5.1

Drawer (D'er) issues a check on April 1st (a month with 30 days) and each of the subsequent transferors (P, X, Y and Z) indorses the check and negotiates it on the date indicated for each of them. Holder (H) presents the check for payment to the drawee bank on May 10th. The presentment is not timely with respect to the D'er and the indorsers P and X, as it was presented outside of the 30-day period. Presentment is timely for Z, and is just within the time limit for Y. The general rule of contract law is to include the day the event is to occur but to exclude the day time is to begin.

[B] Dishonor — § 3-502

[1] Payment Context

The dishonor of checks presented for payment through the check-collection system is governed by the rules provided in Article 4.[29] Usually a drawee bank will give a settlement for the amount of a check to the presenting bank upon presentment of the check. The drawee bank then can recover the settlement if it returns the check before its midnight deadline.[30] This timely return of an instrument by the drawee bank manifests the

---

[27] U.C.C. § 3-414(f). A check that is given to a depositary bank for collection will be presented shortly thereafter because collecting banks are under obligation to forward checks for collection expeditiously. See § 11.02[C] *infra*.

[28] U.C.C. § 3-415(e).

[29] U.C.C. § 3-502(b)(1). The Article 4 rules are provided in U.C.C. §§ 4-301, 4-302. See § 11.03[A] *infra*.

[30] Midnight deadline is defined in section 4-104(a)(10). Return of instruments in the bank-collection process is explained in Chapter 11. See § 11.04 *infra*.

bank's refusal to pay the instrument and constitutes dishonor.[31] If the check is unavailable for return, the bank can dishonor it by sending written notice of dishonor or nonpayment.[32]

The dishonor of checks presented for immediate payment and of all demand drafts other than checks are governed by a different rule.[33] These drafts are dishonored when presentment for payment is duly made and the draft is not paid on the day of presentment. The same rule determines dishonor of an accepted draft payable on demand that is duly presented for payment to the acceptor.[34]

If a draft is payable on a date stated in the draft, the draft is dishonored if presentment for payment is duly made and payment is not made on the day the draft becomes payable or the day of presentment, whichever is later.[35] This rule also governs dishonor of an accepted draft that is not payable on demand.[36]

A note that is payable on demand by its very nature requires a demand for payment by the person entitled to enforce the instrument in order for a dishonor to occur. Such a note is dishonored if presentment is duly made and payment is not made on the day of presentment.[37] On the other hand, if the note is payable at a definite time, dishonor results automatically if it is not paid on the day it becomes payable.[38] Dishonor is not a condition for the liability of a maker,[39] and the usual commercial expectation is that the maker will send payment to the holder on the date when payment is due. Because presentment traditionally was waived for purposes of retaining the liability of indorsers on these notes, it is sensible simply to dispense with any presentment requirement and have dishonor occur upon nonpayment.[40]

When payment or acceptance is required on the day of presentment, parties upon whom the presentment is made do not have to make an instantaneous decision on whether to comply with the requested acceptance or payment. They have a period of time to determine the status of the drawer's account and to ascertain whether the instrument is properly payable. To facilitate the processing of instruments when payment or acceptance must

---

[31] Reflecting general banking and commercial understanding, returning an instrument because it lacks a necessary indorsement is not dishonor. U.C.C. § 3-501(b)(3); First Nat'l Bank v. Montgomery, 9 Pa. D. & C.3d 491, 27 U.C.C. Rep. Serv. 164 (1979).

[32] U.C.C. §§ 3-502(b)(1), 4-301(a)(2). The check might be unavailable for return because it was retained by the depositary bank under a "truncation" procedure, and the presentment was made electronically.

[33] U.C.C. § 3-502(b)(2).

[34] U.C.C. § 3-502(d)(1).

[35] U.C.C. § 3-502(b)(3)(i).

[36] U.C.C. § 3-502(d)(2).

[37] U.C.C. § 3-502(a)(1).

[38] U.C.C. § 3-502(a)(3). Because presentment is required for them, domiciled instruments are excepted from this rule. U.C.C. § 3-502(a)(2).

[39] U.C.C. § 3-412.

[40] U.C.C. § 3-502, Comment 4.

be made on the day of presentment, the party to whom presentment is made is allowed to set a cut-off hour, which cannot be earlier than 2 p.m., for the receipt of instruments presented.[41] Instruments presented after this cut-off hour can be treated as through they were presented on the next business day.

[2] Acceptance Context

The date for payment of some drafts depends upon an initial presentment for acceptance. By its terms, a draft may be payable a fixed period "after acceptance" or "after sight." For example, a draft payable "30 days after sight" means that it is payable 30 days after the drawee incurs liability on the instrument by signing it. With these terms, the instrument obviously cannot be payable until after it has been presented for acceptance. The drawee who accepts such a draft should date it as well as sign it because an undated acceptance is incomplete.[42] Under these circumstances, the holder is entitled to complete the instrument by supplying the date in good faith.[43] When a draft is payable based on a period of time after acceptance or sight, it is dishonored if it is not accepted on the day that it is duly presented.[44]

If an unaccepted draft is payable on a stated date, the holder of the draft has an option of presenting the draft for acceptance before the day on which it becomes payable. A time draft is like a check because it orders a third party to pay a stated sum of money to the payee. Unlike a check, however, it is not drawn on a bank and it is not payable immediately. The payee can elect to hold the draft until the due date and then present it for payment. This approach leaves the payee uncertain during the entire interim from issue until presentment for payment about the drawee's willingness to pay. Alternatively, the payee can present the draft for acceptance. If the drawee complies, the payee has the drawee's signed assurances of payment. In addition, the draft now has enhanced value for negotiation purposes because it carries the primary liability of the acceptor, as well as the secondary liability of the drawer. If the drawee upon presentment refuses to accept the draft, the payee can pursue rights of recourse against the drawer immediately without waiting for payment to become due. The refusal to accept on the day of a duly-made presentment is a dishonor, which satisfies the conditions to the drawer's liability on the instrument.[45]

The right of optional presentment does not apply to demand drafts. A demand draft is payable immediately. Therefore, if the draft itself does not

---

[41] U.C.C. § 3-501(b)(4).

[42] U.C.C. § 3-409, Comment 3.

[43] U.C.C. § 3-409(c). The court in Clawson v. Berklund, 188 Mont. 48, 610 P.2d 1168, 28 U.C.C. Rep. Serv. 1407 (1980), misapplied this provision by indicating that the payee can provide the date even when the drawee fails to provide a written acceptance. Because the draft was not accepted within the time limits established in section 3-502, the payee was entitled to treat the draft as dishonored.

[44] U.C.C. § 3-502(b)(4).

[45] U.C.C. § 3-502(b)(3)(ii).

require presentment for acceptance, and in the absence of an agreement to the contrary, the holder of a demand draft is entitled to payment, but not acceptance.[46]

[C] Notice of Dishonor — § 3-503(c)

When an instrument is taken for collection by a collecting bank, notice of dishonor must be given by the bank "before midnight of the next banking day following the banking day on which the bank receives notice of dishonor of the instrument."[47] This midnight deadline is midnight of the first banking day following the banking day that the bank receives an instrument or notice of its dishonor.[48] Because banks are in the business of dealing with instruments, they do not need much time to investigate their rights and responsibilities. Furthermore, the midnight deadline is a standard time requirement imposed on banks handling instruments in the collection process.[49]

Non-banking parties are given a considerably longer period of time during which to satisfy the notice of dishonor requirement when the affected instrument has been taken for collection by a collecting bank. These persons are given "30 days following the day on which the person receives notice of dishonor."[50] When an instrument is not introduced into the check-collection system, "notice of dishonor must be given within 30 days following the day on which dishonor occurs."[51]

Consider the facts in Diagram 5.1, and assume that the check is dishonored when it is presented on May 10th. Holder has 30 days, or until June 9th (May has 31 days), to notify any of the prior indorsers.[52] An unexcused failure to provide notification to any of these parties within this time results in Holder's failure to satisfy the condition of notice of dishonor with respect to those parties. Holder cannot impair the rights of recourse of prior indorsers by waiting until the last moment and then notifying only one of the indorsers, such as the immediate transferor Z. Z is granted 30 days from the receipt of notice of dishonor to provide notice to any prior indorsers. To the extent that Holder provides notice to other parties upstream from Z, Z is not required to provide additional notice to those parties in order to retain rights of recourse against them.

---

[46] *See also* U.C.C. § 3-409(d) ("the drawee of a check has no obligation to certify the check, and refusal to certify is not dishonor of the check.").

[47] U.C.C. § 3-503(c).

[48] U.C.C. § 4-104(a)(10); Wells Fargo Bank, N.A. v. Hartford Nat'l Bank & Trust Co., 484 F. Supp. 817, 28 U.C.C. Rep. Serv. 446 (D. Conn. 1980) (notice by depositary bank to customer on banking day following receipt on December 17th of written notice of dishonor held untimely when bank had received notice by telephone, consistent with applicable Federal Reserve operating circular, on December 10th).

[49] *See* § 11.03[A][1] *infra*.

[50] U.C.C. § 3-503(c).

[51] U.C.C. § 3-503(c).

[52] As will be seen in the next section of this chapter, P and X were already discharged because of untimely presentment, so notice to them will not retain their liability on the instrument.

§ 5.04 Consequences of Failure to Satisfy the Conditions

[A] Indorsers — § 3-415(c)

If a required presentment or notice of dishonor is delayed, without excuse, beyond the time it is due, any indorser is discharged.[53] The provision operates as an absolute termination of the indorser's liability on the instrument. An indorser who can establish that presentment or notice of dishonor was required but not accomplished in proper form during the applicable time period can defend against a recourse action on the grounds of discharge.[54]

Indorsers are discharged in order to protect their rights of recourse. Each successive indorser who is required to pay the instrument will look upstream to pass the loss to a prior party. Indorsers have rights of recourse against the maker of a note, the drawer or acceptor of a draft, and any prior unqualified indorsers who are given timely notice of dishonor. The discharge provision is premised on the rationale that undue delays seriously impair the indorser's right of recourse. Parties who are able and willing to stand behind their liability on the instrument today might not be in the same posture later. Timely action is generally prudent in matters involving the collection of money. Therefore, a holder must not delay in satisfying the conditions if the holder wishes to retain the liability of an indorser. An indorser's right of recourse is considered to be so valuable that an unexcused delay will result in complete discharge, even if the indorser did not suffer any actual loss because of the delay.

[B] Drawers — § 3-414(f)

A drawer is not automatically discharged upon an unexcused delay in presentment. A drawer can achieve discharge only in a limited set of circumstances.[55]

Different rules of discharge apply to indorsers and drawers because the potential for unjust enrichment differs markedly between the two parties. In exchange for the transfer of an instrument to them, indorsers generally give their transferors something that approximates the value of the instrument. They also generally receive something of similar value when they later negotiate the instrument. If they also have to pay the instrument under their indorsement contract, their right of recourse against prior parties on the instrument is protected. When the holder impairs that right of recourse through undue delay, the indorser is not unjustly enriched upon discharge because the indorser initially paid value to obtain the instrument.

---

[53] U.C.C. §§ 3-415(e), 3-503(c); Hane v. Exten, 255 Md. 668, 259 A.2d 290, 7 U.C.C. Rep. Serv. 35 (1969) (delay in both presentment and notice of dishonor).

[54] Nevada State Bank v. Fischer, 93 Nev. 317, 565 P.2d 332, 21 U.C.C. Rep. Serv. 1384 (1977) (depository bank's remedy was against the collecting bank that caused a nearly 90-day delay and not against the accommodation indorser who was discharged by undue delay in giving notice of dishonor).

[55] U.C.C. § 3-414(f).

The position of a drawer differs considerably. The drawer generally receives something valued at the face amount of the instrument from the payee. Unlike the indorser, however, the drawer executes and issues the instrument but does not pay anything to acquire the value given for it. An indorser pays value to acquire an instrument, but the drawer creates an instrument by simply writing an order to pay. A holder who delays in presentment does not impair rights of recourse of the drawer because drawers do not have these rights. Having initiated the order to pay, the drawer is required to pay if the order is dishonored. The discharge of indorsers is designed to protect their rights of recourse, and is thus not available to drawers. The discharge of drawers under these circumstances would lead to unjust enrichment. They would retain the benefit passed to them by the payee without ever having paid any of their assets.

Nevertheless, discharge is available for drawers of checks who suffer an actual loss occasioned by unexcused delay in presentment. Section 3-414(f) provides that if "(ii) the drawee suspends payments after expiration of the 30-day period [for presentment or initiation of collection] without paying the check, and (iii) because of the suspension of payments, the drawer is deprived of funds maintained with the drawee to cover payment of the check, the drawer to the extent deprived of funds may discharge its obligation to pay the check by assigning to the person entitled to enforce the check the rights of the drawer against the drawee with respect to the funds." The provision gives these parties a method of discharge when the delay causes them to lose funds they entrusted with the drawee to pay the instrument.

The drawer must establish several elements in order to attain discharge under this provision.[56] Suspension of payments by the drawee bank must occur during the delay. If suspension of payments occurred during the 30-day period available to satisfy the presentment requirement, discharge is not possible. The drawer must also establish that the suspension of payments itself deprived the drawer of funds maintained with the drawee for payment of the check. When the suspension results in the loss of some of the drawer's money on deposit with the drawee,[57] or even a significant delay in receiving full payment,[58] this element is satisfied. Under these circumstances the drawer can achieve discharge, but not automatically. The drawer must make an assignment to the person entitled to enforce the check of all of the drawer's rights against the drawee bank with respect to the funds represented by the check. Under the N.I.L., the drawer had to prove the extent of loss caused by the delay. Because the full extent of loss often cannot be ascertained until insolvency proceedings for the drawee are completed, which can take years, drawers were seldom able to meet

---

[56] Wildman Stores, Inc. v. Carlisle Distrib. Co., Inc., 15 Ark. App. 11, 688 S.W.2d 748, 40 U.C.C. Rep. Serv. 1766 (1985) (drawer not discharged just because check was not presented until 17 months after its receipt).

[57] This element generally will not be satisfied because federal bank deposit insurance insures accounts up to $100,000. Some accounts, however, exceed the limit or do not qualify for this insurance or comparable state protection. U.C.C. § 3-415, Comment 6.

[58] U.C.C. § 3-415, Comment 6.

this burden. The written assignment approach is designed to secure prompt discharge for the drawer when the cause of the loss is delay by the person entitled to enforce the instrument.

§ 5.05 Excused Presentment and Notice of Dishonor — § 3-504

[A] Delay

Sometimes a delay in making a necessary presentment or notice of dishonor is excused. The effect is to treat the tardy satisfaction of these conditions as though it had been timely. The excuse of delay is premised upon equitable considerations. A party who innocently delays satisfying a relevant condition should not lose all rights of recourse even though time is generally considered to be of the essence in these transactions.

Delay in giving notice of dishonor "is excused if the delay was caused by circumstances beyond the control of the person giving the notice and the person giving the notice exercised reasonable diligence after the cause of the delay ceased to operate."[59] These circumstances cannot be caused by the party's misconduct or negligence. Applicable events might include war, interruption of communication facilities, or illness.[60]

[B] Complete Excuse

Presentment for payment or acceptance is completely excused in a number of situations.[61] If a person entitled to make presentment cannot present an instrument with due diligence, presentment is excused. The most common circumstance to invoke this provision is the inability of the party desiring to present the instrument to locate the party to whom presentment would otherwise be required. Presentment is also excused when the maker or acceptor has repudiated the obligation to pay or is dead or in insolvency proceedings. When the terms of an instrument preclude the necessity of presenting to enforce obligations of indorsers or the drawer, presentment is not required with respect to the designated obligations. Presentment is also excused if a particular drawer or indorser has waived presentment or if that party does not have any grounds to expect or require payment to be made. For example, a drawer might issue a check against insufficient funds and overdraft coverage or against a non-existent account. Finally, presentment is excused if the drawer has instructed the drawee not to pay or accept the draft or the drawee has no obligation to the drawer to pay the draft.

---

[59] U.C.C. § 3-504(c); New Ulm State Bank v. Brown, 558 S.W.2d 20, 23 U.C.C. Rep. Serv. 389 (Tex. Civ. App. 1977) (but evidence showed bank intentionally delayed return of drafts).

[60] Rich v. Franklin Sav. Bank, 18 U.C.C. Rep. Serv. 451 (N.Y. Sup. Ct. 1975) (assertion that delay caused by unforeseen and unavoidable employee absenteeism was a circumstance beyond the defendant's control raised a triable issue).

[61] U.C.C. § 3-504(a).

Notice of dishonor is excused in a narrower set of circumstances. It is excused when the terms of the instrument dispense with it as a requirement to enforce a payment obligation and when the party against whom enforcement is sought waived notice of dishonor. A waiver of presentment also constitutes a waiver of notice of dishonor.

Chapter 6
HOLDER IN DUE COURSE

SYNOPSIS

§ 6.01   Requirements to Qualify — § 3-302(a)
    [A]   Introduction
    [B]   Value
        [1]   The Article 3 Definition — § 3-303
            [a]   Consideration Performed
            [b]   The Executory Promise Exceptions
            [c]   Security Interest or Lien on Instrument
            [d]   Payment or Security for Antecedent Debt
        [2]   The Article 4 Definition — §§ 4-211, 4-210
    [C]   Good Faith
    [D]   Notice
        [1]   The General Definitions — § 1-201(25),(26)
            [a]   Actual Knowledge
            [b]   Imputed Knowledge
            [c]   Constructive Notice
        [2]   Specifics of Article 3 — § 3-302(a)(2)
            [a]   Notice Instrument is Overdue — § 3-304
            [b]   Notice Instrument Has Been Dishonored
            [c]   Notice of a Claim
            [d]   Notice Any Party Has a Defense or Claim in Recoupment
            [e]   Notice of Unauthorized Signature or Alteration
    [E]   Questionable Authenticity — § 3-302(a)(1)
    [F]   Exclusions — § 3-302(c)
    [G]   Payee as Holder in Due Course

§ 6.02   Rights of Holder in Due Course
    [A]   Free From Claims — § 3-306
    [B]   Free From Defenses — § 3-305(b)
        [1]   Defenses Against the Holder
        [2]   Real Defenses — § 3-305(a)(1)
            [a]   Infancy
            [b]   Other Incapacity, Duress or Illegality
            [c]   Fraud
            [d]   Discharge in Insolvency Proceedings
    [C]   Rights Passed Through Shelter — § 3-203(b)

§ 6.03   Absence of Any Holder-in-Due-Course-Rights

           [A]   Claims and Defenses — § 3-306
           [B]   *Jus Tertii* — Assertion of the Rights of Third
                 Parties — § 3-305(c)
§ 6.04   Negotiation That May be Rescinded — § 3-202
           [A]   Effectiveness of Negotiation
           [B]   The Remedy of Rescission
§ 6.05   Procedural Aspects — § 3-308
           [A]   Effectiveness of Signatures
           [B]   Production of the Instrument
           [C]   Burden to Prove Holder-in-Due-Course Status
§ 6.06   Holders in Due Course and Consumers
           [A]   The Problem
           [B]   The FTC Rule

§ 6.01 Requirements To Qualify — § 3-302(a)

[A] Introduction

The purchaser of an instrument should be concerned about two major types of risk that can adversely affect the purchase. One risk is that someone might assert a superior claim to the instrument. The attractiveness of the purchase will be diminished considerably if the purchaser becomes liable or is forced to relinquish the instrument. The other risk is that the parties who incurred liability on the instrument by signing it may be able to assert successful defenses against their contract liability. The value of the purchased instrument can be substantially diminished if the apparent obligations of some of the parties cannot be enforced.

A purchaser's success against valid claims and defenses often depends upon whether the purchaser can assert the rights of a holder in due course. A purchaser who attains this status will take the instrument free from all claims and claims in recoupment, and also free from most defenses. A holder in due course is also entitled to significant procedural advantages. Accordingly, an understanding of the requirements to qualify as a holder in due course and the consequences of qualifying or not qualifying is essential.

Section 3-302(a) states the elements that are necessary to qualify as a holder in due course. Those elements can be summarized as follows:

   (1)   One must first qualify as a holder of a negotiable instrument;[1]

   (2)   The authenticity of the instrument cannot be called into question;[2]

   (3)   The holder must take the instrument

---

[1] U.C.C. § 3-302(a).

[2] U.C.C. § 3-302(a)(1).

(a) for value;[3]

(b) in good faith;[4]

(c) without notice that the instrument is overdue, that it has been dishonored, or that there is an uncured default with respect to another instrument issued as part of the same series; that the instrument contains an unauthorized signature or has been altered; that there is an adverse claim of ownership to the instrument; or that any party to the instrument has a defense or claim in recoupment;[5] and

(4) The instrument cannot be taken under any "special circumstances" that would preclude the holder from asserting the rights of a holder in due course.[6]

A holder in due course is essentially a special form of a *bona fide* purchaser for value.

The concepts of holder and instrument have been explained extensively in prior chapters, and, therefore, will not be repeated here. "Holder" is a term of art in the Code,[7] and is covered in Chapter 3 as an essential element in a transfer by negotiation.[8] Use of the term "instrument" in Article 3 means a negotiable instrument.[9] Thus, a holder of an instrument that does not meet all of the requisites of negotiability[10] cannot qualify as a holder in due course. The requisites of negotiability are analyzed in Chapter 2.[11] The remaining elements for holder in due course status are covered in this section.

[B] Value

The Code provides a broad definition of general applicability of the term "value." The definition provides in part that "a person gives 'value' for rights if he acquires them . . . (d) generally, in return for any consideration sufficient to support a simple contract."[12] The general definition, however, specifically excludes its applicability to Articles 3 and 4. The concept of value is narrower with respect to negotiable instruments and bank collections.

---

[3] U.C.C. § 3-302(a)(2)(i).

[4] U.C.C. § 3-302(a)(2)(ii).

[5] U.C.C. § 3-302(a)(2)(iii)–(vi).

[6] U.C.C. § 3-302(c).

[7] U.C.C. § 1-201(20).

[8] *See* § 3.04[A] *supra*.

[9] U.C.C. § 3-104(b).

[10] U.C.C. § 3-104(a).

[11] *See* § 2.02 *supra*.

[12] U.C.C. § 1-201(44)(d).

[1] The Article 3 Definition — § 3-303

[a] Consideration Performed

The narrower definition in Article 3 is readily apparent from the first of several methods stated in section 3-303 whereby a holder can take an instrument for value. It provides that "[a]n instrument is issued or transferred for value if: (1) the instrument is issued or transferred for a promise of performance, to the extent the promise has been performed."[13] Thus, the consideration must actually be performed before it constitutes value. Except for two limited exceptions discussed below,[14] an executory promise to give value does not qualify as value,[15] even though an executory promise is a very common form of consideration.

The concepts of consideration and value are both relevant to the law of negotiable instruments, but they serve different purposes. Consideration is required for enforcement of the contract liability of a party to an instrument, and want or failure of consideration can be asserted as a defense against any person who does not have the rights of a holder in due course.[16] "'Consideration' means any consideration sufficient to support a simple contract,"[17] and is important only for the question of whether the payment obligation on an instrument can be enforced against the obligor.[18] Value, on the other hand, is important for the determination of whether the holder of an instrument can qualify as a holder in due course.[19] To qualify as a holder in due course, a holder must take an instrument for value, and value is not the equivalent of consideration in Articles 3 and 4.

The general preclusion against executory consideration as value rests on strong policy grounds. When a transferor who wrongfully acquires an instrument subsequently transfers it and disappears after receiving payment, the Code allocates the resulting loss between two innocent parties — the rightful owner and the purchaser. The allocation depends upon whether the purchaser qualifies as a holder in due course. When a purchaser has not yet paid the transferor, but has only promised to pay, the purchaser has not yet given anything on the purchase transaction other than the

---

[13] U.C.C. § 3-303(a)(1).

[14] *See* § 6.01[B][1][b] *infra*.

[15] Carter & Grimsley v. Omni Trading, Inc., 306 Ill. App. 3d 1127, 716 N.E.2d 320, 39 U.C.C. Rep. Serv. 2d 484 (1999) (because check was taken as a retainer for legal services not yet performed, it was not taken for value); National Sav. & Trust Co. v. Park Corp., 722 F.2d 1303, 37 U.C.C. Rep. Serv. 817 (6th Cir. 1983), *cert. denied*, 466 U.S. 939, 104 S. Ct. 1916 (1984) (executory promise to deliver machinery to buyer-drawer not value).

[16] U.C.C. §§ 3-303(b), 3-305(a)(2),(b); Alarcon v. Ferrari, 490 So. 2d 1047, 1 U.C.C. Rep. Serv. 2d 818 (Fla. Ct. App. 1986); Patterson v. First Nat'l Bank, 47 Ala. App. 98, 251 So. 2d 230, 9 U.C.C. Rep. Serv. 874 (1971).

[17] U.C.C. § 3-303(b).

[18] U.C.C. § 3-303, Comment 1. "The drawer or maker of an instrument has a defense if the instrument is issued without consideration." U.C.C. § 3-303(b).

[19] U.C.C. § 3-303, Comment 1.

promise. If the purchaser learns of prior claims or defenses to the instrument before fulfilling the purchase promise, the appropriate course of action is to refuse to proceed with the purchase. The obligation to pay under the purchase contract will be excused based on failure of consideration from the transferor since delivery by the transferor cannot meet the statutory warranties.[20]

Consider the facts diagramed below:

```
           B.I.
   D'er----▸P────────▸T────────▸H
                theft
```

Diagram 6.1

Drawer (D'er) issues a check to Payee (P). Thief (T) steals the check while it is in bearer form, and negotiates it to Holder (H) in exchange for H's promise to pay for it in two weeks. Even if H satisfies all of the other requirements for holder in due course status, she has not yet taken for value and therefore does not yet qualify. If H learns of the theft prior to paying, holder in due course status will be impossible. She will have notice of a claim to the instrument on the part of P, so if she proceeds to give value by making the payment, her holder-in-due-course status will be precluded under the notice requirement of section 3-302(a)(2). Having received this notice before paying any money on the transaction, the Code will not allow her to proceed knowingly and throw the inevitable loss onto P. T's transfer breached a warranty that the instrument is not subject to a defense that could be asserted against T,[21] which is an ample basis to excuse H's obligation to pay T. H should assert that excuse because P has the superior claim to the instrument and H cannot qualify as a holder in due course to resist the claim.

A purchaser of an instrument might agree to pay in installments and later discover a valid claim or defense after having made some of the payments. In these circumstances, the holder will have taken the instrument for value *to the extent* that the agreed consideration has been paid.[22] If the instrument is taken for a discount, a proportionate share of the discount is covered. Section 3-302(d) states that "the holder may assert rights as a holder in due course only to the fraction of the amount payable under the instrument equal to the value of the partial performance divided by the value of the promised performance." In other words, the ratio of the payments made to the payments promised should be applied to the face

---

[20] *See* 8.03[C][5] *infra*.

[21] U.C.C. § 3-416(a)(4). *See* § 8.03[C][5] *infra*.

[22] U.C.C. § 3-303(a)(1); Halbert v. Horton, 29 Mich. App. 208, 185 N.W.2d 76, 8 U.C.C. Rep. Serv. 1286 (1970) (partial holder in due course as to $8,000 paid on a $20,000 check, but not on the remainder because the promise to cancel a debt was still executory).

amount of the instrument to determine the extent to which the holder can be a holder in due course of the instrument. For example, assume that a note for $10,000 is sold for $9,000, payable in ten equal monthly installments of $900. If the holder has paid five of the installments, the $4,500 paid is 50% of the agreed upon consideration. The holder, therefore, is a holder for value of 50% of the $10,000 note, which is $5,000.[23]

[b] The Executory Promise Exceptions

The policy that justifies restricting value to cases of executed consideration is premised upon the holder's right to be excused from performance upon attaining notice of a problem. Sometimes, however, the holder does not have that option. The drafters thus recognized two circumstances in which an executory promise can nevertheless constitute value.[24] As a result, a holder in either circumstance can proceed with the promised performance and still qualify as a holder in due course if the other requirements of qualification are satisfied.

One of the circumstances arises when a holder who takes an instrument makes an irrevocable commitment to a third person. The Code does not state when a commitment is irrevocable, but the policy involved makes it clear that the only commitment that can qualify is one that the holder cannot rescind upon discovering a claim or defense to the transaction. Very few cases have addressed this provision. The Arizona Court of Appeals found an irrevocable commitment to a third party made by an escrow agent who received checks from the purchaser of real estate and conveyed title to the purchaser.[25] It held that the agent had made an irrevocable commitment to a lender to pay off a first deed of trust on the property.

The classic example involves a bank that issues a letter of credit in exchange for a negotiable instrument.[26] Suppose, for example, that a seller of goods on the east coast enters into a contract with a buyer on the west coast. The seller does not trust the buyer's credit and insists that before shipment the buyer obtain a letter of credit obligating a bank to pay for the goods. The letter will obligate the bank to pay the seller if the seller delivers to the bank certain documents indicating that the proper goods have been shipped, and under Article 5, the bank's duty to honor the letter is independent of the contract between the seller and the buyer.[27] In other words, the bank must pay the seller if the proper documents are presented to it, even if the seller is in breach of the contract between it and the buyer

---

[23] O.P. Ganjo, Inc. v. Tri-Urban Realty Co., Inc., 108 N.J. Super. 517, 261 A.2d 722, 7 U.C.C. Rep. Serv. 302 (1970) (payment of $1,000 of agreed consideration of $2,800 for a $3,000 note resulted in holder in due course status as to $1,073.43 of the note).

[24] U.C.C. § 3-303(a)(4),(5).

[25] Great W. Bank & Trust Co. v. Pima Sav. & Loan Ass'n, 149 Ariz. 364, 718 P.2d 1017, 2 U.C.C. Rep. Serv. 2d 532 (Ariz. Ct. App. 1986). *See also* Schranz v. I.L. Grossman, Inc., 90 Ill. App. 3d 507, 45 Ill. Dec. 654, 412 N.E.2d 1378, 30 U.C.C. Rep. Serv. 1299 (1980) (release of claim against maker of note and placing release in escrow).

[26] The letter of credit is the only illustration specifically mentioned in the Comments. U.C.C. § 3-303, Comment 5.

[27] U.C.C. § 5-108(a).

and the bank has been made aware of that fact. The buyer does not have the resources to repay the bank immediately, and so in exchange for the bank's issuance of the letter of credit, the buyer negotiates to the bank, as security for its repayment obligation, a note issued by a third party. Because the bank's obligation to the seller is irrevocable once the letter of credit has been issued,[28] it is deemed to have given value at that time even though it has not yet paid out any funds.

The other circumstance in which a holder can take for value by giving an executory promise is when the holder issues his or her own negotiable instrument for the instrument being purchased.[29] If, for example, A gives P a check to pay for the purchase of a note issued by M, A's obligation as the drawer, although executory, constitutes value. Value has been given even if A learns that M has a defense against P while A still has time to stop payment on the check. The negotiable instrument would be comparable to an irrevocable commitment if it were negotiated to a holder in due course, because the drawer would be bound and unable to rescind the promise to pay. The Code recognizes value immediately upon issuance, and does not require actual negotiation to a holder in due course. The Comments appropriately indicate that the possibility of such negotiation is sufficient.[30]

[c] Security Interest or Lien on Instrument

A holder who acquires a security interest in an instrument or a lien on it takes for value, provided that the lien is not obtained by judicial proceedings.[31] Attachment, execution and garnishment are methods of lien-acquisition by judicial process, but such methods are invariably commenced after the debt has arisen. In other words, the lienholder does not rely on the existence of the lien at the time the decision to extend credit is made. The type of lien contemplated by the provision is a common-law or a statutory banker's lien.[32] Bankers rely on such liens in making their day-to-day lending decisions, and this reliance provides the theoretical justification for the decision to treat the acquisition of such liens as value.

The most common situation in this category involves a bank that acquires an Article 9 security interest in an instrument as collateral for a loan. Suppose, for example, Bank lends Borrower $10,000 and, as collateral, takes a security interest in a note issued by M and payable to Borrower. In other words, if Borrower defaults to Bank, Bank will be able to enforce the note against M. Bank, of course, will want to take the instrument free of any defenses that M might have against Borrower, and thus it is important that it be treated as having given value.

---

[28] U.C.C. § 5-106(a).

[29] Dalton & Marberry, P.C. v. Nationsbank, N.A., 34 U.C.C. Rep. Serv. 2d 748 (Mo. Ct. App. 1998) (company check exchanged for cashier's check); Green Hills P.C.A. v. R&M Porter Farms, Inc., 716 S.W.2d 296 (Mo. Ct. App. 1986) (check issued in exchange for promissory note).

[30] U.C.C. § 3-303, Comment 5.

[31] U.C.C. § 3-303(a)(2).

[32] U.C.C. § 3-303, Comment 3.

The secured party or other lienholder will be treated as a partial holder in due course if the amount of the instrument exceeds the secured obligation. In the language of section 3-302(e), "the person entitled to enforce the instrument may assert rights as a holder in due course only to an amount payable under the instrument which, at the time of enforcement of the instrument, does not exceed the amount of the unpaid obligation secured." To illustrate, suppose that Bank takes a security interest in a note, issued by M, as collateral for a loan to Borrower. The amount due on M's note is $10,000, but at the time Bank enforces its security interest Borrower's indebtedness has been reduced to $6,000. If M has a valid defense against Borrower, it can assert that defense against Bank to avoid paying Bank more than $6,000.[33] If M does not have a valid defense, Bank can collect the entire $10,000, but must account to Borrower for the surplus.[34]

[d] Payment or Security for Antecedent Debt

A holder takes an instrument for value by taking it in payment of, or as security for, an antecedent claim against any person.[35] This approach encourages creditors to accept an instrument as payment for outstanding debts or as additional security because they can qualify as holders in due course. The holder is not required to give an extension of time or any other concession.[36] The antecedent claim need not be against the person issuing or transferring the instrument, but can be against any person.[37]

[2] The Article 4 Definition — §§ 4-210, 4-211

Article 4 includes provisions on taking for value in the bank-collection process.[38] The holder of a check, wanting to initiate bank collection, deposits the check with a depositary bank. That bank forwards it through intermediary banks for presentment for payment to the payor bank. The depositary bank acts as an agent for the owner/depositor, and the intermediary and presenting banks act as subagents.[39] At common law a collecting agent acquired a possessory lien for advances made on the security of the paper held for collection.[40] Analogizing to this principle, section 4-210(a)

---

[33] U.C.C. § 3-302, Comment 6 (Case #6).

[34] *Id.*

[35] U.C.C. § 3-303(a)(3); Third Nat'l Bank v. Hardi-Gardens Supply of Ill., Inc., 380 F. Supp. 930, 15 U.C.C. Rep. Serv. 853 (M.D. Tenn. 1974) (security for antecedent claim); Bank of Lyons v. Schultz, 22 Ill. App. 3d 410, 318 N.E.2d 52 (1974) (partial payment for loans).

[36] U.C.C. § 3-303, Comment 4; First Nat'l City Bank v. Valentine, 61 Misc.2d 554, 306 N.Y.S.2d 227, 7 U.C.C. Rep. Serv. 53 (Sup. Ct. 1969). When a holder takes an instrument for security of an antecedent debt and does not give anything in exchange, consideration in the traditional sense is not present. Under section 3-303(b), however, consideration has been given because the instrument is issued for value.

[37] Franklin Credit Recovery Fund, XXI, L.P. v. Huber, 487 S.E.2d 825, 33 U.C.C. Rep. Serv. 2d 148 (N.C. App. 1997) (the fact that the makers of a replacement note were not responsible on the prior note was irrelevant because the antecedent claim can be against any person).

[38] U.C.C. §§ 4-210, 4-211.

[39] U.C.C. § 4-201(a). See § 11.02[A] *infra.*

[40] U.C.C. § 4-210, Comment 1; Schnitger v. Backus, 10 Wash. App. 754, 519 P.2d 1315, 14 U.C.C. Rep. Serv. 750 (1974).

gives security interests in an item to banks that extend credit on it in the course of collection.[41] The bank is deemed to give value to the extent of its security interest.[42] If the bank also meets the additional requirements of section 3-302(a), it qualifies as a holder in due course.[43]

Sections 4-210 and 4-211 recognize three situations in which a bank has a security interest in an item and thus gives value. The first situation is "in case of an item deposited in an account, to the extent to which credit given for the item has been withdrawn or applied."[44] When a customer deposits a check for collection, the depositary bank makes a provisional credit to the customer's account. The same policy that justifies denial of executory consideration as value under section 3-303 supports precluding recognition of mere provisional credit as value.[45] The bank has neither given any money for the credit nor become irrevocably committed. The bank is still able to protect its interests in the transaction by debiting the account of the customer to rescind the credit. To the extent that the bank allows the customer to withdraw the credit[46] or applies the credit to discharge other obligations that the customer owes the bank,[47] the bank no longer has a purely executory credit obligation. The bank is like an agent in possession of the principal's property who has advanced money against a security in that property.[48] Allowing the customer to withdraw the credit or applying the credit to the customer's indebtedness thus constitutes giving value. The practical effect of this provision is that a depositary bank will be able to enforce a check against the drawer to the extent that the bank allowed the depositor to draw against uncollected funds. Even if the drawer has discovered a problem in the underlying transaction that induced issuance of the check and has stopped payment on the check, the bank can prevail to the extent that it has given value if it meets the additional requirements for holder-in-due-course status.

---

[41] U.C.C. § 4-208, Comment 1; St. Cloud Nat'l Bank & Trust Co. v. Sabania Const. Co., Inc., 302 Minn. 71, 224 N.W.2d 746, 15 U.C.C. Rep. Serv. 679 (1974).

[42] U.C.C. §§ 3-303(a)(1), (2), 4-211.

[43] U.C.C. § 4-211.

[44] U.C.C. § 4-210(a)(1).

[45] Rockland Trust Co. v. South Shore Nat'l Bank, 366 Mass. 74, 314 N.E.2d 438, 14 U.C.C. Rep. Serv. 1342 (1974) (no value by giving only a provisional credit).

[46] Falls Church Bank v. Wesley Heights Realty, Inc., 256 A.2d 915, 6 U.C.C. Rep. Serv. 1082 (D.C. 1969) (bank held to be holder in due course as to $140 withdrawn of a $1,400 check deposited in bank).

[47] Exchange Nat'l Bank v. Beshara, 236 So. 2d 198, 7 U.C.C. Rep. Serv. 1146 (Fla. Dist. Ct. App. 1970) (proceeds of check applied to a loan); Frantz v. First Nat'l Bank, 584 P.2d 1125, 25 U.C.C. Rep. Serv. 240 (Alas. 1978) (value given as to the part of the check applied to an overdraft).

[48] Authority apart, there is fairness in this majority rule to the effect that there is a presumption that where a bank advances credit to a customer on his drawings . . . both parties intend that the bank may look to the collection item for security up to the amount of the bank's advances. . . . [B]oth parties would ordinarily view this allowance . . . as a bank loan buttressed by the security of the uncollected item.

Universal C.I.T. Credit Corp. v. Guaranty Bank & Trust Co., 161 F. Supp. 790, 793, 1 U.C.C. Rep. Serv. 305, 310 (1958) (pre-Code case with extensive discussion of Code provisions).

Although depositary banks may permit early withdrawals, they are not obligated to allow their customers to withdraw against deposited items until the customers are legally entitled to access to the funds. Therefore, the second situation in which a bank gives value by acquiring a security interest in an item is "in case of an item for which it has given credit available for withdrawal as of right, to the extent of the credit given, whether or not the credit is drawn upon or there is a right of charge-back."[49] When the customer has legal access to the credited funds, the bank is committed to the full extent of the credit, irrespective of the extent to which it has been withdrawn. Because the bank cannot unilaterally debit the account to rescind the credit, it is recognized as having given value.

Although Article 4 has provisions indicating when the credit given by a bank for an item in an account with its customer becomes available for withdrawal as of right,[50] those provisions have been preempted by federal law.[51] The history of the delayed-access policies implemented by banks, the competing policy considerations involved, and the ultimate federal intervention are all explained in detail in Chapter 11.[52] Banks can set their own schedules of funds availability for deposits of different types of items, provided that they do not exceed the maximum times established in the federal schedules of funds availability. Each bank's schedule establishes when provisionally credited funds can be withdrawn as a matter of right. Since the customer may have the right to withdraw the funds before the check clears the payor bank, the security interest granted by section 4-210 is needed to protect the depositary bank.

A bank may cash a check for its customer rather than requiring it to be deposited in the customer's account for collection. Although the bank is not required to provide this service, its election to do so gives the bank a security interest in the check that constitutes giving value.[53] This practice is comparable to allowing early withdrawal against a deposited item. The bank has parted with money, rather than simply giving a provisional credit. Section 4-210(a) refers to this third situation of giving value as "mak[ing] an advance on or against the item."[54] A depository bank that cashes a check that is drawn on another bank *does not pay the check* even though it gives money over the counter to its customer. The bank is a collecting agent and simply is advancing money to its customer against the security of the check.

In *Bowling Green, Inc. v. State Street Bank & Trust Co.*[55] the court held that the three situations in which a security interest can arise under Article

---

[49] U.C.C. § 4-210(a)(2).

[50] U.C.C. § 4-215(e).

[51] Expedited Funds Availability Act, 12 U.S.C. §§ 4001-4010; 12 C.F.R. Part 229 (Regulation CC). The funds availability rules on withdrawal as of right are covered by Subpart B of Regulation CC.

[52] *See* § 11.04[A], [B] *infra*.

[53] Suit and Wells Equip. Co. v. Citizens Nat'l Bank, 263 Md. 133, 282 A.2d 109, 9 U.C.C. Rep. Serv. 1230 (1971); Peoples Bank v. Haar, 421 P.2d 817, 3 U.C.C. 1065 (Okla. 1966).

[54] U.C.C. § 4-210(a)(3).

[55] 425 F.2d 81, 7 U.C.C. Rep. Serv. 635 (1st Cir. 1970).

4 are not exclusive. In that case a payee of a government check indorsed it to a seller of goods for equipment that it never received because the seller filed for bankruptcy. After the seller deposited the check into its bank account, the depositary bank learned that its customer, the seller, had filed a petition in bankruptcy. This knowledge prompted the bank to set off the remaining balance in the account against an outstanding loan owed by the seller. Although this act created a security interest, and constituted value under Article 4, it was too late to support holder-in-due-course status against the payee/indorser because the bank had already received notice of the seller's bankruptcy. In addition to its Article 4 rights, however, the bank had a separate security interest in the seller's equipment under Article 9, and the check, as a proceed of that equipment, was subject to that security interest. Since the Article 9 security interest in the check antedated the disabling notice, the court determined that the bank qualified as a holder in due course.

When a check is ultimately paid by the payor bank upon which it is drawn, the depositary bank's receipt of its final settlement is realization on any security interest that it retained in the check.[56] If the check is returned unpaid, on the other hand, the security interest continues so long as the bank retains possession.[57] The bank will seek reimbursement of the advance from its customer, but if the effort is unavailing, the bank will want to pursue prior parties on their liability on the instrument. The bank has the right to pursue this recovery because it has a possessory lien in the form of a security interest in the check. It also has given value,[58] which is significant if the prior parties assert defenses against the bank. The value requirement for holder-in-due-course status is met and, if the remaining requirements are satisfied, the bank will be able to defeat most of those defenses and recover.

Section 4-210(b) contains two special accounting rules. The first rule, which provides a method for determining when a credit for a specific item has been withdrawn when the account has been credited with several items, is that "credits first given are first withdrawn." For example, assume that the starting balance in an account is $100, a $200 check is deposited on Monday, another check for $500 is deposited on Tuesday, and the depositor withdraws $450 later that same Tuesday. Under the FIFO (first in-first out) rule, the funds withdrawn are considered to be the initial balance of $100, all of the provisional credit for the $200 check, and $150 of the provisional credit for the $500 check. Following the withdrawal, therefore, the bank has given value for the $200 check and to the extent of 30% of the check for $500.[59]

---

[56] U.C.C. § 4-210(c).

[57] U.C.C. § 4-210(c).

[58] "This section completes the thought of the previous section and makes clear that a security interest in an item is 'value' for the purpose of determining the holder's status as a holder in due course." U.C.C. § 4-211, Comment.

[59] Citizens Nat'l Bank v. Fort Lee Sav. & Loan Ass'n, 89 N.J. Super. 43, 213 A.2d 315, 2 U.C.C. Rep. Serv. 1029 (1965) (amount of judgment was based on advances before notice of dishonor of the deposited check less the balance in the account before the check was deposited).

This allocation is adjusted by the second rule of section 4-210(b) for credits that are given simultaneously. This accounting rule provides that "[i]f credit given for several items received at one time or pursuant to a single agreement is withdrawn or applied in part, the security interest remains upon all the items. . . ." When any of the simultaneously deposited checks are affected by the FIFO rule on withdrawals, this provision appears to require a pro rata allocation of the extent of the withdrawal. If the two checks in the example provided above were deposited at the same time, the bank would have given value to the extent of 50% of the $200 check and to the extent of 50% of the $500 check.

[C] Good Faith

A holder in due course is a type of bona fide purchaser for value.[60] Consequently, the requirement that a holder take the instrument in good faith is inevitable. When confronted with the claim of a true owner or with valid defenses of prior parties, the legal system does not favor a subsequent purchaser of an instrument that cannot demonstrate legitimate bona fides, including good faith.

Despite the consensus that good faith is an appropriate prerequisite, a heated debate has raged for over two centuries on the content of the good faith standard.[61] The dispute has been whether the standard should be objective or subjective. An objective test would ask whether a reasonably prudent person would have behaved in the manner that the holder in question acted.[62] A purely subjective test would not address the reasonable-care standard of a prudent person, but instead would focus exclusively on the state of the holder's mind.[63] In other words, a holder who has been negligent in acquiring an instrument could nevertheless be in good faith, and for that reason the subjective test is sometimes referred to derisively as the "pure heart and empty head standard." Even though a prudent individual would have recognized signs that made the transaction highly suspicious, the subjective standard would be satisfied if the individual purchaser did not recognize those signs and believed that the transaction was legitimate.

---

[60] The term "holder in due course" reflects the common-law requirement that only a person who acquired an instrument in the course of his or her business could qualify for the status. K. LLEWELLYN, THE COMMON LAW TRADITION 410-19 (1960); Rightmire, *The Doctrine of Bad Faith in the Law of Negotiable Paper*, 18 Mich. L. Rev. 355, 356-57 (1920). The requirement still exists for comparable status for the holder of a negotiable document. U.C.C. § 7-501(4).

[61] Courts faced the question at least as early as Miller v. Race, 1 Burr. 452, 97 Eng. Rep. 398 (1758). "The [good faith] provision as to holders in due course was perhaps the item most vigorously discussed in the New York hearing." Braucher, *The Legislative History of the Uniform Commercial Code*, 58 Colum. L. Rev. 798, 813 (1958) (citing the 1954 N.Y. Report of the influential New York Law Revision Commission at 203-06, 213-40, 241-43, 424-26).

[62] Gill v. Cubitt, 107 Eng. Rep. 806 (K.B. 1824) (failure to investigate suspicious circumstances).

[63] Goodman v. Harvey, 111 Eng. Rep. 1011 (1836); Goodman v. Simonds, 61 U.S. 343 (1858).

The current version of Article 1 defines "good faith" as "honesty in fact in the conduct or transaction concerned."[64] Clearly, the drafters of this provision opted for a purely subjective standard of good faith. Earlier versions of the Code included an additional objective element of "reasonable observance of the standards of any business or trade in which the purchaser is engaged."[65] Based largely on objections from the American Bar Association and the New York Law Revision Commission,[66] this reference to reasonable commercial standards was deleted from the official text of the Code.[67] The conclusion was that the policy of promoting the free transferability of commercial paper would be advanced further with a purely subjective standard. An objective element, it was thought, could have a dampening effect on the willingness of purchasers to take negotiable instruments because a jury might later determine that the purchaser had not acted reasonably in light of the surrounding circumstances.

A certain academic element pervades the distinction between subjective and objective tests. Even under a purely subjective test, determining a person's state of mind requires the fact finder to make inferences based on objective manifestations.[68] Despite a purchaser's protestations of honesty, a jury might find the surrounding circumstances too suspicious to conclude that the purchaser in fact acted honestly. For example, the purchase of a note at an exceptionally deep discount is clearly a factor that might lead a jury to conclude that the purchaser acted dishonestly,[69] but there is some question as to whether such a discount, standing alone, is a sufficient basis for a finding of bad faith.[70] A jury might also conclude from all the evidence that the purchaser wilfully avoided acquiring

---

[64] U.C.C. § 1-201(19). "From the history of the Uniform Commercial Code it would appear that 'good faith' requires no actual knowledge of or participation in any material infirmity in the original transaction." Kaw Valley State Bank & Trust Co. v. Riddle, 219 Kan. 550, 556, 549 P.2d 927, 932-33, 19 U.C.C. Rep. Serv. 869, 875 (1976). See Anderson, Clayton & Co. v. Farmers Nat'l Bank, 624 F.2d 15, 29 U.C.C. Rep. Serv. 954 (10th Cir. 1980) (absence of good faith because of fraudulent misrepresentations by the holder).

[65] U.C.C. § 1-201(16) (May 1949 Draft); Uniform Commercial Code, Text and Comments Edition § 3-302(1)(b) (Official Draft 1952).

[66] Malcolm, *The Proposed Commercial Code*, 6 Bus. Law. 113, 128 (1951) (report by the Chairman of the Committee on the Proposed Commercial Code of the Section on Corporation, Banking and Business Law of the American Bar Association); 1956 N.Y. Law. Revision Comm'n Rep. 17, 29.

[67] This objective test was added to Article 2 as part of the good-faith standard for merchants. U.C.C. § 2-103(1)(b); Van Gohren v. Pacific Nat'l Bank, 8 Wash. App. 245, 505 P.2d 467, 12 U.C.C. Rep. Serv. 133 (1973) (drafting history shows reasonable care standard was intentionally omitted from Article 1 definition of good faith).

[68] Funding Consultants, Inc. v. Aetna Cas. & Sur. Co., 187 Conn. 637, 447 A.2d 1163, 34 U.C.C. Rep. Serv. 591 (1982) (application of subjective standard of good faith requires reasonable inquiry into the actual known circumstances surrounding the purchase).

[69] Chemical Bank v. Haskell, 68 A.D.2d 347, 417 N.Y.S.2d 541, 26 U.C.C. Rep. Serv. 952 (N.Y. 1979), *rev'd on other grounds*, 51 N.Y.2d 85, 432 N.Y.S.2d 478, 411 N.E.2d 339, 29 U.C.C. Rep. Serv. 1529 (1980) (purchase of notes at substantial discount is a factor to be considered with other factors as evidence of bad faith).

[70] *See* Northwestern Nat'l Ins. Co. v. Maggio, 976 F.2d 320 (7th Cir. 1992) (50% discount standing alone insufficient to support finding of bad faith).

knowledge about the transaction for fear that it would reveal an infirmity.[71] These are problems of proof that always accompany the application of a subjective standard.

The 1990 revisions to Articles 3 and 4 changed the definition of good faith by reintroducing an objective element. Section 3-102(a)(4) defines good faith as "honesty in fact and the observance of reasonable commercial standards of fair dealing." This definition also applies to Article 4.[72] Under this new standard, a purchaser must not only be subjectively honest, but must also act consistently with certain objective criteria.[73] Defining those criteria, however, is not easy. Note that the objective component in the current test for good faith differs from the objective element utilized in the earliest days of the Code. That test, which focused on the standards prevalent in the purchaser's business, was arguably rooted in *Gill v. Cubit*,[74] an English case in which a discount broker purchased a stolen bearer instrument from a stranger and then attempted to enforce it as a holder in due course. In affirming a jury verdict in favor of the defendant, the court in *Gill* noted that the rise in stagecoach robberies, coupled with the unfamiliarity of the seller, should have alerted the broker to ask questions regarding the history of the instrument. In other words, the broker's problem was not that he bought the instrument at a discount from a stranger — it was that he failed to investigate further.

The objective element in the current Code focuses on reasonable commercial standards of fair dealing rather than the standards prevalent in the purchaser's business. The Comments emphasize the concept of fairness:

> Although fair dealing is a broad term that must be defined in context, it is clear that it is concerned with the fairness of the conduct rather than the care with which an act is performed. Failure to exercise ordinary care in conducting a transaction is an entirely different concept than failure to deal fairly in conducting the transaction. Both fair dealing and ordinary care, which is defined in Section 3-103(a)(7), are to be judged in the light of reasonable commercial standards, but those standards in each case are directed to different aspects of commercial conduct.[75]

---

[71] Mid-Continent Nat'l Bank v. Bank of Independence, 523 S.W.2d 569, 16 U.C.C. Rep. Serv. 1286 (Mo. Ct. App. 1975) (previous connivance of holder gave her cause to suspect current transaction).

[72] U.C.C. § 4-104(c).

[73] Hathorn v. Loftus, 726 A.2d 1278, 37 U.C.C. Rep. Serv. 2d 676 (N.H. 1999) (case remanded for consideration of good faith under the new definition as the trial court applied only a subjective standard).

[74] 107 Eng. Rep. 806 (K.B. 1824).

[75] U.C.C. § 3-103, Comment 4; San Tan Irrigation District v. Wells Fargo Bank, 197 Ariz. 193, 3 P.3d 1113, 40 U.C.C. Rep. Serv. 2d 775 (Ariz. Ct. App. 2000) (proper focus of inquiry concerning good faith is not the care with which a transaction is conducted but rather its fairness). Articles 3 and 4 include several provisions that enable a person or a bank taking or paying an instrument to defeat assertions that the instrument has unauthorized signatures or alterations. *See* U.C.C. §§ 3-404 (impostors and fictitious payees), 3-405 (employer responsibility for fraudulent indorsements by employees), 3-406 (negligence contributing to

It is clear under the current formulation that a qualifying purchaser must not only be subjectively honest but also objectively fair. If a trader in instruments of the type at issue would not buy an instrument, it is no longer sufficient to argue that the actual purchaser acted honestly. This change should make it easier, for example, to deny holder-in-due-course status when the only evidence of bad faith is the fact that the instrument was purchased at deep discount. What is not entirely clear is whether the new definition of good faith injects into the formula a duty to inquire further when the purchaser is aware of suspicious circumstances.[76] By indicating that negligence does not preclude a finding of good faith, the Comments suggest that there is no such duty.[77]

Whether there is a duty of inquiry under the good-faith standard is no small matter. As we shall see in the next section, the Code's definition of notice does not encompass inquiry notice. A person is on notice of a fact if, from the universe of facts actually known to that person and without further inquiry, he or she has reason to know that the fact exists.[78] If, as appears likely from the Comments, the definition of good faith in revised Article 3 does not include a duty to inquire when a reasonable commercial buyer would do so, the revision represents only a measured step beyond the subjective test. If it does add a duty of inquiry, it represents a significant theoretical change. Even then, though, it is not likely to change the outcome of many cases because there is no real evidence that traders in negotiable instruments spend the time to inquire into a given instrument's history. The evidence suggests that they decide whether to purchase based solely on the circumstances known to them at the time.

---

forged signature or alteration of instrument), 4-406 (customer's failure to discover and report unauthorized signature or alteration). For discussion of these provisions, see §§ 10.03[B], 10.03[C], 10.02[A] and 10.02[B], respectively. Each of these sections includes two separate requirements. First, successful assertion of any of these sections requires that the person taking the instrument or paying it must do so in good faith. Second, if the first hurdle is passed, a theory of comparative negligence is applied to allocate the loss whenever the person taking the instrument or paying it failed to exercise ordinary care. These sections further demonstrate the distinction between the concepts of "good faith" and "ordinary care" as they are used in Articles 3 and 4. Further, note that "good faith" is defined in section 3-103(a)(4) and "ordinary care" is defined in section 3-103(a)(7).

[76] The defendant in Cadle Co. v. Ginsburg, 51 Conn. App. 392, 721 A.2d 1246, 37 U.C.C. Rep. Serv. 2d 684 (Conn. Ct. App. 1998), contended that the plaintiff did not act in good faith in taking a note because the plaintiff failed to make an inquiry in order to remain ignorant about facts that would disclose a problem in the transaction. The appellate court simply found that the trial court was not clearly erroneous in finding that the defendant did not present any credible evidence to show that the plaintiff purposefully failed to make an inquiry.

[77] A recent decision in Missouri held that the good-faith standard did not impose a duty of inquiry unless the facts known to the holder showed that the failure to inquire revealed an attempt to evade awareness of a defense. Dalton & Marberry, P.C. v. Nationsbank, N.A., 34 U.C.C. Rep. Serv. 2d 748 (Mo. Ct. App. 1998). The court relied for this proposition on caselaw that preceded the revision of Article 3.

[78] U.C.C. § 1-201(25)(c). Notice is discussed in § 6.01[D] *infra*.

[D] Notice

In addition to taking for value and in good faith, in order to qualify as a holder in due course, the holder of a negotiable instrument must also take the instrument without disabling notice. The holder cannot have notice of five things: (1) that the instrument is overdue, (2) that it has been dishonored, (3) that the instrument contains an unauthorized signature or has been altered, (4) that there is a claim to the instrument, or (5) that a party has a defense or claim in recoupment.[79] The Code refers to taking the instrument without notice. Thus, if the purchaser acquires the notice after purchasing an instrument, holder-in-due-course status is not lost.[80]

Section 1-201(25) provides a general definition of "notice." It provides as follows:

A person has "notice" of a fact when

(a) he has actual knowledge of it; or

(b) he has received a notice or notification of it; or

(c) from all the facts and circumstances known to him at the time in question he has reason to know that it exists.

Each of these general provisions are discussed below in the context of holder-in-due-course status, followed by a discussion of each of the forms of disabling notice dictated under Article 3.

[1] The General Definition — § 1-205(25), (26)

[a] Actual Knowledge

A finding of actual knowledge is a determination that the holder did, in fact, know something. It is based on an assessment of the facts developed through direct or circumstantial evidence. Because of the impossibility of exact certitude, the factual inquiry is based on the probability of whether the holder actually knew something. It is a question of fact as to a person's state of mind. A holder who actually knows something has notice of it.[81]

[b] Imputed Knowledge

Even though evidence might be insufficient to establish a holder's actual knowledge, notice can be imputed to a holder.[82] This test establishes notice without showing that the holder was actually aware of all the relevant facts. It imputes knowledge as a matter of law based on the principle that a

---

[79] U.C.C. § 3-302(a)(2).

[80] Morgan v. Depositors Trust Co., 33 U.C.C. Rep. Serv. 1473 (Me. Super. Ct. 1982); Sullivan v. United Dealers Corp., 486 S.W.2d 699, 11 U.C.C. Rep. Serv. 810 (Ky. 1972).

[81] Contrail Leasing Partners, Ltd. v. Executive Serv. Corp., 100 Nev. 545, 688 P.2d 765, 40 U.C.C. Rep. Serv. 161 (1984) (purchaser knew when purchasing note that maker had a cross-claim against payee for damages under a lease agreement); In re Interstate Mfg., Inc., 5 U.C.C. Rep. Serv. 618 (M.D. Ga. 1968) (bank knew corporation did not receive any consideration for note).

[82] U.C.C. § 1-201(25)(c).

person should have additional actual knowledge based on what he or she did know. It focuses on what the holder should have known under the circumstances.

Although imputed notice clearly invokes an objective standard, a careful reading of the Code reveals an applicable subjective element as well. Notice of a fact exists when a person has reason to know that it exists "from all the facts and circumstances *known to him* at the time in question."[83] An initial subjective inquiry must be directed to ascertain what facts and circumstances the holder actually knew. Then an objective inquiry can be made to determine what else a reasonable person would have known based on what was actually known. Establishing only that a reasonable person would have been aware of certain facts is not sufficient. Direct or circumstantial evidence must show what the purchaser actually knew.[84] When it is established that the purchaser actually knew certain facts or circumstances, the objective standard can be applied to impute to the holder such additional knowledge as a reasonable person would have known based on those facts and circumstances.

In addition to holding a person responsible for the additional inferences that should have been drawn based upon information of which the person was aware, some courts have used imputed notice to hold a purchaser responsible for information that would have been acquired if the person had undertaken a reasonable inquiry that the known information should have instigated.[85] According to these courts, the known facts must be sufficient to prompt an investigation; in other words, a holder is not required to be inherently suspicious about every transaction or to pursue inquiries in every case.[86] These courts require signals that are sufficient to alert purchasers that they should further pursue what they already know.

Most courts and commentators limit imputed notice to the reasonable inferences that should be drawn from facts and circumstances actually known, and reject any duty to investigate.[87] A failure to undertake a

---

[83] U.C.C. § 1-201(25)(c) (emphasis added).

[84] Eldon's Super Fresh Stores, Inc. v. Merrill Lynch, Pierce, Fenner & Smith, Inc., 296 Minn. 130, 207 N.W.2d 282, 12 U.C.C. Rep. Serv. 490 (1973).

[85] E. Birhaus & Sons, Inc. v. Bowling, 486 N.E.2d 598, 42 U.C.C. Rep. Serv. 920 (Ind. Ct. App. 1985) (holder had knowledge of prior history of transfers of bad checks and awareness of transferor's extreme financial straits); Salter v. Vanotti, 42 Colo. App. 448, 599 P.2d 962, 26 U.C.C. Rep. Serv. 964 (1979) (purchasers of note did not investigate irregularities in the underlying real property transaction).

[86] Frantz v. First Nat'l Bank, 584 P.2d 1125, 25 U.C.C. Rep. Serv. 240 (Alas. 1978) (depositary bank's knowledge of customer's overdrafts did not impart notice of a defense to a check issued to him by a third party); Slaughter v. Jefferson Fed. Sav. & Loan Ass'n, 538 F.2d 397, 176 App. D.C. 49, 19 U.C.C. Rep. Serv. 171 (D.C. Cir. 1976), *reh'g denied*, 19 U.C.C. Rep. Serv. 534 (1976) (bank's involvement in examining contracts and settlement sheets and in appraisal of houses in connection with receiving notes given by homeowners for loans to finance home improvements did not provide any basis for bank to suspect that the builder was engaged in a fraudulent scheme).

[87] Dalton & Marberry, P.C. v. Nationsbank, N.A., 34 U.C.C. Rep. Serv. 2d 748 (Mo. Ct. App. 1998); Eldon's Super Fresh Stores, Inc. v. Merrill Lynch, Pierce, Fenner & Smith, Inc., 296 Minn. 130, 207 N.W.2d 282, 12 U.C.C. Rep. Serv. 490 (1973).

reasonable investigation could constitute negligence, but it is not construed as imputed notice under the Article 1 definition. Imputed notice is based on what a reasonable person could be held to know from everything that is actually known, and not on what would have been determined through an investigation.

[c] Constructive Notice

The general definition of notice recognizes constructive notice as well by providing that a person has notice of a fact upon receiving notification of it.[88] Section 1-201(26) indicates two methods by which a person receives notification: "(a) it comes to his attention; or (b) it is duly delivered at the place of business through which the contract was made or at any other place held out by him as the place for receipt of such communications." Receipt of the notification establishes a conclusive presumption of notice.[89] Formal compliance with this delivery requirement, or bringing the relevant facts to the person's attention, is sufficient to invoke the presumption, irrespective of whether the person actually appreciates or otherwise assimilates the information.

Although the Code also specifically recognizes instances of publicly recorded information as yet another form of constructive notice,[90] "[p]ublic filing or recording of a document does not of itself constitute notice of a defense, claim in recoupment, or claim to the instrument."[91] This provision eliminates any ambiguity with respect to whether such a filing or recording could preclude holder-in-due-course status on the basis of constructive notice.

[2] Specifics of Article 3 — § 3-302(a)(2)

[a] Notice That Instrument is Overdue — § 3-304

A holder must take an instrument without notice that it is overdue in order to qualify as a holder in due course.[92] Section 3-304 includes several circumstances that determine when an instrument is overdue. It provides separate rules for instruments that are payable on demand and instruments that are payable at a definite time. If a holder takes an instrument with actual, imputed, or constructive notice that the instrument has become overdue, holder-in-due-course status is precluded.[93]

---

[88] U.C.C. § 1-201(25)(b).

[89] Shaffer v. Brooklyn Park Garden Apartments, 311 Minn. 452, 250 N.W.2d 172, 20 U.C.C. Rep. Serv. 1269 (1977) (attorney for the defendants sent letter to bank warning it that conditions established in the underlying transaction from which promissory notes arose had not been satisfied).

[90] For example, *see* Article 9 generally, and specifically Part 5 on filing financing statements.

[91] U.C.C. § 3-302(b).

[92] U.C.C. § 3-302(a)(2)(iii).

[93] Disabling notice also extends to notice that "there is an uncured default with respect to payment of another instrument issued as part of the same series." U.C.C. § 3-302(a)(2)(iii). The provision reaches only instruments in the same series. Ordinarily, even actual knowledge of default on another instrument is not sufficient to constitute notice that an instrument by the same drawer or maker is overdue or subject to a claim or defense.

A demand instrument becomes overdue the day after the day that demand for payment has been made.[94] If demand has not been made, a check becomes stale 90 days after its date.[95] Article 3 provides a flexible standard with respect to other demand instruments, *i.e.*, demand drafts or demand notes. The circumstances of each particular case in light of trade usage and the nature of the instrument must be examined to determined when the instrument has been outstanding after its date for an unreasonably long period of time.[96]

With respect to an instrument payable at a definite time, the instrument is overdue if any part of the principal amount is overdue. An instrument not payable in installments becomes overdue on the day after the due date.[97] An instrument payable in installments becomes overdue on default of an installment payment and stays overdue until the default is cured.[98] Knowledge that there has been a default only in payment of interest on the instrument, as distinguished from principal, does not constitute disabling notice.[99] The distinction is based upon prior law, commercial practices, and the frequency of delayed interest payments.[100]

[b] Notice That Instrument Has Been Dishonored

A holder who takes an instrument with notice that it has been dishonored cannot qualify as a holder in due course. The concept of dishonor is covered in section 3-502 and is discussed extensively in Chapter 5.[101] When the dishonored instrument itself does not show that it has been dishonored, the general tests of notice in section 1-201(25) work well. Holders with actual notice will be barred from holder-in-due-course status, as will holders who received notice of the prior dishonor. Under the imputed notice standard, holders who had reason to know of the dishonor based on facts and circumstances they knew when they purchased the instrument are also disqualified.

Dishonored instruments often are stamped to indicate a dishonor. One would anticipate notice to result from the purchase of an instrument that has been stamped "not sufficient funds," "payment stopped," or "no account." If the purchaser can be shown to have seen the stamped notation on the instrument, the constructive notice provision would be satisfied because it had come to the purchaser's attention. If the purchaser did not see the notation, the imputed notice provision could apply on the premise that a purchaser should examine an instrument before purchasing it.

---

[94] U.C.C. § 3-304(a)(1).

[95] U.C.C. § 3-304(a)(2).

[96] U.C.C. § 3-304(a)(3).

[97] U.C.C. § 3-304(b)(2); Gonderman v. State Exchange Bank, 166 Ind. App. 181, 334 N.E.2d 724, 17 U.C.C. Rep. Serv. 1241 (1975).

[98] U.C.C. § 3-304(b)(1).

[99] U.C.C. § 3-304(c); Cadle Co. v. Ginsburg, 51 Conn. App. 392, 721 A.2d 1246, 37 U.C.C. Rep. Serv. 2d 684 (Conn. Ct. App. 1998).

[100] U.C.C. § 3-304, Comment 6 (original version).

[101] *See* §§ 5.02[B], 5.03[B] *supra*.

[c] Notice of a Claim

A person having the rights of a holder in due course takes free of claims to the instrument.[102] A purchaser who takes an instrument with notice of any claim to it, however, cannot qualify as a holder in due course. The most obvious form of claim is the claim of title asserted by the owner of an instrument that has been stolen. The concept of claim also extends beyond claims of ownership to include "any other claim of a property or possessory right in the instrument or its proceeds, including a claim to rescind a negotiation and to recover the instrument or its proceeds."[103] Equitable claims are made by prior owners of instruments who assert that they issued or transferred the instrument under circumstances that entitle them to rescind the transaction and reacquire title to the instrument. The grounds are based on applicable state law that makes the transaction void or voidable, such as duress, fraud, illegality, or incapacity.[104]

A beneficiary might assert a claim to an instrument because the breach of a fiduciary duty resulted in the proceeds of the instrument being misapplied. Section 3-307 provides rules for determining when a purchaser of an instrument takes with notice of a claim based on breach of a fiduciary duty. The baseline is that "[n]otice of breach of fiduciary duty by the fiduciary is notice of the claim of the represented person."[105]

Knowledge that the person who negotiates an instrument is a fiduciary is not sufficient of itself to give notice of a claim, although knowledge of the fiduciary status is a necessary element of notice.[106] Fiduciaries often have to negotiate instruments in order to fulfill their responsibilities on behalf of the represented person. If knowledge of their fiduciary position constituted disabling notice to prospective purchasers, fiduciaries would find free alienability eliminated on the instruments they hold. With respect to instruments issued by the represented person or by the fiduciary as such, and made payable to the fiduciary personally, purchasers will not be charged with notice unless, in addition to knowledge that the transferor is a fiduciary, they know that the fiduciary has breached the duty to the represented person.[107] The transaction is not unusual because fiduciaries often have the authority to write checks on behalf of the represented person, including the payment for debts and services owed to the fiduciary.[108]

A different set of rules to determine notice of the breach of fiduciary duty applies when the instrument is payable to the represented person or to the fiduciary as such. Disabling notice applies in these transactions when the instrument is "(i) taken in payment of or as security for a debt known by

---

[102] U.C.C. § 3-306. *See* § 6.02[a] *infra*.

[103] U.C.C. § 3-306, Comment.

[104] Bowling Green, Inc. v. State St. Bank & Trust Co., 307 F. Supp 648, 6 U.C.C. Rep. Serv. 1151, *aff'd*, 425 F.2d 81, 7 U.C.C. Rep. Serv. 635 (1st Cir. 1970) (holder in due course took check free from plaintiff's equitable claim of fraudulent inducement to negotiate the check).

[105] U.C.C. § 3-307(b)(1).

[106] U.C.C. § 3-307(b) and Comment 2.

[107] U.C.C. § 3-307(b)(3).

[108] U.C.C. § 3-307, Comment 4.

the taker to be the personal debt of the fiduciary, [or] (ii) taken in a transaction known by the taker to be for the personal benefit of the fiduciary."[109] Notice also results if an instrument payable to the represented person or to the fiduciary as such is deposited in an account other than an account of the fiduciary as such or an account of the represented person.[110] Because an instrument payable to the represented person or to the fiduciary as such is unlikely to be used for the personal benefit of the fiduciary, such use is likely be unlawful and constitutes notice if the represented person asserts a claim.[111]

Although quite expansive, the scope of these rules is undercut substantially by the requirement that the taker have knowledge of the fiduciary status of the fiduciary. Thus, for example, a depositary bank often will not have disabling notice because knowledge of the organization is established by the knowledge of the "individual conducting the transaction,"[112] and the teller involved in the transaction will not have any knowledge of the fiduciary status of the person from whom the instrument is received.[113]

The same set of rules to determine notice of the breach of fiduciary duty applies when the instrument is issued by the represented person or the fiduciary as such to the taker as payee.[114] Companies and other organizations generally do not pay for personal debts or purchases of individuals by issuing checks to the payees of these individuals, which makes it highly likely that the check is being used for unlawful purposes by the fiduciary.[115] This rule could likely change the result in *Eldon's Super Fresh Stores, Inc. v. Merrill Lynch, Pierce, Fenner & Smith, Inc.*[116] In that case an attorney who worked for the drawer of a company check delivered the check to a broker in payment of stock that the attorney had purchased. The check was made out to the broker and was for the exact amount of the stock purchase. The check did not indicate any restrictions on it, and the drawer did not maintain an account with the broker. Under these circumstances, the court ruled that the broker took the check as a holder in due course and not with notice of the drawer's claim that the check was to buy stock for the drawer. The inference drawn by the court was that the attorney had obtained the check from the drawer in payment for legal services and had delivered it to the broker to discharge the debt incurred from his stock purchase. Thus, the court held that the broker lacked knowledge both that the attorney negotiated the instrument as a fiduciary and in breach of that duty.[117] The

---

[109] U.C.C. § 3-307(b)(2).

[110] U.C.C. § 3-307(b)(2)(iii).

[111] U.C.C. § 3-307, Comment 2.

[112] U.C.C. § 1-201(27).

[113] In re Broadview Lumber Co., Inc., 118 F.3d 1246, 33 U.C.C. Rep. Serv. 2d 1 (8th Cir. 1997) (bank teller was unaware even of the depositor's fiduciary status).

[114] U.C.C. § 3-307(b)(4).

[115] U.C.C. § 3-307, Comment 5.

[116] 296 Minn. 130, 207 N.W.2d 282, 12 U.C.C. Rep. Serv. 490 (1973).

[117] *See also* Richardson Co. v. First Nat'l Bank, 504 S.W.2d 812, 14 U.C.C. Rep. Serv. 443 (Tex. Civ. App. 1974) (same holding on comparable facts on delivery by an employee to a bank of a check drawn by employer for the amount of an outstanding auto loan to the employee).

broker would face a substantially greater obstacle under section 3-307(b)(4) of revised Article 3.

[d] Notice That Any Party Has a Defense or Claim in Recoupment

Holder-in-due-course status is not quite as pervasive in its protection against defenses and claims in recoupment as it is in freeing the holder in due course from all claims to the instrument on the part of any person. Nevertheless the status does provide significant protection by cutting off most, but not all, defenses and claims in recoupment of any party to the instrument.[118] A holder who takes an instrument with notice that any party has a defense or a claim in recoupment cannot attain holder-in-due-course status.

Article 3 recognizes defenses based on common-law contract principles.[119] Parties who sign an instrument incur contractual liability.[120] If a subsequent party to whom that liability runs seeks to enforce it, any of the traditional defenses of general contract law might be available to the obligor.[121] The common-law defenses that are most commonly used in this context are fraud, misrepresentation or mistake in the issuance of the instrument.[122]

Additional defenses are specifically stated in Article 3. Some of the defenses relate to issuance of an instrument, and include nonissuance, conditional issuance and issuance for a special purpose.[123] The availability of these defenses in the law of instruments reflects the reified personal-property attributes of negotiable instruments and the requirement of an initial delivery of an instrument by the maker or drawer.[124] The instrument is binding on a maker or a drawer who signs it, but nonissuance of the instrument is a defense to the payment obligation.[125] The delivery of an instrument can be conditioned upon the occurrence of a stated event, such as additional signatures of other parties on the instrument.[126] Failure of

---

[118] U.C.C. § 3-305(b). *See* § 6.02[B] *infra*.

[119] A party's payment obligation is subject to "a defense of the obligor that would be available if the person entitled to enforce the instrument were enforcing a right to payment under a simple contract." U.C.C. § 3-305(a)(2).

[120] *See* § 4.01 *supra*.

[121] Misemer v. Freda's Restaurant, Inc., 961 S.W.2d 120, 34 U.C.C. Rep. Serv. 2d 1097 (Mo. Ct. App. 1998) (lack of consideration is a legitimate defense for a maker of a note, but the performance of consulting services by the payee constituted consideration).

[122] U.C.C. § 3-305, Comment 2.

[123] U.C.C. § 3-105(b).

[124] *See* §§ 1.01, 3.06[A] *supra*.

[125] U.C.C. § 3-105(b).

[126] *Id*; Kelley v. Carson, 120 Ga. App. 450, 171 S.E.2d 150, 7 U.C.C. Rep. Serv. 47 (1969) (agreement that note to raise money for a corporation was not to be used unless four other persons signed notes of the same amount). *See also* Merchants Nat'l Bank v. Professional Men's Assoc., 409 F.2d 600, 6 U.C.C. Rep. Serv. 337 (5th Cir. 1969), *cert. denied*, 396 U.S. 1009 (1970) (note to be repaid only from maker's profits).

the condition is a defense. Sometimes an instrument is delivered to a transferee to be used only for a special purpose. The delivery might be for security [127] or to enable the payee to acquire a specific automobile. [128] A defense of misuse arises when the transferee uses the instrument for some other purpose.

The obligation of a party to an instrument can be supplemented, modified, or nullified by a separate agreement between the obligor and a person entitled to enforce the instrument, and that agreement is a defense to the obligation. [129] The agreement can affect the instrument "if the instrument is issued or the obligation is incurred in reliance on the agreement or as part of the same transaction giving rise to the agreement." [130] Anyone who takes the instrument with notice of the agreement cannot qualify as a holder in due course.

Several other defenses that are provided in Article 3 are discussed in other sections of this text. These defenses include the failure to countersign a traveler's check, [131] payment that violates a restrictive indorsement, [132] and the issuance of an instrument without consideration or for which the promised performance is not given. [133]

Discharge is commonly asserted as a defense to general contract obligations. An obligor may have incurred a contract obligation, but that obligation cannot be enforced if it has been discharged through a manner recognized under contract law. Liability on an instrument can be discharged through a variety of means, [134] but in Article 3 discharge is not expressed as a defense. [135] The reason for this treatment of discharge under Article 3 has to do with its distinctive relationship to the notice concept. Notice of discharge of a party is not a disabling notice that will preclude the attainment of holder-in-due-course status, but the discharge will be effective against a holder in due course who takes an instrument with such notice. [136] Notice of the discharge of fewer than all of the parties to an instrument will not preclude attainment of holder-in-due-course status because the purchaser reasonably can expect the liability of the remaining parties to the instrument to continue.

---

[127] Ventures, Inc. v. Jones, 101 Idaho 837, 623 P.2d 145, 30 U.C.C. Rep. Serv. 1601 (1981) (notes were interim security only, given until adequate security was provided).

[128] American Underwriting Corp. v. Rhode Island Hosp. Trust Co., 111 R.I. 415, 303 A.2d 121, 12 U.C.C. Rep. Serv. 698 (1973) (draft to enable debtor to obtain her repossessed car).

[129] U.C.C. § 3-117.

[130] U.C.C. § 3-117.

[131] U.C.C. § 3-106(c). See § 2.03[B][4] *supra*.

[132] U.C.C. § 3-206(f). See § 3.04[B][2] *supra*.

[133] U.C.C. § 3-303(b). See § 6.01[B][1][a] *supra*.

[134] *See* Chapter 7 *infra*.

[135] U.C.C. § 3-302, Comment 3. The one exception is discharge of the obligor in an insolvency proceeding. See U.C.C. § 3-305(a)(1) and the discussion below.

[136] U.C.C. § 3-302(b). The corollary proposition is stated in section 3-601(b): "Discharge of the obligation of a party is not effective against a person acquiring rights of a holder in due course of the instrument without notice of the discharge."

Article 3 also recognizes certain defenses commonly known as "real defenses" that can be asserted against any person entitled to enforce an instrument.[137] These defenses involve certain aspects of the broader defenses of duress, legal capacity, illegality, fraudulent inducement, and discharge in insolvency proceedings.[138] The real defenses are covered in detail in a subsequent section of this chapter.[139]

The "close-connectedness" doctrine has provided the means for some courts to find that a holder took an instrument with disabling notice.[140] Even though a purchaser of promissory notes might appear to qualify in all respects as a holder in due course, the doctrine enables a court to pierce transactions that are not truly bona fide. When the purchaser of a note has a very close connection with its transferor concerning the transaction between the transferor and the maker of the note, the close-connectedness doctrine enables a court to attribute notice of the payee-transferor to the transferee. The court can thus penetrate sham transactions in which a disreputable seller of goods or services acquires a note from a buyer and promptly negotiates it to another party for the purpose of insulating the buyer's defenses of failure of consideration or breach of warranty from the obligation to pay the instrument. In the most obvious cases, the transferor and transferee clearly were closely affiliated.[141]

The landmark opinion advancing the close-connectedness doctrine is *Unico v. Owen*.[142] A buyer who issued a promissory note to a seller of stereo record albums stopped making payments on the note when he realized that the remaining 128 promised albums would not be delivered. The finance company to which the note had been negotiated sued the buyer for the unpaid time balance, penalties and attorney's fees. The Supreme Court of New Jersey applied the close-connectedness doctrine in refusing to allow the finance company to enforce the note free from the defenses of the buyer. The court stated:

> For purposes of consumer goods transactions, we hold that where the seller's performance is executory in character and when it appears from the totality of the arrangements between dealer and financer that the financer has had a substantial voice in setting standards for the underlying transaction, or has approved the standards established by the dealer, and has agreed to take all or a predetermined or substantial quantity of the negotiable paper which is backed by such standards, the financer should be considered a participant in the original transaction and therefore not entitled to holder in due course status.[143]

---

[137] U.C.C. § 3-305, Comment 1.

[138] U.C.C. § 3-305(a)(1).

[139] *See* § 6.02[B][2] *infra*.

[140] The initial decision was Commercial Credit Co. v. Childs, 199 Ark. 1073, 137 S.W.2d 260 (1940).

[141] Unico v. Owen, 50 N.J. 101, 232 A.2d 405, 4 U.C.C. Rep. Serv. 542 (1967)(finance company was a partnership formed only to finance sales of Universal Stereo).

[142] *Id.*

[143] 50 N.J. at 122, 232 A.2d at 417, 4 U.C.C. Rep. Serv. at 558.

The necessity for the close-connectedness doctrine has been significantly eliminated with the effectiveness in 1976 of the Federal Trade Commission Rule that abrogates the holder in due course doctrine in consumer sales transactions.[144] The Rule, however, does not cover commercial transactions. Some courts have continued to apply the doctrine to transactions between commercial enterprises.[145]

The revision to Article 3 adds the concept of a claim in recoupment in order to state an obligor's rights against a holder more precisely. The concept can be illustrated by assuming that a maker issues a note to a seller who promises to deliver goods at a date in the future. If the seller fails to deliver or delivers goods that the maker properly rejects,[146] the maker will have a defense to the note because the seller's performance will not have been performed when it was due.[147] If the maker instead accepts a nonconforming tender, the maker is obligated to pay for the goods at the contract rate[148] and the maker does not have a defense for failure of consideration.[149] Article 2, however, may give the maker-buyer a claim against the seller for breach of a warranty.[150] The revision to Article 3 refers to such a claim as a claim in recoupment. It operates as a counterclaim to reduce the amount owing on the note.[151] Although the claim for recoupment technically is a claim, it essentially is the same as a defense because it is asserted defensively to reduce or eliminate the obligation to pay the instrument. A purchaser must take an instrument without notice that a party has a claim in recoupment if the purchaser is to qualify as a holder in due course.[152]

[e] Notice of Unauthorized Signature or Alteration

Qualification as a holder in due course also requires the holder to take an instrument "without notice that the instrument contains an unauthorized signature or has been altered."[153] Unauthorized signatures are covered under section 3-403 and are discussed extensively in Chapter 4.[154]

---

[144] Preservation of Consumers' Claims and Defenses, 16 C.F.R. § 433. *See* § 6.06[B] *infra*.

[145] St. James v. Diversified Commercial Fin. Corp., 102 Nev. 23, 714 P.2d 179, 1 U.C.C. Rep. Serv. 2d 121 (1986) (notes given in purchase of debt-collection services); Arcanum Nat'l Bank v. Hessler, 69 Ohio St. 2d 549, 433 N.E.2d 204, 33 U.C.C. Rep. Serv. 604 (1982) (notes given for hogs). Other courts have not extended the close-connectedness doctrine to commercial transactions. Christinson v. Venturi Const. Co., 109 Ill. App. 3d 34, 64 Ill. Dec. 674, 440 N.E.2d 226, 34 U.C.C. Rep. Serv. 1604 (1982).

[146] *See* U.C.C. §§ 2-601, 2-602.

[147] U.C.C. § 3-303(b).

[148] U.C.C. § 2-607(1).

[149] U.C.C. § 3-305, Comment 2.

[150] *See* U.C.C. §§ 2-313 (express warranties), 2-314 (implied warranty of merchantability), 2-315 (implied warranty of fitness for a particular purpose).

[151] U.C.C. § 3-305, Comment 3.

[152] U.C.C. § 3-302(a)(2)(vi).

[153] U.C.C. § 3-302(a)(2)(iv).

[154] *See* § 4.05[B] *supra*.

Alterations of instruments are covered under section 3-407 and are discussed extensively in Chapter 7.[155] Notice of an unauthorized signature or an alteration obviously is notice of a significant infirmity in an instrument that should preclude holder-in-due-course status. It is identified as a separate form of disabling notice because forgery and alteration are not technically defenses under Article 3.[156]

[E] Questionable Authenticity — § 3-302(a)(1)

To be a holder in due course, nothing about the appearance of the instrument can cause the holder to doubt its authenticity. Section 3-302(a)(1) states that a person can be a holder in due course only if "the instrument when issued or negotiated to the holder does not bear such apparent evidence of forgery or alteration or is not otherwise so irregular or incomplete as to call into question its authenticity." The standard does not require the holder's awareness of the incompleteness or irregularity. It must be sufficient, however, to alert a reasonably prudent person.[157]

This provision is based on the simple premise that a prospective payee or purchaser of an instrument ought to examine the instrument before taking it and, therefore, ought to be accountable for any apparent irregularities appearing on either side of the instrument that are sufficient "to call into question its authenticity." The Comments amplify the drafters' intentions with respect to the questionable-authenticity standard: "The term 'authenticity' is used to make it clear that the irregularity or incompleteness must indicate that the instrument may not be what it purports to be."[158]

The revision of Article 3 deviates from the original drafting that used the questionable-authenticity standard to create constructive notice of a claim or defense.[159] Prior to the 1990 revision, facial irregularity or incompleteness gave the holder notice of a claim or defense, but it was not entirely clear whether the claim or defense had to be related to the irregularity. To illustrate the problem, assume that S and B have entered into a contract for aluminum siding for $10,000. S never intended to perform, giving B a defense based on fraud in the inducement. As part of the agreement, B signed a note that erroneously showed the amount due as $9,000. The parties noticed the mistake, crossed through the amount and wrote in $10,000. S then attempted to sell the note to H. Since a reasonably prudent person would have noticed the alteration, H would have been on notice of a claim or defense. However, H might have inquired of B, who, if the fraud has not yet been discovered, would have confirmed that $10,000 was the correct amount. Under the initial Article 3, it was unclear whether H could now be a holder in due course because any suspicion about

---

[155] *See* § 7.02[F] *infra*.

[156] U.C.C. § 3-302, Comment 2.

[157] Western State Bank v. First Union Bank & Trust Co., 172 Ind. App. 321, 360 N.E.2d 254, 21 U.C.C. Rep. Serv. 159 (1977).

[158] U.C.C. § 3-302, Comment 1.

[159] U.C.C. § 3-304(1)(a) (original version).

the alteration had been allayed or whether H, as a result of the alteration, was on notice of B's unrelated fraud defense. Section 3-302(a)(1) makes it clear that questions about authenticity are fatal to holder-in-due-course status. Conceptually, it is as if the irregularity or incompleteness gives notice of all claims and defenses, even those unrelated to the visible problem.

The Code provides no guidance regarding the circumstances that will give rise to an authenticity question. The Comments to the prior version of Article 3 stated that "[a]n instrument may be blank as to some unnecessary particular, may contain minor erasures, or even have an obvious change in the date, as where 'January 2, 1948' is changed to 'January 2, 1949', without even exciting suspicion."[160] Minor problems that can be easily explained from the face of the instrument[161] or from common experience without reference to the parties to the instrument, such as the example of a date change made shortly after the start of a new year, should fall outside the scope of section 3-302(a)(1). However, a person who purchases an instrument with even minor facial problems takes a significant risk.

[F] Exclusions — § 3-302(c)

Section 3-302(c) indicates several circumstances in which a person cannot become a holder in due course even though all of the requirements of section 3-302(a) are satisfied. Acquisitions that do not permit conferral of holder-in-due-course status are: taking an instrument by judicial process or a purchase in an execution, bankruptcy, or other similar proceeding; a purchase as part of a bulk transaction not in the ordinary course of business of the transferor;[162] and taking as a successor in interest to an estate or other organization.[163] These transactions are not the type in which the attributes of negotiability are promoted because the circumstances of acquisition are unusual. The codified exclusions reflect prior case law.

The basic rule on rights acquired by transfer applies to determine the extent of the rights acquired by the transferee in these transactions.[164] The

---

[160] U.C.C. § 3-304, Comment 2 (original version). In Barclays Bank, P.L.C. v. Conkey, 695 So.2d 931, 35 U.C.C. Rep. Serv. 2d 946 (Fla. Dist. Ct. App. 1997), the appellate court reversed a trial court holding that the omission of the date on which installment payments on a note were to begin precluded holder-in-due-court status of the transferee of the note because the note was so incomplete as to call into question its authenticity. The appellate court found that this omission was not sufficient to indicate that the instrument may not be what it purports to be.

[161] See, e.g., National State Bank v. Kleinberg, 4 U.C.C. Rep. Serv. 100 (N.Y. Sup. Ct. 1967) (alteration of principal sum from $41,000 to $42,000 easily explained by the fact that the stated installments totaled $42,000).

[162] Henkin, Inc. v. Berea Bank & Trust Co., 556 S.W.2d 420, 23 U.C.C. Rep. Serv. 1225 (Ky. App. 1978) (purchase by one bank of assets of another bank facing insolvency).

[163] "Subsection (c) would also apply when a new partnership takes over for value all of the assets of an old one after a new member has entered the firm, or to a reorganized or consolidated corporation taking over the assets of a predecessor." U.C.C. § 3-302, Comment 5.

[164] U.C.C. § 3-203(b).

comments make it clear that the transferee who acquires an instrument under the indicated circumstances "is treated as a successor in interest to the prior holder and can acquire no better rights."[165] Of course, if the prior holder is a holder in due course, the transferee acquires the holder-in-due-course rights available to the transferor.[166]

The exceptions of subsection (c) govern the sale of the assets of an insolvent bank by a state banking commission, at least in the absence of contrary state law. The exceptions may be preempted by federal law, however, if the Federal Deposit Insurance Corporation or a similar insurer takes over an insolvent bank. Federal law may give such insurers holder-in-due-course status,[167] and their rights can be transferred to their assignees.[168]

[G] Payee as Holder in Due Course

A payee, like any other holder, can qualify as a holder in due course.[169] The payee simply must satisfy the elements codified in section 3-302(a). The status will not be of any relevance, however, for most payees. If the maker or drawer is the only obligor on the instrument, "the holder-in-due-course doctrine is irrelevant in determining rights between Obligor [maker or drawer] and Obligee [payee] with respect to the instrument."[170] Even a holder in due course is subject to the defenses that an obligor on an instrument has against the holder in due course.[171] Unless other persons are involved in the transaction, so that the defenses of the obligor are against them, the payee's holder in due course status cannot provide the basic benefit of cutting off defenses. Under certain circumstances, such as the use of a remitter or in cases of co-makers or co-payees, the payee will have the necessary insulation to avoid defenses asserted by the party who issued the instrument.[172]

---

[165] U.C.C. § 3-302, Comment 5.

[166] These rights are an application of the shelter principle. For discussion of this principle, see § 6.02[C] *infra*.

[167] *See* 12 U.S.C. 1823(e)(1). The United States Supreme Court decision of O'Melveny & Myers v. F.D.I.C., 510 U.S. 989, 114 S. Ct. 543 (1993), did not deal with the issue directly but did place this area in doubt. *Compare* DiVall Insured Income Fund L.P. v. Boatmen's First Nat'l Bank, 69 F.3d 1398 (8th Cir. 1995) (no federal holder-in-due-course status for nonnegotiable note payable to a bank placed into FDIC receivership), *with* Motorcity of Jacksonville, Ltd. v. Southeast Bank, 83 F.3d 1317 (11th Cir. 1996) (reasoning in support of continued viability of federal doctrine).

[168] U.C.C. § 3-302, Comment 5; Sunbelt Savings, FSB v. Cashin Constr. Co., 737 F. Supp. 41 (E.D. Tex 1990).

[169] U.C.C. § 3-302, Comment 4; McIntyre v. Harris, 304 Ill. App. 3d 304, 709 N.E.2d 982, 39 U.C.C. Rep. Serv. 2d 200 (Ill. Ct. App. 1999) (drawer's assertion that payee cannot be a holder in due course because the instrument has to be negotiated to confer the status is rejected by the court).

[170] U.C.C. § 3-302, Comment 4.

[171] U.C.C. § 3-305(b). *See* § 6.02[B][1] *infra*.

[172] Comment 4 to section 3-302 provides several examples as illustrations.

§ 6.02 Rights of Holder In Due Course

[A] Free From Claims — § 3-306

A person asserts a claim under Article 3 by taking affirmative action to recover an instrument or to impose liability because of someone else's possession of the instrument. A holder in due course takes an instrument free from claims to it.[173] A readily apparent claim is the claim of ownership. An instrument that has been lost by an owner or stolen from the owner can be negotiated to a holder in due course if it is in bearer form.[174] The holder in due course takes the instrument free from the owner's claim of title. The Code does not in so many words confer superior title or ownership status on the holder in due course, but that result follows from granting the holder in due course freedom from the ownership claims of all prior parties. In addition to claims of ownership, a holder in due course takes free of any other claim of a property or possessory right in the instrument or its proceeds. For example, a creditor may claim to have some type of lien on the instrument,[175] or a prior owner of the instrument may claim that a con artist fraudulently induced him to negotiate the instrument.[176]

Article 3 does not provide a holder in due course with absolute immunity with respect to all claims. Because a holder in due course can still be subject to claims that arise against him or her after taking the instrument, section 3-306 is written to provide that a holder in due course "takes" free of the claims of other parties. The purchaser of an instrument has a legitimate concern about achieving freedom from claims that arise before the purchaser takes the instrument. Without these assurances, purchasers would take instruments with the full risk of any of its sordid history prior to the purchase. Prospective purchasers unwilling to incur the risk blindly would have to investigate the relationship of prior parties to the instrument or forgo the purchase. The free transferability of negotiable instruments is dependent on affording protection for bona fide purchasers against these prior claims and defenses. The same considerations do not apply with respect to claims that the holder in due course subsequently creates. Thus, a holder in due course is not free of the claim of ownership of a subsequent purchaser of the instrument from whom possession is wrongfully withheld.

---

[173] U.C.C. § 3-306.

[174] If an instrument is lost or stolen while in order form, holder-in-due-course status can not be attained through a subsequent transfer because the transferee can not qualify as a holder. U.C.C. § 3-302(a).

[175] Bricks Unlimited, Inc. v. Agee, 672 F.2d 1255, 33 U.C.C. Rep. Serv. 989 (5th Cir. 1982) (holder in due course superior to the claim of a garnishing creditor); Farns Assocs., Inc. v. South Side Bank, 93 Ill. App. 3d 766, 417 N.E.2d 818, 30 U.C.C. Rep. Serv. 1729 (1981) (holder in due course of checks payable to its debtor would take free of prior-perfected security interest in debtor's accounts receivable).

[176] Bowling Green, Inc. v. State St. Bank & Trust Co., 307 F. Supp. 648, 6 U.C.C. Rep. Serv. 1151, *aff'd*, 425 F.2d 81, 7 U.C.C. Rep. Serv. 635 (1st Cir. 1970) (holder in due course took check free from plaintiff's equitable claim of fraudulent inducement to negotiate the check).

[B] Free From Defenses — § 3-305(b)

A person asserts a defense under Article 3 to avert personal liability. A holder in due course takes an instrument free from most, but not all defenses. Section 3-305(b) indicates that the right of a holder in due course to enforce the obligation of a party to pay an instrument generally is not subject to common-law defenses, defenses stated in Article 3, or a claim of recoupment of the obligor against the original payee of the instrument. The section, however, also codifies two categories of defenses to which even a holder in due course is susceptible. One of the limitations on freedom from defenses is based on the type of defense asserted. The defenses, commonly known as real defenses, are available to any obligor who can establish them, even when a holder in due course seeks to hold the obligor liable.[177] The other limitation on freedom from defenses logically excludes defenses that the obligor has based on the transaction with the holder in due course.[178] The holder in due course is susceptible to any of these defenses even if they are not classified as real defenses. Such defenses are commonly referred to as personal defenses.

[1] Defenses Against the Holder

The purpose of holder-in-due-course protection is not to insulate the holder from defenses that are caused by the holder. Usually such defenses will preclude holder-in-due-course status because the holder will have notice of the defense at the time of taking the instrument and thus be unable to comply with all of the necessary requirements.[179] A holder might nevertheless qualify as a holder in due course with respect to a transaction in which its transferor would have a viable defense or claim in recoupment.[180] The holder in due course would be susceptible to the defense or the claim in recoupment because section 3-305(b) cuts off only defenses and claims in recoupment "against a person other than the holder."

A holder in due course is protected against the risk that other parties to the instrument might have personal defenses to their apparent liability.[181] Assume that Buyer negotiates to Seller a check that had previously

---

[177] U.C.C. § 3-305(a)(1).

[178] U.C.C. § 3-305(b) ("against a person other than the holder").

[179] Thornton, Sperry & Jensen, Ltd. v. Anderson, 352 N.W.2d 467, 39 U.C.C. Rep. Serv. 525 (Minn. Ct. App. 1984) (notice of excessiveness of fee).

[180] The court misses this point in James Pair, Inc. v. Gentry, 134 Ga. App. 734, 215 S.E.2d 707, 17 U.C.C. Rep. Serv. 801 (1975). An agent of an employment agency, the payee of the note, told the maker that the employer with whom the maker accepted employment would pay the agency's fee after six months on the job, as did the agent for the employer. The maker did not learn otherwise until contacting the home office of the employer over two months later. Nothing in the court's opinion suggests that the payee took the note while aware of this information. For an illustration on a claim in recoupment, see § 6.01[D][2][d] *supra*.

[181] When Buyer and Seller are the only persons involved, "[t]he holder-in-due-course doctrine has no relevance. The doctrine applies only to cases in which more than two parties are involved. Its essence is that the holder in due course does not have to suffer the consequences of a defense of the obligor on the instrument that arose from an occurrence with a third party." U.C.C. § 3-305, Comment 2.

been negotiated to Buyer by the payee. If Seller sued Buyer on the payment obligation, Buyer would be able to assert any of its defenses or claims in recoupment against Seller, even if Seller was a holder in due course. If Seller sued the drawer, or the payee as an indorser, however, those parties could not assert Buyer's defenses or claims in recoupment.[182] Furthermore, if Seller was a holder in due course, they could not assert any personal defense of their own, such as lack of consideration, because their defenses would be against persons other than the holder in due course.[183] Seller would have taken the instrument without notice of their defenses and would be entitled to enforce their liability irrespective of their defenses.

[2] Real Defenses — § 3-305(a)(1)

The real defenses are exceptions to the general rule that protects holders in due course from defenses that they did not cause. The real defenses reflect a policy judgment that, despite the importance of promoting the negotiability of instruments, certain circumstances require greater protection for parties obligated on an instrument. The codification of the real defenses should be read carefully, because they are narrower in their scope than they might at first appear.

[a] Infancy

Infancy is a defense against even a holder in due course "to the extent it is a defense to a simple contract."[184] The Comments state the policy to be "one of protection of the infant even at the expense of occasional loss to an innocent purchaser."[185] The real defense is not, however, blanket protection of infants in all transactions. The defense is available only if the transaction is either void or voidable under applicable state law.

The determination of when infancy is a valid defense is left to state law.[186] Generally, a contract by a person under the age of majority is voidable, enabling the minor to disaffirm or rescind the transaction. Nevertheless, variations among the states in areas such as the age of contractual capacity, misrepresentation of the minor's age, the purchase of necessities, and restoration of property to the other contracting party, mean that the specific law of the applicable jurisdiction must be consulted to determine whether infancy in a particular case is a real or personal defense.[187]

---

[182] Rezapolvi v. First Nat'l Bank, 296 Md. 1, 459 A.2d 183, 35 U.C.C. Rep. Serv. 1559 (1983) (bank could not rely on defenses of third party).

[183] Grand W. Currency Exchange, Inc. v. A:M Sunrise Constr. Co., 163 Ill. App. 3d 51, 516 N.E.2d 486, 5 U.C.C. Rep. Serv. 2d 628 (1987).

[184] U.C.C. § 3-305(a)(1)(i).

[185] U.C.C. § 3-305, Comment 1; Trenton Trust Co. v. Western Sur. Co., 599 S.W.2d 481, 29 U.C.C. Rep. Serv. 921 (Mo. 1980) (by statute, contract pledging minor's assets not binding without approval of probate court).

[186] U.C.C. § 3-305, Comment 1.

[187] Id.

[b] Other Incapacity, Duress or Illegality

All other forms of incapacity to contract are distinguished from infancy in determining whether they constitute real defenses. Whereas infancy is a real defense if it makes the contract either void or voidable, any other incapacity is a real defense only if it "nullifies the obligation of the obligor."[188] Thus, the defense of incapacity other than infancy, such as mental incompetency, guardianship, or lack of corporate capacity, is valid against a holder in due course only if the obligation of the party asserting the defense is entirely null and void.[189] A voidable defense of incapacity in these other categories is only a personal defense and not valid against a holder in due course. Article 3 again defers to state law to determine both the existence and effect of any form of incapacity.[190] An adjudication of incompetency usually makes the subsequent contracts of the incompetent person void, but other forms of incapacity generally do not lead to void transactions.[191]

The same standard of rendering the obligation of a party a nullity also applies to defenses based on duress or illegality of the transaction.[192] Usually duress may render a contract merely voidable, although extreme forms, such as extracting an instrument at gun point, could make the signer's obligation void and constitute a real defense.[193] Although illegality most frequently reaches gambling[194] and usury,[195] a wide range of statutes and interpretations of public policy create substantial variations among the states on illegal transactions.[196] As a rule of thumb, most often the defense of illegality will not constitute a real defense.[197] When a statute or court

---

[188] U.C.C. § 3-305(a)(1)(ii).

[189] U.C.C. § 3-305, Comment 1; Universal Acceptance Corp. v. Burks, 7 U.C.C. Rep. Serv. 39 (D.C. Ct. Gen. Sess. 1969) (statute makes contracts of corporation that lost its articles of incorporation null and void and not merely voidable).

[190] U.C.C. § 3-305, Comment 1.

[191] Katski v. Boehm, 249 Md. 568, 241 A.2d 129, 5 U.C.C. Rep. Serv. 49 (1968) (no defense of incompetency by evidence that signer was distraught, nervous, or under a strain).

[192] U.C.C. § 3-305(a)(1)(ii); Westervelt v. Gateway Fin. Serv., 190 N.J. Super. 615, 464 A.2d 1203, 37 U.C.C. Rep. Serv. 805 (1983) (defense of illegality available against holder in due course because statute rendered secondary mortgage loan transaction from which the note arose "void and unenforceable").

[193] U.C.C. § 3-305, Comment 1; Standard Fin. Co., Ltd. v. Ellis, 657 P.2d 1056, 35 U.C.C. Rep. Serv. 864 (Haw. Ct. App. 1983) (random beatings by husband not sufficiently related to execution of note).

[194] National Recovery Sys. v. Ornstein, 541 F. Supp. 1131, 33 U.C.C. Rep. Serv. 1697 (E.D. Pa. 1982) (checks written for gambling or to cover gambling losses void and unenforceable).

[195] Federal Deposit Ins. Corp. v. Wood, 758 F.2d 156, 40 U.C.C. Rep. Serv. 937 (6th Cir. 1985) (usury defense not valid against holder in due course); Cromwell v. All State Credit Corp., 10 U.C.C. Rep. Serv. 403 (D.C. Super. Ct. 1971) (voidable only).

[196] "The statutes differ greatly in their provisions and the interpretations given them. They are primarily a matter of local concern and local policy. All such matters are therefore left to the local law." U.C.C. § 3-305, Comment 1.

[197] Bankers Trust Co. v. Litton Sys., 599 F.2d 488, 26 U.C.C. Rep. Serv. 513 (2d Cir. 1979) (commercial bribery not a real defense); New Jersey Mortgage & Inv. Corp. v. Berenyi, 140 N.J. Super. 406, 356 A.2d 421, 19 U.C.C. Rep. Serv. 186 (1976) (note issued as part of a transaction in violation of injunctive order not a nullity).

determines that the transaction is void, however, the defense is valid even against a holder in due course.

[c] Fraud

Fraud constitutes a defense for an obligor on an instrument, but again, its availability as a real defense is quite limited. The real defense requires "fraud that induced the obligor to sign the instrument with neither knowledge nor reasonable opportunity to learn of its character or its essential terms."[198] The requirements eliminate the entire category of fraud known as "fraud in the procurement" or "fraud in the inducement."[199] This category of fraud occurs when a person is induced through deceit to issue or to negotiate an instrument. The person signing the instrument may be deceived as to the identity of the other party or some aspect of the underlying transaction, but the person is fully aware that it is a check or note that is being given. Because a negotiable instrument is knowingly passed in the stream of commerce, the transferor runs the risk that it will reach a holder in due course, who can then cut off the personal defense of fraud.[200]

The category of fraud that can qualify as a real defense is known as "fraud in the factum" or "essential fraud." This fraud goes to the nature of the writing or its terms, so that the person signing it either is not aware that an instrument is negotiated or is not aware of its essential terms. The signing party might be duped into believing instead that the form signed was a receipt,[201] a statement of wages earned for tax purposes,[202] or a character reference,[203] or that the amount or due date of the instrument was different from the written terms. Under these circumstances, the signing party did not intend to pass a negotiable instrument, or at least not one with the terms as they were actually written. Under this category of fraud, the defendant in fact signed the instrument, but lacked contractual intent to support liability on the instrument.[204]

This category of fraud *might* create a real defense. An additional requirement must still be met. In addition to fraud that induced the signature and the signer's lack of awareness as to the character or essential terms of the instrument, the signer must not have had a reasonable opportunity to learn

---

[198] U.C.C. § 3-305(a)(1)(iii).

[199] Seinfeld v. Commercial Bank & Trust Co., 405 So. 2d 1039, 32 U.C.C. Rep. Serv. 1137 (Fla. Ct. App. 1981).

[200] Firth v. Farmers-Citizens Bank, 460 N.E.2d 191, 38 U.C.C. Rep. Serv. 212 (Ind. Ct. App. 1984) (check written on misrepresentation that a commission was due to the payee held enforceable by holder in due course); Standard Fin. Co., Ltd. v. Ellis, 657 P.2d 1056, 35 U.C.C. Rep. Serv. 864 (Haw. Ct. App. 1983) (misrepresentation that co-signing was a mere formality and that her husband alone was liable insufficient for real defense).

[201] Federal Deposit Ins. Corp. v. Culver, 640 F. Supp. 725, 1 U.C.C. Rep. Serv. 2d 1585 (D. Kan. 1986).

[202] First Nat'l Bank v. Fazzari, 10 N.Y.2d 394, 223 N.Y.S.2d 483, 179 N.E.2d 493 (1961).

[203] United Bank & Trust Co. v. Schaeffer, 280 Md. 10, 370 A.2d 1138, 21 U.C.C. Rep. Serv. 586 (1977).

[204] U.C.C. § 3-305, Comment 1.

of the instrument's character or terms. Before fraud can be asserted as a real defense against a holder in due course, the party deceived must establish "excusable ignorance of the contents of the writing signed."[205] In assessing the reasonableness of a party's professed ignorance as to the writing, courts should consider all relevant factors, including intelligence, education, business experience, reading ability, nature of the representations, reasons for reliance, and the availability of someone else to explain the instrument.[206]

This final test of reasonableness is generally too difficult to surmount. A party who was not aware of the contents of the writing because of a failure to read it will be unsuccessful against a holder in due course if the party was presented with an adequate opportunity to read it before signing.[207] Unless a party in these circumstances can show that the writing was cleverly switched for another writing,[208] or that the signature was rushed,[209] or that the party was deceived into not reading before signing because the person requesting the signature was in a position of special confidence,[210] the opportunity to read the writing is likely to be considered an adequate opportunity to have avoided the fraud. A party with the capacity to read and understand an instrument is unlikely to establish a real defense,[211] and the lack of such capacity is still likely to be insufficient if the signer has a trusted person available to explain the writing.[212] The other criteria that is generally the most significant in the resolution of these cases is educational and business experience of the signing party.[213]

---

[205] Id.

[206] Id.

[207] Federal Deposit Ins. Corp. v. Culver, 640 F. Supp. 725, 1 U.C.C. Rep. Serv. 2d 1585 (D. Kan. 1986) (maker failed to even read incomplete promissory note that he was directed to sign).

[208] Burchett v. Alied Concord Financial Corp., 74 N.M. 575, 396 P.2d 186, 2 U.C.C. Rep. Serv. 297 (1964) (where salesman filled out different forms from the ones that signers read, court held it was not sufficient to preclude reading the form signed).

[209] American Plan Corp. v. Woods, 16 Ohio App. 2d 1, 240 N.E.2d 886, 5 U.C.C. Rep. Serv. 842 (1968) (seller's representative in a hurry).

[210] United Bank & Trust Co. v. Schaeffer, 280 Md. 10, 370 A.2d 1138, 21 U.C.C. Rep. Serv. 586 (1977) (evidence that accommodation party was nearly illiterate and was told by the accommodated party, then his friend and supervisor, that he was signing a character reference).

[211] The party does not have to understand that the instrument is negotiable or the legal consequences of transferring these instruments, but rather that the instrument involves an obligation for the payment of money.

[212] Christinson v. Venturi Const. Co., 109 Ill. App. 3d 34, 440 N.E.2d 226, 34 U.C.C. Rep. Serv. 1604 (1982) (although unaware of the nature of a trade acceptance, buyer could have consulted with bank before signing); First Nat'l Bank v. Fazzari, 10 N.Y.2d 394, 223 N.Y.S.2d 483, 179 N.E.2d 493 (1961) (although signer could not read English, he was an experienced business person and his wife could read English and was available).

[213] American Plan Corp. v. Woods, 16 Ohio App. 2d 1, 240 N.E.2d 886, 5 U.C.C. Rep. Serv. 842 (1968) (little business experience or knowledge). The court in this case aids the consumer on facts that are not very distinguishable from other cases finding an inadequate defense. First Nat'l Bank v. Fazzari, 10 N.Y.2d 394, 223 N.Y.S.2d 483, 179 N.E.2d 493 (1961) (signer was experienced business man, even though unable to read English).

Relying upon the explanation of a person seeking the signature on the writing is not an action that is sufficiently reasonable to justify passing the resulting loss to a subsequent holder in due course.[214]

[d] Discharge in Insolvency Proceedings

As explained previously, discharge is not expressed as a defense in Article 3.[215] A holder can still qualify as a holder in due course even though the instrument is taken with notice of discharge of prior parties, unless the holder has notice that all of the parties are discharged. When a holder in due course takes an instrument with notice that a party has been discharged, the discharge is effective against even the holder in due course.[216] Conversely, when a holder in due course takes an instrument without notice of the prior discharge of a party, the discharge is not effective against the holder in due course.[217]

Discharge of the obligor in insolvency proceedings is treated differently. Discharge in these proceedings is a real defense, and thus is effective against even a holder in due course, irrespective of prior notice.[218] The bankruptcy goal of rehabilitating the discharged debtor is advanced over protection of a holder in due course by applying the discharge from the debtor's liability even on negotiable instruments.

[C] Rights Passed Through Shelter — § 3-203(b)

Even though a transferee does not qualify as a holder in due course, the transferee might still be able to assert holder-in-due-course rights as its derivative rights. A transferee of an instrument receives any right of the transferor to enforce the instrument,[219] and when the transferor is a holder in due course, the rights received by the transferee are precisely the same holder-in-due-course rights that were available to the transferor.[220] The transferee is thus protected against the same claims, defenses, and claims in recoupment that were cut off under sections 3-305(b) and 3-306 in favor

---

[214] Reading Trust Co. v. Hutchison, 35 Pa. D. & C.2d 790, 2 U.C.C. Rep. Serv. 481 (Pa. Ct. Com. Pl. 1964)(ability to read and write and high degree of intelligence plus lack of any basis to have confidence in the representations made by salesman precluded real defense).

[215] U.C.C. § 3-302(b) (notice of discharge is not notice of a defense for purposes of determining holder in due course status). See § 6.01[D][2][e] supra.

[216] U.C.C. § 3-302(b).

[217] U.C.C. § 3-601(b) and Comment.

[218] U.C.C. § 3-305(a)(1)(iv).

[219] U.C.C. § 3-203(b). The transferee also receives all of the ownership rights of the transferor through the rule of derivative title. These rights are passed through common law. See § 3.03 supra.

[220] U.C.C. § 3-203, Comment 2; Weast v. Arnold, 299 Md. 540, 474 A.2d 904, 38 U.C.C. Rep. Serv. 913 (1984); Nida v. Michael, 34 Mich. App. 290, 191 N.W.2d 151, 9 U.C.C. Rep. Serv. 1380 (1971).

of the transferor.[221] This protection gained from a transfer by a holder in due course is known as shelter.

The shelter transferee's rights, like the rights of all parties that are asserted derivatively, are defined in section 3-203(b). The shelter provision conveys rights, but it does not confer status. Shelter does not make the transferee a holder in due course. Only parties that fully comply with the requirements of section 3-302(a) attain that status. Shelter confers on the transferee the *transferor's rights* of a holder in due course. The transferee thus will be subject to any defenses or claims in recoupment to which the holder in due course transferring the instrument was susceptible.[222] Therefore, the holder-in-due-course rights of the transferor must be determined in order to ascertain the comparable rights of the shelter transferee.[223]

Consider the facts diagramed below:

```
              "P"        "X"
M----▶P────────▶X────────▶Y
                         (HDC)
```

Diagram 6.2

Maker (M) issued a note to Payee (P). The note was subsequently negotiated by P to X, and, in turn, by X to Y. If M were unable to pay the note when it became due, Y could proceed against P on her indorser's liability. As a holder in due course, Y's rights would be governed by sections 3-305 and 3-306, and Y would be able to cut off any personal defense or claim in recoupment that P could have asserted against X, such as breach of warranty on the goods that X delivered in exchange for the note.

---

[221] In Northside Bldg. & Inv. Co. v. Finance Co. of Am., 119 Ga. App. 131, 166 S.E.2d 608, 6 U.C.C. Rep. Serv. 345 (1969), the plaintiff-holder of the note on which the maker had a personal defense of payment could not qualify as a holder in due course. Prior to the pledge of the note to the plaintiff, however, it had been negotiated successively by a bank, a finance company, and an investment company, suggesting the strong possibility of sufficient shelter protection. In a rebuke to plaintiff's counsel, the court noted the following:

Where is it shown that a defense exists, the plaintiff may seek to cut off such defense by establishing itself as a holder in due course or that it has acquired the rights of a prior holder in due course. . . . But in doing so the plaintiff must sustain the burden of proof by a preponderance of evidence. There was no showing made to sustain this burden, that anyone through whom the plaintiff had acquired its rights was a holder in due course.

119 Ga. App. at 134, 166 S.E.2d at 611, 6 U.C.C. Rep. Serv. at 348.

[222] All holders in due course take instruments free from prior claims to the instruments. U.C.C. § 3-306. See § 6.02[A] *supra*.

[223] Great W. Bank & Trust Co. v. Pima Sav. & Loan Ass'n, 149 Ariz. 364, 718 P.2d 1017, 2 U.C.C. Rep. Serv. 2d 532 (Ariz. Ct. App. 1986) (third party to whom check was indorsed was not protected by shelter against personal defenses of the drawer).

Assume now that in the facts diagramed above, Y does not qualify as a holder in due course, but that X did so qualify upon taking the instrument. P could assert her claim in recoupment against Y, and the shelter provision would not assist Y. Through section 3-203(b), Y acquires X's holder-in-due-course rights. Applying section 3-305(a)(3) to X shows that X would be susceptible to P's claim in recoupment. Shelter does not pass greater rights than the transferor had, so Y is also subject to the claim in recoupment.

Assume now that Y must rely upon shelter, but now Y proceeds against M, who resists paying the note because of a personal defense created in the underlying transaction with P. Shelter now is very valuable to Y. Without it, Y would not have any rights of a holder in due course and would thereby be susceptible to the personal defense.[224] Through section 3-203(b), however, Y again acquires X's holder-in-due-course rights. Under section 3-305(b), X cut off the personal defense of M. This right is passed through shelter to Y, enabling Y to take free of the defense. Similarly, if Y were to transfer the instrument to Z, Z would receive X's holder-in-due-course rights.

The Code recognizes shelter, even if the transferee is aware of the defense at the time of taking the instrument, because it protects the holder in due course without imposing additional burdens on the party required to pay the instrument. A holder in due course who retains the instrument can enforce it free of the claims, defenses, and claims in recoupment specified in sections 3-305(b) and 3-306. The substantive rights of other parties will not be affected by allowing the holder in due course to transfer his or her rights to someone else. Because the other parties will not be prejudiced by the transfer, they should not be concerned about the identity of the person entitled to enforce obligations on the instrument. Shelter does protect the holder in due course, on the other hand, by maintaining a market for further transfers of the instrument.[225] If a holder in due course holds an instrument free from a prior party's personal defense, but notice of that defense becomes widely known among prospective purchasers, the market for the instrument would diminish in the absence of shelter for these subsequent purchasers. The holder in due course might be forced to retain the instrument to maturity, thereby impairing the value of the instrument. Shelter thus preserves the marketability of the instrument without prejudicing the rights of anyone else.

The shelter provision does include an exception designed to deny its advantages to undeserving transferees. The exception provides that "the transferee cannot acquire rights of a holder in due course by a transfer, directly or indirectly, from a holder in due course if the transferee engaged in fraud or illegality affecting the instrument."[226] Such transferees cannot "wash the instrument clean by passing it into the hands of a holder in due course and then repurchasing it."[227] For example, a holder who either takes

---

[224] U.C.C. § 3-305(a)(2).
[225] U.C.C. § 3-203, Comment 2.
[226] U.C.C. § 3-203(b).
[227] U.C.C. § 3-203, Comment 2.

an instrument with notice of a defense or fraudulently procures it cannot negotiate the instrument to a holder in due course and then succeed to the shelter rights by reacquiring the instrument.[228] Simply passing the instrument through the hands of a holder in due course does not justify increasing the rights of the transferee who repurchases it. The exception to the shelter provision precludes any advantage from such manipulations.

§ 6.03 Absence of Any Holder-in-Due-Course Rights

[A] Claims and Defenses — § 3-306

While a holder in due course takes an instrument free from all claims to it on the part of any person, a holder without those rights is subject to all valid claims to it.[229] Persons without holder-in-due-course rights include persons that neither qualify personally as holders in due course nor attain holder-in-due-course rights from their transferors through shelter.[230] Anyone with a valid claim of legal title has a superior claim to the instrument over anyone without the rights of a holder in due course. A person without the rights of a holder in due course also takes an instrument subject to equitable claims by which a party wrongfully induced to transfer the instrument seeks to rescind the transfer to recover the instrument.[231]

Although holders in due course are subject only to real defenses and personal defenses against themselves,[232] a person without holder-in-due-course rights takes an instrument subject to all valid defenses of any obligor to the instrument.[233] Parties who sign an instrument incur contractual liability.[234] If a subsequent party to whom that liability runs seeks to enforce it, any of the traditional defenses of general contract law might be available to the obligor. A non-exclusive list of possible defenses includes want or failure of consideration, incapacity, duress, fraud, overreaching, mistake, and breach of warranty.

[B] *Jus Tertii*: Assertion of the Rights of Third Parties — § 3-305(c)

When a defendant obligor on a negotiable instrument does not have an available defense, the defendant might seek to assert a known claim or defense of some other party to the instrument. The assertion of the rights of a third party is known as *jus tertii*. The general rule is that a defendant

---

[228] Petersen v. Roylin Enterprises, Inc., 529 F. Supp. 584, 33 U.C.C. Rep. Serv. 618 (D. Nev. 1982) (reacquisition by seller of goods after making an assignment to a holder in due course).

[229] U.C.C. § 3-306.

[230] *See* § 6.02 *supra*.

[231] Douglas v. Wones, 120 Ill. App. 3d 36, 458 N.E.2d 514, 37 U.C.C. Rep. Serv. 1606 (1983). See § 6.04 *infra* on rescission following an effective negotiation.

[232] U.C.C. § 3-305(b).

[233] U.C.C. § 3-305(a)(1), (2).

[234] *See* § 4.02 *supra*.

cannot raise the claim or defense of another party.[235] The contract of the obligor on an instrument is to pay the person entitled to enforce the instrument, and possible claims that other parties may have against that person do not concern the obligor. Because the obligor often will not have access to adequate evidence to establish the validity of another party's claim, the obligor is neither required nor allowed to assert the claim as a defense.[236] The obligor is fully protected with denial of the option to use the claim as a defense through the corollary general rule that payment of the holder of the instrument discharges the obligor's liability on the instrument.[237]

Article 3 recognizes certain exceptions to these general rules.[238] An obligor is not required to pay an instrument if "the person seeking enforcement of the instrument does not have the rights of a holder in due course and the obligor proves that the instrument is a lost or stolen instrument."[239] Thus, even though an instrument was not stolen from the obligor from whom payment is demanded, the obligor nevertheless can assert the *jus tertii* rights of legal ownership as a defense against payment. The defense is valid against the thief and any subsequent transferees following the theft who do not acquire holder in due course rights. The exception "is based on the policy which refuses to aid a proved thief to recover, and refuses to aid him indirectly by permitting his transferee to recover unless the transferee is a holder in due course."[240] The *jus tertii* exception undercuts the market for instruments acquired by finders and thieves by enabling obligors on the instrument to assert the claim of title of the owner as a defense to their obligations. Because a claim of ownership is cut off by a subsequent holder in due course, the *jus tertii* rights based on theft or loss of an instrument are not available against a person entitled to enforce the instrument who has the rights of a holder in due course.

The other exception to the *jus tertii* rule is that "the other person's claim to the instrument may be asserted by the obligor if the other person is joined in the action and personally asserts the claim against the person entitled to enforce the instrument."[241] If, rather than asserting theft of an instrument from the owner, an obligor seeks to defend against liability by asserting that the holder wrongfully acquired the instrument through fraud

---

[235] "[I]n an action to enforce the obligation of a party to pay the instrument, the obligor may not assert against the person entitled to enforce the instrument a defense, claim in recoupment, or claim to the instrument (Section 3-306) of another person . . . ." U.C.C. § 3-305(c).

[236] Duxbury v. Roberts, 388 Mass. 385, 446 N.E.2d 401, 36 U.C.C. Rep. Serv. 214 (1983); Rezapolvi v. First Nat'l Bank, 296 Md. 1, 459 A.2d 183, 35 U.C.C. Rep. Serv. 1559 (1983).

[237] U.C.C. § 3-602(a). See § 7.02[A][1] *infra*.

[238] The exceptions by which an obligor may assert *jus tertii* claims as a defense are explained in this section. The exceptions on discharge, and their close correlation to the *jus tertii* exceptions, are covered in Chapter 7, § 7.02[A][2] *infra*.

[239] U.C.C. § 3-305(c).

[240] U.C.C. § 3-306, Comment 5 (original version).

[241] U.C.C. § 3-305(c); Osborn v. Chicaro Dev. Corp., 294 S.C. 129, 363 S.E.2d 108, 6 U.C.C. Rep. Serv. 2d 153 (Ct. App. 1987).

against a prior owner, the defense is invalid.[242] The fraud could give the prior owner an equitable claim, however, and that party could defend the action for the obligor. This approach enables the party with the claim to litigate its claim before payment proceeds of the instrument are placed into the hands of the party demanding payment from the obligor. Requiring the prior owner to assert the claim as a defense for the obligor avoids problems with collateral estoppel and brings parties who have the best access to the facts before the court. This third-party defense is available for any legal or equitable claims that the third party can assert against the party seeking to enforce the instrument against the obligor.[243] It cannot be used against a holder in due course because those parties take the instrument free from all claims to it on the part of any party.[244]

The literal language of the exceptions to the shelter provision appear to provide a means to circumvent the *jus tertii* principle. Consider the facts in the following diagram:

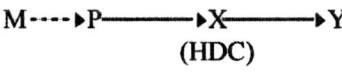

Diagram 6.3

Assume that Y does not qualify as a holder in due course of the note because Y fraudulently induced X to negotiate it to him. Assume also that M has a personal defense of no consideration. M cannot assert that defense against Y because Y acquired the holder-in-due-course rights of X through shelter. M nevertheless might seek to deny shelter to Y by applying the literal language of section 3-203(b) that provides that a transferee who has been a party to fraud affecting the instrument cannot improve his position by taking from a later holder in due course.

The drafting of the exception in section 3-203(b) must be construed in two respects. First, it retains the language used in section 58 of the N.I.L. Courts that interpreted that section did not limit its application only to cases of "fraud or illegality." Instead, the terms were construed to apply to all personal defenses.[245] Second, the exception should apply only to a subsequent party who was actually involved in the activity giving rise to the defendant's defense. The drafters were concerned with a party who negotiates an instrument to a holder in due course and subsequently

---

[242] This result reflects prior common law. Prouty v. Roberts, 60 Mass. 19, 52 Am. Dec. 761 (1850).

[243] University Sav. Ass'n v. Intercontinental Consol. Cos., Inc., 751 S.W.2d 657, 6 U.C.C. Rep. Serv. 2d 788 (Tex. Ct. App. 1988) (fraud).

[244] Williams v. Stansbury, 649 S.W.2d 293, 36 U.C.C. Rep. Serv. 879 (Tex. 1983).

[245] W. BRITTON, HANDBOOK ON THE LAW OF BILLS AND NOTES 324-25 (1961).

reacquires it.[246] The shelter exception should not be used as a backdoor means to circumvent the *jus tertii* principle.

§ 6.04 Negotiation That May be Rescinded — § 3-202

[A] Effectiveness of Negotiation

Even though an instrument is negotiated under circumstances which give rise to a real defense, the negotiation is nevertheless effective. Negotiation is determined exclusively by the requirements of section 3-201,[247] which does not preclude validity of the negotiation based on infirmities in the relationship of the parties or their underlying transaction. Negotiation of an instrument is effective even though the transaction itself is entirely void.[248] Section 3-202(a) affirms this result by providing as follows: "Negotiation is effective even if obtained (i) from an infant, a corporation exceeding its powers, or a person without capacity, (ii) by fraud, duress, or mistake, or (iii) in breach of duty or as part of an illegal transaction."

The essence of negotiability would be greatly compromised if the law allowed a different rule. Negotiation of an instrument creates holder status in the transferee, which confers the right to further negotiate the instrument.[249] The transferor negotiating the instrument may have an equitable claim in the instrument, but until that claim is exercised, the person to whom the instrument was negotiated is a holder.[250] Other parties dealing with the instrument are entitled to deal directly with the holder. If the law withheld the effectiveness of certain negotiations, the transferees in those transactions would not be holders and the transferors would retain rights in the instrument. Prospective subsequent transferees could not rely upon dealing with the holder, which would tend to impair the free alienability of negotiable instruments. Therefore, despite factors that give rise to a real defense or even a void transaction, negotiation of an instrument is nevertheless effective.

[B] The Remedy of Recission

State law in the various jurisdictions will often provide a remedy for an aggrieved transferor who negotiates an instrument under any of the circumstances enumerated under section 3-202(a). The nature of the remedy varies among the states, as does the precise scope of coverage.[251]

---

[246] U.C.C. § 3-203, Comment 2.

[247] *See* § 3.04 *supra*.

[248] Hotel Riviera, Inc. v. First Nat'l Bank & Trust Co., 508 F. Supp. 122, 38 U.C.C. Rep. Serv. 219 (W.D. Okla. 1983), *rev'd on other grounds*, 768 F.2d 1201, 41 U.C.C. Rep. Serv. 363 (10th Cir. 1985) (negotiation of cashier's check valid even though check was for illegal gambling debt).

[249] U.C.C. § 3-201. La Junta State Bank v. Travis, 727 P.2d 48, 2 U.C.C. Rep. Serv. 2d 805 (Colo. 1986).

[250] U.C.C. § 3-202, Comment 2.

[251] The Comments to the original version of Article 3 demonstrated the array of remedies

Generally, however, the enumerated circumstances are sufficient to give rise to an equitable claim, and the aggrieved party can pursue the remedial procedures available locally to enforce the claim. Section 3-202(b) recognizes this approach: "To the extent permitted by other law, negotiation may be rescinded or may be subject to other remedies, but those remedies may not be asserted against a subsequent holder in due course or a person paying the instrument in good faith and without knowledge of facts that are a basis for rescission or other remedy." The provision does not establish any new rights.[252] The Code defers entirely to local law to determine both the rights to an equitable claim and the remedies available to enforce it.

In addition to referencing the applicability of available local remedies to assert claims, the function of section 3-202(b) is to preclude these remedies against a holder in due course. The provision is consistent with the codification of section 3-306. In addition to freedom from claims of legal ownership, a holder in due course takes free from equitable claims of prior parties who may seek to rescind the negotiation and recover the instrument or its proceeds.[253] The equitable claims are valid only against a party who does not have the rights of a holder in due course.[254]

Although a transferor with a valid claim must generally be concerned that the instrument might be acquired by a holder in due course, the concern is alleviated for a maker or drawer who issues an instrument under circumstances that give rise to a real defense. For example, assume that a minor issues an instrument in a transaction that is either void or voidable under local law. The issuance of the instrument is nevertheless effective, and the minor cannot successfully reclaim the instrument from a holder in due course.[255] The minor, however, is in a position as a maker or drawer to resist payment, and thus does not need to reacquire the instrument. A maker can refuse to pay the instrument when it becomes due, and a drawer can initiate a stop-payment order. If sued for nonpayment in either capacity, the minor can successfully defend, against even a holder in due course, by asserting the real defense of infancy.

The case of *Snyder v. Town Hill Motors, Inc.*[256] demonstrates how a minor can lose all control over an instrument when the minor negotiates the instrument as an indorser. In *Snyder*, the minor was the payee of a check. He negotiated the check to an acquaintance as part of a transaction

---

that might be available under the various state laws: "The remedy of any such claimant is to recover the paper by replevin or otherwise; to impound it or to enjoin its enforcement, collection or negotiation; to recover its proceeds from the holder; or to intervene in any action brought by the holder against the obligor." U.C.C. § 3-207, Comment 2 (original version).

[252] U.C.C. § 3-202, Comment 3.

[253] U.C.C. § 3-306; Bowling Green, Inc. v. State St. Bank & Trust Co., 307 F. Supp. 648, 6 U.C.C. Rep. Serv. 1151 (C.D. Mass. 1969), *aff'd*, 425 F.2d 81, 7 U.C.C. Rep. Serv. 635 (1st Cir. 1970) (attempt to hold defendant bank as constructive trustee of funds that were proceeds of a check indorsed to the depositor).

[254] U.C.C. § 3-306; Douglass v. Wones, 120 Ill. App. 3d 36, 76 Ill. Dec. 114, 458 N.E.2d 514, 37 U.C.C. Rep. Serv. 1606 (1983) (claim of rescission of prior negotiation).

[255] U.C.C. § 3-202.

[256] 193 Pa. Super. 578, 165 A.2d 293, 1 U.C.C. Rep. Serv. 231 (1960).

involving the purchase of the transferee's automobile. The check subsequently was negotiated to a used-car dealer in a purchase by the transferee.[257] When the minor discovered that the lien on his purchased automobile exceeded the amount that was represented by his seller, he sought unsuccessfully to recover the check or its proceeds from the car dealer. The car dealer qualified as a holder in due course, thereby cutting off the equitable claim of the minor. Payment of the check to a holder resulted in discharge of the contract liability of the drawer.[258] Even if the minor had discovered the fraud committed by his seller before the check was paid, the minor did not have any direct means to prevent the payment. As an indorser, the minor did not have the authority to stop payment of the check.[259] He might have persuaded the drawer to stop payment, but then the drawer would have been liable to the dealer on its drawer's signature. The minor's claim would not be available as a defense to the drawer, even if the minor himself defended the action. The dealer was a holder in due course, and the *jus tertii* defense is available only against a party who does not have the rights of a holder in due course.[260] The practical significance of taking free from claims can thus be greater in some contexts than it is in others.

§ 6.05 Procedural Aspects — § 3-308

[A] Effectiveness of Signatures

Section 3-308 covers the allocation of the burdens in establishing signatures, defenses, and holder-in-due-course status. The provision is based largely upon empirical considerations of ordinary experiences with most commercial-paper transactions. It seeks to simplify legal actions involving negotiable instruments.

A plaintiff who brings a cause of action to enforce liability on an instrument can generally be successful only against someone who has signed the instrument.[261] A defendant might resist the plaintiff's action by contesting the validity of a signature on the instrument.[262] A defendant choosing this course, however, must specifically deny the contested signatures: "In an action with respect to an instrument, the authenticity of, and authority to make, each signature on the instrument is admitted unless specifically denied in the pleadings."[263] The special denial is required in

---

[257] The court recognized constructive delivery because the minor indorsed the check and delivered it directly to the dealer at the direction of the party with whom the minor was dealing.

[258] U.C.C. § 3-602(a). *See* § 7.02[A][1] *infra*.

[259] U.C.C. § 4-403. *See* § 12.04[A] *infra*.

[260] U.C.C. § 3-305(c). If the holder sued the minor on the minor's indorsement signature, the real defense would be available. The holder can by-pass the minor/indorser, however, and proceed against the drawer or maker of the instrument.

[261] U.C.C. § 3-401(a). *But see* U.C.C. §§ 3-402, 3-403(a), 3-406.

[262] A defendant might contest other signatures upon which the rights of the plaintiff depend, as well as the defendant's own signature.

[263] U.C.C. § 3-308(a); Cadle Co. v. Ginsburg, 51 Conn. App. 392, 721 A.2d 1246, 37 U.C.C. Rep. Serv. 2d 684 (Conn. Ct. App. 1998).

order to alert the plaintiff as to which signatures are contested and to enable the plaintiff to investigate their validity and obtain evidence.[264] A general denial will not be sufficient to contest a signature. This rule is efficient because most signatures are genuine. Admitting signatures in the absence of a specific denial in pleadings saves time and expense.

When the effectiveness of a signature is placed in issue, "the burden of establishing validity is on the person claiming validity."[265] This ultimate burden on the plaintiff is measured under the preponderance of the evidence standard.[266]

The plaintiff, however, is given a significant procedural advantage in meeting the burden. Subject to a narrow exception, the signature is presumed to be authentic and authorized.[267] The presumption requires a finding for the plaintiff until the defendant introduces sufficient evidence to support the denial of the effectiveness of a signature.[268] Once the defendant introduces sufficient evidence to avoid a directed verdict,[269] the presumption drops out and the plaintiff bears the ultimate burden of the preponderance of evidence.[270]

The presumption is based on common experiences and the likely access to evidence. Most signatures on instruments are genuine. A defendant who chooses to contest a signature, therefore, must come forward with evidence to support the challenge before the plaintiff is required to prove the effectiveness of a signature.[271] A defendant who denies the effectiveness of his or her own signature has access to evidence that might not be available to the plaintiff. A defendant contesting signatures of other parties should have evidence to support the position and thus should be required to come forward with it.

The statutory presumption that the signatures on an instrument are authentic and authorized does not apply when "the action is to enforce the

---

[264] U.C.C. § 3-308, Comment 1; First Nat'l Bank v. Blackhurst, 345 S.E.2d 567, 1 U.C.C. Rep. Serv. 2d 820 (W. Va. 1986).

[265] U.C.C. § 3-308(a).

[266] " 'Burden of establishing' a fact means the burden of persuading the triers of fact that the existence of the fact is more probable than its non-existence." U.C.C. § 1-201(8). In re Southern Indus. Banking Corp., 36 B.R. 1010, 38 U.C.C. Rep. Serv. 531 (Bankr. E.D. Tenn. 1984).

[267] U.C.C. § 3-308(a); Gabovitch v. Coolidge Bank & Trust Co., 29 U.C.C. Rep. Serv. 1313 (Mass. Ct. App. 1980).

[268] " 'Presumption' or 'presumed' means that the trier of fact must find the existence of the fact presumed unless and until evidence is introduced which would support a finding of its non-existence." U.C.C. § 1-201(31).

[269] This evidence need not be sufficient to require a directed verdict in the defendant's favor, but rather enough to permit the trier of fact to make a finding in his or her favor. Bates & Springer, Inc. v. Stallworth, 10 Ohio Op. 3d 227, 56 Ohio App. 2d 223, 382 N.E.2d 1179, 26 U.C.C. Rep. Serv. 1181 (1978).

[270] U.C.C. § 3-308, Comment 1; Xanthopoulos v. Thomas Cook, Inc., 629 F. Supp. 164, 42 U.C.C. Rep. Serv. 883 (S.D. N.Y. 1985).

[271] U.C.C. § 3-308, Comment 1; Virginia Nat'l Bank v. Holt, 216 Va. 500, 219 S.E.2d 881, 18 U.C.C. Rep. Serv. 440 (1975).

liability of the purported signer and the signer is dead or incompetent at the time of trial of the issue of validity of the signature."[272] In these two situations, the presumption cannot be supported by the rationale of access to relevant evidence. Evidence that was available to the signer individually will not be available to an executor or guardian who is defending the case. The personal denial of the signer's own signature will not even be available.

[B] Production of the Instrument

When the signatures on an instrument are either admitted or established, the prima facie case of a holder is easy: "If the validity of signatures is admitted or proved and there is compliance with subsection (a), a plaintiff producing the instrument is entitled to payment if the plaintiff proves entitlement to enforce the instrument under Section 3-301, unless the defendant proves a defense or claim in recoupment."[273] By merely producing the instrument with effective signatures, a holder makes a prima facie case and is entitled to recover in the absence of further evidence.[274] The procedural advantage associated with the production of an instrument is available only to a holder. A plaintiff that produces an instrument but does not qualify as a holder must prove that he or she has the rights of a holder before that person is entitled to enforce the instrument.[275]

A person entitled to enforce the instrument can recover payment if the defendant does not establish a defense or a claim in recoupment.[276] The defendant bears the burden of establishing a defense or a claim in recoupment, and the burden applies not only to coming forward with evidence, but also to the ultimate burden of a preponderance of the evidence.[277] The defendant can come forward with evidence to establish any defense or claim in recoupment recognized under section 3-305(a).

[C] Burden to Prove Holder-in-Due-Course Rights

Once a defendant introduces evidence to establish a defense, the plaintiff has several possible courses of action. The plaintiff might seek a directed verdict against the defendant on the grounds that the defendant's presentation was insufficient. An alternative course would be to introduce evidence to rebut the probative force of the defendant's case and rest on the strength

---

[272] U.C.C. § 3-308(a); In re Estate of Carr, 436 Pa. 47, 258 A.2d 628, 7 U.C.C. Rep. Serv. 49 (1969) (died).

[273] U.C.C. § 3-308(b); Camber v. Bridges, 520 A.2d 711, 3 U.C.C. Rep. Serv. 2d 170 (Me. 1987).

[274] U.C.C. § 3-308, Comment 2; Braswell v. Bank of Early, 229 Ga. App. 445, 494 S.E.2d 277, 34 U.C.C. Rep. Serv. 2d 1100 (1997).

[275] U.C.C. §§ 3-308(b), 3-301(ii). "That person must prove a transfer giving that person such rights under Section 3-203(b) or that such rights were obtained by subrogation or succession." U.C.C. § 3-308, Comment 2.

[276] "In the absence of a defense or claim in recoupment, any person entitled to enforce the instrument is entitled to recover." U.C.C. § 3-308, Comment 2.

[277] Bank of N.C. v. Rock Island Bank, 630 F.2d 1243, 30 U.C.C. Rep. Serv. 1036 (7th Cir. 1980).

of the rebuttal. The plaintiff might also seek to cut off the effectiveness of the asserted defenses by establishing applicable holder-in-due-course rights. This approach is viable only against personal defenses of a defendant that were not caused by the holder in due course whose rights are asserted. All of these courses are options available in the discretion of the plaintiff. Establishing holder-in-due-course rights is not required for all of them.[278]

If the defendant does establish a valid defense or claim in recoupment, the only way a plaintiff can succeed is to cut off the defense with holder-in-due-course rights available through his or her own status or through shelter.[279] The plaintiff who pursues this approach bears the burden of proving the necessary holder-in-due-course status. Section 3-308(b) provides that "[i]f a defense or claim in recoupment is proved, the right to payment of the plaintiff is subject to the defense or claim, except to the extent the plaintiff proves that the plaintiff has rights of a holder in due course which are not subject to the defense or claim." The provision requires the plaintiff to establish, by a preponderance of evidence, all of the elements necessary for holder-in-due-course status.[280] The showing must be made with respect to either the plaintiff or to a prior transferor though whom shelter is claimed. Ultimate success also requires that the plaintiff establish holder-in-due-course rights that will take free from the specific defense that has been established. The defense cannot be a real defense or even a personal defense that has been asserted against the party whose holder-in-due-course status is relied upon by the plaintiff.

In actual practice, the plaintiff's burden of proof in establishing holder-in-due-course status can become closely entwined with the substantive law. Courts are well aware that the negotiability of instruments can lead to harsh consequences against some defendants. Before those consequences are allowed to be visited upon a defendant, the plaintiff bears the burden of establishing each element required to achieve holder-in-due-course status. The burden might be particularly hard to meet for the requirements that the holder must take the instrument without notice of a defense or claim to in on the part of any person.[281] A trial court that is left uneasy about the plaintiff's participation in the transaction can rule that the holder did not sustain the burden of proof on this particular element. An appellate court can easily sustain that finding even though the record does not contain facts showing that the holder did take the instrument with specific disabling notice.[282] The burden on establishing holder-in-due-course rights is thus one that should not be taken lightly by either side.

---

[278] U.C.C. § 3-308, Comment 2.

[279] "Until proof of a defense or claim in recoupment is made, the issue as to whether the plaintiff has rights of a holder in due course does not arise." U.C.C. § 3-308, Comment 2.

[280] Funding Consultants, Inc. v. Aetna Cas. & Sur. Co., 187 Conn. 637, 447 A.2d 1163, 34 U.C.C. Rep. Serv. 591 (1982).

[281] U.C.C. § 3-302(a)(2)(v), (vi).

[282] The last paragraph of the decision in Kaw Valley State Bank and Trust Co. v. Riddle, 219 Kan. 550, 549 P.2d 927, 19 U.C.C. Rep. Serv. 869 (1976), is illustrative.

In the present case the court found that the appellant, Kaw Valley, had not sustained its

§ 6.06 Holders in Due Course and Consumers

[A] The Problem

Merchants have often required their customers who purchase items on credit to sign a promissory note in addition to the sales contract. In order to raise the capital necessary to replenish their inventory, the merchants sold the notes at a discount to commercial lenders. Lenders who could qualify as holders in due course were able to enforce the buyers' obligations to pay the notes, even if their sellers had breached the sales contracts and could not have enforced them. The personal defenses of failure of consideration and breach of warranty were cut off in favor of a holder in due course.

An alternative approach used in retail installment sales transactions was the inclusion of a waiver of defenses clause in the contract signed by the consumer.[283] Under this clause the consumer agrees not to assert any claims or defenses against a subsequent assignee of the contract. The waiver clause provides an assignee with a form of contractual protection against consumer grievances that was the practical equivalent of holder-in-due-course status on a promissory note.[284] The consumer's defenses against the payment obligation were ineffective against the lender.[285]

One effect of the holder-in-due-course doctrine, and the corollary waiver-of-defense clause, was to lead lenders in consumer sales transactions to make their decisions primarily on the creditworthiness of the consumer,

---

burden of proving that it was a holder in due course. . . . We cannot say under the facts and circumstances known and participated in by Kaw Valley in this transaction it did not at the time in question have reason to know that the defense existed. This was a question of fact to be determined by the trier of fact which if supported by substantial competent evidence must stand.

219 Kan. at 560, 549 P.2d at 935-36, 19 U.C.C. Rep. Serv. at 879.

[283] Interlocking loans agreements were yet another method. The lender makes the loan directly to the consumer, who uses the proceeds to make the purchase. If consumer dissatisfaction develops, the obligation on the loan is independent of the sale. Some loan transactions, however, were actually precipitated by an established interlocking relationship between the lender and the seller.

[284] Section 9-206(1) provides:

Except as otherwise provided in this section, an agreement between an account debtor and an assignor not to assert against an assignee any claim or defense that the account debtor may have against the assignor is enforceable by an assignee that takes an assignment:

    (1) for value;

    (2) in good faith;

    (3) without notice of a claim or a property or possessory right to the property assigned; and

    (4) without notice of a defense or claim in recoupment of the type that may be asserted against a person entitled to enforce a negotiable instrument under Section 3-305(a).

See Massey-Ferguson Credit Co. v. Wiley, 655 F. Supp. 655, 3 U.C.C. Rep. Serv. 2d 1153 (M.D. Ga. 1987).

[285] For an excellent discussion of the background of these types of transactions, see generally Rohner, *Holder in Due Course In Consumer Transactions: Reform, Revival, or Reformation?*, 60 Cornell L. Rev. 503 (1975).

with little concern over the underlying sales transaction. Lenders did not have to concern themselves with the quality of goods and services provided by the sellers. Holder-in-due-course protection insulated lenders from the claims and defenses of unsuspecting consumers. Sellers could find a readily available market in which to turn their paper, provided only that the credit ratings of their buyers were satisfactory. This readily available line of credit opened the consumer-sales market to sellers who were marginal at best. It also led to another undesirable effect from holder-in-due-course protection: outright fraud and collusion in which promissory notes were promptly negotiated in order to create the illusion of legitimate transfers to achieve protected holder-in-due-course status. Successful operations left the defrauded consumer with only a claim against the seller. That recourse was generally a hollow remedy because the seller was either unavailable for service of process or had become insolvent.

With respect to risk allocations, the holder-in-due-course doctrine was consistent with other major legal approaches at the formative stages of our nation and its legal system. An externalization-of-costs model of risk management was purposely observed. In a desire to encourage industrialization and business expansion, several legal doctrines caused persons injured by economic activities to bear much of the resulting costs.[286] Most significantly, courts retreated from stricter notions of liability embodied in medieval trespass actions and generally applied a less severe fault theory of liability to accidents caused by industry.[287] Consistently, the holder-in-due-course doctrine facilitated economic activity and market entry for new business ventures by promoting increased availability of financing.

The latter half of the twentieth century brought sweeping changes in risk management by increasingly identifying the factors affecting the allocation of costs and incorporating cost considerations into our legal rules.[288] Much of our current law consequently reflects this loss-distribution model of risk management. Workmen's compensation, air and water pollution regulations, the erosion of the doctrine of *caveat emptor*, the adoption of the standard of strict tort liability, the expansion of warranty liability, and the consumer protection movement in general all reflect the more modern premise that businesses should assume greater responsibility for their economic activities.

The use of the holder-in-due-course doctrine and waiver-of-defense clauses in consumer sales transactions came under increasing attack as part of the basic consumer protection movement.[289] It deprived aggrieved

---

[286] M. HOROWITZ, THE TRANSFORMATION OF AMERICAN LAW 1780–1860 71 (1977).

[287] *See generally*, Gregory, *Trespass to Negligence to Absolute Liability*, 37 Va. L. Rev. 359, 365-66 (1951).

[288] Green, *Duties, Risk, Causation Doctrines*, 41 Tex. L. Rev. 42, 43, 55 (1961).

[289] Gilmore, *The Commercial Doctrine of Good Faith Purchase*, 63 Yale L.J. 1057, 1101 (1954) (the doctrine is inequitable because of "inequality of bargaining power and technical knowledge" between the parties); Kripke, *Consumer Credit Regulation: A Creditor-Oriented Viewpoint*, 68 Colum. L. Rev. 445, 469-73 (1968) (the doctrine is unnecessary to transactions involving reputable sellers, products, and financiers); Rosenthal, *Negotiability—Who Needs It?*, 71 Colum. L. Rev. 375, 401 (1971) (subjecting consumers buying on installment contracts to the doctrine can have socially damaging effects).

consumers of the leverage of withholding payment from a breaching seller. It was not consistent with normal consumer expectations and it was often imposed as part of a contract of adhesion. Most commentators came to the conclusion that in the consumer context it produced inequitable results. The dilemma was how to eliminate the inequity.

Initial attempts to deny holder-in-due-course protection to some transferees of consumer paper were undertaken by the courts. They utilized a wide variety of judicial mechanisms to deny the status to transferees who maintained close connections with their sellers-transferors. Some cases held that a lack of necessary good faith could be inferred from a financer's close relationship with a fraudulent seller.[290] Other courts reasoned that the closeness between the seller and financer created an agency relationship between them through which defenses to the seller's actions could be imputed against the financer.[291] The influential case of *Unico v. Owen*[292] established the close-connectedness doctrine, also known as the unity theory. It is based on a finding that the seller and financer are so closely intertwined in their commercial paper transactions that the lender may not be considered a subsequent purchaser. Holder-in-due-course status is denied on the grounds that a transfer did not actually take place, leaving the financer subject to personal defenses of the buyer as though the financer had dealt with the buyer.

Despite some success in individual cases, judicial attacks upon the holder-in-due-course doctrine in consumer-paper transactions were inadequate to address the underlying problem. Results were uneven, as some courts resisted these bold initiatives, and other courts sent conflicting signals with their decisions. The biggest drawback, however, was that it required litigation. The expense and uncertainty associated with litigation created an incentive for lenders to refuse settlements with consumers.

Attempts to curb the doctrine's application to consumer-paper transactions were also made through state and model legislation.[293] Over thirty states ultimately enacted some version of a statutory provision that addressed the holder-in-due-course doctrine or the use of waiver-of-defense clause provisions in consumer sales transactions. The results were far from decisive, however. Most of the statutes did not address all of the techniques that could create the effect of holder-in-due-course protections.[294] The drafting was also extremely inconsistent, and often surprisingly uncertain. As a consequence, judicial and state legislative responses were not making much headway against the problem.

---

[290] Norman v. World Wide Distrib., Inc., 202 Pa. Super. 53, 195 A.2d 115, 1 U.C.C. Rep. Serv. 234 (1963); Commercial Credit Co. v. Childs, 199 Ark. 1073, 137 S.W.2d 260 (1940) (initial judicial decision attacking closeness between transferor and transferee).

[291] Calvert Credit Corp. v. Williams, 244 A.2d 494, 5 U.C.C. Rep. Serv. 607 (D.C. 1968). *See also* Emery-Waterhouse Co. v. Rhode Island Hosp. Trust Nat'l Bank, 757 F.2d 399, 40 U.C.C. Rep. Serv. 737 (1st Cir. 1985) (information known to employee charged to bank).

[292] 50 N.J. 101, 232 A.2d 405, 4 U.C.C. Rep. Serv. 542 (1967).

[293] Uniform Consumer Credit Code § 3.307 (1974); Model Consumer Credit Act § 2.603(3) (1973).

[294] Interlocking loans, in particular, were usually ignored.

[B] The Federal Trade Commission Rule

The Federal Trade Commission (FTC) provided an innovative regulation to address the problem. Its "Trade Regulation Rule Concerning Preservation of Consumer Claims and Defenses" became effective on May 14, 1976.[295] It provides that a seller, who is in the business of selling goods to consumers, commits an unfair or deceptive trade act or practice within the meaning of Section 5 of the Federal Trade Commission Act by taking a consumer credit contract which does not contain the following language in bold-face type:

NOTICE

ANY HOLDER OF THIS CONSUMER CREDIT CONTRACT IS SUBJECT TO ALL CLAIMS AND DEFENSES WHICH THE DEBTOR COULD ASSERT AGAINST THE SELLER OF GOODS OR SERVICES OBTAINED PURSUANT HERETO OR WITH THE PROCEEDS HEREOF. RECOVERY HEREUNDER BY THE DEBTOR SHALL NOT EXCEED AMOUNTS PAID BY THE DEBTOR HEREUNDER.[296]

Knowing violations are punishable by civil penalties.[297]

Inclusion of the language on a promissory note effectively precludes holder-in-due-course status of any subsequent transferee. The status can be achieved only by the holder of a negotiable instrument.[298] One of the prerequisites of a negotiable instrument is that it contain an unconditional promise or order to pay a fixed amount of money.[299] Under the original version of Article 3, including the FTC notice made the consumer's promise to pay conditioned upon the absence of a defense against the seller, thereby destroying negotiability and any opportunity for a subsequent taker to achieve holder-in-due-course status.[300] The revision of Article 3 includes a provision that is designed to preclude holder-in-due-course status with respect to such an instrument, while still keeping the instrument within the scope of Article 3.[301] It accomplishes these results by excluding any language on an instrument that is required by law to preserve claims or defenses as a condition for purposes of determining negotiability, but precluding holder-in-due-course status with respect to such instruments.[302]

---

[295] 16 C.F.R. § 433.

[296] 16 C.F.R. § 433.2(a). Part (b) of the Rule forbids sellers from accepting the proceeds of interlocking loans unless the loan agreement between the buyer and financer contains a similar notice provision.

[297] 15 U.S.C. § 45(m)(1)(A) (maximum fine of $10,000 per violation).

[298] U.C.C. § 3-302(a).

[299] U.C.C. § 3-104(a).

[300] Thomas v. Ford Motor Credit Co., 48 Md. App. 617, 429 A.2d 277, 31 U.C.C. Rep. Serv. 1265 (1981).

[301] U.C.C. § 3-106, Comment 3 (identifies the exclusion of notes bearing the FTC legend from the scope of Article 3 as an unintended effect).

[302] "If a promise or order at the time it is issued or first comes into possession of a holder contains a statement, required by applicable statutory or administrative law, to the effect that

§ 6.06   HOLDERS IN DUE COURSE AND CONSUMERS   167

When the notice is included in a conditional sales contract together with a waiver-of-defense clause, the latter is not enforceable.[303] The two clauses contradict each other. However, the U.C.C. provision validating waiver-of-defense clauses makes them "[s]ubject to law other than this article which establishes a different rule for an account debtor [of consumer goods]."[304] Although the FTC Rule itself is not a statute, its violation constitutes a violation of the Federal Trade Commission Act.[305]

Even when the notice provision required by the FTC Rule is not included in sale or credit agreements, the interaction of the Rule with state law generally will enable consumers to assert underlying contract defenses. A lender who purchases a promissory note knowing that the seller has violated the FTC Rule by not including the preservation-of-defenses notice provision cannot become a holder in due course of the note because the statutory requirement of taking in good faith cannot be met.[306] Moreover, a lender who knows or should know that the promissory note stems from a consumer transaction cannot qualify as a holder in due course because the absence of the federally mandated notice makes the note so irregular or incomplete as to call into question its authenticity.[307] Thus, because most financers will have at least reason to know that the seller dealt with a consumer, financers taking promissory notes will generally be unsuccessful in claiming holder-in-due-course status against consumer debtors.

Lenders purchasing consumer credit contracts with waiver-of-defense clauses that lack the required FTC notice will also find their preferred position undermined.[308] The U.C.C. section validating waiver of defense clauses limits their enforcement to assignees who take the assignment for value, in good faith, and without notice of a claim or defense.[309] The same good faith and notice limitations that deny holder-in-due-course status to the holder of a consumer's promissory note would thus apply to the financer seeking to enforce a waiver-of-defense clause.

The FTC Rule follows the loss-distribution model of risk management. The Rule, like the model, is based upon the premise that costs should be

---

the rights of a holder or transferee are subject to claims or defenses that the issuer could assert against the original payee, the promise or order is not thereby made conditional for the purposes of Section 3-104(a); but if the promise or order is an instrument, there cannot be a holder in due course of the instrument." U.C.C. § 3-106(d).

[303] In a direct loan transaction, the FTC notice is part of the loan agreement between the consumer and the lender. By its terms the lender is subject to the buyer's claims and defenses against the seller.

[304] U.C.C. § 9-403(e).

[305] 15 U.S.C. § 45.

[306] U.C.C. § 3-302(a)(2)(ii).

[307] U.C.C. § 3-302(a)(1).

[308] A lender in an interlocking loan transaction can be precluded from enforcing a consumer's obligation when the lender knows that the required notice is missing from the sales agreement. Each party to a contract governed by common law makes an implied promise to exercise good faith, and under the concept of dependency of covenants, a material breach of the lender's obligation excuses the debtor's performance.

[309] U.C.C. § 9-403(b).

borne by the activities causing them. Initially, therefore, costs are allocated to the party in the best position to shift the ultimate burden onto the appropriate activity.[310] In the context of the FTC Rule, the costs associated with seller misconduct and product failure should be borne by the seller. As between the consumer and the financer, the latter is in a better position, through recourse agreements and controls on the availability of credit, to cast losses back onto the seller. The Rule, therefore, initially allocates the loss to the financer by allowing aggrieved consumers to assert their contract claims and defenses.

Allocation of the initial loss burden to the financer inevitably imposes some costs on lenders that cannot be recovered from sellers. A seller might become bankrupt or otherwise too financially irresponsible. Loss spreading is then utilized as the second tenant supporting the Rule and the loss-distribution model of risk allocation. The principal is to lessen the impact of the loss by spreading the burden over more people and longer periods of time.[311] Between lenders and aggrieved consumers, lenders are in a better position to implement loss spreading. Loss spreading results under the FTC Rule when the future costs for credit are adjusted to reflect the losses that cannot be cast back upon the seller. In promulgating the Rule, the FTC noted that "where certain seller misconduct costs cannot be eliminated from the market we would require that such costs be internalized, so that the prices paid by consumers more accurately reflect the true social costs of engaging in a credit sale transaction."[312]

The FTC thus based its Rule upon the assumption that lenders would act in their own self-interest to reduce their exposure to the increased risks posed in taking consumer paper subject to claims and defenses of the consumer. Lenders should use recourse provisions for losses resulting from deficiencies in sellers' performances. They should also reject the risk of dealing with unscrupulous merchants, thereby driving them from the marketplace. Any remaining losses should be internalized by the credit industry to reflect more accurately the true cost of credit.[313]

---

[310] Calabresi, *Some Thoughts on Risk Distribution and the Law of Torts*, 70 Yale L.J. 499, 505 (1961).

[311] *Id.* at 517.

[312] FTC Statement of Basis and Purpose on Trade Regulation Rule Concerning Preservation of Consumers' Claims and Defenses, 40 Fed. Reg. 53,523 (1975).

[313] The application of the FTC Rule to the credit sales of newly developed products creates a fundamental paradox. The Rule's consumer protection features are particularly attractive to purchasers of innovative products and should thus promote commercialization; however, the Rule actually hinders this commercialization when applied to markets involving new products and sellers with uncertain reputations, because it has an unintended impact that adversely affects credit availability and cost. *See generally* Lawrence & Minan, *The Effect of Abrogating the Holder-in-Due-Course Doctrine on the Commercialization of Innovative Consumer Products*, 64 Boston U. L. Rev. 325 (1984).

Chapter 7
DISCHARGE

SYNOPSIS

§ 7.01 Introduction

§ 7.02 Liability on the Instrument
    [A] Payment — § 3-602
        [1] General Rule
        [2] The Exceptions
            [a] Indemnity or Injunction
            [b] Stolen Instruments
    [B] Tender of Payment — § 3-603
    [C] Cancellation or Renunciation — § 3-604
    [D] Reacquisition — § 3-207
    [E] Discharge of Indorsers and Accommodation Parties — § 3-605
        [1] Rights of Recourse
        [2] Rights in Collateral
    [F] Material Alteration — § 3-407
        [1] Requirements
        [2] Effect
    [G] Acceptance of Draft by Bank — §§ 3-414(c), 3-415(d)
    [H] Acceptance Varying Draft — § 3-410

§ 7.03 Liability on the Underlying Transaction
    [A] Effect of Taking an Instrument — § 3-310
    [B] Accord and Satisfaction — § 3-311

§ 7.01 Introduction

In the law of negotiable instruments, as in general contract law, discharge refers to the termination of contractual liability that has been incurred. Chapter 4 explains how a party incurs liability on the instrument by signing the instrument. Chapters 4 and 5 explain the nature of the liability incurred by signing in different capacities. This chapter explains how those liabilities are brought to an end through discharge.

Article 3 provides a number of different means by which a party's liability on an instrument can be discharged. Most of the provisions are codified in Part 6, which deals explicitly with discharge. Because other means of discharge are so closely tied to specific substantive concepts, however, some discharge provisions are codified in other areas of Article 3.[1] Discharge related to lost, destroyed or stolen cashier's checks, teller's checks or certified checks is explained in Chapter 4,[2] and discharge resulting from an unexcused delay in presentment, notice of dishonor or protest has already been covered in Chapter 5.[3] The other Article 3 means of discharge are covered below.

Although Article 3 includes a number of provisions on discharge, it does not cover all methods by which liability on an instrument may be terminated. Other statutes can provide for discharge, as in the case of bankruptcy or a statute providing discharge on an instrument in a gambling transaction. Discharge can also be effected "by an act or agreement with the party which would discharge an obligation to pay money under a simple contract."[4] For example, an oral agreement for discharge of a party is usually sufficient if supported by consideration.[5]

Discharge by any of these means is the discharge of a party from liability incurred by signing the instrument. Even if the liability of all parties to an instrument is discharged, it is not appropriate to indicate that the instrument itself has been discharged. Parties become liable by signing instruments. Therefore, they are the entities who become discharged from liability on the instrument.

Discharge is not treated as a defense under Article 3.[6] The reason underlying this concept is to avoid treating notice of discharge as notice of a defense that would preclude the attainment of holder-in-due-course status.[7] For example, the discharge of an indorser might be readily apparent because the indorser's signature has been stricken in accordance with section 3-604(a) on cancellation.[8] As long as the signatures of the other parties to the instrument appear valid, however, the transferee can reasonably expect payment from them and can become a holder in due course upon satisfaction of the required elements of section 3-302(a).

A discharge is effective against even a holder in due course if the holder had notice of the discharge at the time of attaining the holder-in-due-course

---

[1] U.C.C. §§ 3-207 (reacquisition); 3-312 (lost, destroyed or stolen cashier's check, teller's check or certified check); 3-407 (fraudulent alteration); 3-410 (acceptance varying draft); 3-414(c) & 3-415(d) (draft accepted by a bank); 3-414(f) & 3-415(c), (e) (unexcused delay in presentment or notice of dishonor).

[2] *See* § 4.06[D] *supra*.

[3] *See* § 5.04 *supra*.

[4] U.C.C. § 3-601(a).

[5] Brannon v. Langston, 375 So.2d 231, 27 U.C.C. Rep. Serv. 758 (Miss. 1979). *See also* Ampex Corp. v. Appel Media, Inc., 374 F. Supp. 1114, 14 U.C.C. Rep. Serv. 980 (W.D. Pa. 1974) (novation as a sufficient discharge). *But see* Wolfe v. Eaker, 50 N.C. App. 144, 272 S.E.2d 781, 30 U.C.C. Rep. Serv. 574 (1980) (oral agreement not supported by consideration not sufficient for discharge). If the agreement to discharge is in writing, it could constitute discharge by renunciation under U.C.C. § 3-604(a) even though it is not supported by consideration. *See* § 7.02[C] *infra*.

[6] U.C.C. §§ 3-302, Comment 3; 3-601, Comment. This concept of discharge is new under the revision of Article 3.

[7] *See* U.C.C. § 3-302(a)(2)(vi) and Comment 3; § 6.01[D][2][d] *supra*.

[8] *See* § 7.02[C] *infra*.

status.[9] Thus, for example, the holder in due course that knew of the cancellation of an indorser's signature when the instrument was taken would be subject to the discharge of that indorser's obligation. On the other hand, a discharge is cut off when a subsequent holder in due course takes the instrument without notice of the discharge: "Discharge of the obligation of a party is not effective against a person acquiring rights of a holder in due course of the instrument without notice of the discharge."[10] For example, if a note is paid early by the maker resulting in discharge under section 3-602,[11] but the maker foolishly leaves the note in the hands of the holder and the holder further negotiates the note to a holder in due course, the holder in due course will take the instrument free from the maker's discharge through prior payment.

Instruments generally are issued as part of an underlying transaction. For example, a check might be issued as part of a purchase transaction, or a note might be issued in exchange for a loan of money. Section 3-310 addresses the relationship between legal obligations created by underlying transactions and the issuance of negotiable instruments. It specifically covers the effect that discharge on the instrument has on the underlying transaction. Section 3-311 covers the use of an instrument to attain discharge of an obligation through accord and satisfaction. This chapter concludes with an explanation of these two sections.

§ 7.02 Liability on the Instrument

[A] Payment — § 3-602

[1] General Rule

Payment is a logical form of discharge. Anyone who signs an instrument incurs contractual liability to pay it. Payment simply constitutes performance of the promise, and with performance comes discharge.[12]

The person paying must take care, however, to pay the proper person. Under section 3-602(a), an instrument is paid to the extent that payment is made "to a person entitled to enforce an instrument."[13] Thus, a maker or acceptor who pays the holder, or who pays a nonholder in possession who has the rights of a holder, thereby achieves discharge. Similarly, payment to these parties by a drawee in accordance with the order of the drawer results in discharge of the drawer. Payment by the drawee is made on behalf of the drawer. An indorser who is required to pay an instrument

---

[9] U.C.C. § 3-601, Comment.

[10] U.C.C. § 3-601(b).

[11] See § 7.02[A] infra.

[12] U.C.C. § 3-602(a).

[13] "'Person entitled to enforce' an instrument means (i) the holder of the instrument, (ii) a nonholder in possession of the instrument who has the rights of a holder, or (iii) a person not in possession of the instrument who is entitled to enforce the instrument pursuant to Section 3-309 or 3-418(d)." U.C.C. § 3-301. See § 3.05 supra.

will also attain discharge by paying a person entitled to enforce the instrument.

Payment made to someone who is not entitled to enforce the instrument does not result in discharge of the payor.[14] This point has recurring relevance when makers and banks pay lost and stolen order instruments over forged indorsements. An indorsement by the finder or thief is not the required indorsement, and no subsequent transferee can qualify as a holder.[15] The payment is improper, and rather than resulting in a discharge, it makes the payor liable to the rightful owner in conversion.[16] Although detection can be difficult in some cases, a person to whom an instrument is presented for payment thus should exercise care to avoid paying over forged indorsements.[17] Because a person entitled to enforce an instrument generally acquires possession of the instrument,[18] the person upon whom presentment is made should also verify that the person presenting has possession. Given established business practices, it is inconceivable that a bank would pay a check without first seeing the check. Makers of notes, however, sometimes foolishly pay the note to the payee without first requiring the payee to exhibit it.[19] If the payee has already negotiated the note, the payee is not a person entitled to enforce it and payment to the payee will not discharge the maker.

Even when payment is made to a person entitled to enforce the instrument, and the payor is discharged under section 3-602(a), the payor should insist upon surrender of the instrument or its cancellation.[20] Payment and discharge alone will not always adequately protect the payor. By leaving a negotiable instrument in the stream of commerce the payor runs the risk that the person entitled to enforce the instrument will negotiate it to someone who qualifies as a subsequent holder in due course. Discharge by payment, like any Article 3 method of discharge, is not effective against

---

[14] Some courts, however, have recognized discharge from a payment when the proceeds from the payment actually reached the holder. Beyer v. First Nat'l Bank, 188 Mont. 208, 612 P.2d 1285, 29 U.C.C. Rep. Serv. 563 (1980); Sullivan v. Wilton Manors Nat'l Bank, 259 So. 2d 194, 10 U.C.C. Rep. Serv. 673 (Fla. Ct. App. 1972).

[15] See § 3.04[B][1][a] *supra*.

[16] U.C.C. § 3-420(a). See § 10.04[A][2] *infra*.

[17] A party that pays over a forged indorsement often will have a breach of warranty claim against other parties. See § 8.04[C][1][a], [2] *infra*.

[18] Holder status requires possession. U.C.C. § 1-201(20). Another person entitled to enforce an instrument is a "nonholder in possession of the instrument who has the rights of a holder. U.C.C. § 3-301. The only persons entitled to enforce an instrument who do not have possession of the instrument are persons entitled to enforce the instrument pursuant to sections 3-309 and 3-418(d).

[19] Unadilla Nat'l Bank v. McQueer, 27 A.D.2d 778, 277 N.Y.S.2d 221, 4 U.C.C. Rep. Serv. 98 (1967) (reliance upon statement by payee that the note was locked in a vault and would be mailed to the maker later). See also Chenowith v. Bank of Dardanelle, 419 S.W.2d 792 (Ark. 1967) (drawer of check settled with payee, but the check had been returned to the depositary bank uncollected after the bank had allowed withdrawal of the funds).

[20] Failure to do so, however, does not preclude discharge. Household Fin. Co. v. Watson, 522 S.W.2d 111, 17 U.C.C. Rep. Serv. 152 (Mo. Ct. App. 1975) (no presumption of nonpayment because holder keeps the instrument; failure to cancel instrument did not affect discharge).

a subsequent holder in due course who takes the instrument without notice of the discharge.[21] Consequently, a maker who pays an instrument to a holder may have to pay the instrument again to a subsequent holder in due course. If the note is a time instrument, paid on the date that it was due, a subsequent purchaser of the note will not likely qualify as a holder in due course because of disabling notice that the instrument is overdue.[22] On the other hand, the risk is significant if payment was made early or if the note is a demand instrument. The party to whom presentment is made can require surrender of the instrument upon its full payment.[23] By acquiring possession, the payor can preclude anyone else from becoming a holder. In the event of partial payments, such as an installment on a note, the payor can require a signed receipt on the instrument.[24] The inclusion of the receipt on the note will give a subsequent purchaser notice of the discharge to the extent of the amount indicated, which will be effective even against a person who becomes a subsequent holder in due course.[25]

Article 3 changes prior law under the N.I.L. by providing that the obligation of the party obliged to pay the instrument is discharged to the extent of the payment "even though payment is made with knowledge of a claim to the instrument under Section 3-306 by another person."[26] Under the N.I.L., discharge depended upon payment being made without notice that the title of the holder was defective.[27] An obligor on the instrument who received notice of a claim of ownership from a prior party was placed in a difficult dilemma. Payment to the holder would not result in discharge. Failure to pay, however, could lead the holder to sue on the contract obligation, and the obligor was either prohibited from defending on the basis of the third-party claim or generally lacked access to the relevant facts to present the defense adequately. The obligor also faced liability to the claimant if the claim could be established as valid. Because the holder and the claimant usually were not parties to the same action, they were not bound by court decisions between the other party and the obligor. Consequently, obligors faced the prospects of double liability. By allowing the obligor to attain discharge by paying the holder, even though the obligor knows of the claim of another person, the general rule of the Code removes this dilemma from the obligor.

[2] The Exceptions

The general rule as it relates to notice of competing claims is not absolute. Section 3-602(b) codifies three exceptions that will preclude discharge even

---

[21] U.C.C. § 3-601(b). See § 7.01 *supra*.

[22] U.C.C. §§ 3-304(b)(2), 3-302(a)(2)(iii). See § 6.01[D][2][a] *supra*.

[23] U.C.C. § 3-501(b)(2)(iii). See § 5.02[A] *supra*.

[24] U.C.C. § 3-501(b)(2)(iii). See § 5.02[A] *supra*.

[25] U.C.C. § 3-302(b).

[26] U.C.C. § 3-602(a). The reference to section 3-306 makes the provision applicable to a claim of ownership or possession, but not a claim in recoupment. For a discussion of the distinction, see § 6.01[D][2][d] *supra*.

[27] N.I.L. § 88.

though payment is made to a party entitled to enforce the instrument. The first two exceptions are based upon two mechanisms through which the third-party claimant protects the obligor against the prospects of double liability. The third exception applies even in the absence of any action by the competing claimant.

[a] Indemnity or Injunction

When an adverse claim to an instrument is asserted by a third party, the dispute is essentially between the claimant and the holder. The claimant asserts an ownership or a possessory right to the instrument that is allegedly superior to the right of the holder. The obligor's interest is to avoid any additional risk or expense because of this dispute. Generally, the claim of a third person to the instrument cannot be used as a defense to the obligor's liability under the *jus tertii* principle.[28] Because the obligor does not have a defense, the general rule on discharge allows the obligor to complete his or her contract obligation and be discharged.

Payment to the holder, however, could greatly imperil the interests of the third-party claimant because paid funds can be quickly dissipated. Consequently, the claimant can take one of two courses to preclude discharge through payment. Payment to the holder will not result in discharge if (1) "the party making payment accepted, from the person having a claim to the instrument, indemnity against loss resulting from refusal to pay the person entitled to enforce the instrument,"[29] or (2) "payment is made with knowledge by the payor that payment is prohibited by injunction or similar process of a court of competent jurisdiction."[30]

In the absence of indemnification or injunction, an exception to the *jus tertii* principle allows the adverse claim to be asserted by the obligor against a party who does not have the rights of a holder in due course, but only if "the other party is joined in the action and personally asserts the claim against the person entitled to enforce the instrument."[31] The indemnification exception can be combined with this aspect of asserting *jus tertii* rights. The obligor generally lacks the means of knowing whether the asserted claim is valid, as well as the evidence to prove it. If litigation is initiated by the holder against the obligor, the indemnification agreement can require the claimant to defend any resulting litigation personally at his or her own expense. The obligor thus serves essentially as a stakeholder in the outcome of that litigation.[32] An indemnification agreement that only protects the obligor against increased expenses in defending against

---

[28] U.C.C. § 3-305(c). See § 6.03[B] *supra*.

[29] U.C.C. § 3-602(b)(1)(ii).

[30] U.C.C. § 3-602(b)(1)(i); Chenowith v. Bank of Dardanelle, 243 Ark. 310, 419 S.W.2d 792, 4 U.C.C. Rep. Serv. 758 (1967) (bank claiming on checks neither supplied indemnity nor sought an injunction against payment, thereby allowing drawer's discharge upon full settlement of the amount of the checks with the holder).

[31] U.C.C. § 3-305(c). See § 6.03[B] *supra*.

[32] The obligor can pay the amount of the instrument into court, and the court will decide whether the payment belongs to the holder or the claimant. U.C.C. § 3-305, Comment 4.

payment to the holder, but does not involve a third-party claimant conducting the defense, eliminates use of the claim for the obligor to resist payment. It would seemingly make practical sense only if the claimant is confident that the obligor has other available defenses.

The exception based on a court injunction gives the claimant an option that does not require as much cooperation with the obligor. The claimant does not have to reach an indemnification agreement with the obligor or incur the additional expense of providing indemnification when the claimant has already pursued legal action to protect his or her interests. The litigation will resolve the dispute between the claimant and the holder, and the obligor again acts as the stakeholder.

The exception to discharge based upon an indemnification agreement does not apply when the applicable instrument is a cashier's check, teller's check or certified check.[33] Thus, payment of such a check, even in violation of an indemnification agreement, "discharges the obligation of the obligated bank on the check to both the holder and the claimant."[34] Any liability of the obligated bank for violation of the indemnity agreement is governed by law outside of Article 3.[35] The reason for the exclusion of these instruments from the scope of the exception to discharge is to conform with section 3-411.[36] That section is intended to discourage obligated banks from refusing payment on checks in which they incur liability for their customers when a claimant to the check provides the bank with indemnity against loss.

Consistent with the exception to the *jus tertii* principle, the indemnification and injunction exceptions to discharge by payment to a holder apply only to assertions of claims by third parties.[37] These claims encompass both legal and equitable claims. Parties with defenses to their own negotiable-instrument contract liability cannot use indemnification or an injunction to prevent discharge of the obligor who pays a holder. Furthermore, holders in due course take instruments free from all claims and thereby acquire superior title over other claimants.[38] Payment to a holder in due course will result in discharge of the obligor.

[b] Stolen Instruments

Theft of an instrument leaves the owner from whom it was stolen with a claim of legal title. Section 3-602 treats this particular claim differently from all others. Usually a third-party claimant cannot preclude discharge of the obligor making payment unless the claimant either indemnifies or enjoins the obligor.[39] Yet merely causing the obligor to know of the claim

---

[33] U.C.C. § 3-602(b)(1)(ii).

[34] U.C.C. § 3-602, Comment.

[35] U.C.C. § 3-602, Comment.

[36] *See* § 12.04[D] *infra*.

[37] The indemnity and injunction exceptions require "a claim to the instrument under Section 3-306 [that] is enforceable against the party receiving payment." U.C.C. § 3-602(b)(1).

[38] U.C.C. § 3-306.

[39] *See* § 7.02[A][2][a] *supra*.

of theft prior to payment *sometimes* prevents discharge. Payment to a holder does not result in the discharge of the liability when "the person making payment knows that the instrument is a stolen instrument and pays a person it knows is in wrongful possession of the instrument."[40]

The unique approach to claims based on theft of an instrument stems from the policy of depriving a thief of opportunities to benefit from the transgression. Obligors are encouraged to refrain from knowingly paying a thief because they will not be discharged. Denying discharge for payment to persons who hold through a thief creates a similar incentive not to pay and restricts the market in which the thief can pass the paper. Even though an instrument is stolen from someone other than the obligor, the claim of legal ownership of that party can still be asserted by the obligor.[41] When this exception to the *jus tertii* principle is available, the obligor should use it rather than pay the party demanding payment, because payment will not discharge the obligor.

The theft exception to the *jus tertii* principle is available only against a party seeking enforcement of the instrument who does not have the rights of a holder in due course.[42] Claims of legal ownership following theft, like all claims, are not valid against a holder in due course. Consistent with this approach, section 3-602(b)(2) allows payment to a person who acquired a stolen instrument nevertheless to discharge the payor, provided that the person paid has the rights of a holder in due course.

To illustrate the discharge by payment rules in the context of a stolen instrument, consider the facts diagramed below:

M----▶P————▶T————▶X·········▶ M
          (theft)

Diagram 7.1

Maker (M) issues a note to Payee (P). Thief (T) steals the note and transfers it to X, who demands payment from M when it becomes due. If the instrument was order paper when it was stolen, M will not be discharged if he pays X because X could not qualify as a person entitled to enforce the instrument. Thus assume that the note was bearer paper when it was stolen and transferred to X. If M pays X while unaware of the theft, M will be discharged. Even though he pays someone who holds the note through a person who acquired it by theft, the payment would be made without knowledge that the note was stolen and the exception of section 3-602(b)(2) thus would not be invoked. If M has prior knowledge of the theft, M's

---

[40] U.C.C. § 3-602(b)(2).
[41] *See* U.C.C. § 3-305(c); § 6.03[B] *supra*.
[42] U.C.C. § 3-305(c).

appropriate response to the demand for payment depends upon whether X is a holder in due course. If X qualifies, the claim of ownership by P is cut off under section 3-306, M cannot successful resist payment to X under section 3-305(c), and payment will discharge M. The same result would apply through the shelter provision for any subsequent transferees if X had decided to transfer the instrument rather than present it for payment. If X is not a holder in due course, M's discharge for a payment with knowledge of the theft will depend upon whether M also knows that the person paid is in wrongful possession of the note. If M knows both that the note was stolen and that X does not have holder in due course rights, M should assert the corollary *jus tertii* principle rather than pay the note.[43] Because obligors often will not have any basis to know the circumstances under which the person entitled to payment acquired the instrument, the exception based on theft of the instrument is likely to be utilized only in relatively rare cases when the instrument was stolen in bearer form.

[B] Tender of Payment — § 3-603

If a person entitled to enforce an instrument refuses to accept a tender of payment of an amount due on the instrument,[44] the party making the tender is discharged only to a limited extent. The party's obligation to pay the instrument is not discharged. The discharge is limited to subsequent liability for interest.[45] To the extent that liability for interest has been incurred prior to the tender, it is not discharged.

The interests of the party making the refused tender can be adequately protected with this limited discharge without awarding the unwarranted windfall that complete discharge would provide. The principle reason why a person entitled to enforce an instrument might be inclined to refuse an offered payment is because the rate of interest on the instrument is particularly attractive and thus desirable to keep running. Once an instrument becomes due, however, a person entitled to enforce it cannot unilaterally continue it and the favorable interest rate by simply refusing to accept tendered payment. The discharge from liability for any further interest creates an incentive for the holder to accept the payment when due.

A refusal to accept a proper tender results in discharge to the extent of the amount tendered of "the obligation of an indorser or accommodation

---

[43] "An obligor is not obliged to pay the instrument if the person seeking enforcement of the instrument does not have rights of a holder in due course and the obligor proves that the instrument is a lost or stolen instrument." U.C.C. § 3-305(c). The circumstances in which an obligor in such a case will be able to prove that the instrument was stolen and that the person seeking enforcement does not have the rights of a holder in due course will be relatively rare. U.C.C. § 3-305, Comment 4.

[44] An obligor is deemed to have made a tender of payment on the due date to the person entitled to enforce the instrument if presentment of the instrument is required and the obligor stands ready and able to pay on the due date at any place indicated on the instrument for payment. U.C.C. § 3-603(c).

[45] U.C.C. § 3-603(c); Guaranty Bank v. Thompson, 632 S.W.2d 338, 33 U.C.C. Rep. Serv. 629 (Tex. 1982); Penny v. Kelley, 528 S.W.2d 330, 18 U.C.C. Rep. Serv. 454 (Tex. Civ. App. 1975). The effect of tender is also governed by "principles of law applicable to tender of payment under a simple contract." U.C.C. § 3-603(a).

party having a right of recourse with respect to the obligation to which the tender relates."[46] These parties would never be liable on the instrument if the holder had accepted the tender.[47] By refusing to accept the tendered payment, the holder in essence wrongfully jeopardizes the freedom from liability that otherwise would result for these parties with recourse against the party making the tender. Although that party was able and willing to pay the instrument upon tendering the payment, the party's ability and willingness to pay may not continue intact in the future. The parties with rights of recourse against the tendering party therefore are granted their discharge even though the holder refused the tendered payment.

[C] Cancellation or Renunciation — § 3-604

A person entitled to enforce an instrument can discharge the obligation of a party to pay the instrument through a process of cancellation or renunciation. The discharge is effective with or without consideration. One method is "an intentional voluntary act, such as surrender of the instrument to the party, destruction, mutilation, or cancellation of the instrument, cancellation or striking out of the party's signature, or the addition of words to the instrument indicating discharge."[48] Instruments commonly are canceled by marking them "Paid." If the entire instrument is canceled, destroyed, or mutilated, the liability of all of the parties to the instrument are thereby discharged.

The more individualized cancellation or striking out of an indorsement will, under this rule, discharge that party's liability on the instrument, while leaving the liability of other parties on the instrument intact.[49] The discharge of the party whose signature is canceled or stricken, however, "does not affect the status and rights of a party derived from the indorsement."[50] So even though a person entitled to enforce an instrument strikes out a signature that was a necessary indorsement for purposes of negotiation,[51] it does not impair subsequent holder status or the rights of subsequent holders. The end result is that this discharge is only effective against the person entitled to payment that intentionally cancels or strikes the signature and against any subsequent parties who take the instrument, including even a subsequent holder in due course.[52]

A holder can also discharge a party "by agreeing not to sue or otherwise renouncing rights against the party by a signed writing."[53] A renunciation

---

[46] U.C.C. § 3-603(b); Guaranty Bank v. Thompson, 632 S.W.2d 338, 33 U.C.C. Rep. Serv. 629 (Tex. 1982) (bank with right of recourse discharged).

[47] *See* § 7.02[D] *infra*.

[48] U.C.C. § 3-604(a)(i).

[49] Another section even states that the contract obligations of indorsers and accommodation parties with rights of recourse against the discharged party are not discharged. U.C.C. § 3-605(b). *See* § 7.02[E][1] *infra*.

[50] U.C.C. § 3-604(b).

[51] U.C.C. § 3-201(b). *See* § 3.04[B][1] *supra*.

[52] U.C.C. §§ 3-302(b), 3-601(b).

[53] U.C.C. § 3-604(a)(ii).

must be in writing signed by the person entitled to enforce the instrument. A renunciation is not relevant to the rights of any other parties, as only the rights of the person making it are involved.

A discharge by cancellation or renunciation can be effective only when it is done by a person entitled to enforce the instrument with an intention to discharge an individual party or all parties to the instrument. Cancellation and renunciation are not effective if they are done by mistake or are otherwise unintentional.

[D] Reacquisition — § 3-207

Sometimes a prior party on an instrument will reacquire it, as when an instrument is negotiated to a prior indorser. A prior party who reacquires an instrument is entitled to cancel all indorsements following the party's initial acquisition of the instrument. Section 3-207 provides in its entirety:

> Reacquisition of an instrument occurs if it is transferred to a former holder, by negotiation or otherwise. A former holder who reacquires the instrument may cancel indorsements made after the reacquirer first became a holder of the instrument. If the cancellation causes the instrument to be payable to the reacquirer or to bearer, the reacquirer may negotiate the instrument. An indorser whose indorsement is canceled is discharged, and the discharge is effective against any subsequent holder.

If the instrument is negotiated to a prior indorser, the negotiation will make the reacquirer a holder, and the reacquirer can further negotiate the instrument or enforce its payment. The contract liability of any indorsers subsequent to the reacquirer's initial indorsement will be meaningless to the reacquirer, as all of those indorsers would, in turn, have a right of recourse against that initial indorsement. Consider the facts diagramed below:

```
                   "Pay X"  "Pay Y"   "Pay P"
                    "P"       "X"       "Y"
   D'er ---- ▶P ─────▶X ─────▶Y ─────▶P
```

Diagram 7.2

Drawer (D'er) issues a check to Payee (P), who negotiates it by indorsement to X. X indorses and negotiates the check to Y and Y signs and negotiates the check back to P. As the holder of the check, P would have rights of recourse against X and Y following a dishonor by the drawee. If P pursued either of these indorsers, however, they in turn would have a right of recourse against P himself based on his prior indorsement.

If an instrument is returned to a prior party without the necessary indorsement, that party will not qualify as a holder. Section 3-207 nevertheless eliminates the need for the prior party to obtain the transferor's indorsement in order to further negotiate the instrument. The party who reacquired the instrument can become a holder again simply by canceling any indorsements that were made after the reacquirer first became a holder of the instrument. Assume that in the facts in the previous diagram Y had not indorsed before transferring the check to P. If P canceled his own indorsement to X and X's indorsement to Y, the instrument would again run to his order and he would be a holder. The cancellation of the indorsements provide notice of the discharge of these indorsers and will be effective against even a subsequent holder in due course.[54]

Reacquisition has particular relevance in transactions that are rescinded or never fully consummated. A party might indorse a cashier's check that is held as a deposit for a transaction that is not completed, or a transferee of an instrument might require the transferor to reacquire a note when the maker of the note misses too many payments.[55] "Section 3-207 is a rule of convenience which relieves [the reacquirer] of the burden of obtaining an indorsement that serves no substantive purpose."[56]

The policy objectives of section 3-207 are important to keep in mind because some literal applications of the section would violate these objectives and thus should not be allowed. The reacquisition of an instrument from a thief or in circumstances in which one of the intervening necessary indorsements was forged is problematic. The reacquiring party should not be allowed simply to cancel the forged indorsement in order to regain holder status. Section 3-207 is intended to enable the reacquiring party to become a holder even though the holder who returns the instrument does not indorse. There is nothing in the section that suggests that a reacquiring party should be able to divest a rightful owner of title to the instrument.

Because section 3-602 provides discharge of a obligor who pays only if the payment is to a person entitled to enforce the instrument, section 3-207 plays an important role when payment is made by an indorser. Consider the following facts:

$$M \cdots \rightarrow P \xrightarrow[\text{"P"}]{\text{"Pay X"}} X \xrightarrow[\text{"X"}]{\text{"Pay Y"}} Y$$

Diagram 7.3

M issues a note to P. Subsequent transfers are made to X and Y, with P and X each providing an indorsement. Assume that Y cannot obtain

---

[54] U.C.C. §§ 3-601, 3-604.

[55] Another illustration is provided in United Credit Corp. v. Necamp, 19 U.C.C. Rep. Serv. 1197 (Pa. Comm. Pl. 1976) (transferor of a note with a "pay any bank" indorsement could cancel the restrictive indorsement upon return of the check by the bank that had tried to collect it).

[56] U.C.C. § 3-207, Comment.

payment from M and provides the necessary notice of dishonor to both of the indorsers. Y then demands payment from X, who pays upon Y's surrender of the note. Under section 3-207 reacquisition of the instrument by X has occurred through transfer of the note to a former holder. At this point, X qualifies as "a nonholder in possession of the instrument who has the rights of a holder,"[57] which qualifies X as a person entitled to enforce the instrument.[58] If X proceeds against P on her indorser's contract, payment by P will be made to the appropriate party for P to attain discharge under section 3-602.[59]

Payment of an instrument by a maker or a drawer does not discharge indorsers. Section 3-602 provides only for discharge of the party that pays the instrument. Payment by the maker or drawer, together with surrender of the instrument, does not constitute reacquisition under section 3-207, both because the instrument would not be transferred and because makers and drawers cannot qualify as former holders of the instrument. The original version of Article 3 would have discharged the liability of all parties to the instrument when any party who did not have a right of action or recourse on the instrument was discharged through any provision.[60] Thus, payment of a note by the maker would discharge the liability of all of the indorsers. Under the revised Code the indorsers would not be discharged, but their liability would never mature because the requirement of dishonor that conditions their liability would not be satisfied.

[E] Discharge of Indorsers and Accommodation Parties — § 3-605

[1] Rights of Recourse

The revision to Article 3 states a rule that deviates from the general principle of suretyship law that a creditor who releases a principal debtor will also be treated as having released the surety.[61] Rather than a discharge of parties in a surety relationship, the revision provides that "[d]ischarge, under Section 3-604, of the obligation of a party to pay an instrument does not discharge the obligation of an indorser or accommodation party having a right of recourse against the discharged party."[62] An

---

[57] U.C.C. § 3-301. The transferor, Y, was a holder, and the transfer "vests in the transferee any right of the transferor to enforce the instrument." U.C.C. § 3-203(b).

[58] Alternatively, X could strike his indorsement under section 3-207, thereby becoming a holder again, and again qualifying as a person entitled to enforce the instrument.

[59] The reacquisition provision will not apply in the context of an anomalous indorsement (see § 4.04 *supra* on establishing accommodation-party status), because the anomalous indorser is not a "former holder." Any accommodation party, however, "is entitled to enforce the instrument against the accommodated party." U.C.C. § 3-419(e). See § 4.04[C] *supra*.

[60] U.C.C. § 3-601(3) (original version).

[61] Where the creditor releases a principal, the surety is discharged, unless
    (a) the surety consents to remain liable notwithstanding the release, or
    (b) the creditor in the release reserves his rights against the surety.

Restatement of Security § 122 (1941). For general background on surety concepts, see L. SIMPSON, HANDBOOK ON THE LAW OF SURETYSHIP §§ 3-17, 63 (1950).

[62] U.C.C. § 3-605(b).

accommodation party essentially signs a negotiable instrument as a surety for the benefit of the principle debtor who also signs the instrument.[63] Even indorsers who are not accommodation parties incur an obligation that is quite comparable to a surety's position, as an indorser essentially is a guarantor of payment.[64] Unlike the general surety, however, indorsers and accommodation parties having recourse against the discharged party are not discharged from their own obligations.

Although the revision in this respect changes the substance of prior law, the practical effect is largely insignificant. Under prior law, the holder of a negotiable instrument usually would expressly reserve its rights against an accommodation party or an indorser at the time that it released the primary obligor. The approach in the revision simply eliminates any requirement for holders to formally reserve rights against accommodation parties and indorsers in order to retain rights of recourse against them.[65]

The approach in Article 3 is designed to facilitate settlements between creditors and principal debtors. A lender who holds a note is unlikely to release gratuitously a borrower who signs a promissory note. The discharge is likely to be the result of a settlement when the borrower experiences financial difficulties, wherein the lender accepts a partial payment in exchange for a release of the borrower. The partial payment at least reduces the obligation of accommodation parties and of indorsers with a right of recourse against the discharged borrower. The rights of these parties against the borrower also remain unimpaired. An accommodation party that has to pay the balance to the lender can obtain reimbursement or enforce the note against the borrower as an accommodated party.[66] An indorser who is not an accommodation party retains its right of recourse against the borrower if it has to pay the balance due on the note.[67] Because "[s]ettlement is in the interest of sureties as well as the creditor,"[68] the lender can settle with the borrower without losing its rights against the sureties.

Section 3-605 also deals with the effect on surety liability that results from modifications to an instrument. One type of modification is an extension in the due date of the obligation of a party to pay an instrument. Such an extension discharges an indorser or an accommodation party having a right of recourse against the party whose obligation is extended, but only to the extent that the indorser or accommodation party proves that the extension caused it loss with respect to the right of recourse.[69] Usually

---

[63] U.C.C. § 3-419(a). See § 4.04[A] supra.

[64] U.C.C. § 3-415(a). See U.C.C. § 3-605, Comment 1. A payee who indorses a note to a holder is comparable to a surety. The principal debtor on the note is the maker, and the holder is in the position of the creditor. The payee/indorser undertakes a form of back-up liability to the obligation of the maker, which is like the obligation assumed by a surety. If required to pay the note to the holder, the indorser has recourse against the maker.

[65] U.C.C. § 3-605, Comment 3.

[66] U.C.C. § 3-419(e). See § 4.04[E] supra.

[67] U.C.C. § 3-604(b). See § 7.02[C] supra.

[68] U.C.C. § 3-605, Comment 3.

[69] U.C.C. § 3-605(c).

an extension in the due date will not result in any discharge because the extension benefits the sureties as well as the principal debtor. If the principal debtor is a borrower who temporarily lacks funds, a surety generally would rather defer paying the instrument to the lender rather than exercising its option to pay right away. Sometimes, however, an extension will reduce the amount that a surety can recover on its right of recourse against the discharged principal debtor because the principal debtor becomes insolvent during the period of insolvency. Under these circumstances, an indorser or accommodation party having a right of recourse can attain discharge to the extent that it proves the loss.[70]

Because other types of modifications to an instrument are less common and are more likely to be detrimental to a surety, they are treated differently than extensions of the due date.[71] These other modifications, when made by a person entitled to enforce the instrument, discharge the obligation of an indorser or accommodation party having a right of recourse against the person whose obligation is modified, again to the extent that the modification causes loss to the indorser or accommodation party.[72] With these other types of modifications, however, the loss is deemed to equal the amount of the right of recourse unless the person enforcing the instrument proves that either no loss or a lesser amount of loss resulted.[73]

The discharge that can be attained through modifications can be waived. Waiver can result from consent of an indorser or an accommodation party to the event or conduct that is the basis of the discharge.[74] Waiver can also result from general or specific language in the instrument or in a separate agreement that the parties waive defenses based upon suretyship.[75] Recognition of these waivers undercuts the practical significance of the suretyship defenses: "It is standard practice to include a waiver of suretyship defenses in notes given to financial institutions or other commercial creditors."[76]

[2] Rights in Collateral

Section 3-605 also provides that if a person entitled to enforce an instrument impairs the value of an interest in collateral that secures the

---

[70] Loss probably could not be proven with respect to accrued interest that results during an extension. The obligation of an accommodation party or an indorser includes interest on a note until it is paid. The accommodation party or the indorser could stop the running of interest by paying the debt. During a delay, these sureties would have the use of the money that they otherwise would have had to pay to the holder of the instrument when it originally became due. Thus, they would not suffer a loss because of the extension of the due date. See U.C.C. § 3-605, Comment 3.

[71] U.C.C. § 3-605, Comment 5. Classic illustrations are an increase in the amount owed or in the rate of interest or changes to the covenants undertaken by the principle obligor.

[72] U.C.C. § 3-605(d).

[73] U.C.C. § 3-605(d).

[74] U.C.C. § 3-605(i)(i).

[75] U.C.C. § 3-605(i)(ii).

[76] U.C.C. § 3-605, Comment 2. See Federal Land Bank v. Taggart, 31 Ohio St. 3d 8, 508 N.E.2d 152, 3 U.C.C. Rep. Serv. 2d 1836 (1987); Farmington Nat'l Bank v. Basin Plastics, Inc., 94 N.M. 668, 615 P.2d 985, 29 U.C.C. Rep. Serv. 1335 (1980).

obligation of a party to pay the instrument, "the obligation of an indorser or accommodation party having a right of recourse against the obligor is discharged to the extent of the impairment."[77] This provision is also based upon fundamental principles of suretyship law in the protection of rights of recourse. A party with a right of recourse is entitled to rights in the collateral upon making payment.[78] Under general suretyship law, a surety who satisfies the obligation is subrogated to the creditor's rights in the collateral. The surety then has the option of proceeding against the principal on the debt or against the collateral. Similarly, under Article 3, a party with a right of recourse against the party that gave the collateral is subrogated to the rights of the holder upon payment of the instrument. The subrogation extends to the holder's rights on both the instrument and the collateral.[79] If the holder has unjustifiably impaired the collateral, however, the party with the subrogation rights is discharged to the extent of the impairment because the holder has wrongfully deprived the party of recourse against the collateral.[80]

Consider the facts diagramed below:

```
        note +
        stock        "P"
   M ------►P ----------►H
```

Diagram 7.4

Maker (M) issues a promissory note to Payee (P), together with collateral in the form of blue chip stocks, in exchange for a loan from P. P indorses the note and delivers it and the stock to Holder (H) for value received from H. A wrongful sale of the stock by H will discharge P. If H returns the collateral to M before the note matures, P will be discharged. H should retain the stock as security against a dishonor of the instrument by M, which would enable H to foreclose against the collateral or proceed against P on her indorsement liability. If P were required to pay the note, she would be entitled to the collateral and could foreclose on it to satisfy M's outstanding obligation. By impairing, rather than preserving the collateral for P's benefit, H will discharge P and be precluded from recovering against her to the extent of the impairment.

---

[77] U.C.C. § 3-605(e). This provision does not apply in favor of any person who is not a party to the instrument. Several cases have denied applicability to a guarantor who signs a separate writing. Simpson v. MBank Dallas, N.A., 724 S.W.2d 102, 3 U.C.C. Rep. Serv. 2d 652 (Tex. Ct. App. 1987); Halpin v. Frankenberger, 231 Kan. 344, 644 P.2d 452, 34 U.C.C. Rep. Serv. 189 (1982).

[78] Restatement of Security § 141(b).

[79] Bank of N.J. v. Pulini, 194 N.J. Super. 163, 476 A.2d 797, 38 U.C.C. Rep. Serv. 1308 (1984); O'Hara v. First Nat'l Bank, 613 S.W.2d 306, 31 U.C.C. Rep. Serv. 743 (Tex. Civ. App. 1980).

[80] Federal Deposit Ins. Corp. v. Blue Rock Shopping Center, Inc., 599 F. Supp. 684, 40 U.C.C. Rep. Serv. 555 (D. Del. 1984) (accommodation maker); Huey v. Port Gibson Bank, 390 So. 2d 1005, 31 U.C.C. Rep. Serv. 637 (Miss. 1980) (indorser).

Prior to the revision of the Code, most courts denied availability of this discharge to co-makers because of the absence of a surety relationship.[81] The revision adds an explicit provision that addresses the effect of impairment of collateral on the rights of a party who is jointly and severally liable:

> If the obligation of a party is secured by an interest in collateral not provided by an accommodation party and a person entitled to enforce the instrument impairs the value of the interest in collateral, the obligation of any party who is jointly and severally liable with respect to the secured obligation is discharged to the extent the impairment causes the party asserting discharge to pay more than that party would have been obliged to pay, taking into account rights of contribution, if impairment had not occurred.[82]

Assume that two parties sign a $10,000 note as co-makers, neither is an accommodation party, and Maker 1 gives a security interest in collateral worth $15,000 in order to secure the loan. If Maker 2 were required to pay the entire obligation, she would be entitled to proceed against the collateral to the extent of $5,000 in order to satisfy her right of contribution. Thus, if the payee of the note impairs the total value of the collateral, Maker 2 will be discharged to the extent of $5,000.

The revision of Article 3 includes a non-exclusive list of examples that constitute an impairment in value of an interest in collateral. Heading the list is the "failure to obtain or maintain perfection or recordation of the interest in collateral."[83] The failure to perfect a security interest has been the most common method of impairment of collateral. Courts have discharged parties because creditors have failed to take any actions to perfect[84] or have taken inappropriate steps.[85]

Delay in perfecting a security interest, thereby permitting the priority of subsequent liens, also constitutes unjustifiable impairment of collateral.[86] Another listed example of impairment of collateral is the "release of

---

[81] Wohlhuter v. St. Charles Lumber & Fuel Co., 25 Ill. App. 3d 812, 323 N.E.2d 134, 16 U.C.C. Rep. Serv. 792 (1975); Common Wealth Ins. Sys., Inc. v. Kerstan, 40 Cal. App. 3d 1014, 115 Cal. Rptr. 653, 15 U.C.C. Rep. Serv. 133 (1974).

[82] U.C.C. § 3-604(f).

[83] U.C.C. § 3-604(g)(i).

[84] Huey v. Port Gibson Bank, 390 So. 2d 1005, 31 U.C.C. Rep. Serv. 637 (Miss. 1980) (failure to file); Shaffer v. Rawlins Fin. Co., 445 P.2d 13, 5 U.C.C. Rep. Serv. 772 (Wyo. 1968) (failure to file or secure notation on certificate of title).

[85] First New Haven Nat'l Bank v. Tirkot, 25 U.C.C. Rep. Serv. 795 (Conn. Super. Ct. 1978) (filed in wrong state); Executive Bank v. Tighe, 66 A.D.2d 70, 411 N.Y.S.2d 939, 25 U.C.C. Rep. Serv. 786 (1978) (filed in wrong office); In re Estate of Voelker, 252 N.W.2d 400, 21 U.C.C. Rep. Serv. 817 (Iowa 1977) (failed to include legal description of real estate upon which corn crop was growing).

[86] El-Ce Storms Trust v. Svetahor, 223 Mont. 113, 724 P.2d 704, 2 U.C.C. Rep. Serv. 2d 1593 (1986). Discharge will not follow a failure to perfect, however, when the collateral is taken pursuant to a lien or interest that had achieve priority before the time that perfection could have been accomplished. Ramsey v. First Nat'l Bank & Trust Co., 683 S.W.2d 947, 40 U.C.C. Rep. Serv. 1769 (Ky. Ct. App. 1984) (preexisting lien); Beneficial Fin. Co. v. Lawrence, 301 N.W.2d 114, 30 U.C.C. Rep. Serv. 1358 (N.D. 1980) (prior perfected security interests).

collateral without substitution of collateral of equal value."[87] For example, the release of the collateral,[88] release of insurance proceeds,[89] and release of an insurance company from its contract[90] have all been held to constitute impairment. Similar judicial results have applied to the return of a certificate of title to the owners[91] and authorization for the debtor to sell the collateral.[92] Another listed example of impairment is the "failure to comply with applicable law in disposing of collateral."[93]

A final listed example of impairment is the "failure to perform a duty to preserve the value of collateral owed under Article 9 or other law, to a debtor or surety or other person secondarily liable."[94] The general standard of care stated in Article 9 is that "[a] secured party must use reasonable care in the custody and preservation of collateral in his possession."[95] The occasional court has construed this provision to limit the question of impairment of collateral only to cases in which the holder is in possession of the collateral.[96] Most courts would reject that limitation in favor of analyzing whether the actions of the creditor have unreasonably diminished the value or the availability of the collateral.[97] Duties that are created by the parties' agreement also establish a standard to which the holder is accountable. Many cases have found that the holder was not responsible for losses of collateral or its value. For the most part, the duty to preserve collateral is only an obligation to maintain its physical safety while it is within the custody of the secured party. Consequently, holders have often avoided discharge when the loss of collateral was not attributable to their actual conduct. In the absence of a contrary agreement, the creditor does not have a duty to insure the collateral.[98] The holder is not responsible for the dishonesty of the debtor.[99] Similarly, a holder is not responsible for

---

[87] U.C.C. § 3-604(g)(ii).

[88] Guida v. Exchange Nat'l Bank, 308 So. 2d 148, 16 U.C.C. Rep. Serv. 1062 (Fla. Ct. App. 1975).

[89] Godfrey State Bank v. Mundy, 90 Ill. App. 3d 142, 412 N.E.2d 1131, 30 U.C.C. Rep. Serv. 1070 (1980).

[90] Tennessee Farmers Mut. Ins. Co. v. Scott, 8 U.C.C. Rep. Serv. 399 (Tenn. Ct. App. 1970).

[91] McHenry State Bank v. Y&A Trucking, 117 Ill. App. 3d 629, 454 N.E.2d 345, 37 U.C.C. Rep. Serv. 509 (1983).

[92] Beneficial Fin. Co. v. Marshall, 551 P.2d 315, 18 U.C.C. Rep. Serv.1014 (Okla. Ct. App. 1976).

[93] U.C.C. § 3-605(g)(iv).

[94] U.C.C. § 3-604(g)(iii).

[95] U.C.C. § 9-207.

[96] Commercial Credit Equip. Corp. v. Hatton, 429 F. Supp. 997, 22 U.C.C. Rep. Serv. 118 (N.D. Tex. 1977).

[97] Ramsey v. First Nat'l Bank & Trust Co., 683 S.W.2d 947, 40 U.C.C. Rep. Serv. 1769 (Ky. Ct. App. 1984); Beneficial Fin. Co. v. Marshall, 551 P.2d 315, 18 U.C.C. Rep. Serv. 1014 (Okla. Ct. App. 1976).

[98] Forest-All Corp. v. New England Merchants Nat'l Bank, 509 F. Supp. 1264, 31 U.C.C. Rep. Serv. 183 (D. Mass. 1981).

[99] Williams v. Lafayette Prod. Credit Ass'n, 508 N.E.2d 579, 4 U.C.C. Rep. Serv. 2d 1489 (Ind. Ct. App. 1987) (debtor absconded with the collateral and sold it without the lender's consent).

vandalism to the real property collateral or the general decline of real estate values in the area.[100] Additional cases have held that a holder does not have a duty to proceed against collateral before pursuing other rights on the instrument,[101] to prevent the debtor from moving the collateral out of the jurisdiction,[102] to object to the listing of its debt in a bankruptcy proceeding as unsecured,[103] or to demand additional collateral from a defaulting principal obligor.[104]

A holder's action or inaction that has been recognized in cases as giving rise to an unjustifiable impairment of collateral does not alone result in any discharge. A party seeking the discharge bears the burden of proving the impairment, as well as the amount of the loss incurred.[105] Discharge under section 3-605 is allowed only "to the extent" that the collateral is impaired.[106] The revision of Article 3 includes a provision that sets a standard for determining the extent of impairment: "The value of an interest in collateral is impaired to the extent (i) the value of the interest is reduced to an amount less than the amount of the right of recourse of the party asserting discharge, or (ii) the reduction in value of the interest causes an increase in the amount by which the amount of the right of recourse exceeds the value of the interest."[107] In several cases defendants have failed to carry the burden.[108] In *Mitchell v. Ringston*,[109] for example, the court stressed that the guarantor did not present any evidence of impairment due to the plaintiff allowing the perfection of the security interest to lapse. If the collateral was not lost or subordinated to another claim, the guarantor was not harmed.[110]

---

[100] Federal Deposit Ins. Corp. v. Kirkland, 272 S.C. 310, 251 S.E.2d 750, 26 U.C.C. Rep. Serv. 110 (1979) (not results of acts of the payee). *See also* Bank of Boston Int'l v. Arguello Tefel, 644 F. Supp. 1423, 3 U.C.C. Rep. Serv. 2d 1069 (E.D. N.Y. 1986) (holder not responsible for loss in value of pledged stock that resulted from expropriation by the new government in Nicaragua).

[101] Commercial Fin., Ltd. v. American Resources, Ltd., 737 P.2d 1120, 5 U.C.C. Rep. Serv. 2d 1172 (Haw. Ct. App. 1987).

[102] American Discount Corp. v. Glover, 391 So. 2d 853, 30 U.C.C. Rep. Serv. 1067 (La. Ct. App. 1980).

[103] Chemical Bank v. Valentini, 84 A.D.2d 801, 444 N.Y.S.2d 154 (1981).

[104] First State Bank v. Raiton, 377 F. Supp. 859, 15 U.C.C. Rep. Serv. 420 (E.D. Pa. 1974).

[105] Mitchell v. Ringston, 169 Ga. App. 88, 311 S.E.2d 516, 38 U.C.C. Rep. Serv. 234 (1983); Christensen v. McAtee, 256 Ore. 333, 473 P.2d 659, 8 U.C.C. Rep. Serv. 66 (1970).

[106] Van Balen v. Peoples Bank & Trust Co., 3 Ark. App. 243, 626 S.W.2d 205, 33 U.C.C. Rep. Serv. 1046 (1981) (discharge is only *pro tanto*).

[107] U.C.C. § 3-604(e).

[108] Lyons v. Citizens Commercial Bank, 443 So. 2d 229, 37 U.C.C. Rep. Serv. 1214 (Fla. Ct. App. 1983) (no evidence of value); Van Balen v. Peoples Bank & Trust Co., 3 Ark. App. 243, 626 S.W.2d 205, 33 U.C.C. Rep. Serv. 1046 (1981) (no showing of extent to which the security was impaired).

[109] 169 Ga. App. 88, 311 S.E.2d 516, 38 U.C.C. Rep. Serv. 234 (1983).

[110] *Compare* First Bank & Trust Co. v. Post, 10 Ill. App. 3d 127, 293 N.E.2d 907, 12 U.C.C. Rep. Serv. 512 (1973) (guarantor discharged when creditor's failure to perfect security interest resulted in the subordination of the security interest to the trustee in bankruptcy). *See also* Guida v. Exchange Nat'l Bank, 308 So. 2d 148, 16 U.C.C. Rep. Serv. 1062 (Fla. Ct. App. 1975) (value of collateral released by bank sufficient to satisfy outstanding indebtedness).

The exceptions based on consent or waiver are also available to a person entitled to enforce an instrument against a discharge based on impairment of collateral.[111] Parties can give consent to allow the holder wide discretion in dealing with collateral.[112] Consent can be given before or after the release or other impairment of collateral.[113] Provisions indicating consent are often included in language in the instrument.[114]

[F] Material Alteration — § 3-407

Fraudulent alteration of an instrument can result in the discharge of any party whose obligation on the instrument is changed.[115] Parties who sign instruments incur contracts that obligate them to the pay according to the terms at specified times.[116] Subsequent parties thus cannot unilaterally change the liability of prior parties simply by altering terms on the instrument. In addition, however, a fraudulent alteration can discharge parties whose contracts have been changed. Elimination of the right to enforce the instrument against these parties creates an incentive to parties entitled to enforce an instrument to refrain from perpetuating this type of fraud with negotiable instruments.

[1] Requirements

Discharge under section 3-407(b) requires "an alteration fraudulently made." One form of alteration is "an unauthorized change in an instrument that purports to modify in any respect the obligation of a party."[117] The addition or deletion of words that do not affect a contract of any previous

---

[111] U.C.C. § 3-605(i).

[112] National Acceptance Co. of Am. v. Demes, 24 U.C.C. Rep. Serv. 197 (N.D. Ill. 1977). Many courts have construed the language of an express consent to deny the particular form of impairment that resulted. First New Haven Nat'l Bank v. Tirkot, 25 U.C.C. Rep. Serv. 795 (Conn. Super. Ct. 1978) (consent to exchange or surrender the collateral was not consent to impair collateral by failure to file); White v. Household Fin. Corp., 302 N.E.2d 828, 13 U.C.C. Rep. Serv. 858 (Ind. Ct. App. 1973) (release of interest in title to car after accident was not consent to release of insurance proceeds).

[113] Ramsey v. First Nat'l Bank & Trust Co., 683 S.W.2d 947, 40 U.C.C. Rep. Serv. 1769 (Ky. Ct. App. 1984) (retroactive consent to sale of part of the collateral).

[114] H&H Operations, Inc. v. West Ga. Nat'l Bank, 181 Ga. App. 766, 353 S.E.2d 633, 3 U.C.C. Rep. Serv. 2d 1054 (1987) (promissory note stated that bank could "release any security . . . without affecting [debtor's] obligation to pay the loan"); Etelson v. Suburban Trust Co., 263 Md. 376, 283 A.2d 408, 9 U.C.C. Rep. Serv. 1371 (1971) (language in indorsement consented to "any modification in the terms of the note or the release or exchange of any collateral without notice").

[115] U.C.C. § 3-407(b); Logan v. Central Bank, 397 So. 2d 151, 31 U.C.C. Rep. Serv. 1029 (Ala. Ct. App. 1981) (co-maker discharged); Peppers v. Citizens & S. Nat'l Bank, 127 Ga. App. 16, 192 S.E.2d 409, 11 U.C.C. Rep. Serv. 796 (1972) (guarantor discharged).

[116] Makers and drawers are obliged to pay according to the terms of the instrument at the time it was issued or, if not issued, at the time it first came into possession of a holder. U.C.C. §§ 3-412, 3-414(b). An acceptor is obliged to pay a draft according to its terms at the time it was accepted. U.C.C. § 3-413(a). An indorser is obliged to pay according to the terms of the instrument at the time it was indorsed. U.C.C. § 3-415(a). See § 4.02 supra.

[117] U.C.C. § 3-407(a)(i).

party is not an alteration and thus does not result in any discharge. The most common form of alteration is an increase in the amount payable. Other additions or deletions can also qualify, however, including a change in the date of payment, the date of execution, the place of payment, or a term on interest.[118] The number and relations of the parties to the instrument can also be relevant, as when the name of the payee is changed.[119] Adding a co-maker or surety is not a material alteration because it does not change the contracts of the parties who have already signed.[120]

Alteration also includes "an unauthorized addition of words or numbers or other change to an incomplete instrument relating to the obligation of a party."[121] An incomplete instrument is "a signed writing, whether or not issued by the signer, the contents of which show at the time of signing that it is incomplete but that the signer intended it to be completed by the addition of words or numbers."[122] If the instrument is completed in accordance with authority granted, it may be enforced according to the terms as augmented by the completion.[123] For example, a drawer of a check might authorize the payee to write in the sum payable for a specific amount. If that sum is written, the check can be enforced in the stated amount. If the payee writes in a higher amount, the completion constitutes an alteration.

An alteration must be fraudulent in order to result in a discharge. The person making the alteration must have a dishonest or deceitful intent to secure a personal gain to which he or she is not entitled. Discharge under section 3-407(b) is aimed as a punishment against fraud, so an alteration in the absence of fraudulent intent does not discharge any party.[124] Consequently, a change or completion made with a honest but mistaken belief that it was authorized does not invoke discharge.[125] Discharge also does not result from a change made with a benevolent motive.[126]

---

[118] Hughes v. Talley, 400 So. 2d 253, 31 U.C.C. Rep. Serv.1419 (La. Ct. App. 1981).

[119] Hanover Ins. Co. v. Brotherhood State Bank, 482 F. Supp. 501, 28 U.C.C. Rep. Serv. 430 (D. Kan. 1979) (changing payee's name on check).

[120] Reagan v. City Nat'l Bank, 714 S.W.2d 425, 2 U.C.C. Rep. Serv. 2d 537 (Tex. Ct. App. 1986) (addition of co-maker).

[121] U.C.C. § 3-407(a)(ii). *See also* U.C.C. § 3-115(c) ("If words or numbers are added to an incomplete instrument without authority of the signer, there is an alteration of the incomplete instrument under Section 3-407"); E. Bierhaus & Sons, Inc. v. Bowling, 486 N.E.2d 598, 42 U.C.C. Rep. Serv. 920 (Ind. Ct. App. 1985) (unauthorized completion of signed check); State v. Ravin, 21 Ariz. App. 216, 518 P.2d 579, 14 U.C.C. Rep. Serv. 1177 (1974) (stealing and completing a blank but signed check).

[122] U.C.C. § 3-115(a). *See* § 2.02[E][2] *supra*.

[123] U.C.C. § 3-115(b).

[124] "No other alteration discharges a party, and the instrument may be enforced according to its original terms." U.C.C. § 3-407(b).

[125] Citizens Nat'l Bank v. Taylor, 368 N.W.2d 913, 41 U.C.C. Rep. Serv. 516 (Minn. 1985), *aff'd*, 387 N.W.2d 451 (Minn. Ct. App. 1986) (bank thought it was entitled to renew overdue demand notes at current interest rates).

[126] Logan v. Central Bank, 397 So. 2d 151, 31 U.C.C. Rep. Serv. 1029 (Ala. Ct. App. 1981) (alterations beneficial to makers). *But see* U.C.C. § 3-407, Comment 1 (although changes favorable to the obligor are unlikely to be motivated by fraudulent intent, a finding of such intent can lead to discharge).

[2] Effect

A fraudulent alteration "discharges a party whose obligation is affected by the alteration unless that party assents or is precluded from asserting the alteration."[127] The discharge is personal to the party whose contract is changed in any respect by the alteration. The comments indicate that "if an alteration discharges a party there is also discharge of any party having a right of recourse against the discharged party because the obligation of the party with the right of recourse is affected by the alteration."[128] Actually, contract liability runs downstream to subsequent parties. Stating the proposition of the comments more accurately, discharge under section 3-407(b) of a party against whom another party has a right of recourse will discharge the subsequent party under section 3-605(d) because of impairment of the recourse right.[129]

Consider the facts diagramed below:

$$M \dashrightarrow P \xrightarrow{\text{"P"}} X \xrightarrow{\text{"X"}} H$$

Diagram 7.5

Maker (M) issues a note to payee (P), who negotiates it with an indorsement in blank to X. X indorses in blank and negotiates the note to Holder (H). If H fraudulently adds the words "collection guaranteed" to P's signature, P will be discharged because the material alteration changes his contract.[130] X would also be discharged because her right of recourse against P was impaired. If H were to pass the instrument to A, A would also take subject to the prior discharges under the shelter principle if A had to rely on the rights of his transferee.

Even though an alteration changes a party's obligation, discharge will not result if the party assents or is precluded from asserting the

---

[127] U.C.C. § 3-407(b); Citizens Nat'l Bank v. Taylor, 368 N.W.2d 913, 41 U.C.C. Rep. Serv. 516 (Minn. 1985), aff'd, 387 N.W.2d 451 (Minn. Ct. App. 1986) (maker consented to change in interest rates); Fairfield County Trust Co. v. Steinbrecher, 5 Conn. Cir. Ct. 405, 255 A.2d 144, 6 U.C.C. Rep. Serv. 682 (1968) (indorser agreed to changes in note after indorsement).

[128] U.C.C. § 3-407, Comment 1; Merchants Nat'l Bank v. Blass, 282 Ark. 497, 669 S.W.2d 195, 39 U.C.C. Rep. Serv. 242 (1984)(indorser discharged after alteration discharged maker).

[129] "[A] material modification of the obligation of a party other than an extension of the due date . . . discharges the obligation of an indorser or accommodation party having a right of recourse against the person whose obligation is modified to the extent the modification causes loss to the indorser or accommodation party with respect to the right of recourse." U.C.C. § 3-605(d). Note that the rule of section 3-505(b), providing that discharge of the obligation of a party to pay the instrument does not discharge the obligation of an indorser or accommodation party having a right of recourse against the discharged party, does not apply as it is relevant only to discharge through cancellation or renunciation under section 3-604. See § 7.02[E][1] supra.

[130] See § 4.04[F] supra.

alteration.[131] The assent essentially operates as a modification of the contractual terms, and it can be given before or after the alteration.[132] Estoppel analysis can create a means to preclude assertion of the discharge.[133] Section 3-406 also codifies the extent to which a person's negligence that substantially contributes to an alteration will preclude assertion of the alteration.[134]

An alteration to an instrument under circumstances that are not fraudulent does not discharge anyone on the instrument. Anyone entitled to enforce the instrument can enforce it according to its original terms.[135] For example, if the payee raised the amount of a check while under the mistaken belief that he was authorized to do so by the drawer, the action would not be fraudulent and the payee could enforce the check for the original amount. An incomplete instrument can be enforced according to the authority given for its completion.[136]

Discharge will not be effective against a person who pays a fraudulently altered instrument or who takes it for value, in good faith, and without notice of the alteration.[137] The person paying or taking the instrument can enforce his or her rights with respect to the instrument according to its original terms. If an incomplete instrument is altered by unauthorized completion, the person paying or taking the instrument can enforce his or her rights according to the terms as completed.[138]

---

[131] U.C.C. § 3-407b); Estate of Pickard, 97 A.D.2d 61, 468 N.Y.S.2d 264, 37 U.C.C. Rep. Serv. 181 (1983).

[132] U.C.C. § 3-407, Comment 1; Bluffstone v. Abrahams, 125 Ariz. 42, 607 P.2d 25, 27 U.C.C. Rep. Serv. 349 (1979) (alteration after consent).

[133] U.C.C. § 3-407, Comment 1; Federal Deposit Ins. Corp. v. Newton, 737 S.W.2d 278, 4 U.C.C. Rep. Serv. 2d 1483 (Tenn. Ct. App. 1987) (estopped from claiming alteration on note after receiving money from note); Fairfield County Trust Co. v. Steinbrecher, 5 Conn. Cir. Ct. 405, 255 A.2d 144, 6 U.C.C. Rep. Serv. 682 (1968) (indorser estopped after indorsing note with deliberate blank spaces, subject to being completed on terms approved by the payee, which he later accepted on being informed of them).

[134] For discussion of section 3-406, see § 10.02[A] *infra*.

[135] U.C.C. § 3-407(b).

[136] U.C.C. § 3-115(b).

[137] U.C.C. § 3-407(c).

[138] This provision places resulting losses on the person who left the instrument incomplete. U.C.C. § 3-407, Comment 2.

The facts diagramed below can be used to illustrate these provisions:

$100 $1,000
D'er ---- ▶P————▶X————▶Y

Diagram 7.6

Drawer (D'er) issues a check in the amount of $100 to payee (P), who negotiates it to X. X fraudulently raises the amount of the check to $1,000 before negotiating it to Y. Both D'er and P incurred liability to the extent of $100, whereas the indorser's contract of X was for $1,000. The fraudulent alteration by X discharges the liability of both D'er and P. That discharge can be asserted against X, and also against Y if Y did not take the check for value, in good faith, or without notice of the alteration. If Y were to qualify as a holder in due course, the discharge defense will not be valid against Y. Y would be able to enforce the contract obligation of either D'er or P, but only for the $100 term of the instrument at the time of their contractual undertakings.

[G] Acceptance of Draft by Bank — §§ 3-414(c), 3-415(d)

The drawer of a draft is discharged if the draft is accepted by a bank.[139] Since a certified check is "a check accepted by the bank on which it is drawn,"[140] drawers of certified checks thus are discharged upon acceptance of the check. By accepting a draft, the bank becomes obligated to pay the draft.[141] Because holders of instruments with bank obligations generally do not rely on the drawer as a guarantor for the bank's solvency,[142] the drawer is discharged upon acceptance.

Discharge from the acceptance of a draft by a bank also extends to indorsers who make their indorsements before the acceptance by the bank.[143] As a demand instrument, a check is payable upon presentment. The acceptance discharge provision simply substitutes the liability of the bank for the liability of the former parties.

[H] Acceptance Varying Draft — § 3-410

When a draft is presented for acceptance by the holder and the drawee proposes to accept under terms that are different from the ones stated in the draft, the holder has a choice. Acceptance of the draft as presented can be required, in which case a refusal to accept would constitute dishonor

---

[139] U.C.C. § 3-414(c).
[140] U.C.C. § 3-409(d).
[141] U.C.C. § 3-413(a). See § 4.02[B] supra.
[142] U.C.C. § 3-414, Comment 3.
[143] U.C.C. § 3-415(d).

of the draft.[144] If the holder assents to the acceptance with different terms, the terms of the acceptance become the obligation of the acceptor and can be enforced by the holder.[145] However, when "the holder assents to an acceptance varying the terms of a draft, the obligation of each drawer and indorser that does not expressly assent to the acceptance is discharged."[146] The liability of these parties is discharged because their contractual undertakings were only on the terms of the instrument at the time that they signed and the altered acceptance has changed those terms.

§ 7.03 Liability on the Underlying Transaction

[A] Effect of Taking an Instrument — § 3-310

Although occasionally given to confer a gift, most instruments are negotiated in order to satisfy an underlying obligation, such as payment of a loan or payment for goods or services. The transfer of an instrument does not place money in the hands of the transferee, however, but rather gives the transferee an Article 3 contract obligation for the payment of money. The drafters of the revision to Article 3 addressed the relationship between the underlying obligation and an instrument given for it in section 3-310.

Generally, the transfer of an instrument that is accepted in exchange for the underlying obligation does not discharge the obligation. Instead, "if a note or an uncertified check is taken for an obligation, the obligation is suspended to the same extent the obligation would be discharged if an amount of money equal to the amount of the instrument were taken."[147] In the case of a note, the suspension continues until dishonor of the note or until it is paid.[148] In the case of an uncertified check, the suspension continues until dishonor of the check or until it is paid or certified.[149] Suspension of the obligation means that it cannot be enforced during the stipulated period.[150] Thus, a merchant who takes a buyer's promissory note in payment of merchandise sold cannot subsequently insist on earlier payment by suing to enforce the payment obligation on the sales contract. That obligation was suspended until the due date of the note when the merchant agreed to take it. Similarly, a merchant who agrees to take a

---

[144] U.C.C. § 3-410(a). The drawee under these circumstances can cancel the acceptance. *Id.*

[145] U.C.C. § 3-410, Comment 1.

[146] U.C.C. § 3-410(c). A failure to object does not constitute the required affirmative assent. U.C.C. § 3-410, Comment 1.

[147] U.C.C. § 3-310(b); Balmoral Arms v. Rutkin, 104 N.J. Super. 354, 250 A.2d 50, 6 U.C.C. Rep. Serv. 165 (1969).

[148] U.C.C. § 3-310(b)(2).

[149] U.C.C. § 3-310(b)(1).

[150] Quigley v. Acker, 955 P.2d 1377, 37 U.C.C. Rep. Serv. 2d 1089 (Mont. 1998) (no default on the underlying land-purchase contract because the obligation was suspended); Grumet v. Bristol, 125 N.H. 537, 484 A.2d 1099, 39 U.C.C. Rep. Serv. 1383 (1984) (holder could not claim default of underlying obligation before presentment).

buyer's check for the goods cannot later insist on cash as the buyer is departing the store. The payment obligation for the goods is suspended until the check is presented for payment.[151]

This general rule on the suspension of the underlying obligation is subject to two exceptions. First, the instrument will immediately discharge the obligation for which it is taken if the parties agree to this result.[152] Transferees rarely agree to such a discharge upon taking an instrument. Second, "if a certified check, cashier's check, or teller's check is taken for an obligation, the obligation is discharged to the same extent discharge would result if an amount of money equal to the amount of the instrument were taken in payment of the obligation."[153] Under these circumstances, the instrument is considered to be treated as the equivalent of cash. For example, if the buyer pays for goods with a cashier's check procured by the buyer as a remitter, the obligation for the purchase price is discharged to the extent of the amount of the check.[154]

The exception also operates in the context of a check certified by a bank. Assume that a payee of a certified check indorses it and transfers it to Seller in exchange for goods. By taking the certified check, Seller will discharge payee's obligation on the underlying sales contract in an amount equal to the amount of the instrument. Article 3, however, expressly preserves payee's liability as an indorser of the instrument.[155] If the certified check were dishonored, Seller could pursue payee for liability on the instrument.

An underlying obligation that is suspended when a note or an uncertified check is taken for the obligation is finally discharged upon payment of the note or uncertified check.[156] Thus when a seller of goods takes a check, payment of the check by the payor bank discharges the drawer of liability on the instrument[157] and of liability on the underlying transaction.[158] In the case of an uncertified check, discharge on the underlying obligation also results from certification of the check.[159] A holder who procures certification of the check holds an instrument equivalent to a check that was certified before it was taken.[160]

---

[151] St. Francis Hospital v. Vaughn, 38 U.C.C. Rep. Serv. 459 (Okla. Ct. App. 1998) (payment by insurance company was not made when the company mailed the check but rather when the check was presented for payment and honored by the payor bank).

[152] U.C.C. § 3-310(b) ("[u]nless otherwise agreed").

[153] U.C.C. § 3-310(a).

[154] In re Tri-Power Electronics, 27 U.C.C. Rep. Serv. 1071 (D. Utah 1979).

[155] "Discharge of the obligation does not affect any liability that the obligor may have as an indorser of the instrument." U.C.C. § 3-310(a).

[156] U.C.C. § 3-310(b)(1), (2).

[157] U.C.C. § 3-602(a). See § 7.02[A][1] supra.

[158] U.C.C. § 3-310(b)(1). After the depositary bank placed holds on checks issued in large amounts, the payee in Long v. Cuttle Const. Co., 70 Cal. Rptr. 2d 698, 34 U.C.C. Rep. Serv. 2d 418 (Cal. Ct. App. 1998), argued that the drawer's liability for interest continued to run during this interim period. The court disagreed, construing the provision on "discharge to the extent of the payment" as discharge to the same extent as if payment were made in money.

[159] U.C.C. § 3-310(b)(1).

[160] Taking a certified check results in discharge of the obligor's underlying obligation. U.C.C. § 3-310(a).

An indorser's underlying obligation also will be discharged upon any form of discharge of the indorser's liability on the instrument.[161] For example, assume that a payee of an uncertified check indorses it and transfers it to Seller in exchange for goods. An untimely delay in presenting the instrument for payment would discharge the obligor both on its indorsement contract and on the underlying obligation.[162]

Certain parties will not be allowed to pursue the underlying obligation. An obligee who takes an instrument but subsequently transfers it is such a party.[163] Assume that Seller takes an uncertified check for $750 from the drawer in partial exchange for goods sold for $1,000, and Seller then negotiates the check to X in exchange for services received from X. Having received compensation from X to induce transfer of the check, Seller's right to enforce the underlying obligation against the drawer is terminated to the extent of the $750 represented by the check.[164]

The other party that cannot pursue the underlying obligation is an obligee who is entitled to enforce an instrument but who does not have possession of the instrument because it was lost, stolen or destroyed. Such an obligee cannot enforce the underlying obligation to the extent of the amount that was payable on the instrument.[165] The rights of the obligee against the obligor are limited to enforcement of the instrument.[166]

When the underlying obligation has been suspended under the general rule, dishonor of the instrument entitles the obligee to maintain an action on either the underlying obligation or on the instrument.[167] For example, if a note was taken in exchange for a buyer's purchase obligation, the merchant who still held the note could, upon dishonor by the buyer, sue on the underlying Article 2 obligation to pay for the goods or on the Article 3 obligation on the instrument. Obviously, the merchant could not successfully pursue both actions as it would lead to double recovery. Generally, the Article 3 cause of action is preferable because of the procedural advantages.[168]

---

[161] "In the case of an instrument of a third person which is negotiated to the obligee by the obligor, discharge of the obligor on the instrument also discharges the obligation." U.C.C. § 3-310(b)(3).

[162] U.C.C. §§ 3-415(e), 3-310(b)(3); Greer v. White Oak State Bank, 673 S.W.2d 326, 39 U.C.C. Rep. Serv. 929 (Tex. Ct. App. 1984).

[163] "If the person entitled to enforce the instrument taken for an obligation is a person other than the obligee, the obligee may not enforce the obligation to the extent the obligation is suspended." U.C.C. § 3-310(b)(4).

[164] "Thus, if the seller sold the note or the check to a holder and has not reacquired it after dishonor, the only right that survives is the right to enforce the instrument." U.C.C. § 3-310, Comment 3.

[165] U.C.C. § 3-310(b)(4).

[166] U.C.C. § 3-310(b)(4). On the right to enforce a lost, destroyed or stolen instrument, see U.C.C. § 3-309 and § 4.06 *supra*.

[167] U.C.C. § 3-310(b)(3); Silk v. Merrill Lynch, Pierce, Fenner & Smith, Inc., 437 So. 2d 112, 37 U.C.C. Rep. Serv. 187 (Ala. 1983).

[168] U.C.C. § 3-308. *See* § 6.05 *supra*.

[B] Accord and Satisfaction — § 3-311

Sometimes when parties are in a dispute as to the amount of money that is owed to a claimant, the party upon which the claim is asserted will extend a payment in settlement of the dispute. A common issue has been whether acceptance of the payment ends the claim to any further amount that the claimant asserts. The discharge of a claim upon payment is known as an accord and satisfaction. Common law generally governs a discharge, but when an instrument is tendered by the person against whom the claim is asserted, section 3-311 applies.

The basic rule creates a discharge of the claim if several basic requirements are met.[169] The instrument must be tendered in full satisfaction of the claim. The amount of the claim must be unliquidated or the subject of a legitimate dispute. The claimant must receive payment of the instrument, as by cashing a check. Finally, the instrument or an accompanying writing must provide a conspicuous statement to the effect that the instrument was tendered in full satisfaction of the claim.[170]

The general rule is subject to two possible exceptions. Neither exception, however, will be available if the person against whom the claim is asserted can establish that the claimant knew that the instrument had been tendered in full satisfaction.[171] An organization can send a conspicuous statement to a person against whom a claim is asserted that requires communications with respect to disputed claims to be sent to a designated person or office. If the instrument or other notice of full satisfaction is not sent in compliance with this statement, the discharge as an accord and satisfaction will not apply.[172] This provision is designed to protect organizations that receive large numbers of instruments sent by customers from an inadvertent accord and satisfaction.[173]

The other exception to discharge as an accord and satisfaction allows the claimant to tender repayment of the amount of the instrument within ninety days to the person against whom the claim is asserted.[174] This exception is available to individuals and, as an alternative to the first exception, to organizations. It is not available, however, to an organization that sends the statement that invokes the first exception. This exception also protects claimants against inadvertent accord and satisfactions, but it enables a claimant to proceed with fast, routine processing of all checks received from customers.[175]

---

[169] U.C.C. § 3-311(a), (b).

[170] Futrelle v. Duke University, 127 N.C. App. 244, 488 S.E.2d 635, 35 U.C.C. Rep. Serv. 2d 1283 (1997) (letter accompanying a check sent to a discharged employee mentioned an arbitration proceeding directed toward the dispute as to the amount the employee was to receive).

[171] U.C.C. § 3-311(d).

[172] U.C.C. § 3-311(c)(1).

[173] U.C.C. § 3-311, Comment 5.

[174] U.C.C. § 3-311(c)(2).

[175] U.C.C. § 3-311, Comment 6.

Chapter 8
WARRANTY LIABILITY

SYNOPSIS

§ 8.01 Overview
    [A] Correlations with Other Warranty Law
        [1] Sales of Goods
        [2] Assignments
    [B] Distinct from Liability on the Instrument

§ 8.02 Organization of Warranty Provisions
    [A] Determining the Applicable Category of Warranty
    [B] Determining the Applicable Article

§ 8.03 Transfer Warranties — §§ 3-416, 4-207
    [A] Who Gives the Warranties
        [1] Transfer
        [2] Consideration
    [B] To Whom the Warranties Run
    [C] The Warranties
        [1] In General
        [2] Entitled to Enforce the Instrument
        [3] Signatures Authentic and Authorized
        [4] No Alterations
        [5] No Defense or Claim in Recoupment
        [6] No Knowledge of Insolvency Proceedings

§ 8.04 Presentment Warranties — §§ 3-417, 4-208
    [A] Who Gives the Warranties
    [B] To Whom the Warranties Run
    [C] The Warranties
        [1] When Unaccepted Drafts Are Paid or Accepted
            [a] Entitled to Enforce the Instrument
            [b] No Knowledge Signature of Drawer is Unauthorized
            [c] No Alterations
        [2] When Instruments Other Than Unaccepted Drafts are Paid

§ 8.05 Breach of Warranties — §§ 3-416(b), 3-417(b)

§ 8.01 Overview

Warranty theory provides a distinct basis for imposing liability on parties who deal with negotiable instruments. The Code warranties allocate responsibility for certain injuries that can occur with the circulation of notes and drafts. In addition, warranties protect justifiable reliance by subsequent parties who deal with negotiable instruments.

[A] Correlations with Other Warranty Law

[1] Sales of Goods

The warranty law of negotiable instruments has some close, but by no means exact, correlations with the warranty law of sales under Article 2. The sales article contains four separate sections that cover the creation of warranties: an implied warranty of title, two implied warranties of quality of goods sold, and an express warranty provision on quality.[1] The warranties of Articles 3 and 4 are implied warranties only and include warranties concerning specific attributes that affect the quality of the paper and title to it.[2] Articles 3 and 4 do not draw the same distinction between types of implied warranties of quality that Article 2 makes — essentially a difference based on fitness for ordinary purposes and fitness for particular purposes. Even though instruments can be used for more than one purpose, they are not the type of personal property that is supplied to meet unique, individualized objectives.

The negotiable instrument warranties are narrower in scope than the comparable implied sales warranty of fitness for ordinary purposes. The ordinary purpose of a draft or a promissory note is ultimate payment by the drawee or the maker, but the Code does not include a warranty that any party to the instrument is solvent or will pay the instrument.[3] Instead, Articles 3 and 4 provide assurances against specific defects in the paper, including unauthorized signatures and alterations.

Although the warranties created under Articles 3 and 4 are implied warranties only, additional express warranties can be created under the principle of freedom of contract. Unless they are written on the instrument, express warranties are unlikely to extend to anyone other than the immediate party to whom they are given, as subsequent parties probably would be unaware of them. If subsequent parties were aware, their reliance on the additional warranty would be necessary. Through express agreement,

---

[1] U.C.C. §§ 2-312, 2-314, 2-315, 2-313.

[2] U.C.C. §§ 3-416, 3-417, 4-207, 4-208. Article 4 also includes encoding and retention warranties that have relevance in electronic check collection. U.C.C. § 4-209. Regulation CC provides warranties used in the bank-collection process, primarily with respect to the return of dishonored checks. These warranties are discussed in the chapter on check collection. *See* § 11.04[C][4] *infra*.

[3] "Under subsection (a)(5) the transferor does not warrant against difficulties of collection, impairment of the credit of the obligor or even insolvency. The transferee is expected to determine such questions before taking the obligation." U.C.C. § 3-416, Comment 4.

warranty obligations can be incurred beyond those that arise automatically upon participation in transactions that invoke implied warranties.

[2] Assignments

The implied warranties of Articles 3 and 4 given by persons who transfer instruments roughly approximate the warranties given by assignors under the common law of contracts.[4] A basic distinction is that negotiable instrument warranties generally run to successive parties, whereas an assignor's warranties extend only to the assignee.[5] The more fundamental difference with the law of assignments is the right of recourse on an instrument when the obligor fails or refuses to pay.[6] In the absence of an express warranty, an assignor does not incur comparable contract liability.[7]

[B] Distinct from Liability on the Instrument

Although warranty liability is a facet of contract liability under Article 2 on sales of goods, warranty liability is completely separate from the contract liability that results when a person signs an instrument. A person can incur warranty liability without signing the instrument, whereas only a person who signs an instrument undertakes the contractual duties to pay it. Warranty liability stems either from transferring an instrument or from receiving payment or acceptance. Therefore, circulating an instrument, rather than signing it, is the activity that creates warranty obligations on negotiable instruments.

The distinction between warranty and contract liability can be illustrated best by identifying situations in which a valid cause of action can lie under one theory but not under the other. A cause of action can accrue on a party's contract obligation to pay an instrument without the contracting party having breached any of the applicable warranties. Conversely, when warranties are breached, several situations can preclude the availability of additional contract liability against the party breaching the warranty. A contract might never have been created, either because the prospective defendant did not sign the instrument[8] or because the signature disclaimed contract liability through a qualified indorsement.[9] Similarly, contract liability might have been discharged through payment[10] or through failure

---

[4] An assignor makes the following three warranties: "(a) that he will do nothing to defeat or impair the value of the assignment and has no knowledge of any fact which would do so; (b) that the right, as assigned, actually exists and is subject to no limitations or defenses good against the assignor other than those stated or apparent at the time of the assignment; (c) that any writing evidencing the right which is delivered to the assignee or exhibited to him to induce him to accept the assignment is genuine and what it purports to be." Restatement (Second) of Contracts § 333(1).

[5] Restatement (Second) of Contracts § 333(4).

[6] Contract liability on a negotiable instrument is covered in Chapter 4.

[7] Story v. Lamb, 52 Mich. 525, 18 N.W. 248 (1884); Wippert v. Blackfeet Tribe of the Blackfeet Indian Reservation, 201 Mont. 229, 654 P.2d 512 (1982).

[8] U.C.C. § 3-401(a).

[9] U.C.C. § 3-415(b).

[10] U.C.C. § 3-602.

to satisfy the requirements of presentment or notice of dishonor.[11] In contrast, a cause of action for breach of warranty "accrues when the claimant has reason to know of its breach."[12] An aggrieved party does not have to await satisfaction of the conditions to contract liability or the due date for payment of a time draft or note.

The distinction between contract and warranty liability is illustrated further through disclaimer of the respective liabilities. A qualified indorsement effectively disclaims contract liability of the indorser.[13] With the exception of checks,[14] warranty liability may also be disclaimed with respect to an instrument.[15] However, different terminology is required to disclaim each form of liability. The customary qualified indorsement to disclaim contract liability is an indorsement "without recourse."[16] This language will not disclaim any warranty liability.[17] A disclaimer of warranty liability requires an explicit statement to that effect.[18]

§ 8.02 Organization of Warranty Provisions

Articles 3 and 4 each codify two categories of warranties. The transfer warranties and the presentment warranties of the two articles overlap somewhat in content, but their applicability is mutually exclusive. The substance of both categories of warranties is essentially the same under both Articles 3 and 4, but their applicability again is mutually exclusive.

[A] Determining the Applicable Category of Warranty

The terminology "transfer warranties" and "presentment warranties" can be highly misleading in determining their correct application. It seems to suggest that the transfer warranties are given by anyone who transfers an instrument, whereas only parties who present instruments for payment or acceptance extend the presentment warranties. Scrutiny of the applicable warranty provisions reveals that this assumption is inaccurate because transferors give both the transfer and presentment warranties.[19]

Contrary to what their names suggest, the applicability of the categories of warranties is not distinguished primarily by the parties who give them,

---

[11] U.C.C. §§ 3-414(f), 3-415(c),(e).

[12] U.C.C. §§ 3-416(d), 4-207(e). See § 8.05[A] infra.

[13] U.C.C. § 3-415(b).

[14] U.C.C. §§ 3-416(c), 3-417(e) (disclaimer of Code warranties prohibited with respect to checks). The reason for the special treatment of checks is that they are paid through automated procedures that cannot detect a disclaimer. U.C.C. §§ 3-416, Comment 5; 3-417, Comment 7.

[15] U.C.C. §§ 3-416, Comment 5; 3-417, Comment 7.

[16] See § 4.03 supra.

[17] "The rationale is that while the purpose of a 'no recourse' indorsement is to avoid a guaranty of payment, the indorsement does not clearly indicate an intent to disclaim warranties." U.C.C. § 3-416, Comment 3.

[18] "In the case of an indorser, disclaimer of transferor's liability, to be effective, must appear in the indorsement with words such as 'without warranties' or some other specific reference to warranties." U.C.C. § 3-416, Comment 5.

[19] U.C.C. §§ 3-416(a); 3-417(a), (d)(1); 4-207(a); 4-208(a), (d).

but rather by the parties to whom they run. Presentment warranties run to a person who in good faith pays or accepts the instrument.[20] Until someone accepts or pays, these warranties do not extend to anyone. Upon acceptance or payment, the presenter and all prior transferors make the presentment warranties. The only recipient of these warranties is the entity that pays or accepts. Transfer warranties, on the other hand, run only to transferees. They always run to a transferor's immediate transferee, and often extend further to subsequent transferees.[21]

The correct determination of both the parties who give and who receive each category of warranty is crucial. The identification of proper plaintiffs and defendants on a warranty cause of action depends on this determination. The preamble language preceding the statement of the warranties identifies these parties.[22] The most fundamental distinction between transfer and presentment warranties is the parties to whom the warranties run.

Care must be exercised to avoid another incorrect assumption in determining the appropriate categories of warranties. Based on what happens to the instrument, payment of an instrument appears to involve a transfer. Since the holder voluntarily gives up possession upon payment, the holder appears to transfer the instrument to the payor. This line of reasoning, however, leads to the incorrect conclusion that the transfer warranties run in favor of the party who pays an instrument. Consistent with the common-law approach, the relinquishment of possession of an instrument to the payor upon its payment is surrender of the instrument and not a transfer.[23]

The drafters intended the applicability of the two categories of warranties to be mutually exclusive. Transfer warranties do not run to persons who pay or to payor banks.[24] These paying entities, as well as parties who accept, purposely receive a less-extensive array of presentment warranty protection. The most apparent aspect of the diminished protection is two fewer warranties. The content of the three presentment warranties cover the same subject matter as the corollary transfer warranties, but limitations make one of the warranties less inclusive.[25] The policy supporting

---

[20] U.C.C. §§ 3-417(a), (d)(1); 4-208(a), (d).

[21] U.C.C. §§ 3-416(a); 4-207(a).

[22] U.C.C. §§ 3-416(a) (Article 3 transfer warranties); 3-417(a), (d)(1) (Article 3 presentment warranties); 4-207(a) (Article 4 transfer warranties); 4-208(a), (d) (Article 4 presentment warranties).

[23] National Bank of Commerce v. Seattle Nat'l Bank, 109 Wash. 312, 187 P. 342 (1920). The party upon whom presentment of an instrument is made has the right to require the person making presentment to "surrender the instrument if full payment is made." U.C.C. § 3-501(b)(2). The surrender of the instrument upon payment is excluded from the scope of the definition of transfer of an instrument: "[I]f a check is presented for payment by delivering the check to the drawee, no transfer of the check to the drawee occurs because there is no intent to give the drawee the right to enforce the check." U.C.C. § 3-203, Comment 1. For discussion of the concept of transfer of an instrument, see § 3.03 *supra*.

[24] Florida Frozen Foods, Inc. v. National Commercial Bank & Trust Co., 439 N.Y.S.2d 771, 31 U.C.C. Rep. Serv. 643 (1981); Payroll Check Cashing v. New Palestine Bank, 401 N.E.2d 752, 28 U.C.C. Rep. Serv. 1421 (Ind. Ct. App. 1980).

[25] Furthermore, some payors of instruments receive only one presentment warranty.

the narrower range of presentment warranties is tied to the venerable case of *Price v. Neal*,[26] which is discussed below in footnote 92 and extensively in the next chapter.[27]

From a practical standpoint, payors could constantly evade the limitations and exclusions associated with presentment warranties if they could turn to the comparable but more expansive transfer warranties. For example, one of the transfer warranties is that all signatures are authentic and authorized.[28] The presentment warranty is not absolute but rather assures only that the warranting party has no knowledge that the signature of the drawer is unauthorized.[29] If a payor, upon discovering that the limitations on the scope of this warranty would preclude recovery, could turn to the absolute transfer warranty of authorization of all signatures, the limiting factors on presentment warranties would be rendered ineffectual.[30]

Thus, presentment and payment does not result in a transfer, and the transfer warranties do not run to the party that pays. The diagram below illustrates the distinction between the two categories of warranties. The dotted line in the diagram distinguishes presentment from transfer.

D'er ---- ▶P ──── ▶X ──── ▶Y ·········· ▶ Drawee

Diagram 8.1

The line in the diagram composed of dashes represents issue of the draft from the drawer to the payee. Because issue is also specifically excluded from the definition of transfer of an instrument,[31] the issuer does not extend either transfer or presentment warranties.

[B] Determining the Applicable Article

Articles 3 and 4 codify essentially identical substantive warranties.[32] The duplicative codification is necessary to reflect certain aspects peculiar to

---

[26] 97 Eng. Rep. 871 (K.B. 1762).

[27] *See* § 9.01[C][1] *infra*. A more condensed discussion is provided in § 8.04[C][1][b] *infra*.

[28] U.C.C. §§ 3-416(a)(2), 4-207(a)(2).

[29] U.C.C. §§ 3-417(a)(3), 4-207(a)(3).

[30] Ed Stinn Chevrolet, Inc. v. National City Bank, 28 Ohio St. 3d 221, 503 N.E.2d 524, 2 U.C.C. Rep. Serv. 2d 1565 (1986) (drawee bank cannot use warranties to avoid payment on forged drawer checks when the transferring party had no knowledge of the unauthorized signatures).

[31] "An instrument is transferred when it is delivered by a person *other than its issuer* for the purpose of giving to the person receiving delivery the right to enforce the instrument." U.C.C. § 3-203(a) (emphasis supplied). *See* § 3.03 *supra*.

[32] Article 4 includes one provision in its section on transfer warranties that is not duplicated in Article 3. *See* U.C.C. § 4-207(b); § 8.03[B] *infra*.

the bank-collection process. Because of these differences, determination of the appropriate article is a threshold question when dealing with warranties.[33]

With respect to the transfer warranties, the proper focus is on the persons who give the warranties. Article 4 applies once an item,[34] usually a check, enters the bank-collection process, whereas Article 3 applies to transactions outside of bank collection. An item enters the bank-collection process when a customer either presents the item to the payor bank for payment or deposits it with a collecting bank for purposes of collection. In this context, the term "customer" means "a person . . . for whom a bank has agreed to collect items."[35] In the downstream flow of the check toward payment, Article 4 describes the transfer warranties given by the customer and each of the successive collecting banks.[36]

The codification in section 3-416 covers the transfer warranties given by all other parties to an instrument. Obviously, if the instrument is never introduced into the check-collection process, the Article 3 warranties govern exclusively. This result follows in most cases involving promissory notes. Additionally, Article 3 dictates the transfer warranties of all transferors of an instrument prior to the time that the instrument enters the check-collection process, whereas Article 4 transfer warranties apply only when the instrument enters the banking system.

The diagram below helps illustrate the proper application of the transfer warranty section of each article.

```
              "P"    "X"    "Y"
D'er----▶P──────▶X──────▶Y──────▶DB──────▶IB·········▶PB
                                                      (pays)
```

Diagram 8.2

The Article 4 transfer warranties would commence with Y, the customer, introducing the check into the collection process and continue with the collecting banks, DB (depositary bank) and IB (intermediary bank). The transfer warranties of all of the transferors prior to Y (P and X) are codified in section 3-416.

The presentment warranties of Article 4 apply to items, while Article 3 presentment warranties apply to negotiable instruments that are not items.

---

[33] In the relatively few instances where the warranty provisions of Articles 3 and 4 conflict, the Article 4 provisions control. U.C.C. § 4-102(a).

[34] " 'Item' means an instrument or a promise or order to pay money handled by a bank for collection or payment." U.C.C. § 4-104(a)(9).

[35] U.C.C. § 4-104(a)(5); Marine Midland Bank, N.A. v. Price, Miller, Evans & Flowers, 57 N.Y.2d 220, 455 N.Y.S.2d 565, 441 N.E.2d 1083 (1982) (definition satisfied even though payee of check did not have an account with the collecting bank).

[36] The Article 4 transfer warranties govern "[a] customer or collecting bank that transfers an item and receives a settlement or other consideration." U.C.C. § 4-207(a).

Article 4 presentment warranties apply to the check indicated in Diagram 8.2. Because the presentment warranties of Articles 3 and 4 are identical, the selection of the appropriate Article is not as critical.

§ 8.03 Transfer Warranties — §§ 3-416, 4-207

Because the transfer warranties are more numerous and more expansive in scope than the presentment warranties, they are discussed first. The subsequent discussion of presentment warranties will develop their limitations and the rationales underlying their narrower scope.

[A] Who Gives the Warranties

Section 3-416(a) provides that "[a] person who transfers an instrument for consideration" makes five transfer warranties. The same warranties are made under section 4-207(a) by "[a] customer or collecting bank that transfers an item and receives a settlement or other consideration." The requisite elements under both articles are transfer and receipt of consideration.

[1] Transfer

Persons who transfer instruments give the transfer warranties. Article 3 provides that an instrument is transferred "when it is delivered by a person other than its issuer for the purpose of giving to the person receiving delivery the right to enforce the instrument."[37] The transfer warranties relate to various attributes of the instrument and its transfer that can affect the value of the instrument in the hands of the transferee. Transfer of an instrument results in transfer warranties, irrespective of indorsement. A transfer without indorsement precludes creation of contract liability, but does not escape the transfer warranties. Conversely, a person who makes an anomalous indorsement does not give the warranties because this indorser does not transfer the instrument.[38]

[2] Consideration

Only those persons who receive consideration for their transfer of an instrument give transfer warranties. The requirement of consideration precludes applying transfer warranty liability against parties who make donative transfers or against accommodation parties who are not compensated for providing their signatures.[39] For purposes of Article 4 warranties, any settlement is sufficient.

Although the requirement of consideration seems to result from the conceptualization of warranty recovery as a contract or sales remedy, a

---

[37] U.C.C. § 3-203(a). See § 3.03 supra.

[38] See U.C.C. § 3-205(d); § 4.04[D] supra; First Nat'l Bank v. Montgomery, 9 Pa. D. & C.3d 491, 27 U.C.C. Rep. Serv. 164 (C.P. 1979).

[39] Oak Park Currency Exchange, Inc. v. Maropoulos, 48 Ill. App. 3d 437, 363 N.E.2d 54, 21 U.C.C. Rep. Serv. 1380 (1977).

consistent underlying rationale remains elusive. A donor who signs an instrument incurs contract liability. Admittedly, the lack of consideration is a defense against a person who does not have the rights of a holder in due course.[40] However, a subsequent holder in due course cannot successfully assert a breach of a transfer warranty against a donor who transfers by indorsement, even though the subsequent party may have relied upon the indorsement and have had no means of knowing that the donor's transfer was without consideration. Nevertheless, the same donor-transferor who is exempted from transfer warranties extends the presentment warranties because consideration is not included as an element of a transferor's liability for presentment warranties. As a result, a donor-transferor's warranty liability depends on the fortuity of whether the aggrieved payor seeks recovery directly from the donor as a prior transferor for breach of presentment warranties or elects to pursue a different party.

[B] To Whom the Warranties Run

The Article 3 transfer warranties always run to immediate transferees. They also extend beyond to subsequent transferees if the transfer is by indorsement. With an indorsement the warranty is not just personal to the transferee, but rather runs with the instrument. This extension of warranties allows warranty causes of action against distant upstream parties, thus avoiding a multiplicity of lawsuits.[41] Even though most aggrieved parties are likely to look to their immediate transferor for relief, the additional prospective defendants can be very beneficial when the transferor is insolvent or cannot be found.

The Article 4 transfer warranties operate somewhat differently. They always run from the transferor "to the transferee and to any subsequent collecting bank."[42] Article 4 does not specifically require an indorsement for the warranties to run with the instrument. All transfers within the check-collection process thus include transfer warranties that run to all of the subsequent collecting banks.[43]

The latter provision was included to alleviate the necessity of the banking practice of express warranties that developed prior to adoption of the Code. Payor banks that made payments by mistake because they had not detected a forged indorsement used a restitution theory to recover. The case of *National Park Bank v. Seaboard Bank*[44] held that if an agent collecting bank paid the money it collected to its principal, the collecting bank would no longer be liable to the payor bank, because "an agent who has received money paid by mistake cannot be compelled to repay it where he has paid it over to his principal without notice."[45] In order to avoid requiring the

---

[40] U.C.C. §§ 3-303(b), 3-305(a)(2),(b).

[41] U.C.C. § 3-416, Comment 1.

[42] U.C.C. § 4-207(a).

[43] Guaranty Bank & Trust Co. v. Federal Reserve Bank, 454 F. Supp. 488, 24 U.C.C. Rep. Serv. 932 (W.D. Okla. 1977).

[44] 114 N.Y. 28, 20 N.E. 632 (1889).

[45] 114 N.Y. at 35, 20 N.E. at 634.

payor bank to proceed against the transferor of the presenting bank, rather than against the presenter itself, banks began stamping their indorsements "P.E.G." or "prior endorsements guaranteed."[46] This indorsement preserved a cause of action against the presenting bank with which the payor bank had conducted its business.[47] Although the Code uses an underlying warranty theory of recovery rather than restitution, the Article 4 transfer-warranty codfication is intended to preserve the same relationships that developed in check collection without the necessity of providing the P.E.G. indorsement.

Article 4 goes even further than allowing the five standard transfer warranties to run with the instrument even in the absence of an indorsement. Section 4-207(b) provides a further engagement that also arises notwithstanding the absence of indorsement: "If an item is dishonored, a customer or collecting bank transferring the item and receiving settlement or other consideration is obliged to pay the amount due on the item (i) according to the terms of the item at the time it was transferred, or (ii) if the transfer was of an incomplete item, according to its terms when completed as stated in Sections 3-115 and 3-407." This "obligation of a transferor is owed to the transferee and to any subsequent collecting bank that takes the item in good faith."[48] It is an obligation that is comparable to an indorser's contract liability that is incurred upon signing an instrument.[49] It is stated as a transfer warranty because conceptually it cannot be imposed as a contract obligation if the customer or collecting bank does not indorse the instrument. The five standard transfer warranties and an obligation comparable to an indorser's contract obligation thus arise automatically as part of the bank-collection process, and they also automatically run with the instrument. Retaining these standard liabilities without requiring signatures enables intermediary banks to bypass actually indorsing the large bundles of checks they receive or having to return a check to a customer who forgets to indorse.

In Diagram 8.2,[50] Y and DB (the depository bank), irrespective of whether they indorse, extend the Article 4 transfer warranties that run with the check to all subsequent transferees. By comparison, P's transfer warranties under Article 3 would run only to X if P did not indorse. With an indorsement, P's warranties run to all of the subsequent transferees, including the collecting banks.

---

[46] "Even without the warranty sections of the U.C.C., the universal banking practice that collecting banks stamp the word 'Prior Endorsements Guaranteed,' or an abbreviation thereof (e.g., PEG) . . . gives a guarantee against forged endorsements to the drawee or payor bank." Society Nat'l Bank v. Capital Nat'l Bank, 30 Ohio App. 2d 1, 281 N.E.2d 563, 10 U.C.C. Rep. Serv. 831 (1972).

[47] A collecting bank that stamped P.E.G. on a check created an express warranty of genuineness of prior indorsements. Lewittes Furniture Enter., Inc. v. Peoples Nat'l Bank, 82 Misc. 2d 1013, 372 N.Y.S.2d 830, 17 U.C.C. Rep. Serv. 1265 (Sup. Ct. 1975). The indorsement has now been abolished for intermediary banks by federal regulation. See § 11.04[C][3] *infra*.

[48] U.C.C. § 4-207(b).

[49] *Compare* U.C.C. § 3-415(a).

[50] *See* § 8.02[B] *supra*.

Even when the warranties run with the instrument, they still warrant the state of facts at the time of transfer only. For example, some of the transfer warranties cover the absence of forged indorsements and the absence of any material alterations. If these defects exist in the paper upon transfer, the warranties are breached in favor of any subsequent party to whom they run. On the other hand, if the instrument was altered after the transfer, the breach of warranty could be traced only to transferors who transferred following the alteration.[51]

[C] The Warranties

[1] In General

Each transferor of an instrument warrants that

(a) the warrantor is a person entitled to enforce the instrument,

(b) all signatures on the instrument are authentic and authorized,

(c) the instrument has not been altered,

(d) the instrument is not subject to a defense or claim in recoupment of any party which can be asserted against the warrantor, and

(e) the warrantor has no knowledge of any insolvency proceeding commenced with respect to the maker or acceptor or, in the case of an unaccepted draft, the drawer.[52]

[2] Entitled to Enforce the Instrument

The first transfer warranty is related directly to the legal consequence of the transfer of an instrument. A transfer vests in the transferee any right of the transferor to enforce the instrument.[53] The first transfer warranty is a warranty that the transferor is a person entitled to enforce the instrument.[54] Satisfaction of the warranty requires the transferor to be a holder of the instrument or, if a nonholder in possession of the instrument, the transferor must have the rights of a holder.[55] If the transferor is not entitled to enforce the instrument, the transferee also will not be entitled to enforce it, and the warranty will be breached upon the transfer. This warranty protects the transferee against the risk that it will not be able to enforce the instrument and against the warranty liability that the transferee will incur if it further transfers the instrument.

In essence, the first transfer warranty is "a warranty that there are no unauthorized or missing indorsements that prevent the transferor from

---

[51] American Nat'l Bank & Trust Co. v. St. Joseph Valley Bank, 389 N.E.2d 379, 26 U.C.C. Rep. Serv. 1174 (Ind. Ct. App. 1979) ("obvious that an endorser does not warrant against future forgeries or alterations").

[52] U.C.C. §§ 3-416(a), 4-207(a). The Article 4 warranty section also includes an obligation to honor an item upon its dishonor. See § 8.03[B] supra.

[53] U.C.C. § 3-203(b). See § 3.03 supra.

[54] U.C.C. § 3-416, Comment 1.

[55] U.C.C. § 3-301. See § 3.05 supra.

making the transferee a person entitled to enforce the instrument."[56] In order to enforce the instrument in the absence of attaining holder status, the transferee must be able to trace derivative enforcement rights through successive transfers back to a holder of the instrument. Consider the facts in the following diagram.

$$\text{D'er} \dashrightarrow \text{P} \xrightarrow{\substack{\text{"Pay X"}\\\text{"P"}}} \text{X} \longrightarrow \text{Y} \longrightarrow \text{Z}$$

Diagram 8.3

X attained holder status through negotiation of the instrument with the special indorsement. Even though X did not indorse to enable Y to become a holder, Y nevertheless derivatively acquired X's right to enforce the instrument, because the instrument was transferred to Y by the holder X. Z subsequently took by transfer and thus derivatively acquired the rights of Y, which include X's rights as a holder to enforce the instrument. The transfers by X and Y both enabled the respective transferees to become a person entitled to enforce the instrument, so neither transferor breached the first warranty.

Assume now that Y stole the instrument from X. X's right to enforce the instrument now did not vest in Y because Y did not take the instrument through transfer. Y subsequently transferred the instrument to Z, but Z received only Y's rights and those rights now do not include the right of X to enforce the instrument. Because Y did not take the instrument by transfer, Y could neither attain or nor pass any derivative right to enforce the instrument. The only way left for Y to be entitled to enforce the instrument would be to qualify as a holder. Because the instrument continues to run to X, however, Y cannot qualify as a holder.[57] Thus, irrespective of whether X's indorsement is missing or forged, Y breaches the first warranty upon transferring the instrument to Z following the theft. If Z subsequently were to transfer the instrument, Z would also breach the same warranty.

---

[56] U.C.C. § 3-416, Comment 2.

[57] If the instrument had been stolen in bearer form, Y would have qualified as a holder, and thereby would have been empowered to enforce the instrument. Because no further indorsement would have been required to attain this status, Y could transfer the instrument to Z without breaching the first transfer warranty.

Note that following a forged indorsement of order paper, all subsequent transferors of the instrument will breach the first transfer warranty. If there are multiple transferees following transfer by the forger, ultimate liability should lie on the forger. Since forgers generally cannot be found or do not have the financial capacity to satisfy a judgment, ultimate liability often stops at the first solvent party downstream from the forger.[58] This relationship of the parties is shown in the diagram provided below.

```
           O.I.
       M----▶P
            |
            ▼   "P"  "T"         "X"
            T ─────────▶X─────────▶Y
```

Diagram 8.4

Y is in possession of a note that still runs to Payee (P) because the forgery of P's signature by Thief (T) is not P's indorsement. Both T and X breached the first transfer warranty because neither of them is a person entitled to enforce the instrument. Every transferor of this note following the forgery by T will breach this warranty. Ultimate liability should fall on the scoundrel T, but if T cannot or will not pay, X will be stuck with the ultimate liability.

[3] Signatures Authentic and Authorized

The second transfer warranty is that all signatures are authentic and authorized.[59] Obviously, a breach of this warranty overlaps with breach of the warranty that a person is entitled to enforce the instrument whenever someone transfers an instrument with a forged indorsement in the chain of transfer. However, this warranty reaches a broader array of forgeries. It covers the authenticity of signatures in any capacity, including drawers, makers, acceptors, and even indorsers whose signatures are not necessary for negotiation of an instrument.[60]

The transfer warranty on signatures protects a transferee's reliance on the appearance that prior parties have incurred liability on the instrument. A transferee seeking to collect on that apparent contract liability will be unsuccessful if the signature was forged. The warranty on authenticity of signatures can be breached if the signature was made by someone other than the person indicated by the signature. The warranty, however, has two components. The warranty is that each signature is authentic *and*

---

[58] Girard Bank v. Mount Holly State Bank, 474 F. Supp. 1225, 26 U.C.C. Rep. Serv. 1210 (D. N.J. 1979); Bank of the West v. Wes-Con Dev. Co., Inc., 15 Wash. App. 238, 548 P.2d 563, 19 U.C.C. Rep. Serv. 593 (1976).

[59] U.C.C. §§ 3-416(a)(2), 4-207(a)(2).

[60] First Nat'l City Bank v. Bankers Trust Co., 4 U.C.C. Rep. Serv. 324 (N.Y. Sup. Ct. 1967) (forged draft).

authorized. Even though a person named did not sign, the warranty is not breached if that person authorized the signature, even if the agency role is not disclosed on the instrument.[61]

Even a holder in due course who transfers an instrument with an unauthorized signature breaches this warranty. The subsequent transferee cannot enforce the instrument against the person named in the forged signature. The shelter principle does not aid the transferee because even the holder in due course does not acquire rights against the person named in the forgery.

Consider the facts diagramed below:

```
             "E"      "P"
        D'er ----▶P ────────▶DB ────────▶IB
```

Diagram 8.5

Dishonest Employee (D) forges the name of his employer (E) on a check and issues the check to Payee (P). P then indorses in blank and transfers the check to Depositary Bank (DB), which in turn transfers the check in the collection process to Intermediary Bank (IB). Neither of the transferors (P and DB) breach their warranty that they are a person entitled to enforce the check. The unauthorized use of the employer's name does not constitute the signature of the employer, and the employer does not incur liability on the instrument. The forged drawer's signature operates as the signature of the thief.[62] The resulting instrument is the forger's check, not the employer's. For purposes of contract liability and the first transfer warranty, issuance of the check with the forged drawer's signature is equivalent to issuance of the check in the forger's own name. Transfer of the check with a forged drawer's signature, however, breaches the warranty that all signatures are authentic and authorized. In the diagram above, this warranty is breached by both P and DB, even if they qualified as a holder in due course of the check.

[4] No Alterations

The third transfer warranty is that the instrument has not been altered. In addition to relying on the authenticity of signatures that appear on an instrument, transferees are likely to rely on the terms of the instrument. This warranty provides protection to transferees when an alteration discharges prior parties, or limits their liability to the original tenor of the

---

[61] U.C.C. § 3-402. *See* § 4.05[A] *supra*; First Nat'l Bank v. Nunn, 628 P.2d 1110, 31 U.C.C. Rep. Serv. 1041 (Mont. 1981).

[62] U.C.C. § 3-403(a). *See* § 4.05[B] *supra*.

instrument or to the terms of authority given in the case of incomplete instruments.[63]

A transferor who alters the instrument and any subsequent transferor breach this warranty.[64]

$100 $1,000
M----▶P————————▶X————————▶Y————————▶Z
                         (HDC)

Diagram 8.6

In the diagram above, both X and Y breach. As a holder in due course, Y can enforce the note against M or P only according to its original terms of $100,[65] assuming that neither of these parties negligently contributed to the alteration.[66] In transferring the note that had been altered to $1,000 to Z, Y (like X) would breach the warranty. Z's reasonable assumption that he will receive $1,000 from M is erroneous. The transfer warranty protects that reasonable expectation.

If, in Diagram 8.6, P had been the party who acted improperly by writing an amount of $1,000 on an incomplete note when the authority given by M was only for $100, Y could use her holder-in-due-course status to enforce the instrument as completed against M.[67] As a subsequent transferee from a holder in due course, Z could use the shelter principle to demand the same payment. Nevertheless, each transferor of the instrument, beginning with P and including Y as a holder in due course, would breach the warranty against alteration. The warranty is absolute, and the completion of an incomplete instrument other than as authorized is an alteration.[68] Just as a transferor to a holder in due course cannot require the transferee to assert the rights of that status, the holder in due course cannot require a subsequent transferee to rely upon the shelter principle. These transferees take an instrument to acquire expected rights on it, not to buy into a lawsuit.

---

[63] U.C.C. § 3-407. For discussion on the effects of alteration of instruments, see § 7.02[F] *supra*.

[64] Garnac Grain Co., Inc. v. Boatmen's Bank & Trust Co., 694 F. Supp. 1389, 7 U.C.C. Rep. Serv. 2d 505 (W.D. Mo. 1988) (each transferor breached); Morgan Guar. Trust Co. v. Chase Manhattan Bank, N.A., 36 U.C.C. Rep. Serv. 584 (N.Y. Sup. Ct. 1983) (collecting bank entitled to recover from depository bank; depository bank entitled to recover against customer who altered check).

[65] U.C.C. § 3-407(c)(i). If Y took the instrument without the requisite bona fides of value, good faith, and absence of notice of the alteration, M and P would be discharged on their obligations. U.C.C. § 3-407(b). See § 7.02[F] *supra*.

[66] U.C.C. § 3-406. For discussion of the effect of negligence contributing to the alteration of an instrument, see § 10.02[A] *infra*.

[67] U.C.C. § 3-407(c)(ii).

[68] U.C.C. § 3-407(a)(ii).

[5] No Defense or Claim in Recoupment

The fourth transfer warranty is that the instrument is not subject to a defense or a claim in recoupment that can be asserted against the warrantor.[69] The warranty is absolute, covering all defenses and claims in recoupment. The warranty is personal to the transferor, however, because it covers only defenses that would be effective against the transferor. It does not warrant the absence of effective defenses against other parties to the instrument. The warranty essentially is that if the transferor were to bring an action to enforce the contract of any party that extends to the transferor, none of the parties would have a defense or claim in recoupment that could be asserted successfully against the transferor.

Note the relationship between the first and the fourth transfer warranties. The first transfer warranty provides assurances that the transferor is a person entitled to enforce the instrument because the transferee will then, as a minimum through the derivative rights acquired, also be someone who can enforce the instrument. That warranty does not provide adequate protection, however, because the availability of valid defenses can make a party's liability on an instrument unenforceable. The fourth warranty, therefore, provides assurances that no one can successfully assert a defense or a claim in recoupment against the transferor because, through the shelter principle, the transferee would also be insulated from defenses and claims in recoupment.[70] Due to the personal nature of this warranty, the availability of holder-in-due-course rights must be considered with respect to each transferor.

Consider the application of these concepts to the facts diagramed below:

```
                 B.I.              "X"
            M----▶P────────▶X────────▶Y
          (infant)         (HDC)
```

Diagram 8.7

The maker (M) is an infant who issues a note in bearer form to Payee (P), who is aware of M's infancy status. P transfers the note without indorsement to X, who qualifies as a holder in due course. X indorses the note and transfers it to Y. If M's infancy is a real defense,[71] M could assert that defense against either P or X if they were to attempt to enforce M's contract liability. P and X thus would have breached the transfer warranty against valid defenses.

If M's defense of infancy were not a real defense, Y could exercise X's holder-in-due-course rights that were attained through shelter to cut off the defense and successfully assert a contract claim against M.[72] If M

---

[69] U.C.C. §§ 3-416(a)(4), 4-207(a)(4).

[70] U.C.C. § 3-203(b). *See* § 6.02[C] *supra*.

[71] *See* § 6.02[B][2][a] *supra*.

[72] M's defense would be valid only against an enforcement action brought as a right of recourse by P.

dishonors the note, however, Y would probably prefer to proceed against X. X did not breach the fourth transfer warranty because, as a holder in due course, M's defense of infancy could not be asserted against X. X nevertheless did indorse the note, and Y could pursue her right of recourse, as the conditions to X's contract liability can be satisfied. X, in turn, would not have an action on the instrument against P because P did not sign the note. A warranty cause of action, however, would lie against P. P transferred an instrument that was subject to a defense of infancy that could be asserted against P. Even though X took the note as a holder in due course free of M's defense, P still breached the warranty. M would have already dishonored the note, so X surely would prefer the option of proceeding against P on the breach of warranty.[73]

[6] No Knowledge of Insolvency Proceedings

The fifth and last transfer warranty concerns insolvency.[74] It encompasses far less than a general guarantee of the solvency of the parties to the instrument because three limitations substantially narrow the scope of this warranty. First, the warranty is only that insolvency proceedings have not been commenced.[75] It covers both voluntary and involuntary proceedings, but does not warrant against insolvencies in the absence of an initiated proceeding. Second, the warranty covers only proceedings instituted with respect to a maker, an acceptor, or a drawer of an unaccepted draft. It does not reach insolvency proceedings commenced against indorsers. Finally, the warranty is not absolute, but is that the transferor lacks knowledge that an insolvency proceeding has been commenced against the requisite parties.[76]

The scope of protection that this warranty is designed to provide is limited. The buyer of an instrument is allocated the burden of ascertaining most of the factors relevant to solvency. Consequently, the transferor does not warrant anyone's credit worthiness or solvency in a commercial sense. The warranty protects merely against a transferor fraudulently concealing specified knowledge that unquestionably would deter most informed purchasers from proceeding.[77]

---

[73] "Even if the transferee takes as a holder in due course who takes free of the defense or claim in recoupment, the warranty gives the transferee the option of proceeding against the transferor rather than litigating with the obligor on the instrument the issue of the holder-in-due-course status of the transferee." U.C.C. § 3-416, Comment 3.

[74] U.C.C. §§ 3-416(a)(5), 4-207(a)(5).

[75] A.I.C. Fin. Corp. v. Walter E. Heller & Co., 59 Wis. 2d 508, 208 N.W.2d 446, 12 U.C.C. Rep. Serv. 1162 (Wis. Ct. App. 1973).

[76] If a party to an instrument has been discharged through an insolvency proceeding, the transferor breaches the warranty that no defenses are good against him. Discharge in insolvency proceedings is a real defense that is good even against a holder in due course. U.C.C. § 3-305(a)(1)(iv). See § 6.02[B][2][d] supra.

[77] U.C.C. § 3-416, Comment 4.

§ 8.04 Presentment Warranties — §§ 3-417, 4-208

[A] Who Gives the Warranties

Section 3-417(a) and section 4-208(a) both provide that if an unaccepted draft is presented to the drawee for payment or acceptance, "(i) the person obtaining payment or acceptance, at the time of presentment, and (ii) a previous transferor of the draft, at the time of the transfer" make three presentment warranties. Section 3-417(d)(1) and section 4-208(d) both state one presentment warranty, with essentially the same persons giving the warranty: the person obtaining payment and a prior transferor of the instrument. A person receiving payment or acceptance gives only the presentment warranties. All transferors give both the transfer and the presentment warranties on instruments that are ultimately accepted or paid.

[B] To Whom the Warranties Run

The three presentment warranties run under both Article 3 and Article 4 only to the drawee making payment or accepting an unaccepted draft in good faith.[78] Until the unaccepted draft is paid or accepted, the presentment warranties do not run to anyone. The drawee is the party ordered to pay a draft, and the other parties dealing with the draft expect the drawee to pay it.

Only one presentment warranty applies when the payor is the drawer or an indorser of a dishonored draft or is the party obliged to pay any other instrument.[79] This single warranty applies in all cases of payment other than the payment of an unaccepted draft,[80] which means it applies to the payment of notes (maker obligated to pay) and accepted drafts (acceptor obligated to pay), as well as the payment of dishonored drafts by the drawer or an indorser.[81] The reasons for the more-limited warranty coverage in these cases is explained below.[82]

It is important to remember that the transfer of an instrument downstream for value does not constitute payment of the instrument. Thus, even if a depositary bank gives its customer cash over the counter for the face value of a check drawn on another bank, the depositary bank has not paid the check.[83] The bank has agreed to collect the check and has made a cash advance against it.[84] The transaction between the bank and its customer

---

[78] U.C.C. §§ 3-417(a), 4-208(a).

[79] U.C.C. §§ 3-417(d)(1), 4-208(d).

[80] Payment of an unaccepted draft by the drawee results in the three presentment warranties of sections 3-417(a) and 4-207(a).

[81] U.C.C. § 3-417, Comment 4.

[82] See § 8.04[C][2] infra.

[83] Stone & Webster Engineering Corp. v. First Nat'l Bank & Trust Co., 345 Mass. 1, 184 N.E.2d 358, 1 U.C.C. Rep. Serv. 195 (1962) (bank that cashed check drawn on another bank was not the payor bank).

[84] U.C.C. § 4-210(a)(3). See § 6.01[B][2] supra; Cooper v. Union Bank, 9 Cal.3d 123, 107 Cal. Rptr. 1, 507 P.2d 609, 12 U.C.C. Rep. Serv. 209 (1973) (money paid over the counter by a collecting bank is "the bank's own money").

is a transfer, not a payment. Therefore, the customer gives the transfer warranties to the depositary bank rather than the presentment warranties. A visualization of this relationship is provided in the diagram below. The presentment for payment is distinguished from prior transfers through use of a dotted line. In the diagram, only the payor bank paid the check.

```
              "P"
D'er ---- ▶P ────▶DB ────▶IB ········▶PB
                                     (pays)
```

Diagram 8.8

[C] The Warranties

The presentment warranties are narrower in scope than the transfer warranties. Three presentment warranties are extended when a drawee pays or accepts an unaccepted draft. These warranties cover the same subject matter as the first three transfer warranties, but they do not include comparable warranties of no valid defense and no knowledge of insolvency proceedings. Furthermore, the three presentment warranties are somewhat narrower in substantive coverage than their transfer-warranty counterparts. When an instrument other than an unaccepted draft is paid, only a single presentment warranty applies.

The coverage of the presentment warranties reflects two major policy determinations. One objective is to advance the finality doctrine, which is addressed in the next chapter of this book.[85] The other policy is based on risk allocation. When the payor or acceptor would not suffer a loss, or when either of these parties is in the best position to protect against losses, they do not receive the benefit of warranties. For example, a payor does not need a warranty that no valid defenses are available against the party presenting for payment because payors do not enforce the instruments that they pay.[86] Also, since a payor or acceptor can determine better than the presenter whether a drawer's account is in proper order, presenters do not warrant the sufficiency of funds in the account or that a stop-payment order has not been issued. Additional examples of how the policy is applied through codification of the presentment warranties are discussed below.

[1] When Unaccepted Drafts are Paid or Accepted

[a] Entitled to Enforce the Instrument

The first presentment warranty given to a drawee who pays or accepts an unaccepted draft is a warranty that the transferors at the time of their transfers were persons entitled to enforce the draft and that the presenter

---

[85] *See* § 9.01[C] *infra*.

[86] Furthermore, if the draft is properly payable, the drawee is entitled to charge the account of the drawer for the amount of the draft. U.C.C. § 4-401(a). *See* § 12.02[B] *infra*.

is either a person entitled to enforce the draft or is authorized to obtain payment or enforcement on behalf of a person who is entitled to enforce the draft.[87] The substance of the first presentment warranty is identical to the comparable transfer warranty.[88] Like the transfer warranty, it "in effect is a warranty that there are no unauthorized or missing indorsements."[89] A forged indorsement on order paper means that the instrument is not properly payable and a drawee who pays such a draft can be required to recredit the drawer's account.[90] This absolute warranty is needed to protect the drawee against such mistaken payments.

[b] No Knowledge Signature of Drawer is Unauthorized

Another presentment warranty given to the drawee who pays or accepts an unaccepted draft is narrower than the corollary transfer warranty that all signatures are authentic and authorized. This presentment warranty is not an absolute guarantee of the authenticity of any signature. The first presentment warranty is the only one that absolutely warrants the validity of a signature, and its effect is limited to indorsements of order paper. The presentment warranty with respect to the drawer's signature is only that the warrantor has no knowledge that the signature of the drawer of the draft is unauthorized.[91] Thus, transfer or presentment of a draft with a forged drawer's signature will not breach this warranty in the absence of knowledge of the forgery.

The reason for the disparate treatment of a forged drawer's signature and a forged indorsement on an unaccepted draft is that a drawee can verify a drawer's signature with the signature card in its possession, but the drawee has no similar method to verify indorsement signatures.[92] On the

---

[87] U.C.C. §§ 3-417(a)(1), 4-207(a)(1).

[88] *Compare* U.C.C. § 3-417(a)(1), *with* U.C.C. § 3-416(a)(1); U.C.C. § 4-208(a)(1), *with* U.C.C. § 4-207(a)(1). The additional language in the first presentment warranty simply addresses the potential agency relationship involved at the presentment stage.

[89] U.C.C. § 3-417, Comment 2; First Nat'l Bank of Chicago v. Midamerica Fed. Sav. Bank, 303 Ill. App. 3d 176, 707 N.E.2d 673, 37 U.C.C. Rep. Serv. 2d 1104 (1999).

[90] U.C.C. § 4-401(a). See § 12.02[B][2] *infra*.

[91] U.C.C. §§ 3-417(a)(3), 4-207(a)(3).

[92] The different treatment of the two types of forgeries reflects the results of pre-Code case law. A payor who paid on a forged drawer's signature was not allowed to recover in Price v. Neal, 97 Eng. Rep. 871 (K.B. 1762). The court in Canal Bank v. Bank of Albany, 1 Hill 287 (N.Y. Sup. Ct. 1841) permitted the payor bank to recover after it had paid on a forged indorsement. Sections 3-417(a) and 4-208(a) essentially codify the results of these decisions. "Subsection (a)(1) retains the rule that the drawee does not admit the authenticity of indorsements and subsection (a)(3) retains the rule of Price v. Neal, 3 Burr. 1354 (1762), that the drawee takes the risk that the drawer's signature is unauthorized unless the person presenting the draft has knowledge that the drawer's signature is unauthorized." U.C.C. § 3-417, Comment 3. The reference in the Comment to the authenticity of indorsements clearly is drawn from the concept of the *Canal Bank* opinion: "Neither acceptance nor payment, at any time, nor under any circumstances, is an admission, that the first, or any other endorser's name is genuine." 1 Hill at 289. For more detailed discussion of the rationales behind these decisions, see § 9.01[C][1], [D] *infra*.

other hand, the genuineness of each transferor's signature can be ascertained best by each succeeding transferee.[93] Careful examination of the instrument and reasonable identification procedures can be employed to minimize the chances of forged indorsements. Because drawees have the best opportunity to detect forged drawer's signatures and transferees can best detect forged indorsements, the presentment-warranty provisions allocate any resulting losses accordingly.

The same rationale explains why the first presentment warranty is breached when a necessary indorsement on order paper is missing or when a transferor or presenter exceeds delegated authority when acting on behalf of another person. Each transferee taking an instrument is in the superior position to detect the absence of a missing necessary indorsement.[94] Similarly, agents are in the best position to know the extent of their authority, and their transferees are in the best position to verify that authority.

Although transferors and presenters are generally relieved from any Code warranty on the genuineness of the drawer's signature, they are subject to warranty liability to a drawee who pays or accepts an unaccepted draft when they know that the signature was unauthorized. Transferring or presenting the instrument with such knowledge is fraudulent, and the drawee is protected against such fraud through the warranty.

[c] No Alterations

A final presentment warranty given to a drawee who pays or accepts an unaccepted draft is an absolute warranty that the draft has not been altered.[95] It is thus comparable to the transfer warranty that the instrument has not been not altered.[96] The presentment warranty is needed to protect a drawee who pays an instrument according to terms that are an alteration to the terms provided by the drawer, as the drawee's right to charge the drawer's account in such a case will be limited.[97] Unlike its drawer's signature, the drawee does not have a readily available means to verify the accuracy of the terms to the agreement. The drawee is just as vulnerable with respect to an alteration as it is to a forged indorsement. Hence the presentment warranty protection is extended.

---

[93] Stapleton v. First Security Bank, 675 P.2d 83, 37 U.C.C. Rep. Serv. 847 (Mont. 1983); First Nat'l Bank v. Trust Co., 510 F. Supp. 651, 32 U.C.C. Rep. Serv. 909 (N.D. Ga. 1981).

[94] A purpose of the rule embodied in the first presentment warranty is "to speed up the collection and transfer of checks and to take the burden off each bank to meticulously check the endorsements of each item transferred." Federal Deposit Ins. Corp. v. Marine Nat'l Bank, 303 F. Supp. 401, 403, 6 U.C.C. Rep. Serv. 762, 765 (M.D. Fla. 1969).

[95] U.C.C. §§ 3-417(a)(2), 4-207(a)(2).

[96] See § 8.03[C][4] supra.

[97] U.C.C. § 4-401(d). See § 12.02[B][3] infra.

[2] When Instruments Other Than Unaccepted Drafts are Paid

Only the first presentment warranty applies with respect to the payment of any instrument other than payment of an unaccepted draft by the drawee.[98] Payors of these instruments thus do not receive a warranty against alterations, and the only warranty that they receive concerning signatures is a warranty that there are no missing or unauthorized indorsements. The reasons for this restricted warranty coverage for these payors are explained below.

The limited warranty protection is readily understandable with respect to makers and drawers. These parties ought to know their own signatures when they are asked to pay. They are in a better position than the presenter and prior transferors to know whether they signed the instrument or authorized their signature. They can scrutinize the signature to detect forgeries and they should consult records, which they ought to keep, indicating the instruments they have issued. Therefore, makers and drawers do not receive any warranties concerning the authenticity of their own signatures.

The same rationale explains why they do not receive any warranties against alterations. The contract liability of makers and drawers is based on the terms of the instrument at the time it is issued. These parties ought to be aware of the terms of the instruments that they sign, as well as the authenticity of their signatures.

Makers and drawers, on the other hand, generally do not have the means to detect a forged indorsement. They nevertheless incur a risk in paying instruments with indorsements because they will not be discharged from their liability on the instrument unless they pay a person who is entitled to enforce the instrument.[99] They are, therefore, protected against this risk through the presentment warranty that the warrantor was a person entitled to enforce the instrument or authorized to obtain payment on behalf of a person entitled to enforce the instrument.

An indorser's liability on the instrument is based on the terms of the instrument at the time it was indorsed. An indorser should know what those terms were, and thus does not require warranty protection against a subsequent alteration of those terms. By transferring an instrument after signing it, an indorser makes a transfer warranty on the authenticity of all signatures on the instrument at the time of the transfer.[100] No comparable presentment warranty, therefore, is extended back if that indorser is required to pay the instrument. The indorser's transfer warranty of authenticity of signatures, however, covers only the signatures that are on the instrument at the time of the transfer. If a subsequent indorsement in the chain of transfer were forged, the indorser's payment would not be made to a person entitled to enforce the instrument, meaning that the indorser's

---

[98] U.C.C. §§ 3-417(d)(1), 4-207(d).

[99] U.C.C. § 3-602(a). See § 7.02[A][1] *supra*.

[100] U.C.C. §§ 3-416(a)(2), 4-207(a)(2).

obligation would not be discharged. Because the indorser has no reliable means of detecting such a forgery, the protection of the warranty against such forged indorsements is extended.

An acceptor of a draft receives the three presentment warranties at the time of acceptance,[101] but only the warranty against forged and missing indorsements at the time of payment.[102] Having received warranties with respect to alteration and lack of knowledge that the drawer's signature is unauthorized upon accepting the draft, the drawee can use breach of either warranty as a defense to its obligation to pay the instrument when it is later presented for that purpose. If the drawee nevertheless pays the accepted instrument, it can recover from any warrantor who breached a warranty when the draft was accepted. Repeating these warranties in subsection (d) of sections 3-417 and 4-208 would simply be redundant.[103] The drawee who pays an instrument that is altered after having accepted it is not protected by additional warranty protection against the subsequent alteration. The acceptor should know the terms of the drafts that it accepts.

§ 8.05 Breach of Warranties — §§ 3-416(b), 3-417(b)

[A] Accrual and Termination of Cause of Action

A cause of action for breach of warranty can be brought immediately upon discovery of the breach. This opportunity can be advantageous in circumstances where a cause of action for liability on the instrument will be delayed on a time instrument or by requirements of presentment and notice of dishonor. The cause of action for breach of a warranty "accrues when the claimant has reason to know of the breach."[104] Thus, the cause of action for a breach of a transfer warranty would accrue after transfer of the instrument to the claimant and the claimant had reason to know of the breach. The cause of action for a breach of a presentment warranty would accrue after the instrument is accepted or paid and the payor had reason to know of the breach.

Provisions in the warranty sections of Articles 3 and 4 affect the timeliness of warranty claims. The claimant has thirty days from the time he or she has reason to know of the breach and the identity of the warrantor to give notice of a claim for breach of warranty to the warrantor.[105] Otherwise, the warrantor's liability for damages is discharged to the extent of any loss caused by the delay in giving notice of the claim. The section does not act as a statute of frauds for setting the outside time limit for commencing a cause of action. It is a notification procedure for allowing transferors and presenters an opportunity to avoid or minimize their losses

---

[101] U.C.C. §§ 3-417(a), 4-207(a).
[102] U.C.C. §§ 3-417(d), 4-207(d).
[103] U.C.C. § 3-417, Comment 4.
[104] U.C.C. §§ 3-416(d), 3-417(f), 4-207(e), 4-208(f).
[105] U.C.C. §§ 3-416(c), 3-417(e), 4-207(d), 4-208(e).

stemming from claims that they have breached warranties.[106] Failure to assert the claim in timely fashion can operate as a partial or complete discharge of liability for the breach.

Even if a claimant delays in providing notice of a claim for breach of warranty, the delay does not result in any discharge if it does not cause any loss to the breaching party. Thus, a New Jersey court held that an excessive delay did not cause loss to the collecting bank because the account that the forger (an attorney) maintained at the bank was an escrow account of funds held in trust for clients, to which the bank's set-off rights did not extend.[107] The court in another case held that the depositary bank could not have suffered any loss from a delayed claim by the payor bank because the drawer notified both the payor bank and the depositary bank on the same day that the check was missing and the collecting bank proceeded immediately to freeze the proceeds of the check that remained in its depositor's account.[108] In yet another opinion a court determined that an excessive delay did not occasion any loss to the breaching collecting bank because the bank still controlled most of the proceeds of the deposit to cover the customer's overdrafts and the funds actually withdrawn by the customer were taken before the expiration of the time for notice of the claim.[109] Although surmounting the burden of establishing a loss caused by the delay can be difficult, the defense occasionally has been successful.[110]

Statute of limitations provisions in Articles 3 and 4 establish the time by which an action for breach of warranty must be commenced.[111] The period stated is three years and, consistent with general law, runs from the time that the cause of action accrues. Thus, an action for breach of warranty must be commenced within three years from the time that the claimant has reason to know of the breach.

[B] Damages

Articles 3 and 4 include provisions that state the measure of damages for breach of warranty. The damages for breach of transfer warranties do not apply unless the claimant took the instrument in good faith.[112] If a transferee purchases an instrument fully aware of defenses that are good

---

[106] Home Indem. Co. v. First Nat'l Bank, 659 F.2d 796, 31 U.C.C. Rep. Serv. 1664 (7th Cir. 1981) ("codification of the prior law which required those with knowledge of a fraud to notify those who might be liable as soon as possible in order to avoid or lessen any loss").

[107] Clarkson v. Selected Risks Ins. Co., 170 N.J. Super. 373, 406 A.2d 494, 27 U.C.C. Rep. Serv. 1366 (1979).

[108] Girard Bank v. Mount Holly State Bank, 474 F. Supp. 1225, 26 U.C.C. Rep. Serv. 1210 (D. N.J. 1979).

[109] First Nat'l Bank v. Trust Co., 510 F. Supp. 651, 32 U.C.C. Rep. Serv. 909 (N.D. Ga. 1981).

[110] Phoenix Assurance Co. v. Davis, 126 N.J. Super. 379, 314 A.2d 615, 13 U.C.C. Rep. Serv. 1105 (1974) (loss of $200 deducted from claimant's recovery because the bank's offset rights were adversely affected by the delay when the customer closed the account).

[111] U.C.C. §§ 3-118(g), 4-111.

[112] U.C.C. §§ 3-416(b), 4-207(c).

against the transferor, or knowing that a prior signature is not genuine, the transferee cannot have relief for breach of the transfer warranties.

The claimant under a transfer warranty is entitled to recover "an amount equal to the loss suffered as a result of the breach," subject to specified limitations.[113] This measure is consistent with the basic warranty-law principle of protecting the legitimate expectations of the aggrieved party. Recovery should cover actual damages that will place the injured party in the same monetary position that would have resulted had the warranties not been breached. The applicable measure will not always be the face amount of the instrument. For example, if the only parties liable on the instrument are insolvent, the actual value of the instrument as warranted is less than face value because the solvency of parties is not warranted. If the breach of warranty is based on a material alteration of the amount payable on the instrument, the damages should be limited to the extent of the alteration.[114]

The amount recoverable for a breach of warranty claim cannot exceed an explicit limitation. The limitation is the amount of the instrument plus expenses and the loss of interest that was incurred because of the breach. The "expenses" referred to include ordinary collecting expenses in the bank-collection process and, in appropriate cases, can include expenses such as attorney fees.[115]

The basic measure of damages for breach of a presentment warranty is an amount equal to the amount paid plus expenses and loss of interest resulting from the breach.[116] Expenses for attorney fees again are not expressly included, but they can be granted in the discretion of the court.[117] When the payment is made by the drawee of an unaccepted draft, the amount that the drawee received or is entitled to receive from the drawer because of the payment is deducted from the amount paid by the drawee.[118]

---

[113] U.C.C. §§ 3-416(b), 4-207(c).

[114] Under section 4-401(d)(1), a drawee bank can charge its customer's account according to the original terms of the altered item.

[115] Several courts have allowed recovery of attorney fees. See, e.g., Southern Provisions, Inc. v. Harris Trust & Sav. Bank, 96 Ill. App. 3d 745, 422 N.E.2d 33, 31 U.C.C. Rep. Serv. 460 (1981). Some courts, on the other hand, have denied recovery of attorney fees. First Nat'l Bank v. Plymouth-Home Nat'l Bank, 553 F. Supp. 448, 35 U.C.C. Rep. Serv. 1240 (D. Mass. 1982) (attorney fees not awarded because defendant had not behaved egregiously in forcing plaintiff to litigate its claim); Riedel v. First Nat'l Bank, 287 Or. 285, 598 P.2d 302, 27 U.C.C. Rep. Serv. 503 (1979) (historical antipathy toward attorney fees absent express authority).

[116] U.C.C. §§ 3-417(b), (d)(2), 4-208(b), (d).

[117] U.C.C. §§ 3-417, Comment 5; Grasso v. Crow, 57 Cal. App. 4th 847, 67 Cal. Rptr. 2d 367, 35 Rep. Serv. 2d 1288 (1997)(attorney fees denied because California law requires that attorney fees be specifically provided for by statute or agreement of the parties).

[118] U.C.C. § 3-417(b), 4-208(b). The amount that the bank is entitled to charge against its customer's account is determined under section 4-401. For discussion of the provisions in this section, see § 12.02[B] infra.

Chapter 9
PREVENTION OF UNJUST ENRICHMENT

SYNOPSIS

§ 9.01 Restitution: Recovery of Payments Made by Mistake
    [A] Introduction
    [B] Pre-Code Law
        [1] Restatement of Restitution
        [2] The Dominant Case Law
    [C] U.C.C. — § 3-418
        [1] Warranties and Finality
        [2] Problems With Customers' Accounts
        [3] Beneficiaries of Finality
        [4] The Double-Forgery Problem
    [D] Rationales for Finality

§ 9.02 Subrogation: Recovery by Assertion of Rights of Others
    [A] The Subrogation Concept — § 4-407
    [B] Stop-Payment Orders
    [C] Other Grounds for Objection by Drawers
    [D] Burden of Proof — § 4-403(3)

§ 9.01 Restitution: Recovery of Payment Made by Mistake

[A] Introduction

The previous chapter explains why a bank or other payor that pays a negotiable instrument with a forged drawer's signature cannot recover from the presenter or prior transferors on a breach of warranty theory.[1] Breach of the applicable warranty requires actual knowledge that the signature was forged,[2] and presenters and prior transferors are not likely to be in violation.

Contract theories do not improve the plight of someone who pays over a forged drawer's signature. Payment precludes satisfaction of the requirement of dishonor that conditions the liability of drawers and indorsers.[3] The ostensible drawer whose name is forged never incurs liability on the instrument.[4] Furthermore, the checking-account contract between the

---

[1] See § 8.04[B][1][b] supra.
[2] U.C.C. §§ 3-417(a)(3), 4-208(a)(3).
[3] U.C.C. §§ 3-414(b), 3-415(a).
[4] U.C.C. §§ 3-401(a), 3-403(a).

ostensible drawer and a bank does not authorize the bank to debit the account unless the authorized drawer's signature appears on the check. Because a check with a forged signature is not properly payable, the payor bank will be required to recredit the account.[5]

An option possibly available to the payor bank is a claim in restitution against the presenter to recover money paid by mistake. The mistake is obvious when a bank pays a forged check. Because instruments bearing forgeries are not properly payable, thus precluding the bank from debiting a customer's account for payment, banks will not pay them knowingly. When payment is made innocently in the mistaken belief that the instrument is properly payable, payors will desire to recover from the party who received the mistaken payment.

The drafters of the U.C.C. affected the law in this area in two major ways. They changed the general underlying theory for recovery for certain categories of cases from the pre-Code approach of recovery in restitution of money paid by mistake to a theory of implied warranties. In the revision to Article 3 they also codified the right to restitution in certain cases and deferred to general law governing mistake and restitution in others. The combined effect of these rules closely reflects the results achieved under prior restitution law, which by no means recognized a right of recovery for all payments made by mistake on negotiable instruments. The denial of a claim in restitution with respect to negotiable instruments is known historically as the finality doctrine. The doctrine is well-named because it allocates the ultimate loss on some instruments to the party who pays them, thus making the payment final.

The discussion below explains the restitution principle as it applies to mistaken payments on negotiable instruments. It demonstrates that warranty theory and the finality doctrine operate in conjunction to allow payors generally to recover mistaken payments on instruments with forged indorsements or alterations, but not payments of instruments containing forgeries of other parties. It also analyzes the rationales underlying this disparate treatment. The discussion addresses as well the application of the finality doctrine to payments made because of mistakes in determining the state of a customer's account and includes an analysis of the problem of double forgeries.

[B] Pre-Code Law

[1] *Restatement of Restitution*

Although the specifics concerning the right to restitution for payment by mistake vary from state to state, the *Restatement of Restitution* provides the general principles. As with all cases in which restitution is authorized, the purpose is to prevent unjust enrichment.[6] The *Restatement* includes

---

[5] U.C.C. § 4-401(a). The provisions of this section are developed in Chapter 12. *See* § 12.02[B] *infra*.

[6] "A person who has been unjustly enriched at the expense of another is required to make restitution to the other." RESTATEMENT OF RESTITUTION § 1 (1937).

both general provisions concerning money paid by mistake and special rules for bills (drafts and checks in modern parlance) and notes.[7] A substantial array of exceptions and limitations precludes restitution from operating as a universal principle that entitles one to recover all payments made in mistake.

The general *Restatement* provisions for recovery of mistaken payments would be broad enough if applied alone to cover all payors who pay over forged signatures by drawers, makers, acceptors, or indorsers. Restitution is recognized in circumstances in which payment was made in either a mistaken belief in the existence of a contract with the person paid[8] or in the mistaken belief that the terms of the contract required such payment.[9] Restitution also applies when a payor makes payment in the mistaken belief that a third person owes the duty to the person paid.[10] The special rules of the *Restatement* that apply to bills and notes recognize these same general principles, subject to significant modifications.[11]

The special rules alter the expansive availability of restitution that is otherwise indicated in the general provisions. In one major instance they create a specific duty of restitution — when payment has been received on a negotiable instrument with a break in the chain of title due to a forged or unauthorized indorsement.[12] Generally, however, the special rules deny the existence of a duty of restitution by bona fide purchasers. A holder who qualifies as a bona fide purchaser for value does not owe a duty of restitution to a payor who pays an instrument on which the payor's name was forged as a party or to a drawee who pays an instrument with a forged drawer's signature.[13] Another rule similarly precludes restitution recovery when a drawee pays under a mistaken belief concerning the state of the drawer's account, such as the sufficiency of funds to cover the check, the issuance of a stop-payment order, or whether the account actually exists.[14] Yet another provision precludes much of the duty of restitution following the receipt of payment on a negotiable instrument on which the amount for payment was raised fraudulently.[15]

The right to retain the payment under all of the special rules enumerated above that deny a duty of restitution by a bona fide purchaser, however, is subject to a critical condition. If a holder makes a misrepresentation causing the mistake, or suspects or has reason to know of the payor's

---

[7] RESTATEMENT OF RESTITUTION, Title A and Title B of Topic 2, Ch. 2.

[8] RESTATEMENT OF RESTITUTION § 15. This provision would reach payments by makers or acceptors over their own forged signatures.

[9] RESTATEMENT OF RESTITUTION § 18. This provision would cover payments made over a forged indorsements.

[10] RESTATEMENT OF RESTITUTION § 23(1)(a),(b). This provision would cover payments made over forged drawers' signatures.

[11] RESTATEMENT OF RESTITUTION § 29.

[12] RESTATEMENT OF RESTITUTION §§ 35, 37.

[13] RESTATEMENT OF RESTITUTION § 30.

[14] RESTATEMENT OF RESTITUTION § 33 and Comment *a*.

[15] RESTATEMENT OF RESTITUTION § 31(a).

mistake at the time of payment, the holder incurs a duty of restitution.[16] The comments to the provision creating this duty explain that a "duty of care to detect a possible deception" commences from the time the instrument is taken and continues until payment is received.[17] Negligence in taking a check, therefore, can make a holder who receives payment liable in restitution if the drawer's name was forged.[18]

[2] The Dominant Case Law

The most celebrated decision in the law of negotiable instruments, and perhaps in all of commercial law, is Lord Mansfield's opinion in *Price v. Neal*.[19] The case has been extremely influential since it was decided in 1762. The principle that the case established still is commonly referred to as the rule of *Price v. Neal*.

The case involved the payment of two drafts, each of which had been issued with a forged drawer's signature. One of the drafts was accepted by Price, the drawee, and subsequently paid by his representative pursuant to his instructions when Neal presented it for payment. The other draft was not accepted by Price, but as the drawee, he also paid it to Neal. Price did not learn until after both payments that the drafts had not been signed by the ostensible drawer, but rather were forged by an individual named Lee. Price's opportunity to pursue his legal claim against Lee was clearly unavailable because Lee had been hanged for his offense. Price, therefore, brought suit against Neal "for money had and received" in an attempt to recover the money paid by mistake.

Lord Mansfield advanced the principle of unjust enrichment as the basis for recovery of the money. He found that "the plaintiff can not recover the money, unless it be against conscience in the defendant, to retain it. . . ."[20] He then held that it would not be unjust for the defendant to retain the money when he gave fair and valuable consideration for the instrument, in good faith and without any suspicion of the forgery. The court reasoned that between the two innocent parties, the drawee is in a better position to know the drawer's signature and thereby detect the forgery.[21] "If there was no neglect in the [drawee], yet there is no reason to throw off the loss from one innocent man upon another innocent man: but, in this case, if there was any fault or negligence in any one, it certainly was in the [drawee], and not in the [person paid]."[22] The rule of *Price v. Neal* thus

---

[16] RESTATEMENT OF RESTITUTION § 34(a),(b).

[17] RESTATEMENT OF RESTITUTION § 34, Comment *a*, *b*. The holder also is under a duty to notify the payor of subsequently discovered facts or suspicious circumstances that might lead the payor to make a mistaken payment. *Id.* § 34(c).

[18] RESTATEMENT OF RESTITUTION § 34, Comment *a*, Illustration 1.

[19] 94 Eng. Rep. 871 (K.B. 1762).

[20] 97 Eng. Rep. at 872.

[21] "It was incumbent upon the plaintiff, to be satisfied 'that the bill drawn upon him was the drawer's hand,' before he accepted or paid it: but it was not incumbent upon the defendant, to inquire into it." *Id.*

[22] *Id.*

is that a drawee who pays or accepts a draft with a forged drawer's signature cannot recover the payment from the person paid if that person acquired the instrument as a bona fide purchaser.

A subsequent leading case provided a different result for an instrument with a forged indorsement. Recognizing that "[t]he plaintiffs paid their money under the mistaken belief thus induced, that the name was genuine," the court in *Canal Bank v. Bank of Albany*[23] permitted the payor bank to recover after it had paid the instrument. The court refused to apply the rule of *Price v. Neal*, noting that "it is sufficient to distinguish the case, that it goes on the superior negligence of the party paying or accepting."[24] Drawees were not presumed to know the signatures of indorsers, whereas payment or acceptance carried an effect of recognition of the drawer's signature. "Neither acceptance nor payment, at any time, nor under any circumstances, is an admission that the first, or any other endorser's name is genuine."[25]

The reasoning of both the rule and the exception also led to different treatments on liability for payment of altered instruments. In *Bank of the United States v. Bank of Georgia*,[26] Justice Story drew an analogy to *Price v. Neal* in precluding a maker from recovering the excessive payment made on a note that had been raised by someone in the chain of transfer prior to the recipient of the payment. Story noted that the principle requiring drawees to know the signatures of their drawers requires that makers are "bound to know their own notes."[27] On the other hand, the Court of Appeals of New York used the reasoning underlying *Canal State Bank* to allow drawees recovery for the excessive amounts paid on alterations. Conceding the reasonableness of requiring a drawee to recognize the signature of its drawer, the court in *Bank of Commerce v. Union Bank*[28] stated the difference precisely: "There is no ground for presuming the body of the bill to be in the drawer's hand-writing, or in any hand-writing, known to the acceptor" so that "to require the drawee to know the hand-writing of the residue of the bill, is unreasonable."[29]

The rule of *Price v. Neal* became a generally accepted principle of common law in this country,[30] as did the exception in favor of recovery for money paid over a forged indorsement and the different approaches to altered instruments.[31] Many courts, however, grafted onto the rule of *Price v. Neal*

---

[23] 1 Hill 287 (N.Y. 1841).

[24] *Id.* at 290.

[25] *Id.* at 289 (citation omitted).

[26] 10 Wheat. (23 U.S.) 333 (1825).

[27] *Id.* at 355.

[28] 3 N.Y. 230 (1850).

[29] 3 N.Y. at 235, 236.

[30] See W. BRITTON, HANDBOOK ON THE LAW OF BILLS AND NOTES 376 (2nd. ed. 1961) and the cases cited therein. The earliest opinions adopting the rule in this country were Young v. Adams, 6 Mass. 181 (1810) and Levy v. Bank of United States, 1 Binn. 27 (Pa. 1802).

[31] See W. BRITTON, HANDBOOK ON THE LAW OF BILLS AND NOTES 392, 399 (2nd ed. 1961) and the cases cited therein.

by requiring that a holder seeking to preclude recovery by a drawee must be free from negligence as well as bad faith. The principle form of negligence recognized in the cases is the failure to require adequate identification from a stranger who forges a check.[32] Yet the cases present hopeless confusion concerning a consistent standard by which to determine negligence in these transactions.[33] *Price v. Neal* and its progeny, including the judicial expansion on negligence, are reflected in the provisions of the *Restatement of Restitution*.[34]

The N.I.L. provided very little direct coverage on these subjects,[35] so the common-law approaches predominated even under that codification. They were easily applicable under section 196 of the N.I.L.,[36] which operated like section 1-103 of the U.C.C. to supplement the text of the codification with principles of common law.[37] These common-law principles governing claims of restitution for money paid by mistake on negotiable instruments also supplement the U.C.C., but the codification of the U.C.C. brought certain changes that now will be examined.

[C] U.C.C. — § 3-418

The U.C.C. does not radically alter the substance of the commmon-law approach to restitution; rather it changes the underlying theory of recovery of *Price v. Neal* and its progeny from one based on restitution to one founded on implied warranties. The presentment warranties of Articles 3 and 4 reflect the results of the dominant case law concerning forged signatures and alterations. Even though these claims by the payor are now based on a warranty cause of action, the substance of these claims is similar to the original restitution claim for recovery of payments made by mistake.

The original enactment of Article 3 did not include a provision that recognized a cause of action for restitution for payment or acceptance by

---

[32] *See e.g.*, Cairo Banking Co. v. West, 187 Ga. 666, 2 S.E.2d 91 (1939); Canadian Bank of Commerce v. Bingham, 30 Wash. 484, 71 P. 43 (1902).

[33] For example, Pennington County Bank v. First State Bank, 110 Minn. 263, 125 N.W. 119 (1910), holds that it is not negligence to take a check from a stranger, whereas Hutcheson Hardware Co. v. Planters State Bank, 26 Ga. App. 321, 105 S.E. 854 (1921), found negligence in cashing a check for a stranger after having gone to the drawee bank to ascertain if the drawer's signature was valid.

[34] RESTATEMENT OF RESTITUTION §§ 30, 35, 37, 31, 34. *See* § 9.01[B][1] *supra*.

[35] Section 62 of the N.I.L. deprived an acceptor of any defense on grounds of a forged drawer's signature because it provided that the acceptor admitted the genuineness of the signature upon acceptance. No section, however, addressed the effect on recovery of payment over a forged drawer's signature. Sections 65 and 66 of the N.I.L. established warranties that were given by indorsers. These warranties, however, were considered to run generally to subsequent transferees only, and not to parties who paid instruments.

[36] "In any case not provided for in this act the rules of the law merchant shall govern." N.I.L. § 196.

[37] "The courts assume that the doctrine of Price v. Neal, with all its common law exceptions real or apparent, have been carried into the Act, or are available through Section 196." W. BRITTON, HANDBOOK ON THE LAW OF BILLS AND NOTES 384 (2nd ed. 1961) (discussing decisions under the N.I.L.).

mistake. Rather, the restitution principle supplemented the Code[38] and Article 3 included a provision that limited its applicability in negotiable instruments transactions.[39] Payment and acceptance of any instrument was made final in favor of a holder in due course or a person who in good faith changed position in reliance on the payment. These designated beneficiaries of finality could not be liable for payments received by mistake unless they breached a presentment warranty.

The revision of Article 3 alters this structure somewhat. Section 3-418 now specifically states a right of restitution. Subsection (a) allows the remedy in the two most-common cases in which the issue arises: payment or acceptance of forged checks and checks on which the drawer has stopped payment.[40] It allows the drawee to revoke acceptance in these cases and to recover the payment it made on the check. Similar recoveries are authorized in subsection (b) for all other cases, "to the extent permitted by the law governing mistake and restitution." Care must be exercised in these latter cases to ascertain any local variations in how these legal principles are applied.

Consistent with the original version of Article 3, however, section 3-418 excludes the availability of the restitution remedy against two designated classes of beneficiaries: "a person who took the instrument in good faith and for value or who in good faith changed position in reliance on the payment or acceptance."[41] These designated beneficiaries nevertheless still remain liable for any presentment warranties that they breach.[42]

The Code approach of conceptualizing the cases under both implied warranties and restitution based on mistake thus continues under the Article 3 revision. The traditional common-law approach to recovery in these cases also essentially remains intact.

[1] Warranties and Finality

Neither payment nor acceptance is final in favor of anyone when a presentment warranty has been breached. Because breach of warranty is codified as an exception to the defense of finality in an action even against the beneficiaries designated in section 3-418, presentment warranties are the logical starting point for analysis.

The limited scope of the presentment warranty on drawer's signatures preserves the rule of *Price v. Neal*.[43] If persons receiving payment were held to warrant to payors that all signatures are genuine, payors could

---

[38] U.C.C. § 1-103.
[39] U.C.C. § 3-418 (original version).
[40] U.C.C. § 3-418, Comment 1.
[41] U.C.C. § 3-418(c).
[42] U.C.C. § 3-418(c).
[43] *See* § 9.01[B][2] *supra*. "[S]ubsection (a)(3) [of section 3-417] retains the rule of Price v. Neal, 3 Burr. 1354 (1762), that the drawee takes the risk that the drawer's signature is unauthorized unless the person presenting the draft has knowledge that the drawer's signature is unauthorized." U.C.C. § 3-417, Comment 3.

recover losses caused by a forged drawer's signature.[44] As the discussion in the previous chapter explains, however, the absolute transfer warranties do not run to persons that pay instruments, and the applicable presentment warranties are more limited.[45] Persons receiving payment warrant only that they have no knowledge that the signature of the drawer is unauthorized. If they do not breach the warranty and if they qualify as a designated beneficiary, payment is final in their favor under section 3-418. Consequently, payment over a forged drawer's signature generally leaves the ultimate loss on the payor.[46]

The finality doctrine also binds a drawee who accepts an instrument on which the signature of the drawer has been forged. A holder who takes a draft in good faith and for value after it has been accepted does not, when the instrument is paid by the acceptor, extend a presentment warranty of no knowledge that the signature of the drawer is unauthorized.[47] A holder who presents an unaccepted draft for acceptance does warrant an absence of knowledge of the drawer's forged signature, but the warranty applies only "at the time of presentment."[48] This time limitation on the warranty means that any qualified holder who learns of the forgery after the acceptance will not breach the warranty upon obtaining payment, and the payment made will be final under section 3-418. If the drawee-acceptor resists payment, the acceptance is final in favor of the holder under section 3-418 and can be enforced. Hence, finality of acceptance will impose upon the drawee the same losses that would be incurred had the instrument been paid rather than accepted.

The presentment warranty that the warrantor is a person entitled to enforce the instrument is a codification of the rule in the *Canal Bank* case.[49] This absolute warranty constitutes a guarantee that the instrument does not contain forged indorsements. If a drawee pays or accepts an instrument with such a forgery, the exception based on breach of the warranty precludes the payment or acceptance from being final under section 3-418.[50]

The codification of the final presentment warranty reflects the rules drawn by analogy from *Price v. Neal* and *Canal Bank* that were developed at early common law for cases of alterations.[51] Breach of the warranty

---

[44] "If the warranty of [§ 4-207(a)(2)], i.e., that all signatures are 'genuine or authorized,' were to run to payors, the doctrine of *Price v. Neal*, alive in the Code, would be obliterated." Payroll Check Cashing v. New Palestine Bank, 401 N.E.2d 752, 756, 28 U.C.C. Rep. Serv. 1421, 1426 (Ind. Ct. App. 1980).

[45] *See* § 8.04[B] *supra*.

[46] The payor might also subrogate to the rights of the forging drawer against the payee on his or her underlying transaction. *See* § 9.02 *infra*. Those rights will be of little solace, however, when the drawer has resorted to forgery.

[47] U.C.C. §§ 3-417(d), 4-208(d).

[48] U.C.C. §§ 3-417(a)(3), 4-208(a)(3).

[49] *See* § 9.01[B][2] *supra*.

[50] U.C.C. §§ 3-418(c); 3-417(a)(1), (d)(1); 4-208(a)(1), (d).

[51] *See* § 9.01[B][2] *supra*.

allows a drawee of an unaccepted draft, who does not have access to information indicating the correct amount of the instrument, to recover the excessive portion of the payment.[52] The warranty is not made, however, when payment is received from the maker of a note, from the drawer of a draft, or from the acceptor of a draft that was raised after acceptance.[53] These categories of payors should know the terms of the instrument at the time they incur their contractual liability on the instrument. Without a breach of warranty, the finality doctrine runs in favor of the holder who took the instrument in good faith and for value, which precludes the payor from recovering the excessive amount paid when the amount payable on the instrument has been altered.

Finality and warranties thus impose the harsh consequence that payors in certain circumstances will not be able to recover payments made by mistake from anyone else and acceptors will not be able to resist the obligation to make payment. Payors and acceptors are freed of ultimate responsibility for forged indorsements and some classes of alterations, but they bear a heavy burden for forged instruments and the other alterations. If they can detect these forgeries and alterations early, the solution obviously is to not pay or accept the instrument.[54] Once these instruments are accepted or paid, however, the limitation on a restitution claim makes that acceptance or payment final in favor of the identified beneficiaries.[55]

[2] Problems With Customers' Accounts

Mistaken payments can be made for reasons other than the frauds reflected in the rule of *Price v. Neal* and its progeny. Payors also make mistaken payments because they commit errors concerning the state of their customers' accounts. A drawee bank might confuse its customers and charge the wrong account, or even pay an instrument drawn by a person who does not have an account with the bank. Alternatively, the bank might pay a check because a breakdown in internal communications did not draw sufficient attention to a stop-payment order. Mistakes in determining the balance in a customer's account lead to payments of checks drawn on nonsufficient funds (NSF checks).

The *Restatement of Restitution* recognizes all of these categories of mistaken payments.[56] The common-law rule that it reflects provides that the holder who acquires the instrument as a bona fide purchaser and receives payment without knowledge of the payor's mistake does not incur

---

[52] A drawee bank is entitled to charge its customer's account only for the amount of "the original terms of the altered item." U.C.C. § 4-401(d)(1).

[53] U.C.C. §§ 3-417(d), 4-208(d).

[54] "A check or other draft does not of itself operate as an assignment of funds in the hands of the drawee available for its payment, and the drawee is not liable on the instrument until the drawee accepts it." U.C.C. § 3-408.

[55] When payment or acceptance is made by mistake and the payor or acceptor successfully recovers the payment or revokes the acceptance, the instrument is then treated as dishonored and not paid or accepted. The person from who payment is recovered has the rights of a person entitled to enforce the dishonored instrument. U.C.C. §§ 3-418(d), 3-301.

[56] RESTATEMENT OF RESTITUTION § 33. *See* § 9.01[B][1] *supra*.

a duty of restitution to the payor even though the payment was induced by mistake. The burden of these mistakes thus lies with the mistaken payor.

The Article 3 codification carries forward this same principle. Section 3-418 recognizes a restitution remedy for payment by a drawee over a stop-payment order and defers to the general law of mistake and restitution in the other cases. These remedies cannot be asserted, however, against the two designated classes of beneficiaries.[57] Analysis of these cases lies exclusively within these principles of restitution, as the warranty provisions do not include any warranties that can be exceptions to finality in these cases. Presentment warranties do not extend to the sufficiency of the drawer's account or to whether a stop-payment order has been issued. Unlike the presenter and prior transferors, payors and acceptors are in the best position to determine the state of a drawer's account.

Cases of checks drawn on insufficient funds pose a unique consideration. The mistake on payments of checks with forgeries or checks subject to valid stop-payment orders is obvious; they are not properly payable, so the drawer can assert a claim against the payor bank to recredit the drawer's account.[58] The bank can properly charge the account, however, for charges that create an overdraft.[59] The check constitutes the drawer's authorization to charge the account and it includes an implied promise to reimburse the drawee for over-charges. In effect, the payor bank extends a loan to its drawer-customer. Consequently, mistake by the payor bank often is not involved in payment of NSF checks. In an exercise of business judgment, payor banks frequently make intentional payment on these checks. Some modern checking accounts with "overdraft insurance" features even obligate the payor bank to pay NSF checks up to an indicated amount.

The distinction between knowing and mistaken payments of overdrafts is critical to restitutionary recovery. The claim is established in common-law principles, and it arises for payments on an instrument only if they are made by mistake. A payor bank that knowingly pays an overdraft simply does not have a claim in restitution to recover the payment.[60] The

---

[57] Gentner & Co., Inc. v. Wells Fargo Bank, 76 Cal. App. 4th 1165, 90 Cal. Rptr. 2d 904, 40 U.C.C. Rep. Serv. 2d 38 (Cal. Ct. App. 1999) (bank that mistakenly paid a check over a stop payment order could not recover the payment from a person who took the instrument in good faith and for value). A bank that mistakenly paid a $75,000 check drawn on insufficient funds successfully challenged the summary denial of its claim in restitution by establishing that the corporation that received payment did not qualify as either of the beneficiaries designated in section 3-418. The corporation still possessed the machinery it promised to deliver under its executory contract with the drawer, so it had not given value. Its payment of a sales commission was not in good-faith reliance on final payment of the check because it was not made until after the drawee bank informed the corporation of its payment by mistake. The Code, therefore, did not bar the claim in restitution. National Sav. & Trust Co. v. Park Corp., 722 F.2d 1303, 37 U.C.C. Rep. Serv. 817 (6th Cir. 1983), *cert. denied*, 466 U.S. 939 (1984).

[58] U.C.C. § 4-401.

[59] U.C.C. § 4-401(a).

[60] Demos v. Lyons, 151 N.J. Super. 489, 376 A.2d 1352, 22 U.C.C. Rep. Serv. 754 (1977) (payor bank paid check knowing it would produce an overdraft of over $9,600 in anticipation that the drawer would make a deposit to his account to cover the check).

bank then can look only to its drawer-customer on its implied promise of reimbursement.[61]

[3] Beneficiaries of Finality

When a presentment warranty is not breached, acceptance or payment is final only in favor of designated beneficiaries. Section 3-418 identifies them as persons who took the instrument in good faith and for value and as persons who in good faith changed their position in reliance on the payment or acceptance. The shelter principle also confers the benefit of finality on transferees of the protected parties.[62]

The requirement of taking an instrument in good faith provides the bona fides that are considered essential to swing the balance of competing equities against the party seeking recovery of the payment. The effect of imposing finality is to preclude recovery for restitution. If the holder took the instrument in bad faith, the holder lacks equities against the drawee. The contest under these circumstances is not between two equally-innocent parties, and enrichment of the recipient of the payment at the expense of the payor who paid by mistake would be unjust.

If the holder did not give value for the instrument, enrichment also will not be allowed at the expense of the mistaken payor. A holder who has given only an executory promise or credit[63] can extricate himself or herself from the transaction and liability on the instrument by rescinding when notified of the forgery or other irregularity, while a holder who received the instrument as a donee does not have any personal assets at stake in the transaction.[64]

The shelter principle confers the rights attained by a transferor on subsequent transferees, so finality also applies in their favor. Consider the following fact situation:

```
          "E"
          D'er ---- ▶P ──────▶X ──────▶Y ......... ▶ Bank
                           (HDC)              (pays)
```

Diagram 9.1

Drawer (D'er) forged his employer's (E's) signature on the check and issued it to Payee (P). Payee negotiated the check to X, who qualified as a holder in due course and, in turn, negotiated the check to Y. Assuming the last transfer was a gift, which would preclude Y from qualifying as a holder in due course, Y nevertheless acquired X's holder-in-due-course rights.

---

[61] See § 12.02[B][1] infra.

[62] U.C.C. § 3-203(b).

[63] Although executory promises constitute consideration, they are not value. U.C.C. § 3-303. See § 6.01[B][1][a] supra.

[64] U.C.C. § 3-303, Comment 2. See § 6.01[B][1][a] supra.

Consequently, Bank's payment to Y is final, provided that Y did not breach the warranty of no knowledge of the unauthorized drawer's signature.

The principle case identifying a person "who in good faith changed position in reliance on the payment or acceptance" is *First National City Bank v. Altman*.[65] The defendant Altman was a wholesale diamond dealer. He entered into two transactions with an individual who falsely identified himself as a buyer for a reputable company. In each instance the alleged agent selected several unset diamonds that were placed in a sealed envelope and retained by Altman. Each time the defrauding buyer also sent a check, which Altman promptly deposited in his bank, for the purchase price of the selected diamonds. The checks were forgeries drawn on the account of the company that supposedly had authorized the buyer to make these purchases on its behalf. The two transactions differed in one critical respect. Altman did not release the first envelope of diamonds until he learned from his bank that the drawee bank had paid the first check. He gave the forger the second envelope without first ascertaining that the check was paid, although in fact the drawee bank had paid it before the release. When the drawee bank learned of the forgeries, it sought recovery of the payments from Altman on grounds that the checks were paid by mistake in the belief that the drawers' signatures were authorized. Altman moved to dismiss the complaint on the basis of the finality doctrine.

The court made different rulings concerning the two checks. Altman qualified as a person who changed his position in reliance on the drawee's payment of the first check because he kept the merchandise in his possession until he knew payment had been made.[66] As to the second check, however, he again changed his position by releasing the diamonds, but he did not act in reliance on payment by the drawee because he did not know the check was paid.[67] Therefore, the court held that finality could not preclude recovery of the payment on the second check.

Before ruling against Altman on the second check, the court should have analyzed whether he was a holder in due course. Altman did not have any knowledge of the forged drawer's signature, so his defense on the finality doctrine should not have failed unless he could not qualify under either class of designated beneficiary. Careful examination of the facts suggests that actually he did not qualify as a holder in due course. Although he was unaware of it, the second check in fact was paid before he released the second group of selected diamonds. Therefore, prior to the payment on his behalf he had not given value because he had not yet performed his consideration on the transaction with the diamond buyer. Because he could not

---

[65] 3 U.C.C. Rep. Serv. 815 (N.Y. Sup. Ct. 1966), *aff'd*, 27 A.D.2d 706, 277 N.Y.S.2d 813 (1967).

[66] Similarly, a depositary bank that allows its customer to withdraw the proceeds of a deposited check only after it knows that the drawee has paid it has changed its legal position in reliance on the payment. Fireman's Fund Ins. Co. v. Security Pac. Nat'l Bank, 85 Cal. App. 3d, 149 Cal. Rptr. 883, 25 U.C.C. Rep. Serv. 495 (1978). Alternatively, the depositary bank had also gave value for holder-in-due-course purposes. The customer's credit was available for withdrawal as of right under the applicable time for funds availability.

[67] Altman appears to have released the second envelope, as well as the first packet of diamonds, in reliance on payment of only the first check.

qualify as either of the designated beneficiaries, the finality doctrine did not preclude the bank's recovery for restitution.

Although case law has not provided much additional guidance on what actions are sufficient to constitute a good faith change of position in reliance on payment for purposes of section 3-418,[68] general principles of restitution law provide relevant considerations on when a change of position through consumption or expenditure is an adequate defense.[69] The recipient's use of the payment to meet ordinary expenses and debts generally should not be sufficient. Reliance on payment in the sense of incurring additional expenses that otherwise would not have been incurred should be required.[70] General restitution principles on depreciation also can provide guidance.[71] When transferred property depreciates in value before the restitution claim is asserted, the innocent recipient generally can avoid the loss from the depreciation by returning the property itself.[72] By analogy, a recipient of a mistaken payment who relied on it by making an extraordinary purchase might nevertheless be required to return the current value of the item purchased.

The change of position must not only be in reliance on the payment; it also must be incurred in good faith. Simply making an extraordinary purchase with the proceeds of the payment cannot alone assure the recipient of finality. For example, a recipient of payment who knows that the drawer's signature on a check is forged breaches the second presenter's warranty. Even if the warranty is not breached, but rather the recipient learns of the bank's mistake before changing position in reliance on the payment, the recipient who proceeds with the purchase would not act in good faith and could not qualify as a protected beneficiary.[73]

The Code deviates sharply in one respect from the development of prior law. The Code seeks to avoid the conflicts and uncertainties associated with the negligence criteria that developed under common law by eliminating its relevance to finality of payment or acceptance. Prior cases on negligence in taking an instrument are no longer valid. The allocation of losses due to taking instruments with forgeries is done without regard to fault under the Code.[74] A drawee can charge a customer's account only for items that

---

[68] *See* Richardson Co. v. First Nat'l Bank, 504 S.W.2d 812, 14 U.C.C. Rep. Serv. 443 (Tex. Civ. App. 1974) (release of collateral securing a loan following receipt of final payment held sufficient under § 3-418).

[69] III G. PALMER, THE LAW OF RESTITUTION 523-27 (1978).

[70] *Id.* at 524-25. Under the same principle, payment should be final if the recipient makes a gift that would not have been made but for the payment, provided that the gift is irrevocable. *Id.* at 527.

[71] *Id.* at 527-29.

[72] *Id.* at 528.

[73] National Sav. & Trust Co. v. Park Corp., 722 F.2d 1303, 37 U.C.C. Rep. Serv. 817 (6th Cir. 1983), *cert. denied*, 466 U.S. 939 (1984) (recipient of payment from the payor bank did not pay a commission to his sales agent until two weeks after having been informed by the bank that it had paid the check by mistake).

[74] *See generally*, Phillips, *The Commercial Culpability Scale*, 92 Yale L.J. 228 (1982). The effect of negligence in contributing to the forgery is covered in the next chapter. *See* § 10.02[A] *infra*.

are "properly payable"; the implied warranties are based on standards of strict liability; and the defense of final payment or acceptance to an action for restitution is determined without regard to the holder's negligence in taking the instrument.[75]

[4] The Double-Forgery Problem

Occasionally a check can have both a forged drawer's signature and a forged indorsement. Payment of the check by the drawee bank raises an issue concerning the appropriate application of the finality doctrine. The drawee bank would like to focus on the forged indorsement so that it can pass liability upstream on a breach of warranty theory. The conflicting applicability of the rule of *Price v. Neal* to the forged drawer's signature would generally leave liability on the drawee bank. A fundamental question is whether to focus on the forgery of the instrument or on the forged indorsement.

The case with the greatest renown in this area is *Perini Corp. v. First National Bank*.[76] Perini Corp., located in Massachusetts, had checking accounts with two New York banks on which the authorized signature was provided by a facsimile-signature machine. An unknown individual gained access to the machine and prepared seventeen checks totaling in excess of a million dollars. These checks were deposited over a period of time in a rural bank in Georgia by an individual who represented himself as Jesse D. Quisenberry. He opened accounts in the name of "Quisenberry Contracting Co." and "Southern Contracting Co." on sole proprietorship signature cards for which he was the only authorized signer. The checks were all payable to one of the two companies and deposited accordingly, but the indorsements were only in the individual name of Quisenberry. Proceeds of the checks were withdrawn in cash over the period of a month, and the individual posing as Quisenberry disappeared.

Perini's claim against the drawee banks was precluded because the corporation had given the bank a resolution by which it authorized the bank to honor all checks that were signed on the facsimile-signature machine.[77] Perini, together with a drawee bank who joined the cause of action, proceeded against the depositary bank and the collecting bank. A federal district court dismissed most of the claims, and the Fifth Circuit affirmed, leaving only the issue of the good faith of the Georgia depositary bank in dealing with Quisenberry.

The Fifth Circuit, as well as most courts that have addressed the issue, treated the case as one involving a forged check loss, but not an indorsement

---

[75] Perini Corp. v. First Nat'l Bank, 553 F.2d 398, 403-06, 21 U.C.C. Rep. Serv. 929, 937-41 (5th Cir. 1977).

[76] 553 F.2d 398, 21 U.C.C. Rep. Serv. 929 (5th Cir. 1977).

[77] Even without the resolution, the corporation in Perini might have been estopped to assert the improper payment by the drawee banks because of negligence in allowing unauthorized persons to gain access to the signature machine. U.C.C. § 3-406. *See* § 10.02[A][3] *infra*. A very difficult factual issue would have been raised, however, because the identity of the wrongdoer remained a mystery.

loss.[78] It drew this conclusion through an analysis of loss-allocation principles of Article 3. A payee has a rightful claim against the payor bank when a check that is properly issued is paid over a forged indorsement.[79] In these cases, the payee has a right to payment, and the natural expectation is that the payee will assert that right upon discovering the loss of the instrument. In a case like *Perini*, however, the payee on the forged check does not have a legitimate claim to payment by the payor bank, and, in all probability, does not even exist. Payees on forged checks cannot successfully assert claims against either the purported drawer or the payor bank. The loss that these double-forgery checks cause the drawer or the banks is not the result of improper indorsements, but rather is a consequence of the forgery of the drawer's signature. Therefore, a cause of action based on breach of the warranty of no forged indorsements was not available.[80]

The despository bank and collecting banks had to qualify as holders in due course in order to invoke the benefits of the finality doctrine. The Fifth Circuit held in *Perini* that the banks qualified, despite some difficulties with the requirements of holder status. The checks were issued in the name of corporations, but the indorsements were in the individual name of "Quisenberry" and without any indication of representative capacity. The court turned to a combination of factors in ruling that the banks became a "holder" of the forged checks. Several of the checks included a bank stamp guaranteeing the absence of indorsements. The court held that this stamp was sufficient under section 4-205 to constitute the customer's indorsement and to remedy the omission of representative capacity.[81] The depositary bank also credited the accounts of the companies named on the checks as the payees. The court also found that the banks could even be holders of the checks that the bank did not indorse by relying primarily on the fictitious payee provision of Article 3 that makes the indorsements effective.[82] The essential role that the fictitious payee rule should play in most double forgery cases is developed further in the discussion of that rule in the next chapter of this book.[83]

[D] Rationales for Finality

Two distinct justifications support the continuation of the principles associated with the rule of *Price v. Neal* that generally leave the loss of

---

[78] Ed Stinn Chevrolet, Inc. v. National City Bank, 28 Ohio St. 3d 221, 503 N.E.2d 524, 2 U.C.C. Rep. Serv. 2d 1565 (1986) (payor bank not allowed to charge customer's account); Cumis Ins. Soc'y, Inc. v. Girard Bank, 522 F. Supp. 414, 32 U.C.C. Rep. Serv. 877 (E.D. Pa. 1981) (same); Aetna Life & Cas. Co. v. Hampton State Bank, 497 S.W.2d 80, 13 U.C.C. Rep. Serv. 876 (Tex. Ct. App. 1973) (payor bank not allowed to recover payment upstream).

[79] U.C.C. § 3-420(a) (cause of action in conversion). *See* § 10.04[B] *infra*.

[80] The Fifth Circuit also utilized the fictitious payee rule to find that the indorsements were effective. U.C.C. § 3-404. For discussion of this rule, see § 10.03[B][1][b] *infra*.

[81] The decision on this point is slippery. A bank's indorsement on behalf of its customer under section 4-205 can be effective only to the extent that the representative is an authorized agent. *See* § 11.02[A][1] *infra*.

[82] U.C.C. § 3-404.

[83] *See* § 10.03[B][1][b] *infra*.

payments of forged instruments on the payor, but not the loss from paying an instrument with a forged indorsement. One justification is found in loss-allocation principles that place the ultimate loss on the innocent party in the best position to have detected the forgery. The other justification stems from the finality doctrine with the view that it is better to end the transaction on the instrument when it is paid rather than to reopen a series of transactions once the forgery is discovered.[84]

Each of these rationales has been criticized. Loss allocation to the payor as the best risk-avoider for forged instruments allegedly requires an exception in favor of the payor when the forgery is accomplished so skillfully that careful comparison with a signature card would not reveal the unauthorized signature. The same rationale has been attacked also on the grounds that it does not comport with modern banking practices. With the high volume of checks that are presented for payment each day and the adoption of mechanized procedures, payor banks realistically cannot scrutinize the signature on every check, and, therefore, arguably should not be expected to know them or to compare them to signature cards. The criticism directed toward finality as a rationale centers on its inconsistency. Although the transactions on a forged instrument end on its payment to a holder, payment over a forged indorsement is not final.

These criticisms, as the discussion below explains, are all wide of the mark. Both of these policies operate together to provide valid justifications for a continuation of the finality principle in modern commercial transactions.

The liability rules create incentives to encourage parties that deal with negotiable instruments to behave in ways that will minimize the risks of fraudulent activities like forgeries. This approach obviously is realistic only to the extent that the potentially liable party can do something to detect or prevent the frauds. Passing the ultimate liability on an instrument with a forged indorsement from the payor to the party who took the instrument from the forger reflects this reality. The payor lacks any means to determine the genuineness of signatures of parties with whom it does not have any dealings. The party taking the instrument from the forger, which often is a depositary bank, at least can reduce the opportunities for these frauds with practices as simple as requiring adequate identification.[85] The allocation of liability to these parties is not premised on the inaccurate assumption that they can eliminate all of the risk of this fraud in their transactions. Rather, it is based on creating incentives to enact preventive measures that will lessen the extent of fraud.

In the case of forged instruments, many critics of the Code's finality rationales fail to perceive the extent to which the codified scheme creates incentives for the payees who take these instruments. A merchant who receives a check in payment for a sale of merchandise incurs the risk that

---

[84] *See* U.C.C. § 3-418, Comment 1 (original version).

[85] Girard Bank v. Mount Holly State Bank, 474 F. Supp. 1225, 1230-31, 26 U.C.C. Rep. Serv. 1210, 1216 (D. N.J. 1979) (person taking from the forger is "normally in the best position to detect the forgery [of the indorsement] and prevent the fraud").

the check will be returned unpaid for a variety of reasons, including insufficient funds, nonexistence of the account, issuance of a stop-payment order, or a forged drawer's signature. The fact that the Code limits the merchant in these situations only to recourse against the drawer of the check creates an incentive for payees to implement preventive practices that will minimize fraudulent activities in the issuance of the check.

The imposition of additional incentives on payors is realistic in cases of forged instruments or irregularities in a customer's account. Payor banks have a means within their control to compare the authorized signature of their drawers with the signatures that appear on the instruments presented for payment. They also have exclusive control over the accounts of their customers and access to all of the information they need to make accurate determinations on whether the state of the account justifies payment. Imposing liability on payors for mistaken payments in these categories of cases creates an incentive for payors to utilize this available information to minimize these frauds. Elimination of the incentive would lead to a tendency for drawees and other payors simply to make prompt processing and payment their sole concern.

Modern check-collection methods and volume unquestionably preclude many payor banks from verifying every check they pay against their customers' signature cards. Even if verification were practical, the cost involved surely would exceed the risk exposure. These considerations, however, are not sufficient to justify shifting the risk to other parties.[86] They are simply factors that affect the ultimate business judgment of the payor bank on how to operate its business in light of its prospects for liability. Some losses can be absorbed at less cost than would be required for detection.[87] The payor bank nevertheless can implement specific measures to give special scrutiny to instruments on which potential losses would be excessive. For example, special processing can be devised for all checks above a particular amount or drawn on designated accounts.[88] The payor bank has means available that can be utilized to minimize certain classes of fraud. The bank's decision not to use them is a conscious business judgment to assume the risk of loss.

Use of the available measures of fraud detection by a payor bank certainly does not ensure complete success, but the risk-allocation rules are not premised on that exalted goal. None of the parties to a negotiable instrument

---

[86] Concerns about large volumes of checks and the utilization of modern mechanized procedures are even less of a problem in the context of mistakes concerning the state of customers' accounts because the computers can be programmed to detect them.

[87] Affidavits submitted by a bank in a case in Oregon showed that reviewing checks for unauthorized signatures resulted in the detection of a small number of forgeries. This benefit was outweighed greatly by the approximate annual cost of $200,000. The bank implemented a system of always reviewing all signatures only on checks of $5,000 or more. Medford Irrigation Dist. v. Western Bank, 66 Or. App. 58, 676 P.2d 329, 38 U.C.C. Rep. Serv. 411 (1984).

[88] Read v. South Carolina Nat'l Bank, 286 S.C. 534, 335 S.E.2d 359, 42 U.C.C. Rep. Serv 974 (1985) (in the absence of special instructions from the customer or an alert on the account, signatures compared only on checks over $10,000); Community Bank v. United States Nat'l Bank, 276 Or. 471, 555 P.2d 435, 20 U.C.C. Rep. Serv. 589 (1976) (payor bank procedure to visually verify drawers' signatures against signature cards on all checks for more than $1,000).

have absolutely fool-proof methods to detect all forms of fraud; consequently, losses that must be borne by innocent parties are inevitable. The Code scheme is to allocate those losses to parties in the best position to detect and prevent each of the different types of fraud. The prospect of ultimate liability creates an incentive to undertake measures to minimize the losses.

Loss-distribution principles further justify placing the ultimate loss on payor banks in cases of forged instruments. These banks can insure against their losses and in turn distribute the cost to their customers who use checks. Despite the preventative efforts, some fraud losses from mistaken payment are inevitable.[89] In effect they are unavoidable costs imposed on the checking system, and, therefore, ought to be borne by the users of that system. The payor bank is the party best situated to cover those costs through insurance and to distribute them to its customers.

The finality rationale, which supports finality from the perspective that ending a transaction upon payment is more desirable than upsetting the prior series of transactions on the instrument, does not by itself explain the results that are codified in the U.C.C. The disparate treatment of payments of forged instruments and payments of instruments with forged indorsements demonstrates the obvious contradictory applications of this rationale. These results, however, do not mean that the professed desirability of ending transactions upon payment is faulty. Rather, it simply is not the only value to be advanced, and thus it is not the sole rationale. The desirability of finality operates in conjunction with the loss-allocation principles. Thus, to the extent that it operates consistently with loss-allocation principles, ending the transaction at the payment stage is highly desirable. The strength of that desirability is not sufficient to relieve parties who take instruments by indorsement from all responsibility for any preventative measures to avoid forged indorsements.

An additional factor further reinforces the desirability of finality upon payment of a forged instrument. The willingness of merchants and other payees to accept checks as a method of payment could lessen if they were to remain liable for forged drawers' signatures even after checks are paid. Such a rule would extend their potential liability until the applicable statute of limitations runs. Payees currently run the risk that the check will be returned unpaid. This exposure is for a relatively short period, however, which enhances a payee's position in pursuing the drawer. Modern commercial practices are not similarly concerned with promoting the transfer of checks by indorsement. Depositary banks are the most likely subsequent transferees of checks, and to the extent that they face ultimate losses from forged indorsements, they are in a position to redistribute them as part of the cost of using the banking system. This perspective thus also demonstrates that the desirability for finality is not an overriding rationale of universal applicability.

---

[89] An individual bank's premiums can be affected by its experience rating, however. The desired incentive for care thus is continued even when the bank insures. *See* Farnsworth, *Insurance Against Check Forgery*, 60 Colum. L. Rev. 284, 302-03 (1960).

§ 9.02 Subrogation: Recovery by Assertion of Rights of Others

[A] The Subrogation Concept — § 4-407

The finality doctrine[90] does not necessarily result in the finality of a drawee bank's options to relieve itself of the loss incurred in paying a check by mistake. Finality alone is not sufficient to address all aspects of unjust enrichment in the check-collection process. It balances the equities between the party paid and the payor bank, allowing the party paid to retain a mistaken payment when the qualifications for one of the designated beneficiaries of section 3-418 are satisfied. The finality doctrine, however, does not address the potential for unjust enrichment of other parties. That concern is the domain of the equitable remedy of subrogation. Subrogation enables the drawee bank to prevent its loss by asserting the rights of other parties either on the instrument or on the underlying transaction that led to issuance of the instrument.

The prospect for additional unjust enrichment in bank collections is readily discernable. If the drawee bank pays by mistake under circumstances in which it is not entitled to charge the payment against the account of its customer and in which it cannot recover the payment itself, the bank faces a certain loss. Furthermore, some other party involved with the instrument and the transaction leading to its issuance may secure a windfall if the bank is not allowed any further recourse. For example, assume that the drawer had issued a stop-payment order on a check without any defense either under Article 3 or on the purchase for which the check was issued. If the bank mistakenly paid the check but was not allowed to subrogate to the seller's contract action for payment, the drawer would be left in possession of the goods and the bank would have paid for them. On the other hand, assume that the drawer issued the stop-payment order because the seller-payee breached the sales contract. If the drawee bank were not permitted to subrogate to the drawer's contract rights against the seller, the bank would have to recredit the drawer's account, but the breaching seller would be left with a windfall in the form of the bank's payment.

The subrogation principle stems from common law. The provision on subrogation in the *Restatement of Restitution* provides as follows: "Where property of one person is used in discharging an obligation owed by another . . ., under such circumstances that the other would be unjustly enriched by the retention of the benefit thus conferred, the former is entitled to be subrogated to the position of the obligee. . . ."[91] Subrogation is a specialized form of restitution given to a plaintiff to prevent unjust enrichment of the defendant when the plaintiff's property has been used to discharge an obligation owed by the defendant.[92] The equitable procedure is used to

---

[90] *See* § 9.01 *supra*.
[91] RESTATEMENT OF RESTITUTION § 162 (1937).
[92] RESTATEMENT OF RESTITUTION § 162, Comment *a*.

revive the defendant's discharged obligation for the benefit of the plaintiff; the plaintiff is subrogated to the position of the obligee.[93] For example, if A owes $50 to B, but C believes that she owes B the $50 and pays B, C can be subrogated to B's right against A for the $50.

Section 4-407 codifies this subrogation principle for application by payor banks. It provides as follows:

> If a payor bank has paid an item over the order of the drawer or maker to stop payment, or after an account has been closed, or otherwise under circumstances giving a basis for objection by the drawer or maker, to prevent unjust enrichment and only to the extent necessary to prevent loss to the bank by reason of its payment of the item, the payor bank is subrogated to the rights
>
> (1) of any holder in due course on the item against the drawer or maker;
>
> (2) of the payee or any other holder of the item against the drawer or maker either on the item or under the transaction out of which the item arose; and
>
> (3) of the drawer or maker against the payee or any other holder of the item with respect to the transaction out of which the item arose.

Section 4-407 enables a bank to prevent several forms of unjust enrichment to the extent necessary to prevent the loss that the bank incurred through its mistaken payment. Because section 4-407 refers directly to drawee bank payments over valid stop-payment orders, the discussion below will initially explain the bank's subrogation rights in this context. It then will explore subrogation rights in the additional circumstances that give drawers and makers a basis to object to payment by the bank. Finally, difficult questions concerning the burden of proof will be posed and analyzed.

[B] Stop-Payment Orders

A drawee bank cannot avoid potential losses from failures to observe stop-payment orders by refusing to accept the orders or through exculpatory clauses.[94] The checking-account customer has a right to issue stop-payment orders for any reason, and that right cannot be negated.[95] Clauses in the contracts with its customers or on stop-payment forms that purport to excuse the bank for improper payment are invalid.[96] The subrogation rights of section 4-407, however, give a drawee bank that improperly pays over a stop-payment order a choice of a number of parties whose rights might assist the bank.

---

[93] RESTATEMENT OF RESTITUTION § 162, Comment c.

[94] This discussion of stop-payment orders is limited to the subrogation context. Chapter 12 on the relationship between the payor bank and its customer provides further treatment of stop-payment orders. See § 12.04 *infra*.

[95] U.C.C. § 4-403(a) and Comment 1.

[96] U.C.C. §§ 4-103(a), 4-403, Comment 7.

§ 9.02   RECOVERY BY ASSERTION OF RIGHTS OF OTHERS   243

The drawee bank can assume the rights of a holder in due course of the check against the drawer.[97] The bank assumes the rights that the holder in due course would have had if the bank had observed the stop-payment order and the holder in due course had sued on the drawer's contract liability.[98] Any defenses that the drawer would have that are valid against the holder in due course are available against the subrogating bank, but all other defenses are cut off.[99] A drawer who loses would have been required to pay the holder in due course anyway, so the bank's improper payment was not a cause of any loss to the drawer. Subrogation denies the drawer the windfall of avoiding its legal obligation to the holder in due course at the expense of the drawee bank.[100]

In the bank-collection process, the availability of a holder in due course often will depend upon whether the depositary bank has given value. These banks generally will meet the good faith and notice elements for holder-in-due-course status, so the issue is likely to be whether they have given value. As a federal court in a Massachusetts case properly indicated, the depositary bank that allowed its customer to draw on the full amount of the credit before it had been collected was a holder in due course for the full amount,[101] and the drawee bank that paid over a stop-payment order was allowed to subrogate to the depositary bank's rights against the drawer.[102]

Additional parties may have valid rights against the drawer even though they do not attain holder-in-due-course status. The drawee bank can also subrogate to the rights of a payee or any other holder of the item. In addition to Article 3 rights on the check itself, the payee's rights on the underlying transaction that led to the drawer's issuance of the check are subrogable.[103]

---

[97] Section 4-407 specifically indicates that this right can also be asserted against the maker of an instrument. Stop-payment orders most commonly are made only on checks, but a maker also can stop payment of a note payable at a bank. In addition, "[b]y analogy the rule extends to drawees other than banks." U.C.C. § 4-403, Comment 3. For convenience of expression, the explanation in this chapter will be limited to checks.

[98] A holder in due course can recover from the drawer who successfully stops payment on a check. McIntyre v. Harris, 304 Ill. App. 3d 304, 709 N.E.2d 982, 39 U.C.C. Rep. Serv. 2d 200 (Ill. Ct. App. 1999); Vail Nat'l Bank v. J. Wheeler Constr. Corp., 669 P.2d 1038, 36 U.C.C. Rep. Serv. 883 (Colo. Ct. App. 1983).

[99] U.C.C. § 3-305(b).

[100] Ordering the drawee bank to stop payment does not discharge the drawer's liability on the instrument. Sawgrass Builders, Inc. v. Realty Coop Inc., 172 Ga. App. 324, 323 S.E.2d 243, 40 U.C.C. Rep. Serv. 159 (1984).

[101] See § 6.01[B][2] supra.

[102] Universal C.I.T. Credit Corp. v. Guaranty Bank & Trust Co., 161 F. Supp. 790, 795, 1 U.C.C. Rep. Serv. 305, 312 (D. Mass. 1958) (drawer "suffered no loss because it would have been liable to [depositary bank] as a holder in due course in any event"). The U.C.C. was not yet effective in Massachusetts, but the court nevertheless applied its relevant provisions in the case analysis. See also Lynnwood Sand & Gravel, Inc. v. Bank of Everett, 29 Wash. App. 686, 630 P.2d 489, 33 U.C.C. Rep. Serv. 1703 (1981) (subrogation allowed when holder-in-due-course status was created in the depositary bank by applying proceeds of deposited check against an existing overdraft in the depositor's account).

[103] Seigel v. Merrill Lynch, Pierce, Fenner & Smith, Inc., 745 A.2d 301, 40 U.C.C. Rep. Serv. 2d 819 (D.C. Ct. App. 2000) (drawee subrogated to rights of casino payees who had the right to enforce checks issued for gambling activity); McIntyre v. Harris, 304 Ill. App. 3d 304, 709

Acceptance of goods by the buyer under a sales contract, for example, obligates the buyer to pay the contract price for the goods.[104] If the goods were defective, giving rise to a claim for breach of warranty,[105] the payee-seller would be entitled only to the portion of the purchase price that exceeds the damages claim, and the drawee bank's subrogation claim against the drawer would be limited accordingly. If the underlying contract claim of the payee-seller exceeds the purchase price of the goods because of additional incidental damages, the bank's subrogation claim would be limited under section 4-407 to the amount that it paid on the instrument.[106]

Finally, the drawee bank may assert the rights of the drawer against the payee or any other holder of the check.[107] These rights must stem from the transaction that induced the drawer to issue the check. If the payee defrauded the drawer, the drawee bank would have to recredit the drawer's account after paying over the stop-payment order, but it could subrogate to the drawer's rights to recover against the fraudulent payee.[108] The bank has the option of pursuing any subsequent holders of the check to the extent that the drawer's rights would be valid against them as well, which is important to the bank if the payee is either unavailable or insolvent.

The Tenth Circuit correctly applied subrogation to a settlement agreement between the drawer and the payee.[109] The drawer stopped payment on a check to an art dealer because he believed the deal for the purchase of a sculpture was unfavorable. The dealer sued for payment, and the

---

N.E.2d 982, 39 U.C.C. Rep. Serv. 2d 200 (1999) (underlying agreement allowed payee to cash the check if the project was not completed on a specified date); Chute v. Bank One of Akron, N.A., 10 Ohio App. 3d 122, 460 N.E.2d 720, 38 U.C.C. Rep. Serv. 949 (1983) (drawer's proof of fraud failed, leaving a valid claim in the payees on their sale of goods); First Nat'l Bank v. Ward, 29 U.C.C. Rep. Serv. 200 (N.M. Ct. App. 1980) (bank successfully subrogated to rights of payee against guarantors of the drawer once the drawer filed for bankruptcy).

[104] U.C.C. § 2-607(1).

[105] U.C.C. § 2-714.

[106] The drawee bank is granted subrogation rights "only to the extent necessary to prevent loss to the bank by reason of its payment of the item." U.C.C. § 4-407.

[107] Southeast First Nat'l Bank v. Atlantic Telec, Inc., 389 So. 2d 1032, 30 U.C.C. Rep. Serv. 1629 (Fla. Dist. Ct. App. 1980) (payee breached contract with drawer by failing to provide technical information and sales assistance required by the contract).

[108] The drawee bank sometimes will subrogate to the interests of two parties. Assume that Buyer issues a check for $1,000 to Seller for goods delivered to Buyer. Buyer promptly stops payment on the check after discovering that the goods have a defect, but the drawee bank pays the check to Seller by mistake. Buyer's breach of warranty claim on the goods she accepted is worth $250. Drawee Bank should be required to recredit Buyer's account for only $250, as the remaining $750 could be recovered from Buyer by Seller if the drawee bank had in fact stopped payment. Drawee Bank could also subrogate to Buyer's warranty claim for $250 against Seller in order to prevent Seller from being unjustly enriched by receipt of full payment for defective goods. If Seller had deposited the check for collection rather than presenting directly to the drawee bank, the depositary bank might qualify as a holder in due course for the full amount of the check, in which case the drawee bank could subrogate to those rights and Buyer would be forced to assert its breach of warranty claim against Seller.

[109] Swiss Credit Bank v. Balink, 614 F.2d 1269, 28 U.C.C. Rep. Serv. 479 (10th Cir. 1980). For a settlement case in which the payor bank subrogated to the rights of the payee against the drawer, see Manufactures Hanover Trust Co. v. Ava Indus., Inc. 98 Misc. 2d 614, 414 N.Y.S.2d 425, 26 U.C.C. Rep. Serv. 747 (Sup. Ct. 1978).

drawer counterclaimed for damages from alleged false advertising. The dealer deposited the check a second time, and the Swiss payor bank paid it by mistake over the stop-payment order. Under Swiss law the bank had to recredit the drawer's account upon learning of its error. Subsequently, the drawer and the payee settled their suit. Because the payee had refused the bank's earlier demand to return the money paid, the bank sued the payee in federal court in New Mexico. The court held that the bank could subrogate to the rights of the drawer against the payee. Although the payee asserted that he depended upon the payment already received from the bank in agreeing to the settlement, the court found on the record that the payee could not reasonably believe he held the bank's payment free and clear.[110]

[C] Other Grounds for Objection by Buyers

The payor bank's right to subrogation does not apply only when the bank makes an improper payment in disregard of a stop-payment order. Its subrogation right also applies to any circumstances in which the bank has paid an item but cannot properly charge its customer's account. Any case in which the payor bank is required to recredit its customer's account under section 4-401 is a potential case for subrogration.

Premature payment on a postdated check has been a traditional occasion for subrogation. Despite improper payment of the check, the bank could assert a subrogation claim for any rights that entitled the payee to the funds. The amendments to Article 4, however, have changed the circumstances under which a postdated check is considered to be not properly payable. Automated check-collection systems generally cannot detect the date of a check. In order to accommodate this reality of check collections, the amendments require an additional procedure that a customer must observe in order to make early payment on a postdated check improper. Following a procedure comparable to the issuance of a stop-payment order, the customer must give the bank advance notice of the postdating with sufficient time for the bank to have a reasonable opportunity to act upon it.[111] Thus, a payor bank now will be concerned about subrogation rights only if the bank pays early on a check on which the customer has provided the required notification.

A payor bank also does not have any authority to charge its customer's account when it pays a check that does not have the drawer's required signature. Even in these circumstances, however, the bank occasionally can assert a legitimate subrogation claim. In *American Communications Telecommunications, Inc. v. Commerce North Bank*,[112] the bank improperly

---

[110] The bank had demanded return of the payment two months prior to the settlement. The payee-dealer received $11,500 from payment of the check. In the settlement with the drawer, the dealer received paintings worth $9,400 plus $500 cash. The court concluded that the difference of $1,600 could have been the reasonable worth of the dismissal of an apparently legitimate claim of false advertising. Essentially the court found that the dealer had been paid twice and would be unjustly enriched if allowed to retain the payment from the bank.

[111] U.C.C. § 4-401(c).

[112] 691 S.W.2d 44, 41 U.C.C. Rep. Serv. 909 (Tex. Ct. App. 1985).

paid a check signed by only one authorized employee, even though the account agreement required two signatures. The check had been issued, however, to pay for advertising services that had been provided under a valid contract to the drawer company. The payor bank was subrogated to the rights of the advertising firm against the drawer company for this underlying contract obligation.[113]

The case of *Dozier v. First Alabama Bank*[114] demonstrates the devastating impact on a payor bank's subrogation rights when a drawer's signature is not authorized and, thus, does not bind the purported principal. The payor bank sought to subrogate to its corporate customer's rights against the holder of the check who presented it and received payment, despite the undisputed lack of authority of the signatory drawer to sign checks on the account. The court easily found that the corporate customer was not a drawer of the check, so the bank could not subrogate to any rights its customer might have against holders of the check. A bank facing a similar ruling could not be any more successful in seeking to subrogate to the rights of any other party, because every option in section 4-407 on a check involves subrogation to the rights of the drawer or to the rights of other parties against the drawer.

In cases of forged drawers' signatures, rights of payor banks generally apply only with respect to the individual who signed the check.[115] A warranty cause of action will not lie against the forging drawer, even though the drawer obviously knows that the signature of the purported drawer is unauthorized, because the drawer is not a transferor of the draft.[116] Subrogation rights apply to these checks, as the forging drawer is unjustly enriched by the payor bank's payment by mistake. The payor bank has a restitution claim, as money of the bank was used to discharge an obligation owed by the forging drawer.[117] The practical limitations of enforcing valid claims against forgers constrains recovery on these claims.

Subrogation could also apply conceptually in some cases to preclude a drawer's insistence that the deposit account be recredited following payment over a forged indorsement. If the payee's signature is forged on a check that is paid by the drawee bank to the forger, the payee has a valid cause of action for conversion against the bank.[118] If the bank pays the payee

---

[113] Even though the check did not contain the two signatures required by the agreement to make the check properly payable, the one signature was authorized and indicated representative capacity sufficient to bind the company as a drawer of the check. U.C.C. §§ 3-401(a), 3-402.

[114] 363 So. 2d 781, 25 U.C.C. Rep. Serv. 802 (Ala. Ct. App. 1978).

[115] If the purported drawer received and retained benefits from the underlying transaction, ratification principles would allow recovery against the indicated drawer. Similarly, if negligence of the purported drawer contributed to the unauthorized signature, the drawer would be precluded from denying the signature. U.C.C. § 3-406(a).

[116] U.C.C. § 4-208(a). The forging drawer issues the instrument, but does not transfer it. U.C.C. §§ 3-105(a), 3-203(a).

[117] *See* RESTATEMENT OF RESTITUTION § 162 (1937); § 9.02[A] *supra*.

[118] U.C.C. § 3-420(a).

in recognition of that liability, the drawer's right to complain that the check was not properly payable becomes irrelevant. If the drawer chose to press a claim against the bank under section 4-401, the bank could defend by subrogating to the rights of the payee, who in the absence of payment from the bank on the check would have been entitled to enforce the instrument against the drawer.[119]

[D] Burden of Proof — § 4-403(c)

Although subrogation rights can be very valuable to a payor bank because of their extensive nature, the predicament for the bank is that its rights can depend upon the rights of the drawer, the payee, or other holders against each other. For example, a drawer of a check might issue a stop-payment order because of an alleged defect in the goods delivered under the applicable sales contract. The payor bank that improperly pays over the drawer's stop-payment order can subrogate to the rights of either the drawer or the payee, or both, but selection of the correct party for subrogation is predicated on resolution of the breach of warranty claim. An opportunity to implead third parties, therefore, can be very important to the bank.[120] If both the drawer and the payee can be joined in one suit and their dispute litigated, the bank's alternative subrogation rights resolve much of its dilemma.[121]

Payor banks have successfully impleaded third parties in subrogation cases. In *Mitchell v. Republic Bank & Trust Co.*,[122] the appointed receiver of the drawer instituted an action against the payor bank for failure to observe a stop-payment order. The bank claimed subrogation rights of the payee against the drawer, and subsequently filed a third-party complaint against the payee based on subrogation to the rights of the plaintiff drawer. In *Sunshine v. Bankers Trust Co.*,[123] the bank paid a check by not returning it to the depositor-payee before its midnight deadline. It nevertheless debited the payee's account to comply with a stop-payment order, and the payee sued to recover the chargeback. The bank then impleaded the drawer. In both cases the payor bank was at odds with its drawer.

---

[119] U.C.C. §§ 3-309(a), 3-310(b)(4).

[120] Third-party practice involves several devices to bring other involved parties into a single case, including impleader, interpleader, vouching, and joinder of parties. See U.C.C. §§ 2-607(5); 3-803. Jurisdiction problems still can present obstacles. Hughes v. Marine Midland Bank, 127 Misc. 2d 209, 484 N.Y.S.2d 1000, 40 U.C.C. Rep. Serv. 998 (City Ct. N.Y. 1985) (N.Y. court lacked jurisdiction over Florida payee).

[121] Professional Sav. Bank v. Galloway Farm Nursery, Inc., 514 So. 2d 76, 5 U.C.C. Rep. Serv. 2d 138 (Fla. Ct. App. 1987) (error to dismiss claim against drawer in restitution action brought by bank against both payee and drawer). Courts have ruled that motions by plaintiffs for summary judgment against payor banks are incorrect in part on the grounds that the pending joinder of a third party was necessary to secure the availability of the bank's rights of subrogation. Kupersmith v. Manufacturers Hanover Trust Co., 15 U.C.C. Rep. Serv. 696 (N.Y. Civ. Ct. 1974).

[122] 35 N.C. App. 101, 239 S.E.2d 867, 23 U.C.C. Rep. Serv. 712 (1978).

[123] 34 N.Y.2d 404, 358 N.Y.S.2d 113, 314 N.E.2d 860, 14 U.C.C. Rep. Serv. 1416 (Ct. App. 1974).

Article 4 creates two apparently irreconcilable burdens of proof for cases in which a drawer and its bank contest the consequences of the bank's failure to observe a stop-payment order. A bank that defends its actions by asserting section 4-407 subrogation rights seemingly would bear the burden of proof on the asserted rights. Yet section 4-403(c) places a contrary burden of proof on the bank's customer. It provides that "[t]he burden of establishing the fact and amount of loss resulting from the payment of an item contrary to a stop-payment order or order to close an account is on the customer." The question posed is whether loss must be proved by the drawer or the absence of loss must be proved by the payor bank.

Several courts have reconciled the apparent conflict between sections 4-403(c) and 4-407 by dividing the burden of proof. The Court of Appeals of New York indicated in *Sunshine* that the bank acting as subrogee has the burden of moving forward. A subsequent opinion of the New York Supreme Court, *Thomas v. Marine Midland Tinkers National Bank*,[124] affirmed that opinion and stated that the burden includes "presenting evidence which would show an absence of actual loss sustained by a plaintiff depositor. . . ."[125] The supreme court went on to indicate that when the bank meets its burden of moving forward, the ultimate burden on loss must be sustained by the drawer.

This same approach was followed by the court in *Mitchell*. It stated precisely the allocations of proof when the drawer sues the bank:

> We are aware that the two sections [4-403(3) and 4-407] may present a question as to who has the ultimate burden of proof. The better rule, we believe, is to place the ultimate burden of proof as to loss on the customer. A prima facie case is established by the customer when he shows that the bank paid a check contrary to a valid stop payment order. Then the bank, exercising its subrogation rights created by [4-407], has the burden of coming forward and presenting evidence of an absence of actual loss sustained by the customer. When the bank meets the burden of coming forward, the customer must sustain the ultimate burden of proof.[126]

Because a material issue of fact existed concerning the plaintiff's actual loss, the court appropriately ruled that the trial court had erred in granting the plaintiff's motion for summary judgment.

---

[124] 381 N.Y.S.2d 797, 801, 18 U.C.C. Rep. Serv. 1273, 1278 (N.Y. Sup. Ct. 1976).

[125] 381 N.Y.S.2d at 801, 18 U.C.C. Rep. Serv. at 1278.

[126] 239 S.E.2d at 869, 23 U.C.C. Rep. Serv. at 714. *Accord*, Southeast First Nat'l Bank v. Atlantic Telec, Inc., 389 So. 2d 1032, 30 U.C.C. Rep. Serv. 1629 (Fla. Dist. Ct. App. 1980). This approach differs from the one indicated by the court in Siegel v. New England Merchants Nat'l Bank, 386 Mass. 672, 437 N.E.2d 218, 33 U.C.C. Rep. Serv. 1601 (1982). The *Siegel* court reduces the extent of the bank's burden. It requires the bank to identify the status of the parties to whose rights it subrogates, but specifically relieves the bank of any requirement to establish a claim in favor of its subrogee against the drawer when the rights asserted are based on the underlying transaction. It places all of this responsibility entirely on the drawer because the drawer, unlike the bank, participated in the transaction and knows of the relevant facts. Although the facts in *Siegel* involved premature payment of a postdated check, the court applied section 4-403(3) on stop-payment orders by analogy.

Chapter 10
TORT CONCEPTS

SYNOPSIS

§ 10.01 Introduction

§ 10.02 Negligence
- [A] Negligence Contributing to Forgeries or Alterations — § 3-406
  - [1] The Doctrine of *Young v. Grote*
  - [2] Preclusion
    - [a] Rationale
    - [b] Applying the Preclusion
  - [3] Negligence
    - [a] Tort Standard
    - [b] Substantially Contributes
  - [4] Comparative Negligence
- [B] Customer Negligence With Respect to Statement of Account — § 4-406
  - [1] The Customer's Duty
  - [2] Consequences of Customer Noncompliance
  - [3] Comparative Negligence of the Bank
  - [4] Time Limits on Customer's Rights

§ 10.03 Strict Liability
- [A] Introduction
- [B] Impostors and Nominal or Fictitious Payees — § 3-404
  - [1] Applicable Rules
    - [a] The Impostor Rule
    - [b] The Nominal or Fictitious Payee Rule
  - [2] The Indorsement
  - [3] Comparative Negligence
- [C] Fraudulent Indorsements by Employees — § 3-405

§ 10.04 Conversion — § 3-420
- [A] The Proper Defendant
  - [1] Thieves, Finders and Their Transferees
  - [2] Collection, Payment and Indorsements
  - [3] Representatives: Depositary and Collecting Banks
- [B] The Proper Plaintiff
  - [1] Payees and Indorsees: Delivery
  - [2] Issuers and Acceptors Excluded
- [C] Damages

[D] The Case of Restrictive Indorsements — § 3-206(c)

§ 10.01 Introduction

The Code utilizes torts concepts in its loss-allocation rules. The legal position of persons who do not observe ordinary standards of care can change because of their negligence. Section 3-406 determines the legal effect of negligence that "substantially contributes" to a forged signature on an instrument or an alteration of an instrument. Section 4-406 addresses the duty of a customer to examine bank statements and returned checks and to notify the bank of discovered alterations and unauthorized signatures. Sections 3-404 and 3-405 cover circumstances in which indorsements can be effective even though they are unauthorized. The sections are premised on the responsibility of an employer and principles of enterprise liability. In addition, section 3-420 recognizes circumstances in which a person is liable for conversion of a negotiable instrument. All of these concepts are discussed in this chapter.

§ 10.02 Negligence

[A] Negligence Contributing to Forgeries or Alterations — § 3-406

[1] The Doctrine of *Young v. Grote*

A husband, who planned to be away from home for an extended period, left a number of signed blank checks with his wife so that she could complete them when payments were necessary. She gave one of these checks to her husband's clerk to be completed for fifty pounds. The clerk filled in the blanks for the amount by beginning the writing far toward the right on each of the blanks. The clerk showed the wife the completed check in the amount of fifty pounds, and she instructed him to cash the check at the bank. Before presenting the check, the clerk, by inserting additional writing in the spaces he purposely left open, raised the amount of the check to 350 pounds. The court denied the husband recovery against the bank for the amount of the alteration because of the negligence of the husband and wife in the drawing and delivery of the check prepared in a manner that easily facilitated the insertion of the additional language.[1]

The drafters of the Code adopted the doctrine of *Young v. Grote* in codifying a provision on the effect of negligence contributing to forged signatures or alterations. The provision states as follows:

> A person whose failure to exercise ordinary care substantially contributes to an alteration of an instrument or to the making of a

---

[1] Young v. Grote, 4 Bing. 253, 130 Eng. Rep. 764 (1827).

forged signature on an instrument is precluded from asserting the alteration or the forgery against a person who, in good faith, pays the instrument or takes it for value or for collection.[2]

The Comments to the provision state that the early English case upon which the section is patterned "held that a drawer who so negligently draws an instrument as to facilitate its material alteration is liable to a drawee who pays the altered instrument in good faith."[3] The Code section extends the doctrine in three significant respects. First, it expands the doctrine to all instruments, not just drafts. Second, it applies the negligence principle to the facilitation of forged signatures as well as to alterations. Third, in addition to drawees who pay the instrument, it designates as beneficiaries of the provision a person who pays the instrument or who takes it for value or for collection.

[2] Preclusion

[a] Rationale

Although negligence under section 3-406 is clearly the standard tort concept, it does not operate to create tort liability for the negligent party.[4] Instead the negligent party is precluded from asserting a forged signature or an alteration against the designated protected parties. Rather than making negligent parties liable in tort, the section estops them from asserting the acts that their negligence facilitates. As a result, the parties designated in section 3-406 can treat the altered instrument as though it had been issued in its altered form, and they can preclude a negligent party from asserting that a signature is forged.

The reason for applying negligence through an estoppel basis stems from the problem of proof associated with the traditional form of tort liability.[5] Tort recovery would allow damages only for the loss occasioned by the negligence, which would be limited to the amount that the payor or the person who took the instrument could not recover from the wrongdoer. The damages of the negligent party thus could not be ascertained until remedies against the wrongdoer were pursued. The drafters favored estopping the negligent party, thereby allowing full recovery for the payor or person who took the instrument and leaving the negligent party as the one to be faced with pursuing recovery against the wrongdoer.

[b] Applying the Preclusion

The preclusion associated with negligence facilitating a forged signature should be read in conjunction with section 3-403.[6] That section provides

---

[2] U.C.C. § 3-406(a).

[3] U.C.C. § 3-406, Comment 1.

[4] *Id.*

[5] U.C.C. § 3-406, Comment 5 (original version). Section 3-406(a) is based on the original version.

[6] The term forged signature, rather than unauthorized signature, is used in section 3-406

dual legal consequences for unauthorized signatures: they operate as the signature of the unauthorized signer, but they are inoperative as the signature of the person whose name is signed.[7] Section 3-406(a), however, can impact the latter consequence. When the negligence of the person whose name is signed substantially contributes to a forgery of that person's name, section 3-406 can preclude that person from asserting the forgery. With the preclusion stemming from the negligence of the person whose name is signed, the forged signature can be treated as through it were the signature of the named person, but only by payors in good faith and persons who in good faith take the instrument for value or collection.[8]

Section 3-403 does not apply to all cases of preclusion due to negligence contributing to a forged signature. The negligence of a party can contribute to the forgery of a signature other than his or her own. For example, negligence of drawers has led to their preclusion to deny the effectiveness of an indorsement.[9]

In cases of alteration, section 3-406 should be read together with section 3-407 on alteration.[10] When the alteration consists of the improper completion of an incomplete instrument, negligence under section 3-406 does not add anything to the rights of a subsequent holder in due course or a payor bank or drawee that pays the instrument, as these parties are always entitled to enforce rights with respect to the instrument as it has been completed.[11] The Code does not specifically state that persons who prepare incomplete instruments are prima facie negligent, but that is the thrust of the provisions. The comments to the section dealing with incomplete instruments indicates that "[t]he loss should fall upon the party whose conduct in signing blank paper has made the fraud possible, rather than upon the innocent purchaser."[12] When the alteration consists of changing or adding to the terms of a complete instrument, the negligence of a party

---

because it focuses more precisely on the scope of the section. In addition to forgeries, unauthorized signatures also include signatures without the authority to bind the principal. U.C.C. § 1-201(43). These latter signatures are governed by the law of agency.

[7] U.C.C. § 3-403(a). See § 4.04[B] supra.

[8] "Good faith" is defined in Article 3 to mean "honesty in fact and the observance of reasonable commercial standards of fair dealing." U.C.C. § 3-103(a)(4). For discussion of the content of this definition, see § 6.01[C] supra. San Tan Irrigation District v. Wells Fargo Bank, 197 Ariz. 193, 3 P.3d 1113, 40 U.C.C. Rep. Serv. 2d 775 (Ariz. Ct. App. 2000) (remand necessary to establish the record concerning the fairness of the bank's conduct for purposes of section 3-406).

[9] A drawer who negligently mails a check to the wrong person having the same name as the payee could substantially contribute to a forged indorsement. U.C.C. § 3-406, Comment 3 (Illustration #2). See Koerner & Lambert v. Allstate Ins. Co., 374 So. 2d 179, 27 U.C.C. Rep. Serv. 478 (La. Ct. App. 1979) (insurer entrusted drafts to repair facility in name of insured without notifying the insured); Fidelity & Cas. Co. v. Constitution Nat'l Bank, 167 Conn. 478, 356 A.2d 117, 16 U.C.C. Rep. Serv. 439 (1975) (failure to verify loan application information).

[10] For discussion of section 3-407, see § 7.02[F] supra.

[11] U.C.C. § 3-407(c). A payor bank can charge the drawer's account according to the tenor of the completed check. U.C.C. § 4-401(d)(2). See § 12.02[B] infra.

[12] U.C.C. § 3-115, Comment 4 (original version). Section 3-115 of the revision carries forward the rules set forth in the original version.

who contributes to the alteration is relevant to a holder in due course or a person who pays the instrument in good faith. Absent the negligence, these parties are entitled to enforce rights with respect to the instrument, against a party whose contract has been changed by the alteration, only according to its original terms.[13] If that same party is negligent under section 3-406, however, preclusion to assert the alteration entitles these parties to treat the altered instrument as though it had been issued in its altered form.

When an altered instrument is taken by a person other than a subsequent holder in due course, section 3-407(b) allows discharge of any person whose contract has been fraudulently changed. The section, however, provides an exception when "that party assents or is precluded from asserting the alteration."[14] The language on preclusion "recognizes the possibility of an estoppel or other ground barring the defense which does not rest on assent."[15] Thus, a party whose negligence substantially contributes to the alteration of an instrument cannot achieve discharge against any person who, in good faith, takes the instrument for value or for collection.

The estoppel principle generally operates effectively with the other Code liability rules to pass the loss, or at least the necessity of pursuing the wrongdoer, from the party who would face ultimate liability to the party whose negligence substantially contributed to the wrongdoing. The estoppel can be exercised as a defense when the negligent party seeks recovery against one of the protected parties stipulated under section 3-406. Sometimes it can also be used to defeat a defense asserted by the negligent party when a protected party brings an action.

Consider the negligence of a drawer that substantially contributes to an alteration or an unauthorized signature on a check. If the drawer wants the checking account recredited under section 4-401 because the check was not properly payable, the drawee bank has a good defense based on the drawer's negligence. By estopping the drawer from asserting the alteration or forgery, the bank is entitled to retain the charge against the customer's account for the full amount of the check as paid.[16] If the check is dishonored by the payor bank rather than paid, a holder in due course can enforce the drawer's contract, using section 3-406 in conjunction with either section 3-404 or section 3-407(3) to estop the drawer's defense of unauthorized signature or alteration.

A payor bank's successful use of section 3-406 to resist recrediting its customer's account does not convert forgeries into good signatures or alterations into unaltered instruments. The negligence provides a defense, and the estoppel operates only against the negligent party and in favor of

---

[13] U.C.C. § 3-407(c).

[14] U.C.C. § 3-407(b).

[15] U.C.C. § 3-407, Comment 1.

[16] Insurance Co. of N. Am. v. Purdue Nat'l Bank, 401 N.E.2d 708, 28 U.C.C. Rep. Serv. 766 (Ind. Ct. App. 1980); Stone & Webster Engineering Corp. v. First Nat'l Bank & Trust Co., 345 Mass. 1, 184 N.E.2d 358, 1 U.C.C. Rep. Serv. 195 (1962).

the designated protected parties.[17] Consequently, prior transferors and the recipient of payment may have breached presentment warranties to the payor bank.[18] Their breach means they are liable for any damages beyond the amount of the item that the breach causes to the payor bank. The most significant possible damages are the costs of defense against the customer-drawer, including attorney fees.[19]

Although a drawee bank clearly can raise section 3-406 against its negligent customer who contends under section 4-401 that the bank paid an item that was not properly payable, the drawee bank might choose to waive its defense and recredit its customer's account. The bank might prefer this approach out of deference to its business relationship with the customer or because it wishes to avoid becoming embroiled in a dispute over the customer's negligence. If the drawee bank follows this option, the question then becomes whether the bank can recover its loss by pursuing a warranty cause of action. Breach of warranty will be relatively easy to establish against a collecting bank in cases of material alteration or forged indorsements.[20] The negligence of the drawer-customer in facilitating the act that led the collecting banks to breach their warranties cannot be asserted against the drawee bank, because the estoppel operates only against the negligent party.

The problem with this approach is that it allows the drawer or maker whose negligence substantially contributes to the alteration or the unauthorized signature to avoid responsibility for the negligence. It also places the drawee bank in the position of deciding who bears the loss. The collecting banks can pass liability upstream under transferors' warranties until liability rests on the party who took from the wrongdoer. That party would then have to proceed against the wrongdoer for breach of warranty, although the scoundrel is most likely insolvent or unavailable. Even when facing ultimate liability for the breach of warranty, that party could not pursue a drawer whose negligence created this predicament. A contract cause of action would not lie because the instrument was paid and not dishonored, and the issuer of an instrument does not extend transfer warranties. Section 3-406 furthermore does not provide a cause of action against the customer for the negligence.

The drafters resolved this dilemma by creating a defense against a presentment-warranty claim by the drawee. When the warranty claim asserted by a drawee is based on a forged indorsement or alteration of the draft, the warrantor can defend on the grounds that the drawer is precluded under section 3-406 from asserting the forged indorsement or alteration against the drawee.[21] This defense "gives to the warrantor the benefit of rights that the drawee has against the drawer" under section 3-406.[22]

---

[17] A California case inaccurately indicates that negligence operates to preclude the negligent party from denying that the forged signatures are operative indorsements. Cooper v. Union Bank, 9 Cal. 3d 371, 107 Cal. Rptr. 1, 507 P.2d 609, 12 U.C.C. Rep. Serv. 209 (1973).

[18] U.C.C. § 4-208(a).

[19] See § 8.05[B] supra.

[20] U.C.C. § 4-208(a)(1), (2).

[21] U.C.C. §§ 3-417(c), 4-208(c).

[22] U.C.C. § 3-417, Comment 6.

The negligence of a maker or an acceptor can also lead to an estoppel. A maker or an acceptor who pays the instrument and then seeks to recover on a presentment warranty may face the section 3-406 defense of negligence from a party who had taken the instrument for value or for collection. The maker or acceptor who refuses to pay because its signature was forged or because the instrument was altered will lose its defense if its negligence was a substantial contributing factor. Two lower courts in New York completely misapplied the negligence provision to the contract of an acceptor, reasoning erroneously that, because an acceptor is liable according to the terms of the instrument at the time is was accepted, a certifying bank cannot be liable for a subsequent alteration caused by its negligence.[23] The bank's negligence estops it from asserting the alteration, and the bank is bound on its contract for the altered amount.[24]

Negligence of the payee that substantially contributes to a forged indorsement also poses a straightforward application of section 3-406. Causes of action based on a theory of conversion are explained later in this chapter,[25] but one of the clearest applications of the theory allows the owner to sue when an instrument is paid over a forged indorsement.[26] If the negligent payee were to bring this suit against a drawee bank or other payor, the defense of negligence would preclude the payee from asserting the forgery, thereby undermining the validity of the claim.[27]

[3] Negligence

[a] Tort Standard

The U.C.C. does not undertake to define specific actions that constitute a "failure to exercise ordinary care [that] substantially contributes" to an alteration or a forgery. It only defines "ordinary care" in broad terms applicable to a person engaged in business.[28] Nevertheless, negligence is

---

[23] Wallach Sons, Inc. v. Bankers Trust Co., 62 Misc. 2d 19, 307 N.Y.S.2d 297, 7 U.C.C. Rep. Serv. 141 (1970) (bank's negligence consisted of certifying a check drawn so that it was possible to insert two zeros after the numerical "29" and the word "hundred" after the written "twenty nine" to raise the check from $29 to $2900); Sam Goody, Inc. v. Franklin Nat'l Bank, 57 Misc. 2d 193, 291 N.Y.S.2d 429, 5 U.C.C. Rep. Serv. 502 (1968) (check certified for $16 raised to $1,600).

[24] In a subsequent federal decision in New York, the district court stated that it did not believe that the Court of Appeals of New York would follow the two lower court opinions cited in the previous footnote and it denied summary judgment for the certifying bank against a professed holder in due course. Brower v. Franklin Nat'l Bank, 311 F. Supp. 675, 7 U.C.C. Rep. Serv. 1021 (S.D. N.Y. 1970) (certification of checks for $10 and $8 with spaces that facilitated their alteration to $10,000 and $28,600 respectively).

[25] See § 10.04 *infra*.

[26] U.C.C. § 3-420(a).

[27] Cooper v. Union Bank, 9 Cal. 3d 371, 107 Cal. Rptr. 1, 507 P.2d 609, 12 U.C.C. Rep. Serv. 209 (1973).

[28] " 'Ordinary care' in the case of a person engaged in business means observance of reasonable commercial standards, prevailing in the area in which the person is located, with respect to the business in which the person is engaged." U.C.C. § 3-103(a)(7). This definition is applicable to all businesses, including banks. An additional sentence of the definition has relevance only to banks processing instruments for collection or payment by automated means. For discussion of this part of the definition, see § 10.02[A][4] *infra*.

a tort concept based on a violation of a duty of reasonable care owed to the injured party. Section 3-406 extends the negligence principle adopted in *Young v. Grote*[29] to benefit persons who take an instrument for value or for collection, as well as drawees and other payors. It "rejects decisions holding that the maker of a note owes no duty of care to the holder because at the time the instrument is issued there is no contract between them."[30] The responsibility to exercise due care is justified by the actions of drawers and makers in allowing an instrument to enter the stream of commerce.

Although the possible forms of negligence are myriad, the cases show several patterns that have been raised repeatedly. The classic facts of *Young v. Grote*, wherein the drawer of a check leaves ample spaces on the lines showing the amount of the check, has repeatedly led to a finding of negligence.[31] Leaving critical spaces completely blank is an even more obvious case.[32] On the other hand, a reasonably careful person does not protect against leaving any spaces on an instrument. Even though provisions can be added, it generally is not negligence to leave spaces between lines or at the end of an instrument. Even though space following the name of a payee allows an alteration by the addition of the word "or" and an additional payee's name, leaving the space is not likely to constitute negligence given the common practices of check preparation and the lessened likelihood for this type of alteration compared with changes in the amount. Drawers and makers do not have a duty to use sensitized paper, indelible ink, or a protectograph, but the use of a pencil or easily erased ink probably constitutes negligence.

A person who uses a rubber stamp or an automatic signing device must exercise reasonable care to secure it. If access to the stamp or machine is available to unauthorized persons, together with blank check forms, the drawer is likely to be held negligent.[33] One case drew a distinction concerning a protectograph that was kept in an unlocked desk drawer of a company's office.[34] The business was burglarized and a number of the company's blank checks were stolen after being filled in with the amount

---

[29] *See* § 10.02[A] *supra*.

[30] U.C.C. § 3-406, Comment 1.

[31] U.C.C. § 3-406, Comment 3 (Case # 3). *See* J. Gordon Neely Enters., Inc. v. American Nat'l Bank, 403 So. 2d 887, 32 U.C.C. Rep. Serv. 1525 (Ala. 1981); Williams v. Montana Nat'l Bank, 167 Mont. 24, 534 P.2d 1247 (1975). The Supreme Court of Texas reversed a lower court and refused to find negligence that substantially contributed to the alteration under this fact pattern, but the decision is a classic example of "widow's law." Ray v. Farmers State Bank, 576 S.W.2d 607, 25 U.C.C. Rep. Serv. 779 (Tex. 1979).

[32] E. Bierhaus & Sons, Inc. v. Bowling, 486 N.E.2d 598, 42 U.C.C. Rep. Serv. 920 (Ind. Ct. App. 1985) (issuing a blank check).

[33] U.C.C. § 3-406, Comment 3 (Case # 1). *See* Commercial Credit Equip. Corp. v. First Alabama Bank, 636 F.2d 1051, 30 U.C.C. Rep. Serv. 1185 (5th Cir. 1981) (drawer negligently hired a forger and gave forger access to checks and embossing equipment). General access to the customer's checkbook each time the grandson visited his residence, however, was held not, without more, to constitute a lack of ordinary care. Marx v. Whitney Nat'l Bank, 713 So. 2d 1142, 38 U.C.C. Rep. Serv. 2d 488 (La. 1998).

[34] Fred Meyer, Inc. v. Temco Metal Prods. Co., 267 Or. 230, 516 P.2d 80, 13 U.C.C. Rep. Serv. 853 (1973).

set on the protectograph machine. The court did not allow recovery by the retail store chain where the checks were cashed because the drawer's signature was forged manually and not by use of a facsimile signature machine.

Placing a check in the hands of someone other than the payee sometimes constitutes negligence. The most obvious case is when a check is mailed to the wrong person who has the same name as the payee.[35] Other cases must be analyzed in terms of the risk of fraudulent actions by the person to whom the check is entrusted. For example, courts have found a lack of negligence in sending a check to someone other than the payee,[36] but not when the check was sent directly to a person who had promised to repair an insured party's boat.[37] A drawer has been found negligent in sending checks to an attorney, however, because the authority for the attorney to open the account in his client's name and to conduct the transactions on her behalf was never verified, and in fact, did not exist.[38] Once a drawer is determined to be negligent in issuing a check, the question turns on whether the negligence substantially contributed to the subsequent forgery. As the discussion in the next subsection indicates, the courts are split on the issue in these types of cases.

Employers must exercise care in their hiring and supervision of employees. In a number of cases, employers have hired individuals with known backgrounds of gambling or embezzlement or have failed to investigate their backgrounds before hiring them.[39] When these individuals are placed in a position where they can forge or alter instruments of the company or forge indorsements on checks payable to the company, the employer has generally been found to be negligent. The revision to Article 3 precludes any necessity of establishing negligence with respect to fraudulent indorsements made by employees who have been assigned responsibilities to deal

---

[35] U.C.C. § 3-406, Comment 3 (Case # 2). *See* Park State Bank v. Arena Auto Auction, Inc., 59 Ill. App. 2d 235, 207 N.E.2d 158, 2 U.C.C. Rep. Serv. 903 (1965).

[36] Guardian Life Ins. Co. v. Chemical Bank, 47 A.D.2d 608, 363 N.Y.S.2d 820, 16 U.C.C. Rep. Serv. 786 (1975) (check sent to payee's broker); Gast v. American Gas. Co., 99 N.J. Super. 538, 240 A.2d 682, 5 U.C.C. Rep. Serv. 155 (1968) (check sent to attorney of purchasers of damaged property).

[37] Koerner & Lambert v. Allstate Ins. Co., 374 So. 2d 179, 27 U.C.C. Rep. Serv. 478 (La. Ct. App. 1979). *See also* Fidelity & Deposit Co. v. First Nat'l Bank, 98 Wis. 2d 474, 297 N.W.2d 46, 30 U.C.C. Rep. Serv. 253 (Ct. App. 1980) (check payable to borrower and contractor was sent directly to the contractor).

[38] Bagby v. Merrill Lynch, Pierce, Fenner & Smith, Inc., 491 F.2d 192, 13 U.C.C. Rep. Serv. 1069 (8th Cir. 1974). *See also* Fidelity & Deposit Co. v. Chemical Bank N. Y. Trust Co., 65 Misc. 2d 619, 318 N.Y.S.2d 957, 8 U.C.C. Rep. Serv. 541 (App. Div. 1970), *aff'd*, 39 A.D.2d 1019, 333 N.Y.S.2d 726, 10 U.C.C. Rep. Serv. 1080 (1972).

[39] Fireman's Fund Ins. Co. v. Bank of N.Y., 146 A.D.2d 95, 539 N.Y.S.2d 339, 8 U.C.C. Rep. Serv. 2d 410 (1989) (relied on fictitious resume and placed individual with extensive criminal record in management of millions of dollars of funds); Flagship Bank v. Complete Interiors, Inc., 450 So. 2d 337, 38 U.C.C. Rep. Serv. 957 (Fla. Dist. Ct. App. 1984) (hired person on probation for the felony of check kiting to be bookkeeper); J. Gordon Neely Enters., Inc. v. American Nat'l Bank, 403 So. 2d 887, 32 U.C.C. Rep. Serv. 1525 (Ala. 1981) (cursory inquiry despite rumors the employee embezzled in another state); Prudential Ins. Co. v. Marine Nat'l Exchange Bank, 55 F.R.D. 436, 11 U.C.C. Rep. Serv. 129 (E.D. Wis. 1972) (hired known gambler in position where he could submit false loan applications to employer).

with instruments in the course of their employment. The strict liability of employers in these cases is covered in a subsequent section of this chapter.[40]

[b] Substantially Contributes

To operate as a preclusion, negligence must substantially contribute to an alteration or an unauthorized signature. Although a question arose under the original version of Article 3 of whether this requirement of substantial contribution eases the causation burden by restricting it to cause in fact or whether it continues the concept of proximate cause, the issue is resolved under the revision. The Comments clarify that the proximate cause test is not intended: "Conduct 'substantially contributes' to a material alteration or forged signature if it is a contributing cause of the alteration or signature and a substantial factor in bringing it about."[41]

The Comments of the revision approve the analysis provided in the earlier case of *Thompson Maple Products v. Citizens National Bank*.[42] In its opinion, the court held that the Code "shortened the chain of causation which the defendant bank must establish."[43] The plaintiff-drawer was found to be negligent in the issuance of several checks that were prepared on the basis of falsified delivery slips indicating that an independent driver had delivered logs to the company from several timber sellers. The company issued the checks to the wrongdoing driver, who, rather than giving them to the supposed sellers, forged the indorsements and cashed them at the drawee bank. The negligence of the drawer that substantially contributed to the forgeries involved several aspects of the way the company conducted its business. Rather than retaining the duplicate delivery slip, the company employees who checked in the logs often allowed the drivers to take both slips to the office. Blank sets of slips were also easily accessible, and they were not numbered consecutively. This absence of adequate internal controls left the company unable to prevent fraud by the drivers and be sure that proper parties were paid for logs received. In addition, the company gave the checks to the wrongdoer-driver to deliver to the payees. The appellate court concluded that these practices in their entirety supported the trial court's decision that the drawer's negligence substantially contributed to the forgeries.

[4] Comparative Negligence

The analysis of the negligence concept under section 3-406 does not end with the determination that a particular person is precluded from asserting the alteration or the forgery. The concept of comparative negligence may also apply. If the person precluded can establish that the person asserting

---

[40] *See* § 10.03[C] *infra*.

[41] U.C.C. § 3-406, Comment 2. Travelers Indemnity Co. v. Good, 325 N.J. Super. 16, 737 A.2d 690, 39 U.C.C. Rep. Serv. 2d 625 (1999) ("substantially contributes" refers to the contribution toward the forgery and not that the negligence must be substantial).

[42] 211 Pa. Super. 42, 234 A.2d 32, 4 U.C.C. Rep. Serv. 624 (1967).

[43] 211 Pa. Super. at 47, 234 A.2d at 34; 4 U.C.C. Rep. Serv. at 627.

the preclusion failed "to exercise ordinary care in paying or taking the instrument and that failure substantially contributes to loss," the loss can be allocated between the two parties under the principles of comparative negligence.[44] The extent of the loss will be allocated to each party according the extent that the lack of ordinary care of each contributed to the loss.

The standard of care requires some basic detection efforts when a customer deals directly with a depositary bank or presents a check for payment directly to the payor bank. The bank employee should certainly exercise care to identify the person undertaking the transaction and to take note of any apparent alterations to a check.[45] The bank employee should scrutinize the indorsements for proper appearance,[46] and a drawee bank can verify the drawer's signature against the signature card in cases of direct presentment.[47] Banks should also exercise care in ascertaining the authority of agents to sign and cash checks for their principals.[48] They should be particularly careful about paying checks to individuals when the checks run to an organization or a government agency.[49]

Prior to the revision of Article 3, most courts that addressed the issue found that drawee banks do not follow reasonable commercial banking standards when they fail to verify the signature card, which adversely affects the ability of these banks to assert the preclusion based on negligence against a party facilitating a forgery or alteration.[50] When pressed on the impracticality of signature verifications on all checks under modern banking methods, the courts responded by holding that the banks had not demonstrated the commercial reasonableness of the practice.

The revision to Article 3 changes this approach with respect to instruments taken for processing for collection or payment by automated

---

[44] U.C.C. § 3-406(b).

[45] Owensboro Nat'l Bank v. Crisp, 608 S.W.2d 51, 30 U.C.C. Rep. Serv. 240 (Ky. 1980) (bank allowed party unknown at the bank to cash check raised from $12.50 to $6,212.50 upon showing a driver's license that was not in the standard form of the state).

[46] National Bank v. Refrigerated Transp. Co., 147 Ga. App. 240, 248 S.E.2d 496, 25 U.C.C. Rep. Serv. 528 (1978) (indorsement irregular enough require bank to ascertain presenter's authority).

[47] Mortimer Agency, Inc. v. Underwriters Trust Co., 73 Misc. 2d 970, 341 N.Y.S.2d 75, 13 U.C.C. Rep. Serv. 270 (1973) (bank negligent when it certified forged check signed by rubber stamp not authorized for use on checks).

[48] Aetna Cas. & Sur. Co. v. Hepler State Bank, 6 Kan. App. 2d 543, 630 P.2d 721, 32 U.C.C. Rep. Serv. 187 (1981) (bank allowed deposit of corporate checks into personal account without questioning presenter's authority); Bank of S. Md. v. Robertson's Crab House, 39 Md. App. 707, 389 A.2d 388, 24 U.C.C. Rep. Serv. 702 (1978) (apparent authority must relate back to principal and not solely to statements and actions of agent).

[49] Commonwealth Fed. Sav. & Loan Ass'n v. First Nat'l Bank, 513 F. Supp. 296, 34 U.C.C. Rep. Serv. 218 (E.D. Pa. 1979) (bank allowed deposit of check payable to a state agency in the account of an individual); Seattle-First Nat'l Bank v. Pacific Nat'l Bank, 22 Wash. App. 46, 587 P.2d 617, 25 U.C.C. Rep. Serv. 821 (1978) (bank allowed checks payable to a corporation to be deposited in the account of a different business entity).

[50] The original version of Article 3 was more detrimental to the drawee bank's position than the revision because it applied contributory negligence principles to deny a bank that did not observe reasonable commercial standards any opportunity to assert the facilitating negligence. See U.C.C. § 3-406 and Comment 6 (original version).

means.[51] In this context only, reasonable commercial standards for purposes of the definition of ordinary care under the revision do not require a bank to examine the instrument "if the failure to examine does not violate the bank's prescribed procedures and the bank's procedures do not vary unreasonably from general banking usage not disapproved by [Article 3] or Article 4."[52] This approach leaves a customer free to prove that a bank's procedures are unreasonable, unfair, or arbitrary,[53] but it alters the blanket approach that had been embraced by many courts prior to the revision.

The result achieved under the revision is desirable. When negligence is not involved, drawee banks are absolutely accountable for the checks on which they make final payment.[54] If they make a business decision to incur increased risks by not manually inspecting every check before payment, their accountability remains appropriate, but not to the extent of alleviating prior parties of the burden of their negligence. Placing any loss on the drawee bank in these cases either results in passing the ultimate loss to an innocent party under the warranty provisions, often the depositary bank, or leaves the loss in cases like forged checks on the drawee bank. Increasing the loss on the banks results in higher costs to all users of banking services. Rather than subsidization of negligent acts by users who are not negligent, the better approach is to recognize that automated collection and payment can be consistent with reasonable commercial standards, while at the same time permitting affected customers to challenge specific aspects of such practices as unfair.

[B] Customer Negligence With Respect to Statement of Account — § 4-406

[1] The Customer's Duty

Article 4 imposes some very specific duties on a customer with respect to paid checks and bank statements. The customer is required to "exercise reasonable promptness in examining the statement or the items."[55] The return of cancelled checks and the bank statement is not simply for the customer's records or to provide receipts in the event of a dispute over whether the customer made a particular payment. The purpose of the customer's examination is also "to determine whether any payment was not authorized because of an alteration of an item or because a purported signature by or on behalf of the customer was not authorized."[56] The duty simply reflects the fact that the drawer is in the best position to detect these types of frauds on checks paid from his or her account by reconciling the

---

[51] For a discussion of automated check collection and payment, see §§ 11.02[B] and 11.03[A] infra.

[52] U.C.C. § 3-103(a)(7).

[53] U.C.C. § 3-103, Comment 5.

[54] See § 11.03[C] infra.

[55] U.C.C. § 4-406(c).

[56] U.C.C. § 4-406(c).

information in the statement and on the checks with the records any careful drawer maintains on the check stubs or carbonized copies of checks.[57] Even if the forgery of the drawer's signature is so accomplished that even the drawer cannot spot it as a forgery from the signature alone, the drawer should be able to determine whether he or she issued that particular check to the designated payee. When alterations are skillful, the drawer again should have records showing the date of the check, the payee, and the amount. In other words, drawers should have information that can be used to detect forged and altered checks that is not available to their banks. This duty requires drawers to apply such information to discover forgeries and alterations that have escaped detection by the banks.

The duty of reasonable examination is not satisfied with making only a mathematical verification of the balances on the bank statement and the customer's records.[58] A customer in Missouri who followed this procedure allowed forty-three checks with forged signatures and seven checks with altered names of payees to go undetected.[59] In addition to reconciling balances, the returned checks should be examined to make certain that the signatures that appear are authorized. The name of the payee, the amount of the check, and the number of the check should also be compared with the information recorded on the check stubs or shown on the retained carbonized copies.

Customers also must "promptly notify the bank of the relevant facts" of an unauthorized payment that the customer should reasonably have discovered.[60] It is clearly in the customer's own best interest to notify the bank about these matters because these checks are not properly payable and the customer will want the deposit account recredited for the appropriate amount. The statutory duty, however, provides some protection for the drawee bank by requiring that the customer give the notification promptly after its discovery. The bank's rights of recovery, and the prospect of ultimate detection and apprehension of the wrongdoer, are best enhanced when timely action is taken. If the wrongdoer plans a repetition of the fraudulent activity with the same account, the bank's prompt awareness of the problem is particularly crucial for its efforts to stem similar future activities.

Ideally, a business should segregate the responsibilities for check preparation and bank statement reconciliation among different employees. With access to the statement and returned checks, a dishonest employee who

---

[57] The absence of access to any better information than is available to the banks with respect to indorsements explains why section 4-406 does not create a duty on the customer to discover unauthorized indorsements. U.C.C. § 4-406(b) imposes the duty to determine whether the customer's purported signature was unauthorized. Clarkson v. Selected Risks Ins. Co., 170 N.J. Super. Ct. 373, 406 A.2d 494, 27 U.C.C. Rep. Serv. 1366 (1979); East Gadsden Bank v. First City Nat'l Bank, 50 Ala. App. 576, 281 So.2d 431, 13 U.C.C. Rep. Serv. 275 (1973).

[58] George Whalley Co. v. Nat'l City Bank, 55 Ohio App. 2d 205, 9 Ohio Op. 2d 363, 380 N.E.2d 742, 24 U.C.C. Rep. Serv. 1234 (1977).

[59] Nu-Way Serv., Inc. v. Mercantile Trust Co., N.A., 530 S.W.2d 743, 18 U.C.C. Rep. Serv. 748 (Mo. Ct. App. 1975).

[60] U.C.C. § 4-406(c).

prepares checks is in a better position to perpetuate fraud. Efforts by a dishonest employee to conceal forgeries and alterations do not release a customer from the duty to examine the statement and checks and to discover the wrongdoing.[61] Nearly all courts that have addressed the issue under the U.C.C. have held that the customer is charged with whatever information would have been obtained if the reconciliation process had been conducted by an honest employee who performed the task in a competent and reasonable manner.[62]

These duties of examination and notification by customers do not apply unless the bank makes a statement of account or the items paid available to the customer.[63] A common method of invoking the customer's duty is a monthly mailing of a bank statement, together with canceled checks. As long as it properly addresses the envelope and provides proper postage, the bank sends the statement and checks upon their deposit in the mail.[64] If the correspondence is lost in the mail, the obligation of the customer nevertheless begins to run. The opinions of courts that have found a depositor negligent under section 3-406 in not inquiring about the nonreceipt of statements[65] suggest the appropriate response for depositors in this circumstance as well. The customer is the party in the best position to avoid losses attributable to nonreceipt of the items when they are sent properly by the bank.

A customer can request that the bank hold the statement and checks rather than sending them.[66] The request is practical when the customer

---

[61] K & K Mfg., Inc. v. Union Bank, 129 Ariz. 7, 628 P.2d 44, 31 U.C.C. Rep. Serv. 177 (Ariz. Ct. App. 1981); Pine Bluff Nat'l Bank v. Kesterson, 257 Ark. 813, 520 S.W.2d 253, 16 U.C.C. Rep. Serv. 805 (1975).

[62] "[T]he employer, though not imputed with knowledge of the fraud of his faithless agent, is, as principal, chargeable with such information as an honest employee, unaware of the wrongdoing, would have acquired from the examination of the canceled checks and bank statements." Kiernan v. Union Bank, 55 Cal. App. 3d 111,117, 127 Cal. Rptr. 441, 445, 18 U.C.C. Rep. Serv. 1026, 1031 (1976), citing Basch v. Bank of Am., 22 Cal.2d 316, 327 (1943). See also Jensen v. Essexbank, 396 Mass. 65, 483 N.E.2d 821, 41 U.C.C. Rep. Serv. 1366 (1985); Dean v. Centerre Bank, 684 S.W.2d 373, 39 U.C.C. Rep. Serv. 1416 (Mo. Ct. App. 1984).

[63] The duties of the customer are subject to a proviso: "If a bank sends or makes available a statement of account or items pursuant to subsection (a). . . ." U.C.C. § 4-406(c). A bank is not under a statutory duty to send or otherwise provide bank statements or canceled checks, although its agreement with the customer may require it to do so. U.C.C. § 4-406, Comment 1. If the bank does not provide either the checks or a statement, however, the customer does not incur the duties provided in subsection (c). Mac v. Bank of Am., 76 Cal. App. 4th 562, 90 Cal. Rptr.2d 476, 40 U.C.C. Rep. Serv. 2d 1 (Cal. Ct. App. 1999) (held that time limits of section 4-406 were not given effect when the monthly statement was returned to a customer who had died because they were not then sent to a person who was the customer and the person who had died was not in a position to detect the forgeries).

[64] U.C.C. § 1-201(38). The bank can also send them "by any other usual means of communication." Id; Kiernan v. Union Bank, 55 Cal. App. 3d 111, 127 Cal. Rptr. 441, 18 U.C.C. Rep. Serv. 1026 (1976).

[65] Westport Bank & Trust Co. v. Lodge, 164 Conn. 604, 325 A.2d 222, 12 U.C.C. Rep. Serv. 450 (1973); Myrick v. National Sav. & Trust Co., 268 A.2d 526, 7 U.C.C. Rep. Serv.1139 (D.C. App. 1970).

[66] Alternatively, the customer can give special instructions on where to send them. McMickle v. Girard Bank, 356 Pa. Super. 521, 515 A.2d 16, 2 U.C.C. Rep. Serv. 2d 250 (1986) (bank complied with its duty by sending statements and canceled checks to an attorney in accordance with the customer's instructions).

wishes to avoid the delays associated with delivery or is moving. Sometimes employers who are concerned about defalcations on the part of employees instruct their banks to hold the statements and canceled checks to prevent access to them by a wrongdoer whose scheme might be furthered by such possession.[67]

The provisions of section 4-406 were revised in the amendments to Article 4 to accommodate practices of check truncation. Under a system of payor-bank truncation, the payor bank does not return the canceled checks to the customer; instead it sends a statement of the account, but it stores the checks or it destroys them and keeps photocopies of both sides of the check. The advantage of the system is one less step in moving the mountain of paper that checks represent in the payment system, which results in significant cost savings. The advantage is magnified substantially with depository-bank truncation because the physical movement of the checks themselves stops at the bank in which they are deposited. The depositary bank keeps the photocopies and transmits the payment order contained in the check directly to the payor bank electronically. Again, the customer receives a statement of the account from the payor bank, but does not get the canceled checks.

Bank truncation is facilitated under the amendment of section 4-406 because it clarifies that the canceled checks themselves do not have to be returned or even made available to the customer.[68] If the canceled checks are not returned, the person retaining them must do so for seven years, or, if the checks are destroyed, the ability to provide legible copies must be maintained for seven years.[69] If a customer requests a paid item, the payor bank must provide it, or a legible copy in the event the item was destroyed or is otherwise not obtainable, within a reasonable time.[70]

The implementation of check-truncation practices can affect the scope of the customer's duty under section 4-406(c). The customer must promptly notify the bank as to unauthorized payments that the customer should reasonably have discovered "based on the statement or items provided."[71] When a bank provides only a statement of the account, but not the actual canceled checks, the ability of the customer to detect unauthorized payments is limited somewhat. For example, a customer cannot detect the alteration of the name of the payee on a check when the account statement does not include this information. Customers therefore will be excused from the duty to discover alterations that could be detected only with access to

---

[67] *See* Ossip-Harris Ins., Inc. v. Barnett Bank, 428 So. 2d 363, 35 U.C.C. Rep. Serv. 1604 (Fla. Dist. Ct. App. 1983). *But see*, Henrichs v. Peoples Bank, 26 Kan. App. 2d 582, 992 P.2d 1241, 41 U.C.C. Rep. Serv. 2d 894 (Kan. Ct. App. 1999) (bank protected when it followed instructions of customer to send statements to another individual, even though that individual was the person perpetuating the fraud).

[68] The obligation can nevertheless apply under the deposit agreement with the customer. Banks that desire to implement truncation practices should secure the customer's agreement through the terms of the deposit contract.

[69] U.C.C. § 4-406(b).

[70] *Id.*

[71] U.C.C. § 4-406(c).

the checks themselves. The statement of account provided by the bank will provide enough information to invoke a customer's duties if, as a minimum, it describes each paid item by item number, amount, and date of payment.[72] This information can be read by bank computers from the MIRC line on each check, and thus can be provided economically. Other relevant information, such as the name of the payee and the date of the item, cannot be read electronically under existing technology. The duty of a customer thus would not extend to alterations of these parts of a paid item when the bank's statement does not include this relevant information and the bank does not return the item itself.

[2] Consequences of Customer Noncompliance

The effects of a customer's failure to comply with the duties to discover and report unauthorized signatures of the customer or alterations are twofold. The first consequence is that "the customer is precluded from asserting against the bank: (1) the customer's unauthorized signature or any alteration on the item, if the bank also proves that it suffered a loss by reason of the failure."[73] The customer's failure to observe the duties imposed constitutes negligence that the bank can establish as a defense to an action to recredit the deposit account. However, the preclusion against the customer does not reach all forgeries and alterations that fall within the scope of the duty. The bank must prove that it suffered some loss as a result of the customer's failure. Because banks pay checks with alterations or forgeries before the duty of their customers arises, banks generally will have difficulty in proving a causal connection between their loss on a check and their customer's negligence.[74]

The second consequence of a customer's failure is premised on a "repeat-offender rule." The preclusion that it invokes is stated as follows: "If the bank proves that the customer failed, with respect to an item, to comply with the duties imposed on the customer by subsection (c), the customer is precluded from asserting against the bank: . . . (2) the customer's unauthorized signature or alteration by the same wrongdoer on any other item paid in good faith by the bank if the payment was made before the bank received notice from the customer of the unauthorized signature or alteration and after the customer had been afforded a reasonable period of time, not exceeding 30 days, in which to examine the item or statement of account and notify the bank."[75]

This rule addresses what the drafters considered to be the worst aspect of a customer's failure to examine the bank statement and returned checks.[76] The customer's inaction is a key element in the perpetuation of

---

[72] U.C.C. § 4-406(a).

[73] U.C.C. § 4-406(d)(1).

[74] Commercial Cotton Co., Inc. v. United Cal. Bank, 163 Cal. App. 3d 511, 209 Cal. Rptr. 551, 40 U.C.C. Rep. Serv. 234 (1985) (eighteen-month delay in notifying bank of unauthorized signatures did not affect the bank's negligence or its wrongful payment of the check).

[75] U.C.C. § 4-406(d)(2).

[76] U.C.C. § 4-406, Comment 2.

many fraudulent schemes. A wrongdoer is more likely to avoid detection if the customer does not reconcile the bank statement. Even if the customer's discovery of wrongdoing does not identify the perpetrator, notification to the bank alerts it to be more vigilant concerning payment of checks drawn on the account. Because the customer is in the best position to discover forged drawer signatures or alterations to the instrument, the losses from repeated similar misdeeds by the same wrongdoer are passed to the customer once the customer should have become aware of the problem. The bank first has to make the statement and the canceled checks available. The customer would not be responsible under the repeat-offender rule for multiple forged checks all appearing for the first time on a single statement, even though the same perpetrator forged them all.[77] In addition, the customer needs a reasonable time in which to carry out the duties, which is codified to not exceed thirty calendar days.[78] Once given the means and the time for detection, a customer who does not comply is precluded from asserting against the bank any subsequent forgeries or alterations by the same wrongdoer.[79]

[3] Comparative Negligence of the Bank

Even though a customer is negligent with respect to its section 4-406 duties, the bank's attempt to preclude the customer from asserting an unauthorized signature or alteration can be impaired if the customer shows that the bank was negligent in paying the check. If "the customer proves that the bank failed to exercise ordinary care in paying the item, and that the failure substantially contributed to loss," the loss is allocated between the bank and the customer on the principle of comparative negligence.[80] This standard is comparable to the similar provision in section 3-406.[81]

Many courts have found payor banks to have been negligent when they paid over a forged instrument without verifying the drawer's signature against the signature card.[82] As it does with respect to the comparable issue

---

[77] Winkler v. Commercial Nat'l Bank, 42 Mich. App. 740, 202 N.W.2d 468, 11 U.C.C. Rep. Serv. 1031 (1972).

[78] Flagship Bank v. Complete Interiors, Inc., 450 So. 2d 337, 38 U.C.C. Rep. Serv. 957 (Fla. Ct. App. 1984) (summary judgment not proper to preclude bank's opportunity to show that less than fourteen days was a reasonable time to notify bank of altered checks). Prior to the amendment of section 4-406, the statutory limitation was fixed at fourteen days.

[79] Marx v. Whitney Nat'l Bank, 713 So. 2d 1142, 38 U.C.C. Rep. Serv. 2d 488 (La. 1999); Winkie, Inc. v. Heritage Bank, 99 Wis. 2d 616, 299 N.W.2d 829, 31 U.C.C. Rep. Serv. 163 (1981).

[80] U.C.C. § 4-406(e). Assertions against the bank are not precluded at all because of the customer's negligence if the bank did not pay an item in good faith. *Id.*

[81] *See* § 10.01[A][4] *supra.*

[82] Federal Ins. Co. v. Bank of N.Y., 2 U.C.C. Rep. Serv. 2d 580 (N.Y. Civ. Ct. 1986) (ruled against the bank for failure to present evidence that it had compared the signature card even though the customer had not offered any evidence concerning the bank's lack of care); G & R Corp. v. American Security & Trust Co., 523 F.2d 1164, 18 U.C.C. Rep. Serv. 33 (D.C. Cir. 1975). *See also* Wilder Binding Co. v. Oak Park Trust & Sav. Bank, 173 Ill. App. 3d 34, 527 N.E.2d 354, 7 U.C.C. Rep. Serv. 2d 134 (1988) (failure to have forgery detection procedures for checks of $1,000 or less held to be lack of ordinary care as a matter of law).

concerning negligence under section 3-406,[83] the revision changes this approach with respect to instruments taken for processing for collection or payment by automated means.[84] The Tennessee Supreme Court foresaw this change, which is implemented in the definition of "ordinary care" in revised Article 3,[85] when it determined that a bank makes a sufficient showing when it demonstrates its compliance with customary banking practices, unless the customer shows that the practices of the industry are so careless as to constitute a lack of ordinary care on the part of all banks.[86] Although the finality doctrine generally will leave liability on the payor bank in cases of forged drawers' signatures,[87] the negligence of the bank's customer should alter that outcome without regard to the information the bank might have acquired had it physically examined the check and the customer's signature card, provided the bank's actions conform to general practices in the banking industry[88] and the customer does not show the practice was unreasonable, arbitrary, or unfair in the particular case.

The adoption of particular practices is not alone sufficient to insulate a bank against claims of contributory negligence. The bank must also exercise ordinary care in applying those practices.[89] Consequently, a bank that compared the drawer's signature on checks against the signature card was nevertheless negligent in failing to detect an obvious misspelling of the drawer's name.[90] Similarly, a bank that physically examined the checks was found liable for checks on which egregious alterations had been made.[91]

[4] Time Limits on Customer's Rights

Section 4-406 imposes an absolute bar to the right of a customer to make a claim for payment over an unauthorized customer's signature or alteration "[w]ithout regard to care or lack of care of either the customer or the bank."[92] The customer must notify the bank of unauthorized drawer

---

[83] See § 10.01[A][4] supra.

[84] Karmin Door Co. v. BankBoston, N.A., 2000 Mass. Super. LEXIS 94, 41 U.C.C. Rep. Serv. 2d 1191 (Mass. Super. Ct. 2000). For discussion of automated check collection and payment, see §§ 11.02[B] and 11.03[A] infra.

[85] U.C.C. § 3-103(a)(7).

[86] Vending Chattanooga, Inc. v. American National Bank & Trust, 730 S.W.2d 624, 4 U.C.C. Rep. Serv. 2d 506 (Tenn. 1987).

[87] See § 9.01[C][1] supra.

[88] Testimony in one case indicated that nine out of every ten banks in the country do not verify all checks by signature. Curtis v. Hibernia Nat'l Bank, 522 So. 2d 705, 6 U.C.C. Rep. Serv. 2d 476 (5th Cir. 1988).

[89] Travelers Indemnity Co. v. Good, 325 N.J. Super. 16, 737 A.2d 690, 39 U.C.C. Rep. Serv. 2d 625 (1999) (subrogee of bank customer was entitled to explore through discovery whether the actual practice of the bank was consistent with its policy and whether the training provided for its employees was adequate to discover forged signatures).

[90] American Security Bank, N.A. v. American Motorists Ins. Co., 538 A.2d 736, 5 U.C.C. Rep. Serv. 2d 1413 (D.C. 1988) (last "s" clearly omitted in forgery of the name "Sellers").

[91] Nu-Way Serv., Inc. v. Mercantile Trust Co., N.A., 530 S.W.2d 743, 18 U.C.C. Rep. Serv. 748 (Mo. Ct. App. 1975).

[92] U.C.C. § 4-406(f).

signatures and altered checks within one year from the time the bank statement or the canceled checks are made available to the customer.[93] When this time limit expires,[94] the noncomplying customer is precluded from asserting the unauthorized signature or alteration against the bank, irrespective of anyone's negligence.

The absolute time limits to customers' claims do not set the time frame for customer compliance with the duty to exercise reasonable promptness to discover forged and altered checks and to notify the bank promptly after their discovery. When the customer does not act, the negligence triggers the dual consequences of subsection (d). The applicability of that subsection depends upon negligence of the customer. The absolute notice bar, however, operates to terminate any potential outstanding customer claims against the bank. The bar is absolute; even claims that could not have been discovered during the time limit are nevertheless barred.[95] Furthermore, the absolute bar can operate in conjunction with the repeat-offender rule to deny a customer any recovery. For example, in a case involving forged checks over a fourteen-month period, the one-year absolute bar precluded bank liability on the initial forgeries and the repeat-offender rule left the customer liable for the continuation of the series of forgeries.[96]

Most courts have not addressed the question of whether a bank can alter the statutory time periods by requiring the customer to report any irregularities in a returned bank statement within a shorter period of time. New York courts have consistently upheld such agreements between banks and their depositors.[97] The courts uphold them as legitimate variations allowed under the Code because they do not excuse the bank for its negligence or its obligations of good faith and ordinary care. They also do not consider the agreements to be contracts of adhesion. A court in Ohio, on the other hand, has held that a printed instruction of a bank statement requiring notification of errors within ten days did not excuse a bank for paying a

---

[93] Lowenstein v. Barnett Bank of South Florida, N.A., 35 U.C.C. Rep. Serv. 2d 1314 (Fla. Cir. Ct. 1998) (claim on forged drawer's signatures valid for checks paid within one year prior to notice but lost as to all prior checks); Spancom Services, Inc. v. Southtrust Bank, N.A., 744 So.2d 931, 39 U.C.C. Rep. Serv. 2d 823 (Ala. Ct. Civ. App. 1999) (customer barred from suing banks on unendorsed checks because of a failure to notify its bank within one year).

[94] Several states have altered the time periods indicated in the uniform codification.

[95] Mesnick v. Hempstead Bank, 106 Misc. 2d 624, 434 N.Y.S.2d 579, 30 U.C.C. Rep. Serv. 1376 (1980) (husband kept wife's monthly statements from her attention); Davis Aircraft Prods. Co. v. Bankers Trust Co., 36 A.D.2d 705, 319 N.Y.S.2d 379, 7 U.C.C. Rep. Serv. 1039 (1972) (plaintiff's employee manipulated the account to cover up forgeries).

[96] Karmin Door Co. v. BankBoston, N.A., 2000 Mass. Super. LEXIS 94, 41 U.C.C. Rep. Serv. 2d 1191 (Mass. Super. Ct. 2000); Dean v. Centerre Bank, 684 S.W.2d 373, 39 U.C.C. Rep. Serv. 1416 (Mo. Ct. App. 1984).

[97] Parent Teacher Ass'n v. Manufacturers Hanover Trust Co., 138 Misc. 2d 289, 524 N.Y.S.2d 336, 5 U.C.C. Rep. Serv. 2d 679 (1988) (14 days from delivery or mailing of statement); Coine v. Manufacturers Hanover Trust Co., 16 U.C.C. Rep. Serv. 184 (N.Y. Sup. Ct. 1975) (14 days from receipt of statement); New York Credit Men's Adjustment Bureau, Inc. v. Manufacturers Hanover Trust Co., 41 A.D.2d 912, 343 N.Y.S.2d 538, 12 U.C.C. Rep. Serv. 717 (1973) (30 days from delivery or mailing of statement). *See also* Borowski v. Firstar Bank Milwaukee, N.A., 35 U.C.C. Rep. Serv. 2d 221 (Wis. Ct. App. 1998) (14 days); W.J. Miranda Const. Corp., Inc. v. First Union Nat. Bank, 40 U.C.C. Rep. Serv. 2d 8 (Fla. Cir. Ct. 1999) (60 days).

check that had been erroneously encoded as payable for $10,000 more than the actual amount.[98]

The absolute time limits imposed under section 4-406 do not constitute a statute of limitations.[99] Claims against the payor bank are barred under this section because of the customer's failure to notify the bank of its unauthorized signature or alterations within the applicable time limits. Section 4-406 does not impose limits on when a law suit must be commenced to enforce these claims. Timely notice of the claim will preserve the availability of the full statute of limitations period,[100] which under the amendments to Article 4 is within three years after the cause of action accrues.[101] Some courts, nonetheless, have erroneously described the absolute time limits for notice as a statute of limitations.[102]

The absolute time periods of section 4-406 commence with each bank statement. Once the bank makes the statement or the canceled checks available to the customer,[103] the time period begins.[104] The repeat-offender rule does not apply in determining the absolute time limits.[105]

Cases have split on the question of whether the one-year notice period applies to cases in which banks have paid checks on fewer than the required number of drawer's signatures. Several courts have held that the requirement applies as much to cases with missing signatures as it does to outright forgeries.[106] Other courts have concluded that a missing signature does not constitute an "unauthorized signature" and that the one-year bar therefore does not apply.[107]

---

[98] State ex rel. Gabalac v. Firestone Bank, 46 Ohio App. 2d 124, 346 N.E.2d 326, 19 U.C.C. Rep. Serv. 219 (1975).

[99] W.J. Miranda Const. Corp., Inc. v. First Union Nat. Bank, 40 U.C.C. Rep. Serv. 2d 8 (Fla. Cir. Ct. 1999); Euro Motors, Inc. v. Southwest Fin. Bank & Trust Co., 297 Ill. App. 3d 246, 696 N.E.2d 711, 38 U.C.C. Rep. Serv. 2d 167 (1998); Spears Carpet Mills, Inc. v. Central Nat'l Bank, 88 Bankr. 86, 6 U.C.C. Rep. Serv. 2d 503 (W.D. Ark 1988).

[100] American Home Assurance Co. v. Scarsdale Nat'l Bank & Trust Co., 96 Misc. 2d 715, 409 N.Y.S.2d 608, 25 U.C.C. Rep. Serv. 534 (N.Y. Cty. Ct. 1978).

[101] U.C.C. § 4-111.

[102] Garnac Grain Co., Inc. v. Boatmen's Bank & Trust, 694 F. Supp. 1389, 7 U.C.C. Rep. Serv. 2d 505 (W.D. Mo. 1988); Far West Citrus, Inc. v. Bank of Am., 91 Cal. App. 3d 913, 154 Cal. Rptr. 464, 26 U.C.C. Rep. Serv. 464 (1979); Kraftsman Container Corp. v. United Counties Trust Co., 169 N.J. Super. 488, 404 A.2d 1288, 26 U.C.C. Rep. Serv. 1240 (1979).

[103] Cooley v. First Nat'l Bank, 276 Ark. 387, 635 S.W.2d 250, 33 U.C.C. Rep. Serv. 1736 (1982) (statements reasonably available when sent to post office box indicated on signature card); Mesnick v. Hempstead Bank, 106 Misc. 2d 624, 434 N.Y.S.2d 579, 30 U.C.C. Rep. Serv. 1376 (1980) (available from date of mailing despite interception by forger).

[104] Neo-Tech Sys., Inc. v. Provident Bank, 43 Ohio Misc. 31, 72 Ohio Op. 2d 329, 335 N.E.2d 395, 17 U.C.C. Rep. Serv. 1079 (1974).

[105] Exchange Bank & Trust Co. v. Kidwell Constr. Co., 463 S.W.2d 465, 8 U.C.C. Rep. Serv. 1079 (Tex. Civ. App. 1971), aff'd, 472 S.W.2d 117, 9 U.C.C. Rep. Serv. 482 (Tex. 1971); Hardex-Steubenville Corp. v. Western Pa. Nat'l Bank, 446 Pa. 446, 285 A.2d 874, 10 U.C.C. Rep. Serv. 448 (1971).

[106] Provident Sav. Bank v. United Jersey Bank, 207 N.J. Super. 303, 504 A.2d 135, 1 U.C.C. Rep. Serv. 2d 184 (1985); Rascar, Inc. v. Bank of Or., 87 Wis. 2d 446, 275 N.W.2d 108, 25 U.C.C. Rep. Serv. 1414 (1978).

[107] In re Florida Airlines, Inc., 57 B.R. 113, 1 U.C.C. Rep. Serv. 2d 507 (M.D. Fla. 1986); Far West Citrus, Inc. v. Bank of Am., 91 Cal. App. 3d 913, 154 Cal Rptr. 464, 26 U.C.C. Rep. Serv. 464 (1979).

The second line of cases is clearly in error. The drafters carefully avoided limiting the concept of "unauthorized signature" to include only forgeries. "'Unauthorized' signature or indorsement means one made without actual, implied or apparent authority and includes a forgery."[108] Even though a check issued with fewer than the required signatures does not contain a forgery, the signature is unauthorized if it is executed as a purported check of the drawer without the requisite authority. The reasoning advanced by one court that the customer should prevail because detection of a missing signature should be easier for the bank than a forged signature is equally fallacious.[109] The absolute one-year time limit to report an unauthorized signature applies "[w]ithout regard to care or lack of care of either the customer or the bank."[110]

A payor bank that does not assert the one-year bar that it has against a claim of its customer is denied any right to pursue a breach of warranty action against collecting banks or any prior party based upon an unauthorized signature or an alteration affected by the bar.[111] Without this limitation a valued customer of a payor bank could bring pressure on the payor bank to pass losses attributable to its negligence upstream to the collecting banks. The payor bank might well acquiesce in the interest of maintaining a good business relationship with its customer, and the customer could escape the consequences of noncompliance with the one-year bar.

The effect on a breach of warranty claim by the payor bank operates differently with respect to a customer's negligence in failing to promptly examine a statement of account or canceled checks sent by the bank. In these cases, the provisions on presentment warranties in Articles 3 and 4 provide the warrantor with a defense based upon section 4-406 negligence of the customer.[112] The policy advanced is to prevent a payor bank from shifting the loss from a drawer to the warrantor when the conduct of the drawer contributed to a its unauthorized signature or an alteration.[113]

§ 10.03 Strict Liability

[A] Introduction

Article 3 uses principles of strict liability to reallocate losses associated with certain types of indorsements. When unauthorized indorsements are made in the absence of any negligence, the ultimate loss generally is directed to the person who took the instrument from the forger. The strict-liability provisions make unauthorized indorsements associated with

---

[108] U.C.C. § 1-201(43).
[109] Madison Park Bank v. Field, 64 Ill. App. 3d 838, 381 N.E.2d 1030, 25 U.C.C. Rep. Serv. 542 (1978).
[110] U.C.C. § 4-406(f).
[111] *Id.*
[112] U.C.C. §§ 3-417(c), 4-208(c).
[113] U.C.C. § 3-417, Comment 6.

stipulated frauds effective in favor of good-faith takers and payors of the instrument.

Section 3-404 applies strict liability to two situations. The first situation involves impostors. A thief impersonates another person, persuading a drawer to issue a check naming that person as the payee. The thief forges the indorsement of the check and receives payment for it or negotiates it for value before disappearing with the proceeds. Upon discovering the deception, the drawer insists that the drawee recredit the drawer's account on the grounds that the payee was the party that the drawer intended rather than the thief. The imposter rule makes "an indorsement of the instrument by any person in the name of the payee effective as the indorsement of the payee" in favor of designated parties.[114]

The second situation where section 3-404 applies is with respect to indorsements of nominal or fictitious payees. As part of a dishonest scheme, a company official with authority to issue checks on the company account prepares a check in the name of a payee that does not exist. The dishonest official then indorses the check to himself, deposits the check, and withdraws all of the proceeds once the check clears payment. Upon discovery of the defalcation, the company insists that the check was not properly payable because it ran to the order of the fictitious payee and had not been indorsed by that party. The fictitious payee rule makes the dishonest official, as the person in possession of the instrument, its holder, and makes the indorsement in the name of the payee effective as the indorsement of the payee in favor of the bank that paid the check. The same result would apply if, rather than naming a fictitious payee, the dishonest official issued a check in the name of an actual creditor of the company, but with the intention that the named creditor identified as the payee would not have any interest in the check. In the latter scheme, the payee is nominal only — just in name and not in fact.

The loss is placed on drawers and makers in imposter and fictitious payee cases because they are in the best position to have avoided the loss.[115] Requiring adequate identification from the impersonator or verifying the authority of the impersonating agent would contribute significantly to avoidance of impostor fraud.[116] Proper selection and supervision of employees can do a great deal to prevent fraud in the fictitious-payee context.

Article 3 also uses strict liability to reallocate losses associated with fraudulent indorsements made by employees who have been assigned responsibilities to deal with instruments in the course of their employment. Indorsements made by these dishonest employees are deemed to be effective, which has the effect of allocating the loss to the employer. The rationale that underlies section 3-405 is based on loss allocation to the best risk avoider. The Comments explain as follows:

---

[114] U.C.C. § 3-404(a).

[115] U.C.C. § 3-404, Comment 3.

[116] Client's Security Funds v. Allstate Ins. Co., 219 N.J. Super. 325, 530 A.2d 357, 5 U.C.C. Rep. Serv. 2d 127 (1987).

Section 3-405 adopts the principle that the risk of loss for fraudulent indorsements by employees who are entrusted with responsibility with respect to checks should fall on the employer rather than the bank that takes the check or pays it, if the bank was not negligent in the transaction. Section 3-405 is based on the belief that the employer is in a far better position to avoid the loss by care in choosing employees, in supervising them, and in adopting other measures to prevent forged indorsements on instruments payable to the employer or fraud in the issuance of instruments in the name of the employer.[117]

[B] Imposters and Nominal or Fictitious Payees — § 3-404

[1] Applicable Rules

[a] The Impostor Rule

Section 3-404(a) states the imposter rule as follows:

> If an imposter, by use of the mails or otherwise, induces the issuer of an instrument to issue the instrument to the imposter, or to a person acting in concert with the impostor, by impersonating the payee of the instrument or a person authorized to act for the payee, an indorsement of the instrument by any person in the name of the payee is effective as the indorsement of the payee in favor of the person who, in good faith, pays the instrument or takes it for value or for collection.

The impostor rule is nicely illustrated in *Covington v. Penn Square National Bank*.[118] A schemer name Beaird convinced a prospective investor in an oil lease that he was an individual named Baird employed by a company in the business of selling leases. After calling the company and verifying that a man named Baird did work for it, the investor gave the impostor a cashier's check drawn to the order of Baird. Beaird then cashed the check at a bank where he was known after indorsing the check twice in the names Baird and Beaird. The remitter-investor's suit against the depositary and the payor banks was unsuccessful. The remitter had been duped by an impostor to purchase the cashier's check for delivery to the impostor as the intended payee. The impostor rule, therefore, was applicable and the indorsement by Beaird was effective.

Although pre-Code law also generally recognized an impostor rule, many of the courts distinguished face-to-face impersonations from other impostures, such as through the mail. The drawer's or maker's intent in face-to-face transactions was considered to be the desire to deal with the individual impersonator, whereas in a mail imposture the dominant intent was held to be to deal with the person impersonated. When the impersonation was not face-to-face, the impostor rule did not apply and indorsement by the

---

[117] U.C.C. § 3-405, Comment 1.
[118] 545 P.2d 824, 17 U.C.C. Rep. Serv. 1048 (Okla. Ct. App. 1975).

impersonator was consider a straight forgery. The U.C.C. rejects the cases that drew this distinction on the grounds that the dominant intent concept is a fiction.[119] The Code impostor rule applies equally to impersonation "by use of the mail or otherwise."[120]

Not all cases in which a person pretends to be someone else in order to further a fraudulent scheme with negotiable instruments invoke the impostor rule. Thieves often represent themselves as the payees on the paper they steal in attempts to cash it or to sell it. Section 3-404(a) does not apply to these ordinary forged-indorsement cases, however, because the person assuming the identity of the payee did not induce "the issuer of an instrument to issue the instrument to the imposter, or to a person acting in concert with the impostor, by impersonating the payee of the instrument."[121] The motivations that induced issuance of the instrument are unrelated to the forger's assumption of the payee's identity. An impostor has to acquire the instrument through impersonation.[122]

Under the original version of Article 3, the imposter rule was not invoked when the imposter did not impersonate the payee but rather falsely claimed to be an agent of the payee.[123] Consequently, the indorsements in these cases were considered forged rather than effective, and the drawee bank was generally liable for the payment on the forged indorsement. The revision of Article 3 expands the scope of the imposter rule to include impersonations of "a person authorized to act for the payee" as well as impersonations of the payee.[124]

---

[119] U.C.C. § 3-405, Comment 2 (original version). In the eyes of the defrauded drawer or maker, the imposter and the named payee are one and the same.

[120] U.C.C. § 3-404(a). *See* Franklin Nat'l Bank v. Shapiro, 7 U.C.C. Rep. Serv. 317 (N.Y. Sup. Ct. 1970) (imposter-by-mail case in which wife posed as her husband).

[121] Franklin Nat'l Bank v. Chase Manhattan Bank, 68 Misc. 2d 880, 328 N.Y.S.2d 25, 16 U.C.C. Rep. Serv. 173 (1972) (no impersonation when buyer forged indorsement of seller on check issued for car-purchase loan payable to the buyer and the seller).

[122] First Nat'l Bank of Chicago v. Midamerica Fed. Sav. Bank, 303 Ill. App. 3d 176, 707 N.E.2d 673, 37 U.C.C. Rep. Serv. 2d 1104 (1999) (no impersonation when nephew returned a maturity notice on a certificate of deposit sent to the uncle and subsequently stole the cashier's check mailed to the uncle as the proceeds of the certificate); Client's Security Fund v. Allstate Ins. Co., 219 N.J. Super. 325, 530 A.2d 357, 5 U.C.C. Rep. Serv. 2d 127 (1987) (no impersonation when attorney received checks payable jointly to the attorney and client after the attorney forged claim releases to an insurance company).

[123] U.C.C. § 3-404, Comment 1. *See* Maddox v. First Westroads Bank, 199 Neb. 81, 256 N.W.2d 647, 22 U.C.C. Rep. Serv. 743 (1977) (attorney portrayed himself as agent of the guardian rather than as the guardian).

[124] U.C.C. § 3-404(a).

When the impostor rule does apply, an indorsement in the name of the payee is effective as the indorsement of the payee in favor of anyone who, in good faith, pays the instrument or takes it for value or for collection.[125] The consequences that flow from this rule can be illustrated with the following diagram:

$$\text{D'er} \cdots \blacktriangleright \overset{P}{I} \overset{"P"}{\longrightarrow} H \longrightarrow DB \cdots\cdots\cdots \overset{PB}{\blacktriangleright(\text{pays})}$$

Diagram 10.1

Imposter (I) fraudulently induces Drawer (D'er) to give a check to Impostor (I) that names P as the payee. I forges the indorsement of P's name and negotiates the check to H. H deposits the check in his account at Depositary Bank (DB), which presents the check to Payor Bank (PB) and receives payment. Under the impostor rule, I's indorsement is effective as the indorsement of P with respect to H (takes the check for value), DB (takes the check for collection), and PB (pays the check), assuming that each of these subsequent parties acted in good faith. The effect is to place the loss on D'er by leaving I as the only party against whom D'er can succeed. The check was properly payable, so PB need not recredit D'er's account. If D'er had discovered the fraud before the check was presented and successfully stopped payment, D'er would be liable in contract to either DB or H. With the indorsement by I deemed to be effective as P's indorsement, H and DB can both qualify as holders, and either or both of them are likely to qualify as a holder in due course, in which case D'er's claim to the instrument and defenses against payment upon notice of dishonor will be cut off. Because H and DB could both qualify as a person entitled to enforce the draft, neither of them would breach a presentment warranty upon receiving payment from D'er.

[b] The Nominal or Fictitious Payee Rule

Section 3-404(b) states the nominal or fictitious payee rule as follows:

> If (i) a person whose intent determines to whom an instrument is payable . . . does not intend the person identified as payee to have any interest in the instrument, or (ii) the person identified as payee of an instrument is a fictitious person, the following rules apply until the instrument is negotiated by special indorsement:
>
> (1) Any person in possession of the instrument is its holder.
>
> (2) An indorsement by any person in the name of the payee stated in the instrument is effective as the indorsement of the payee in favor of a person who, in good faith, pays the instrument or takes it for value or for collection.

---

[125] "Good faith" is defined in U.C.C. § 3-103(a)(4). For discussion of this definition, see § 6.01[C].

The case of *Braswell Motor Freight Lines, Inc. v. Bank of Salt Lake*[126] illustrates the application of the nominal or fictitious payee rule. An accomplice of the assistant comptroller of a corporation opened a checking account under a name identical to the name of the corporation except for the omission of the term "Inc." The assistant comptroller drew checks to the order of this entity which were deposited in the account by the accomplice. When the corporation discovered this chicanery it sued to recover from the bank that accepted the checks on deposit. The fictitious payee rule prevented recovery. The assistant comptroller signing on behalf of the corporate drawer did not intend the entity designated as the payee to have any interest in the checks, so the indorsements of the accomplice were effective.

Although the fictitious payee rule originally derived its name from the requirement that the named payee be fictitious, the requirements have changed. The rule also applies to cases in which the drawer or maker of an instrument does not intend the payee to have any interest in the instrument.[127] Section 3-404(b)(i) is written in terms of the "person whose intent determines to whom an instrument is payable." That person is determined in subsections (a) and (b) of section 3-110 on the identification of the person to whom an instrument is payable. Section 3-110(a) provides as follows:

> The person to whom an instrument is initially payable is determined by the intent of the person, whether or not authorized, signing as, or in the name or on behalf of, the issuer of the instrument. The instrument is payable to the person intended by the signer even if that person is identified in the instrument by a name or other identification that is not that of the intended person.

The issuer is the drawer or the maker of an instrument.[128] The intent of the drawer or the person acting on behalf of the drawer of a check thus will determine the identification of the payee, even if the signature is unauthorized.

---

[126] 28 Utah. 2d 347, 502 P.2d 560, 11 U.C.C. Rep. Serv. 1020 (1972).
[127] U.C.C. § 3-404, Comment 2.
[128] U.C.C. § 3-105(a).

The application of the nominal or fictitious payee rule can be explained in the context of the following diagram.

```
                   "Pay H"
      Co.      P     "P"      "H"
      D'er----▶D'er───────▶H───────▶DB·········▶PB
                                                (pays)
```

Diagram 10.2

Drawer (D'er) draws a check of Company that is payable to Payee (P). D'er subsequently indorses the check in P's name to H and delivers it to H, and D'er then disappears. H indorses in blank and deposits the check in his account at Depositary Bank (DB), which presents the check to Payor Bank (PB) and receives payment. Assume initially that the check is not forged, *i.e.*, that D'er had authority to draw checks on behalf of Company. When the nominal or fictitious payee rule applies in such a case, the drawer will face the loss if the subsequent parties have acted in good faith. Consider the following possibilities:

(1) P is a nonexistent person.[129] The rule applies because P is fictitious. As the person in possession of the check, D'er qualified as the holder of the check until it was negotiated. D'er's indorsement is effective as the indorsement of P with respect to H (takes the check for value), DB (takes the check for collection), and PB (pays the check), assuming that each of these subsequent parties acted in good faith.[130] DB qualified as a holder and thus a person entitled to enforce the instrument. The check was properly payable, meaning that Company cannot require its account to be recredited. Company can proceed only against D'er.

(2) P is an actual supplier of Company, but D'er intended to steal the check when the check was drawn.[131] The rule applies because P is nominal. D'er is the person whose intent determines to whom the check is payable, because D'er signed as drawer in the name of Company. At the time of signing, D'er did not intend for P to have any interest in the check because D'er intended to steal it. The results then are the same as under illustration (1) above.[132]

(3) P is an actual supplier of Company; D'er signs the check in order to pay money that Company owes to P, but D'er later decides to steal the

---

[129] U.C.C. § 3-404, Comment 2 (Illustration # 1). Meng v. Maywood Proviso State Bank, 702 N.E.2d 258, 36 U.C.C. Rep. Serv. 2d 1106 (Ill. Ct. App. 1998).

[130] "Good faith" is defined in U.C.C. § 3-103(a)(4). For discussion of this definition, see § 6.01[C].

[131] U.C.C. § 3-404, Comment 2 (Illustration # 2).

[132] Illustration (1) falls under section 3-404(b)(ii) as a case of a fictitious payee. Illustration (2) falls under section 3-404(b)(i) as a case of a nominal payee.

check.[133] The rule does not apply because P is not fictitious and D'er did intend P to have an interest in the check when it was drawn.[134]

(4) P is an actual supplier of Company, D'er intended to steal the check when it was drawn, and President of Company also signed the check as the drawer in the belief that Company owes the money to P.[135] The rule applies because P is nominal. D'er still qualifies as a "person whose intent determines to whom an instrument is payable," and D'er does not intend P to have any interest in the check. D'er thus qualified as a holder of the check through his possession, and the indorsement was effective, producing the same result as under illustration (1) above.

(5) D'er prepared the check with the intent to steal it but did not sign the check. The check was signed by President as the only authorized representative of Company. The rule applies only if P is a fictitious person. If P is a real person the rule does not apply even though D'er did not intend P to have an interest in the check. As the person signing in the name of Company, President, and not D'er, is the person whose intent determines to whom the check is payable.[136]

Assume now that the check is forged, *i.e.*, that D'er did not have any authority to issue the check. When the nominal or fictitious payee rule applies in these cases, the loss will fall on the drawee bank unless the bank has some other means to pass the loss to another party. Consider the following possibilities:

(1) After stealing a blank check from Company, D'er draws the check naming P as the payee, but with the intent to steal the check, and forging President's name as the only authorized person to sign checks for Company as drawer.[137] D'er then forges P's indorsement and disappears with the funds received. The rule applies because P is nominal. D'er signed as drawer in the name of Company while intending that P not have any interest in the check. As possessor of the check, D'er was a holder, and D'er's indorsement was effective as the indorsement of P in favor of H, DB, and PB. PB thus was protected through the fictitious payee rule with respect to the indorsement, but not with respect to the forged drawer's signature. Because the check was not properly payable with a forged drawer's signature, PB was not entitled to charge Company's account. PB could not successfully pursue a warranty action against either H or DB. With an effective indorsement by D'er, they were both persons entitled to enforce the check and their warranty on the signature of D'er extended only to the absence of knowledge that the signature was unauthorized. PB's payment also was final in favor of DB because DB took the check in good faith and gave value when the credit for the check

---

[133] U.C.C. § 3-404, Comment 2 (Illustration # 2).

[134] This case would be decided under section 3-405, however, and the result will be the same. *See* U.C.C. § 3-405, Comment 3 (Illustration # 6); § 10.03[C] *infra*.

[135] U.C.C. § 3-404, Comment 2 (Illustration # 3).

[136] This case would be decided under section 3-405, however, and the result will be the same. *See* U.C.C. § 3-405, Comment 3 (Illustration # 7); § 10.03[C] *infra*.

[137] U.C.C. § 3-404, Comment 2 (Illustration # 5).

was withdrawn. PB can proceed against Company only if it can establish Company's negligence under sections 3-406 or 4-406. Otherwise, PB can look only to the wrongdoer D'er for its losses.

(2) D'er acts without any authority in causing Company's check-writing machine to prepare a check payable to P. D'er does not intend for P to have any interest in the check.[138] The rule applies because P is nominal. D'er is the person whose intent determines to whom an instrument is payable because, under section 3-110(b), when the signature of the issuer is made by automated means "the payee of the instrument is determined by the intent of the person who supplied the name or identification of the payee, whether or not authorized to do so." The analysis is thus the same as in the previous illustration in which D'er forged the drawer's signature on a stolen check form. Ultimately, however, in this illustration, PB would probably be able to pass the loss back to Company on the basis of an agreement. Banks are likely to insist on an agreement with their customers using check-writing machines that allows the bank to debit the customer's account for all checks produced by the machine that are paid, even if the checks are forged.

[2] The Indorsement

The applicability of the rules of section 3-404 requires "an indorsement of the instrument by any person in the name of the payee."[139] The indorsement does not have to be made by the impostor or other person who caused the check to the issued. An indorsement by any person is effective if it is made in the payee's name. Obviously, the person who initiates the fraud or a confederate is the person most likely to indorse. The indorsement nevertheless is effective even if made by a subsequent thief of the instrument or by someone else who acquires the instrument by the means of a secondary fraud. Because a depositary bank becomes a holder of a check that it receives for collection, whether or not the customer indorses the check,[140] the rules of section 3-404 apply even when a check, whether or not indorsed, "is deposited in a depositary bank to an account in a name substantially similar to that of the payee."[141]

Several courts applying the original version of Article 3 required the indorsement to be an exact duplication of the name of the payee. Some of these cases carried the point to an extreme. For example, a case in Missouri denied applicability to two checks because the indorsements omitted the abbreviations "Co." and "Inc." from the designations of the names indicated on the checks as the payees.[142] The revision rejects such a precise application by indicating that an indorsement is made in the name of a payee if

---

[138] U.C.C. § 3-404, Comment 2 (Illustration # 4).

[139] U.C.C. § 3-404(a). Subsection (b)(2) is comparable.

[140] U.C.C. § 4-205(1).

[141] U.C.C. § 3-404(c)(ii).

[142] Consolidated Pub. Water Supply Dist. No. C-1 v. Farmers Bank, 686 S.W.2d 844, 40 U.C.C. Rep. Serv. 955 (Mo. Ct. App. 1985).

"it is made in a name substantially similar to that of the payee."[143] As long as the indorsement is reasonable to create a normal appearance and not arouse suspicions, it meets the objective that section 3-404 is intended to serve.

[3] Comparative Negligence

Sometimes the person taking a check might have detected the fraud encompassed under the impostor and the fictitious payee rules. Because an approach that creates incentives for all parties to exercise reasonable care is preferable, the drafters of the revision impose a standard of ordinary care on persons who take or pay instruments affected by these rules.[144] If their failure to exercise such care "substantially contributes to loss resulting from payment of the instrument, the person bearing the loss may recover from the person failing to exercise ordinary care to the extent the failure to exercise ordinary care contributed to the loss."[145] This provision enables the person who suffers the loss imposed by the rules to recover from the person who failed to exercise ordinary care.[146]

The most likely defendant under this ordinary care standard is a depositary bank that takes a check and does not exercise ordinary care.[147] An illustration of the type of facts that could lead to liability is provided in the Comments.[148] It supposes that a dishonest employee opens an account in the name of a well-known company and the bank personnel handling the transaction do not require the employee to produce any evidence of authorization for the employee to act for the company. The employee later deposits a check for a large amount into the account and, after the check is paid, orders the bank to wire the proceeds to an account in a bank in a foreign country. A trier of fact might determine a failure on the part of the depositary bank to exercise ordinary care that substantially contributed to the loss incurred by the company. The allocation of the loss between the company and the depositary bank would be left to the trier of fact.[149]

If a depositary bank or any other transferor or presenter does not violate this standard of care, they have a defense available if an action for breach

---

[143] U.C.C. § 3-404(c)(i). For a case influenced by the approach of the revision prior to its effective date, see Basse Truck Line, Inc. v. First State Bank, 949 S.W.2d 17, 34 U.C.C. Rep. Serv. 2d 82 (Tex. Ct. App. 1997) (indorsement was made in the name "Texas Insurance," while the name of the payee was stated as "Texas Insurance Agency, Inc.").

[144] "'Ordinary care' in the case of a person engaged in business means observance of reasonable commercial standards, prevailing in the area in which the person is located, with respect to the business in which the person is engaged." U.C.C. § 3-103(a)(7).

[145] U.C.C. § 3-404(d). The standard of "substantially contributes" refers to factual causation, but not proximate causation, and is comparable to use of the same standard in section 3-406. U.C.C. § 3-406, Comment 2. See § 10.02[A][3][b] supra.

[146] U.C.C. § 3-404, Comment 3; Gina Chin & Associates, Inc. v. First Union Bank, 500 S.E.2d 516, 35 U.C.C. Rep. Serv. 2d 1069 (Va. 1998) (allegations by company of failure of the depositary bank to exercise ordinary care were sufficient to state a cause of action under section 3-404 and 3-405).

[147] U.C.C. § 3-404, Comment 3.

[148] U.C.C. § 3-405, Comment 4.

[149] U.C.C. § 3-404, Comment 3.

of the presentment warranty against forged indorsements is asserted against them. The warrantor can defend against the warranty claim by proving that the indorsement is effective under either the impostor rule or the fictitious or nominal payee rule.[150]

In addressing the standard of ordinary care, the drafters of the revision have recognized the modern practice of processing instruments for collection and payment by automated means. As a concession to these realities, the definition of ordinary care specifically excludes a requirement for the bank to examine the instrument, subject to the caveat that the failure to examine does not violate the bank's prescribed procedures and that those procedures not vary unreasonably from general banking usage consistent with the provisions of Articles 3 and 4.[151]

[C] Fraudulent Indorsements by Employees — § 3-405

Section 3-405(b) states the rule with respect to fraudulent indorsement by employees as follows:

> For the purpose of determining the rights and liabilities of a person who, in good faith, pays an instrument or takes it for value or for collection, if an employer entrusted an employee with responsibility with respect to the instrument and the employee or a person acting in concert with the employee makes a fraudulent indorsement of the instrument, the indorsement is effective as the indorsement of the person to whom the instrument is payable if it is made in the name of that person.

This provision covers two types of situations.[152] One situation is employee theft and indorsement of checks sent to the employer by parties owing money to the employer. An example would be a bookkeeper, whose assigned tasks include the collection and deposit of checks payable to the employer, stealing one of the incoming checks, forging an indorsement to herself, and depositing it into her own account. The other situation is employee theft of a check issued by the employer. An example would be the same dishonest bookkeeper who steals a payroll check prepared in the name of one of the employer's workers, forging an indorsement to herself, and depositing it into her own account. Section 3-405 includes provisions that are comparable to the provisions in section 3-404 concerning the nature of the required indorsement[153] and the liability of a person paying an instrument or taking it for value or for collection without exercising ordinary care.[154] The effectiveness of the indorsement in these situations

---

[150] U.C.C. §§ 3-417(c), 4-208(c).

[151] U.C.C. § 3-103(a)(7).

[152] U.C.C. § 3-405(a)(2).

[153] U.C.C. § 3-405(c). *See* § 10.03[B][2] *supra.*

[154] U.C.C. § 3-405(b). *See* § 10.03[B][3] *supra;* United States Fidelity & Guar. Co. v. Bank of Bentonville, 29 F. Supp. 2d 553, 37 U.C.C. Rep. Serv. 2d 1081 (W.D. Ark. 1998) (bank's motion to dismiss denied because facts could establish bank's failure to exercise ordinary care); Hunter's Modern Appliance, Inc. v. Bank IV Oklahoma, N.A., 34 U.C.C. Rep. Serv. 2d 426

also requires that the person taking the instrument or paying it do so in good faith.[155]

The rule of section 3-405 is new with the revision to Article 3. It serves to increase employer responsibility for selection and supervision of employees entrusted with responsibilities concerning negotiable instruments. Under prior law the negligence provisions were sometimes used to preclude employers from asserting a forged indorsement by an employee whom they entrusted to deal with negotiable instruments but failed to supervise. Section 3-405 eliminates any need for an analysis under the negligence provisions because it makes the employer strictly liable for the risk associated with fraudulent indorsements by employees entrusted with responsibilities with respect to negotiable instruments.[156]

Obviously, section 3-405 has some overlap with section 3-404(b) on the nominal or fictitious payee rule. The latter rule is not limited to just employees, but it does represent a type of fraud that generally is committed by an employee. Section 3-405 is likely to eclipse the nominal or fictitious payee rule in importance both because it is tends to be easier to prove and because it covers a considerably wider range of employee fraud.

Note, however, that section 3-405 does not cover all fraudulent indorsements by employees on instruments issued to or by their employers. Most importantly, an employee must have been entrusted with responsibility with respect to instruments. A janitor, for example, who finds a check payable to the employer while the janitor is cleaning the desk of the bookkeeper will not invoke section 3-405 by stealing the check and fraudulently indorsing it.[157] On the other hand, section 3-406 would apply if the janitor's access to the check was determined to be negligence on the part of the employer.[158] Similarly, a janitor who wrongfully causes a check-writing machine of the employer to prepare a check in the name of a

---

(Okla. Ct. App. 1997) (summary judgment on behalf of the bank was improper because substantial issues of material fact remained as to whether the bank exercised ordinary care). The "substantially contributes" standard refers to factual causation, but not proximate causation, and is comparable to use of the same standard in section 3-406. U.C.C. § 3-406, Comment 2. See § 10.02[A][3][b] supra.

[155] "Good faith" is defined in U.C.C. § 3-103(a)(4). For discussion of this definition, see § 6.01[C]. San Tan Irrigation District v. Wells Fargo Bank, 3 P.3d 1113, 197 Ariz. 193, 40 U.C.C. Rep. Serv. 2d 775 (Ariz. Ct. App. 2000) (remand necessary to establish the record concerning the fairness of the bank's conduct for purposes of section 3-405). The court in Cable Cast Magazine v. Premier Bank, N.A., 729 So. 2d 1165, 39 U.C.C. Rep. Serv. 2d 159 (La. Ct. App. 1999), found that an employer was erroneous in its assertion that the bank acted in bad faith when it deposited checks payable to the company into the personal account of an employee. The company had not reserved its trade name with the state, and the employee represented to the bank that she was the company. The bank did not know of her employee status, and the company had its business accounts at a different bank.

[156] "The provision [§ 3-405] applies regardless of whether the employer is negligent." U.C.C. § 3-405, Comment 1.

[157] U.C.C. § 3-405, Comment 3 (Illustration # 1).

[158] If the employer was not negligent in safeguarding the check, it can successfully assert an action in conversion against the payor bank. For discussion of the conversion action, see § 10.04 infra.

fictitious payee which the janitor then indorses in the name of the payee will invoke section 3-404(b), but not section 3-405.

Section 3-405 defines the type of responsibility delegated to an employee that will make the employer responsible for fraudulent indorsements of the employee.[159] It includes authority in the following areas:

- To sign or indorse instruments on behalf of the employer.[160] For example, assume that an attorney's secretary is given the task of indorsing checks that are sent to the attorney at her office before they are taken to the bank by another employee. The secretary steals one of these checks, forges an indorsement to himself, deposits the check in his own account, and later withdraws the proceeds. Because the forged indorsement of the check is deemed to be effective, neither the depositary bank nor the payor bank will be liable to the attorney for conversion.[161]

- To process instruments received by the employer for bookkeeping purposes, for deposit to an account, or for other disposition.[162] For example, assume that the secretary in the previous example had the duty of depositing checks sent to the attorney in the attorney's account. The secretary steals one of these checks, forges an indorsement to himself, deposits the check in his own account, and later withdraws the proceeds.

- To prepare or process instruments for issue in the name of the employer.[163] For example, assume that a corporate official has the authority to draw checks on behalf of the corporation. The official draws a check to pay a supplier the amount of money owed by the corporation. The official later decides to steal the check, forges the indorsement of the supplier, and obtains payment through check collection. The indorsement is effective under section 3-405, but section 3-404 does not apply.[164]

- To supply information determining the names or addresses of payees of instruments to be issued in the name of the employer.[165] For example, assume that a payroll clerk has the duty of preparing a list of names of employees who are to receive payroll checks and the amounts owed on any given week. One week he includes an extra name and amount on the list with the intention of stealing the check that would be prepared. He forges the indorsement in the name of the payee, deposits the check in his account, and receives the proceeds of the check. Section 3-405

---

[159] U.C.C. § 3-405(a)(3).

[160] Cable Cast Magazine v. Premier Bank, N.A., 729 So. 2d 1165, 39 U.C.C. Rep. Serv. 2d 159 (La. Ct. App. 1999) (employee entrusted with responsibility to indorse incoming checks and to arrange for their deposit at the bank).

[161] For discussion of the conversion action, see § 10.04 *infra*. If the bank decided to recredit the attorney's account and proceed against prior parties on a breach of the implied warranty against forged indorsements, the defendants could defend against the action by proving that the indorsement is effective under section 3-405. U.C.C. §§ 3-417(c), 4-208(c).

[162] U.C.C. § 3-405(a)(3) (Illustration # 3); Halla v. Norwest Bank Minnesota, N.A., 601 N.W.2d 449, 39 U.C.C. Rep. Serv. 2d 1104 (Minn. Ct. App. 1999).

[163] *See* U.C.C. § 3-405, Comment 3 (Illustration # 6).

[164] For discussion of the inapplicability of section 3-404(b), see § 10.03[B][1][b] *supra*.

[165] *See* U.C.C. § 3-405, Comment 3 (Illustration # 7).

makes the indorsement effective because of the entrusted responsibility. Section 3-404(b)(i) does not apply because the clerk is not a person whose intent determines to whom the check is payable. If the payee was nonexistent, section 3-404(b)(ii) applies, although the result is the same.

- To control the disposition of instruments to be issued in the name of the employer. For example, assume that once the payroll checks are prepared each week, a payroll clerk has the responsibility to deliver them to employees in the office. One week she keeps two of the checks, forges an indorsement on them to herself, and deposits the checks in her account. The indorsement is effective.

§ 10.04 Conversion — § 3-420

[A] The Proper Defendant

[1] Thieves, Finders and Their Transferees

The personal-property attributes of negotiable instruments are relevant to the concept of conversion. Like other property, an instrument can be stolen from the rightful owner, or someone can exercise other dominion and control over the instrument inconsistent with the owner's rights. Consistent with the common-law tort concept, parties who wrongfully exert dominion over an instrument that belongs to someone else can be held liable for conversion. The liability of parties who receive a converted instrument is comparable to the liability of buyers of stolen goods. Even if the property is purchased by a person who is completely unaware that the owner was wrongfully deprived of the property, the buyer nevertheless can be liable for converting the property.

Article 3 identifies several parties who can incur conversion liability with respect to a negotiable instrument. Section 3-420 provides initially that "[t]he law applicable to conversion of personal property applies to instruments."[166] This reference to the common law will cover a person who steals an instrument or a finder of a negotiable instrument if the finder appropriates the instrument for his or her own use. The thief is the most obvious defendant in conversion.[167]

The common-law concept of conversion will also cover some transferees of thieves and finders, but because instruments are negotiable, their conversion sometimes differs significantly from the conversion of nonnegotiable property. If a thief steals an instrument in bearer form, the thief can negotiate the instrument.[168] If the transferee gives value, and takes the instrument in good faith and without any disabling notice, the transferee will become a holder in due course.[169] The transferee then takes free of

---

[166] U.C.C. § 3-420(a).

[167] Moore v. Richmond Hill Sav. Bank, 120 Misc. 2d 488, 466 N.Y.S.2d 131 (N.Y. Civ. Ct. 1983).

[168] U.C.C. § 3-201(b).

[169] U.C.C. § 3-302(a).

the owner's claim of conversion.[170] Upon payment of the instrument to a holder, the liability on the instrument of the drawer or maker will be discharged,[171] as will the liability on the underlying obligation that led to issuance of the instrument.[172] The owner will be left with only a conversion cause of action against the thief.[173] The owner of a negotiable instrument loses both the rights on the instrument and the conversion claim against a subsequent transferee when the instrument reaches a holder in due course, whereas with nonnegotiable property, the bona fides of a recipient generally are insufficient insulation against a conversion claim.[174] A holder to whom bearer paper is negotiated who does not have the rights of a holder in due course is similarly situated to the latter circumstance and thus liable in conversion.[175]

Conversion of an instrument also results "if it is taken by transfer, other than a negotiation, from a person not entitled to enforce the instrument."[176] Thus, a person who receives a lost or stolen instrument also will incur conversion liability when both of these requirements are met. The provision is included to address situations when an indorsement on order paper is either forged or missing.[177] For example, assume that a thief of an order instrument forges the indorsement of the payee and sells the instrument to a buyer. The requirement of taking by transfer would be met because the instrument was delivered by a person other than the issuer (the thief) for the purpose of giving the recipient of the delivery (the buyer) the right to enforce the instrument.[178] Furthermore, the transfer would not be by negotiation because, with a forged indorsement of the payee, the buyer could not become a holder.[179] The final requirement for conversion liability

---

[170] U.C.C. § 3-306.

[171] U.C.C. § 3-602(a).

[172] U.C.C. § 3-310(b).

[173] U.C.C. § 3-420(a).

[174] In a dispute between the rightful owner of personal property and a subsequent bona fide purchaser, the true owner will have the superior claim at common law. The true owner has the best claim to the property. First State Bank v. Perryman, 746 P.2d 706 (Okla. Ct. App. 1987). The possessory and ownership interest of the subsequent BFP is superior to everyone except for the interest of the true owner. Snethen v. Oklahoma State Union of Farmers Ed. & Co-op., 664 P.2d 377 (Okla. 1983). The main reason that the claim of the true owner is superior to the claim of the subsequent BFP is that the BFP cannot have an interest in the property greater than the interest held by his or her transferor. *Id.*; Mercer v. Braziel, 746 P.2d 702 (Okla. Ct. App. 1987). When the personal property is converted, the thief has no valid possessory or ownership interest against the owner. Anderson Contracting Co., Inc. v. Zurich Ins. Co., 448 So. 2d 37 (Fla. Ct. App. 1984). Therefore, a subsequent BFP who purchases from a thief or from someone who had previously purchased from a thief, has no defensible interest in the property that can defeat the claim of the true owner. *Id.*; State v. Warren, 450 So. 2d 1249 (Fla. Ct. App. 1984) (dicta).

[175] U.C.C. § 3-306. An owner of an instrument can enforce its claim either by seeking to replevy the instrument or by seeking damages for conversion of the property.

[176] U.C.C. § 3-420(a).

[177] U.C.C. § 3-420, Comment 1.

[178] U.C.C. § 3-203(a).

[179] U.C.C. § 3-201 (requires indorsement by the holder).

of the transferee would also be met. The transfer was made by the thief, and the thief would not be entitled to enforce the instrument.[180]

Assume now that, rather than a theft situation, the payee of the order instrument transferred the instrument without indorsing it, and that the transferee subsequently indorsed her own name and sold it to the buyer. The delivery to the buyer would still constitute a transfer that was not a negotiation, thus satisfying the first requirement for conversion liability of the buyer. The second requirement, however, now would not be met. Even though the transferee from the payee could not qualify as a holder, because the instrument would still run to the payee in the absence of the payee's indorsement, the transferee would qualify as a person entitled to enforce the instrument because she had the rights of the holder through the transfer.[181] The buyer was purchasing these rights to enforce the instrument, and thus could not be liable in conversion.

[2] Collection, Payment, and Indorsements

Section 3-420 includes another provision identifying appropriate defendants for a cause of action in conversion: "An instrument is also converted if . . . a bank makes or obtains payment with respect to the instrument for a person not entitled to enforce the instrument or receive payment."[182] This provision will reach a payor bank that pays an instrument with a forged indorsement and a depositary bank that takes for collection such an instrument that is paid.[183] Such collection and payment are considered to be an exercise of dominion and control over the instrument that is inconsistent with the rights of the owner.

The provision also addresses cases involving missing indorsements. If the customer that deposits a check is a person entitled to enforce the instrument, even though a prior indorsement required for negotiation was inadvertently omitted, the instrument would not be converted by the depositary bank or the payor bank. A different result would apply, however, to an instrument that is payable to two persons and not in the alternative. For example, a check payable to Seigfried and Roy is enforceable only by both parties acting together. If a depositary bank takes the check for deposit to one of these persons' account, the bank will be liable to the other person, unless that person consented to the transaction.[184]

In addition to payor banks, any person that pays an instrument to a person not entitled to enforce the instrument is liable for conversion.[185]

---

[180] U.C.C. § 3-301 (would not qualify as a holder and would not have the rights of a holder).

[181] U.C.C. § 3-301(ii).

[182] U.C.C. § 3-420(a).

[183] Another provision generally will insulate any other collecting bank that is not also a depositary bank. See § 10.04[a][3] infra.

[184] Stefano v. First Union Nat'l Bank of Virginia, 981 F. Supp. 417, 34 U.C.C. Rep. Serv. 2d 11 (E.D. Va. 1997).

[185] U.C.C. § 3-420(a) (common-law conversion concept); Robbins v. First Fed. Sav. Bank, 363 S.E.2d 418, 5 U.C.C. Rep. Serv. 2d 1420 (S.C. Ct. App. 1987) (payment over a forged indorsement constitutes common-law conversion).

Payors can include the drawee of a check or draft,[186] an acceptor of a draft,[187] and the maker of a note.[188] Payment that is made to a person not entitled to enforce the instrument will not discharge a party obliged to pay the instrument.[189]

[3] Representatives: Depositary and Collecting Banks

Section 3-420(c) creates a defense to a conversion cause of action for a person who deals with an instrument only as a representative. The provision provides as follows:

> A representative, other than a depositary bank, who has in good faith dealt with an instrument or its proceeds on behalf of one who was not the person entitled to enforce the instrument is not liable in conversion to that person beyond the amount of any proceeds that it has not paid out.

"'Representative' includes an agent, an officer of a corporation or association, and a trustee, executor or administrator of an estate, or any other person empowered to act for another."[190] Depositary and collecting banks act as agents for the collection of deposited checks.[191] Depositary banks, however, are expressly excluded from availability of the defense of section 3-420(c).

Although representatives can be liable for conversion when they deal with an instrument on behalf of someone who is not the person entitled to enforce the instrument, the imposition of such liability would be unfair in many instances. Section 3-420(c) therefore allows a representative to assert a defense to liability for conversion if the representative acted in good faith in dealing with the instrument. A representative who qualifies is liable to the person entitled to enforce the instrument only for any proceeds of the instrument still in the representative's possession. When proceeds are still retained, the representative is required to pass them to the party with the rightful claim rather than to his or her principal.

The exclusion of depositary banks from the defense available to representatives is supported by strong policy considerations that reveal the desirability of allowing a direct cause of action in conversion against the depositary bank. Pursuit of the depositary bank avoids circuitous causes of action. Consider a check with a forged indorsement that passes through the check-collection process and is paid by the drawee bank. The person entitled to enforce the instrument has a valid cause of action in conversion

---

[186] Larkin Gen. Hosp., Ltd. v. Bank of Florida, 464 So. 2d 635, 40 U.C.C. Rep. Serv. 985 (Fla. Dist. Ct. App. 1985) (bank held liable as drawee on checks and insurance company held liable as drawee on drafts).

[187] Reynolds-Wilson Lumber Co. v. People's Nat'l Bank, 699 P.2d 146, 40 U.C.C. Rep. Serv. 1319 (Okla. 1985).

[188] Guaranty Nat'l Bank v. Beaver, 738 P.2d 1336, 3 U.C.C. Rep. Serv. 2d 1027 (Okla. 1987).

[189] U.C.C. § 3-602.

[190] U.C.C. § 1-201(35).

[191] U.C.C. § 4-201(1). *See* § 11.02[A] *infra*.

against the drawee bank. That bank will pass the liability upstream under breach of the presenters' warranty of entitlement to enforce the draft,[192] and applications of warranty law under the Code will place the ultimate liability on the depositary bank that took the check from the thief.[193] The policy reasons underlying the finality doctrine justify placing this liability on depositary banks because they have the best opportunity to minimize losses by implementing practices of careful identification of persons seeking to cash or deposit checks and of determining their authority to deal with the instrument. Precisely the same rationale supports a direct cause of action in conversion against the depositary bank. It is the only bank that dealt with the thief and, therefore, it had the best opportunity to prevent the fraud. The liability of depositary banks is inevitable for breach of warranty, and nothing beneficial is achieved by forcing a circuity of actions in this particular context.[194]

The desirability of a direct conversion action against the depositary bank extends beyond the preclusion of nonfunctional circuitous actions. An opportunity to proceed directly against the depositary bank is likely to be significantly more convenient for the person entitled to enforce the instrument. Forgers often convert a check by depositing it or cashing it at a bank in the same general locale where the rightful party resides. When the check is drawn on a bank located a considerable distance away, it would be easier for the owner to proceed against a local depositary bank. When the forger has converted several checks, the convenience of a direct cause of action against the depositary bank is even greater. If an employee of the payee of several checks forges the employer's name and cashes them all at a local bank, the employer-payee can press the conversion claim on all of the checks in just one law suit. Otherwise, the employer would be required to pursue multiple causes of action against drawee banks or drawers located potentially in different jurisdictions when the ultimate liability under each case will be passed to the single depositary bank located precisely where the employer's business is located.

[B] The Proper Plaintiff

It is readily apparent, given the nature of the action, that the true owner of a negotiable instrument is a proper plaintiff in a conversion cause of action. In the case of instruments, the owner is the payee or a subsequent transferee in the chain of title.[195] A conversion claim is available to protect property interests in personal property. Because multiple parties can be

---

[192] U.C.C. § 4-208(a)(1). The warranty essentially is one that there are no unauthorized or missing indorsements. See § 8.04[B][1][a] *supra*.

[193] *See* § 8.03[C][2] *supra*.

[194] New Jersey Lawyers' Fund for Client Protection v. First Fidelity Bank, N.A., 303 N.J. Super. 208, 696 A.2d 728, 33 U.C.C. Rep. Serv. 2d 19 (1997) (because the depositary bank is strictly liable for conversion by taking checks with forged indorsements, there can be no defense based on the bank's innocence).

[195] Morgan Guaranty Trust Co. v. Chase Manhattan Bank, 36 U.C.C. Rep. Serv. 584 (N.Y. Sup. Ct. 1983); Riggs Nat'l Bank v. Security Bank, N.A., 10 U.C.C. Rep. Serv. 460 (D.C. 1972).

involved in transactions with negotiable instruments, a number of issues concerning proper plaintiffs in conversion claims arose under the initial version of Article 3. The revision includes explicit provisions designed to eliminate the uncertainty that was created.

[1] Payees and Indorsees: Delivery

The revision of Article 3 clarifies that "a payee or indorsee who did not receive delivery of the instrument either directly or through delivery to an agent or a co-payee" is not entitled to bring a cause of action in conversion.[196] The point can be illustrated with a check that is prepared in the name of a designated payee. If the check is stolen from the drawer or is intercepted from the mail before reaching the payee's mailbox, the payee does not have a conversion cause of action. The demarcation of delivery of the check to the payee [197] is appropriate, because "[u]ntil delivery, the payee does not have any interest in the check."[198] Just as delivery is a necessary element for a property claim in a gift transfer of personal property, delivery is required for any property interest to arise in a negotiable instrument.[199] Absent delivery of the instrument to the payee, the payee cannot have a conversion action against any transferees or payors of the instrument.[200]

The designated payee's rights in the prior illustration are adequately protected through other provisions. Assume that the drawer intended the check to be delivered to the named payee to satisfy an underlying obligation that the drawer owed to the payee. If the check was not delivered to the payee, the underlying obligation would be unaffected, even if the thief forged the payee's signature and received payment from the drawee bank.[201] The payee could still enforce the underlying obligation against the drawer. On the other hand, if the check were delivered to the payee prior to the theft, the underlying obligation could not be enforced to the extent of the amount payable on the instrument, and the obligee's rights against the obligor would be limited to that extent to enforcement of the instrument.[202] The

---

[196] U.C.C. § 3-420(a)(ii).

[197] "The payee receives delivery when the check comes into the payee's possession, as for example when it is put into the payee's mailbox. Delivery to an agent is delivery to the payee. If a check is payable to more than one payee, delivery to one of the payees is deemed to be delivery to all of the payees." U.C.C. § 3-420, Comment 1; Stefano v. First Union Nat'l Bank of Virginia, 981 F. Supp. 417, 34 U.C.C. Rep. Serv. 2d 11 (E.D. Va. 1997) (although one of the co-payees was deceased, the deceased's executor received each of the checks as an agent of the estate).

[198] U.C.C. § 3-420, Comment 1.

[199] Merely being named as a payee on the instrument is not enough. See § 3.06[A] *supra*.

[200] Delivery is a similar prerequisite for a conversion cause of action by any subsequent indorsees. Assume that Payee indorses a check to A, but the check is stolen before ever reaching A. The thief forges A's signature and obtains payment of the check through the collection system. Because delivery was never made to A, A would not have any rights in the check. At the time of the theft, Payee was the owner of the property, not A. Payee would have a conversion action, but not A. Any underlying obligation that Payee owed to A would be unaffected.

[201] U.C.C. § 3-310 (designated effects on the underlying obligation would not occur because the check was not taken by the payee for the obligation).

[202] U.C.C. § 3-310(b)(4). See § 7.03 *supra*.

theft now would affect the property rights of the payee adversely, so a cause of action lies in conversion.[203]

[2] Issuers and Acceptors Excluded

As the preceding subsection establishes, if a check is stolen before it is delivered to the designated payee, the payee does not have a conversion action, but rather should look to the drawer on the unaffected underlying obligation. Even if the check is stolen directly from the drawer, the drawer also will not have an action in conversion. The revision resolves the prior conflict of authority by providing that a conversion action may not be brought by "the issuer or acceptor of the instrument."[204]

The approach taken in the revision reflects the rule stated in *Stone & Webster Engineering Corp. v. First National Bank & Trust Co.*[205] The plaintiff-drawer in that case prepared three checks payable to Westinghouse Electric Corporation to pay an indebtedness owed. Prior to delivery of the checks to the payee, an employee of the plaintiff forged Westinghouse's indorsement and cashed the checks at the depositary bank. The checks were forwarded for collection and ultimately paid by the payor bank. The plaintiff sued the depositary bank. The court tied the conversion cause of action to interference with rights of ownership and precluded recovery for the drawer. The drawer's rights of ownership in a check do not extend beyond the piece of paper at best, and certainly do not reach the right to payment.[206] Ownership rights in a check accrue upon delivery to the designated payee and to subsequent transferees to whom the rights are passed.[207]

The drawer is adequately protected if a check that it draws is stolen and paid by the drawee bank over a forged indorsement, because the drawer can require the drawee bank to recredit its account for the amount of the improper payment.[208] The drawee bank, in turn, will be able to send the liability upstream on breach of a presentment warranty. Ultimate liability

---

[203] U.C.C. § 3-420, Comment 1.

[204] U.C.C. § 3-420(a)(i). *See* IBP, Inc. v. Mercantile Bank of Topeka, 6 F. Supp. 2d 1258, 36 U.C.C. Rep. Serv. 2d 270 (D. Kan. 1998). *See also* Sebastian v. D & S Express, Inc., 61 F. Supp. 2d 386, 39 U.C.C. Rep. Serv. 2d 475 (D. N.J. 1999) (because issuer of disputed checks was the corporation, not the fraudulent officer that signed, the action for conversion was barred).

[205] 345 Mass. 1, 184 N.E.2d 358, 1 U.C.C. Rep. Serv. 195 (1962).

[206] "Since, as we have seen, [the drawer] did not have the right of a payee or subsequent holder to present them to the drawee for payment, the value of its rights was limited to the physical paper on which they were written, and was not measured by their payable amounts." 345 Mass. at 8, 184 N.E.2d at 362, 1 U.C.C. Rep. Serv. at 202.

[207] "The check represents an obligation of the drawer rather than property of the drawer." U.C.C. § 3-420, Comment 1. The same observation applies to any issuer and to an acceptor of a draft.

[208] U.C.C. § 4-401(a). *See* § 12.02[B][2] *infra*; Pamar Enterprises, Inc. v. Huntington Banks of Michigan, 228 Mich. App. 727, 35 U.C.C. Rep. Serv. 2d 1298 (1998) (drawer may not maintain an action in conversion but can require its account to be recredited by the payor bank after payment of a check on which the indorsement of one of the co-payees was missing).

will lie on the forger or, from the practical sense, most likely the person who took the check from the forger.

[C] Damages

In a conversion action brought under section 3-420 "the measure of liability is presumed to be the amount payable on the instrument."[209] The presumption is rebutted when the defendant introduces evidence that is sufficient to support a contrary finding.[210] For example, the defendant can introduce evidence of a defense or of insolvency to show that the obligation on the instrument is worth less than face value or is even valueless.[211]

Windfalls are prevented for payees making conversion claims in multiple-payee situations by a provision that "recovery may not exceed the amount of the plaintiff's interest in the instrument."[212] If one of the payees forged the indorsement of other payees, a payee whose signature was forged will be able to recover from the bank that converted the check only the amount of the proceeds of the check to which that payee was entitled.

[D] The Case of Restrictive Indorsements — § 3-206(c)

A separate provision in Article 3 covers conversion liability with respect to restrictive indorsements. The provisions on restrictive indorsements are included in section 3-206, and cover cases in which the indorsement is in terms such as "pay any bank," "for deposit," and "for collection."[213] Intermediary banks, and a payor bank that pays an item presented by a collecting bank, are not affected by the restrictive indorsements.[214] Restrictive indorsements bind depositary banks,[215] a payor bank upon which the customer makes direct presentment,[216] and any other person.[217] These parties must honor the restrictive indorsement or they will be liable for conversion. This requirement means that the proceeds given to purchase the instrument, to take it for collection, or to pay it must either be received by the indorser or applied consistently with the indorsement.[218]

Because intermediary banks and payor banks process checks in bulk with automated equipment that cannot read written indorsements, they are not

---

[209] U.C.C. § 3-420(b).

[210] U.C.C. § 1-201(31); Mohr v. State Bank, 241 Kan. 42, 734 P.2d 1071, 3 U.C.C. Rep. Serv. 2d 1459 (1987) (depositary bank held liable for face amount of checks when it did not introduce evidence to mitigate damages).

[211] Tette v. Marine Midland Bank, 78 A.D.2d 383, 435 N.Y.S.2d 413, 30 U.C.C. Rep. Serv. 1059 (N.Y. Sup. Ct. 1981) (presumption rebutted by demonstrating proceeds reached the intended payee).

[212] U.C.C. § 3-420(b).

[213] U.C.C. §§ 3-206(c), 4-201(b).

[214] U.C.C. § 3-206(c)(4).

[215] U.C.C. § 3-206(c)(2).

[216] U.C.C. § 3-206(c)(3).

[217] U.C.C. § 3-206(c)(1).

[218] See § 3.04[B][2][c] supra.

affected by a restrictive indorsement. Section 3-206(c)(4) simply precludes conversion liability against these banks if the liability would be based solely on the failure to apply the proceeds of an instrument in accordance with the restrictive indorsement. Depositary banks, on the other hand, are required to apply value given consistently with a restrictive indorsement.[219] These banks take instruments from their customers over the counter and they should scrutinize them for compliance with restrictive indorsements. This requirement provides protection for the indorser. A depositary bank that does not comply is liable for conversion.[220]

---

[219] U.C.C. § 3-206(c)(2).

[220] Brite Lite Lamps Corp. v. Manufacturers Hanover Trust Co., 34 U.C.C. Rep. Serv. 1221 (N.Y. Sup. Ct. 1982); C.S. Bowen Co., Inc. v. Maryland Nat'l Bank, 36 Md. App. 26, 373 A.2d 30, 21 U.C.C. Rep. Serv. 1387 (1977).

Chapter 11

CHECK COLLECTION AND PAYMENT

SYNOPSIS

§ 11.01 Overview
    [A] Article 4
    [B] Regulation CC
    [C] Amendments to Article 4

§ 11.02 Forward Collection
    [A] Agency Status of Collecting Banks
        [1] Rights as Special Agents — § 4-201(a)
        [2] Collecting Bank as Holder — § 4-205(1)
    [B] Ways that Checks are Collected
        [1] Collection Through the Federal Reserve
        [2] Direct Presentment by Collecting Banks
        [3] Collection Through Clearinghouses
        [4] Collection Through Transmission of Information: Truncation
        [5] Presentment by the Customer
    [C] Duties of Collecting Banks in Forwarding Checks — §§ 4-202, 4-204

§ 11.03 Payor Banks
    [A] Deferred Posting — § 4-301
        [1] Statutory Authorization
        [2] Noncompliance With Time Limits
    [B] Over-the-Counter Presentment for Cash
    [C] Final Payment — § 4-215(a)
        [1] Introduction
        [2] The Definition
    [D] Competing Claims to a Drawer's Account Balance — § 4-303
        [1] The Priorities Approach
        [2] When Payment Attains Priority

§ 11.04 The Return Process
    [A] The Reasons for Regulation CC
        [1] Inefficient Check-Return Procedures
        [2] Check-Hold Practices
    [B] Funds Availability
    [C] Revised Check Return
        [1] Expeditious Return
        [2] Notice of Nonpayment
        [3] Indorsements

[4] **Warranties**

---

§ 11.01 Overview

[A] Article 4

A check is a drawer's order to the payor bank to pay; the holder of a check has to collect from that bank in order to be paid. The holder can present the check directly to the payor bank upon which the check is drawn. Often, however, it is more convenient simply to take the check to one's local bank to initiate check collection. The banking network has established a variety of relationships among banks that are devoted to check collection and payment. The legal structure in which they operate is known as the check-collection process.

The enactment of Article 4 of the U.C.C. represented the first widespread adoption of a comprehensive statutory treatment of check collections. The N.I.L. included a few provisions dealing with presentment and notice of dishonor, but it addressed few of the problems raised in modern check collection. Several states enacted a variety of different statutes to cover parts of the collection process. The Bank Collection Code of the American Bankers Association was the first comprehensive draft, but it was enacted ultimately by only eighteen states. The legislative approach was fragmented and haphazard, and common-law principles of contracts, agency, and torts had to be relied upon to fill the gaps.

The business of bank collections operated with amazing efficiency despite the absence of a uniform legal backdrop. This operation is particularly interesting in light of the obvious interstate nature of bank collections, as well as the increase in volume that the system had to absorb. The enactment of Article 4 nevertheless was a welcome development. For the most part, it reflected the check-collection practices that already had been implemented, but it provided a comprehensive and uniform legal basis to govern the relationships.

The bank-collection process will be divided into three convenient segments for purposes of the discussion in this Chapter. The first segment is the forward-collection process. It starts with a customer's introduction of a check into the process through a depositary bank and traces its flow through presentment for payment. The second segment covers the response by the payor bank through the ultimate payment or dishonor of the check. The final segment is the process of payment to the customer of the depositary bank or the return of the dishonored check to the customer.

[B] Regulation CC

Federal law also plays a role in the check-collection process. The Federal Reserve System was created in 1913.[1] Through regulations and operating letters, the Federal Reserve (the "Fed") established requirements that affected primarily collections that utilize the services of Federal Reserve Banks. Until recently, the most important of these federal rules was Regulation J.[2] Because the regulations of the Federal Reserve essentially reflect requirements of Article 4 on check collection, they did not change much state law, but rather supplemented it.

True federal preemption came in 1988 with the effectiveness of Regulation CC.[3] The Regulation is the product of authority delegated in the Expedited Funds Availability Act, which was signed into law on August 11, 1987[4] as Title VI of the Competitive Equality Banking Act of 1987.[5] The federal legislation resulted from increasing consumer dissatisfaction with the practice of banks placing "holds" on checks deposited for collection so that the depositor was denied access to the proceeds of the check for long periods of time.

The legislation that resulted extends far beyond merely addressing concerns over check-holds. Congress mandated the implementation of specific rules concerning the availability of funds to customers, but in addition it delegated extensive regulatory authority to the Federal Reserve. The enacted legislation includes three distinct levels of authority. The first requirement is a mandatory instruction to the Fed to issue regulations "to carry out the provisions of this [Act]."[6] This instruction empowered the Fed to implement the funds-availability rules that were spelled out already with significant detail in the legislation itself. The second level of delegation instructs the Federal Reserve to consider several specified aspects of check collection and authorizes it to promulgate regulations "to improve the check processing system."[7] The areas listed for consideration by the Fed concern potential ways to improve, and, in particular to accelerate, the return of dishonored checks. The final level of delegated authority grants the Federal Reserve the power and responsibility to regulate "any aspect of the payment system, including the receipt, payment, collection, or clearing of checks" and "any related function of the payment system with respect to checks."[8]

---

[1] Federal Reserve Act, Ch. 6, 38 Stat. 251 (1913), codified in scattered sections of 12 and 31 U.S.C.

[2] 12 C.F.R. Part 210.

[3] 12 C.F.R. Part 229.

[4] 12 U.S.C. §§ 4001-4010; Pub. L. No. 100-86.

[5] Pub. L. No. 100-86.

[6] 12 U.S.C. § 4008(a).

[7] 12 U.S.C. § 4008(b).

[8] 12 U.S C. § 4008(c)(1). Another provision empowers the Fed to "impose on or allocate among depository institutions the risks of loss and liability in connection with any aspect of the payment system. . . ." 12 U.S.C. § 4010(f). For an excellent evaluation of the regulatory techniques utilized in the Act, see Cooter & Rubin, *Orders and Incentives as Regulatory Methods: The Expedited Funds Availability Act of 1987*, 35 U.C.L.A. L. Rev. 1115 (1988).

The Expedited Funds Availability Act represents a milestone in the law of check collections. Whereas the enactment of Article 4 as state law essentially codified the established practices of bank collection, this federal legislation allows the Federal Reserve to impose entirely new sets of rules. In addition, the prospects for federal preemption under the delegated authority are pervasive. The Fed now has authority over the entire check-collection system of this country, rather than authority limited to collections utilizing services of the Federal Reserve System. The third level of delegation is sufficiently broad enough that the Federal Reserve Board could preempt Articles 3 and 4 of the Code in their entirety insofar as they govern checks.

Regulation CC is the Federal Reserve's first exercise of its new powers. Beyond implementing the funds-availability regulations mandated by Congress, it also applied some of its discretionary authority by promulgating rules affecting the check-collection process.[9] Nearly all of the collection rules are designed to affect the dishonor and return process, so essentially the Fed's response thus far has been to utilize the first two levels of delegated authority. Although the collection rules of Regulation CC do not displace all of the provisions of Article 4, they nevertheless are so pervasive as to make the Regulation the primary source of law on the return process of checks. The Regulation also may well signal future federal preemption.[10]

Because the substantive provisions of Regulation CC and the motivations that led to federal legislation both primarily concern the return process, detailed explanations are reserved for the parts of this chapter that cover check return. The discussion explains the perceived inadequacies of the Article 4 coverage on returns and the response of Regulation CC. The Regulation does have some peripheral effects on both forward collection and payor banks' actions of payment or dishonor. The explanation of these effects is integrated throughout the description of the check-collection process in the next two sections of this Chapter.

[C] Amendments to Article 4

A major impetus for amendment of Article 4 was the desire to modernize its provisions to reflect the automated processing methods that were introduced shortly after Article 4 was originally promulgated. The use of Magnetic Ink Character Recognition encoding and high-speed sorters and computers posed some issues that the codification based on manual processing simply did not address adequately. The amendments to Article 4 were promulgated at the same time as the revision to Article 3.

In working on the amendments to Article 4, the Drafting Committee developed proposals for several provisions designed to improve the check-return process. Those provisions were abandoned once Regulation CC was

---

[9] Subpart B of Regulation CC contains the rules on expedited funds availability. Subpart C states the rules on check collection.

[10] Professor Rubin has provided an insightful analysis into the rationales underlying federal preemption in this area in Rubin, *Uniformity, Regulation, and the Federalization of State Law: Some Lessons From the Payment System*, 49 Ohio St. L.J. 1251 (1989).

promulgated to include most of them. An effort was then made to revise the interbank settlement provisions of Article 4 to conform to Regulation CC. This effort was also abandoned because of concern that the Federal Reserve Board would extend Regulation CC to forward check collection. The amended version of Article 4 thus contains several provisions that are preempted. As federal law, Regulation CC is the binding source of law on check returns and customer funds availability. Amended Article 4 covers forward collection and final payment by payor banks, as long as the Fed does not decide to preempt those areas as well.[11]

§ 11.02 Forward Collection

[A] Agency Status of Collecting Banks

[1] Rights as Special Agents — § 4-201(a)

Article 4 creates a presumption that each collecting bank "is an agent or sub-agent of the owner of the item."[12] The provision does not make the banks general agents of the owner, but rather agents only for purposes of check collection. The owner of a check could travel personally to a distant city to present a check directly to the payor bank or send a personal agent to accomplish the task. Instead most check holders initiate collection through their own local bank. When the depositary bank agrees to collect the check, the holder is a customer[13] on the transaction, and the depositary bank[14] is an agent for collection on behalf of the customer. All subsequent collecting banks[15] act as sub-agents for the customer. Throughout the collection process, the customer of the depositary bank retains ownership of the check. Regulation CC preserves this agency relationship between the customer and banks in the collection process.[16]

The agency relationship between the owner of the check and collecting banks has several practical consequences. Several fundamental risks remain on the owner of a check in collection, including loss.[17] The owner

---

[11] One important aspect of forward collection under Article 4 is also preempted. Article 4 provides that initial settlements by collecting and payor banks are provisional. U.C.C. §§ 4-201(a), 4-301((a). Regulation CC, however, makes these settlements final when made. 12 C.F.R. § 229.36(d). See § 11.02[B][1] supra.

[12] U.C.C. § 4-201(a). A bank can purchase a particular item and become the owner of it, but it bears the heavy burden of establishing this purpose. Id.

[13] For purposes of check collection, a "customer" means "a person . . . for whom a bank has agreed to collect items, including a bank that maintains an account at another bank." U.C.C. § 4-104(a)(5).

[14] "Depositary bank" means "the first bank to take an item even though it is also the payor bank, unless the item is presented for immediate payment over the counter." U.C.C. § 4-105(2).

[15] "Collecting bank" means "a bank handling an item for collection except the payor bank." U.C.C. § 4-105(5).

[16] 12 C.F.R. § 229.36, Commentary (d).

[17] U.C.C. § 4-201, Comment 4; Mercantile Bank & Trust Co. v. Hunter, 501 P.2d 486, 11 U.C.C. Rep. Serv. 545 (Colo. Ct. App. 1972) (depositary bank was only an agent for collection purposes when customer withdrew deposit before check cleared).

bears the risk that the check will not be paid.[18] No bank assumes liability for the insolvency, neglect, misconduct, mistake, or default of any other bank or person or for loss or destruction of an item in transit or in possession of others.[19]

Even in their capacity as agents, collecting banks have certain rights in a check that is being collected or in its proceeds. Section 4-201(a) provides that "the continuance of ownership of an item by its owner and any rights of the owner to proceeds of the item are subject to rights of a collecting bank, such as those resulting from outstanding advances on the item and rights of recoupment and set-off." The reference to advances on the item indicate the circumstances in section 4-210(a) in which a bank attains a security interest in an item.[20]

[2] Collecting Bank as Holder — § 4-205(1)

The agency status of a collecting bank does not preclude it from being a holder of a check deposited for collection. Anyone in possession of an instrument that runs to that person is a holder.[21] Obviously a holder of a check can negotiate it to a depositary bank. If the check is in bearer form, it can be negotiated to the bank by transfer of possession alone, whereas indorsement by the holder will be required if the check is payable to an identified person.[22]

A customer need not actually negotiate the instrument, however, for the depositary bank to become a holder. When a customer delivers a check to a depositary bank for collection "the depositary bank becomes a holder of the item at the time it receives the item for collection if the customer at the time of delivery was a holder of the item, whether or not the customer indorses the item."[23] As a holder, the depositary bank is a person entitled to enforce the instrument and to pass that status on to others in the collection process.[24] This provision helps to speed up the collection process by eliminating the need to return a check to a customer when the check has been given to the depositary bank without the customer's indorsement.

[B] Ways that Checks are Collected

When a depositary bank receives a check for collection from its customer, it has several methods by which it can initiate collection. This section will discuss three of the most common approaches taken to move the check forward to presentment for payment to the payor bank, as well as another

---

[18] *Id.*

[19] U.C.C. § 4-202(c).

[20] This provision is discussed in conjunction with section 4-211 in § 6.01[B][2] *supra*. It explains how a bank can satisfy the "taking for value" requirement to attain holder-in-due-course status.

[21] U.C.C. § 1-201(20).

[22] U.C.C. § 3-201(b).

[23] U.C.C. § 4-205(1).

[24] U.C.C. § 3-301.

method that the Board of Governors of the Federal Reserve System is encouraging. These methods include collection through the Federal Reserve System, direct presentment by a collecting bank, collection through clearinghouses, and collection through transmission of information. In addition, a customer can present a check directly to a payor bank.

[1] Collection Through the Federal Reserve

Assume that a customer takes a check drawn on a bank in Boston to her bank in Kansas City and deposits it in her account for collection. During the same day, the Kansas City bank is likely to receive deposits of other customers drawn on hundreds of other distant banks. The cost and burden of sending each check to these separate banks scattered throughout the country would be prohibitive. In addition, the remittance of payment from those banks would pose a problem. The Kansas City bank would not be likely to maintain an account with most of these distant banks because the infrequency of business with them would not justify it. Payment by the distant bank, therefore, cannot be accomplished through crediting of accounts, and sending cash, of course, is too risky. Most nonlocal checks, therefore, will be cleared through the Federal Reserve System.

The Federal Reserve System includes twelve Federal Reserve Banks, as well as branches, that provide check-collection services for their members. Instead of sending each nonlocal check directly to the payor bank, the Kansas City bank can forward all of them to the Federal Reserve Bank in Kansas City, provided it maintains a reserve account. The Federal Reserve Bank then acts as a collecting bank, and credits the Kansas City Bank (its customer) for all of the checks forwarded to it. The Kansas City Bank will have met its responsibility of forwarding its customers' checks for collection. It also receives a credit from the Federal Reserve that equals the amount of credits it has given its customers in receiving each individual check, thus keeping its books in balance.

The Federal Reserve Bank in Kansas City will have received huge quantities of checks from throughout its multi-state district. It will sort all of the checks received and route them toward the Federal Reserve district in which the various payor banks are located. So the check drawn on the Boston bank will be forwarded in a heavy bundle with other checks drawn on banks in the New England area to the Federal Reserve Bank in Boston. The Interdistrict Settlement Fund is used to settle accounts among Reserve Banks. Each Reserve Bank maintains an account with the Fund, which is located in Washington, D.C. On a daily basis, the Fund transfers net credit balances among the accounts of the Reserve banks. The Fund compares the credit for the total amount of items forwarded by the Kansas City Fed to the Boston Fed with the credit that the Boston Fed is entitled to for items forwarded to the Kansas City Fed, and makes the net settlements between the two Federal Reserve Banks.

The Federal Reserve Bank in Boston then sorts the checks it has received from Kansas City, as well as from other locales. The checks are sorted according to the payor banks upon which they are drawn and are sent to each payor bank for payment, provided that the payor bank has an account with the district Federal Reserve Bank. The Boston Fed also debits the account of each payor bank for the total amount of the items that are forwarded to it for payment.

Checks are collected in this manner by the transfer of credit balances from one account to another. Consequently, the system depends upon the existence of accounts between banks forwarding a check for collection and the bank to which it is forwarded. The forwarding bank is entitled to a credit for each check sent, and the recipient bank therefore must make a corresponding debit in its account. By providing settlements through their respective accounts, collecting banks eliminate any need for cash transfers in the collection process. By maintaining an account with the Federal Reserve Bank in the geographic area where it is located, a collecting bank can enjoy the benefits of collection through account balancing without having to maintain multiple accounts.

Fewer than half of the banks in the nation, however, have an account with the Federal Reserve Bank in their district.[25] Non-member banks nonetheless can clear their checks through the Federal Reserve System by entering into a correspondent relationship with a bank that does maintain a Reserve account with the district Fed Bank. This arrangement simply adds an additional step in the forwarding process. The depositary bank sends its nonlocal checks to its correspondent bank, with the applicable debits and credits by both banks for the total amount of checks forwarded. The correspondent bank then continues the bank-collection process by forwarding all of these checks with the others its has for collection through the Federal Reserve System to the Reserve Bank with which it has its account. If a check is drawn on a bank that does not have an account with a Reserve Bank, the Reserve Bank cannot forward it for payment to the payor bank, but rather must forward it to the correspondent bank of the payor bank. The latter then presents it for payment.

The following diagram illustrates the check collection process through the Federal Reserve System, with a correspondent bank on each end of the trail.

D'er ····▶P—▶DB—▶CB(1)—▶FRB(KC)—▶FRB(BO)—▶CB(2)·····▶PB

Diagram 11.1

Correspondent Bank Number 1 (CB(1)) routes the check from the depositary bank (DB) to the Federal Reserve Bank in Kansas City (FRB(KC)). Correspondent Bank Number 2 (CB(2)) receives the check from the Federal

---

[25] Banks must maintain reserve accounts if they use the Federal Reserve System check-clearing services. 12 U.S.C. §§ 461-466.

Reserve Bank in Boston (FRB(BO)) and presents it for payment to the payor bank (PB).

Although several banks can be involved in the forward-collection process, the system is highly automated and streamlined. Checks are encoded with Magnetic Ink Character Recognition (MICR) numbers, the wiggly numbers located along the bottom of a check, that can be read by the sorting machines at the collecting banks. Fast methods of transportation also speed the bundles of checks forward to the next stop in the collection process.

Under Article 4, the credits given by each collecting bank for the items forwarded to it by other banks are provisional.[26] The Code scheme envisions all of these provisional settlements becoming finalized upon final payment of the item by the payor bank.[27] If the payor bank dishonored the item rather than make final payment on it, the item was sent back through the collection system, retracing its journey through each of the banks used in forward collection. In this situation, each collecting bank would reverse the provisional entries on its books and return the check to the bank that had forwarded it. Ultimately the check reached the depositary bank, which returned it to its customer and reversed the credit given to the customer.

The biggest impact of Regulation CC on the forward-collection process is its elimination of provisional credits by collecting banks.[28] A primary function of the Regulation is to speed the return of checks to depositary banks. It seeks to accomplish this objective in part by dispensing with the need to return checks by sending them back through each bank involved in the collection process. The Regulation, therefore, makes settlements between collecting banks final when they are made during forward collection. With additional changes in the return process described below in the discussion on returns,[29] Regulation CC is able to shorten the collection chain on returns.

[2] Direct Presentment by Collecting Banks

A depositary bank has the option of short-circuiting the collection chain by making direct presentment. Article 4 specifically recognizes the right of collecting banks to send an item directly to the payor bank.[30] Despite the authorization for direct presentment, the method is rarely utilized between distant banks. The disadvantages for the collecting bank are substantial, including special handling of the item and increased expense. Widespread use of direct routing would deprive collecting banks of the efficiencies that the Federal Reserve System are designed to provide. Consequently, direct presentment on a distant bank generally is provided only as a special service to a customer who specifically requests it. For example, a customer who is suspicious about the collectability of a check might want

---

[26] U.C.C. § 4-201(a).
[27] U.C.C. § 4-215(c).
[28] 12 C.F.R. § 229.36(d).
[29] *See* § 11.04 *infra*.
[30] U.C.C. § 4-204(b)(1).

the fastest response possible on the payor bank's willingness to honor the check.

[3] Collection Through Clearinghouses

Even in a small community with only a few banks, greater efficiency in the collection process is likely if a clearinghouse is established rather than relying on direct presentment.[31] Instead of chasing all over town to present checks drawn on each of the local banks directly to those banks, it is more convenient to send all of these checks to one central clearinghouse. The clearinghouse can be a separate facility or simply a designated room of one of the bank participants. Member banks that join in this association present all of the checks drawn on other member banks to the clearinghouse rather than directly to each payor bank. The checks are exchanged, with each payor bank taking physical possession of the checks drawn upon it. Presentment through the clearinghouse constitutes presentment on the payor bank. Settlements for the checks also are made through the clearinghouse. The account of each bank is credited for the checks it presents for payment and debited for the checks drawn against it, and the clearinghouse provides a daily net settlement among the associated banks. A clearinghouse enables its members to replace a series of bilateral collections with a more efficient multilateral collection process.

[4] Collection Through Transmission of Information: Truncation

Rather than presentment of the check itself, the depositary bank can send information on the check electronically to the payor bank with a demand to pay it.[32] This process is known as depositary bank truncation.[33] Presentment occurs when the payor bank receives the transmitted information. Elimination of the forward routing of the paper itself can allow substantial savings of time and money for check collection.

Check truncation by collecting banks raises interesting questions under the finality doctrine.[34] The payor bank never receives the check in this form of truncation. This approach to check collection substantially undercuts the rationales that support placing finality on payor banks in certain classes of cases. The ultimate liability of payor banks is premised in large measure on their opportunity to compare the drawer's signature on the check with the signature cards in their possession. The designation of payor banks as the best risk avoider dissolves when these banks do not receive the checks themselves. It could continue if technological developments allow depositary banks a cost-effective means to transmit electronic facsimiles of

---

[31] "'Clearing house' means an association of banks or other payors regularly clearing items." U.C.C. § 4-104(a)(4).

[32] Electronic presentment is authorized under both Article 3 and Regulation CC. U.C.C. § 3-501(b)(1); 12 C.F.R. § 229.36(c).

[33] Compare this form of truncation with payor bank truncation discussed in Chapter 10. See § 10.02[B][1] supra.

[34] See § 9.01[C], [D] supra.

drawers' signatures. In the interim, payor banks are well-advised to negotiate specific risk-allocation provisions when entering into these forms of truncation agreements.

[5] Presentment by the Customer

Rather than utilizing the services of collecting banks, a customer can present a check for payment directly to the bank on which the check is drawn. This method of collection generally occurs when the check is drawn on the same bank at which the customer maintains an account. Because collecting banks are not used, the only bank involved is both the depositary bank and the payor bank. These checks thus are referred to as "on us" items. The customer may demand either cash payment or an account deposit. The bank maintains the accounts of both the drawer and the customer, so it clears the check internally through entries in the respective accounts.

[C] Duties of Collecting Banks in Forwarding Checks — §§ 4-202, 4-204

Collecting banks are granted expansive discretion in selecting the method to forward items for collection. Because of the many methods available and the desire to preserve flexibility, the Code simply establishes a general standard to send items "by reasonably prompt method."[35] The emphasis is on avoidance of routing methods that would result in unreasonable delay in forwarding an item for collection.[36] Forwarding by a "reasonably prompt method" is not equivalent to sending by the fastest or most direct route.[37]

The Code imposes additional responsibilities on collecting banks in the check-collection process. They are subject to the pervasive standard of good faith.[38] In addition, collecting banks must exercise ordinary care in presenting checks or in forwarding them for presentment.[39] Collecting banks thus must exercise care in selecting sub-agent banks for purposes of forwarding checks.[40] Collecting banks are responsible for errors made in encoding checks.[41] A collecting bank must also exercise ordinary care to notify its

---

[35] U.C.C. § 4-204(a).

[36] Werting v. Manufacturers Hanover Trust Co., 461 N.Y.S.2d 157, 36 U.C.C. Rep. Serv. 242 (N.Y. Civ. Ct. 1983).

[37] Gulf Coast State Bank v. Emenhiser, 562 S.W.2d 449, 23 U.C.C. Rep. Serv. 1259 (Tex. 1978) (improper jury charge to suggest that collecting bank required to forward sight draft directly to payor bank).

[38] U.C.C. § 1-203.

[39] U.C.C. § 4-202(a)(1).

[40] Nesso Surgical Prods., Inc. v. Long Island Trust Co., 51 A.D.2d 733, 379 N.Y.S.2d 128 (1976) (summary judgment denied because of question whether defendant bank had followed general banking practices in choosing and giving instructions to a collecting bank).

[41] United States v. Hibernia Nat'l Bank, 841 F.2d 592, 5 U.C.C. Rep. Serv. 2d 1392 (5th Cir. 1988), is illustrative. The customer deposited a check for collection that was typed ". . . 24844 DOLLARS/50CENTS," which conformed with the amount on the deposit slip. The figure on the right-hand side of the check appeared as "$244844.50." During encoding the proofing machine signaled an error of $220,000. The proof operator looked only at the deposit slip and

transferor of loss or delay in transit a reasonable time after its discovery.[42]

The exercise of ordinary care includes timely handling of items in the check-collection process. Article 4 includes a standard on seasonal action. A collecting bank acts seasonably if it forwards a check for collection before its midnight deadline following receipt of the check.[43] A reasonably longer time will also be allowed, but the bank has the burden to establish that it acted seasonably.[44] In this context, the bank's "midnight deadline" is "midnight on its next banking day following the banking day on which it receives the relevant item."[45] For example, if a depositary bank receives a check for collection from its customer on Wednesday morning, it should forward the check before midnight on Thursday. Similarly, if an collecting bank receives a check from the depositary bank on Friday, its deadline would be midnight of the following Monday.

§ 11.03 Payor Banks

[A] Deferred Posting — § 4-301

[1] Statutory Authorization

When a check is presented for payment to a payor bank, the bank must determine whether to pay it. Because the bank can debit the account of the drawer only when the check is properly payable,[46] it must exercise caution in making this decision. The large volume of checks presented daily means that payor banks must develop methods to streamline their decision-making on which checks to pay and which to dishonor. Fortunately for payor banks, they do not have to make a decision immediately upon presentment.

Acute shortages of banking personnel during the Second World War led to the practice of deferred posting. Upon receipt of checks drawn upon it, a payor bank would provide initial credits to the presenting banks. It would then defer the processing of the checks presented until the following day. This approach allowed it all of the next day to process the checks received rather than having to rush to complete the processing before midnight on the day of receipt. It allowed the banks an extra day by moving the deadline

---

the right-hand side of the check, decided the customer made an error, and prepared a correction slip for a $220,000 credit. The customer withdrew the funds credited, and, after the overpayment was discovered, was placed in involuntary bankruptcy. The depositary bank's improper coding was determined to be a failure to exercise ordinary care, and the bank was held liable to the drawer.

[42] U.C.C. § 4-202(a)(4).

[43] U.C.C. § 4-202(b).

[44] U.C.C. § 4-202(2); Pan Am. World Airways v. Bankers Trust Co., 99 A.D.2d 712, 472 N.Y.S.2d 315, 37 U.C.C. Rep. Serv. 1636 (1984) (summary judgment proper for recovery of face amounts of checks that would have been collected if defendant depositary bank acted seasonably because defendant gave no acceptable explanation for the inordinate delay).

[45] U.C.C. § 4-104(a)(10).

[46] U.C.C. § 4-401(a). See § 12.02[B] *infra*.

for the return of unpaid checks to midnight of the next banking day after receipt. Increased volume in the check-collection process justified the allowance of the additional day even after the war, and the practice was legitimized through state statues, clearinghouse rules, and Federal Reserve regulation.

Deferred posting greatly facilitates efficiency of operation for payor banks. Modern business practices include the adoption of high-speed automated procedures. The mechanical steps of posting are now accomplished in all but the smallest rural banks through automation. High-speed machines can both read and sort the checks fed into it. A batch of checks can be fed into it from a source like a courier from the Federal Reserve Bank, and the reader-sorter can proof the total indicated on the cash letter[47] with the reading of the checks themselves. The reader-sorters can also photograph both sides of a check, affix a paid stamp on the check, and transmit information directly to the bank computers to debit the appropriate accounts automatically.[48]

In modern banking practices, the judgment in determining to pay a check is most often exercised through established procedures focusing on steps taken to prevent payment on checks that the bank does not want to pay. A bank's computer might be programmed to reject checks that the bank always wishes to dishonor, such as checks drawn on non-existent accounts or on accounts that have been closed. Computer printouts reflecting the activity in accounts maintained by the payor bank might also be scrutinized by bank officials to identify checks that the bank may wish to dishonor. Checks drawn on insufficient funds are nevertheless properly payable,[49] so the bank might make specific decisions on whether to create overdrafts by paying particular checks. A bank might target particular accounts or types of accounts for special scrutiny. It might choose to implement a practice of examining checks drawn over a particular amount to detect problems concerning proper payability that would not be detected by the high-speed reader-sorters.[50] A bank also might include random selection and screening of all accounts maintained with the bank.[51] Procedures oriented toward detecting checks that the bank wishes to dishonor means, of course, that some checks will be paid without direct scrutiny or an affirmative decision to proceed with payment.

---

[47] The cash letter is prepared by the bank forwarding a batch of checks. It accompanies the checks and indicates the total amount of the checks.

[48] Automation in banking operations has reached the stage where some banks have computers and machines that prepare the monthly account statements and place the statement and canceled checks into envelopes for mailing to the drawer.

[49] U.C.C. § 4-401(a). See § 12.02[B][1] infra.

[50] The machines do not read the signatures, so a bank might implement procedures to examine them on certain checks.

[51] The automated mechanical steps of posting show a clear circumstance in which the reversal of an entry or action can be necessary. A check might initially be debited against a drawer's account and the check might even be stamped "paid." If, in the subsequent course of review of the check, a bank official decides that the check should not be paid, the debit entry can be reversed and the "paid" stamp can be cancelled. Van Senus Auto Parts, Inc. v. Michigan Nat'l Bank, 116 Mich. App. 342, 323 N.W.2d 391, 35 U.C.C. Rep. Serv. 570 (1982).

Article 4 also authorizes the practice of deferred posting in all cases except when presentment is made for immediate payment over the counter.[52] Payor banks must comply with two specific time prescriptions. An initial settlement in favor of the presenter must be made no later than midnight of the banking day on which the check is received by the payor bank. If during processing the check, the bank decides it should dishonor the check, section 4-301(a) authorizes it to revoke the settlement given if the bank returns the check before it makes final payment[53] and before its midnight deadline.[54] Thus under the Code scheme of deferred posting, a provisional settlement is given for a check before midnight on the date that it is received, and the bank then decides before midnight of the next banking day whether to make final payment or to return the check and revoke the provisional credit.

Regulation CC does not preclude deferred posting, but it does alter its operation somewhat. The provisional settlement approach of Article 4 is preempted because the Regulation provides that "settlements between banks for forward collection of a check are final when made."[55] Finality is required in forward collection because of the sweeping changes made for the return of unpaid checks to the customer of the depositary bank. By making the settlement between banks final in forward collection, Regulation CC dispenses with the need to route returned checks back through each collecting bank that handled them.

Final settlement by a payor bank under Regulation CC does not constitute final payment, however. Equating final settlement for the check presented with its final payment would destroy the availability of deferred posting. Final payment by a payor bank terminates its right to return the item and recover its settlement, even if it occurs prior to the expiration of the midnight deadline.[56] The bank has the right under deferred posting to return a check for which a timely settlement has been made only until final payment or its midnight deadline, whichever occurs first.[57] The Commentary to Regulation CC therefore stresses that in order to preserve the payor bank's right to recover its settlement upon return of a check, "[s]ettlement by a paying bank is not considered to be final payment."[58]

[2] Noncompliance With Time Limits

Section 4-302 establishes the liability of a payor bank that does not comply with the time limits prescribed for taking action upon the receipt

---

[52] U.C.C. § 4-301.

[53] See § 11.03[C] infra.

[54] U.C.C. § 4-104(a)(10).

[55] 12 C.F.R. § 229.36(d).

[56] Section 4-301(a) stipulates that the payor bank's rights are contingent upon it taking the requisite action "before it has made final payment." See also U.C.C. § 4-301, Comments 2, 3 (section 4-301 has no operation if the item is finally paid).

[57] Actually, as the discussion in the next section shows, expiration of the midnight deadline itself will constitute final payment if an earlier method has not already occurred.

[58] 12 C.F.R. § 229.36, Commentary (d).

of checks payable by the bank. The general rule is that if the bank either retains the check beyond midnight of the banking day of its receipt without settling for it or does not pay or return the check before its midnight deadline, the bank is "accountable" for the amount of the check.[59] In other words, the bank is strictly liable if it fails to comply with either of the successive midnight time requirements.[60] Uncollectability of the presented check does not diminish the payor bank's responsibility. The payor bank that delays is accountable for the amount of the check "whether properly payable or not."[61]

The payor bank's accountability for a check simply establishes its liability. Its actions with regard to a check presented for payment cannot be construed as liability "on the instrument" because that form of liability is limited to contractual liability incurred by signing an instrument. When a payor bank becomes accountable for a check, as it does under section 4-302 by delays, it becomes liable for the face amount of the check. Through its accountability for the check (and ultimately its final payment of the check)[62] the drawer's liability is essentially replaced by the payor bank's liability.

[B] Over-the-Counter Presentment for Cash

When a customer presents a check for cash over the counter, a payor bank has considerably less time to decide whether to pay it than when it simply credits an account for the customer. The bank is granted a reasonable time to examine a check to determine if it is properly payable, but the payment must be made before the close of business on the day of presentment.[63] If the bank does not pay during this time period, it will have dishonored the check. When customers request checks to be deposited in their accounts, payor banks can reverse a credit given if, subsequently during the posting process, they discover a reason why a check should not be paid.

Banks are likely to exercise more caution in responding to presentments for cash. As the discussion in the section below explains, payment in cash is final payment and the opportunity for the bank to recover it is severely curtailed. Before passing cash over the counter, the bank teller will examine the check in accordance with instructions from bank officials. Payment will be denied if irregularities are noted on the check. The balance of the account upon which the check is drawn will be determined by contacting the

---

[59] U.C.C. § 4-302(a)(1); Lombardo v. Mellon Bank, N.A., 454 Pa. Super. 403, 685 A.2d 595, 33 U.C.C. Rep. Serv. 2d 154 (1996) (payor bank did not return check until ten days after its midnight deadline).

[60] The strict accountability consequence of untimely action by a payor bank "is subject to defenses based on breach of a presentment warranty (Section 4-208) or proof that the person seeking enforcement of the liability presented or transferred the item for the purpose of defrauding the payor bank." U.C.C. § 4-302(b).

[61] U.C.C. § 4-302(a)(1); State & Sav. Bank v. Meeker, 469 N.E.2d 55, 39 U.C.C. Rep. Serv. 1391 (Ind. Ct. App. 1984).

[62] *See* U.C.C. § 4-215(a)(3); § 11.03[C] *infra*.

[63] U.C.C. § 3-502(b)(2).

bookkeeping department, usually by telephone or computer, to determine that it contains sufficient funds to cover the check and that a stop payment has not been issued on the check or a freeze upon the account. Other personnel within the bank might be consulted by the teller for final authority to pay. In exceptional cases, the drawer might even be contacted to seek confirmation on the order to pay. If the check is paid, an immediate hold on the account for the amount of the check might also be noted in the drawer's account.

[C] Final Payment — § 4-215(a)

[1] Introduction

Final payment is a pivotal concept in the check-collection process. It has a pervasive effect upon rights and liabilities of several parties. Payment to a person entitled to enforce the instrument discharges the party obliged to pay the instrument.[64] The payor bank loses the right to dishonor the check and recover its prior settlement by returning the check, even if the check is not properly payable.[65] The payor bank that makes final payment by mistake and does not have a basis to recover on a presentment warranty, restitution claim, or subrogation claim will have to absorb the loss.[66] Final payment also plays a decisive role in determining priorities of competing claims to the account balance of the drawer[67] and in fixing preferential rights.[68]

Regulation CC somewhat alters the extent of the legal consequences of final payment. Under the Code scheme, provisional credits provided in the check-collection process became final automatically upon final payment, and the agency status of collecting banks converted to a debtor-creditor relationship. Because Regulation CC requires the initial settlements between collecting banks to be final even in the forward-collection process, the creditor relationship commences on the credit entry and final payment no longer plays its role of "firming up" the provisional line of credits. The agency status is continued, however, and even extended, through the check-return process.

Section 4-215(a) describes when a payor bank makes final payment. It occurs at the first of three different events: (1) payment of an item in cash; (2) settlement for the item without a right to revoke the settlement; and (3) failure to make timely revocation of a provisional settlement. Although some of these events utilize the concept of provisional settlements, the Board of Governors of the Federal Reserve System does not intend for Regulation CC to displace the concept of final payment. The adaptation of the codification of section 4-215(a) to the requirements of Regulation CC is explained below.

---

[64] U.C.C. §§ 3-602(a).
[65] U.C.C. § 4-302(a)(1).
[66] U.C.C. §§ 4-208(a), 3-418, 4-407.
[67] U.C.C. § 4-303.
[68] U.C.C. § 4-216.

[2] The Definition

When a payor bank pays a check in cash, its payment is final.[69] If the bank should later discover some reason why it should not have paid the check, it cannot simply insist that the recipient give the money back. The bank also cannot debit the amount paid against an account that the recipient of the payment maintains with the payor bank.[70] The bank's right to dishonor and return the check terminated when it paid cash. Courts have recognized that final payment also occurs when a bank gives a cash equivalent, such as a cashier's check in the same amount as the check presented for payment.[71]

A payor bank also makes final payment if it has "settled for the item without having a right to revoke the settlement under statute, clearinghouse rule, or agreement."[72] The idea behind the provision is that if the payor bank does not retain any basis to revoke its settlement, it cannot return the check and recover the settlement. Its position with respect to prior parties is the same as if it had paid cash for the check.

Banking practices, however, traditionally have utilized statutes, rules, and agreements to preclude almost any applicability of this provision. If a payor bank provides a credit at least by midnight of the day of receipt of a check, Article 4 recognizes the right to revoke the settlement by returning the check before the midnight deadline. Most clearinghouse rules have also provided that settlements between their members are provisional, with a right to return the check and revoke the credit in accordance with prescribed time limits. Deposit contracts entered into between a bank and its customer have also generally established by private agreement that items deposited into the account are settled provisionally and subject to revocation.[73]

A literal application of Regulation CC in this context would alter the legal concept of final payment considerably. The Regulation makes settlements final when they are made during forward collection of checks, and a payor bank does not have any right to revoke those settlements. On the other hand, a payor bank is granted a right to recover settlements from a returning[74] or depositary bank.[75] In preservation of this right, the Commentary

---

[69] U.C.C. § 4-215(a)(1).

[70] Kirby v. First & Merchants Nat'l Bank, 210 Va. 88, 168 S.E.2d 273, 6 U.C.C. Rep. Serv. 694 (1969).

[71] Howard Bank v. Iron Kettle Restaurant of Bolton, Inc., 428 A.2d 1138, 33 U.C.C. Rep. Serv. 1734 (Vt. 1981) (final payment when payor bank gave cashier's check in same amount as a presented counter check); Banco Ganadero y Agricola, S.A. v. Society Nat'l Bank, 418 F. Supp. 520, 21 U.C.C. Rep. Serv. 233 (N.D. Ohio 1976) (final payment upon receipt of cashier's check by payee).

[72] U.C.C. § 4-215(a)(2).

[73] First Georgia Bank v. Webster, 168 Ga. App. 307, 308 S.E.2d 579, 37 U.C.C. Rep. Serv. 1643 (1983).

[74] "Returning bank" means "a bank (other than the paying or depositary bank handling a returned check or notice in lieu of return." 12 C.F.R. § 229.2(cc).

[75] 12 C.F.R. §§ 229.31(c), 229.32(b).

to Regulation CC states that the payor bank's settlement is not considered to be final payment for purposes of U.C.C. section 4-215(a)(2).[76] The critical factor now is not the right of the payor bank to revoke settlement, but rather the bank's right to recover it. Through the force of federal law, Regulation CC provides that right. Consequently, invocation of final payment through section 4-213(a)(2) will continue to be rare.

The third, and most common method by which a payor bank makes final payment is when it has "made a provisional settlement for the item and failed to revoke the settlement in the time and manner permitted by statute, clearing-house rule, or agreement."[77] Article 4 has recognized the practice of deferred posting by which a provisional credit for a check is provided by midnight of the day of receipt.[78] The bank then may revoke its settlement if it returns the check before expiration of its midnight deadline.[79] The bank that does not return the check before the deadline makes final payment of the check.[80] Clearinghouse rules allowing the return of checks by a stated hour the next business day to revoke the provisional initial settlement have also been common. Final payment results by default when payor banks fail to comply with applicable time restrictions for the return of checks.

The application of this provision again has to be adjusted to conform to the requirements of Regulation CC. On its face, the Code provision could no longer apply because payor bank settlements are now final rather than provisional. Just as it does with section 4-215(a)(2), however, the Commentary of the Regulation stresses that the payor bank's settlement is not considered to be final payment for purposes of section 4-215(a)(3).[81] The deferred-posting approach of section 4-301 is preserved, although the midnight deadline can be extended in some circumstances to facilitate expeditious returns.[82]

[D] Competing Claims to a Drawer's Account Balance — § 4-303

[1] The Priorities Approach

Although checking accounts are opened for the purpose of paying checks issued by the drawer, competing interests may intervene during the payment process in order to suspend or terminate the payor bank's right

---

[76] 12 C.F.R. § 229.36, Commentary (d).

[77] U.C.C. § 4-215(a)(3).

[78] *See* § 11.03[A] *supra*.

[79] U.C.C. § 4-301(a)(1).

[80] Kimberly A. Allen Trust v. Firstbank of Lakewood, N.A., 989 P.2d 203, 40 U.C.C. Rep. Serv. 2d 1048 (Colo. Ct. App. 1999) (when payor bank's midnight deadline was on March 18th, but bank did not return the check until March 25th, the depositary bank could not charge-back the check against the customer's account). A collecting bank cannot charge-back the credit given when a settlement for the item becomes final. U.C.C. § 4-214(a).

[81] 12 C.F.R. § 229.36, Commentary (d).

[82] 12 C.F.R. § 229.30(c).

or duty to pay. The intervening events, known collectively as "the four legals," include the following: (1) the payor bank's knowledge or notice of bankruptcy,[83] death, or incompetence of its customer;[84] (2) receipt of a stop payment order from the customer;[85] (3) legal process served upon the payor bank;[86] and (4) setoff exercised by the payor bank.[87] The effect of some of these legals is to preclude the payor bank from proceeding to pay at least some checks that are otherwise properly payable from the customer's account. In other instances the intervening legal operates to remove funds from the customer's account and thereby perhaps leave an insufficient amount to meet all of the checks issued by the drawer.

The inevitable issue posed by the four legals is the determination of when their intervention is sufficient to preclude payment on a check or other item that is properly payable. Section 4-303 addresses this issue by codifying a priority provision, consistent with the general priority principle of the Code, of first in time, first in right.[88] If the processing of a check has progressed sufficiently, an intervening notice, stop payment, legal process, or setoff arrives too late to interfere with payment; priority lies with payment of the check. Timely arrival of an intervening legal, on the other hand, gives it priority over payment of the check and affects the payor bank's rights and duties to pay it. Because the competition between payment of a check and an intervening legal is resolved essentially by the race to achieve priority, the determination of the timeliness of the competing actions is critical.

Under the terms of section 4-303, the time factor for the legals varies by their nature. Stop payment orders must be received; legal process has to be served. The payor bank must have either knowledge or notice of death or incompetence of its customer. In all of these instances the bank must have a reasonable time to act upon the legal.[89] A setoff is determined from

---

[83] The basis of intervention stems from section 542(b) of the Bankruptcy Reform Act of 1978, Pub. L. No. 95-598, 92 Stat. 2594, 11 U.S.C. § 542(b) (control of the customer's account is in the trustee upon bankruptcy petition).

[84] The effect of death or incompetence of a bank's customer is governed by U.C.C. § 4-405. *See* § 12.06 *infra*.

[85] Stop payment orders are governed by U.C.C. §§ 4-403, 4-405. *See* §§ 12.04, 12.06 *infra*.

[86] Legal process includes actions like garnishment that enable a creditor other than the payor bank to reach the funds a customer maintains in the account. It is a statutory remedy and varies somewhat from state to state. Legal process includes a court enjoining payment, such as an injunction envisioned in section 3-602, as a means to preclude discharge on an instrument even though payment is made to a holder. *See also* Citizens & Peoples Nat'l Bank v. United States, 570 F.2d 1279, 23 U.C.C. 984 (5th Cir. 1978) (service of notice of tax levy by the IRS).

[87] Setoff is the means by which a payor bank reaches funds in its customer's account for the purpose of satisfying a debt the customer owes to the bank on another transaction, such as a mortgage obligation or an overdue personal property loan.

[88] *See* U.C.C. §§ 9-317(a), 9-322(a), 9-334(d).

[89] Nautilus Leasing Serv., Inc. v. Crocker Nat'l Bank, 147 Cal. App. 3d 1023, 195 Cal. Rptr. 478, 37 U.C.C. 217 (1983).

the time at which it is exercised, as for example, by making a bookkeeping entry.[90]

[2] When Payment Attains Priority

Any of the legals that arrive after the payor bank has made final payment on a check arrive too late to interfere with payment of that check. Section 4-303 reiterates the same events constituting final payment that are listed in section 4-215(a).[91] Therefore, payment of a check achieves priority over any subsequent competing legal once the payor bank has paid the check in cash,[92] settled for it without a right to recovery,[93] or failed to return the check in time.[94] The occurrence of any of these events with respect to a check before the effective time for a competing legal allows the check to prevail.

Section 4-303 also recognizes a few events that occur prior to final payment by the payor bank that nevertheless operate to establish the time at which payment of the check will have priority over any subsequent legal. A competing legal arrives too late, for example, if the check has already been accepted or certified.[95] Priority based on certification is logical because the payor bank will generally place a hold on the funds in the drawer's account sufficient to cover the check.

Another event that precedes final payment, but nevertheless enables payment of the check to defeat a subsequent legal, is payor bank accountability for the check under section 4-302.[96] A bank must provide a settlement for the check by midnight of the day of receipt of the item, and failure to do so makes the bank accountable for the amount of the check. Although the deferred posting arrangement traditionally envisioned an initial provisional payment, Regulation CC now requires this settlement to be final.[97]

---

[90] Aspen Indus., Inc. v. Marine Midland Bank, 74 A.D.2d 59, 426 N.Y.S.2d 620, 28 U.C.C. 1456 (1980) (overt, binding act required of bank for setoff in order to counter unsupported internal declarations that are self-serving); Baker v. National City Bank, 511 F.2d 1016, 16 U.C.C. 298 (6th Cir. 1975) (accord; applying Ohio law). *But see*, Pittsburgh Nat'l Bank v. United States, 657 F.2d 36, 31 U.C.C. 1217 (3d Cir. 1981) (applying Pennsylvania law of automatic setoff under which setoff is viewed as exercised at the moment of the customer's default).

[91] U.C.C. § 4-303(a). These events of final payment are explained, together with the few necessary adjustments to accommodate Regulation CC, in § 11.03[C], *supra*.

[92] First Nat'l Bank v. Continental Bank, 138 Ariz. 194, 673 P.2d 9938, 37 U.C.C. Rep. Serv. 523 (1983).

[93] Citizens & S. Nat'l Bank v. Youngblood, 135 Ga. App. 638, 219 S.E.2d 172, 18 U.C.C. Rep. Serv. 180 (1975).

[94] *Compare* Raymer v. Bay State Nat'l Bank, 384 Mass. 310, 424 N.E.2d 515, 31 U.C.C. Rep. Serv. 537 (1981) (bank's exercise of setoff came too late when not exercised until after the bank's midnight deadline), *with* Nautilus Leasing Serv., Inc. v. Crocker Nat'l Bank, 147 Cal. App. 3d 1023, 195 Cal. Rptr. 478, 37 U.C.C. Rep. Serv. 217 (1983) (setoff executed before bank midnight deadline held effective and timely).

[95] U.C.C. § 4-303(a)(1); Kaufman v. Chase Manhattan Bank, N.A. 370 F. Supp. 276, 13 U.C.C. Rep. Serv. 477 (S.D. N.Y. 1973) (stop payment too late when received after bank accepted the item).

[96] U.C.C. § 4-303(a)(4); Raymer v. Bay State Nat'l Bank, 384 Mass. 310, 424 N.E.2d 515, 31 U.C.C. Rep. Serv. 1537 (1981).

[97] *See* § 11.03[A][1] *supra*.

Regulation CC does not change the accountability of a payor bank failing to make the timely settlement, however, so the priority result remains the same.

The last basis by which an event can precede final payment but still enable payment of the check to defeat a subsequent legal applies only with respect to checks. The bank can fix an hour on the day after the check is received.[98] The hour selected can not be earlier than one hour after the opening of the applicable banking day and no later than the close of that banking day.

§ 11.04 The Return Process

[A] The Reasons for Regulation CC

The payor bank's handling of a check presented for payment is the turnaround point in the check-collection process. For every check presented, the payor bank must either return it in time or become accountable for final payment. These contradictory responses pose further distinct issues. If the payor bank returns the check, how does it arrive back in possession of the depositary bank so that it can be returned to the customer? Alternatively, if the payor bank pays a check, when does the customer who deposited the check for collection have the right to draw on those funds from the depositary bank? Regulation CC provides substantially different answers than Article 4 to both of these questions because of perceived inadequacies in the Code approaches. The discussion of the return process, therefore, commences with a brief outline of the Article 4 approach that is designed to reveal the deficiencies that led to federal preemption. Current law under Regulation CC is developed subsequently.

[1] Inefficient Check-Return Procedures

Article 4 allows a payor bank to return a check if the bank has not become accountable for it. The bank can comply by returning the check before midnight of the day of receipt.[99] More commonly, however, banks would provide a provisional settlement before midnight of that day, and then make a return before their midnight deadline.[100] The payor bank would return the dishonored check back to the presenter. Return of a check entitled the payor bank to revoke a provisional credit for the check that had been given to the presenter.[101]

The collecting bank could revoke a provisional settlement that it gave to a forwarding bank or customer by returning the check to its transferor by its midnight deadline.[102] In this manner, dishonored checks were

---

[98] U.C.C. § 4-303(a)(5).
[99] U.C.C. § 4-302(a).
[100] U.C.C. § 4-301(a).
[101] U.C.C. § 4-301(b).
[102] U.C.C. § 4-212(a).

returned back upstream by precisely the same route through which they had been forwarded. This course of action enabled each collecting bank to revoke the provisional settlement that it granted for the check in forward collection. Eventually, the dishonored check would reach the depositary bank. That bank also would revoke the provisional credit that it had given to its customer and would return the check to the customer. If the bank had already allowed the customer to draw against the credit, the depositary bank was entitled to a refund from the customer.[103]

While the forward-collection process enabled the two to five banks that are generally involved to process checks very quickly, the return process was considerably slower. Forward collection uses high-speed sorters to sort and route checks automatically,[104] special couriers for pickups and delivery, and jet aircraft for volume transfers. The opportunity to use provisional credits granted for checks in forward collection to meet reserve requirements of the forwarding bank to the Federal Reserve System and to invest the excess in the federal funds market created an economic incentive for prompt forward collection.

Following dishonor, however, the return routing of a check was extremely tortuous. It had to retrace its steps back through each bank that had forwarded the check so that the provisional credits granted by each bank could be reversed. Each return had to be performed manually, however, as the MICR numbers only routed checks forward to the payor bank. To make matters worse, banking practices made it difficult to determine the bank that had forwarded the check. Each bank handling a check would place its indorsement anywhere on the back of the check. With several banks involved in forward collection, the indorsement stamps of the several banks often overlapped one another, making them extremely difficult to read. As a result, specially trained personnel had to be employed to decipher the indorsement as the only means of identifying the bank to which the check should be returned. The economic incentives that spurred speedy forward collection were also undone with returns. The return of a check resulted in reversal of the provisional credit, thereby eliminating the satisfaction of reserve requirements and the interest earnings that had been attained temporarily. Banks lacked any incentive to speed this reversal. Their sole incentive was the legal requirement to get the returned check out of their control before they became accountable for it. Generally, they simply mailed the check to the next bank at some point prior to their midnight deadline. Thus the mechanics and incentives that promoted fast, efficient forward collection did not apply to check returns under Article 4.

[2] Check-Hold Practices

Inefficiencies in the check-return process and the legal incentives that helped to perpetuate them combined to extend the necessary time before a depositary bank could have confidence that a check had been honored. When a payor bank paid a check, it did not notify any of the banks that

---

[103] U.C.C. § 4-212(a).
[104] Machines can process up to 120,000 checks each hour.

handled it for collection. It simply debited the account of the drawer and generally returned the cancelled check to the drawer, together with a statement of account activity and other cancelled checks drawn on the account, at the end of each month. The only time the depositary bank actually received information about the disposition of a check that it forwarded was when the check was returned because it was unpaid. This actual practice of the check-collection process gave rise to the saying that for depositary banks "no news is good news."

The right of a customer to withdraw funds represented by a check that was deposited for collection was not tied to final payment by the payor bank. Other banks in the collection process cannot be aware of the payor bank's payment of a given check at the moment it occurs. Article 4 thus provided that the customer did not have a right of withdrawal until a provisional settlement became final *and* the customer's bank had an opportunity to learn that the settlement was final.[105] This approach meant that the legal standard governing a customer's right of access to the funds represented by a check deposited for collection was measured by the time that would be required for the check to retrace its way back to the depositary bank as if it had been dishonored rather than paid. Only with the passage of the time that would be required to receive the "bad news" of return could the bank infer the "good news" that payment must have occurred instead. Of course, this legal standard meant that the right of customers to be paid would be delayed on all checks until the time associated with the slow return process could elapse. The fact that this standard applied to all checks deposited for collection, even though only two-thirds of one percent of all checks presented for payment are actually returned,[106] serves to further highlight the inefficiencies of the check-collection process under Article 4.

In order to provide greater assurance that funds would be in a customer's account for a chargeback in the event that a check was dishonored and returned, many depository banks initiated check holds.[107] This policy of delayed funds availability meant that the money represented by the check was not available to the depositor until passage of the time indicated by the bank's availability schedule. Checks drawn on local banks were generally held between a day to a week, whereas out-of-state check holds usually extended between seven and ten days. Holds extending between two weeks to thirty-eight days for local checks and between twenty-three to forty-five days on out-of-state checks applied by some banks greatly fueled consumer ire.

---

[105] U.C.C. § 4-213(1), (4)(a) (1989) (amended at U.C.C. § 4-215(a), (e)(1) (1990). Final payment automatically converted all provisional settlements in the collection chain to final settlements. U.C.C. § 4-213(c), (d). These provisions are preempted by federal law. *See* § 11.02[B][1] *infra.*

[106] Wechsler, *Delayed Funds Availability*, 35 Syracuse L. Rev. 1117, 1341 (1984) (citing Bank Admin. Inst., The Impact of Exception Items on the Check Collection System 23 (1974)).

[107] See *id.* for a much-more detailed account of check holds. The article cites numerous hearings and surveys and the statistics used in this subsection on check holds are taken from them.

Consumer advocates pointed to several aspects of extended check-hold practices in support of their argument that new regulation was required. Because banks often did not adequately inform their customers concerning their check-hold policies, customers often were unaware of the practice until their own checks bounced after being drawn against deposited amounts still under hold, resulting in loss of reputation, impaired credit, and overdraft charges. The extensive hold periods imposed by some banks also appeared to exceed any period that would be necessary to ensure the bank that the funds of a deposited check would not have been withdrawn before the bank learned that the check had been dishonored. These banks were also charged with basic greed because the practice enabled a bank to receive earnings from the investment of provisional credits received by the depository bank in collecting payment on a deposited check while the proceeds of the check were not yet available to the customer.

While the check-holds imposed by many depository banks were clearly excessive, the banks had a legitimate argument based on their exposure to delays inherent in the procedures for returning checks.[108] The primary concern of depository banks is outright fraud by their customers because the defrauding depositor usually disappears after the scam, leaving the loss on the bank. In check kiting a depositor opens two or more accounts with a small amount of money in each account. Subsequent deposits are made in each account by checks drawn on the other accounts. Before any check can bounce, it is covered with a check for a larger amount drawn on one of the other accounts. Eventually, the thief withdraws a large amount in one of the accounts and disappears. MICR fraud results from a false encoding of the routing characters on a check, so that rather than being routed directly to the payor bank it is sent in another direction to an incorrect bank. The objective is to delay the forward-collection process so that the depositary bank will assume that the payor bank paid the fraudulent check once the usual time for a return has elapsed.[109]

[B] Funds Availability

The Board of Governors of the Federal Reserve Board implemented the specific requirements that Congress mandated on funds availability in Subpart B of Regulation CC. They include specific rules concerning the availability of funds from deposits, disclosure requirements to inform customers of funds availability, requirements for payment of interest on deposits, and remedies for violations of the regulation.

In certain specified situations in which the risk exposure of the depository bank is considered to be minimal, the bank must provide next-day availability. It is required for cash deposits, electronic payments, postal money

---

[108] Although the number of returned checks was low as a percentage comparison with all checks, the volume was still substantial–between 267 million and 360 million a year.

[109] United States Fidelity & Guar. Co. v. Federal Reserve Bank, 590 F. Supp. 486, 39 U.C.C. 944 (S.D. N.Y. 1984), *aff'd*, 786 F.2d 77, 42 U.C.C. 1715 (1986) (check with fraudulent MICR symbols routed over two weeks through five banks, while depositary bank after ten days allowed fraudulent depositor to draw $755,000 against the check).

orders, and low-risk categories of checks, including various government checks; cashier's, certified, or teller's checks; and some "on us" checks. Under next-day availability, the funds must be "available for withdrawal not later than the business day after the banking day" of the deposit. Business days are calendar days excluding weekends and bank holidays,[110] whereas banking days are days when the bank is open to the public for carrying on substantially all of its banking functions.[111] Thus deposits made at automatic teller machines or even at a drive-in window when the bank is closed to the public for other functions, like loans or opening accounts, is considered to have been received by the bank on the next banking day.

Since September 1, 1990, all checks not subject to next-day availability are subject to permanent availability schedules. Local checks (ones payable at or through a paying bank located in the same check-processing region as the depositary bank)[112] must be "available for withdrawal not later than the second business day following the banking day on which funds are deposited."[113] Thus, a deposit made on Monday would require availability on Wednesday. Nonlocal checks must be "available for withdrawal not later than the fifth business day following the banking day on which funds are deposited."[114] A Monday deposit would require availability on the following Monday.

The regulation also includes exceptions to the required availability of deposits.[115] These exceptions address areas in which the risk of fraud poses a genuine concern to depositary banks. The first exception relates to the first thirty calendar days after opening a new account. The permanent schedules on availability do not apply and next-day availability applies only to cash deposits and wire transfers. All other items generally subject to first-day availability require such availability only up to the first $5,000 deposited during any one banking day, with the remainder available on the ninth business day after the day of deposit.

For the additional exceptions the depository bank can delay availability for a "reasonable period of time," which is presumed to be four business days.[116] The exceptions provide the depositary banks with more protection by granting them additional time to ascertain whether a check will be returned by a payor bank. The permanent schedules apply only to the first $5,000 deposited on one banking day. Another exception precludes applicability of the availability schedules to checks that are redeposited for collection after being returned unpaid. The availability schedules also do not apply to any of the accounts of a customer who has repeatedly overdrawn an account. Depositary banks also have an exception when they have reasonable grounds to believe that a particular check is uncollectible. A

---

[110] 12 C.F.R. § 229.2(g).
[111] 12 C.F.R. § 229.2(f).
[112] 12 C.F.R. § 229.2(r), (s).
[113] 12 C.F.R. § 229.12(b).
[114] 12 C.F.R. § 229.12(c).
[115] 12 C.F.R. § 229.13.
[116] 12 C.F.R. § 229.13(h).

final exception is based on emergency conditions, such as interruptions of communications or other equipment, a suspension of payments by another bank, or war.

The mandated time periods stated in Regulation CC operate as maximum times for funds availability. Depository banks are free to implement schedules that advance availability, but they cannot exceed the stated time periods.[117] The banks can follow the statutory schedules for some types of deposits and advance availability for other categories. Each depository bank is required to establish its own policy concerning funds availability, within the regulatory limits, and then to observe it in practice.[118]

Depository banks must disclose their funds-availability policies to their customers. Customers need to know when their deposited funds can be withdrawn so that they will not attempt to draw them too soon by issuing checks that will bounce. The expectation is that consumers will be able to compare availability schedules among different banks, perhaps leading banks to compete by voluntarily providing even quicker availability than the Regulation mandates. Appendix C to Regulation CC contains several model disclosure forms that reflect a variety of different policies that a depository bank might choose to implement. The contents of a bank's disclosure of its specific policy must include a summary of the bank's availability policy, a description of the relevant categories of checks and deposits under its policy and how to identify them, a description of any of the statutory exceptions that the bank may invoke, and its case-by-case policy for delaying availability beyond its normal practice of making funds available before times required in the Regulation.[119]

In the case of an interest-bearing account, a depository bank must begin to accrue interest or dividends on deposited funds no later than the business day on which the depository bank receives credit for the funds.[120] This requirement to pay interest serves to eliminate the float advantage that some banks attained though delayed funds availability policies. If a check is returned unpaid, the depository bank can cancel the interest that had accrued on it during the collection process.

Regulation CC provides an incentive in the form of civil liability for depository banks to comply with funds-availability requirements.[121] Individual plaintiffs can sue for actual damages plus statutory damages between $100 and $1,000. In cases of a class action, a cap of total damages is fixed at the lesser of $500,000 or one percent of the net worth of the bank. Costs and reasonable attorney's fees also are recoverable by successful plaintiffs.

---

[117] The regulation uses the term "not later than" in describing the applicable time periods. 12 C.F.R. §§ 229.10, 229.12.

[118] 12 C.F.R. § 229.16(a).

[119] 12 C.F.R. § 229.16(b).

[120] 12 C.F.R. § 229.14(a).

[121] 12 C.F.R. § 229.21.

[C] Revised Check Return

Although the federal legislation required the Federal Reserve Board to issue regulations to implement the funds-availability rules that Congress had already spelled out in considerable detail, the Board went further and exercised its discretionary authority to promulgate regulations to improve the check-processing system. Subpart C of Regulation CC imposes new rules that primarily concern returns in the check-collection process. Its inclusion in the Regulation provides vivid proof of the Board's belief that shortened funds availability periods had to be accompanied by measures to reduce the risk exposure of depositary banks. Subpart C is designed to achieve this objective through the implementation of new requirements that will speed the return of dishonored checks to depositary banks.

[1] Expeditious Return

Banks engaged in the return of checks are now under an obligation to return them in an "expeditious manner."[122] Previously, these banks only had to be concerned with meeting their midnight deadline. They could meet their responsibilities if they initiated or continued the return process by sending the check back to the next applicable bank in the forward-collection chain before expiration of their respective deadlines. These deadlines of the Code and Regulation J are continued under Regulation CC to determine when the banks have acted timely in sending returned checks.[123] The additional requirement of Regulation CC requires the banks to concern themselves with the manner, as well as the timeliness, of the return. Returns must be made in ways that will improve the efficiency of the return process. Expeditious return generally envisions a return process that is "as fast as the forward collection process."[124]

One of two tests must be met in order for the expeditious-return requirement to be satisfied. The forward-collection test is met if a paying or returning bank[125] initiates a return that would be just as fast as a similarly situated bank normally would use for forward collection of a check of the same amount drawn on the depositary bank.[126] The standard is not based on the forward-collection practices of the individual paying bank, but rather on a general community standard. A "similarly situated bank" means "a bank of similar size, located in the same community, and with similar check handling activities as the paying bank or returning bank."[127] A paying bank whose forward collection path or transportation methods are not as swift as the measures used by similarly situated banks will have to improve its procedures in order to comply with this return test. Thus, a paying bank

---

[122] 12 C.F.R. §§ 229.30(a) (paying banks); 229.31(a) (returning banks).

[123] 12 C.F.R. §§ 229.30(c); 229.31(a)(2).

[124] 12 C.F.R. § 229.30, Commentary (a).

[125] A "paying bank" essentially is the bank by, at, or through which a check is payable and to which it is sent for payment or collection. 12 C.F.R. § 229.2(z). A "returning bank" is a bank other than a depositary or paying bank that handles a returned check. 12 C.F.R. § 229.2(cc).

[126] 12 C.F.R. § 229.30(a)(1),(2).

[127] 12 C.F.R. § 229.2(ee).

that uses the mail to forward checks for collection in order to avoid courier delivery costs would be required to use the faster couriers for its returns if similarly situated banks use them in their forward collections. The paying bank has the option of using any alternative method of return, so long as it results in delivery as quick as would be accomplished in forward collection by similarly situated banks.

Because the forward-collection test entails some degree of vagueness and can present difficult issues of proof of compliance, the Fed included an alternative test based on fixed days.[128] Compliance with the applicable fixed time period conclusively establishes expeditious return. When a paying bank is located in the same check-processing region as the depositary bank, the time period is no later than 4:00 p.m. of the second business day after the banking day on which the check was presented to the paying bank. For example, a check presented on Monday would have to be returned to the depositary bank by 4:00 p.m. on Wednesday. For nonlocal check processing, the time period is extended to four business days. For example, a check presented on Monday would have to be returned by Friday. The paying bank must utilize a return measure that will normally satisfy these receipt deadlines. The paying bank is not responsible for unanticipated delays that arise during transit.

Failure to comply with the requirement of expeditious return will enable an aggrieved party to invoke the general liability provision for Part C of Regulation CC.[129] If the failure to comply is a result of the lack of ordinary care, the measure of damages is "the amount of the loss incurred, up to the amount of the check, reduced by the amount of the loss that party would have incurred even if the bank had exercised ordinary care."[130] If the bank failed to act in good faith, it "may be liable for other damages, if any, suffered by the party as a proximate consequence."[131] Although a paying bank and a returning bank must exercise due care and good faith in selecting a means of return, "the bank is not liable for the insolvency, neglect, misconduct, mistake, or default of another bank or person, or for loss or destruction of a check or notice of nonpayment in transit or in the possession of others."[132]

Regulation CC drastically changes the routing of checks that are returned. The requirement of expeditious return would have been impossible to satisfy in most cases utilizing the return process that preceded the regulation. Paying and returning banks now can return a check directly to the depositary bank;[133] otherwise it must be sent to a returning bank. Generally, however, it can be sent only to a returning bank "agreeing to

---

[128] 12 C.F.R. §§ 229.30(a)(1), 229.31(a)(1).

[129] 12 C.F.R. § 220.38. Liability can extend to the depository bank, the depository bank's customer, the owner of a check, or another party to the check. § 229.38(a).

[130] 12 C.F.R. § 220.38(a).

[131] Id.

[132] Id.

[133] 12 C.F.R. §§ 229.30(a)(2), 229.31(a)(2).

handle the returned check expeditiously."[134] A check cannot be returned generally to a bank in the forward-collection process that does not agree to accept returns. Certain banks will provide their services as a return conduit, whereas other banks will elect not to receive returns. The financial incentive for returning banks is the regulatory authorization to charge a fee on the bank sending a returned check.[135] The services of returning banks are assured by an agreement of all Federal Reserve Banks to handle returned checks expeditiously.[136]

Through this procedure, returned checks no longer have to retrace the forward-routing trail through all of the collecting banks. Returned checks now can be rerouted much more directly and actually bypass all of the collecting banks except for the depository bank. The other collecting banks now have no need to know of the return of a dishonored check because Regulation CC, in one of the few provisions dealing with forward collection, eliminates the provisional-credit concept and treats credits given against collection as firm obligations from the outset.[137]

With checks returned by routes different than they followed during forward collection, and with final settlements required during the forward-collection process, a revised system for settlements and payment became necessary. Now a returning bank must settle for a returned check and the depository bank must pay for it. A returning bank is required to "settle with a bank sending a returned check to it for return by the same means that it settles or would settle with the sending bank for a check received for forward collection drawn on the depository bank," and the settlement is final when made.[138] A depositary bank is obligated to pay a returning bank or a paying bank that returns a check to it, and payment is final when made.[139] Paying and returning banks do not recover against a depositary bank through charge back, but rather "by, in effect, presenting the returned check to the depositary bank."[140] The return process again is designed to reflect aspects of forward collection.

Regulation CC creates an incentive for paying and returning banks to convert a check to a "qualified returned check."[141] A "qualified returned check" is "a returned check that is prepared for automated return to the depositary bank by placing the check in a carrier envelope or placing a strip on the check and encoding the strip or envelope in magnetic ink."[142] The advantage of qualifying a check is that it enables returning banks to use their high-speed sorters in routing the returned check to the depositary bank. Encoding the necessary data for the return is how a check is qualified.

---

[134] 12 C.F.R. §§ 229.30(a)(2), 229.31(a)(2).
[135] 12 C.F.R. § 229.31(d).
[136] 12 C.F.R. § 30, Commentary (a).
[137] 12 C.F.R. § 229.36(d).
[138] 12 C.F.R. § 229.31(c).
[139] 12 C.F.R. § 229.32(b).
[140] 12 C.F.R. § 229.32, Commentary (b).
[141] 12 C.F.R. §§ 229.30(2) (paying bank), 229.31(2) (returning bank).
[142] 12 C.F.R. § 229.2(bb).

A returning bank is granted an extension of one day for both expeditious return under the forward-collection test and its midnight deadline in order to qualify a check. The extra day is allowed because the return will be handled more efficiently by subsequent returning banks.

[2] Notice of Nonpayment

Regulation CC imposes an obligation on a paying bank to provide notice of its decision not to pay certain checks that is comparable to a similar provision added by amendment in 1985 to Regulation J.[143] The notice requirement applies only to checks for $2,500 or more.[144] The Regulation CC requirement shortens the time period for receipt of the notice by the depository bank from the original forty-eight hours after the midnight deadline to "4:00 p.m. (local time) on the second business day following the banking day on which the check was presented to the paying bank."[145] The other basic difference from the former Regulation J provision is that the requirement now applies to all checks of the stated amount rather than only checks collected through the Federal Reserve System.

This provision provides significant protection for depository banks. The notice is not a substitute for the requirement to return the dishonored check in a timely fashion, but prompt communication of nonpayment on large-dollar checks gives the depository bank a basis to continue to withhold availability of the funds represented by the check.[146] If the mandated notice is not provided correctly by a paying bank, that bank can be held liable for any actual damages that its noncompliance causes.[147]

[3] Indorsements

Regulation CC establishes new uniform indorsement standards. Any bank that handles a check during forward collection or during its return is required to indorse the check in accordance with the requirements of Appendix A.[148] The indorsement standards are designed to alleviate the problem of identifying prior collecting banks because of insufficient information or because indorsement stamps of several collecting banks overlap. The identification of the depository bank is of utmost importance because it is the bank to which a returned check must ultimately be sent. Provisions of the indorsement standards are included to improve the ease and accuracy of depository-bank identification.

Depositary-bank indorsement specifications include both mandatory and optional information. The indorsement is required to include the bank's

---

[143] First Am. Sav., F.A. v. M & I Bank, 865 F.2d 561, 7 U.C.C. Rep. Serv. 2d 609 (3d Cir. 1989) (payor bank liable for failure to notify depository bank of decision to dishonor).

[144] 12 C.F.R. § 229.33.

[145] 12 C.F.R. § 229.33(a).

[146] The notice gives the depository bank a basis to invoke the statutory exception based on a reasonable cause to doubt collectability of the check. 12 C.F.R. § 229.13(e).

[147] 12 C.F.R. § 229.38.

[148] 12 C.F.R. § 229.35(a).

nine-digit routing number, the bank's name and location, and the indorsement date. The routing number must be marked with arrows at each end of the number that point toward it. Depositary banks have the option of including a telephone number for receipt of notification of large-dollar returned checks. Depositary banks must indorse in dark purple or black ink.

Subsequent collecting banks are limited to including in their indorsements only their nine-digit routing number (without arrows), the indorsement date, and an option/trace sequence number. This limitation helps avoid clutter in the indorsements.

These indorsements must be made in an ink color other than purple to facilitate the distinction of the depositary bank indorsement. The same objective of removing unnecessary language to ensure readability of indorsements underlies the elimination of two common aspects of collecting-bank indorsements. Guarantee language like "prior endorsements guaranteed" ("P.E.G.") is unnecessary under the Code because the presentment warranties include this guaranty.[149] Although depositary banks are discouraged from using the indorsement, subsequent collecting banks are prohibited from including it, because when more information is included in an indorsement it is likely to be in a smaller print that is harder to read.[150] On the same grounds, subsequent collecting banks are prohibited from including the words "pay any bank." This language operated as a restrictive indorsement that kept the check in the bank collection system once it was deposited by a customer.[151] Regulation CC simplifies the approach by making every indorsement by a bank a restrictive indorsement to the same effect without having to add the additional words.[152]

A specific zone on the back of checks is reserved for the depositary bank's indorsement. The area is designated as the space on the back of the check three inches from the leading edge of the check (the right side of the check looking at it from the front) to one and a half inches from the trailing edge of the check (the left side of the check looking at it from the front). Imagine the back of a check as divided into four equal spaces by lines running parallel with the sides of the check. The depositary bank zone is the second of these spaces from the trailing edge. Payees are expected to indorse in the first space from the trailing edge. The third and fourth spaces are available for collecting and returning banks subsequent to the depositary bank. The reservation of an exclusive zone for the depositary bank's indorsement allows banks to program their equipment to locate their indorsements so that the depositary bank's routing number will always remain legible.

Regulation CC allocates responsibility between the paying bank and depositary bank to keep the back of the check clear for bank indorsements.[153]

---

[149] U.C.C. §§ 3-417(a)(1), 4-208(a)(1). *See* § 8.03[B] *supra.*

[150] 12 C.F.R. § 229.35(a).

[151] U.C.C. §§ 3-206(c), 4-201(b). *See* § 3.04[B][2][c] *supra.*

[152] The Regulation imposes precisely the same legal consequences codified in U.C.C. § 4-201(b), *see id.*, "[a]fter a check has been endorsed by a bank." 12 C.F.R. § 229.35(c).

[153] 12 C.F.R. § 229.38(d).

Paying banks are made responsible for the condition of checks when they are issued by the bank or its customers. Paying banks thus should preclude the inclusion of material that would infringe upon the reserved zones, or contract with its customers concerning such liability. Depositary banks are responsible for damages that result from the conditions on the back of the check that arise after its issuance and before the bank accepts the check for collection. If the back of the check is unreasonably obscured by entries of its customer or prior indorsers, the bank can refuse to accept the check or contract with its customer concerning the liability.

[4] Warranties

Regulation CC creates warranties that run with check returns. One set of warranties relates to the dishonored check and is given by the paying bank and returning banks that transfer the returned check and receive a settlement on it.[154] The warranties run to each party in the return process down to the owner of the check. The first three warranties are: the paying bank returned the check within its deadline, the return is authorized, and the check has not been materially altered.

Regulation CC also includes warranties by paying banks with respect to the requirement of notifying the depository bank when it decides not to pay a check for $2,500 or more.[155] The paying bank warrants that it is authorized to send the notice, that the check has not been materially altered, and that it returned or will return the check within its deadlines.[156] The warranty protects the depository bank if the paying bank later pays the check after having sent a notice of nonpayment.

---

[154] 12 C.F.R. § 229.34(a).
[155] *See* § 11.04[C][2] *supra*.
[156] 12 C.F.R. § 229.34(b).

Chapter 12
RELATIONSHIP BETWEEN A PAYOR BANK AND ITS CUSTOMER

SYNOPSIS

§ 12.01 Introduction

§ 12.02 Contractual Basis of the Relationship
    [A] The Deposit Contract
    [B] The Implicit Contract — § 4-401
        [1] Items Creating an Overdraft
            [a] Joint Accounts
            [b] Dishonor Following Pattern of Honoring
            [c] Service Charges
        [2] Unauthorized or Missing Signatures
        [3] Alterations
        [4] Stop-Payment Orders; Postdated Checks

§ 12.03 Wrongful Dishonor — § 4-402
    [A] Liability
        [1] Payor Bank
        [2] Customer
        [3] Dishonor That is Wrongful
    [B] Damages

§ 12.04 Customer's Right to Stop Payment — § 4-403
    [A] The Right
    [B] Reasonable Opportunity to Act
        [1] Timeliness
        [2] Manner
    [C] Oral or Written
    [D] The Bank as Acceptor or Drawer

§ 12.05 Stale Checks — § 4-404

§ 12.06 Customer Death or Incompetence — § 4-405

§ 12.01 Introduction

In addition to the customer status created by introducing a check into the bank-collection process, a different customer relationship is created with a drawee-payor by opening a deposit account. The Code provisions that govern this relationship are found primarily in Part 4 of Article 4. A few of these provisions are covered in other chapters of this text. The payor bank's right to subrogation in section 4-407 is covered in Chapter 9 on the prevention of unjust enrichment.[1] Because section 4-403(3) on the burden of proving loss due to a bank's failure to observe a valid stop-payment order are so closely tied to the subrogation concept, it also is covered in Chapter 9.[2] Section 4-406, which covers the effect of a customer's negligent failure to report forged checks and alterations that are discernible from an examination of returned checks and bank statements, is treated in Chapter 10 on tort principles.[3] All of the remaining provisions of Part 4, as well as an explanation of the nature of the relationship between a payor bank and its customer, is covered in this chapter.

§ 12.02 Contractual Basis of the Relationship

[A] The Deposit Contract

A customer opens a checking account by entering into a contract with a bank.[4] The customer signs a signature card that the bank keeps on file to determine the party or parties authorized to issue checks on the account. The bank can use the card as a means to compare signatures on checks in an effort to detect unauthorized signatures in the name of an appropriate drawer. A customer must also sign the deposit contract, either as part of the signature card or as a separate form. This express contract generally includes fairly standard terms that vary depending primarily upon the type of account, such as personal, corporate or partnership, and whether more than one person is permitted to draw checks on the account. Many of the terms reflect provisions codified in Article 4. Article 4 includes statutory regulations that cover specific aspects of the relationship between a bank and its customer.

Sometimes, however, the bank attorneys that draft the form contract seek an advantage by including terms that are particularly favorable to the bank. When they alter the applicability or effect of provisions included in the U.C.C., an issue is raised concerning the enforceability of the drafted terms. Three broad principles, all codified in section 4-103(a), provide the guidance on this issue: (1) Freedom of contract is facilitated by allowing parties to vary the effect of Article 4 provisions through agreement; (2) agreements that allow a bank to disclaim responsibility for its lack of good faith or its failure to exercise ordinary care or the measure of damages for such violations are unenforceable; and (3) parties may by agreement define the standards of such bank responsibility, provided they are not manifestly unreasonable.

Cases that have litigated the enforceability of deposit contract terms that vary provisions of Article 4 have involved primarily exculpatory clauses in

---

[1] *See* § 9.02 *supra.*

[2] *See* § 9.02[B] *supra.*

[3] *See* § 10.02[B] *supra.*

[4] "Customer" means "a person having an account with a bank. . . ." U.C.C. § 4-104(a)(5).

§ 12.02   CONTRACTUAL BASIS OF THE RELATIONSHIP   325

night-depositary agreements and significant limitations on the time for depositors to notify the bank about forgeries or errors in the bank statement. Customers argue that exculpatory clauses in night-depository agreements constitute a disclaimer of any bank negligence in policing its employees who handle the deposits, whereas the banks respond that their exculpation is necessary to counter fraudulent claims concerning deposits or their amounts allegedly made during non-business hours. The cases have been decided both ways.[5] Several New York decisions have upheld a term in the deposit contract of Manufacturers Hanover Trust Co. that reduces the time period to notify the bank about forgeries and alterations from the statutory one year[6] to as few as fourteen days.[7]

The deposit contract between a bank and its customer creates a debtor-creditor relationship between them. The customer is a creditor to the extent of the balance maintained in the checking account. The deposited funds do not create a legal bailment.[8] The bank is not obligated to keep each customer's funds separated from other monies. The bank is free to use the money as it sees fit, so long as it does not imperil its ability to pay in accordance with its customer's order. The customer issues its payment orders to the bank by issuing checks. Each time the bank pays money that correctly complies with its customer's order, it fulfills its role of the debtor in repaying some of the money credited to the customer's account.[9] Although the Code does not specifically identify the debtor-creditor relationship that is created by the deposit contract, the courts have recognized the relationship in cases decided under the Code.[10]

[B] The Implicit Contract — § 4-401

Even though the contractual relationship between a bank and its customer is formalized in an express deposit contract, the terms of that contract generally do not spell out the fundamental duties of the bank to its customer. The most basic duty of the bank is governed by its implicit

---

[5] Real Good Food Stores, Inc. v. First Nat'l Bank, 276 Or. 1057, 557 P.2d 654, 20 U.C.C. Rep. Serv. 1253 (1976) (disclaimer not effective); Valley Nat'l Bank v. Tang, 18 Ariz. App. 40, 499 P.2d 911, 11 U.C.C. Rep. Serv. 164 (1972) (disclaimer effective).

[6] U.C.C. § 4-406(f).

[7] See § 10.04[B][4] supra.

[8] "A special deposit is a bailment, which implies a setting apart of the special money to be itself returned on demand. [citation omitted] To create a special deposit, special instructions or an agreement between a bank and its depositor to use the funds for a special purpose is necessary." In re Smith, 51 Bankr. 904, 41 U.C.C. Rep. Serv. 804, 812 (M.D. Ga. 1985). Deposits into general checking accounts are not special deposits.

[9] Hennesy Equip. Sales Co. v. Valley Nat'l Bank, 25 Ariz. App. 285, 543 P.2d 123, 18 U.C.C. Rep. Serv. 151 (1975).

[10] Cincinnati Ins. Co. v. First Nat'l Bank, 63 Ohio St. 2d 220, 17 Ohio Ops. 3d 136, 407 N.E.2d 519, 29 U.C.C. Rep. Serv. 1581 (1980) (section 4-401 is based on debtor-creditor relationship because the bank must obey the orders of the creditor before making payment); Stone & Webster Engineering Corp. v. First Nat'l Bank & Trust Co., 345 Mass. 1, 184 N.E.2d 358, 1 U.C.C. Rep. Serv. 195 (1962) (creditor-debtor contractual relationship at common law was not changed by the U.C.C.).

contract with the customer that is statutorily established in section 4-401(a).[11] That section provides that "[a] bank may charge against the account of a customer an item that is properly payable from that account even though the charge creates an overdraft." By converse reading, a bank cannot charge its customer's account for the payment of a check that is not properly payable, and courts have recognized an implicit cause of action under section 4-401 in favor of the customer against the bank for breach of this contractual relationship.[12] Thus the most fundamental aspects of the relationship between a payor bank and its customer are governed by the implicit contract of section 4-401. Its application turns on the determination of which checks are properly payable.

[1] Items Creating an Overdraft

Items that would create an overdraft if paid are clearly properly payable under the terms of section 4-401(a).[13] Unlike other properly payable items, however, the payor bank is not under any statutory obligation to pay these items. The Code gives the payor bank the option of paying any item that would create an overdraft.[14]

This option to pay can be changed through terms in the express deposit contract between the bank and its customer. These agreements are now common and becoming even more widely utilized as banks compete for new business. The payor bank often agrees to honor all overdrafts within specified limits either from its own funds or even as a charge against a customer's credit card. The agreement is often desired by the customer to provide a source of temporary credit, to save the expense of service charges, and to avoid the stigma and embarrassment associated with dishonored checks. Rather than the specialized service that in the past was available only to certain favored customers, overdraft agreements now provide more customers with a pre-arranged line of credit available upon demand.

In the absence of an express overdraft agreement, or when the credit limit of the agreement is exceeded, the legal relationship of the bank and the customer on an overdraft is implicit in the provisions of section 4-401(a)

---

[11] Walker v. Texas Commerce Bank, 635 F. Supp. 678, 1 U.C.C. Rep. Serv. 2d 1261 (S.D. Tex. 1986) (relationship of bank and customer governed by implied contract under common law and the Code); Fireman's Fund Ins. Co. v. Security Pac. Nat'l Bank, 85 Cal. App. 3d 797, 149 Cal. Rptr. 883, 25 U.C.C. Rep. Serv. 495 (1978) (bank has implied contract with depositor to discharge its indebtedness by honoring checks issued by the customer); Taylor v. Equitable Trust Co., 269 Md. 149, 304 A.2d 838, 12 U.C.C. Rep. Serv. 922 (Md. Ct. App. 1973) (section 4-401 codifies underlying contract implied between bank and its customer).

[12] C&R Corp. v. American Sec. & Trust Co., 173 App. D.C. 215, 523 F.2d 1164, 18 U.C.C. Rep. Serv. 33 (D.C. Ct. App. 1975). Refusal to pay checks that are properly payable results in bank liability to the customer for wrongful dishonor. U.C.C. § 4-402. *See* § 12.03 *infra*.

[13] Pulaski State Bank v. Kalbe, 122 Wis. 2d 663, 364 N.W.2d 162, 40 U.C.C. Rep. Serv. 1794 (Wis. Ct. App. 1985).

[14] Mercantile-Safe Deposit & Trust Co. v. Delp & Chapel Concrete & Constr. Co., 44 Md. App. 34, 408 A.2d 1043, 28 U.C.C. Rep. Serv. 465 (1979) (no affirmative obligation on payor bank to pay an item creating an overdraft); Continental Bank v. Fitting, 114 Ariz. 98, 559 P.2d 218, 20 U.C.C. Rep. Serv. 1263 (Ct. App. 1977) (payor bank has the option of paying an overdraft).

and the check itself. The check authorizes the payor bank to make the payment and to charge the drawer's account and it carries an implied promise to reimburse the drawee of any payment in excess of the balance.[15] In the absence of an explicit agreement between the parties covering overdrafts, the courts have treated the payment of overdrafts as analogous to the payor bank giving the customer an unsecured loan for the amount necessary to cover the draft.[16] The bank is free to pursue all of the usual means necessary for repayment of the loan.[17] One of the primary ways that a payor bank can recover if the customer does not reimburse the bank for the overdraft amount is to set off the amount owed from another source of funds that the customer has at the bank. For example, the payor bank can set off the amount owed from the customer's savings account or a certificate of deposit held by the customer.[18]

[a] Joint Accounts

In the absence of an enforceable express agreement in which one customer on a joint account agrees to assume responsibility for overdrafts of the other customer, the issue has arisen whether the bank can recover the amount of the overdraft from the customer who did not issue the check. Courts that faced the issue considered a variety of factors in determining whether the nonsignatory customer on joint accounts could be charged for an overdraft. The revision to Article 4 precludes a customer's liability for the amount of an overdraft unless the customer signed the instrument or benefitted from the proceeds of the instrument.[19]

[b] Dishonor Following Pattern of Honoring

Customers sometimes have argued that when their banks have routinely honored overdrafts in the past, the banks cannot unilaterally change their position and start bouncing their customers' overdrafts. The case of *Schaller v. Marine National Bank*[20] is illustrative. The customer-partnership had overdrawn its account thirty-six times during a period exceeding six years,

---

[15] Connecticut Bank & Trust v. Dadi, 182 Conn. 530, 438 A.2d 733, 30 U.C.C. Rep. Serv. 580 (1980) (customer implicitly agrees to cover all overdrafts honored by the bank); City Bank v. Tenn, 52 Haw. 51, 469 P.2d 816, 7 U.C.C. Rep. Serv. 1150 (1970) (customer issuing overdraft impliedly authorized bank to pay it and must bear ultimate responsibility for the amount of the item).

[16] Sayan v. Riggs Nat'l Bank, 544 A.2d 267, 6 U.C.C. Rep. Serv. 2d 1211 (D.C. Ct. App. 1988); First Citizens Bank & Trust Co. v. Perry, 40 N.C. App. 272, 252 S.E.2d 288, 26 U.C.C. Rep. Serv. 1269 (1979).

[17] United States v. Christo, 614 F.2d 486, 28 U.C.C. Rep. Serv. 777, *reh'g denied*, 618 F.2d 1390 (5th Cir. 1980) (bank may enforce the debt in the same manner as any other loan).

[18] Lincoln Nat'l Bank & Trust Co. v. Peoples Trust Bank, 177 Ind. App. 312, 379 N.E.2d 527, 24 U.C.C. Rep. Serv. 1229 (1978) (bank set off overdraft amount against customer's certificate of deposit). Setoff is not available, however, against all funds of the customer. Central Bank v. Butler, 517 So. 2d 507, 5 U.C.C. Rep. Serv. 2d 1046 (Miss. 1987) (bank not free to set off overdraft amount from customer's trust fund).

[19] U.C.C. § 4-401(b).

[20] 131 Wis. 2d 389, 388 N.W.2d 645, 1 U.C.C. Rep. Serv. 2d 1283 (Wis. Ct. App. 1986).

and the bank had unfailingly honored all of the checks to create overdrafts. The bank reversed its position and decided to dishonor a number of checks that would have created a sizeable overdraft, and subsequently dishonored a number of additional checks. The customer sued for alleged injuries to its credit reputation that resulted in substantial business losses. Rather than asserting that the bank wrongfully dishonored the checks, the customer argued that prior notice of the intention to dishonor was required because of an implied contract, an established prior course of dealing between the parties, and breach of the bank's duty of good faith.

In granting the bank's motion for summary judgment, the court held that absent an agreement requiring the bank to continue honoring overdrafts,[21] the bank's prior practice did not create any rights in the customer. In short, an implied contract was not involved. The court rejected the claim of a course of dealing because the parties did not have any dealings before entering the express contract creating the checking account. Course of performance could not apply, in the court's view, because its codification in Article 2 confines its applicability to contracts for sales of goods,[22] and the duty of good faith in the context of a purely subjective standard was not considered to have been violated.

The facts of the case were particularly weak to advance the plaintiff's case, even in the absence of these conceptual difficulties. Most of the prior overdrafts had been small, although some were for more than $30,000. The initial dishonors, however, were for checks that would have created an overdraft of $143,000; the subsequently dishonored checks would have overdrawn the account by $635,000. Even if the court accepted a theory of implied contract or course of performance, the bank's prior actions in creating overdrafts did not create legitimate expectations on overdrafts in these substantially larger amounts. In the absence of an agreement by the bank, the customer cannot unilaterally escalate repeated creations of small overdrafts into assurances of a massive line of credit.[23]

[c] Service Charges

Cases deciding class actions in California and Oregon that challenged the fees charged to customers by their banks for writing checks against insufficient funds have several parallels. The California Supreme Court, in *Perdue v. Crocker National Bank*,[24] after holding that the signature card

---

[21] In Thiele v. Security State Bank, 396 N.W.2d 295, 3 U.C.C. Rep. Serv. 2d 686 (N.D. 1986), the court felt that language in the deposit agreement with the customer to the opposite effect–that honoring overdrafts, irrespective of frequency, would not bind the bank to pay future overdrafts–further strengthened the bank's right to decide in its discretion whether to continue paying overdrafts.

[22] U.C.C. § 2-208.

[23] *But see* Murdaugh Volkswagen, Inc. v. First Nat'l Bank, 801 F.2d 719, 2 U.C.C. Rep. Serv. 2d 25 (4th Cir. 1986) (court determined that the bank's sudden reversal of its agreement to honor checks against deposited funds resulted in wrongful dishonor of the checks that it returned, that the bank had acted in bad faith, and that the substantial damages awarded by the jury were supported by sufficient evidence).

[24] 38 Cal. 3d 913, 216 Cal. Rptr. 345, 702 P.2d 503 (1985), *app. dismissed*, 475 U.S. 1001, 106 S. Ct. 1170, 89 L.Ed.2d 290 (1986).

is a valid, enforceable contract,[25] remanded for additional consideration on the question of whether the NSF-check charges were per se unconscionable. It utilized a statutory version of section 2-302 that extends the unconscionability doctrine to contracts for services. The Oregon Supreme Court, in *Best v. United States National Bank*,[26] did not have a similar statute available. Furthermore, the court determined that unconscionability was not an appropriate cause of action because the plaintiffs sought restitution of fees paid rather than cancellation of a contract or term in a contract. The Oregon Supreme Court also remanded the case to the trial court, but by ruling that the allegation of bad faith in setting the fee raised a material issue of fact that was sufficient to overturn the trial court's grant of the bank's motion for summary judgment. Both courts virtually ignored an interpretive ruling by the Comptroller of Currency that permits national banks to establish service fees based upon a competitive basis as a business decision of each bank, freed of the constraints of state regulation.

A different approach was taken by the New York Court of Appeals in *Howard L. Jacobs, P.C. v. Citibank, N.A.*[27] Because the deposit agreement incorporated a schedule of service charges, the court found that the charges were authorized by the contract with the customer. A customer who draws a check against insufficient funds does not breach any duty, so the service charge imposed cannot constitute a penalty within the meaning of section 1-106. In assessing the argument that the charge imposed exceeded the cost incurred by the bank to process NSF checks, the court determined that the customers did not show that the bank imposed the fees in bad faith or that the fee was grossly disproportionate to ordinary processing costs. The court also rejected the argument on unconscionability because the customers had not shown a lack of choice in dealing with other banks or that the fees unreasonably favored the bank. Finally, the court recognized the ruling of the Comptroller of Currency and held that judicial limitations on service charges on national banks would violate federal regulation.

The U.C.C. does not regulate the fees that banks charge their customers for any of the services covered under its provisions. The Comments, however, note the availability of legal principles like good faith and unconscionability to review fees and the discretion of banks to set them.[28]

[2] Unauthorized or Missing Signatures

The general rule is that a check with a forged drawer's signature is not properly payable.[29] If the payor bank pays the check, the customer has a

---

[25] The signature card used by Crocker National Bank provided that customers were subject to "all applicable laws, to the bank's present and future rules, regulations, practices and charges." The bank used this clause to implement its rule of a six-dollar NSF charge.

[26] 78 Or. App. 1, 714 P.2d 1049, 1 U.C.C. Rep. Serv. 2d 6 (1986), *aff'd*, 303 Or. 557, 739 P.2d 554, 4 U.C.C. Rep. Serv. 2d 8 (1987).

[27] 61 N.Y.2d 869, 474 N.Y.S.2d 464, 462 N.E.2d 1182, 37 U.C.C. Rep. Serv. 1648 (1984).

[28] U.C.C. § 4-401, Comment 3.

[29] Fireman's Fund Ins. Co. v. Security Pac. Nat'l Bank, 85 Cal. App. 3d 797, 149 Cal. Rptr. 883, 25 U.C.C. Rep. Serv. 495 (1978).

cause of action under section 4-401(a) to require the bank to recredit the deposit account for the amount of the improper debit.[30] The payor bank breaches its implicit contract with its customer when it pays a check with a forged drawer's signature.[31] The forged check does not constitute the customer's order to pay,[32] and therefore the check is not properly payable against the customer's account. The same principles apply to cases of other unauthorized drawers' signatures that do not constitute forgeries[33] and to cases of a missing drawer's signature.[34]

Checks that have necessary indorsements that are forged are also not properly payable.[35] The drawer's order to the bank in essence is to pay the payee or whomever the payee, through proper indorsement, orders payment to be made. With the indorsement forged, the check cannot be negotiated and subsequent transferees cannot become holders.[36] No subsequent transferee of the check can even have the rights of a holder.[37] Consequently, no subsequent transferee can qualify as a person entitled to enforce the check[38] or make proper presentment for payment.[39] Payment to anyone under these circumstances is not proper and subjects the bank to liability under section 4-401.[40] The same considerations mean that a check that is paid over a missing necessary indorsement is also not properly payable.[41] A check that is not indorsed by all of the joint payees is not properly payable.[42] When a depositary bank properly exercises its option under

---

[30] G.F.D. Enterprises, Inc. v. Nye, 37 Ohio St. 3d 205, 525 N.E.2d 10, 6 U.C.C. Rep. Serv. 2d 460 (1988) (dicta, as no drawee banks were parties to the case).

[31] Cumis Ins. Soc., Inc. v. Girard Bank, 522 F. Supp. 414, 32 U.C.C. Rep. Serv. 877 (E.D. Pa. 1981).

[32] U.C.C. § 3-403(a).

[33] " 'Unauthorized' signature or indorsement means one made without actual, implied or apparent authority and includes a forgery." U.C.C. § 1-201(43); La Sara Grain Co. v. First Nat'l Bank, 673 S.W.2d 558, 38 U.C.C. Rep. Serv. 963 (Tex. 1984) (payor bank held to have breached an implied term in the contract between the bank and its customer in paying corporate checks on an unauthorized signature).

[34] German Educational Television Network, Ltd. v. Bankers Trust Co., 109 A.D.2d 684, 487 N.Y.S.2d 26, 40 U.C.C. Rep. Serv. 997 (1985) (check not properly payable when one of two required signatures was missing).

[35] First Nat'l Bank v. Plymouth-Home Nat'l Bank, 553 F. Supp. 448, 35 U.C.C. Rep. Serv. 1240 (D. Mass. 1982); Girard Bank v. Mount Holly State Bank, 474 F. Supp. 1225, 26 U.C.C. Rep. Serv. 1210 (C.D. N.J. 1979).

[36] U.C.C. §§ 3-201; Ford Motor Credit Co. v. United Serv. Automobile Ass'n, 11 U.C.C. Rep. Serv. 361 (N.Y. Civ. Ct. 1972); Perley v. Glastonbury Bank & Trust Co., 170 Conn. 691, 368 A.2d 149, 19 U.C.C. Rep. Serv. 188 (1976).

[37] U.C.C. § 3-203(b).

[38] U.C.C. § 3-301.

[39] U.C.C. § 3-501(a).

[40] First Nat'l Bank v. Price, 553 F. Supp. 448, 35 U.C.C. Rep. Serv. 1240 (D. Mass. 1982).

[41] National Credit Union Admin. v. Michigan Nat'l Bank, 771 F.2d 154, 41 U.C.C. Rep. Serv. 1573 (6th Cir. 1985).

[42] Murray Walter, Inc. v. Marine Midland Bank, 103 A.D.2d 466, 480 N.Y.S.2d 631, 39 U.C.C. Rep. Serv. 972 (1984); Cincinnati Ins. Co. v. First Nat'l Bank, 63 Ohio St. 2d 220, 17 Ohio Ops. 3d 136, 407 N.E.2d 519, 29 U.C.C. Rep. Serv. 1581 (1980) (signatures of all payees are required to negotiate or enforce the instrument when it is payable to two or more persons not in the alternative).

section 4-205 to supply the necessary indorsement of a payee, however, the check is properly payable.

In several circumstances the bank can properly charge the account of the customer even though the required signatures are not in proper order. The bank can defend its charge against the account of the customer when the customer ratifies the signature.[43] The bank can also prevail when negligence of the drawer precludes assertion of the forgery[44] or when the customer is precluded from asserting its unauthorized signature because of the customer's failure to discover and report it.[45] Forged indorsements are also made effective in favor of a bank that pays a check in good faith under circumstances that invoke the impostor rule,[46] the fictitious or nominal payee rule,[47] or the rule on employer responsibility for fraudulent indorsements by employees.[48]

[3] Alterations

Section 4-401(d) establishes the authority of a bank to charge its customer's account for items that have been altered. It provides as follows:

> A bank that in good faith makes payment to a holder may charge the indicated account of its customer according to:
>
> (1) the original terms of the altered item; or
>
> (2) the terms of the completed item even though the bank knows the item has been completed unless the bank has notice that the completion was improper.

Thus section 4-401(d) protects a payor bank to the same extent that section 3-407(c) protects a holder in due course.[49]

Limiting the amount by which a deposit account may be charged to the original terms of an altered check means that the check is properly payable only in that amount.[50] Any payment beyond the original amount by the drawer is not properly payable and can be recovered in an action by the customer against the bank. Thus, if a drawer prepares a check for $1.50 that is subsequently raised to $1,851.50, the original term of the check that is chargeable against the drawer's account is only $1.50.[51] That amount constitutes the order issued by the customer. On the other hand, a drawer whose negligence substantially contributes to the alteration can be

---

[43] U.C.C. § 3-403(a).

[44] U.C.C. § 3-406. *See* § 10.02[A] *supra*.

[45] U.C.C. § 4-406. *See* § 10.02[B] *supra*.

[46] U.C.C. § 3-404(a). *See* § 10.03[B][1][a] *supra*.

[47] U.C.C. § 3-404(b). *See* § 10.03[B][1][b] *supra*.

[48] U.C.C. § 3-405. *See* § 10.03[C] *supra*.

[49] U.C.C. § 4-401, Comment 4. *See* § 7.02[F][2] *supra*.

[50] *See also* Hanover Ins. Cos. v. Brotherhood State Bank, 482 F. Supp. 501, 28 U.C.C. Rep. Serv. 430 (D. Kan. 1979) (payor bank not entitled to charge payment of check to customer's account when the name of the payee had been altered).

[51] Ray v. Farmers State Bank, 576 S.W.2d 607, 25 U.C.C. Rep. Serv. 779 (Tex. 1979).

precluded from asserting the alteration against the bank's payment in the altered amount.[52]

Consistent with the policy of section 3-115 on incomplete instruments, a bank acting in good faith and without notice of improper completion is entitled to charge the account of its customer in the amount of the completed check.[53] The underlying policy is that the conduct of the drawer in signing an incomplete instrument created the opportunity for a loss from an unauthorized completion, so the drawer should incur any such losses. Thus, if the bank with the requisite bona fides pays the full $125 on a check that the payee wrongfully completed in that amount rather than the authorized $25, the full $125 can be charged against the drawer's account.

[4] Stop-Payment Orders; Postdated Checks

When a customer meets specified requirements of notification to the payor bank, neither checks subject to stop-payment orders nor postdated checks are properly payable.[54] To be effective, a stop-payment order must describe the item with reasonable certainty and be received in a manner that gives the bank a reasonable opportunity to act on it in timely fashion.[55] Comparable requirements are imposed on a customer to notify the bank that a check has been postdated.[56] A bank that uses automated check collection and payment cannot detect a check that has been postdated in the absence of prior notification from the customer.[57] Payor banks that fail to observe effective notice of stop-payments or postdating may be liable for damages for resulting losses.[58] The practical importance of a bank making these types of improper payments is greatly minimized, however, because the payor bank is generally able to assert its subrogation rights and thereby avoid having to recredit its customer's account.[59]

---

[52] U.C.C. § 3-406. *See also* U.C.C. § 4-406; Ray v. Farmers State Bank, 576 S.W.2d 607, 25 U.C.C. Rep. Serv. 779 (Tex. 1979) (bank liable for amount of alteration when probative evidence supported trial court finding that customer had not been negligent).

[53] Newman v. Manufacturers Nat'l Bank, 7 Mich. App. 580, 152 N.W.2d 564, 4 U.C.C. Rep. Serv. 630 (1967) (bank allowed to charge customer's account for two checks dated April 17, 1964 that it honored on April 22, 1964 which the customer had issued, undated, in 1955).

[54] U.C.C. § 4-401(c) (bank entitled to charge customer's account in the absence of notice to the bank of the postdating). "A payment in violation of an effective direction to stop payment is an improper payment, even though it is made by mistake or inadvertence." U.C.C. § 4-403, Comment 7. By making a stop-payment order, a customer countermands the order to pay the indicated check, so its payment can no longer be proper. Section 3-113(a) provides that the time when a postdated check is payable is determined by the stated date.

[55] U.C.C. § 3-403(a). For discussion of these requirements, see § 12.04[b] *infra*.

[56] U.C.C. § 4-401(c).

[57] U.C.C. § 4-401, Comment 3.

[58] Losses in both instances can include damages for dishonor of subsequent items under section 4-402. U.C.C. §§ 4-403(c), 4-401(c). For discussion of bank liability for wrongful dishonor, see § 12.03 *infra*.

[59] Siegel v. New England Merchants Nat'l Bank, 386 Mass. 672, 437 N.E.2d 218, 33 U.C.C. Rep. Serv. 1601 (1982) (appropriateness of subrogation claims on improper payment of postdated check recognized); Manufacturer & Traders Trust Co. v. Murphy, 369 F. Supp. 11, 13 U.C.C. Rep. Serv. 1064 (W.D. Pa. 1974) (bank failing to observe stop-payment order subrogated to rights of holder in due course). For discussion of a payor bank's right of subrogation, see § 9.02 *supra*.

§ 12.03 Wrongful Dishonor — § 4-402

[A] Liability

If a check is properly payable upon presentment, the payor bank that dishonors it rather than paying it makes a wrongful dishonor.[60] Under the provisions of section 4-402, "[a] payor bank is liable to its customer for damages proximately caused by the wrongful dishonor of an item."[61] The appropriate plaintiff and defendant and the basis of the liability are all delineated in this section.

[1] Payor Bank

Liability for wrongful dishonor can apply only against payor banks. Prior transferors and collecting banks are never appropriate defendants in a cause of action based on this liability. A payor bank is "a bank that is the drawee of a draft."[62] Only the payor bank can pay a check drawn upon it. Conversely, only the payor bank can dishonor the check upon presentment for payment. As a consequence, the payor bank is the only entity in position to wrongfully dishonor a check, and the Code explicitly indicates that it is the only entity that can incur liability under section 4-402.

[2] Customer

The liability of a payor bank for wrongful dishonor does not run to anyone except the bank's customer. Consequently, even if a payor bank has no legitimate reason to dishonor a check, the payee or other holder cannot successfully sue the bank for wrongful dishonor.[63] The check itself is not an assignment of funds available in the drawer's account.[64] Similarly, a depositary bank does not qualify as a customer for purposes of a wrongful dishonor cause of action.[65]

An issue litigated with some degree of frequency has arisen in the context of partnership and corporate accounts. The question posed is whether individuals, such as the founder, stockholders, or officers, can assert damages that are proximately caused by the wrongful dishonor of checks issued on these accounts. The argument advanced to allow the cause of action is that section 4-402 is available in large part to compensate drawers for the loss to their reputations when checks they issue are dishonored without good reason, and often an individual in certain positions within

---

[60] U.C.C. § 4-402(a).

[61] U.C.C. § 4-402(b).

[62] U.C.C. § 4-105(3).

[63] C&K Petroleum Prods., Inc. v. Equibank, 839 F.2d 188, 6 U.C.C. Rep. Serv. 2d 180 (3d Cir. 1988) (holder); Bon Bon Productions, Ltd. v. Xanadu Productions, Inc., 32 U.C.C. Rep. Serv. 253 (D. Mass. 1981) (payee).

[64] U.C.C. § 3-408. *See also* Da Silva v. Sanders, 600 F. Supp. 1008, 40 U.C.C. Rep. Serv. 945 (D. D.C. 1984) (third-party beneficiaries not customers for purposes of section 4-402).

[65] First Am. Nat'l Bank v. Commerce Union Bank, 692 S.W.2d 642, 41 U.C.C. Rep. Serv. 1339 (Tenn. Ct. App. 1985).

an organization can also be adversely affected by the payor bank's wrongful act.

For the most part, attempts to include these individuals as customers of the bank have proven to be unsuccessful. Many courts have taken a very literal approach to construing the term "customer." "Customer" is defined to mean "a person having an account with a bank,"[66] and "person" includes an organization, such as a corporation or partnership.[67] Based on a literal reading of these terms, many courts have held that when the person that maintained the account is an organization, individuals affiliated with the organization do not qualify as customers.[68]

[3] Dishonor That is Wrongful

The duty of a payor bank to its customer includes payment of checks that are properly payable. When a bank breaches this duty, it becomes liable to its customer for wrongful dishonor. When the bank does not have a legitimate reason for dishonoring a check, it is susceptible to a cause of action under section 4-402. For example, if the bank refuses to pay certain checks because it has reduced the account balance through a set-off that is determined to be improperly exercised[69] or because it has improperly frozen the account,[70] the bank is liable to its customer for wrongful dishonor. The bank's liability also extends to dishonors that occur simply due to the bank's mistake, such as computer error or making a deposit to the wrong account.[71] On the other hand, "a bank may dishonor an item that would create an overdraft unless it has agreed to pay the overdraft."[72]

---

[66] U.C.C. § 4-104(a)(5).

[67] U.C.C. § 1-201(30), (28).

[68] Thrash v. Georgia State Bank, 189 Ga. App. 21, 375 S.E.2d 112, 8 U.C.C. Rep. Serv. 2d 767 (1988) (officer and shareholder not customer); Koger v. East First Nat'l Bank, 443 So. 2d 141, 37 U.C.C. Rep. Serv. 531 (Fla. Ct. App. 1983) (principle shareholder not a customer); Farmers Bank v. Sinwellen Corp., 367 A.2d 180, 20 U.C.C. Rep. Serv. 1267 (Del. Super. 1976) (corporate president not a customer for a check drawn on the corporate account); Loucks v. Albuquerque Nat'l Bank, 76 N.M. 735, 418 P.2d 191, 3 U.C.C. Rep. Serv. 709 (1966) (individuals doing business as a corporation were not customers). *But see* Murdaugh Volkswagen, Inc. v. First Nat'l Bank, 801 F.2d 719, 2 U.C.C. Rep. Serv. 2d 25 (4th Cir. 1986) (primary shareholder who controlled the corporation's affairs held to be customer when bank looked to her to meet fiscal responsibility and provide personal guarantees); First Nat'l Bank v. Hobbs, 248 Ark. 76, 450 S.W.2d 298, 7 U.C.C. Rep. Serv. 323 (1970) (individual considered customer on account in the name "Holiday Inn–Operating Account" because he opened the account and directed the manner in which it was to be handled).

[69] Hansman v. Imlay City State Bank, 121 Mich. App. 424, 328 N.W.2d 653, 35 U.C.C. Rep. Serv. 927 (1982) (summary judgment improper when questions of fact raised concerning propriety of set-off); Raymer v. Bay State Nat'l Bank, 384 Mass. 310, 424 N.E.2d 515, 31 U.C.C. Rep. Serv. 1537 (1981) (right to set-off was exercised too late).

[70] Landrum v. Security Nat'l Bank, 104 N.M. 55, 716 P.2d 246, 1 U.C.C. Rep. Serv. 2d 827 (N.M. Ct. App. 1985) (wrongful dishonor to be determined on whether payor bank placing hold on customer account was proper).

[71] Zatal v. First Nat'l City Bank, 9 U.C.C. Rep. Serv. 1098 (N.Y. Sup. Ct. 1971) (cause of action stated in complaint alleging deposit of a check for $8,500 that was credited to the customer's account for only $850).

[72] U.C.C. § 4-402(a); Modoc Meat & Cattle Co. v. First State Bank, 271 Or. 276, 532 P.2d 21, 16 U.C.C. Rep. Serv. 1083 (1975) (no wrongful dishonor of bill of sale drafts in excess of the approved line of credit).

The bank is entitled to determine the sufficiency of funds in the drawer's account based on the time that it makes its initial determination.[73]

[B] Damages

The standard measure of damages codified in Article 4 does not apply to cases of wrongful dishonor. The general standard is stated in section 4-103(e):

> The measure of damages for failure to exercise ordinary care in handling an item is the amount of the item reduced by an amount that could not have been realized by the exercise of ordinary care. If there is also bad faith it includes any other damages the party suffered as a proximate consequence.

The maximum amount recoverable under this standard, in the absence of bad faith, is the amount of the item.[74] Wrongful dishonor, however, is "different from 'failure to exercise ordinary care in handling an item',"[75] so section 4-103(e) does not apply.

The measure of damages for wrongful dishonor is stated in section 4-402(b), which provides in full as follows:

> A payor bank is liable to its customer for damages proximately caused by the wrongful dishonor of an item. Liability is limited to actual damages proved and may include damages for an arrest or prosecution of the customer or other consequential damages. Whether any consequential damages are proximately caused by the wrongful dishonor is a question of fact to be determined in each case.

The customer is entitled to recover the damages that can be proven to have resulted factually and proximately from the wrongful dishonor. Provided that they are proximately caused, provable consequential damages are recoverable, including damages for false arrest and prosecution stemming from issuing allegedly bad checks.[76] A court's holding that, as a matter of law, a customer could not recover for lost wages, illness, or inconvenience in the absence of malice by the bank because they do not constitute actual damages within the meaning of section 4-402 was clearly erroneous.[77] If they could have been actually proven, they would be recoverable consequential damages,[78] and the issue of whether they were proximately caused by

---

[73] U.C.C. § 4-402(c).

[74] U.C.C. § 4-103, Comment 6.

[75] U.C.C. § 4-402, Comment 2.

[76] The language of the section specifically "reject[s] decisions holding that as a matter of law the dishonor of a check is not the 'proximate cause' of the arrest and prosecution of the customer." U.C.C. § 4-402, Comment 3.

[77] Bank of Louisville Royal v. Sims, 435 S.W.2d 57, 7 U.C.C. Rep. Serv. 234 (Ky. 1968).

[78] U.C.C. § 4-402(b) (second sentence); Murdaugh Volkswagen, Inc. v. First Nat'l Bank, 801 F.2d 719, 2 U.C.C. Rep. Serv. 2d 25 (4th. Cir. 1986) (value of dealership assets, loss of a home, and personal defamation); Allison v. First Nat'l Bank, 85 N.M. 283, 511 P.2d 769, 12 U.C.C. Rep. Serv. 885 (N.M. Ct. App. 1973),*rev'd on other grounds*, 85 N.M. 511, 514 P.2d 30, 13 U.C.C.

the wrongful dishonor is a question of fact.[79]

Several courts have also indicated a willingness to award compensatory damages for emotional distress and mental suffering in appropriate cases of wrongful dishonor. They are cautious in this area because these claims are easily fabricated and it is difficult to control juries on these awards. Therefore, the courts have added additional requirements that help assure the validity of the claim. One court, for example, indicated that the customer must show objectively verifiable events following the dishonor that would have induced mental suffering in any reasonable person.[80] Another court similarly indicated that the cause and existence of these damages must be established by credible evidence rather than conjecture or opinions, but that they will not be denied simply because they are difficult to assess with exactness.[81] Other courts have looked for personal injury,[82] as well as some form of outrageous conduct on the part of the bank.[83]

Section 4-402 clearly abolishes the pre-Code "trader rule" in cases of mistaken wrongful dishonor. The trader rule originated at the turn of the century in *Wiley v. Bunker Hill National Bank*.[84] The court in that case decided that because the check that was wrongfully dishonored was issued by a business, rather than by an individual, damages resulting from the wrongful dishonor could be presumed. The trader rule evolved into the principle that whenever a check drawn by a merchant is dishonored, the merchant is "defamed in his business, trade or profession by a reflection on his credit and hence that substantial damages may be awarded on the basis of defamation 'per se' without proof that damage has occurred."[85] The comments to the section on wrongful dishonor indicate that the trader rule

---

Rep. Serv. 291 (1973) (seizure of assets in Mexico, threat of imprisonment, and ruin of credit standing); Skov v. Chase Manhattan Bank, 407 F.2d 1318, 6 U.C.C. Rep. Serv. 170 (3d Cir. 1969) (award of three years of lost profits).

[79] U.C.C. § 4-402(b) (last sentence); Shaw v. Union Bank & Trust Co., 640 P.2d 953, 32 U.C.C. Rep. Serv. 508 (Okla. 1981) (wrong to strike allegations of allowable consequential damages); Loucks v. Albuquerque Nat'l Bank, 76 N.M. 735, 418 P.2d 191, 3 U.C.C. Rep. Serv. 709 (1966) (question of fact raised on damages to partnership's credit standing).

[80] Kendall Yacht Corp. v. United Cal. Bank, 50 Cal. App. 3d 949, 123 Cal. Rptr. 848, 17 U.C.C. Rep. Serv. 1270 (1975) (criminal and administrative investigations and charges and acts of harassment and vandalism).

[81] Twin City Bank v. Isaacs, 283 Ark. 127, 672 S.W.2d 651, 39 U.C.C. Rep. Serv. 35 (1984) (denied use of money frozen in account for four years, loss of credit standing in the community, precarious financial position, loss of house because of dishonor of earnest money check, repossession of automobiles, and strain on the marriage leading to filing of a divorce suit).

[82] Buckley v. Trenton Sav. Fund Soc'y, 111 N.J. 355, 544 A.2d 857, 6 U.C.C. Rep. Serv. 2d 1040 (1988) (plaintiff did not make adequate showing that bank's conduct was reckless or outrageous and the distress severe or the cause of bodily injury).

[83] Farmers & Merchants State Bank v. Ferguson, 617 S.W.2d 918, 31 U.C.C. Rep. Serv. 198 (Tex. 1981) ($25,000 award for mental anguish upheld on jury finding that wrongful dishonor was malicious).

[84] 183 Mass. 495, 67 N.E. 655 (1903).

[85] U.C.C. § 4-402, Comment 3 (original version).

is not retained.[86] Business persons are placed on equal footing with other individuals.

Punitive damages have been available in tort causes of action, but traditionally have not been awarded in breach of contract cases. An argument occasionally advanced, therefore, is that punitive damages should not be available because an action for wrongful dishonor is essentially one for breach of contract. Because the bank's obligation to honor properly payable items stems from its contractual relationship with its customer, the position certainly has some conceptual validity. On the other hand, in additional to breach of contract, the liability of a drawee for dishonor in pre-Code law was sometimes stated in terms of a variety of tort actions, including negligence, defamation, and breach of other tort duties. The drafters purposely left it to the courts of each state to determine issues concerning the availability of specific types of damages.[87]

§ 12.04 Customer's Right to Stop Payment — § 4-403

[A] The Right

Customers who open checking accounts retain the right to control the flow of money into and out of their accounts. Money moving into their accounts is determined by the amounts that they deposit. Control over funds paid from their accounts results in part from the issuance of checks, which constitute orders to the bank to make payments and the corresponding right of the bank to charge an account consistent with an order. Customers can also control payments through the exercise of their right to stop payment on an issued check. A stop-payment order in essence countermands the earlier order to pay money from the account that was embodied in the issuance of the check.[88]

The order to pay embodied in a check, as well as the countermanding order to stop payment, runs from the customer-depositor to the payor bank.[89] The issuance of a check does not constitute an assignment to the payee of funds that the drawer has on deposit with the payor bank.[90] Consequently, a holder who does not receive payment upon proper presentment does not have a cause of action against the drawee/payor bank irrespective of the reasons for the bank's refusal to pay and irrespective

---

[86] U.C.C. § 4-402, Comment 1.

[87] "Whether a bank is liable for noncompensatory damages, such as punitive damages, must be decided by Section 1-103 and Section 1-106 ("by other rule of law").

[88] Revocation of authority to execute checks modifies the agreement between the bank and the depositor as to who has authority to draw funds from the account, but it is not a stop-payment order. The stop order focuses on specific items drawn and countermands that individual order. First Piedmont Bank & Trust Co. v. Doyle, 97 Idaho 700, 551 P.2d 1336, 19 U.C.C. Rep. Serv. 1189 (1976).

[89] Whitmire v. Woodbury, 154 Ga. App. 159, 267 S.E.2d 783, 29 U.C.C. Rep. Serv. 963 (1980) (no right in payee of check to impair right of drawer to stop payment).

[90] U.C.C. § 3-408.

of whether a stop-payment order has been issued.[91] On the other hand, the issuance of a stop-payment order does not rescind the drawer's promise to pay.[92] Upon satisfying the condition of dishonor, the holder can proceed against the drawer on the contractual liability incurred in signing as a drawer.[93]

Section 4-403 assures bank customers of the right to stop payment. It provides in pertinent part that "[a] customer or any person authorized to draw on the account if there is more than one person may stop payment of any item drawn on the customer's account."[94] Even though banks may find that complying with stop-payment orders is a burden, the drafter's policy of assuring customers of the right is clear: "The position taken by this section is that stopping payment or closing an account is a service which depositors expect and are entitled to receive from banks notwithstanding its difficulty, inconvenience and expense."[95] Consequently, banks should not be allowed to evade providing the service or incurring responsibility for their errors through exculpatory clauses. Banks should also be precluded from frustrating the purpose of the Code provision by including conditions to the customer's right to stop payment.[96] Payor banks cannot even insist that the customer provide reasons for wanting to stop payment because the right to stop payment does not depend upon the validity of any obligations that the drawer owes to other parties to the check.[97]

[B] Reasonable Opportunity to Act

In order to invoke its right to stop payment, a drawer must provide "an order to the bank describing the item . . . with reasonable certainty received at a time and in a manner that affords the bank a reasonable opportunity to act on it before any action by the bank with respect to the item described in Section 4-303."[98] Section 4-303 establishes priorities in

---

[91] "[T]he drawee is not liable on the instrument until the drawee accepts it." U.C.C. § 3-408.

[92] First Nat'l Bank v. McKay, 521 S.W.2d 661, 16 U.C.C. Rep. Serv. 1294 (Tex. Civ. Ct. App. 1975) (stop-payment order does not affect liability of drawer to holder in due course); Citizens Nat'l Bank v. Fort Lee Sav. & Loan Ass'n, 89 N.J. Super. 43, 213 A.2d 315, 2 U.C.C. Rep. Serv. 1029 (1965) (right to stop payment did not excuse liability on the check against the depositary bank). Comment 8 states:

It has sometimes been said that payment cannot be stopped against a holder in due course, but the statement is inaccurate. The payment can be stopped but the drawer remains liable on the instrument to the holder in due course (Sections 3-305, 3-414) and the drawee, if it pays, becomes subrogated to the rights of the holder in due course against the drawer. Section 4-407.

U.C.C. § 4-403, Comment 8.

[93] U.C.C. § 3-414(b).

[94] U.C.C. § 4-403(a). Any of these parties may also close the account. Id.

[95] U.C.C. § 4-403, Comment 1. "The inevitable occasional losses through failure to stop or close should be borne by the banks as a cost of the business of banking." Id.

[96] McLaughlin v. Franklin Soc. Fed. Sav. & Loan Ass'n, 6 U.C.C. Rep. Serv. 1183 (N.Y. Civ. Ct. 1969) (requirement of indemnification agreement from customer held to be improper condition).

[97] Whitmire v. Woodbury, 154 Ga. App. 159, 267 S.E.2d 783, 29 U.C.C. Rep. Serv. 963 (1980).

[98] U.C.C. § 4-403(a). The same requirements apply to the description of an account that is ordered to be closed. Id.

competing claims to the balance of a drawer's account by indicating the circumstances under which one of the "four legals" can intervene in the payment process to terminate a payor bank's right or duty to pay a check.[99] A stop-payment order is one of the recognized four legals. The requirement that effectiveness of the stop-payment order depends upon it being received under circumstances that give the payor bank a reasonable opportunity to act on it is entirely consistent with the requirements codified in section 4-303 to give priority to the stop order over the order to pay embodied in the check.[100]

[1] Timeliness

As the discussion in Chapter 11 explains,[101] section 4-303 identifies several acts by a payor bank that will preclude the effectiveness of a subsequently arriving legal like a stop-payment order. Most of these actions constitute the methods of final payment described in section 4-215(a).[102] In addition, certain acts that precede final payment, such as accepting or certifying a check, also give priority to payment of a check when they occur prior to receipt of the stop-payment order.[103] A stop-payment order that arrives after the payor bank has taken any of the enumerated actions simply arrives too late.

Timeliness for the arrival of a stop-payment order also includes sufficient time for the bank to act upon the information. The stop order is not self-executing upon arrival at the bank. The information has to be communicated to tellers who are in the position to pay cash for the check over the counter. Dissemination of the order to several branch offices might be required.[104] The bookkeeping department should be notified, and automated equipment might have to be programmed to observe the stop order. The cases demonstrate that to escape liability the courts generally require prompt action on the part of banks in acting upon a stop-payment order.[105]

---

[99] For discussion of the four legals, see § 11.03[D] *supra*.

[100] "Any . . . stop-payment order received by . . . a payor bank comes too late . . . if [it] is received . . . and a reasonable time for the bank to act thereon expires. . . ." U.C.C. § 4-303(a).

[101] *See* § 11.03[D] *supra*.

[102] *See* § 11.03[C][2] *supra*.

[103] New Covenant Community Church v. Federal Nat'l Bank & Trust Co., 734 P.2d 1318, 3 U.C.C. Rep. Serv. 2d 190 (Okla. Ct. App. 1987) (drawer's right to issue a valid stop-payment order extinguished when drawee accepted draft prior to receipt of stop-payment order).

[104] Texaco, Inc. v. Liberty Nat'l Bank & Trust Co., 464 F.2d 389 (10th Cir. 1972) (stop-payment order had not reached bank when check was presented for payment at drive-in branch of bank).

[105] Dunbar v. First Nat'l Bank, 63 A.D.2d 755, 404 N.Y.S.2d 722, 23 U.C.C. Rep. Serv. 1266 (1978) (stop order made at 9:05 A.M.; teller informed at 12:30 P.M.; teller paid cash for the check around 10:15 A.M.); Tusso v. Security Nat'l Bank, 76 Misc. 2d 12, 349 N.Y.S.2d 914, 13 U.C.C. Rep. Serv. 1131 (1973) (stop order placed at 9 A.M.; check certified at 10:40 A.M.).

[2] Manner

Drawers can issue multiple checks on their accounts. Consequently, if they issue a stop-payment order on one check, they must provide adequate information for the payor bank to identify the intended check. Unless the check can be identified with sufficient accuracy, a payor bank will not have a reasonable opportunity to act on it and will not be held responsible for proceeding with payment. A New York court applying this standard had little difficulty in ruling against a customer whose stop-payment order incorrectly stated the number of the check, the amount, the date, and the name of one of the joint payees.[106] Of course, most cases do not involve such multiple errors by the drawer.

The extensive use of computers in the check-payment process has led to a very restrictive interpretation by many payor banks of when they are given a reasonable opportunity to act. Because they program their computers to search for checks that are subject to stop-payment orders only by the amount of the check, payor banks assert that they have a reasonable opportunity to act on a stop-payment order only when the customer is completely accurate with respect to the amount of the issued check. A deviation by even one cent will foil a successful search. A few courts have acceded to this position by holding that the bank's computer could not reasonably be expected to find a check with an incorrectly described amount.[107]

The argument, however, has not been successful with most courts.[108] The minor nature of some of the errors seems to influence several courts. In addition, courts have been blunt in their assessment that banks should be able to program their computers when they receive information that is substantially correct.[109] The courts certainly should be alert to preclude banks from undercutting the right to stop payment through the adoption of restrictive procedures. One court appropriately noted the drafter's intention to place the stop-payment burden on payor banks "notwithstanding its difficulty, inconvenience and expense."[110] If the purpose of section 4-403 is to be upheld, payor banks cannot be allowed to dictate the meaning of "reasonable opportunity to act" simply from the perspective of their convenience and cost considerations.

Some courts have demonstrated a greater willingness to require an exact statement of the amount of the check on a stop-payment order if the

---

[106] Marine Midland Bank v. Berry, 123 A.D.2d 254, 506 N.Y.S.2d 60, 1 U.C.C. Rep. Serv. 2d 1606 (1986).

[107] Poullier v. Nacua Motors, Inc., 108 Misc. 2d 913, 439 N.Y.S.2d 85, 32 U.C.C. Rep. Serv. 258 (1981).

[108] Kunkel v. First Nat'l Bank, 393 N.W.2d 265, 2 U.C.C. Rep. Serv. 2d 576 (N.D. 1986) (material issue of fact as to whether stop-payment order misstating amount as $7,400 rather than $7,048.27 gave bank a reasonable opportunity to act); Parr v. Security Nat'l Bank, 680 P.2d 648, 38 U.C.C. Rep. Serv. 275 (Okla. Ct. App. 1984) (50¢ error).

[109] Migden v. Chase Manhattan Bank, 32 U.C.C. Rep. Serv. 937 (N.Y. Civ. Ct. 1981) (2¢ error).

[110] First State Bank v. Dixon, 21 Ark. App. 17, 728 S.W.2d 192, 3 U.C.C. Rep. Serv. 2d 1473 (1987).

customer is advised adequately of the necessity of absolute precision.[111] The approach is an attempt to avoid a purely objective standard that totally ignores the particular search methods adopted by individual banks and instead to favor a balancing of the bank's procedure against the rights of individual customers. These courts begin with recognition that payor banks might avoid liability for paying over stop-payment orders by informing the customer of the need for complete accuracy.[112] Like most disclosure standards, however, the issue evolves into a question concerning the adequacy of the notification. A court in New Jersey held that a generalized warning that all information must be accurate was insufficient to impress upon the customer the need for the only essential information, which was the amount.[113] The court also indicated that the bank should explain why the information is required, perhaps in order to overcome the human tendency to believe that a faulty description of only a few cents could not prevent the bank from finding the check. In another case the drawer could not remember whether the amount was $235 or $250, and he guessed wrong in filling out the stop-payment order.[114] Under these circumstances the court indicated that if he had been informed of the consequences of guessing wrong, in light of the nominal fee charged he could have filled out two forms. The court held the bank liable.

The lessons to payor banks should be evident from these cases. Banks that insist on programming their computers to read only for the encoded amount of a check run a risk that courts will not consider their search procedures or will hold them to be unreasonable against some errors of amount on a stop-payment form. Of course, this system also leaves banks vulnerable to encoding errors when the correct amount is reported on a stop form. Banks concerned with this risk exposure can program their computers to search additional categories, such as the check number.[115] They can also program the computers to search for checks within a range both above and below the reported amount on a stop-payment order. Finally, they can inform the customers of the importance of and reasons for requiring precision in stating the amount of checks on which they wish to stop payment.

[C] Oral or Written

Article 4 authorizes the use of both oral and written stop-payment orders, but it provides substantial differences in the respective periods of

---

[111] *But see* First State Bank v. Dixon, 21 Ark. App. 17, 728 S.W.2d 192, 3 U.C.C. Rep. Serv. 2d 1473 (1987) (held for customer unsure of amount even though bank informed customer that precise amount was required for a successful search).

[112] Parr v. Security Nat'l Bank, 680 P.2d 648, 38 U.C.C. Rep. Serv. 275 (Okla. Ct. App. 1984); Delano v. Putnam Trust, 33 U.C.C. Rep. Serv. 635 (Conn. Super. 1981).

[113] Staff Serv. Associates, Inc. v. Midatlantic Nat'l Bank, 207 N. J. Super. 327, 504 A.2d 148, 42 U.C.C. Rep. Serv. 968 (1985) (check for $4,117.12 incorrectly indicated as $4,117.72).

[114] Rimberg v. Union Trust Co., 12 U.C.C. Rep. Serv. 527 (D.C. Super. 1973).

[115] Hughes v. Marine Midland Bank, 127 Misc. 2d 209, 484 N.Y.S.2d 1000, 40 U.C.C. Rep. Serv. 998 (City Ct. 1985) (affidavit of bank employee indicated check could be stopped by check number, dollar amount, or a combination of both).

duration.[116] An oral stop-payment order lapses after only fourteen calendar days unless it is confirmed in writing within that period. Written stop-payment orders are effective for six months, and can be renewed in writing within that period for additional six-month periods. Due undoubtedly to the precision with which these time periods are set out, little litigation has centered on these provisions.

[D] The Bank as Acceptor or Drawer

A bank customer's right to stop payment on a check is one concern that sometimes makes creditors or prospective sellers unwilling to take a personal check. They may insist instead on a check on which a bank incurs contractual liability. The bank can certify a customer's check by signing it as an acceptor. Alternatively, the bank can issue a cashier's check, on which it is also the drawee, or a teller's check, on which a second bank is the drawee. The use of these instruments raises the question of whether the bank's customer that procures certification or purchases one of these instruments can initiate a stop-payment order.

The Comments to section 4-403 explicitly state that a bank customer does not have the right to stop payment with respect to any of these instruments.[117] A person who purchases a cashier's check or a teller's check is a remitter,[118] but is not a customer on that check. The check is drawn by the bank from which it is purchased on the account of the issuing bank itself rather than the account of the customer.[119] Because a remitter is not the customer, the purchaser of the check does not have the right under section 4-403 to order stop payment of the check.[120] Certification constitutes acceptance by the drawee bank,[121] and the bank thereby incurs its own liability on the instrument.[122] An attempted stop-payment order from the drawer as the customer in the transaction would arrive too late once the check is certified. Priority between the stop order and the bank's obligation on payment of the check goes to the payment obligation.[123] The bank incurs its own contractual liability by signing the drawer's check, and the drawer does not have authority to require the bank to breach its commitment.[124]

---

[116] U.C.C. § 4-403(b).

[117] U.C.C. § 4-403, Comment 1.

[118] U.C.C. § 3-103(a)(11).

[119] See § 2.03[B][1] supra.

[120] Fur Funtastic, Ltd. v. Kearns, 120 Misc. 2d 794, 467 N.Y.S.2d 499, 41 U.C.C. Rep. Serv. 862 (1983); Santos v. First Nat'l Bank, 186 N.J. Super. 52, 451 A.2d 401, 35 U.C.C. Rep. Serv. 518 (1982).

[121] U.C.C. § 3-409(d). See § 4.02[B] supra.

[122] U.C.C. § 3-413.

[123] U.C.C. § 4-303(1)(a). See § 11.03[D] supra on priorities against the four legals.

[124] "The acceptance is the drawee's own engagement to pay, and it is not required to impair its credit by refusing payment for the convenience of the drawer." U.C.C. § 4-403, Comment 4.

Because a bank customer cannot stop payment on a cashier's check, a teller's check, or a certified check, the customer might seek to persuade the bank itself either to stop payment or to refuse to pay the check. The customer is often motivated by an underlying dispute with the party to whom the customer has delivered the check. Even with notice of the customer's adverse claim to the check, the bank can discharge its obligation on a check that it drew on itself or that it certified by paying the holder.[125] Banks nevertheless sometimes refuse payment or make a stop-payment order as an accommodation to their customers. Section 3-411 of the revision is provided to discourage this practice.[126]

Section 3-411 imposes additional liability on any bank that is the issuer of a cashier's check or a teller's check and that is the acceptor of a certified check when the bank wrongfully stops payment or refuses to pay.[127] The bank's liability then extends to pay for expenses and the loss of interest stemming from the refusal to pay, including possible recovery of attorney's fees.[128] If the bank refuses to pay after receiving notice of particular circumstances giving rise to the damages, consequential damages may be awarded. Section 3-411 also provides some defenses to the bank that will preclude the recovery of expenses or consequential damages.[129]

A certifying bank does not have any right to stop payment on a check that it certifies. In addition to the priority afforded to certification over a stop payment, the bank is not a customer in the transaction[130] and thus does not acquire stop-payment rights under section 4-403. On the other hand, the bank might be in a position to cancel its certification. The finality doctrine of section 3-418 applies to finality of an acceptance as well as to payments. In the absence of a breach of presentment warranties, acceptance of a check is final only in favor of a person who took the instrument in good faith and for value or a person who in good faith changes position in reliance on the acceptance.[131] Thus, a payor bank could accede to a drawer-customer's request to resist payment of a certified check and escape liability on its certification signature if the holder of the instrument does not qualify as either of the two designated beneficiaries of section 3-418.[132] On the other hand, the payor bank cannot just routinely assert defenses available to the drawer as a successful defense to its contract liability. The

---

[125] U.C.C. § 3-602(a). *See* § 7.02[A] *supra.*

[126] U.C.C. § 3-411, Comment 1.

[127] U.C.C. § 3-411(b); DRP, Inc. v. Burgess, 730 So. 2d 474, 39 U.C.C. Rep. Serv. 2d 165 (La. Ct. App. 1999).

[128] U.C.C. § 3-411, Comment 2.

[129] U.C.C. § 3-411(c); DRP, Inc. v. Burgess, 730 So. 2d 474, 39 U.C.C. Rep. Serv. 2d 165 (La. Ct. App. 1999) (bank that stopped payment of its teller's check as an accommodation to its customer did not have a defense to protect itself and was held liable for payment of the storage fees incurred by the customer).

[130] U.C.C. § 4-104(a)(5).

[131] U.C.C. § 3-418(c). For discussion on the finality doctrine, see § 9.01 *supra.*

[132] Rockland Trust Co. v. South Shore Nat'l Bank, 366 Mass. 74, 314 N.E.2d 438, 14 U.C.C. Rep. Serv. 1342 (1974) (holder bank had not given value for the check).

availability of defenses of third parties is limited under the *jus tertii* principle, and they are never applicable against a holder in due course.[133]

The *jus tertii* principle will also present a major difficulty for a bank that wants to stop payment on a teller's check or to refuse payment on its cashier's check based on defenses that the remitter would like to assert. A bank that issues a teller's check has the authority to stop payment for any reason it chooses, including requests by the remitter to stop payment because of wrongs allegedly done to the remitter. As with any stop payment, however, the order does not cancel the bank's contract liability as a drawer.[134] When the item purchased by the remitter is a cashier's check, the drawer of the cashier's check incurs the same obligation to pay the instrument as the maker of a promissory note.[135] The *jus tertii* principle operates again with respect to these instruments to limit severely the availability of the remitter's defenses to the bank even against someone who is not a holder in due course.[136]

§ 12.05 Stale Checks — § 4-404

The drafters decided to leave the choice of whether or not to pay checks that are stale to the banks themselves. Section 4-404 states in full that "[a] bank is under no obligation to a customer having a checking account to pay a check, other than a certified check, which is presented more than six months after its date, but it may charge its customer's account for a payment made thereafter in good faith." Because checks are demand instruments subject to immediate payment upon presentment, the section is based on a general suspicion of checks that are in circulation for an extended period of time.

The option of the bank to pay a stale check is subject to the limitation that it must pay in good faith. The comment to section 4-404 indicates the existence of the applicable banking standard: "The time limit is set at six months because banking and commercial practice regards a check outstanding for longer than that period as stale, and a bank will normally not pay such a check without consulting the depositor."[137] The comment also recognizes a circumstance in which the bank is excused from prior consultation with its customer. This option is quite constrained, however, because it depends upon the bank otherwise knowing that the drawer wants the payment to be made.[138]

---

[133] U.C.C. § 3-305(c). See § 6.03[B] *supra*.

[134] Peoria Sav. & Loan Ass'n v. Jefferson Trust & Sav. Bank, 81 Ill. 2d 461, 410 N.E.2d 845, 29 U.C.C. Rep. Serv. 1305 (1980) (even though savings and loan could stop payment on its check, bank that took it for value still might recover on it).

[135] U.C.C. § 3-412.

[136] U.C.C. § 3-305(c); DRP, Inc. v. Burgess, 730 So. 2d 474, 39 U.C.C. Rep. Serv. 2d 165 (La. Ct. App. 1999) (bank that issued a teller's check could not assert any alleged defense or claims of its customer when the customer did not join in the assertion).

[137] U.C.C. § 4-404, Comment; AmSouth Bank, N.A. v. Spigener, 505 So. 2d 1030, 4 U.C.C. Rep. Serv. 2d 115 (Ala. 1986).

[138] "It [the bank] is therefore not required to do so [consult with the depositor], but is given the option to pay because it may be in a position to know, as in the case of dividend checks, that the drawer wants payment made." U.C.C. § 4-404, Comment.

For the most part the courts have intuitively recognized the need to apply a commercial standard in stale-check payment cases. A lower court in New York granted summary judgment in favor of the drawer against the bank for payment on a stale check.[139] The check in question was ten years stale, written on different paper than checks the depositor currently used, and written on an account that had been closed seven years earlier. The bank was also aware of the staleness. In the absence of any explanation by the bank, the court found that these allegations were sufficient to constitute bad faith based on reckless lack of due care.[140]

These cases on the bank's duty to consult with its customer before paying a stale check do not explain one element that should be addressed. Courts should ascertain whether the bank knew or should have known that the check was stale. Modern banking practices by which most checks are paid through automated procedures are again relevant.[141] Banks should not be held to a standard that requires them to examine every check physically before they pay it, and the bank computers cannot read the date written on a check.[142] If the customer wants assurances against automated payment of a check in circulation, it should issue and renew stop-payment orders. On the other hand, when the payor bank should be aware of the staleness of a check, such as when the check is presented for payment over the counter or when the bank computer rejects initial payment of the check, the bank ought to be required to consult with its customer before proceeding to pay the check, except in rare cases in which the bank already knows that the drawer still wants it paid.

§ 12.06 Customer Death or Incompetence — § 4-405

Section 4-405(a) sets out the effect that death or incompetence of a customer will have on the authority of the payor bank. It provides in full as follows:

> A payor or collecting bank's authority to accept, pay, or collect an item or to account for proceeds of its collection, if otherwise effective, is not rendered ineffective by incompetence of a customer of either bank existing at the time the item is issued or its collection is undertaken if the bank does not know of an adjudication of incompetence. Neither death nor incompetence of a customer revokes the

---

[139] New York Flameproofing Co., Inc. v. Chemical Bank, 15 U.C.C. Rep. Serv. 1104 (N.Y. Civ. Ct. 1974).

[140] In specifically addressing the question of whether the bank had a duty of inquiry before paying the check, the court in Granite Equip. Leasing Corp. v. Hempstead Bank, 68 Misc. 2d 350, 326 N.Y.S.2d 881, 9 U.C.C. Rep. Serv. 1384, 1387 (N.Y. Sup. Ct. 1971), entered summary judgment for the bank after noting "the absence of any facts that could justify a finding of dishonesty, bad faith, recklessness, or lack of ordinary care."

[141] See § 11.03[A][1] supra.

[142] Scott D. Leibling, P.C. v. Mellon PSFS (NJ) N.A., 35 U.C.C. Rep. Serv. 2d 590 (N.J. Super. Ct. 1998) (payment of 19-month-old check was in accordance with reasonable commercial standards by using an adequate computer system and in good faith because the oral stop-payment order had expired).

authority to accept, pay, collect, or account until the bank knows of the fact of death or of an adjudication of incompetence and has reasonable opportunity to act on it.

This provision is unique because, in addition to a payor bank and its customer-drawer, it also applies to collecting banks and their customers who initiate bank collection.

Due to the impossibility for a bank to verify the continued life and competency of its customers, the bank must have actual knowledge of death or incompetency before its authority is revoked. In the case of incompetence, however, the bank must know that the customer has been adjudicated to be incompetent. In *Lincoln National Bank & Trust Co. v. People's Trust Bank*[143] a customer of Lincoln National Bank had written several checks just before he died. His mind was alleged to have been somewhat unstable, even reaching the point that he was considered incompetent. His attorney informed the bank of his condition and ordered the bank to place holds on certain checks. Before the actual hold was placed on the account, a check that had been drawn by the customer for nearly $9,000 was presented for payment. The bank cashed the check, and the plaintiffs sued, charging the bank with payment of an improperly payable item. One of the theories relied upon was that the bank did not have the authority to pay this check because it had prior notice of the customer's incompetence. The only notice that the bank had received, however, was the statement of the attorney. The court correctly ruled that payment of the check did not violate section 4-405(a) because the record did not contain any showing that the customer had been adjudged to be incompetent.

The requirement that the bank have actual knowledge of its customer's death or adjudication of incompetency undercuts any argument that death or an adjudication of incompetency is constructive notice to all the world.[144] Banks do not have to remain on constant lookout for postings of this type of information.[145] Instead the bank must have actual knowledge. The Code includes a specific standard to determine when the knowledge received by an organization is effective.[146] Under this standard the information concerning death or adjudication of incompetency of a customer has to be communicated to persons in the bank who have the duty and authority to implement the measures necessary to take required action. These persons are the ones with authority on accounts and on decisions to cash or pay items. These individuals will be held to have knowledge in any event from the time that the information would have been brought to their attention if the bank had acted diligently.

---

[143] 379 N.E.2d 527 (Ind. 1978).

[144] U.C.C. § 4-405, Comment 1.

[145] *Id.*

[146] "Notice, knowledge or a notice or notification received by an organization is effective for a particular transaction from the time when it is brought to the attention of the individual conducting that transaction, and in any event from the time when it would have been brought to his attention if the organization had exercised due diligence." U.C.C. § 1-201(27).

Once a bank knows of the death or adjudication of incompetency of a customer, it must also have a reasonable opportunity to act upon the knowledge before its authority to accept, pay, or collect an item is revoked. The courts have not amplified this requirement, but it is comparable to the similar provision in section 4-403(a) dealing with stop-payment orders issued by customers to payor banks.[147] It recognizes that effective action by a bank in response to the knowledge acquired by its responsible employees can require dissemination of orders to tellers and to the accounts department. The provision should be interpreted to require prompt action upon attaining the knowledge.

Section 4-405(b) states a rule that enables persons holding checks that were issued shortly before a deceased customer's death to cash them without having to file a claim in the probate of the estate.[148] The subsection provides that "[e]ven with knowledge, a bank may for 10 days after the date of death pay or certify checks drawn on or before that date unless ordered to stop payment by a person claiming an interest in the account." The subsection only relieves the bank from liability for payment; it does not affect any law on gifts in contemplation of death or that allows executors to recover payments made to holders.[149]

The authorization to pay or certify checks is subject to the right of any person claiming an interest in the account to order stop payment. The limitation allows other persons with an interest in the deceased's account to prevent dissipation of funds from the account. The bank does not have to ascertain the validity of any claim "or even whether it is 'colorable'."[150] The obvious response, therefore, should be for the bank to follow any stop order upon learning of a customer's death.

---

[147] *See* § 12.04[B] *supra*.

[148] "The justification is that these checks normally are given in immediate payment of an obligation, that there is almost never any reason why they should not be paid, and that filing in probate is a useless formality, burdensome to the holder, the executor, the court and the bank." U.C.C. § 4-405, Comment 2.

[149] U.C.C. § 4-405, Comment 2.

[150] U.C.C. § 4-405, Comment 3.

Chapter 13
PAYMENT BY CASH

SYNOPSIS

§ 13.01   Development of the Concept of Cash
§ 13.02   Legal Tender
§ 13.03   Free Transferability of Cash
§ 13.04   Allocation of Loss

§ 13.01 Development of the Concept of Cash

The facilitation of money in exchange relationships is readily apparent. In the absence of money a society must rely upon barter, in which one commodity is exchanged directly for another commodity. Reliance upon a barter economy is nigh impossible for any society that has developed more than a minimal level of division of labor. Money is the great facilitator because it serves as an intermediary by enabling a seller to dispose of commodities to buyers who desire them without having to be concerned with the types of commodities or services that these buyers can offer in return. By taking money for the sale, the seller can then use it to deal directly with other persons who provide what the seller wants.

Commentators have identified several features of money based on the functions that it serves. These functions include money serving as a medium of exchange, a unit of value, a standard of deferred payment, and a store of value.[1] These functions interrelate. When money serves as a common medium of exchange within a society, sellers offer their goods and services in exchange for this medium, which results in placing a value on their offerings that is measurable by this common medium and which makes the medium the obvious measure for deferred payments.[2]

The earliest forms of money were ones in which its value was determined through its own intrinsic worth. Certain commodities served as an exchange medium and were prized because of their own inherent value. Particular commodities emerged in this role because of the willingness of members of the trading community to accept them in exchanges. Corn, tobacco, beaver pelts and gold dust all served significant roles as commodity money in the development of this country.

---

[1] J. LAUGHLIN, THE PRINCIPLES OF MONEY 2 (2nd ed. 1919).
[2] A. NUSSBAUM, MONEY IN THE LAW 3 (1939).

The inconveniences associated with commodity paper led to the evolution of a more sophisticated money system. Merchants in London who dealt in gold as an exchange medium were well aware of the burden and risk of lugging around pouches of the heavy metal. The practice developed for merchants to leave their gold supplies with goldsmiths who issued notes indicating an indebtedness for the amount owed.[3] These notes began serving as money because the commercial community had confidence in the goldsmiths and recognized that the notes could be redeemed for their stated value in gold. The success of this system led to banking enterprises in which banks issued bearer notes that could be redeemed for the valued gold upon presentment.[4]

Money becomes symbolic when it cannot be redeemed for a valued commodity held by the issuer. Government action generally creates this money, but government edicts alone do not suffice. The sense of the value of the monetary unit and its acceptability are dependent upon a group psychological process within an applicable community that permits the symbolic money system to become part of the social norm.[5] The United States witnessed aborted efforts to establish a symbolic money system,[6] but genuine success did not endure until passage of the Federal Reserve Act in 1913.[7] This legislation empowered the Federal Reserve System to issue Federal Reserve notes,[8] the instruments that currently constitute our supply of paper currency.[9] These notes were originally secured by gold or gold certificates for forty percent of their value and the remainder by commercial paper.[10] The percentage of gold security was reduced during the Second World War to twenty-five percent. Federal Reserve notes are obligations of the United States government.[11] The notes are a first and

---

[3] *See* § 1.03 *supra*.

[4] In responding to the argument that bank notes were legally comparable to goods, Lord Mansfield stated in the leading case of Miller v. Race, 97 Eng. Rep. 398 (K.B. 1758):

But the whole fallacy of the argument turns upon comparing bank notes to what they do not resemble, and what they ought not to be compared to, viz. to goods, or to securities, or documents for debts.

Now they are not goods, not securities, nor documents for debts, nor are so esteemed: but are treated as money, as cash, in the ordinary course and transaction of business, by the general consent of mankind; which gives them the credit and currency of money, to all intents and purposes. They are as much money, as guineas themselves are; or any other current coin, that is used in common payments, as money or cash.

[5] A. Nussbaum, Money in the Law 6, 8, 28 (1939).

[6] On the development of money in this country, see J. Hurst, A Legal History of Money in the United States, 1744-1970 (1973).

[7] 38 Stat. 251, Ch. 6 (1913) (codified in scattered sections of 12 and 31 U.S.C.).

[8] 12 U.S.C. § 411.

[9] Federal Reserve notes initially were issued only in denominations of $5 of more. The $1 and $2 bills were silver certificates, which were a form of redeemable money against U.S. Treasury silver until 1963. Silver coins were a form of commodity money until 1965, when all silver was removed from their contents in favor of a combination of nickel and copper. 31 U.S.C. § 5112(b).

[10] A provision of the Federal Reserve Act that permitted redemption of Federal Reserve notes in gold was omitted in an amendment passed in 1934.

[11] 12 U.S.C. § 411.

paramount lien on all of the assets of the Federal Reserve Bank that places them in circulation,[12] as well as against the collateral required by law.[13]

§ 13.02 Legal Tender

Legal tender is money that cannot be rightfully refused when it is tendered for a debt. Payment in legal tender discharges an outstanding debt. By way of comparison, payment by check generally suspends but does not discharge the underlying obligation until the liability incurred on the check itself is discharged, generally through presentment and payment.[14] A creditor is both entitled to insist upon legal tender and required to accept it, unless the parties have specifically agreed upon some other form of payment.[15] Although broad acceptability of legal tender in this country might lead one to imagine that legal tender is the most favorable form of money payment,[16] historically many legal tender laws have been enacted to force a form of payment on reluctant recipients. In these contexts the terminology of legal tender appropriately emphasizes the unilateral tender of the debtor.

In the United States cash is legal tender. Federal law provides that "United States coins and currency (including Federal Reserve notes and circulating notes of Federal Reserve banks and national banks) are legal tender for all debts, public charges, taxes, and dues."[17] Federal Reserve notes all include the following inscription: "This note is legal tender for all debts, public and private." The government also is bound through this law to accept legal tender in discharge of debts owed to it.

§ 13.03 Free Transferability of Cash

Cash is a readily transferable form of personal property. It can be passed from one person to another as a means of payment without imposing the necessity of further collection and without the involvement of anyone else. The free transferability of cash is primarily dependent on its form. The government issues currency payable to bearer.[18] Bona fide recipients can take cash without preoccupation with the circumstances under which their transferors acquired it. In the absence of this attribute, cash would lose its serviceability as a circulating medium of exchange. In establishing the requisites of negotiability for commercial paper, the law generally has set cash as the high standard of comparison: the goal has been to create paper

---

[12] 12 U.S.C. § 414.

[13] 12 U.S.C. § 412.

[14] U.C.C. § 3-310. See § 7.03[A] *supra*.

[15] *See* U.C.C. § 2-304(1) ("The price [in a contract for the sale of goods] can be made payable in money or otherwise.").

[16] A sign posted near a cash register stating "In God we trust; all others pay cash" reflects this sentiment.

[17] 31 U.S.C. § 5103. The same provision specifically excludes foreign gold or silver coins as legal tender for debts.

[18] 31 U.S.C. § 5115(a)(1).

that as much as possible is as freely transferable as cash.[19] In this respect, cash is the paramount exception to the rule of derivative title.[20] In short, no property is more negotiable than cash.

When I am told by a store owner that an item I desire to purchase costs $100, the dollar monetary system is being used, as distinct from some other system, such as British pounds or Japanese yen. The store owner uses the dollar as a unit of value to indicate the worth placed on the proposed exchange transaction. If I decide that the item is worth the quoted price, the question of how to make payment remains. If I give the store owner a $100 Federal Reserve note, or a combination of smaller denominations totaling $100, I will have paid in cash, thereby electing to use official U.S. currency as the medium of exchange. Assuming the store owner is amenable, however, I alternatively might pay by check, credit card, or debit card. Cash payment is one of the alternatives, and substantial numbers of transactions, particularly for payments of smaller amounts, are conducted regularly in cash.

Even though cash has the sterling attributes of free transferability, legal tender, the credit of the government behind it, and no further need to pursue collection, it by no means is always the preferred method of payment. Payment of cash means that the payor must replenish the supply, which can mean inconvenient trips to the bank or to an automated teller machine. Withdrawals of larger amounts to minimize these trips increase security concerns and preclude further payment of interest on all of the withdrawn amount. The risks associated with the use of cash[21] preclude it as a sensible choice of payment method in many transactions. The primary use of cash payments in our modern economy is for transactions of relatively small amounts.[22]

§ 13.04 Allocation of Loss

The risks to an owner of cash are significant. Cash is in bearer form, and as the discussion above indicates, it can be readily transferred. It can also be stolen and used by the thief to make payments, and the same risk applies to lost money that someone other than the owner finds. Paper money in particular is vulnerable to complete or partial destruction. Transferees can also learn to their dismay that the coins or notes that they have taken are not cash at all but rather counterfeits.

---

[19] "The very object in view, in making negotiable securities, is, that they may serve the purposes of cash." Peacock v. Rhodes, 99 Eng. Rep. 402 (K.B. 1781) (holding bearer draft not governed by the rule of derivative title).

[20] See § 2.01[B] supra.

[21] The nature of the risks in the use of cash are covered in the next section of this chapter. See § 13.04 infra.

[22] A primary area in which large cash payments are still made is in criminal activities. For efforts of the government to combat crime through regulation affecting cash flow, see the Bank Secrecy Act, Pub. L. No. 97-258, 96 Stat. 995, 31 U.S.C. §§ 5311-5322 and the Money Laundering Control Act, 18 U.S.C. 1956.

A thief cannot acquire good title to someone else's cash simply by taking it. The thief, however, can easily transfer it to another person. As long as the subsequent transferee gives value for it and is a bona fide holder of the cash, the transferee receives the rights of ownership in the cash.[23] This legal approach is justified on the grounds of the need for continuance in the flow of business and commerce without interruptions to determine the source of transferred cash, a determination which in many instances would be impossible to discover. Although the protected status of the bona fide holder for value of cash is comparable to the position of a holder in due course of commercial paper, the protection of the cash holder is somewhat better. A holder in due course must bear the burden of establishing all of the necessary elements for that status,[24] whereas the burden of disproving the bona fides of a holder of cash lies upon the plaintiff.[25] Its free transferability and this additional burden serve to increase the risk of loss through theft to the owner of cash. Precisely the same risk applies when the owner loses cash and it is found by someone.

A holder of cash is also very vulnerable to loss caused by destruction of the coins or currency. When a seller takes a promissory note or a check in payment for a sale and a fire destroys the negotiable instrument, the seller as the owner can insist upon a replacement note or check.[26] The assets of the issuer are not yet diminished, so the instrument is still enforceable. A seller that receives cash in the sales transaction does not have a similar right against the buyer to demand additional Federal Reserve notes. The buyer's payment in cash discharges the underlying sales obligation and the seller assumed the risk attendant upon subsequent destruction of the cash.

Because cash is issued by the federal government and represents its obligation, the owner who loses cash by destruction might seek to require replacement of the loss by the government. Some early cases held that state banks that issued notes continued obligated to replace them for the last owner provided that the evidence of total destruction of the notes was sufficiently compelling and that the owner posted an indemnity bond against the reappearance of the notes in circulation.[27] The issue is now governed

---

[23] "It is a rule of law that title to currency passes with delivery to the person who receives it in good faith and for valuable consideration." Transamerica Ins. Co. v. Long, 318 F. Supp. 156, 160 (1970) (proceeds of bank robbery used to pay tax liability to the Internal Revenue Service). Halla v. Norwest Bank Minnesota, N.A., 601 N.W.2d 449, 39 U.C.C. Rep. Serv. 2d 1104 (Minn. Ct. App. 1999) (bank not liable for conversion based on cash that a dishonest employee collected from employer's customers and deposited in the employee's personal account). This rule has a long history. "So, in case of money stolen, the true owner can not recover it, after it has been paid away fairly and honestly upon a valuable and bona fide consideration: but before money has passed in currency, an action may be brought for the money itself." Miller v. Race, 97 Eng. Rep. 398 (K.B. 1758).

[24] U.C.C. § 3-308(b). See § 6.05(C) supra.

[25] Wyer v. Dorchester and Milton Bank, 11 Cush. (65 Mass.) 51 (1853).

[26] U.C.C. § 3-309. See § 4.06 supra.

[27] Wade v. New Orleans Canal & Banking Co., 8 Rob. (La.) 140 (1844). Cf. Hinsdale v. The Bank of Orange, 6 Wend. (N.Y. 378 (1831). The similarity of these requirements with the elements of section 3-309 is readily apparent.

by federal regulations governing the exchange of mutilated paper currency. The lawful holder of mutilated paper currency[28] is entitled to have it exchanged at face amount if clearly more than one-half of the original whole note remains.[29] Whenever the portion is not clearly more than one-half, the exchange will be made at face value only if a designated government official in the Department of the Treasury is satisfied that the missing portions have been totally destroyed, and that official's decision is final.[30] No relief is available when paper currency has been totally destroyed.[31]

When a party makes payment with counterfeit cash, payment has not been made at all and the transferee is still entitled to a valid form of payment. This means theoretically that the ultimate loss stemming from transfers of counterfeit cash should lie upon the criminal who introduced the counterfeits into the stream of commerce.[32] As with their counterparts who make illegal uses of other payment systems, however, these individuals can be difficult to locate and recover from. Another difficulty can be in establishing that the counterfeit cash was passed in a particular transaction. Consequently, an innocent transferee often takes the ultimate loss associated with counterfeit cash payments. Once transferees know that the cash they hold is counterfeit, they cannot further transfer it without violating federal criminal law.[33] The counterfeits are forfeited to the United States.[34]

---

[28] "Mutilated currency is currency which has been damaged to the extent that (i) one-half or less of the original note remains or (ii) its condition is such that its value is questionable and the currency must be forwarded to the Treasury Department for examination by trained experts before any exchange is made." 31 C.F.R. § 100.5(a)(1). "Unfit currency is currency which is unfit for further circulation because of its physical condition such as torn, dirty, limp, worn or defaced. Unfit currency should not be forwarded to the Treasury, but may be exchanged at commercial banks." 31 C.F.R. § 100.5(a)(2).

[29] 31 C.F.R. §§ 100.5(a), 100.7(a)(1).

[30] 31 C.F.R. §§ 100.5(a), 100.7(a)(2),(b)(2).

[31] 31 C.F.R. § 100.6.

[32] Persons who fraudulently make or pass counterfeits are subject to federal criminal sanctions of a fine and imprisonment up to fifteen years. 18 U.S.C. §§ 471, 472.

[33] "Whoever buys, sells, exchanges, transfers, receives, or delivers any false, forged, counterfeited, or altered obligation or other security of the United States, with the intent that the same shall be passed, published, or used as true and genuine, shall be fined under this title or imprisoned not more than ten years, or both." 18 U.S.C. § 473.

[34] 18 U.S.C. § 492.

Chapter 14

PAYMENT BY CREDIT CARD

SYNOPSIS

§ 14.01   Relationship of the Participants

§ 14.02   Federal Legislation
- [A] Background
- [B] Scope
- [C] Disclosure
  - [1] Solicitation and Application Disclosures
  - [2] Initial Disclosure Statement
  - [3] Periodic Statements
- [D] Sanctions
- [E] Card Issuance
- [F] Unauthorized Use
- [G] Criminal Liability for Fraud
- [H] Treatment of Credits
- [I] Error-Resolution Procedures
- [J] Claims and Defenses of Cardholders
- [K] Anti-Setoff Provision

§ 14.01 Relationship of the Participants

The number of participants in credit card systems varies depending upon the structure of the system. Two-party cards are cards issued by the supplier of goods or services that are purchased with the card by the cardholder. Cards issued by retailers, oil companies, and telephone companies to their charge account customers are two-party cards. Travel and entertainment cards exemplify three-party cards. Companies like American Express, Diners Club, and Carte Blanche issue cards that are honored primarily by merchants in businesses related to travel and entertainment, such as airlines, car rental agencies, hotels, and restaurants. They are three-party cards because the card issuer is independent from both the customer and the merchant. Bank credit cards are similar to travel and entertainment cards except that they add revolving credit by not requiring the customer to pay the entire balance each billing period. Bank credit cards often are four-party cards because the cardholder and the merchant are participants in a national bank credit card system through agreements with two different banks. The predominant national bank credit card companies are MasterCard and Visa, with the relatively recent market entrant, Discover, also enjoying substantial success.

Unlike some payment systems, the use of a bank credit card serves two functions. In addition to serving as a means of payment for goods and services, it also enables the cardholder to draw upon a revolving line of credit. The combination of these two functions is comparable to a checking account with an overdraft feature that enables the customer to draw against a line of credit by issuing checks that exceed the amount on deposit in the account.

MasterCard and Visa are bank-owned corporations in which voting rights and profits are distributed among members on the basis of the value of payments that they collect through the system. Member banks of the credit card association issue cards that can be used to make payments with merchants willing to accept the card. The merchants discount the sales slips created by these purchases with their merchant banks, which are also members of the credit card association. The merchant banks collect payment for the sales slips, through an interchange process, from each bank that issued the card used to create each of the sales slips. The card-issuing bank then periodically bills the cardholder for all of the charges billed to the cardholder's account.

The relationship of these participants is established through a number of necessary agreements. The issuing bank and the cardholder enter into a written agreement that establishes the revolving line of credit and the party responsible for the account. The agreement authorizes the issuer to purchase the sales drafts and to extend cash advances, and obligates the cardholder to pay for these amounts, plus finance charges and other charges like membership fees, to the card issuer. Federal legislation regulates these agreements, both in requiring specific provisions to be included in the agreements and in requiring disclosure of other terms of the agreement. These requirements are covered in the next section of this chapter.

The sales agreement between the cardholder and the seller of goods and services is governed by usual sales law. Sales of goods are within the scope of Article 2 of the Uniform Commercial Code and other sales agreements are covered by general contract law. To the extent that an outstanding credit card balance remains to be paid on a disputed sales transaction, federal legislation preserves the sales defenses of the cardholder by allowing them to be asserted against the card issuer.[1]

A separate agreement governs the relationship between the merchant and the merchant bank. The merchant agrees to honor the card of the association when it is presented by customers who wish to use the card for payments. The merchant bank agrees to purchase the sales slips generated by the merchant's sales in transactions using the association's credit card. It is a discount agreement that has similarities to factoring of accounts receivable.[2] The sales slips transferred to the merchant bank are

---

[1] *See* § 14.02[J] *infra*.

[2] The payment obligation, however, runs from the card-issuer directly to the merchant bank, so that the agreement between the merchant and the merchant bank does not lead to an assignment of rights by the merchant.

discounted, generally within a range of less than one to seven percent, either upon receipt or according to periodic billing periods. The discount means that the merchant does not receive the full purchase price for credit sales. In exchange, the merchant is relieved of both the need to extend credit to its customers and the burden and expense of collection on credit sales, together with the attendant risks of nonpayment. A recourse feature is commonly included for the merchant bank to require the merchant to repurchase sales slips from transactions in which the cardholder has asserted a claim or defense against the merchant. In order to reduce the chances for losses from fraudulent and other wrongful uses of credit cards, the agreement between the merchant and the merchant bank generally also conditions the bank's obligation to purchase sales slips upon the merchant's compliance with requirements like ascertaining that the card presented for use is still valid, obtaining preauthorizations before completing transactions exceeding a stated amount, and verifying that the card number does not appear on the distributed hot list of cards that have been reported lost or stolen.[3] Merchant banks also are generally excused from the obligation to purchase sales slips that are illegible or which do not adequately identify the cardholder account.

The national bank credit card company has agreements with a number of banks across the nation that are willing to serve as card issuers and accept the sales slips from transactions resulting from the use of the issued cards. These banks bill their cardholders and thereby initially receive all of the fees and interest charged. The credit card company also has agreements by which banks are willing to sign up merchants and purchase their sales slips that result from credit card transactions. The merchant bank discounts the merchant's sales slips, and thus receives the value of the discount. In order to equalize the benefits for issuing cards and enrolling merchants, the merchant banks are required to pay part of the profitable merchant discount to the card-issuing bank through an Interchange Reimbursement Fee. The fee is about seven cents per item plus 1.7% of the face value of the item.

An interchange agreement is necessary in order for a merchant bank to collect on sales slips from separate card-issuing banks when the cards issued by those banks are used to make purchases. The interchange operates by presentment through clearing channels in which the credit card association acts as a clearing house. Bank credit card clearance originally involved forwarding the actual payment slips to the issuing bank, which then returned them to the cardholder together with the monthly statement. Just as with the clearance of checks,[4] however, substantial savings can be realized by reducing the flow of paper through the clearing system. Complete truncation therefore was quickly implemented, so that electronic messages on amounts payable are forwarded through the system rather than the sales slips. Electronic information for each sales slip is forwarded

---

[3] Much of this verification is now determined electronically through pre-authorizations attained in advance of completion of the sales transaction.

[4] *See* § 11.02[B][4] *supra.*

by the merchant bank to a clearing bank that has the capacity within the credit card system to communicate directly with the central computer facility of the system, known as the switch. The information for the transaction is communicated by the switch through a clearing member bank to the card-issuing bank, and the latter bank adds the transaction to the cardholder's periodic statement. Service fees of about one-half cent per item are assessed by the computer against the clearing banks sending and receiving the message to cover the switching cost.

Settlements between the banks involved in collection of credit card sales slips are determined each evening by the central computer facility. The net position of each clearing bank is determined with respect to all other banks in the system by totalling the amounts owed and the credits due. Each bank that owes more than the credits to which it is entitled pays the difference. The clearing banks maintain accounts with a settlement bank that is designated by the credit card system. Settlements between the clearing banks are accomplished by debits and credits to these accounts in accordance with their net settlement positions as computed by the central computer.

§ 14.02 Federal Legislation

[A] Background

The Truth in Lending Act (TIL Act) was passed by Congress in 1968 and became effective on July 1, 1969.[5] This original federal incursion into the field of consumer credit was directed primarily toward disclosure requirements rather than regulation of the transactions themselves. The objective was to provide consumers with information reported in a uniform manner to explain the cost of credit and charges that can be imposed by the creditor.[6] The disclosure approach was relatively unique at the time because most state enactments concerning consumer credit regulated practices and rates.

The TIL Act was not aimed only at credit card transactions, but rather at nearly all types of consumer-credit transactions. In fact, there was still relatively little experience with credit card transactions at the time of the original enactment. Most consumer financing was still closed-end credit, rather than the open-end credit plans, such as credit cards, under which repeated transactions are anticipated and finance charges are based on the outstanding unpaid balance. The explosive growth in credit card usage accompanied the enactment of the TIL Act and revealed several unforeseen consumer problems.

---

[5] The Truth in Lending Act was enacted as Title 1 of the Consumer Credit Protection Act, Pub. L. No. 90-321, 82 Stat. 146, 15 U.S.C. §§ 1601–1641.

[6] The original enactment provided as follows: "It is the purpose of this title to assure a meaningful disclosure of credit terms so that the consumer will be able to compare more readily the various credit terms available to him and avoid the uninformed use of credit." 15 U.S.C. § 1601.

Over the years Congress has passed many substantial amendments to the TIL Act, and several of these amendments are significant to credit cards. With the amendments in 1970[7] Congress went beyond mere disclosure in credit card transactions and started regulating the marketplace. These amendments include prohibitions on sending unsolicited cards, limitations on liability for unauthorized use of a credit card, and the addition of criminal liability for credit card frauds. Several substantive provisions governing billing matters in credit card transactions were added in 1974 in the form of the Fair Credit Billing Act, which was enacted as Chapter 4 of the TIL Act.[8] These provisions include requirements for entering credits to a cardholder's account, mandatory error-resolution procedures, preservation of the cardholder's claims and defenses, and limitations on the right of the card issuer to setoff against a deposit account.[9] Congress also enacted the Truth in Lending Simplification and Reform Act of 1980,[10] but it dealt primarily with closed-end consumer credit transactions and had practically no effect on credit cards. Open-end credit received congressional attention again in 1988. The Fair Credit and Charge Card Disclosure Act[11] imposes disclosure requirements on solicitations and applications for credit and charge cards.

The Board of Governors of the Federal Reserve Board adopted Regulation Z pursuant to a directive in the Truth in Lending Act to implement the Act through regulations. The original regulation, enacted in 1969, was rewritten in 1981 to reflect the changes of the Simplification and Reform Act. The Board amends the regulation fairly frequently. With the exception of the provisions on sanctions for noncompliance, Regulation Z restates all of the requirements of the Act. In several respects, however, the content of Regulations Z differs from provisions in the TIL Act. Congress granted the Board broad authority to make necessary changes to carry out the objectives of the legislation.[12] The most updated and comprehensive source of requirements is thus Regulation Z rather than the statute.

When Regulation Z was rewritten in 1981 the Board of Governors of the Federal Reserve Board issued an Official Commentary on the Regulation

---

[7] Pub. L. No. 91-508, 84 Stat. 1126, 15 U.S.C. §§ 1642-1644.

[8] Pub. L. No. 93-495, 88 Stat. 1511, 15 U.S.C. § 1666.

[9] An additional objective was included in the statement of purpose of the TIL Act: "to protect the consumer against inaccurate and unfair credit billing and credit card practices." 15 U.S.C. § 1601(a). During the early 1970s, Congress protected consumers in a variety of other contexts involving credit: Fair Credit Reporting Act, Pub. L. No. 91-508, 84 Stat. 1127 (1970), 15 U.S.C. § 1681 (consumer credit reports); Equal Credit Opportunity Act, Pub. L. No. 93-495, 88 Stat. 1521 (1974), 15 U.S.C. § 1691, as amended, Pub. L. No. 94-239, 90 Stat. 251 (1976) (forbids discriminatory granting of credit); Fair Debt Collection Practices Act, Pub. L. No. 95-109, 91 Stat. 874 (1977), 15 U.S.C. § 1692 (places limitations on debt collections by independent parties).

[10] It was enacted as Title VI of the Depository Institutions Deregulation and Monetary Control Act of 1980. Pub. L. No. 96-221, 94 Stat. 168.

[11] Pub. L. No. 100-583, 102 Stat. 2960.

[12] 15 U.S.C. § 1604(a). This power was affirmed in Mourning v. Family Publications Serv., Inc., 411 U.S. 356, 93 S. Ct. 1652 (1973).

to provide additional guidance.[13] The Board provides updates annually. The TIL Act protects anyone who follows the official advice contained in the Commentary from being subjected to sanctions.[14] The Supreme Court has also held that the Commentary controls in civil litigation unless the interpretations of the staff are "demonstrably irrational."[15] The Commentary thus is an important source for interpretation of Truth in Lending requirements.

[B] Scope

Regulation Z provides a concise statement concerning the scope of its coverage.

> In general, this regulation applies to each individual or business that offers or extends credit when four conditions are met: (i) The credit is offered or extended to consumers; (ii) the offering or extension of credit is done regularly; (iii) the credit is subject to a finance charge or is payable by a written agreement in more than 4 installments, and (iv) the credit is primarily for personal, family, or household purposes.[16]

These requirements reflect the consumer orientation of the regulation and the exemption of isolated, nonrecurring consumer credit transactions. Payments by consumers using bank credit cards clearly fall within the scope of this provision.

The provision does not encompass all credit card transactions. Purchases by credit card can also be made for business purposes. In addition, travel and entertainment card agreements and thirty-day charge plans do not allow payments to be extended over installments and do not impose finance charges, thereby failing another of the indicated conditions. Partial coverage nevertheless applies to these transactions, as the general coverage provisions of Regulation Z also indicate as follows: "If a credit card is involved, however, certain provisions apply even if the credit is not subject to a finance charge, or is not payable by a written agreement in more than 4 installments, or if the credit card is to be used for business purposes."[17]

The disclosure requirements of Regulation Z differ for the two types of credit arrangements that it distinguishes: open-end credit and closed-end credit. Open-end credit means "consumer credit extended by a creditor under a plan in which:

> (i) The creditor reasonably contemplates repeated transactions;
>
> (ii) The creditor may impose a finance charge from time to time on an outstanding unpaid balance; and

---

[13] Official Staff Commentary on Regulation Z Truth in Lending, 46 Fed. Reg. 50,288 (1981).
[14] 15 U.S.C. § 1640(f).
[15] Ford Motor Credit Co. v. Milhollin, 444 U.S. 555, 100 S. Ct. 790 (1980).
[16] 12 C.F.R. § 226.1(c)(1).
[17] 12 C.F.R. § 226.1(c)(2). See §§ 14.02[E], 14.02[F].

(iii) The amount of the credit that may be extended to the consumer during the term of the plan (up to any limit set by the creditor) is generally made available to the extent that any outstanding balance is repaid."[18]

A plan that does not include the possibility of a periodic finance charge being applied against the outstanding balance does not qualify.[19] A plan that enables a customer to avoid all finance charges by paying within a stated period of time can still qualify because the standard is that the creditor may impose a finance charge.[20] The other essential feature is recurring availability of the established line of credit when the balance is reduced below the established limit.[21] If the line of credit can be reused by the consumer and the creditor reasonably anticipates its repeated use,[22] this feature of open-end credit is satisfied. The Regulation Z rules on open-end credit are contained in Subpart B of the regulation.

Credit card transactions that are structured on open-end plans are the transactions that use either two-party credit cards or bank cards. The card issuer and the customer enter into a written contract that specifies the terms of their agreement, including the customer's credit limit.[23] The card issuer reasonably contemplates that the customer will use the card to make repeated payments for purchases. The issuer will impose a finance charge on the outstanding balance of the customer's account that is not paid within any designated grace period. To the extent that the customer repays the outstanding balance, that amount of the line of credit is available for the consumer to reuse by initiating additional card payment transactions.[24]

Closed-end credit is defined under Regulation Z to mean "consumer credit other than *open-end credit*."[25] It essentially is a single credit transaction and all aspects of the transaction are known at the time the agreement is consummated. Direct loans from a bank or finance company, including a home mortgage, provide one typical example of closed-end credit. The other traditional closed-end credit transaction is the installment sales transaction

---

[18] 12 C.F.R. § 226.2(a)(20). "The Definition requires that there be a plan, which connotes a contractual arrangement between the creditor and the consumer." 12 C.F.R. § 226.2, Commentary 2(a)(20)-2.

[19] 12 C.F.R. § 226.2, Commentary 2(a)(20)-4.

[20] 12 C.F.R. § 226.2, Commentary 2(a)(20)-4.

[21] This requirement does not mandate an absolute right to borrow up to the established limit. "The creditor may reduce a credit limit or refuse to extend new credit in a particular case due to changes in the economy, the creditor's financial condition, or the consumer's creditworthiness." 12 C.F.R. § 226.2, Commentary 2(a)(20)-5.

[22] The fact that a particular consumer elects to use the plan only once does not affect the open-end nature of the credit plan because the standard is based on the reasonable expectations of creditor that the consumer will make repeated use of the plan. 12 C.F.R. § 226.2, Commentary 2(a)(20)-3.

[23] *See* § 14.01 *supra*.

[24] Revolving credit plans and check overdraft plans can also be open-end credit arrangements for purposes of Truth in Lending. This chapter does not address them, however, because the focus is on credit card payments.

[25] 12 C.F.R. § 226.2(a)(10) (emphasis provided).

in which the balance of the price for goods or services is financed. The Regulation Z rules on closed-end credit are contained in Subpart C of the regulation. These transactions do not involve the use of credit cards[26] and therefore are not covered in this book.

Plans using travel and entertainment cards do not fit neatly into either of the two categories of credit. Despite the recurring use of the card against a replenished line of credit to the extent of repayment of the outstanding balance, these plans do not meet the requirement for open-end credit that the creditor may impose a finance charge on the outstanding balance, because they generally require payment in full for each billing period and thus do not impose finance charges. The plans also are not comparable to closed-end credit transactions in which the amount financed is known at the time the creditor and customer enter into their agreement. Regulation Z purposefully brings travel and entertainment cards within the scope of Subpart B on open-end credit.[27] Thus, even though travel and entertainment card plans do not themselves qualify as open-end credit plans, creditors in these plans nevertheless must comply with the regulations directed toward open-end credit.[28]

The Truth in Lending Act and Regulation Z address only part of credit card operations. They are essentially a federal package of consumer protection regulation. The regulation addresses protection of the customer by governing the relationship between the card issuer and its customers. It has virtually nothing to do with relationships with other participants in credit card transactions.[29] The relationship between the cardholder and the party honoring the card is established by the law governing the type of sales transactions involved, and truth in lending law has only a very limited relevance.[30] The federal legislation also does not govern the agreement

---

[26] See the discussion below on travel and entertainment cards for the potential applicability of Subpart C of Regulation Z to some transactions involving these cards.

[27] The inclusion is accomplished through a special definition of the term "creditor" for purposes of Subpart B. In addition to card issuers that extend open-end credit, the term includes card issuers that extend "credit that is not subject to a finance charge and is not payable by written agreement in more than 4 installments." 12 C.F.R. § 226.2(a)(17)(iii).

[28] Some travel and entertainment card plans allow a customer the choice of paying for some purchases in installments. Regulation Z subjects issuers of these cards that extend closed-end credit to provisions of both Subpart B and Subpart C if the credit is subject to a finance charge or is payable by written agreement in more than four installments. 12 C.F.R. § 226.2(a)(17)(iv).

[29] Truth in Lending enables a cardholder who has a dispute with the merchant who honored the credit card to assert that defense against the card issuer for payment of any of the outstanding balance attributable to the disputed transaction. 12 C.F.R. § 226.12(c)(1). See § 14.02[I] infra.

[30] Congress purposefully intended to preserve possible benefits to consumers who make their payments in cash. Truth in lending law forbids a card issuer from prohibiting persons who honor credit cards from offering a price discount to induce the customer to pay by another means, such as cash. 15 U.S.C. § 1666f(a); 12 C.F.R. § 226.12(f)(1). Payments by cash rather than by credit card can benefit a merchant whose sales slips from credit card transactions would be discounted substantially. The discount from the regular price that is offered to induce payments by cash or other means does not constitute a finance charge under truth in lending law if the discount is offered to all prospective buyers and its availability is clearly disclosed. 15 U.S.C. § 1666f(b).

between the merchant and the merchant bank or the operation of the credit card corporation.

Although Truth in Lending regulation is fairly comprehensive on the relationship between a credit card issuer and its customers, it does not cover all aspects of that regulation. The TIL Act and Regulation Z do not impose any price of credit requirements on these transactions.[31] Usury laws of the states persist as the source of law concerning the legal limits on interest rates for credit transactions. This book does not deal with the usury question because the focus is on credit cards as a payment mechanism rather than their use as a means to extend credit. The book does cover the requirements of the TIL Act on disclosure, including disclosures of items affecting credit aspects from the use of the card, because these items still must be disclosed even though the cardholder never incurs finance charges and thus uses the card only as a payment device. The discussion is not very involved concerning these finance elements, however, because their application is relevant to credit aspects of the cards rather than payment purposes.

Although federal law on disclosure and billing practices for credit transactions preempts some prior state disclosure law, the preemption is limited. The statutory approach calls for preemption to the extent that state provisions are inconsistent.[32] With respect to disclosure requirements, Regulation Z provides that a state requirement is inconsistent if it contradicts requirements of federal law.[33] The Commentary establishes a basic principle of interpretation: "Generally, State law requirements that call for the disclosure of items of information not covered by the Federal law, or that require more detailed disclosures, do not contradict the Federal requirements."[34] Regulation Z has two sets of preemption standards for the fair credit billing procedures of truth-in-lending law. It provides that state-law requirements are inconsistent with federal law concerning the correction of billing errors or the regulation of credit reports "if they provide rights, responsibilities, or procedures for consumers or creditors that are different from those required by the Federal law."[35] It also provides that inconsistency and preemption with respect to other fair credit billing provisions in the TIL Act result "if the creditor cannot comply with State law without violating Federal law."[36] Indications of some of the typical state

---

[31] A usury law provision was deleted from the bill before the TIL Act was enacted.

[32] 15 U.S.C. §§ 1610(a)(1), 1666j(a).

[33] 12 C.F.R. § 226.28(a)(1). "A state law is contradictory if it requires the use of the same term to represent a different amount or a different meaning than the federal law, or if it requires the use of a term different from that required in the federal law to describe the same item." *Id.*

[34] Regulation Z Commentary ¶ 226.28(a)-3. An example of additional requirements would be a warning to read the form before signing and an indication that the signer is entitled to a copy of the contract. *Id.*

[35] 12 C.F.R. § 226.28(a)(2)(i). An exception is allowed for state provisions that extend the time for consumers to initiate inquiries about accounts. Thus, a state law provision that allows a consumer to initiate a bill resolution procedure beyond the 60 days allowed under federal law would not be preempted, but a state approach that allowed additional time for response to the consumer would be preempted. Regulation Z Commentary ¶ 226.28(a)-5.

[36] 12 C.F.R. § 226.28(a)(2)(ii). For example, a state law allowing a card issuer to make setoffs against a cardholder's deposit account would be preempted. Regulation Z Commentary ¶ 226.28(a)-6.

law approaches are included in the notes that accompany the discussion below on the substance of the federal law.[37]

Some credit cards are issued so that they can also serve as an access devise for debit transactions. The latter transactions are governed by the Electronic Fund Transfer Act (EFT Act)[38] and Regulation E,[39] which in some instances provide rules that are less strict than comparable rules under truth in lending.[40] Regulation E addresses the scope question that arises when the same card can be used in transactions governed by the two different legal regimes.[41] The TIL Act applies only to a credit card transaction that does not involve an electronic fund transfer; otherwise the transaction is covered by the EFT Act. For example, the use of a bank credit card to access an automated teller machine to receive cash is governed by the latter Act.

[C] Disclosure

The disclosure requirements of Subpart B of Regulation Z are imposed on the creditor.[42] In the context of three-party card transactions, several entities might potentially qualify as a creditor, specifically the card issuer, the merchant who accepts the card, and the national card system company. The definition of creditor in Regulation Z specifies the person who extends credit and to whom the obligation is initially payable,[43] which designates the card issuer. The person that honors the credit cards is also considered to be a creditor for purposes of a few rules,[44] but these rules do not include the disclosure requirements. Amendments to the Truth in Lending Act in 1982 removed some uncertainty so that clearly the national card company is not a creditor.[45] The disclosure requirements of Truth in Lending thus fall directly on the card issuer.

---

[37] A primary source of state law regulation of consumer credit transactions is the Uniform Consumer Credit Code. Even states that have not enacted the U.C.C.C. itself have passed requirements that are based on provisions of this Code.

[38] Title XX of the Financial Institutions Regulatory and Interest Rate Control Act of 1978, Pub. L. No. 95-630, 92 Stat. 3728, 15 U.S.C. §§ 1693-1693r.

[39] 12 C.F.R. Part 205.

[40] One illustration is card-issuance rules. *Compare* § 14.02[E], *with* § 15.02[C].

[41] 12 C.F.R. § 205.5(d).

[42] The Uniform Consumer Credit Code incorporates the federal disclosure requirements by reference rather than trying to establish a parallel set of state disclosure requirements. U.C.C.C. § 3.201.

[43] Creditor means a person "(A) who regularly extends consumer credit that is subject to a finance charge or is payable by written agreement in more than 4 installments (not including a downpayment), and (B) to whom the obligation is initially payable, either on the face of the note or contract, or by agreement when there is no note or contract." 12 C.F.R. § 226.2(a)(17)(i).

[44] The rules have to do with discounts, finance charges imposed at the time of the transaction, and prompt notification of returns and crediting of refunds. 12 C.F.R. § 226.2(a)(17)(ii).

[45] Garn-St. Germain Depository Institution Act of 1982, § 702, Pub. L. No. 97-320, 96 Stat. 1469. The term "arranger of credit" was removed from the definitions of Regulation Z and from the definition of "creditor."

The original Truth in Lending approach required two primary disclosures: initial disclosure and periodic disclosure.[46] The initial disclosure statement is required when the account is opened. This disclosure must be provided "before the first transaction is made under the plan."[47] This disclosure thus might not come until the customer receives the card. Periodic statements of account activity must be sent to the cardholder for any billing cycle in which the account has a debit or credit balance exceeding one dollar or on which a finance charge is imposed.[48] If the plan provides a grace period during which the balance can be paid to avoid finance charges,[49] the periodic statement must be sent at least fourteen days before the end of the period to enable the customer to take advantage of it.[50]

The original disclosure approach led to dissatisfaction with its adequacy because a consumer often was not notified under initial disclosure until the decision was already made to accept the card of a particular issuer. As a result, amendments to the Truth in Lending Act passed in the Fair Credit and Charge Card Disclosure Act added further requirements of disclosure at earlier stages. Effective August 31, 1989, these disclosures became required with card applications and solicitations of cardholders.[51] They should further the goal of comparison shopping of credit card terms by consumers.

[1] Solicitation and Application Disclosures

Section 226.5a was added to Regulation Z to deal with disclosures with credit and charge card applications and solicitations. Solicitation means "an offer by the card issuer to open a credit or charge card account that does not require the consumer to complete an application."[52] The offer in a solicitation is for a pre-approved account. A consumer contact that requires an application by the consumer is not a solicitation and does not invoke the disclosure requirements. The disclosure requirements affect solicitations and applications made through the communication modes of direct mail, telephone, and availability to the general public through posters or publications.

The card issuer who sends an application or solicitation through the mail to the consumer must disclose ten specific items on or with the application or solicitation.[53] The first seven of these disclosures must be presented in tabular form.[54] The required items are the following:

---

[46] Additional subsequent disclosure requirements are imposed for supplemental credit devices and additional features to a plan and when a creditor changes terms of the plan. 12 C.F.R. § 226.9(b),(c)(1).

[47] 12 C.F.R. § 226.5(b)(1).

[48] 12 C.F.R. § 226.5(b)(2)(i).

[49] 12 C.F.R. § 226.7(j).

[50] 12 C.F.R. § 226.5(b)(2)(ii).

[51] 12 C.F.R. § 226.5a.

[52] 12 C.F.R. § 226.5a(a)(1).

[53] 12 C.F.R. § 226.5a(c). The items of required disclosure are enumerated as subsections (1) through (10) of 12 C.F.R. § 226.5a(b).

[54] 12 C.F.R. § 226.5a(a)(2).

(1) Annual percentage rate. This rate is the periodic rate charged, such as daily or monthly, multiplied by the number of periods in a year.[55]

(2) Fees for issuance or availability. These fees include annual or other periodic fees, but a periodic fee must be expressed in an annualized amount. Fees that are imposed based on account activity or inactivity are also included.

(3) Minimum finance charge. Minimum or fixed finance charges that can be imposed during a billing cycle must be disclosed.

(4) Transaction charges. These charges are any fee that the card issuer charges for using the card to make purchases.

(5) Grace period. The card issuer must state the date by which or the period within which a credit that was extended for purchases must be paid in order to avoid finance charges. If a grace period is not allowed, the disclosure must state this fact.

(6) Balance computation method. Regulation Z defines six methods by which the balance for an account can be computed. If the card issuer uses one of these methods, the disclosure requires only that the name of the method be indicated in the tabular part of the disclosure form.

(7) Statement on charge card payments. Issuers of charge cards must include a statement that the charges incurred are due when the periodic statement is received by the cardholder. Credit card issuers do not include this statement.[56]

(8) Cash advance fee. Finance charges that can be imposed for an extension of credit in the form of cash must be disclosed.

(9) Late payment fee. A fee that the card issuer imposes for making late payments also must be disclosed.

(10) Over-the-limit fee. If the card issuer can impose a fee on the consumer for exceeding the credit limit established for the account, the fee must be disclosed.

If a card issuer initiates an application or solicitation contact by telephone, the card issuer generally must disclose orally the information required in the first seven items for disclosure in direct mailings.[57] The oral disclosure is not required, however, if the card issuer either does not impose a fee for issuing the card or making it available or does not impose the fee unless the consumer uses the card.[58] Thus a card issuer who imposes an annual membership fee immediately upon opening the account would have to give oral disclosure in a telephone conversation in which the consumer makes the application, whereas the card issuer who defers

---

[55] 12 C.F.R. § 226.14(b).

[56] 12 C.F.R. § 226.5a(b). The charge card issuer is required to disclose items (2), (4) and (7) through (10). *Id.*

[57] 12 C.F.R. § 226.5a(d)(1).

[58] 12 C.F.R. § 226.5a(d)(2).

applying the membership fee until the consumer uses the card could avoid oral disclosure. In addition to these limitations on the choice of not making oral disclosure, the option is also conditioned on providing a subsequent written disclosure that provides all of the same information required in direct mailings and that states that the consumer does not have to accept the card or pay any of the fees disclosed unless the consumer uses the card.[59]

When an application or solicitation is available to the general public through magazines or other publications or on tear-off forms placed on posters, the card issuer has three choices concerning disclosure. The first option is full disclosure.[60] Disclosure on all of the items required for direct mailings must be provided in a prominent location on the application or solicitation. The second option is to disclose certain of the information required in the initial disclosure statement.[61] The discussion of the requirements of initial disclosure are provided below.[62] The third option is to provide a toll-free number or address that the consumer can contact concerning costs associated with the card.[63]

[2] Initial Disclosure Statement

The creditor is required to provide an initial disclosure statement prior to the time that the first transaction is made under the plan.[64] Card issuers often include this disclosure in the cardholder agreement that is sent together with the card itself. To the extent that they apply, the creditor is required to disclose four items: (1) the finance charge, (2) other charges, (3) security interests, and (4) a statement of billing rights. Each of these items of disclosure is considered below in the credit card context.

A creditor must indicate the "circumstances under which a finance charge will be imposed and an explanation of how it will be determined."[65] Several features of the calculation must be disclosed, including the following:

(1) The circumstances under which finance charges can be imposed, including an indication of whether or not a grace period exists.

(2) Each periodic rate used to compute the finance charge (such as daily or monthly),[66] the range of balances to which it applies, and the resulting annual percentage rate, which is determined by multiplying the periodic rate by the number of periods in a year.

(3) An explanation of the method used to determine the balance upon which a finance charge can be imposed.

---

[59] 12 C.F.R. § 226.5a(d)(2)(i), (ii).
[60] 12 C.F.R. § 226.5a(e)(1).
[61] 12 C.F.R. § 226.5a(e)(2).
[62] See § 14.02[C][2] infra.
[63] 12 C.F.R. § 226.5a(e)(3).
[64] 12 C.F.R. § 226.5(b)(1).
[65] 12 C.F.R. § 226.6(a).
[66] 12 C.F.R. § 226.2(a)(21).

(4) An explanation of the calculation of the amount of any finance charge,[67] including a description of how finance charges other than the periodic rate are determined.[68]

An initial disclosure statement must also cover charges other than a finance charge that may be imposed under a credit card plan.[69] Charges included in this category include annual membership fees, late payment and over-the-credit-limit charges, and fees for providing documentary evidence of transactions requested as part of the billing-error resolution procedures.[70] The disclosure of these charges must include the amount of the charge or an explanation of how the charge will be determined.[71]

Creditors must also make initial disclosure about any security interests that have been or will be acquired.[72] Little specificity is required in this disclosure. It must indicate that the security interest is in the property purchased under the plan or in other property identified by item or type. A general prohibition under Regulation Z against a card issuer making a setoff of the cardholder's indebtedness against an account of the cardholder held by the issuer[73] can be avoided if the cardholder takes a security interest in the account.[74]

The final disclosure that must appear on an initial disclosure statement is a statement of the rights of the consumer and the responsibilities of the creditor concerning the resolution of billing errors.[75] These error-resolution procedures are set forth in other sections of Regulation Z[76] and are covered later in this discussion.[77] The disclosure statement must outline these rights and responsibilities in a form that is substantially similar to the statement provided in Appendix G-3 of Regulation Z.

[3] Periodic Statements

On a periodic basis the creditor must provide the consumer with a statement indicating the activity in the account during the billing period and certain other account and credit terms information.[78] Credit card

---

[67] Common examples are the monthly rate applied to an average daily balance and the annual percentage rate divided by 365 days to provide a daily rate that is applied to balances.

[68] This description would have to cover charges like minimum charges that must be made by the consumer, fixed charges, and charges based on use of the card or on specific transactions.

[69] 12 C.F.R. § 226.6(b).

[70] Regulation Z Commentary ¶ 226.6(b)-1. Charges specifically excluded as "other charges" include fees charged for documentary evidence of transactions for income tax purposes, amounts payable by a consumer for collection activity after default, attorney's fees, foreclosure costs, and post-judgment interest rates imposed by law. *Id.* ¶ 226.6(b)-2.

[71] 12 C.F.R. § 226.6(b).

[72] 12 C.F.R. § 226.6(c).

[73] *See* § 14.02[K] *infra*.

[74] 12 C.F.R. § 226.12(d)(2).

[75] 12 C.F.R. § 226.6(d).

[76] 12 C.F.R. § 226.13.

[77] *See* § 14.02[I] *infra*.

[78] 12 C.F.R. § 226.7.

issuers usually provide statements for a monthly billing cycle. Some of the required information duplicates items required in prior disclosures. The objective is to provide the consumer with sufficient information to make a reasoned decision to avoid an uninformed use of credit. All of the following items are required to be disclosed on the periodic statement: previous balance, identification of transactions, credits, periodic rates, balance on which finance charges are computed, amount of finance charge, annual percentage rate, other charges, closing date and new balance, free-ride period, and address for notice of billing errors.

[D] Sanctions

The cause of action made available to consumers under the TIL Act encouraged a substantial volume of litigation. Although actual damages for nondisclosures or incorrect disclosures can be extremely difficult to establish, the Act also enabled a cardholder to recover a civil penalty of twice the finance charge, as well as costs and reasonable attorney fees.[79] The civil penalty has a cap of $1,000 and a floor of $100.[80] The creditor's liability was absolute whenever a violation occurred, irrespective of its technical nature. The creditor's efforts and good faith in attempting to comply were irrelevant. Consumers who defaulted on their obligations utilized the combination of the strict nature of creditor liability and automatic recoveries as an effective basis for a defense or as the means to extract a settlement.

The Truth in Lending Simplification and Reform Act of 1980 eased the creditor's exposure to liability somewhat. The cardholder's cause of action for established violations remains the same, but the impact of technical violations has been softened and expanded defenses grant recognition to a creditor's compliance efforts. The amendments eliminate the availability of the statutory penalty for certain disclosure violations, thereby restricting penalty recoveries to the more serious violations.[81] A creditor also is not to be held liable if the creditor "shows by a preponderance of evidence that the violation was not intentional and resulted from a bona fide error notwithstanding the maintenance of procedures reasonably adapted to avoid any such error.[82]

Class actions for disclosure violations by credit card issuers were quite popular following the initial enactment of the TIL Act. With a statutory

---

[79] 15 U.S.C. § 1640(a).

[80] 15 U.S.C. § 1640(a)(2)(A)(ii).

[81] *See* S. Rep. No. 73, 96th Cong., 1st Sess. 7 (1979). The sanction provisions are not limited only to violations of the disclosure requirements of the TIL Act. They also clearly apply to the credit billing provisions of Chapter 4 of the Act. 15 U.S.C. § 1640(a). A special liability provision for noncompliance with error resolution procedures is provided at 15 U.S.C. § 1666(e).

[82] 15 U.S.C. § 1640(c). "Examples of a bona fide error include, but are not limited to, clerical, calculation, computer malfunction and programming, and printing errors, except that an error of legal judgment with respect to a person's obligations under this title is not a bona fide error." *Id.*

penalty of $100 for each cardholder in the class, a substantial recovery was possible. The same disclosure form generally is used for all cardholders, so an issuer who made an error was likely to face a class composed of all of its cardholders. An issuer with 100,000 outstanding cards could face strict liability for $10 million, even though the error was innocent and relatively unimportant.[83] Because the liability exposure of card issuers under class actions was considered to be so disproportionate to the nature of the violations, class actions generally were not well received by the courts. The courts, therefore, undertook to restrict the availability of class actions under the TIL Act, often on procedural grounds.[84]

Congress addressed the class action issue by amending the TIL Act. Minimal recovery of the civil penalty is no longer available for each member of the class.[85] Class action recoveries are limited to actual damages plus such amount as the court may allow, not exceeding the lesser of $500,000 or one percent of the net worth of the creditor.[86]

[E] Card Issuance

The initial amendments to the Truth in Lending Act in 1970 were largely in response to marketing practices of card issuers. As three-party cards gained wider consumer acceptance, issuers began sending cards to consumers who had not applied for them or even indicated they wanted them. Disputes arose over liability for transactions in which these cards had been used improperly. The amendments to the Truth in Lending Act responded to the consequences of this new competitive environment.[87]

One of the responses was to prohibit the issuance of unsolicited credit cards. The amendment provided that "[n]o credit card shall be issued except in response to a request or application therefore."[88] This amendment provided a significant competitive advantage to the two major systems (now known as Visa and MasterCard) because they had greatly expanded consumer acceptance of their cards through unsolicited issuances. The prohibition on issuing unsolicited cards has made market entry difficult for other three-party card systems.

The required request or application must be made explicitly for a credit card, and not for some other service feature, such as a request for overdraft

---

[83] *See* Ratner v. Chemical N.Y. Trust Co., 329 F. Supp. 270 (S.D. N.Y. 1971) (finding of liability for failure to disclose the nominal annual percentage rate on periodic statements to 130,000 Master Charge customers who had not incurred new finance charges during the prior month but did have outstanding balances; liability exposure equaled $13 million).

[84] The court rejected the class action approach as inappropriate in a second *Ratner* decision. Ratner v. Chemical Bank of N.Y. Trust Co., 54 F.R.D. 412 (S.D. N.Y. 1972).

[85] 15 U.S.C. § 1640(a)(2)(B).

[86] 15 U.S.C. 1640(a)(1), (2)(B).

[87] For additional background material on the congressional decision to prohibit unsolicited issuance of credit cards, see Weistart, *Consumer Protection in the Credit Card Industry: Federal Legislative Controls*, 70 Mich. L. Rev. 1475, 1485-1508 (1972).

[88] 15 U.S.C. § 1642. This prohibition applies equally to consumer and nonconsumer card recipients.

privileges on a checking account.[89] The form of the request is not limited, so it can be written or oral, as in response to a telephone contact.[90] Card issuers do not need a specific request from a consumer in order to issue a credit card that renews or replaces a card that has already been accepted by the consumer.[91]

[F] Unauthorized Use

An additional response to early credit card market activities that is reflected in the 1970 amendments is a limitation on cardholder liability for unauthorized use of the card. Some creditors had attempted to hold the cardholder liable for charges that had been made by thieves of cards or by other persons who had not been authorized to make the charges. The amendments limit a cardholder's liability for unauthorized use of his or her card to the lesser of $50 or the value obtained by the unauthorized user.[92] The $50 sum thus is the maximum potential liability for unauthorized use that a cardholder faces.[93]

In order to impose any liability on the cardholder for unauthorized use of a card, the card issuer must establish that several conditions have been satisfied. First, the credit card must be an accepted card. An accepted credit card is "any credit card that a cardholder has requested or applied for and received, or has signed, used, or authorized another person to use to obtain credit."[94] Second, the card issuer must have provided the cardholder with adequate notice concerning the cardholder's potential liability and the means by which to notify the issuer of loss or theft of the card. Finally, the card issuer must provide a means to identify the cardholder or the authorized user of the card. The means could be by signature, photograph, fingerprint, or a mechanical or electronic confirmation.[95] If an unauthorized person makes a purchase by telephone by using a credit card account number only, this condition is not satisfied and the cardholder does not incur any liability for the transaction.[96]

Cardholders can avoid any liability for the unauthorized use of their cards by notifying the card issuer before the unauthorized use occurs.[97] Notification requires taking the steps to provide the card issuer with the pertinent information about loss, theft, or possible unauthorized use of a credit card.[98] It can be given in person, by telephone, or in writing, and is effective

---

[89] Regulation Z Commentary ¶ 226.12(a)(1)-1.

[90] Regulation Z Commentary ¶ 226.12(a)(1)-4.

[91] 12 C.F.R. 226.12(a) and n.21. *See also* Regulation Z Commentary ¶ 226.12(a)(2).

[92] 15 U.S.C. § 1643; 12 C.F.R. § 226.12(b).

[93] The small amount at stake generally means that most card issuers will not pursue litigation. For one of the rare cases, see Martin v. American Express, Inc., 361 So. 2d 597 (Ala. Civ. App. 1978).

[94] 12 C.F.R. § 226.12 n.21.

[95] Regulation Z Commentary ¶ 12(b)(2)(iii)-1.

[96] Regulation Z Commentary ¶ 226.12(b)(2)(iii)-3.

[97] 12 C.F.R. § 226.12(b)(1).

[98] 12 C.F.R. § 226.12(b)(3).

whether or not it is received by any particular officer or employee of the card issuer.[99] The purpose of notifying the card issuer is to enable the issuer to circulate information through "hot sheets" and alerts to warn merchants not to accept the card for purchase transactions.

The limitation on liability applies, however, only if the use of the card is unauthorized. An unauthorized use is "the use of a credit card by a person, other than the cardholder, who does not have actual, implied, or apparent authority for such use, and from which the cardholder receives no benefit."[100] Both actual and implied authority are based on manifestations of the principal to the agent.[101] They differ in the degree of specificity of the manifestations. A father who gives a card to his son to make a specific purchase has conferred actual authority to use the card for that purpose. Giving the son the card to use on a trip to Florida is a more general direction that confers implied authority. It can raise an issue concerning the scope of implied authority. For instance, the authorization probably covers transportation expenses and food and lodging to and from Florida, but it may not apply to an extension of the trip to the Bahamas. Irrespective of the breadth or narrowness of the scope of implied authority in the case, apparent authority probably has been created. The manifestations of this form of authority run to the person with whom the agent deals and reasonably lead that person to believe that the principal will be bound by the actions of the agent.[102] Despite a lack of direct contact between the cardholder and a merchant who honors it, the entrustment of the card to the control of the user appears to be sufficient to give rise to apparent authority, thereby making the cardholder responsible for charges made by the user even though they were outside the scope of either actual or implied authority.[103] The absence of any consent to the transfer and use of a card, however, precludes apparent authority when the card is used by someone who has stolen it.[104]

The case of *Walker Bank & Trust Co. v. Jones*[105] raises the issue of whether notification to the card issuer can terminate apparent authority created by entrusting a card to a person who refuses to return it. Mrs. Jones opened an account and authorized the issuance of a duplicate card in her husband's name. When the couple became estranged, Mrs. Jones wrote to the card-issuing bank indicating that her husband was no longer authorized

---

[99] 12 C.F.R. § 226.12(b)(3).

[100] 12 C.F.R. § 226.12 n.22.

[101] RESTATEMENT (SECOND) OF AGENCY § 7 (1957).

[102] RESTATEMENT (SECOND) OF AGENCY § 8.

[103] Mastercard v. Town of Newport, 396 N.W.2d 345 (Wis. Ct. App. 1986) (card issued to town clerk for official purchases but used for personal expenses not an unauthorized use); Transamerica Ins. Co. v. Standard Oil Co., 325 N.W.2d 210 (N.D. 1982) (use of business credit card for personal uses was not an unauthorized use).

[104] Vaughan v. United States Nat'l Bank, 79 Or. Ct. App. 172, 718 P.2d 769 (1986) (unauthorized use when card was taken without permission to make cash withdrawals that were kept by the user); Society Nat'l Bank v. Kienzle, 463 N.E.2d 1261 (Ohio Ct. App. 1983) (unauthorized use when wife stole card from estranged husband).

[105] 672 P.2d 73 (Utah 1983).

to use the card. The bank insisted upon the return of both cards, referring to such a requirement in the cardholder agreement. Both spouses continued to use their cards, until ultimately the bank sued Mrs. Jones for the unpaid balance.

The court held that the $50 limitation under the Truth in Lending Act did not apply because the husband's use of the card was not unauthorized. The husband had apparent authority because the wife had consented to the issuance of the card in his name and merchants honoring the card would not have reason to suspect unauthorized use. The court felt that the notice to the bank did not affect the authorization for use, but rather only eliminates subsequent liability within the $50 limitation for uses that are unauthorized.

The dissenting opinion raises good points concerning the burden that the majority places on the cardholder. It can be very difficult for a cardholder to retrieve a card from someone to whom its was entrusted when the relationship between the parties has soured. The task might prove to be even impossible in circumstances in which the individual with the card disappears. The dissent also argued that the issuer is in the better position to take actions to protect affected parties. Following notification from the cardholder, the issuer can close the account and include the card number on the list distributed to merchants that indicates cards that they should not accept. Admittedly, the issuer cannot apprise merchants of this information instantaneously and some time might elapse during which further charges are made on the account. The alternative approach of the majority, however, creates cases in which persons who open accounts can not terminate their liability for charges made by a person who will not voluntarily return an entrusted card unless they bring legal action against the person entrusted with the card, and even that option is unavailable when the person with the card cannot be located.

The truth in lending rules limiting liability for unauthorized use apply irrespective of any negligence of the cardholder that contributes to the improper use. They differ from the approach to checks taken under the U.C.C. in which a customer whose negligence substantially contributes to unauthorized withdrawals bears the entire resulting loss.[106] The cardholder's liability for the initial $50 of unauthorized use prior to notification is included as an incentive to cardholders to be vigilant in reporting loss of the card and to be careful with their cards to avoid loss. The initial liability, however, is a form of strict liability that applies equally to cardholders irrespective of whether they actually exercised appropriate care. If a mugger inflicts bodily harm resulting in the hospitalization of a cardholder and uses the credit card taken in the mugging to make several charges before the cardholder is physically capable of notifying the issuer of the

---

[106] U.C.C. § 3-406. The negligence rules of section 4-406 also are not applied in the credit card context. For discussion of these negligence rules in the context of checks, see § 10.02 *supra*.

theft, the cardholder is nevertheless liable for the first $50 of the unauthorized charges.[107]

The limitation on unauthorized use of credit cards is another one of the provisions of the Truth in Lending Act that applies to business credit cards.[108] Thus, the $50 upper limit also applies to both business and consumer cardholders. However, a card issuer can enter into a separate agreement with any organization that supplies ten or more cards issued by the same card issuer for use by its employees.[109] The agreement on liability for unauthorized use cannot result in any liability being imposed on an employee of the organization beyond what is imposed on consumer cardholders.

[G] Criminal Liability for Fraud

The initial amendments to the Truth in Lending Act also provided penalties for fraudulent use of credit cards. Further amendments in 1974 expanded the enumerated prohibitions, decreased the amount required to constitute a federal violation, and increased the maximum punishment. A fine and imprisonment of not more than ten years can be imposed on anyone who obtains anything of value aggregating $1,000 in value during a one-year period through the use of a counterfeit, fictitious, altered, forged, lost, stolen, or fraudulently obtained credit card.[110] The prohibition also reaches attempts and conspiracies to make such fraudulent uses of credit cards, as well as transporting such cards in interstate commerce or using instrumentalities of interstate commerce to sell such cards. The same penalties apply to anyone who knowingly receives or uses anything purchased by fraudulent card transactions if the aggregate value during any one-year period is $1,000 or more.[111] Finally, persons who provide anything in credit card transactions that aggregates a value of at least $1,000 during a one-year period is also liable if they know that the card they accept is counterfeit, fictitious, altered, forged, lost, stolen, or fraudulently obtained.[112]

Congress provided additional means to attack fraudulent card use with the enactment as part of the federal criminal code of the Credit Card Fraud

---

[107] If the mugger took the victim's checkbook and forged checks that were debited to the victim's account, the bank would have to recredit the entire amount of the forged checks. U.C.C. § 4-401. *See* § 12.01[B] *supra*.

[108] 15 U.S.C. § 1645.

[109] 15 U.S.C. § 1645; 12 C.F.R. § 226.12(b)(5).

[110] 15 U.S.C. § 1644(a); United States v. Bice-Bey, 701 F.2d 1086 (4th Cir.), *cert. denied*, 464 U.S. 837 (1983) (unauthorized use of account number held to be a violation in order not to defeat congressional purpose of the provision); United States v. Callihan, 666 F.2d 422 (9th Cir. 1982) (unauthorized use of account number held not to violate the provision). *See also* United States v. Kasper, 438 F. Supp. 1208 (E.D. Pa. 1980) (despite fraudulent intent to not pay for charges made on a card, defendants held not to have violated the provision by purchasing the card from a cardholder who later reported the card as lost or stolen, because the card was acquired without using fraud).

[111] 15 U.S.C. § 1644(d); United States v. Mikelberg, 517 F.2d 246 (5th Cir. 1975), *cert. denied*, 424 U.S. 909 (1976) (aggregated purchases from more than one credit card).

[112] 15 U.S.C. § 1644(f).

Act of 1984.[113] It applies to access devices, which, in addition to credit cards, includes other means to access an account to obtain property or services or to transfer funds.[114] Prohibited conduct, which always requires an intent to defraud[115] and involvement of interstate commerce, includes producing, using or trafficking in counterfeit access devices; using or trafficking in unauthorized access devices and obtaining during any one-year period anything of value aggregating $1,000 or more through such devices;[116] possessing fifteen or more counterfeit or unauthorized access devices; and producing, possessing, or trafficking in device-making equipment.[117] Acts in furtherance of an offense and conspiracies to commit the offenses are also made criminal violations.[118] The penalties include fines and imprisonment up to twenty years.[119]

[H] Treatment of Credits

The Fair Credit Billing Act, which was added as Chapter 4 to the Truth in Lending Act in 1974, addresses credit card billing practices. One of the areas covered is the handling of credits to a cardholder's account. These procedures are important under credit card plans that allow grace periods during which a balance can be paid in full to avoid finance charges and in plans that apply finance charges on daily balances. A creditor is required to credit a payment to a consumer's account as of the date of receipt.[120] Date of receipt is defined to mean "the date that the payment instrument or other means of completing the payment reaches the creditor."[121] For example, payment by check is received the day the creditor receives the check rather than the collected funds for the check.

Regulation Z also addresses the crediting process for returned goods. A creditor other than the card issuer must send a credit statement through normal channels to the card issuer within seven days after accepting a return of goods or forgiving a debt for services that is to be reflected as a credit on the cardholder's account.[122] The card issuer must then credit

---

[113] Chap. XVI, Title II of the Continuing Appropriations and Crime Control Act, Pub. L. No. 473, 98 Stat. 2183 (1984) (adds § 1029 to Chap. 47 of Title 18 of United States Code).

[114] 18 U.S.C. § 1029(e)(1). Cards, plates, codes and account numbers are all included.

[115] The requirement to establish that an access devise was "obtained with intent to defraud" eliminates the scope problem of the "fraudulently obtained" requirement of the TIL Act that was revealed in the *Kasper* case. See n. 110 *supra*.

[116] The aggregation is made irrespective of the number of cards involved in the criminal's activity.

[117] 18 U.S.C. § 1029(a).

[118] 18 U.S.C. § 1029(b)(2).

[119] 18 U.S.C. § 1029(c). Nearly all of the states also have credit card fraud statutes. For the citations to these statutes and a broad overview of their content, see Comment, *Credit Card Fraud: The Neglected Crime*, 76 J. of Crim. L. & Criminology 746, 748-50 (1985).

[120] 12 C.F.R. § 226.10(a).

[121] Regulation Z Commentary ¶ 226.10(a)-2.

[122] 12 C.F.R. § 226.12(e); Federal Trade Comm'n v. World Travel Vacation Brokers, Inc., 861 F.2d 1020 (7th Cir. 1988) (merchant purposely retained credit slips longer than allowed to improve cash flow position).

the cardholder's account within three days of receiving the credit statement.[123]

[I] Error-Resolution Procedures

Another major feature that the Fair Credit Billing Act added was mandatory error-resolution procedures.[124] The computerization of the billing process led to heightened consumer frustrations as attempts to resolve errors often proved difficult. The new amendment extended consumer protection by requiring credit card issuers to investigate alleged errors and to respond promptly to the customer.[125] The card issuer is required to disclose the billing-error-resolution procedures to customers at regular intervals.[126] The TIL Act and Regulation Z prescribe several inclusions or omissions, which if reflected on or with a periodic statement, constitute billing errors.[127]

To invoke the error-resolution procedures the consumer must send a written notice that is received by the creditor within sixty days after the creditor transmitted the first periodic statement that reflected the billing error.[128] Unless the creditor completes its required error-resolution procedures sooner, the creditor must respond with a written acknowledgment to the consumer within thirty days of receiving notice from the consumer.[129] Following an acknowledgment, the creditor must finish its required procedures within two complete billing cycles after receiving the notice from the consumer, but in no event more than ninety days.[130] A consumer's notice of an error essentially triggers a suspension of the disputed obligation because the creditor does not have to pay any portion of the obligation that the consumer believes is related to the disputed amount, including related

---

[123] 12 C.F.R. § 226.12(e)(2).

[124] State enactments preceded federal regulation in setting error-resolution responsibilities on card issuers. *See* California Song-Beverly Credit Card Act of 1971, Cal. Civ. Code §§ 1747.40, 1747.50.

[125] These rules do not extend to cards issued for business purposes. American Express Co. v. Koener, 452 U.S. 233 (1981). The rules do apply to all forms of credit card accounts, however, including travel and entertainment cards that do not qualify as open-end credit plans because they do not utilize finance charges. *See* Gray v. American Express Co., 743 F.2d 10 (D.C. Cir. 1984).

[126] *See* § 14.02[C][2], [3] *supra*.

[127] 15 U.S.C. § 1666(b); 12 C.F.R. § 226.13(a). These errors include extensions of credit that are not made to the consumer or a person authorized to use the consumer's credit card, credit charges that are not properly identified, extensions of credit for property or services not accepted by or delivered to the consumer, the failure to properly credit a payment or other credit issued to the consumer's account, computational errors, and charges for which the consumer requests additional clarification or documentary evidence. In addition, the failure to deliver a periodic statement to the consumer at least twenty days before the end of the billing cycle is a billing error that invokes the mandatory error resolution procedures.

[128] 12 C.F.R. § 226.13(b)(1); Himelfarb. v. American Express Co., 301 Md. 698, 484 A.2d 1013 (1984) (notice by telephone insufficient).

[129] 12 C.F.R. § 226.13(c)(1).

[130] 12 C.F.R. § 226.13(c)(2).

finance charges, and the creditor may not try to collect it.[131] In addition, the creditor is prohibited from making an adverse credit report concerning any of the disputed amount.[132]

A creditor's investigation of an alleged billing error will lead it to conclude that the error occurred as asserted, that a different billing error occurred, or that no error occurred. When the determination is that the error was correctly asserted, the creditor must, within the time limits indicated above, correct the error, credit the consumer's account with any disputed amount, including finance and other charges, and send a corrective notice to the consumer.[133] When the creditor determines, within the time limits and after a reasonable investigation, that an error did not occur or that the error differed from the one indicated by the consumer, the creditor must send the consumer an explanation for its belief, correct any different billing error it determined to exist, and provide the consumer upon request copies of documentary evidence of the consumer's indebtedness.[134] When the creditor determines that the consumer owes an obligation that was suspended pending resolution, the creditor must send the consumer written notification of the amount that the consumer still owes, including finance and other charges, and a statement of when the payment is due.[135]

When a creditor complies with its obligation to investigate and respond promptly to the consumer, it has no further error-resolution responsibilities, even if the consumer reasserts that the error did occur.[136] The creditor is prohibited from reporting the account delinquent until the consumer has the opportunity to pay during any applicable grace period or ten days, whichever is longer.[137] If the consumer reasserts the error in writing during this time frame, the creditor must indicate on any adverse creditor report that the amount or account is in dispute and must provide the consumer with a written notice of each person to which the report is sent.[138] The creditor also must promptly report subsequent resolutions of the dispute to each person to which the unfavorable credit report is sent. Other than these restrictions on reporting delinquency on the disputed account, the creditor is free to pursue collection. The error-resolution procedures are simply designed to force creditors to investigate alleged errors and to respond about them promptly. They are not determinative on the consumer's liability. Once they are properly completed, the creditor can pursue it collection rights and the consumer can assert its legal position.[139]

---

[131] 12 C.F.R. § 226.13(d)(1).

[132] 12 C.F.R. § 226.13(d)(2). On the opportunity for the creditor to cancel an account, compare Gray v. American Express Co., 743 F.2d 10 (D.C. Cir. 1984), with Smith v. Federated Dep't Stores, 165 Ga. App. 459, 301 S.E.2d 652 (1983).

[133] 12 C.F.R. § 226.13(e).

[134] 12 C.F.R. § 226.13(f).

[135] 12 C.F.R. § 226.13(g)(1).

[136] 12 C.F.R. § 226.13(h).

[137] 12 C.F.R. § 226.13(g)(3).

[138] 12 C.F.R. § 226.13(g)(4).

[139] A creditor who does not comply with the error-resolution procedures is subject to forfeiture of the amount of the claimed billing error, up to a maximum of $50. 15 U.S.C. § 1666(e).

[J] Claims and Defenses of Cardholders

Truth-in-lending law also addresses the extent to which claims and defenses that a cardholder has against the seller of goods or services can be asserted against the payment obligation to the card issuer. The general rule is that "[w]hen a person who honors a credit card fails to resolve satisfactorily a dispute as to property or services purchased with the credit card in a consumer credit transaction, the cardholder may assert against the card issuer all claims (other than tort claims) and defenses arising out of the transaction and relating to the failure to resolve the dispute."[140] The cardholder can withhold payment for the amount of credit that is outstanding for the transaction that gave rise to the dispute. Neither the Truth in Lending Act nor Regulation Z, however, determines whether an asserted claim or defense is valid against a merchant.[141] The assertion against the card issuer of a claim or defense that is not valid against the merchant who honored the credit card leaves the cardholder in default on the payment due to the card issuer. Truth-in-lending law preserves valid cardholder claims and defense that are available against the merchant.

The general rule is comparable to the FTC Rule that abrogates the holder in due course doctrine by preserving claims and defenses of consumers who issue negotiable instruments.[142] The FTC Rule requires the inclusion of a legend on the consumer paper indicating that any holder of the paper is subject to the claims and defenses that the debtor could assert against the seller of goods or services obtained with the paper. The general rule in the Truth in Lending Act and Regulation Z similarly preserves consumer cardholder claims and defenses against the card issuer who otherwise would enforce the payment obligation. The rationale underlying the general rule on credit cards also is similar to the reasoning that supports the FTC Rule. Card issuers are in a better position than consumers to cast losses back onto sellers of goods and services. The card issuer can exert control over business practices of merchants through recourse agreements and the denial of credit card services to unscrupulous merchants. Furthermore, as to the losses that cannot be cast back to the seller because of bankruptcy or other financial irresponsibility, the card issuer is also in a better position to implement loss spreading. The internalized costs of seller misconduct will cause the price paid by consumers for credit card services to rise and more accurately reflect the true social cost of these transactions.

The truth-in-lending rules also include some specific limitations not found in negotiable instruments law.[143] One requirement is that the cardholder must have made a good-faith effort to resolve the dispute with the person who honored the credit card.[144] Another limitation to a cardholder's right

---

[140] 12 C.F.R. § 226.12(c)(1).

[141] Determination of the validity of asserted claims and defenses is made under state or other applicable law that governs the underlying transaction. Regulation Z Commentary ¶ 226.12(c)-2.

[142] 16 C.F.R. Part 433. See § 6.06[B] *supra*.

[143] *See generally* Brandel & Leonard, *Bank Charge Cards: New Cash or New Credit*, 59 Mich. L. Rev. 1033 (1971).

[144] 12 C.F.R. § 226.12(c)(3)(i).

to assert a claim or defense against the card issuer based on an unresolved dispute with the person who honors the credit card is that the credit extended in the disputed transaction must exceed $50.[145] It would be uneconomical for card issuers to investigate and attempt to resolve disputes involving lesser amounts. The cardholder also does not have much money at risk in these transactions.

A geographical limitation also affects cardholders' rights to assert their claims and defenses. The disputed transaction must have occurred either within the same state as the cardholder's designated address or within 100 miles from that address.[146] This limitation is designed to confine the scope of the general rule to an area in which the card issuer has an opportunity to police the credit card practices of merchants who honor the card, although realistically the mechanism most likely to be relied upon by card issuers is a charge-back through the card system against the merchant for disputed transactions. The latter mechanism can be utilized just as effectively against merchants located outside the artificial geographic boundary.

When the cardholder is able to assert a relevant claim or defense against the card issuer, the cardholder is allowed to withhold payment of the amount of credit that is outstanding for the transaction that gave rise to the dispute.[147] When a cardholder does not pay an amount outstanding on a disputed transaction, the card issuer is prohibited from reporting that amount as delinquent until the dispute is settled or until judgment is rendered.[148] The prohibition does not preclude the card issuer from pursuing normal collection approaches for delinquent accounts.[149]

[K] Anti-Setoff Provision

State law generally allows a financial institution to setoff the amount owed on an account like a credit card account against money that had been deposited in another account maintained by the same financial institution. The Fair Credit Billing Act includes a provision that prohibits most of the opportunity for a card issuer to follow this practice for a cardholder's indebtedness that arises from a consumer credit transaction under the relevant credit card plan.[150] The covered indebtedness includes purchases, cash advances, check overdraft lines of credit, finance charges, or any other charges to an account incurred through a credit card plan.[151] Placing a hold on the account or freezing funds in an account are considered to be

---

[145] 12 C.F.R. § 226.12(c)(3)(ii).

[146] 12 C.F.R. § 226.12(c)(3)(iii); Hyland v. First USA Bank, 1995 U.S. Dist. LEXIS 14794 (E.D. Pa. 1995) (claim for breach of warranty against seller in a foreign country is not applicable, but trial was required to determine whether bank had waived the geographic limitation).

[147] 12 C.F.R. § 226.12(c)(1).

[148] 12 C.F.R. § 226.12(C)(2).

[149] Regulation Z Commentary ¶ 226.12(c)(2)-1.

[150] 15 U.S.C. § 1666h. *See also* 12 C.F.R. § 226.12(d)(1).

[151] Regulation Z Commentary ¶ 226.12(d)(1)-3.

functional equivalents of a setoff, and thus are also subject to the same general prohibition.[152]

The anti-setoff provision includes several exceptions.[153] The cardholder can provide written authorization for the credit card balance to be deducted from a deposit account held by the card issuer. A card issuer who obtains and enforces a consensual security interest in the funds on deposit is not subject to the prohibition against setoffs. State law collection remedies are retained for bank creditors by excluding the setoff prohibition to attachment or levy upon deposited funds. Finally, a card issuer is still entitled to obtain and enforce court orders directed toward deposited funds.

---

[152] Regulation Z Commentary ¶ 226.12(d)(1)-1.
[153] 12 C.F.R. § 226.12(d)(2), (3).

Chapter 15

ELECTRONIC FUND TRANSFERS

SYNOPSIS

§ 15.01   The Systems
    [A]   Introduction
    [B]   Automated Clearinghouses (ACHs)
    [C]   Bill Payment by Telephone
    [D]   Automated Teller Machines (ATMs)
    [E]   Point-of-Sale Systems (POS)
    [F]   Check Guarantee
    [G]   Wire Transfers
    [H]   Smart Cards

§ 15.02   The Electronic Fund Transfer Act and Regulation E
    [A]   Background
    [B]   Scope
    [C]   Card Issuance
    [D]   Disclosure
    [E]   Liability for Unauthorized Transfers
    [F]   Documentation
    [G]   Error Resolution
    [H]   Stop Payment
    [I]   Financial Institution Liability
    [J]   Enforcement

§ 15.03   Operating Rules and Regulation J
    [A]   Automated Clearinghouses (ACHs)
    [B]   Debit Cards
    [C]   Wire Transfers

§ 15.04   Article 4A of the U.C.C.
    [A]   Scope
    [B]   Transfer Relationships
        [1]   Acceptance
            [a]   By a Receiving Bank Other Than the Beneficiary's Bank
            [b]   By the Beneficiary's Bank
        [2]   Rejection
        [3]   Payment
    [C]   Allocation of Loss
        [1]   Erroneous Execution
        [2]   Erroneous Payment Orders
        [3]   Unauthorized Transfers

[4] Insolvency

§ 15.01 The Systems

[A] Introduction

The means of making payments has evolved through several extremely significant historic developments. Exchanges initially were possible only through a simple barter system. That system was largely surpassed with the introduction of money systems, which in turn have been displaced to a significant extent by a banking and commercial paper system. The next evolutionary stage is currently in the process of development and implementation. It involves electronic fund transfers. The transfer and processing of paper is replaced in these systems by the electronic transmission, processing and storage of data. Several different systems are in use already and are expected, along with new technological developments, to be expanded for both commercial and consumer use.

[B] Automated Clearing Houses (ACHs)

Regional automated clearing houses were established in the early 1970s. Several of these regional clearing houses formed the National Automated Clearing House Association (NACHA) in 1974. In 1978 the Federal Reserve System made its communications network available to connect NACHA and other institutions.[1] All of the United States is now included in the service area of an automated clearing house association.

Instead of clearing checks, an automated clearing house processes electronic items. Debit and credit entries from originating institutions are received by the ACH either recorded on magnetic tape or transmitted electronically.[2] The ACH uses data-processing equipment to sort and balance the entries that it receives. Data from the entries relevant to each receiving institution is sent by magnetic tape or paper list, or also can be transmitted electronically.

When the originating and receiving institutions are both in the same service area, settlements are effected by the ACH through debits and credits in the accounts that the institutions maintain with the ACH. When the institutions are located in different service areas, the originating institution generally sends the entries to its local ACH. The Federal Reserve's interdistrict network then can be utilized by the ACH to forward the entries to the ACH located in the receiving institution's service area.

---

[1] 43 Fed. Reg. 17,402 (Apr. 24, 1978).

[2] The New York Clearing House Association, one of the largest processors, set January 1990 as its date to become fully electronic, at which time it would not deal with paper, magnetic tape, or messenger deliveries. *N.Y. Automatic Clearing House Nears Goal of Paperless Payments*, AMERICAN BANKER, Jan 13, 1989, at 2.

An ACH greatly increases the efficiency of a program like direct deposit of payrolls. In order to decrease mailing costs and the risk of theft of checks prior to their deposit, some employers in the 1970s began offering their customers direct deposit of their payroll checks. The employer issued a check to each participating financial institution for the payroll of all of its employees who kept their accounts at that institution. The institution, in turn, credited each employee's account for the amount of payroll payment indicated by instructions from the employer. The use of an ACH enables the employer to send the credit entries for all of its participating employees only to its own bank, rather than to each of its employee's financial institutions.

The employee must elect to participate in the preauthorized payroll deposit program by authorizing the employer to initiate credits for direct deposit and authorizing his or her financial institution to receive the credits.[3] Prior to the date on which the payroll payments are due, the employer prepares a magnetic tape indicating the payroll credits to be made for every employee who has agreed to participate in the program and delivers that tape to the employer's bank. The bank runs the tape through its data-processing equipment to remove all of the "on-us" entries, so that it can credit the accounts of employees who also happen to maintain accounts at the same bank, and forwards the resulting tape to the ACH. The ACH then sorts the entries, balances the accounts between the originating and the receiving institutions, and transmits the applicable entries to each of the receiving institutions so that they can credit the individual accounts of the respective employees as of the date that the payroll is due. The receiving institution notifies the employee that the credit has been made as scheduled and the preauthorized credit is reflected on the monthly statement of account activity that is sent by the receiving institution to each of its customers.

The federal government has an extensive direct deposit program under which recurring payments can be deposited directly in the recipient's bank account. The biggest element of the Federal Direct Deposit Program is social security payments, but it includes many other payments, such as military service payments, certain federal agency salaries, civil service retirement and annuity, and revenue sharing payments. Some nonrecurring payments, like payments to federal contractors, also can be authorized for direct deposit in the recipient's account.

A customer can also give prior authorization for ACH debit transfers. These preauthorizations are most commonly given for recurring payments in the same amount, such as mortgage or insurance payments. Authorization for variable recurring bills, such as utilities, is also sometimes given. For each billing cycle, the company prepares a magnetic tape that indicates the customer accounts and amounts to be debited for each customer who has signed a debit authorization form. The tape is sent to the billing

---

[3] A 1988 survey found that almost half of the employees who have been offered direct payroll deposits utilize the service. *52% of Firms Use Direct Deposit*, AMERICAN BANKER, Aug. 31, 1988, at 1.

company's bank, and the data processing equipment at the bank removes all of the "on-us" entries and debits the accounts of these customers according to the indicated amounts. The tape with all of the other entries is sent to the ACH, where the entries are sorted, settlements are made, and the respective debit entries are forwarded to each financial institution where customers who authorized the debits maintain their accounts.

[C] Bill Payment by Telephone

Telephone transfer systems can be implemented to provide customers with a convenient way to make payments of non-recurring bills. When bills are received, the customer can call his or her bank with instructions to pay individual payees. With a touch-tone telephone, the information can be transmitted electronically. The customer's account number and identification number are entered, as well as the identification number of the merchant and the amount and date of the payment. Rotary-dial telephones require a human operator to orally receive the order or a tape recorder for the instructions which are later processed. When the customer and the merchant maintain accounts at the same financial institution, the transfer of funds can be made directly between the accounts. If the payee banks at a different institution, direct payment by bank check can be used to transfer the funds. A more efficient approach, however, is to transfer funds to the payee's financial institution through an ACH. The customer receives a monthly statement that indicates all of the payments made and the payees.

Although banking by telephone can offer services in addition to bill paying, such as balance requests and transfers of funds between accounts, its lack of two features has diminished its consumer acceptance. Many consumers prefer to obtain a receipt of the transaction at the time that it is conducted. Furthermore, banking by telephone cannot disburse cash, so the customer is still required to visit a bank or automated teller machine to obtain money. Projects of home banking using home computers are seeking solutions to these problems, but the high investment costs have left many financial institutions reluctant to proceed. Home banking services are continuing to grow, but at a slower rate than had been anticipated.

[D] Automated Teller Machines (ATMs)

An automated teller machine is a terminal that enables a consumer to conduct several banking service transactions without the assistance of a teller. ATMs free bank personnel from these routine transactions, as well as provide access to the services at locations remote from the financial institution and at all hours of the day and night. Automated teller machines can supplement the cash payment system by disbursing cash to consumers. They also operate as EFT systems by taking deposits, transferring funds between accounts, answering balance inquiries, and making payments. They also can be used for credit transactions by disbursing cash for small loans against credit cards or overdraft services on checking accounts. The versatility of these machines accounts for the substantial growth in machine availability and usage that occurred during the 1980s.

A customer's account is accessed by inserting a pre-approved credit or debit card into the terminal and typing the customer's personal identification number (PIN) on the keyboard. The customer responds to instructions displayed on a television screen to enter the appropriate transaction information. Once all of the information is entered and verified by the customer, the terminal completes the transaction, and returns the customer's card and printed receipt of the transactions, along with any cash withdrawn by the customer.

[E] Point-of-Sale Systems (POS)

Like the ATM, point-of-sale systems utilize a debit card issued by the customer's financial institution. Use of the card enables customers to pay for retail goods and services through automatic debiting of their accounts, rather than paying cash or by check. Point-of-sale terminals are located at participating merchants' businesses and operated by their employees. The systems are likely to be economically feasible only at businesses with a high volume of transactions.

A point-of-sale system operates somewhat like an automated teller machine. When the total price is tallied at the merchant's check-out counter, the customer inserts the debit card into the terminal and enters his or her personal identification number. The merchant also enters an identification number and the relevant data on the proposed transaction. This information is transmitted electronically to the customer's bank. If the account contains sufficient funds to cover the transaction, an approval is transmitted back to the merchant and the transaction is closed. The customer's account is immediately debited in the amount of the transaction, and the merchant's account is credited for the same amount. If the customer's account does not have enough money to cover the transaction, a rejection is transmitted back to the merchant and the customer cannot complete the purchase by debit card.

A POS system would be relatively straight-forward if the customer and the merchant both maintained their accounts with the same financial institution. Such a requirement, however, would greatly limit the availability of the system to many prospective customers. Shared POS systems enable several financial institutions to tie into a single network. A switch is utilized in these systems to route the transaction messages from each participating merchant to the financing institution with which the customer maintains an account.

[F] Check Guarantee

Check-guarantee systems utilize some of the electronic equipment used in point-of-sale transactions, but they are designed to facilitate the acceptability of checks to merchants. The person desiring to write a check to pay for a purchase inserts an identification card in the terminal at the merchant's location. The transaction data is transmitted through an ACH to a depositor account data base, which in turn transmits back an authorization or rejection, depending upon the state of the customer's account. These systems generally guarantee the payment of the check issued in accordance with the transmitted information. The systems sometimes are tied only to a centralized negative file to determine if bad risk information is on file about the drawer. Other systems simply verify that the drawer has an account with the drawee bank and that there are currently sufficient funds to cover the check, but without guarantees of payment.

[G] Wire Transfers

Financial institutions and commercial enterprises require the means to transfer large sums of money quickly for payment and settlements for their own accounts or the accounts of their customers. Two primary systems are used for these purposes. Fedwire is the Federal Reserve Wire Network, a system operated by the Federal Reserve System. The Clearinghouse Interbank Payment System (CHIPS) is operated by the New York Clearing House Association. In addition, the Society of Worldwide Interbank Financial Telecommunication (SWIFT) is a privately-operated international communications system for financial messages.

Although the Federal Reserve System from its inception in 1913 initially sent messages through Western Union, it quickly established its own system, which progressed from a Morse code system, to a teletype system, and finally to an automatic message system. The current system was fully automated in 1973, utilizing a central switch facility. With additional communications switches in district offices and each Federal Reserve Bank, nearly instantaneous communications and transfers of funds can be made among institutions participating in the network.[4]

Money transfers are made on Fedwire by means of credit transfers of account balances. A financial institution with a Federal Reserve account instructs its Federal Reserve Bank to transfer funds to another institution with a Federal Reserve account. Institutions and other customers who do not maintain accounts with the Federal Reserve can ask an institution that has an account to transfer funds by Fedwire. If the sending and receiving banks each maintain their accounts with the same Reserve bank, their accounts are debited and credited respectively. Otherwise, the sender's Federal Reserve Bank debits the account of the sender and credits the account of the receiver's Federal Reserve Bank, while the latter Reserve bank in turn debits the account of the sender's Reserve Bank and credits the receiver's account.

Fedwire does more than simply transmit financial messages; it makes transfers of actual funds. The transfer results through the settlement of accounts described above. Fedwire transfers are settled as the transactions are made. Irrespective of who initiates the transfer, a fund transfer through the Federal Reserve System is considered to be paid on receipt of the communication from Fedwire, and that payment is guaranteed by the full credit

---

[4] The average daily value transferred over Fedwire by the end of 1986 was $700 billion. AMERICAN BANKER, Dec. 15, 1980.

of the U.S. government. Settlement of the banks with the Fed is not accomplished, however, until the end of the day. It results through a netting of the debit and credit positions of the banks for transactions conducted during the day, and balances in member accounts maintained with the Fed are adjusted accordingly.

CHIPS also clears electronic fund transfers of large dollar amounts. The system is owned by the twelve New York banks that comprise the New York Clearing House. A party who wishes to transfer funds by CHIPS requests its bank to effectuate the transfer to the recipient's bank. The sending bank makes the transfer over CHIPS if it is a member of the system; otherwise it must use a correspondent associate. The transmittal of the transfer through CHIPS does not result in an actual change in deposits as occurs in a Fedwire transfer. CHIPS participants send payment messages during the day. The central computer constantly records the transactions and messages as they are made, and at the end of the day it produces a balance position report showing the daily new debit and credit position for all participants. CHIPS participants settle with one another on a daily basis in the early evening. Settlement payments are accumulated and distributed by means of an escrow account of the system maintained in the New York Federal Reserve Bank. CHIPS participants who send more payments during a day than they receive must transfer funds by Fedwire to this account to cover the difference owed. Funds are not actually moved through any part of this network until the end of the day.

SWIFT is a nonprofit cooperative society that provides international transmission of messages related to fund transfers among its members. It has more than 1,200 members in more than fifty countries. SWIFT is solely a message-communications system concerning funds-transfer transactions among its members. These messages result in debits and credits on bank books, but the system does not effect actual transfer of funds or provide any settlement capacity. SWIFT does not require members to maintain funds on deposit for settlement and it does not compute the net positions of members banks. Settlement is accomplished through bilateral agreements between member institutions. SWIFT is designed to provide its members with the necessary facilities for the telecommunication, transmission, and routing of international financial messages.

[H] Smart Cards

The use of smart cards has increased substantially in recent years. A stored value of funds is maintained on a computer chip or magnetic strip on the card itself. The card can then be used to purchase goods or services without any prior authorization required from a central database. The amount for each use is deducted from the card as each transaction is completed. The more simple applications have only a single use, such a public transit or telephone services, and the card is disposed of after it is depleted. More sophisticated cards can have a greater variety of uses and they can be reloaded with additional value, either by a teller or an ATM machine. The legal framework that will regulate these transactions is still uncertain because they do not fit neatly into any of the existing legal regimes.

§ 15.02 The Electronic Fund Transfer Act and Regulation E

[A] Background

Electronic fund transfers are not within the scope of Articles 3 or 4 or any other provisions of the U.C.C. Article 3 covers negotiable instruments, and to be negotiable, the promise to pay money must be in writing.[5] "Written" means an "intentional reduction to tangible form,"[6] and consistent with the treatment of negotiable instruments as a type of indispensable paper, verbal and electronic orders or promises to pay money do not constitute instruments.[7] Article 4 deals with bank collection of "items," which are defined as "an instrument or a promise or order to pay money handled by a bank for collection or payment."[8] Payment orders governed by Article 4A, as well as credit and debit card slips are specifically excluded from the scope of the definition.[9]

An effort was undertaken to provide one comprehensive statutory scheme that would apply, to the extent possible, a uniform set of principles to all forms of payment systems.[10] The approach was based on the premise that the rights and liabilities of participating parties should not vary a great deal depending on the type of payment system utilized.[11] Although skepticism that common principles could be applied to all payment systems ultimately caused the project to fail, its demise was also hastened by an unwillingness to reduce consumer protections provided by applicable law outside of the Uniform Commercial Code. As with the case of credit card payments, a substantial body of federal law governs consumer rights and liabilities in electronic fund transfers.

---

[5] U.C.C. §§ 3-104(a), 3-103(a)(6), (9).

[6] U.C.C. § 1-201(46).

[7] *See* § 2.02[c][1] *supra*.

[8] U.C.C. § 4-104(a)(9).

[9] *Id.*

[10] The 3-4-8 Committee of the Permanent Editorial Board of the Uniform Commercial Code spearheaded the project. Its efforts culminated in the issuance for public comment of Permanent Editorial Board Draft No. 3 of a proposed Uniform New Payments Code. If it had been enacted, this Code would have replaced most of U.C.C. Article 4 and the federal legislation on electronic fund transfers that is discussed in this Chapter. In addition it would have superceded substantial portions of U.C.C. Article 3 and the federal Truth in Lending Act.

[11] For commentary on the ill-fated proposed New Payments Code, see Ellis, *The Uniform New Payments Code: Highlights of Proposed Changes in U.C.C. Articles 3 and 4*, 23 Am. Bus. L.J. 617 (1986); Leary & Fry, *A "Systems" Approach to Payment Modes: Moving Toward a New Payments Code*, 16 U.C.C. L.J. 283 (1984); Miller, *A Report on the New Payments Code*, 39 Bus. Law. 1215 (1984); Scott, *Corporate Wire Transfers and the Uniform New Payments Code*, 83 Colum. L. Rev. 1664 (1983).

The primary federal legislation is the Electronic Fund Transfer Act (the EFT Act), which was enacted in 1978.[12] Pursuant to the enabling authority of the Act, the Federal Reserve Board promulgated Regulation E to implement the statute.[13] Regulation E became effective on May 10, 1980. Congress determined that the use of electronic systems to transfer funds can be to the advantage of consumers, but was concerned about the application of consumer protection to the unique aspects of the new electronic technologies.[14] Thus, the primary purpose of the EFT Act "is the provision of individual consumer rights."[15]

[B] Scope

The EFT Act regulates electronic fund transfers. The term "electronic fund transfer" is defined in the Act to mean:

> any transfer of funds, other than a transaction originated by check, draft, or similar paper instrument, which is initiated through an electronic terminal, telephonic instrument, or computer or magnetic tape so as to order, instruct, or authorize a financial institution to debit or credit an account. Such term includes, but is not limited to, point-of-sale transfers, automated teller machine transactions, direct deposits or withdrawals of funds, and transfers initiated by telephone.[16]

The definition requires a transfer of funds initiated by one of the specified electronic means that results in a debit or credit to an account.[17]

The definition of "electronic fund transfer" was amended in Regulation E in 1984 to include "[t]ransfers resulting from debit card transactions, whether or not initiated through an electronic terminal."[18] This extension of the definition effectively picks up point-of-sale transactions initiated through a paper sales draft similar to bank credit card transactions when the customer uses a debit card. The Federal Reserve Board reasoned that these transactions can be conceived as being electronically initiated because most of the sales slips are truncated and converted to electronic form for further transmission. Although its approach does considerable violence to the original concept of an electronic fund transfer, the Board was motivated by concerns that a legal vacuum of consumer protection for debit card transfers not involving electronic terminals would exist if these transactions were not brought within the scope of the EFT Act and Regulation E.[19]

---

[12] Title XX of the Financial Institutions Regulatory and Interest Rate Control Act of 1978, Pub. L. No. 95-630, 92 Stat. 3728, 15 U.S.C. §§ 1693-1693r.

[13] 12 C.F.R. Part 205.

[14] For coverage of the legislative history of the EFT Act, see Brandel & Oliff, *The Electronic Fund Transfer Act: A Primer*, 40 Ohio St. L.J. 531, 538-40 (1979).

[15] 15 U.S.C. § 1693 (findings and purpose).

[16] 15 U.S.C. § 1693a(6).

[17] Check truncation systems are not covered because the fund transfer is initiated by the issuance of a check.

[18] 12 C.F.R. § 205.3(b)(5).

[19] 49 Fed. Reg. 40,794-95 (1984).

The term account is also defined. It means "a demand deposit (checking), savings, or other consumer asset account (other than an occasional or incidental credit balance in a credit plan) held either directly or indirectly by a financial institution and established primarily for personal, family, or household purposes."[20] The EFT Act thus does not cover transactions involving only commercial accounts. Only consumer asset accounts are within the scope of the Act. Payments made by placing money into an automated teller machine would not be covered because a credit account would be involved.

The EFT Act and Regulation E specifically exclude several transfers of funds that involve some use of electronic transmissions. Any check guarantee or authorization service is excluded if it does not directly result in a debit or credit to the consumer's account.[21] If the funds for the check are not actually paid until it is received, the fund transfer is paper initiated and the Act does not apply. On the other hand, if the funds are paid from the customer's account upon authorization or guarantee, the payment transfer is triggered by the electronic transmission and the EFT Act would apply. Wire transfers also are specifically excluded.[22] The use of any wire network that is used primarily for transfers between businesses or financial institutions does not qualify, even though the wire transfer of funds is for a consumer.[23] Another exclusion is for transfers whose primary purpose is the purchase or sale of securities or commodities regulated by the Securities and Exchange Commission or the Commodity Futures Trading Commission.[24] Electronic payment of interest and dividends to a consumer's account would not be excluded, however, because it does not involve the purchase or sale of securities.

The EFT Act further specifically excludes from its scope "any automatic transfer from a savings account to a demand deposit account pursuant to an agreement between a consumer and a financial institution for the purpose of covering an overdraft or maintaining an agreed upon minimum balance in the consumer's demand deposit account."[25] The exclusion depends upon automatic transfers pursuant to an agreement between the consumer and financial institution, so that an individual request for fund transfers is not covered by the exclusion. Regulation E also excludes certain categories of individual transfers initiated without a specific request from the consumer, including transfers between a consumer's accounts within the financial institution, such as a transfer from a checking account to a savings account, and transfers from a consumer's account to an account of another family member held in the same financial institution.[26] Transfers of funds that are initiated by a telephone conversation between a consumer

---

[20] 12 C.F.R. § 205.2(b)(1).
[21] 15 U.S.C. § 1693a(6)(A); 12 C.F.R. § 205.3(c)(2).
[22] 15 U.S.C. § 1693(a)(6)(B); 12 C.F.R. § 205.3(b).
[23] 12 C.F.R. § 205.3(c)(3).
[24] 15 U.S.C. § 1693a(6)(C); 12 C.F.R. § 205.3(c)(4).
[25] 15 U.S.C. § 1693a(6)(D).
[26] 12 C.F.R. § 205.3(c)(5).

and personnel of a financial institution, provided that they are not made under a telephone bill payment plan or other prearranged agreement under which the parties contemplate periodic or recurring transfers, are also excluded from the scope of the EFT Act.[27]

An additional exclusion was made available for small institutions. They do not have to comply with Regulation E for preauthorized transfers to and from their customer's accounts if they have assets of $100 million or less.[28] The burden of compliance on these institutions was considered excessive because the only electronic fund transfers they receive are often from federal recurring payment programs. Any other electronic funds services offered by these institutions, such as ATMs, are subject to the EFT Act and Regulation E.

[C] Card Issuance

The EFT Act includes limitations on the opportunity for companies and financial institutions to issue EFT cards or other access devices to consumers.[29] Rather than following the approach taken in response to the concerns over unsolicited credit cards, which precludes issuance of a card unless it is requested by the consumer,[30] Congress steered a middle course on the issuance of debit cards. Its choice was an attempt to provide consumer protection while avoiding the unfavorable competitive advantage that accrued to credit card issuers who had already distributed unsolicited cards prior to federal regulation.

EFT cards and access devices can be sent to consumers under the general rule only in response to a request or an application or as a renewal of or substitution for a card or devise that has been previously accepted.[31] Notwithstanding the general rule, unsolicited cards and access devices can be issued when four conditions are satisfied.[32]

(1) The access device is not validated;

(2) The distribution is accompanied by a complete disclosure . . . of the consumer's rights and liabilities that will apply if the access device is validated;

(3) The distribution is accompanied by a clear explanation that the access device is not validated and how the consumer may dispose of the access devise if validation is not desired; and

(4) The access devise is validated only in response to the consumer's oral or written request or application for validation and after

---

[27] 15 U.S.C. § 1693a(6)(E); 12 C.F.R. § 205.3(c)(6).

[28] 12 C.F.R. § 205.3(c)(7).

[29] Regulation E defines an "access device" to mean "a card, code, or other means of access to a consumer's account, or any combination thereof, that may be used by the consumer to initiate electronic fund transfers." 12 C.F.R. § 205.2(a)(1).

[30] 15 U.S.C. § 1642. See § 14.02[E] supra.

[31] 15 U.S.C. § 1693i(a); 12 C.F.R. § 205.5(a). On the acceptance of an access device, see 15 U.S.C. § 1693a(1) and 12 C.F.R. § 205.2(a)(2).

[32] 15 U.S.C. § 1693i(b); 12 C.F.R. § 205.5(b).

verification of the consumer's identity by any reasonable means, such as by photograph, fingerprint, personal visit, or signature comparison.

Under this approach, an unsolicited card or access device can be sent to a consumer, provided that it is not validated.[33] A request or application by the customer is required before the card or device can be operational.

[D] Disclosure

The EFT Act and Regulation E impose disclosure requirements on financial institutions that are patterned on the Truth-in-Lending Act disclosure requirements for credit cards.[34] Initial disclosure is required at the time that the consumer contracts for the EFT services or before the first electronic fund transfer is made involving a consumer's account.[35] Regulation E indicates ten different subjects that must be included in an initial disclosure.[36]

(1) A summary of the consumer's liability for unauthorized electronic fund transfers.

(2) Address and telephone number of office to notify in the event of an unauthorized transfer.

(3) The business days of the financial institution.

(4) The type of electronic fund transfer the consumer is entitled to make, including any limitations on frequency and dollar amounts of transactions.

(5) Charges assessed for electronic fund transfers (such as a per-transfer charge) or for the right to make them (such as a monthly EFT service charge).

(6) A summary of the consumer's right to receive documentation for electronic fund transfers.

(7) A summary of the right and procedure to stop payment of a preauthorized EFT.

(8) A summary of the financial institution's liability to the customer for failure to make or stop certain transfers.

(9) The circumstances under which the financial institution in the ordinary course of business will disclose information to third parties concerning the consumer's account.

---

[33] An access device is considered validated when a financial institution has performed all procedures necessary to enable a consumer to use it to initiate an electronic fund transfer. 15 U.S.C. § 1693i(b); 12 C.F.R. § 205.5(b)(1).

[34] 15 U.S.C. § 1693c; 12 C.F.R. § 205.7. See § 14.02[C] supra.

[35] 12 C.F.R. § 205.7(a).

[36] 12 C.F.R. § 205.7(b). Most of these disclosure requirements are also included in 15 U.S.C. § 1693c(a). Model disclosure clauses available for optional use by financial institutions are provided for all of these subjects in Appendix A to Regulation E.

(10) A notice describing error-resolution procedures and the consumer's rights under them.

The EFT Act and Regulation E also include subsequent disclosure requirements. The error-resolution notice must be sent to consumers at least annually.[37] A shorter form of the notice can be used, provided it is substantially similar to the shorter form included in Regulation E and provided that it is included with a periodic statement sent to consumers. Financial institutions must also send subsequent disclosures to notify consumers of changes in terms or conditions concerning any subject on which initial disclosure is required. The EFT Act requires the disclosure to be in a disseminated writing at least twenty-one days prior to the effective date of the change when "such change would result in greater cost or liability for such consumer or decreased access to the consumer's account."[38]

[E] Liability for Unauthorized Transfers

The EFT Act and Regulation E limit the liability that can be imposed on consumers for unauthorized transfers. The term "unauthorized electronic fund transfer" is defined to mean "an electronic fund transfer from a consumer's account initiated by a person other than the consumer without actual authority to initiate such transfer and from which the consumer receives no benefit."[39] The reference to actual authority only, particularly following the reference to actual, implied or apparent authority in Regulation Z on unauthorized transactions with credit cards,[40] suggests that the Federal Reserve Board intended for purposes of Regulation E that an unauthorized transfer can be found even though it was made with apparent authority.

When a customer provides an access device to another person and that person initiates a transfer in accordance with the authority granted, the transfer is with actual authority of the consumer and it does not constitute an unauthorized electronic fund transfer.[41] Yet the Federal Reserve Board has also determined that if the person who is furnished the access device exceeds the actual authority granted, the consumer cannot successfully assert that the transfers are unauthorized but rather remains liable for them.[42] The definition of unauthorized transfer creates an exception to furnished-access-device cases, however, when "the consumer has notified

---

[37] 12 C.F.R. § 205.8(b).

[38] 15 U.S.C. § 1693c(b). *See also* 12 C.F.R. § 205.8(a).

[39] 15 U.S.C. § 1693a(11); 12 C.F.R. § 205.2(m).

[40] 12 C.F.R. § 226.12. *See* § 14.02[F] *supra*.

[41] The court in Ognibene v. Citibank, 112 Misc. 2d 219, 446 N.Y.S.2d 845 (N.Y. Civ. Ct. 1981), held that a customer who allowed a scam artist to use his ATM card in an adjoining machine in the belief that the bank wanted him to try the card to "unjam" the machine, did not preclude finding that the subsequent withdrawals by the scam artist were unauthorized. The customer did not provide the PIN that was needed to access the customer's account. Rather, that number was learned surreptitiously by the scam artist.

[42] 12 C.F.R. Part 205 Supp. I, 2(m) (unauthorized electronic fund transfer).

the financial institution involved that transfers by such other person are no longer authorized."[43] The Board has also clarified that a consumer is not considered to have furnished an access device for purposes of determining whether a transfer is unauthorized when the device is given up by fraud or robbery[44] or if the consumer is forced to initiate the transfer.[45]

Before a financial institution can impose any liability on a consumer for an unauthorized transfer, it must have satisfied three requirements.[46] First, the access device used to initiate the transfer must have been accepted by the consumer. Second, the financial institution must have provided a means to identify the consumer to whom the access devise was issued. Finally, the financial institution must have provided specific disclosure information to the consumer in writing.

When a financial institution has satisfied these requirements and can impose liability on a consumer for unauthorized transfers, The EFT Act and Regulation E control the extent of the liability that can be imposed. The general rule limits the consumer's liability to the lesser of $50 or the amount of transfers made before the consumer notifies the financial institution that they were unauthorized.[47] Two exceptions, however, can increase the extent of the consumer's liability substantially.

The first exception applies when the consumer fails to notify the financial institution within two business days after learning that the access device has been lost or stolen.[48] The maximum liability that can ever be imposed because of this failure to notify is $500. Liability cannot exceed the lesser of $500 or the sum of unauthorized transfers that occur before the close of the two business days up to a top limit of $50 plus the amount of unauthorized transfers that occur during the period after those two days and before notification and that the financial institution can establish would not have occurred if the consumer had notified it within two business days after learning of the loss or theft of the access device.[49] Note that the two-day

---

[43] 15 U.S.C. § 1693a(11); 12 C.F.R. § 205.2(m).

[44] 12 C.F.R. Part 205 Supp. I, 2(m) (unauthorized electronic fund transfer).

[45] Id.

[46] 12 C.F.R. § 205.6(a). See also 15 U.S.C. § 1693g(a). The financial institution bears the burden of proof to establish that these requirements have been satisfied. 15 U.S.C. § 1693g(b). Alternatively, the financial institution is required to prove that the electronic fund transfer was authorized. Id. The bank could not succeed in meeting this latter burden in Judd v. Citibank, 107 Misc. 2d 526, 435 N.Y.S.2d 210 (N.Y. Civ. Ct. 1980), where a consumer sued for $800 allegedly charged to her account in error. The customer testified that she was at work during the indicated withdrawal times from an ATM and that she had not allowed anyone to use the card or revealed her PIN to anyone. The bank countered only with evidence concerning their computerized records.

[47] 15 U.S.C. § 1693g(a); 12 C.F.R. § 205.6(b).

[48] 15 U.S.C. § 1693g(a); 12 C.F.R. § 205.6(b)(2).

[49] Assume that on Day 1 consumer's card is stolen and a $100 unauthorized transfer is made on June 2. Consumer learns of the theft on Day 3, and the next day another $25 unauthorized transfer is made. Day 5 is the close of two business days after consumer learned of the theft, but an additional $600 of unauthorized transfers are made on Days 7 and 8 that could have been prevented had notice been given by Day 5. Consumer notifies the bank on Day 9. Consumer's liability is calculated as follows: Although $125 of unauthorized transfers were

period designated in this exception is not based from the time that the access device is lost or stolen but rather from the time that the customer learns of the loss or theft.[50]

The second exception applies when the consumer fails to report any unauthorized electronic fund transfer that appears on a periodic statement within sixty days of the transmittal of the statement.[51] The failure to report leaves the consumer liable for any subsequent unauthorized transfers that occur thereafter and that the financial institution can establish would not have occurred if the consumer had notified it within the sixty-day period. This liability is potentially unlimited because it does not include a cap.[52] Furthermore, both of the exceptions can apply simultaneously under the right circumstances,[53] with unauthorized transfers occurring during the sixty-day period covered by the first exception and subsequent unauthorized transfers covered by the second exception.

With its three levels of liability for unauthorized transfers, the EFT Act and Regulation E do not adhere to either the U.C.C. or the Truth-in-Lending approaches. The unlimited liability exception creates an incentive comparable to section 4-406 to examine periodic statements and to report unauthorized transactions.[54] On the other hand, the EFT regulatory approach does not adopt the principles of section 3-406 which makes the customer liable for the entire loss if the customer's negligence substantially contributes to the loss of an access device.[55] The $50 limit for initial wrongful use constitutes a form of consumer protection that applies even when the consumer is negligent.[56] Even the obvious negligence of writing a personal identification number on the debit card itself does not increase the limited liability of the consumer.[57] The exceptions, however, do deviate

---

made before the close of two business days, $50 is the maximum liability for this period. Consumer is also liable for $450 of the $600 transferred after the close of business and prior to notice being given by Consumer, because the maximum total liability is $500. If the unauthorized transfers had all been made before Day 6, total liability could not exceed $50. See 12 C.F.R. Part 205 Supp. I, ¶ 6(b)(2).

[50] In many instances it will be an insurmountable burden for the financial institution to be able to establish when the consumer learned of the loss or theft. 15 U.S.C. § 1693g(b) (burden of proof on the financial institution).

[51] 15 U.S.C. § 1693g(a); 12 C.F.R. § 205.6(b)(3).

[52] Kruser v. Bank of America, 230 Cal. App. 3d 741, 281 Cal. Rptr. 463 (Cal. Ct. App. 1991) (cardholders liable for $9,020 for failure to notify bank).

[53] An access device must be involved in the unauthorized transfer for the consumer to be liable under the $50 and $500 tiers. 12 C.F.R. § 205.6(b)(3).

[54] See § 10.02[B][1] supra.

[55] See § 10.02[A][1] supra.

[56] The initial liability level of up to $50 is also a form of strict liability that applies even to customers who act with care.

[57] 12 C.F.R. Part 205 Supp I, (6)(b) (limitations on amount of liability); Russell v. First of Am. Bank-Mich., N.A., 1988 U.S. Dist. LEXIS 17226 (W.D. Mich. 1988) (because the consumer reported the loss or theft of her ATM card and PIN within the two-day time period, her extent of liability for unauthorized transfers was limited to $50 even if the PIN was written on or near the ATM card and an agreement with the bank that purported to increase the consumer's liability was unenforceable).

from the consumer protection model of truth-in-lending for credit cards by increasing the extent of consumer liability in certain circumstances. The periodic statement received by the consumer indicates debits already made to the account rather than the bill for payment that a credit card statement represents, thus justifying the requirement for consumers to verify their statements on debit card transactions and to notify the financial institution of unauthorized transfers. The other exception encourages prompt notification concerning lost and stolen access devices once the consumer learns that the loss or theft has occurred. The additional liability possible for unauthorized EFTs thus follows from the consumer's failure to provide timely notice to the financial institution.[58]

[F] Documentation

The EFT Act and Regulation E include requirements concerning the documentation of electronic fund transfers initiated by consumers.[59] Congress considered adequate information on account activity to be important for consumers to be able to keep track of their transactions and to ascertain any problems concerning electronic funds transfers. The documentation requirements cover receipts for transactions and periodic account statements.

A financial institution must make a receipt available at the time that an electronic fund transfer is initiated at an electronic terminal by a consumer.[60] Transfers that are initiated by most telephones are not covered by the receipt requirement.[61] Providing receipts in these circumstances would be quite burdensome and costly. The receipts required at electronic terminals must include six points of information "clearly set forth": (1) the amount of the transfer, (2) the date of the transfer, (3) the type of transfer and the consumer's accounts affected, (4) the number or code that uniquely identifies the consumer initiating the transfer, the customer's accounts, or the access device used, (5) the location of the terminal, and (6) the name of any third party to or from whom funds are transferred.

A financial institution must also provide periodic statements indicating the activity in any account to or from which electronic funds can be made.[62] The statement must include the amount of fees assessed, the account balances at the beginning and the close of the statement period, and the

---

[58] Required notice is given "when a consumer takes steps reasonably necessary to provide the institution with the pertinent information," whether or not the notice is actually received. 12 C.F.R. § 205.6(b)(5). *See also* 15 U.S.C.§ 1693g(a)(2). Written notice is governed by the traditional mailbox rule under which it is effective upon dispatch. Even though the consumer does not take affirmative action, "[n]otice may be considered constructively given when the institution becomes aware of circumstances leading to the reasonable belief that an unauthorized transfer to or from the consumer's account has been or may be made." *Id.*

[59] 15 U.S.C. § 1693d; 12 C.F.R. § 205.9.

[60] 15 U.S.C. § 1693d(a); 12 C.F.R. § 205.9(a).

[61] Telephones operated by a consumer are excluded from the definition of "electronic terminal." 15 U.S.C. § 1693a(7); 12 C.F.R. § 205.2(h).

[62] 15 U.S.C. § 1693d(c); 12 C.F.R. § 205.9(b).

address and telephone number to be used for inquiry or notice of errors, in addition to all of the information required on a receipt for EFTs initiated by a consumer at an electronic terminal. Statements must be sent on a monthly or shorter cycle for periods in which an electronic fund transfer has occurred, and at least quarterly if no transfer has been made.[63]

[G] Error Resolution

Errors are inevitable in the operation of any payment system, and the EFT Act and Regulation E provide a set of procedures to resolve them when they arise in electronic fund transfers.[64] The concept of error is defined very expansively in the regulation. The term "error" includes unauthorized transfers, incorrect transfers to or from the customer's account, omissions in periodic statements, computational or bookkeeping errors made by a financial institution, receipt of the incorrect amount of money from an electronic terminal, transfers that are not documented properly, and consumer requests for required documentation or additional information or clarification.[65] Routine consumer requests for information, like an account balance or information for tax or other record-keeping purposes, do not constitute a request that is sufficient to invoke the error-resolution procedures.[66]

A consumer who believes that an error has occurred must notify the financial institution within sixty days of the time that the periodic statement reflecting the error is transmitted.[67] The financial institution can require the customer to provide written confirmation of an oral notice within ten days, provided the consumer is advised of the requirement at the time the oral notice is given.[68] Notice by the consumer must include specified information. It must be sufficient to identify the consumer's name and account number. In addition, it must indicate that the consumer believes that an error exists in the account or documentation and the reasons for the belief, and, to the extent possible, the notice should indicate the type, the date, and the amount of the error.[69]

When it has received notice of an error from a consumer, the financial institution must investigate the alleged error promptly and make a determination within 10 business days.[70] Because some investigations might require more than ten days to properly investigate, a financial institution can pursue an alternative approach that will allow it forty-five days for investigation. A financial institution that utilizes the protracted error-resolution procedure, however, can not continue to deny the consumer

---

[63] Certain exceptions apply. 12 C.F.R. § 205.9(c).

[64] For a critique of the error resolution procedures, see Budnitz, *Federal Regulation of Consumer Disputes in Consumer Banking Transactions*, 20 Harv. J. on Legis. 31 (1983).

[65] 15 U.S.C. § 1693f(f); 12 C.F.R. § 205.11(a)(1).

[66] 12 C.F.R. § 205.11(a)(2).

[67] 15 U.S.C. § 1693f(a); 12 C.F.R. § 205.11(b)(1).

[68] 15 U.S.C. § 1693f(a); 12 C.F.R. § 205.11(b)(2).

[69] 15 U.S.C. § 1693f(a); 12 C.F.R. § 205.11(b)(1)(ii), (iii).

[70] 12 C.F.R. § 205.11(c)(1).

access to the disputed funds. To invoke the additional time for investigation the financial institution generally must provisionally recredit the consumer's account in the amount of the alleged error within ten days of receiving notice of the error.[71] The financial institution can withhold up to $50 from the amount recredited if it has reasonable grounds to believe that an unauthorized transfer occurred and that it has satisfied the requirements that make the consumer liable.[72]

When a financial institution determines that an error has occurred it must promptly correct the error, and the maximum time allowed is one day.[73] The financial institution must also notify the consumer about the correction within 3 business days of completing the investigation.[74] If the consumer's account was provisionally recredited under the forty-five day extended period for investigation, the notice to the consumer following determination of the error by the financial institution must indicate that the provisional credit granted has been made final.

Procedures are also required for when the financial institution determines that an error did not occur. The written report on the results of the investigation must include an explanation of the institution's findings and indicate that the consumer can request the documents the institution relied upon in making its determination.[75] If the financial institution had utilized the forty-five day period by provisionally crediting the consumer's account in the amount of the alleged error, it can debit the account for the recredited amount. It must notify the consumer of the debit and, in addition, inform the consumer of its obligation to continue to honor checks or drafts payable to third parties or preauthorized transfers from the account against the provisionally credited funds for five business days following transmittal of the notice.[76]

The statute provides for treble damages in certain civil actions for violation of the error-resolution procedures.[77] One circumstance for this recovery is when the financial institution does not provide a timely provisional recrediting of a consumer's account and the institution either fails to make a good faith investigation of the error or does not have a reasonable basis to believe that an error had not been made in the consumer's account. The other circumstance that triggers treble damages is when the financial institution knowingly concludes that an error had not been made in a consumer's account when that conclusion cannot be reasonably supported by the evidence available during the investigation.

---

[71] 15 U.S.C. § 1693f(c); 12 C.F.R. § 205.11(c)(2)(i).

[72] 12 C.F.R. § 205.11(c)(2)(i). On consumer liability for unauthorized transfers, see 12 C.F.R. § 205.6 and § 15.02[E] *supra*.

[73] 15 U.S.C. § 1693f(b); 12 C.F.R. § 205.11(c)(1), (2)(iii).

[74] 12 C.F.R. § 205.11(c)(1), (2)(iv).

[75] 15 U.S.C. § 1693f(d); 12 C.F.R. § 205.11(d)(1).

[76] 12 C.F.R. § 205.11(d)(2). The financial institution cannot charge any overdraft charges for any payments during this time against the provisionally credited funds. There is no requirement to honor items that would create an overdraft beyond the amount of provisionally recredited funds that have been debited.

[77] 15 U.S.C. § 1693f(e).

[H] Stop Payment

The EFT Act does not create a right for a consumer to reverse a completed transfer. Allowing such a right would leave the risk of nonpayment on the seller by enabling the consumer to undo the payment initiated by an electronic fund transfer. Instead, the position of the consumer who initiates an EFT transaction is comparable to payment made by cash. The consumer who is disappointed with the completed transaction must turn to available seller warranties or the willingness of the seller to correct deficiencies.

A consumer does have the right, however, to stop payment of a preauthorized electronic fund transfer from the consumer's account.[78] Thus, if a customer has signed a preauthorization debit agreement for payment of recurring utility bills, the customer is entitled to counter the payment authorization by issuing a stop-payment order. The order must be given up to three business days before the scheduled date of the transfer. It can be oral or in writing, but the financial institution can require written confirmation of an oral notice within fourteen days, provided that the requirement is disclosed at the time of the oral notification. When written confirmation is properly required, an oral stop-payment order ceases to be binding fourteen days after it is made. Once a stop-payment order is issued, the financial institution can suspend all subsequent payments to the designated payee until the consumer advises that payments should resume.[79]

[I] Financial Institution Liability

A financial institution incurs liability to a consumer for all of the damages that are proximately caused by the failure of the institution to make a properly initiated electronic fund transfer in the correct amount and in a timely manner.[80] The liability is comparable to the liability of a payor bank for wrongful dishonor of a properly issued check.[81] Several exceptions preclude liability of a financial institution. Again, like a payor bank under Article 4,[82] the financial institution does not have to make a transfer if the customer's account has insufficient funds or if the transfer would exceed an established credit line.[83] If the financial institution fails to make a transfer because of insufficient funds, it is liable if the inadequate funds are the result of its failure to credit a deposit of funds to the consumer's account that would have provided sufficient funds to cover the transfer.[84] Another exception to financial-institution liability for not completing a transfer results from a legal process or other encumbrance that restricts

---

[78] 15 U.S.C. § 1693e(a); 12 C.F.R. § 205.10(c).
[79] 12 C.F.R. Part 205 Supp. I, 10(c) (consumer's right to stop payment).
[80] 15 U.S.C. § 1693h(a)(1).
[81] U.C.C. § 4-402. See § 12.03[A][1] *supra*.
[82] U.C.C. § 4-401. See § 12.02[B][1] *supra*.
[83] 15 U.S.C. § 1693h(a)(1)(A), (C).
[84] 15 U.S.C. § 1693h(a)(2).

the transfer.[85] This exception also reflects the relationship between a payor bank and its customer under Article 4.[86] A financial institution also is excused from liability if the electronic terminal at which it is conducted has insufficient cash to complete the transaction.[87] Finally, an act of God or other circumstances beyond its control excuses a financial institution if it exercises due diligence,[88] and a consumer who knows of a technical malfunction but proceeds to initiate a transfer cannot hold the financial institution liable for failure to complete it.[89]

In addition to liability for failing to make a properly initiated electronic fund transfer, a financial institution is liable for all damages proximately caused by its failure to comply with a proper stop-payment order concerning a preauthorized transfer.[90] Yet again, the parallel to Article 4 is apparent.[91]

[J] Enforcement

The EFT Act provides both individual and class actions against any person or financial institution that fails to comply with its provisions.[92] The measure of recovery in an individual action is the sum of actual damages incurred, a civil penalty of not less than $100 nor greater than $1,000, costs of the action, and reasonable attorney fees.[93] Recovery in a class action is the sum of actual damages, such amount as the court may allow not exceeding the lesser of $500,000 or one percent of the net worth of the defendant, costs, and reasonable attorney's fees.[94] In any case the court is required to consider the frequency and persistence of noncompliance, the nature of noncompliance, and the extent to which noncompliance was intentional.[95] In addition to these factors, the court in determining damages in a class action should consider the resources of the defendant and the number of persons adversely affected.[96]

---

[85] 15 U.S.C. § 1693h(a)(1)(B).

[86] U.C.C. § 4-303(a) (legal process as one of the four legals). *See* § 11.03[D] *supra*.

[87] 15 U.S.C. § 1693h(a)(1)(D).

[88] Provided that the person to be paid has agreed to accept payment by EFT, the consumer's obligation to that person is suspended when the initiated transfer cannot be completed because of a system malfunction. The suspension lasts until the malfunction is corrected, unless the person to be paid makes a subsequent written demand for payment by means other than electronic fund transfer. 15 U.S.C. § 1693j.

[89] 15 U.S.C. § 1693h(b).

[90] 15 U.S.C. § 1693h(a)(3).

[91] U.C.C. § 4-402. *See* § 12.04 *supra*. *But see* § 9.02[B] *supra*.

[92] 15 U.S.C. § 1693m. The liability provisions of the EFT Act are patterned after similar provisions in the Truth In Lending Act. *See* § 14.02[D] *infra*.

[93] When a court determines that an unsuccessful action was brought in bad faith or to harass the defendant, it must award costs and reasonable attorney's fees to the defendant. 15 U.S.C. § 1693m(f).

[94] A minimum civil penalty is not provided for class actions. 15 U.S.C. § 1693m(a)(2)(B).

[95] 15 U.S.C. § 1693m(b)(1).

[96] 15 U.S.C. § 1693m(b)(2).

Civil liability can be avoided under several circumstances enumerated in the EFT Act. A defendant who can show by a preponderance of the evidence that the violation was not intentional and was the result of a bona fide error can escape liability, provided that the defendant used procedures that were reasonably designed to avoid such an error.[97] This exception does not preclude liability for actual damages proved, however, for cases in which a financial institution fails to complete a properly initiated electronic fund transfer or to comply with a proper stop-payment order.[98] Civil liability can also be avoided if the defendant acted in good faith compliance with any rule, regulation, or interpretation by the Federal Reserve Board or utilized an appropriate model disclosure form issued by the Board.[99] A person can also avoid civil liability by settling with the consumer prior to the initiation of legal action.[100] To qualify under this exception the prospective defendant must, before an action is commenced, notify the consumer of the failure, institute corrective measures for compliance, adjust the consumer's account, and, when applicable, pay any damages of actual loss for not completing a proper transfer or for not complying with a proper stop-payment order.

Knowing and wilful failure to comply with provisions of the EFT Act and knowingly and wilfully give false information or failing to provide required information can result in criminal liability.[101] The applicable penalties are a fine of not more than $5,000 or imprisonment for not more than one year, or both. The Act also includes the same provisions on fraudulent activities that are codified in the Truth In Lending Act, setting criminal penalties at up to $10,000, imprisonment up to ten years, or both.[102] The increased penalties for fraudulent traffic in access devices that become effective in 1984 also covers debit cards and other electronic fund transfer access devices.[103]

§ 15.03 Operating Rules and Regulation J

The Electronic Funds Transfer Act and Regulation E do not provide comprehensive treatment of the full range of electronic fund transfer activities. Consistent with the approach taken in the Truth in Lending Act for credit card transactions,[104] the federal legislation governing electronic funds transfers is oriented toward consumer protection. It controls the relationship between the consumer who sends the order and that consumer's financial institution. It does not control the transfer system itself or its participants, including the receiving financial institution, its customer, and

---

[97] 15 U.S.C. § 1693m(c).

[98] 15 U.S.C. § 1693m(c). These violations are indicated in 15 U.S.C. § 1693h(a). *See* § 15.02[I] *supra*.

[99] 15 U.S.C. § 1693m(d).

[100] 15 U.S.C. § 1693m(e).

[101] 15 U.S.C. § 1693n(a).

[102] 15 U.S.C. § 1693n(b). *See* § 14.02[G] *supra*.

[103] 18 U.S.C. § 1029. *See* § 14.02[G] *supra*.

[104] *See* § 14.02[A] *supra*.

the intermediaries. Transactions involving commercial accounts and wire transfers are excluded from all coverage of the EFT Act.[105] Having satisfied the perceived need for consumer protection that the EFT Act provides, Congress has not felt compelled to impose further controls but rather has preferred to allow these relatively novel services to develop competitively.

Because significant aspects of EFT operations have been left unregulated, operation of the systems and the relationship of the participants for the most part have been shaped by private contract. Most of the systems have developed their own sets of operating rules. The applicable rights and obligations of participants are generally indicated in these operating rules and in a membership agreement. The operating rules have the legal force of a mutilateral contract because through the membership agreement each participant agrees to be bound by the operating rules. The Federal Reserve Board has taken an administrative approach to Fedwire operations through provisions promulgated in Regulation J.[106]

[A] Automated Clearing Houses (ACHs)

Each of the regional automated clearing house associations, as well as the National Automated Clearing House Association (NACHA), have developed their own operating rules.[107] These rules cover the operation of the ACH and include timing requirements. They also specify the rights and obligations of sending and receiving institutions. The regional associations have patterned their rules more closely to the NACHA rules as interregional transfers have increased through the national association.[108] The NACHA rules have distinct provisions for consumer payments and corporate payments. For example, consumer depositors are allowed a return of funds pending resolution of an alleged unauthorized transfer, whereas a similar rule is not included in the corporate payments provisions.

An operating circular developed by NACHA and the Federal Reserve Banks deals with the capacity of Reserve Banks as automated clearing houses. It governs clearing and settlement of items, as well as the respective rights and obligations of these banks and other institutions that utilize the Fed's ACH services. Liability of a Federal Reserve Bank is specifically limited to losses from failure to exercise good faith or reasonable care.

A receiving bank faces potential liability to its depositor when credit or debit activity to the depositor's account is improper. The depositor enters into a standard debit or credit authorization agreement with a company or employer under which it agrees to the indicated debits or credits to its account and the receiving bank agrees to accept these entries. The receiving bank can incur liability for effecting entries without proper authorization, failing to execute required entries, making untimely debits or credits, or making entries in the incorrect amount.

---

[105] 15 U.S.C. § 1693a(6)(B); 12 C.F.R. §§ 205.2(b), 205.3(c)(3). See § 15.02[B] *supra*.

[106] 12 C.F.R. Part 210, Subpart B.

[107] National Automated Clearing House Ass'n, Operating Rules (1987).

[108] The NACHA rules are largely patterned on the rules developed in 1972 by California bankers for the Special Committee on Paperless Entries (SCOPE).

A company that receives an executed authorization must send a prenotification to the receiving bank, and actual transfer orders cannot be sent until ten days elapse after sending it. A new notification must be sent under a similar rule whenever a preauthorized electronic fund transfer from a consumer's account varies in amount from the previous transfer based on the same authorization, unless the consumer has specifically agreed to receive notice only if the transfer does not fall within a stated range of amounts or when the transfer differs from the most recent transfer by a stated amount.[109] This time period allows the receiving bank to verify the prospective order with its customer and to reject the prenotification if the depositor revokes the authorization.

NACHA operating rules allocate some risks back to the originating bank by establishing warranties that run from those banks to receiving banks and to the automated clearing house. For consumer payment transactions the warranties cover areas like the correctness of transmitted entries, the timeliness of these entries, the execution of an authorization by the depositor, compliance with prenotification requirements, and lack of knowledge of depositor revocation of the authorization. The originating bank is required to indemnify the receiving bank for any liability occasioned by breach of these warranties. The NACHA rules impose these warranty requirements on originating banks rather than the companies who initiate the credit or debit entries because it assures receiving banks that the warranties run from a regulated financial institution rather than from a company whose character and solvency are unknown to the receiving institution. Originating banks, having been allocated the risks associated with these warranties, have an incentive to screen the companies that they deal with and to enter into contractual provisions with these companies that will provide necessary protection.

[B] Debit Cards

Private contracts also govern many of the relationships in debit card transactions. Automated teller machine (ATM) and point-of-sale (POS) transactions ultimately involve many participants, including financial institutions, parties who process the transactions, and merchants, as well as the cardholder who initiates the transfer. The use of shared facilities by several financial institutions increases the interrelationship of parties in these transactions. Like the ACH approach, the rights and obligations of the financial institutions, the system, and the processors is largely determined through membership agreements and the operating rules that are incorporated through those agreements.

The card issuer is generally the participant that is allocated the risk associated with fraud and credit loss. When the electronic fund transfer

---

[109] This rule was originally set at seven days, but it was changed in 1980 to correspond to a comparable requirement in the adoption of Regulation E that specifies ten days. 12 C.F.R. § 205.10(d). The original NACHA operating rules preceded the enactment of the EFT Act, and therefore had to be modified to reflect the consumer protection requirements of the Act and Regulation E.

system is fully operational the authorization of the card issuer is required before a transaction can be completed. The card issuer is in the best position, therefore, to determine that the transaction is being initiated with someone using an appropriate access device with the corresponding personal identification number and that there are sufficient funds in the cardholder's account. Card issuers usually can chargeback losses that they incur when the system is fully operational only when a prior participant or components of the system owned by other participants make a processing error. On the other hand, a merchant might proceed with a transaction even though part of the system is temporarily inoperable, thereby preventing direct authorization by the card issuer. The merchant is allowed to proceed by preparing written sales drafts or by storing the transaction data and transmitting it later when the system becomes operational again. The lack of prior authorization by the card issuer, however, generally means that the merchant bears the risk of loss in these transactions.

Because of the importance of being able to rely upon the transmission of authorizations for debit card transactions, the operating rules of EFT networks generally impose performance standards on members of the system. The standards are directed in part toward the dependability of each member's electronic processing equipment. The equipment must be operative and available to complete transactions in a very high percentage of the system operating time in order to comply. The equipment must also have sufficient capability to be able to respond to transmitted messages within just seconds. This standard is included to assure that debit card transactions can be completed quickly so that they can be promoted as a convenient alternative to other payment systems. The EFT system generally levies charges against participants who do not comply with the performance standards, and persistent substandard performance can lead to expulsion from the system.

In most EFT systems merchants who employ POS terminals at their checkout counters are participants in the system but are not members of the system. Merchants generally are brought into the system through a sponsoring bank member. Assurances that nonmember merchants will comply with the operating procedures of the system are attained by various means. Sometimes the system dictates that agreements between sponsoring bank members and merchants must provide a binding commitment on the part of the merchant to observe system rules or include certain of the rules themselves. Other systems require the merchant-sponsoring member bank to assume the risk of loss associated with their merchants' failure to conform to system rules, thereby creating the incentive for the sponsoring members to include provisions in their contracts with merchants to pass such losses back to the noncomplying merchant.

[C] Wire Transfers

The rules and procedures that govern wire transfers on Fedwire are contained in Subpart B of Regulation J[110] and operating circulars that are

---

[110] 12 C.F.R. Part 210, Subpart B.

issued by Federal Reserve Banks.[111] The initial version of these rules covered settlement and the procedures and mechanics for conducting transactions on the wire network. Regulation J fixes the extent of liability of the Federal Reserve System for the operation of Fedwire.[112] Consequential damages are precluded, even if they are foreseeable.[113]

The New York Clearing House has adopted rules to govern the operation of the CHIPS system.[114] These rules cover operational procedures and settlement requirements, as well as loss-allocation principles.[115] The primary focus is on the liabilities of the CHIPS system itself, rather than on the participants in the system. Any losses that occur because of mistakes made within the system are not borne by CHIPS but rather must be settled directly between the involved participants. Losses caused because of fraud fall on the entity in which the fraud occurred, either a participant or the Clearing House. The liability of the CHIPS system, however, is limited to the extent of its $25 million insurance coverage. Any additional fraud losses occasioned within the Clearing House are allocated pro rata to each participant based on dollar amounts of wire transactions during the prior month.

Although payment obligations become final once they are sent by a CHIPS participant, the rules include a special settlement procedure for use when a CHIPS participant is unwilling or unable to meet is commitments by the deadline for settlements. All of the transfers to and from that participant are deleted from the system and the settlement is made without that bank. This process is known as "unwinding." The affected parties are left to their own private agreements to work out settlements of the deleted transactions.

Under rules adopted by SWIFT,[116] the system incurs liability for direct losses up to a maximum amount of insurance coverage for losses caused by negligence or fraud of SWIFT employees. Losses beyond the maximum are apportioned among participants making claims for recovery. The rules also allocate interest loss that arises because of delays in processing among SWIFT and transaction participants. Because SWIFT provides message services, without settlement services, participants must make arrangements among themselves for settlement. The SWIFT rules do allocate responsibilities of both sending and receiving banks in using the SWIFT

---

[111] Regulation J authorizes each Reserve Bank to issue these operating circulars. 12 C.F.R. § 210.25(c).

[112] 12 C.F.R. § 210.32(a).

[113] 12 C.F.R. § 210.38(b). This provision was added as an amendment in reaction to Evra v. Swiss Bank Corp., 673 F.2d 951 (7th Cir. 1982). The Seventh Circuit held that the common-law rule on foreseeability adopted in *Hadley v. Baxendale* applies to wire transfers, thereby exposing institutions who mishandle wire transfers to the possibility of consequential damages.

[114] Rules Governing the Computerized Clearing House Interbank Payments System (as amended, April 1986).

[115] On loss allocation, see generally Lingl, *Risk Allocation in International Interbank Electronic Funds Transfers: CHIPS & SWIFT*, 22 Harv. Int'l L.J. 621 (1981).

[116] S.W.I.F.T., User Handbook (1979).

network, but they do not include any provisions concerning failures to execute these responsibilities.

As the discussion above indicates, the primary focus of the wire-system rules and of Regulation J on wire transfers is on liability of the system and not on allocation of losses among participants of the system. The relationship between originators of transfers and intended recipients of wire-transfer proceeds with their respective financial institutions supposedly has been covered by contracts between these participants, but actual practice has revealed deficiencies in this approach. These contracts often do not exist, and when they do, they fail to address many fundamental risk-allocation issues.[117] The lack of established industry standards in this area makes the achievement of consensus among the various participants difficult to attain through private contract. Both customers and banks have proven to be hesitant to assume purposely the risks that are associated with wire-transfer transactions. The uncertainty as to whether the courts would accept the private risk-allocation aspects of an agreement also created a disincentive to undertake efforts to include them in agreements with customers.

In the absence of applicable system rules and relevant private contract provisions, the common law has been the only remaining source by which to resolve litigated issues between wire-system participants. This body of law is inadequate to provide much of the needed guidance because most of the cases involve telegraph companies and the cases simply do not address many of the issues that have arisen in wire transfer transactions. The common law simply never developed much in the context of bank transfers because the relatively small number of participants in these transactions historically tended to resolve their disputes through gentlemen's agreements. That approach withered, however, in the face of increased participants, new technological innovations, and increased monetary values transferred by wire.

The combination of these forces joined to create an environment that was neatly summarized by a noted commentator as follows: "Ironically, . . . , the payment system transferring the greatest value is governed by a poorly developed framework of legal rules."[118] This need for a legal framework led to the promulgation of Article 4A of the Uniform Commercial Code, which is discussed below. The Federal Reserve Board revised Subpart B to Regulation J substantially to make it conform with Article 4A.[119]

---

[117] Scott, *Corporate Wire Transfers and the Uniform New Payments Code*, 83 Colum. L. Rev. 1164, 1674 (1983), citing Bank Administration Institute, Studies in Funds Transfer, Operations and Automation Survey Findings (1982). The discussion of the deficiencies of private contract and the common law in the wire transfer context draws on Professor Scott's fine article. Common law case citations are also included. *See id.* at 1674-78.

[118] Scott, *Corporate Wire Transfers and the Uniform New Payments Code*, 83 Colum. L. Rev. 1664 (1983). Based on figures for 1980, $19 trillion was transferred by check and $49 billion by bank credit card, compared with $117 trillion of funds transferred by wire transfers. *Id.*, citing Arthur D. Little, Inc., Issues and Needs in the Nation's Payment System 12 (1982).

[119] 12 C.F.R. § 210, Subpart B (1991).

§ 15.04 Article 4A of the U.C.C.

[A] Scope

Article 4A deals with funds transfers.[120] It "governs a method of payment in which the person making payment (the 'originator') directly transmits an instruction to a bank either to make payment to the person receiving payment (the 'beneficiary') or to instruct some other bank to make payment to the beneficiary."[121] Payments by check and credit card are excluded from this coverage because the order to the bank to pay the payee is not given directly to the bank but rather is delivered to the payee who must then collect it from the drawee bank.[122] Article 4A covers payments in which the payor issues the payment order directly to his or her bank. Section 4A-108 specifically excludes application of the new Article to funds transfers that are in any manner governed by the Electronic Funds Transfer Act.[123]

The scope of Article 4A encompasses both the overall transaction and the individual series of actions that are necessary to effectuate it.[124] The terms used to represent the full transaction and the incremental steps respectively are "funds transfer" and "payment order." Unless the payor and the payee both have accounts at the same bank, more than one banking institution will be required to complete a funds transfer. Furthermore, because payment orders are settled between banks by debit and credit entries to their accounts, additional correspondent banks may be necessary in order to complete a transfer. Consequently, a funds transfer may require a series of additional payment orders between banks in order to effect the payment ordered by a customer.

As can be anticipated before even examining any of the substantive provisions, some rules will apply in the context of the entire funds transfer transaction, whereas other rules will focus on the narrower relationship of an individual payment order. The drafters thus logically have provided definitions to designate the applicable parties in both of these contexts. Different definitions thus can apply to the same party depending upon the context in which the reference to the party is made.

An illustration of a typical funds transfer that involves three payment orders provides an appropriate means to explain these definitions and the scope of Article 4A.[125] Assume that X owes a large sum of money to Y. X calls his bank (Bank A) and orders the bank to pay this sum to Y's account in Bank B. Because Bank A does not maintain an account with Bank B, it utilizes Bank C, a bank that is a correspondent of both Bank A and Bank

---

[120] U.C.C. §§ 4A-101, 4A-102.

[121] U.C.C. § 4A-104, Comment 1.

[122] U.C.C. § 4A-103(a)(1)(iii) and Comment 5. On check collections and credit cards, see Chapters 11 and 14, respectively.

[123] On coverage of this Act, see § 15.02 *supra*.

[124] U.C.C. § 4A-102, Comment.

[125] Comment 1 to section 4A-104 provides three examples, based on adding further participants. The illustration used here is the third illustration in the comment.

B. Bank A proceeds by issuing an instruction to Bank C to pay the sum to Y's account in Bank B. Bank C in turn instructs Bank B to pay the money to Y's account. The diagram provided below shows the three payment orders comprising the funds transfer, and the relevant terms that apply to the participants.

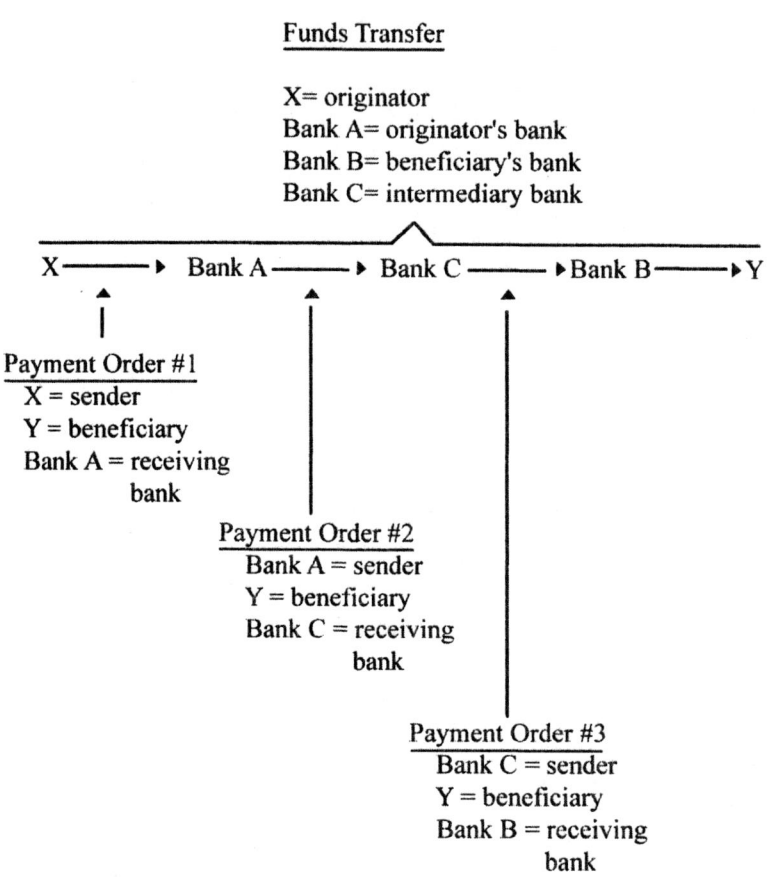

Diagram 15.1

The instruction from X (the sender) to Bank A (the receiving bank) is the first payment order. A payment order is "an instruction of a sender to a receiving bank . . . to pay, or to cause another bank to pay, a fixed or determinable amount of money to a beneficiary."[126] In this illustration, X ("the person giving the instruction to the receiving bank")[127] gives Bank A ("the bank to which the sender's instruction is addressed"),[128] an

---

[126] U.C.C. § 4A-103(a)(1).
[127] U.C.C. § 4A-103(a)(5).
[128] U.C.C. § 4A-103(a)(4).

instruction to cause another bank to pay the beneficiary Y ("the person to be paid by the beneficiary's bank").[129] Bank A complies with the order it receives by sending another payment order with the same instruction to Bank C. In the context of this second payment order, Bank A is the sender, Bank C is the receiving bank, and Y is again the beneficiary. A third payment order is still necessary for Bank C to comply with the order that it received. On this last payment order Bank C is the sender and Bank B is the receiving bank; Y again is the beneficiary. Bank B now is in the position to make the payment to Y's account that motivated X's issuance of the first payment order.

The entire transaction that includes these payments orders is a funds transfer. Funds transfer means "the series of transactions, beginning with the originator's payment order, made for the purpose of making payment to the beneficiary of the order."[130] In the illustration, as "the sender of the first payment order," X is known as the originator of the funds transfer.[131] Each of the banks also has a specific designation for purposes of the funds transfer context. Bank A is the originator's bank because it is "the receiving bank to which the payment order of the originator is issued."[132] Bank B is the beneficiary's bank, "the bank identified in a payment order in which an account of the beneficiary is to be credited pursuant to the order."[133] Bank C is an intermediary bank since it does not qualify as either the originator's bank or the beneficiary's bank.[134]

A funds transfer might involve as few as one payment order. This minimum-payment-order funds transfer is commonly referred to as a "book transfer" because it is accomplished when the originator and the beneficiary both have their accounts in the same bank and the bank effects the payment by debiting the account of the sender and crediting the account of the beneficiary.[135] The bank in a book transfer is both the originator's bank and the beneficiary's bank.

Although the payments covered by Article 4A are commonly referred to as wire transfers, the means of transmission of the payment order do not determine the applicability of Article 4A. The definition of payment order specifically indicates that the instruction of the sender can be "transmitted

---

[129] U.C.C. § 4A-103(a)(2). Bank B is the beneficiary's bank, which means "the bank identified in a payment order in which an account of the beneficiary is to be credited pursuant to the order or which otherwise is to make payment to the beneficiary if the order does not provide for payment of an account." U.C.C. § 4A-103(a)(3).

[130] U.C.C. § 4A-104(a). "The term includes any payment order issued by the originator's bank or an intermediary bank intended to carry out the originator's payment order. A funds transfer is completed by acceptance by the beneficiary's bank of a payment order for the benefit of the beneficiary of the originator's payment order." *Id.*

[131] U.C.C. § 4A-104(c).

[132] U.C.C. § 4A-104(d). This part of the definition applies when the originator is not a bank. When the originator is a bank, it is also the originator's bank. *Id.*

[133] U.C.C. § 4A-103(a)(3).

[134] U.C.C. § 4A-104(b).

[135] U.C.C. § 4A-104, Comment 1.

orally, electronically, or in writing."[136] Payment orders between banks generally are transmitted electronically. An originator who is a bank customer, however, will generally transmit the order by making a telephone call to the originating bank or by delivering a written payment order.

Several provisions in the scope and definition sections purposely restrict the primary focus of Article 4A to payments that are commonly known as wholesale funds transfers. For the most part, the targeted transactions are the low-volume, high-value payment transactions conducted between businesses and financial institutions. Consumer payment transactions are characterized by much lower dollar amounts for each payment but a tremendously higher volume of payment orders. A corporate wire transfer can be for millions of dollars, whereas a check is more likely to be written in the range of hundreds of dollars or less. The exclusion of funds transfers that have any applicability under the Electronic Fund Transfer Act[137] is aimed directly at excluding consumer-related transactions from the scope of Article 4A. The requirement that a payment instruction be sent to a bank to qualify as a payment order[138] and thus invoke Article 4A is similarly motivated. It excludes transfers initiated through Western Union or some other entity outside of the banking system because the excluded transfers are primarily simple consumer transactions involving small amounts of money.[139]

Article 4A also applies only to credit transfers. A payment instruction sent to a receiving bank can qualify as a payment order only if "the receiving bank is to be reimbursed by debiting an account of, or otherwise receiving payment from, the sender."[140] The provision excludes debit transfers under which a company, acting under preauthorization of a customer, issues an instruction to the customer's bank to transfer money from the customer's account to the company's bank. Payment of the debit transfer is made by debiting the account of the bank's customer rather than reimbursement from the sender of the order. Such debit transfers are not within the scope of Article 4A.

[B] Transfer Relationships

[1] Acceptance

Acceptance is a pivotal concept in Article 4A. Rights and obligations do not arise under a payment order until a receiving bank accepts it. A payment order is simply a request by the sender to a receiving bank which

---

[136] U.C.C. § 4A-103(a)(1).

[137] U.C.C. § 4A-108.

[138] U.C.C. § 4A-103(a)(1).

[139] U.C.C. § 4A-104, Comment 2. Another requirement for an instruction to qualify as a payment order is that it "does not state a condition to payment to the beneficiary other than time of payment." U.C.C. § 4A-103(a)(1)(i). This requirement excludes applicability to instructions that require actions by the beneficiary, such as a letter of credit that conditions transfer of funds on delivery of documents.

[140] U.C.C. § 4A-103(a)(1)(ii).

the receiving bank can either accept or reject.[141] The legal consequences of an acceptance vary based upon whether the payment order is issued to the beneficiary's bank or to a bank other than the beneficiary's bank.

[a] By a Receiving Bank Other Than the Beneficiary's Bank

Acceptance of a payment order by a receiving bank other than the beneficiary's bank occurs only when the receiving bank executes the order.[142] It is the exclusive method of acceptance by these banks. The receiving bank executes a payment order that it receives when it issues its own payment order "intended to carry out the payment order received by the bank."[143] Acceptance thus is the receiving bank's compliance with the request to execute the sender's payment order by issuing its own payment order to either the beneficiary's bank or an intermediary bank.

A receiving bank that is not the beneficiary's bank incurs obligations to the sender upon acceptance. Generally, the receiving bank is obligated in issuing its payment order to comply with the sender's order and with instructions on the funds transfer system to be used, the means for transmittal of payment orders in the funds transfer, and the selection of intermediary banks.[144] In the absence of instructions, a receiving bank can use any commercially reasonable funds transfer system and select an intermediary bank through the exercise of ordinary care.[145] The receiving bank is excused from following the sender's instructions on the funds transfer system if the receiving bank determines in good faith that compliance is not feasible or would unduly delay completion of the transfer.[146]

Execution by a receiving bank must also be timely. An originator will often indicate a concern that the funds transfer be completed rapidly by instructing that it be carried out by telephone, by wire transfer, or by the most expeditious means. The receiving bank does not have to comply literally with this instruction so long as it utilizes a commercially reasonable means that is just as expeditious.[147] When the sender's instructions state a payment date, the receiving bank must transmit its order at a time

---

[141] U.C.C. § 4A-209, Comment 1.

[142] U.C.C. § 4A-209(a).

[143] U.C.C. § 4A-301(a).

[144] U.C.C. § 4A-302(a). Instructions of the originator must also be passed along to intermediary banks and observed by them if they accept the payment order. *Id.*

[145] U.C.C. § 4A-302(b).

[146] U.C.C. § 4A-302(b). For example, a computer malfunction that would delay the designated method of transmittal would allow the receiving bank to select in good faith another method. The same flexibility is not available to the receiving bank when the sender designates the intermediary bank for the routing. "The sender's designation of that intermediary bank may mean that the beneficiary's bank is expecting to obtain a credit from that intermediary bank and may have relied on that anticipated credit. If the receiving bank uses another intermediary bank the expectations of the beneficiary's bank may not be realized." U.C.C. § 4A-302, Comment 2.

[147] U.C.C. § 4A-302(a)(2), (c).

and by a means to allow payment to the beneficiary on the indicated date.[148]

If a receiving bank breaches these rules in its execution of a payment order and causes a delay in payment to the beneficiary, the receiving bank must pay interest on the amount of the order for the period of the delay.[149] The interest can be paid to either the originator or the beneficiary. The general practice is to pay the beneficiary to make the beneficiary's position the same as if the funds transfer had been timely.[150]

Acceptance of a payment order by a receiving bank imposes obligations on the sender, as well as upon the receiving bank. Acceptance obligates the sender to pay the bank the amount of the order.[151] However, if the funds transfer is not ultimately completed by acceptance by the beneficiary's bank of the order instructing payment to the beneficiary, the sender's obligation to pay the receiving bank is excused.[152] The receiving bank must refund payment to the sender to the extent that the sender has paid an order that it is not obligated to pay.[153]

[b] By the Beneficiary's Bank

Acceptance by the beneficiary's bank can occur in more than one way. The beneficiary bank can pay the beneficiary[154] or notify the beneficiary of receipt of the order or of the crediting of the account for the amount of the order.[155] The notification will not constitute acceptance, however, if it also indicates that the bank is rejecting the payment order or that the credited funds cannot be withdrawn until the sender of the order settles for it. When the beneficiary's bank does not accept through payment or notice to the beneficiary it accepts when it receives payment of the sender's order.[156] Acceptance by the beneficiary bank is automatic when the payment order is issued by Fedwire because final payment is made by the Federal Reserve Bank upon receipt of the payment order.[157] Acceptance by the beneficiary bank occurs at the earliest time that one of these indicated methods is realized.[158]

---

[148] U.C.C. § 4A-302(a)(2).

[149] U.C.C. § 4A-305(a). See U.C.C. § 4A-506 on the rate of interest.

[150] U.C.C. § 4A-305, Comment 1.

[151] U.C.C. § 4A-402(c); Donmar Enterprises, Inc. v. Southern Nat'l Bank, 828 F. Supp. 1230 (W.D. N.C. 1993) (bank not required to return money to sender when sender indicated the beneficiary in an ambiguous manner).

[152] U.C.C. § 4A-402(c).

[153] The refund must include interest from the date of payment. U.C.C. § 4A-402(d).

[154] U.C.C. § 4A-405(a). See § 15.04[B][3] *infra*.

[155] U.C.C. § 4A-209(b)(1).

[156] U.C.C. § 4A-209(b)(2). On payment by the sender, see U.C.C. § 4A-403 and § 15.04[B][3] *infra*.

[157] U.C.C. § 4A-209, Comment 6.

[158] Yet another method of acceptance is available in cases of book transfers. See U.C.C. § 4A-209(b)(3).

Upon acceptance a beneficiary's bank incurs liability to the beneficiary, but none to either the sender or the originator. Acceptance obligates the beneficiary's bank to pay the amount of the order to the beneficiary.[159] The bank must also notify the beneficiary of receipt of the order when the order instructs payment to the beneficiary's account.[160] Otherwise, notification is required only if the order requires it.[161] Under Regulation CC the bank must make the funds available for electronic payments "not later than the business day after the banking day on which the bank received the electronic payment."[162]

Acceptance of a payment order by the beneficiary's bank establishes liability beyond the duty owed by the beneficiary's bank. The sender of the payment order also becomes liable upon the acceptance of its order to pay the amount of the order to the beneficiary bank.[163] Thus, it should be noted, the payment obligations created under Article 4A for all of the parties is ultimately tied to acceptance by the beneficiary's bank. It establishes liability of the sender to pay the beneficiary's bank, and for the latter to pay the beneficiary. It also precludes excuse of the obligation of a sender to pay a payment order that is accepted by a receiving bank other than a beneficiary's bank.[164]

As the discussion above indicates, a completed funds transfer involves a series of payment orders in which the participants become indebted through the process of acceptance. An originator pays a beneficiary by causing the beneficiary's bank to become indebted to the beneficiary in the amount of the payment.[165] The discussion below explains that the originator pays the beneficiary upon acceptance of a payment order in the funds transfer by the beneficiary bank.[166] The title of Article 4A follows convention, but nevertheless is something of a misnomer. No funds or other property rights of the originator are transferred to the beneficiary. The series of payment orders create payment obligations.

Unlike payment by means of a negotiable instrument, a sender does not become liable by issuing a payment order.[167] The sender's obligation to pay arises only upon acceptance by the receiving bank, and liability of a sender on a payment order does not extend to anyone else. Receiving banks are not comparable to collecting banks under Article 4. "No receiving bank, whether it be an originator's bank, an intermediary bank or a beneficiary's bank, is an agent for any other party in the funds transfer."[168]

---

[159] U.C.C. § 4A-404(a).

[160] U.C.C. § 4A-404(b). The notice must be given "before midnight of the next funds-transfer business day following the payment date." *Id.*

[161] U.C.C. § 4A-404(b).

[162] 12 C.F.R. § 229.10(a), (b).

[163] U.C.C. § 4A-402(b).

[164] *See* § 15.04[B][1] *supra.*

[165] Article 4A, Funds Transfers, Prefatory Note.

[166] *See* § 15.04[C] *infra.*

[167] U.C.C. § 4A-403, Comment 3.

[168] U.C.C. § 4A-212, Comment.

[2] Rejection

The duty of a receiving bank to accept a payment order is determined by an underlying agreement that it has with the sender or through requirements of operating rules of the funds transfer system.[169] These underlying agreements do exist in many instances, and a receiving bank that fails to accept in contravention of the agreement breaches its contract obligation. An issue of particular relevance in these agreements is whether the receiving bank must extend credit to the sender when the payment order exceeds the amount that the sender has on deposit with the receiving bank. Article 4A does provide that a receiving bank that fails to execute a payment order that it was obligated to execute under the terms of a written contract is liable to the sender for the damages stipulated in the contract, including consequential damages.[170] If the contract does not specify damages, recovery is limited to the sender's expenses in the transaction, as well as incidental expenses and interest that are lost because of the failure to execute.[171] In the absence of an agreement by the receiving bank to accept payment orders for funds transfers from a particular sender, the sender does not have any basis for expecting the bank to accept them, and the bank that does not accept does not owe a duty to the sender with respect to the order received.

Even when a receiving bank has an underlying agreement with a sender, it might elect not to accept certain payment orders. The order might lack sufficient clarity for the bank to be certain of the instructions. The instructions might be impossible to carry out because of reasons like equipment failure or credit limitations that apply to the receiving bank. The amount of the payment order might exceed the credit limits that the receiving bank is obligated to extend to the sender. A receiving bank that is not the beneficiary's bank can control most of its own destiny with regard to Article 4A in these circumstances by simply refusing to execute the payment order received. Execution is the exclusive means of acceptance, and, in the absence of a contrary agreement, the receiving bank does not incur liability with respect to the payment order until acceptance.[172] The bank does not have to notify the sender of rejection of the order. The bank simply refuses to accept.

There is one qualification on notification of rejection with respect to the rights of a receiving bank other than the beneficiary's bank. When the sender's account has sufficient money to cover the amount of the payment order, the receiving bank can debit the account and thus be assured of payment. Even if the refusal to accept is not wrongful under the agreement with the sender, the receiving bank still has the use of the money that the sender thought would be used to pay for the funds transfer, and the sender will continue under its misapprehension of payment until it learns that its order was not accepted. In the interest of restitution, the receiving bank

---

[169] U.C.C. § 4A-212.
[170] U.C.C. § 4A-305(d).
[171] U.C.C. § 4A-305(d).
[172] See § 15.04[B][1] infra.

is required to pay interest to the sender on the amount of the order for the number of days from the execution date until the sender learns the order was not accepted.[173] The receiving bank can avoid liability for this interest by providing notice of rejection that the sender receives on the execution date.[174]

In some cases notice of rejection will be required by the beneficiary's bank to prevent an acceptance. When acceptance will occur without any specific action by the beneficiary's bank, the bank must reject before the automatic acceptance occurs. A payment order is rejected when a receiving bank transmits a notice of rejection to the sender.[175] The notice need merely indicate that the receiving bank will not accept the order, and it is effective when it is given if the method of transmission is commercially reasonable.[176] The opportunity to reject is not available for a payment made by Fedwire because final payment, and therefore acceptance, is made when the payment order is received.[177]

[3] Payment

Several parties incur payment obligations in a funds transfer. The originator nearly always utilizes a funds transfer to pay an obligation owed to the beneficiary. Each sender incurs payment obligations to a receiving bank that accepts its payment order.[178] A beneficiary bank that accepts a payment order incurs a payment obligation to the beneficiary.[179] Article 4A therefore includes specific provisions that govern how and when these payment obligations are satisfied.

The obligation of a beneficiary's bank to pay the beneficiary is generally satisfied by crediting the amount of the payment order to the account of the beneficiary and giving the beneficiary notice of the right to withdraw the credit.[180] Rather than paying the beneficiary directly, the beneficiary might also be paid through the benefit attained by the bank's lawful application of the amount of the payment order to a debt of the beneficiary.[181] Two typical examples are setoff by the beneficiary bank or application of the proceeds of the payment order to a garnishment order.[182]

---

[173] U.C.C. § 4A-210(b). The execution date is determined by the instructions of the sender, and is otherwise the day that the order is received. U.C.C. § 4A-301(b).

[174] U.C.C. § 4A-210(b).

[175] U.C.C. § 4A-210(a).

[176] U.C.C. § 4A-210(a). Although it is not an invariable rule, most funds transfers will require a very quick method of communication because of the general importance of speed in these transactions. A notice of rejection is not effective until it is received when the method of transmission is not commercially reasonable. *Id.*

[177] U.C.C. § 4A-209(b)(2). *See* § 15.04[B][2] *supra.*

[178] U.C.C. § 4A-402(b), (c).

[179] U.C.C. § 4A-404(a).

[180] U.C.C. § 4A-405(a)(i).

[181] U.C.C. § 4A-405(a)(ii).

[182] U.C.C. § 4A-405, Comment 1.

The general rule is that payment by the beneficiary's bank to the beneficiary is final.[183] Even if the beneficiary agreed to return the payment if the sender did not ultimately settle with the beneficiary bank or if the bank imposed a similar condition on released funds, the payment cannot be recovered by the bank. If payment resulted from notifying the beneficiary of the right to withdraw a credit, the right to withdraw cannot be revoked. When the beneficiary bank pays the beneficiary before receiving payment from the sender of the payment order, the beneficiary bank assumes the risk of nonpayment by the sender.[184] The beneficiary bank can protect against assumption of this risk by delaying acceptance.[185]

The major exception to the general rule allows a funds transfer system to create a rule that makes payments to beneficiaries provisional until the beneficiary bank receives payment of an accepted payment order.[186] This exception is allowed in recognition of the custom in automated clearing house transactions to release funds to customers early in the payment date even though settlement to the beneficiary bank does not occur until later in the day.[187] To qualify for recovery of a provisional payment from the beneficiary under a funds-transfer-system rule the beneficiary's bank must not have received payment of the accepted payment order, both the originator and the beneficiary must have been given notice of the provisional nature of the rule, and the beneficiary must have agreed to be bound by the rule.[188]

An originator issues a payment order for the purpose of paying a stated sum to the designated beneficiary. Consequently, "the fundamental rule of Article 4A [is stated in section 4A-406(1) and provides] that payment by the originator to the beneficiary is accomplished by providing to the beneficiary the obligation of the beneficiary's bank to pay."[189] Payment by the originator to the beneficiary under the funds transfer thus occurs when the beneficiary's bank accepts a payment order for the benefit of the beneficiary that was part of a funds transfer initiated by the originator.[190]

Payment by the originator through funds transfer also generally discharges the originator on any underlying obligation for which the payment is made.[191] This discharge will not occur if a contract with the beneficiary

---

[183] U.C.C. § 4A-405(c).

[184] U.C.C. § 4A-405, Comment 2.

[185] U.C.C. § 4A-209(b)(1). See § 15.4[B][2] supra.

[186] U.C.C. § 4A-405(d).

[187] The practice is comparable to recovery of funds advanced by a depositary bank against a check in the collection process that is dishonored. U.C.C. § 4A-405, Comment 3.

[188] U.C.C. § 4A-405(d).

[189] U.C.C. § 4A-406, Comment 1.

[190] U.C.C. § 4A-406(a). Because other senders in the transfer process might make errors in the amount of their payment orders, the originator pays the beneficiary "in an amount equal to the amount of the order accepted by the beneficiary's bank, but not more than the amount of the originator's order." Id.

[191] U.C.C. § 4A-406(b). The obligation of the beneficiary's bank is switched for the obligation of the originator. The result is comparable to a debtor paying a credit with a cashier's check under U.C.C. § 3-310(a).

prohibited the funds transfer payment method, the funds are not withdrawn by the beneficiary, the beneficiary notifies the originator of refusal of the payment method within a reasonable time after receiving notice of the receipt of the payment order from the beneficiary's bank, and the beneficiary would suffer a loss that could have been avoided through payment by the correct payment method.[192] This provision precludes the originator from passing the risk of insolvency of the beneficiary's bank to the beneficiary in circumstances in which the beneficiary has specifically contracted for another method of payment.[193] When the statutory conditions are all satisfied to preclude discharge of the originator, the originator is subrogated to the beneficiary's rights to receive payment from the beneficiary's bank,[194] but the originator remains obligated to pay the receiving bank to which it sent its payment order,[195] as well as the beneficiary on the underlying obligation.

A number of rules determine when a sender is determined to have met its payment obligation to its receiving bank for an accepted payment order. If the sender is a bank, payment occurs upon final settlement of the obligation through a Federal Reserve Bank or through a funds transfer system.[196] A Fedwire results in final settlement with a debit to the sender's Federal Reserve account and a credit to the receiving bank's Federal Reserve account when the receiving bank receives the payment order.[197] If the sender and receiving bank are members of a funds transfer system that nets obligations multilaterally among participants, the receiving bank receives final payment upon the completion of settlement under the rules of the system.[198] This provision is based on the CHIPS system of settling at the end of the day according to the net debit and credit position of each participant with other participants after the transmittal of payment orders among participants during the day.[199] A comparable provision provides that if two banks transmit payment orders to each other during the day under an agreement providing for later settlement, the total amount owed by each bank for payment orders transmitted during the settlement period is set off against the amount received, and the amounts setoff are treated as payment that each bank has made to the other bank.[200]

Sometimes a bank does not settle through a Federal Reserve Bank because it does not have access to the system, which is most likely with a foreign bank. In these cases payment is likely to be made through credits and debits in the accounts of two banks. When the sender is a bank that credits an account of the receiving bank that is maintained with the sender

---

[192] U.C.C. § 4A-406(b).
[193] U.C.C. § 4A-406, Comment 3.
[194] U.C.C. § 4A-406(b).
[195] See § 15.04[B][1][a] supra.
[196] U.C.C. § 4A-403(a)(1).
[197] U.C.C. § 4A-403, Comment 1.
[198] U.C.C. § 4A-403(b).
[199] U.C.C. § 4A-403, Comment 4.
[200] U.C.C. § 4A-403(c).

or it causes an account of the receiving bank maintained in another bank to be credited, payment is made by the sender when the credit is withdrawn.[201] If the credit is not withdrawn, payment is considered to be made at midnight of the day on which the credit is withdrawable and the receiving bank learns of that fact.[202] This time period gives the receiving bank an opportunity to reject the payment order of the sender if it so chooses.[203]

A final method of payment by a sender is available to nonbanks, as well as banks. Payment occurs when a receiving bank debits an account of the sender that is maintained with the receiving bank, to the extent that the debit is covered with a withdrawable credit balance in the account.[204] This method of payment is utilized when the originator is an entity other than a bank.

[C] Allocation of Loss

The desire for a body of law to govern loss allocations in wholesale wire transfers was a primary motivating factor leading to the Article 4A codification effort. Losses can occur in a variety of ways in funds transfers, and their losses can be particularly relevant given the large dollar amounts involved. The loss allocation principles codified in Article 4A are discussed below. The price structure of the industry was considered by drafters in determining loss allocation.[205] Wire transfers are made for only a few dollars despite the fact that they carry millions of dollars of value.

[1] Erroneous Execution

Although a sender generally is obligated under section 4A-402(c) to pay the amount of a payment order to the receiving bank that accepts it,[206] section 4A-303 takes precedence over the requirement in several circumstances of erroneous execution of the sender's payment order.[207] One of the mistakes could be for a receiving bank to issue a payment order in an amount greater than the amount of the sender's order. If that erroneous order results in payment of the greater amount to the beneficiary, the receiving bank is entitled to payment from the sender only for the amount of the sender's order.[208] The bank becomes liable for the full amount of its erroneous order upon acceptance of the order,[209] however, which places the initial loss upon the receiving bank making the erroneous execution of the payment order. The bank's remedy is to turn to the law governing mistake

---

[201] U.C.C. § 4A-403(a)(2).
[202] U.C.C. § 4A-403(a)(2).
[203] U.C.C. § 4A-403, Comment 2.
[204] U.C.C. § 4A-403(a)(3).
[205] Article 4A, Prefatory note.
[206] See § 15.04[B][1][a] supra.
[207] U.C.C. § 4A-303, Comment 1.
[208] U.C.C. § 4A-303(a).
[209] U.C.C. § 4A-402(c).

and restitution to recover the excess payment from the beneficiary.[210] Precisely the same rules apply if a receiving bank mistakenly executes two payment orders for the same transaction and both orders are paid to the beneficiary.[211]

If the erroneous payment order results in payment of an amount less than the amount of the sender's order, the receiving bank is entitled to payment from the sender for the amount of the sender's order if the bank corrects its mistake by issuing another payment order for the benefit of the beneficiary.[212] A receiving bank that does not correct its mistake is entitled to payment from the sender only to the extent of the amount of the erroneous order.[213]

Another form of erroneous execution can occur when the receiving bank indicates the wrong beneficiary. If the funds transfer is completed on the basis of that error, the sender of the payment order that was erroneously executed, as well as all of the previous senders, are excused from their obligations to pay the orders that they issued.[214] The receiving bank issuing the erroneous order is relegated to its remedies under the law of mistake and restitution against the beneficiary that received payment.[215]

[2] Erroneous Payment Orders

When a sender makes an error in a payment order and the funds transfer is completed, the sender generally is obligated to pay the order.[216] Security procedures can be implemented, however, that can sometimes detect certain errors.[217] An error in designating the intended beneficiary could be

---

[210] U.C.C. § 4A-303(a). These allocation rules can be illustrated as follows: X orders A Bank to pay $1,000,000 to Y's account in B Bank. A Bank erroneously instructs B Bank to pay $2,000,000 to Y's account. B Bank is entitled following acceptance to receive $2,000,000 from A Bank, but A Bank can receive only $1,000,000 from X. A Bank must proceed against Y for the excess payment.

[211] U.C.C. § 4A-303(a). In Banque Worms v. BankAmerica Int'l, 570 N.E.2d 189 (N.Y. 1991), the bank mistakenly proceeded with a transfer after the originator had canceled the request to make the wire-transfer. The appellate court narrowed the bank's right of restitution from the beneficiary. It allowed the beneficiary to keep the money because the money had been applied to a debt owed to it by the originator that had been the purpose for sending the wire transfer.

[212] U.C.C. § 4A-303(b).

[213] U.C.C. § 4A-303(b). This allocation rule can be illustrated as follows: X orders A Bank to pay $1,000,000 to Y's account in B Bank. A Bank erroneously instructs B Bank to pay $100,000 to Y's account. If A Bank does not correct its mistake by issuing another payment order for the additional $900,000, A Bank is entitled to receive only $100,000 from X.

[214] U.C.C. § 4A-303(c).

[215] U.C.C. § 4A-303(c). This allocation rule can be illustrated as follows: X orders A Bank to pay $1,000,000 to Y's account in B Bank. A Bank erroneously instructs B Bank to pay $1,000,000 to Z's account, and B Bank accepts. A Bank must pay $1,000,000 to B Bank, but X does not have to pay its payment order to A Bank. A Bank must proceed against Z to recover the mistaken payment.

[216] U.C.C. § 4A-402(b), (c).

[217] For this purpose, a security procedure is "a procedure established by agreement of a customer and a receiving bank for the purpose of–(ii) detecting error in the transmission or the content of the payment order or communication." U.C.C. § 4A-201.

determined through a procedure that requires special verification of an order to a beneficiary to which the sender normally does not make funds transfer payments. A security procedure aimed at discovering erroneous dollar amounts of an order could require verification of amounts over a stated maximum or might utilize codes for different dollar amounts. Erroneously transmitted duplicate orders might be detected by a procedure that requires each payment order to include a number that does not apply to any other payment order. With the applicability of security procedures for the purpose of detecting errors, Article 4A adjusts the allocation of risk in some cases.[218]

The risk of loss stemming from the sender's error is shifted to the receiving bank when the sender can establish that it complied with the security procedure and that the error could have been detected if the receiving bank had also complied.[219] Under these circumstances the sender does not have to pay either an erroneously transmitted duplicate order or a payment order indicating the wrong beneficiary.[220] When the error consisted of an instruction to pay a greater amount than intended by the sender, the sender does not have to pay the order to the extent of the excessive amount.[221] The rationale supporting these loss allocation rules is stated succinctly in the comments: "Although the customer may have been negligent in transmitting the erroneous payment order, the loss is put on the bank on a last-clear-chance theory."[222] The receiving bank that did not comply with the security procedure must rely on the general law of mistake and restitution to seek recovery from the beneficiary.[223]

If the risk of loss for an erroneous payment order is shifted to the receiving bank and the bank notifies the sender that the order has been accepted or that the sender's account has been debited for it, the sender has a duty to exercise ordinary care to discover the error and notify the bank of the relevant facts within a reasonable time not exceeding ninety days following receipt of the bank's notification.[224] When the sender fails in this duty, the bank can require the sender to reimburse it for any loss that it can prove resulted from the sender's failure.[225] The bank's success in this showing will depend upon whether the failure to inform the bank impaired the bank's rights against the beneficiary.

---

[218] U.C.C. § 4A-205.

[219] U.C.C. § 4A-205(a)(1).

[220] U.C.C. § 4A-205(a)(2).

[221] U.C.C. § 4A-205(a)(3).

[222] U.C.C. § 4A-205, Comment 2.

[223] U.C.C. § 4A-205(a)(2), (3). These rights are comparable to the rights of a receiving bank to proceed against a beneficiary when the receiving bank erroneously executes a payment order. See U.C.C. § 4A-303; § 15.04[C][1] supra.

[224] U.C.C. § 4A-205(b).

[225] U.C.C. § 4A-205(b).

[3] Unauthorized Transfers

Sections 4A-202 and 4A-203 provide loss-allocation rules for cases in which an unauthorized party fraudulently issues a payment order in the name of a sender or fraudulently alters a payment order before it reaches the receiving bank. If the receiving bank accepts the fraudulent order and incurs liability to pay the beneficiary of the order or a receiving bank, it may suffer a loss if it cannot enforce payment of the payment order that it accepted. The purported sender might resist payment on the basis that the payment order was unauthorized or was fraudulently altered. Specific provisions to allocate these losses thus are desirable.

The principles of agency law provide one possible approach, and it was essentially the only one in the absence of a statute or agreement that addressed the issue. Article 4A also defers to agency law as a residual approach for cases in which a receiving bank does not comply with an alternative, preferred procedure. Quite simply, the person identified as the sender of a payment order is the sender if that person authorized the order or is otherwise bound by principles of agency law or other applicable law.[226] Essentially, the analysis focuses on the actual or apparent authority of the person who caused the order to be issued and on conduct of the customer that is relevant to estoppel against the customer to deny that the order was authorized.[227] These agency law principles would give a receiving bank very little protection, however, particularly when a payment order is transmitted electronically.[228]

The exposure of a receiving bank under the agency law approach creates an incentive for the bank to follow the desired alternative. This approach is based upon verification of payment orders pursuant to security procedures agreed upon by a bank and its customer.[229] Security procedures using codes or identification numbers or words can be implemented to help ensure that the person transmitting a payment order to the receiving bank has proper authority. The general rule under Article 4A is that when a receiving bank accepts a payment order in good faith and in compliance with an agreed upon verification procedure that is commercially reasonable,[230] the

---

[226] U.C.C. § 4A-202(a).

[227] U.C.C. § 4A-203, Comment 1.

[228] Unlike presentment of a check with a forged drawer's signature, the bank does not have a signature that it can scrutinize. U.C.C. § 4A-203, Comment 1.

[229] In this context, security procedure means "a procedure established by agreement of a customer and a receiving bank for the purpose of (i) verifying that a payment order or communication amending or cancelling a payment order is that of the customer." U.C.C. § 4A-201.

[230] "The burden of making available commercially reasonable security procedures is imposed on receiving banks because they generally determine what security procedures can be used and are in the best position to evaluate the efficacy of procedures offered to customers to combat fraud." U.C.C. § 4A-203, Comment 3. A court is to consider a number of factors in deciding as a question of law whether a particular security procedure is commercially reasonable for the particular customer. U.C.C. § 4A-202(c). An informed customer can reject the use of a commercially reasonable security system by agreeing in writing to assume the risk of unauthorized transfers. U.C.C. § 4A-202(c).

payment order it received is effective as an order of the customer irrespective of whether it was actually authorized.[231] If the bank's employees cannot detect a fraudulent transmission of a payment order through proper observance of the security procedure, the bank has complied and the customer must pay the accepted order.[232] If the fraud went undetected because the bank employees did not comply with the security procedures, the customer is not bound.[233]

The general rule that makes a customer responsible for a payment order that is unauthorized but nevertheless effective through compliance with verification procedures is subject to an exception. The customer can avoid the loss if it can establish that the issuance of the order was not caused by an agent of the customer or by a person who obtained confidential security procedure information from a source controlled by the customer.[234] A successful issuance of an unauthorized payment order after commercially reasonable security procedures have been implemented requires knowledge of the procedures and relevant codes. When the customer can prove that the breach of procedures did not occur by a source under its control, the security breach had to occur from within the control of the receiving bank. Although the burden of proof initially appears to be insurmountable in many cases, the customer is expected to have access to sufficient evidence as a result of the criminal investigation which inevitably follows in these types of cases.[235]

[4] Insolvency

With several banks involved in a funds transfer, the risk exists that a bank will suspend payments because of insolvency before complying with its payment obligations. This risk can be particularly great for a bank that has extended credit on the transactions prior to settlement with the insolvent bank. Transfers by Fedwire do not create the risk because a receiving bank does not accept an order from the sender without receiving payment since settlement is final on these payments when the payment order is received by the receiving bank.[236] Multilateral settlements through the CHIPS network operate differently, however, and the approach also differs when two banks send payment orders to each other during the day

---

[231] U.C.C. § 4A-202(b). "In the wire transfer business the concept of 'authorized' is different from that found in agency law. In that business a payment order is treated as the order of the person in whose name it is issued if it is properly tested pursuant to a security procedure and the order passes the test." U.C.C. § 4A-203, Comment 1.

[232] "The burden on the customer is to supervise its employees to assure compliance with the security procedure and to safeguard confidential security information and access to transmitting facilities so that the security procedure cannot be breached." U.C.C. § 4A-203, Comment 3.

[233] As in cases in which agency law applies, if the loss is passed to the receiving bank it can seek recovery from the beneficiary who received payment on the funds transfer initiated by the fraudulent payment order.

[234] U.C.C. § 4A-203(a)(2).

[235] U.C.C. § 4A-203, Comment 5.

[236] See § 15.04[B][1][a] *supra*.

and settle later. Although the credit extended on the payment orders in these latter cases may last only during the day of the transfers, the large amounts carried on some payment orders can pose significant risk exposure when a bank cannot settle for them at the end of the day.

The banks that transmit payment orders over the CHIPS system settle with each other at the end of the day.[237] The net credit and debit position for each bank participant is computed with respect to all other participants on the system, and each bank that is in a debit position with another bank must promptly make a payment in that amount to the other bank through Fedwire. Article 4A provides that the payment obligations of senders are met when these settlements are realized.[238] "This provision is intended to invalidate any argument, based on common-law principles, that multilateral netting is not valid because mutuality of obligation is not present."[239] Another similar provision of Article 4A recognizes that a setoff of debits and credits at the end of the day between two banks that send payment orders to each other satisfies the payment obligations of the sender.[240]

These net settlement provisions become particularly relevant when one of the banks becomes insolvent and suspends payments. They establish that the payment obligation of the failed bank with respect to its issued payment orders is the net amount it owes after the setoff of payment orders that it received. This approach means that the risk in extending credit to a sending bank is based on the net debit position of the sending bank.[241] These rules also provide an incentive for the banking system to retain its current practice of imposing credit limits on banks that issue payment orders.

---

[237] *See* § 15.01[G] *supra.*
[238] U.C.C. § 4A-403(b).
[239] U.C.C. § 4A-403, Comment 4.
[240] U.C.C. § 4A-403(c).
[241] U.C.C. § 4A-403, Comment 4.

TABLE OF CASES

[References are to pages and footnotes.]

A

A. Alport & Sons, Inc. v. Hotel Evans, Inc. 25n89
Adoption of (see name of party)
Aetna Cas. & Sur. Co. v. Hepler State Bank 94n128; 259n48
Aetna Life & Cas. Co. v. Hampton State Bank 237n78
Agaliotis v. Agaliotis 58n67
A.I.C. Fin. Corp. v. Walter E. Heller & Co. 213n75
Alarcon v. Ferrari 120n16
Alleged Contempt of (see name of party)
Allison v. First Nat'l Bank 335n78
American Communications Telecommunications, Inc. v. Commerce North Bank ... 245n112
American Discount Corp. v. Glover 187n102
American Express Co. v. Koener 376n125
American Home Assurance Co. v. Scarsdale Nat'l Bank & Trust Co. 268n100
American Nat'l Bank & Trust Co. v. St. Joseph Valley Bank 207n51
American Oil Co. v. Valenti 89n95
American Plan Corp. v. Woods 150n209, n213
American Security Bank, N.A. v. American Motorists Ins. Co. 266n90
American Underwriting Corp. v. Rhode Island Hosp. Trust Co. . 69n133; 139n128
Ames v. Great S. Bank 37n155
Ampex Corp. v. Appel Media, Inc. 170n5
AmSouth Bank, N.A. v. Spigener 344n137
Anderson, Clayton & Co. v. Farmers Nat'l Bank 129n64
Anderson Contracting Co., Inc. v. Zurich Ins. Co. 283n174
Appeal of (see name of party)
Appeal of Estate of (see name of party)
Application of (see name of applicant)
Arcanum Nat'l Bank v. Hessler 141n145
Aspen Indus., Inc. v. Marine Midland Bank 310n90
Atlantic Cement Co., Inc. v. South Shore Bank 80n47
Atlas Bldg. Supply Co., Inc. v. First Independent Bank 95n132

Available Iron & Metal Co. v. First Nat'l Bank 5n21

B

Bagby v. Merrill Lynch, Pierce, Fenner & Smith, Inc. 257n38
Baker v. National City Bank 310n90
Balmoral Arms v. Rutkin 193n147
Banco Ganadero y Agricola, S.A. v. Society Nat'l Bank 307n71
Bank of Am. v. Superior Court of San Diego County 85n72
Bank of Am., N.T.S.A. v. Security Pac. Nat'l Bank 38n163
Bank of Boston Int'l v. Arguello Tefel ... 187n100
Bank of Commerce v. Union Bank 227n28
Bank of Louisville Royal v. Sims 335n77
Bank of Lyons v. Schultz 124n35
Bank of Miami v. Florida City Express, Inc. 105n13
Bank of N.C. v. Rock Island Bank 161n277
Bank of N.J. v. Pulini 184n79
Bank of Ripley v. Sadler 86n73
Bank of S. Md. v. Robertson's Crab House 259n48
Bank of the United States v. Bank of Georgia 227n26
Bank of the West v. Wes-Con Dev. Co., Inc. 209n58
Bankers Trust Co. v. Litton Sys. 148n197
Banque Worms v. BankAmerica Int'l 419n211
Barclays Bank, P.L.C. v. Conkey 143n160
Barthelmess v. Cavalier 10n2
Barton v. Scott Hudgens Realty & Mortgage, Inc. 32n134
Basch v. Bank of Am. 262n62
Basse Truck Line, Inc. v. First State Bank 278n143
Bates & Springer, Inc. v. Stallworth 160n269
Beal Bank, S.S.B. v. Caddo Parish-Villas South, Ltd. 97n148
Behring Int'l, Inc. v. Greater Houston Bank 56n61

TABLE OF CASES

[References are to pages and footnotes.]

Beneficial Fin. Co. v. Lawrence . . 185n86
Beneficial Fin. Co. v. Marshall . . 186n92, n97
Best v. United States National Bank 329n26
Beyer v. First Nat'l Bank 172n14
Bice-Bey; United States v. 374n110
Bizzocco v. Chinitz 88n90
Bluffstone v. Abrahams 191n132
Bobby D. Assoc. v. DiMarcantonio 99n159
Bon Bon Productions, Ltd. v. Xanadu Productions, Inc. 333n63
Booker v. Everhart 21n58
Borowski v. Firstar Bank Milwaukee, N.A. 267n97
Bowling Green, Inc. v. State St. Bank & Trust Co. 126n55; 136n104; 145n176; 158n253
Brannon v. Langston 170n5
Brannons No. Seven, Inc. v. Phelps 107n23
Braswell v. Bank of Early 161n274
Braswell Motor Freight Lines, Inc. v. Bank of Salt Lake 274n126
Bricks Unlimited, Inc. v. Agee . . 145n175
Brite Lite Lamps Corp. v. Manufacturers Hanover Trust Co. . . 64n106; 290n220
Broadview Lumber Co., Inc., In re 137n113
Brower v. Franklin Nat'l Bank . . . 78n31; 255n24
Brown v. Fifth Third Bank 104n4
Brown & Root, Inc. v. Ring Power Corp. . . 13n14
Buckley v. Trenton Sav. Fund Soc'y 336n82
Buller v. Crips 7n25
Burchett v. Alied Concord Financial Corp. 150n208
Burke v. Burke 89n94
Burke v. First Peoples Bank 41n184

C

C&K Petroleum Prods., Inc. v. Equibank 333n63
C&R Corp. v. American Sec. & Trust Co. 326n12
C & Z, Inc. v. Oklahoma Tax Comm'n . . . 34n142
Cable Cast Magazine v. Premier Bank, N.A. 280n155; 281n160
Cadle Co. v. Ginsburg . . 131n76; 135n99; 159n263
Cairo Banking Co. v. West 228n32

Cairo Cooperative Exchange v. First Nat'l Bank 64n105
Callihan; United States v. 374n110
Calvert Credit Corp. v. Williams 165n291
Camber v. Bridges 161n273
Canadian Bank of Commerce v. Bingham 228n32
Canal Bank v. Bank of Albany . . 216n92; 227n23; 230
Carr, In re Estate of 161n272
Carter & Grimsley v. Omni Trading, Inc. 120n15
Catalina Yachts v. Old Colony Bank & Trust Co. 106n16
Central Bank v. Butler 327n18
Chase Manhattan Bank v. Concord Utilities Corp. 98n154
Chase Manhattan Bank v. Lake Tire Co. 46n10
Chemical Bank v. Haskell 129n69
Chemical Bank v. Valentini . . . 187n103
Chenowith v. Bank of Dardanelle 172n19; 174n30
Chidakel v. Blonder 75n10
Christensen v. McAtee 187n105
Christinson v. Venturi Const. Co. 141n145; 150n212
Christo; United States v. 327n17
Chrysler Credit Corp. v. Friendly Ford, Inc. 35n147
Chute v. Bank One of Akron, N.A. 243n103
Cincinnati Ins. Co. v. First Nat'l Bank . . . 325n10; 330n42
Cissna Park State Bank v. Johnson 89n98
Citizens Nat'l Bank v. Fort Lee Sav. & Loan Ass'n 127n59; 338n92
Citizens Nat'l Bank v. Taylor . . 189n125; 190n127
Citizens & Peoples Nat'l Bank v. United States 309n86
Citizens & S. Nat'l Bank v. Youngblood . . 310n93
City v. (see name of defendant)
City and County of (see name of city and county)
City Bank v. Tenn 327n15
City First Mortgage Corp. v. Florida Residential Prop. & Cas. Joint Underwriting Ass'n 31n125
Clarkson v. Selected Risks Ins. Co. 220n107; 261n57
Clawson v. Berklund 110n43

TABLE OF CASES

[References are to pages and footnotes.]

Client's Security Fund v. Allstate Ins. Co. 270n116; 272n122
Coine v. Manufacturers Hanover Trust Co. 267n97
Coltharp v. Calcasieu-Marine Nat'l Bank 56n58
Commercial Cotton Co., Inc. v. United Cal. Bank 264n74
Commercial Credit Co. v. Childs 140n140; 165n290
Commercial Credit Equip. Corp. v. First Alabama Bank 256n33
Commercial Credit Equip. Corp. v. Hatton 186n96
Commercial Fin., Ltd. v. American Resources, Ltd. 187n101
Commission v. (see name of opposing party)
Commissioner v. (see name of opposing party)
Commissioner of Internal Revenue (see name of defendant)
Common Wealth Ins. Sys., Inc. v. Kerstan 185n81
Commonwealth v. (see name of defendant)
Commonwealth ex rel. (see name of relator)
Commonwealth Fed. Sav. & Loan Ass'n v. First Nat'l Bank 259n49
Community Bank v. United States Nat'l Bank 239n88
Connecticut Bank & Trust v. Dadi 327n15
Conservatorship of (see name of party)
Consolidated Pub. Water Supply Dist. No. C-1 v. Farmers Bank 277n142
Continental Bank v. Fitting 326n14
Contrail Leasing Partners, Ltd. v. Executive Serv. Corp. 132n81
Cooley v. First Nat'l Bank 268n103
Cooper v. Union Bank .. 214n84; 254n17; 255n27
Copple v. Boatman's First Nat'l Bank of Oklahoma 66n115
County v. (see name of defendant)
County of (see name of county)
Covington v. Penn Square National Bank 271
Crawford v. 733 San Mateo Co. ... 98n153
Cromwell v. All State Credit Corp. 148n195
C.S. Bowen Co., Inc. v. Maryland Nat'l Bank 290n220
Cumis Ins. Soc'y, Inc. v. Girard Bank ... 237n78; 330n31
Cundy v. Lindsay 10n2
Curtis v. Hibernia Nat'l Bank ... 266n88
Custody of (see name of party)

D

Da Silva v. Sanders 333n64
Dalton & Marberry, P.C. v. Nationsbank, N.A. 123n29; 131n77; 133n87
Davis Aircraft Prods. Co. v. Bankers Trust Co. 267n95
Dean v. Centerre Bank .. 262n62; 267n96
Delano v. Putnam Trust 341n112
Demos v. Lyons 232n60
DiVall Insured Income Fund L.P. v. Boatmen's First Nat'l Bank 144n167
Don E. Williams Co. v. Commission of Internal Revenue 37n154
Donmar Enterprises, Inc. v. Southern Nat'l Bank 412n151
Douglass v. Wones ... 154n231; 158n254
Dozier v. First Alabama Bank .. 246n114
DRP, Inc. v. Burgess 343n127, n129; 344n136
Dunbar v. First Nat'l Bank 339n105
Duxbury v. Roberts 155n236

E

E. Bierhaus & Sons, Inc. v. Bowling 133n85; 189n121; 256n32
East Gadsden Bank v. First City Nat'l Bank 261n57
Ed Stinn Chevrolet, Inc. v. National City Bank 202n30; 237n78
El-Ce Storms Trust v. Svetahor .. 185n86
Eldon's Super Fresh Stores, Inc. v. Merrill Lynch, Pierce, Fenner & Smith, Inc. .. 133n84, n87; 137
Electrical Distributors, Inc. v. SFR, Inc. .. 29n117
Ellis Canning Co. v. Bernstein ... 23n77
Emery-Waterhouse Co. v. Rhode Island Hosp. Trust Nat'l Bank 165n291
Est. of (see name of party)
Estate of (see name of party)
Estrada v. River Oaks Bank & Trust Co. 55n52
Etelson v. Suburban Trust Co. .. 188n114
Euro Motors, Inc. v. Southwest Fin. Bank & Trust Co. 268n99
European Am. Bank & Trust Co. v. Starcrete Int'l Indus., Inc. 94n127
Evra v. Swiss Bank Corp. 405n113
Ex parte (see name of applicant)
Ex rel. (see name of relator)
Exchange Bank & Trust Co. v. Kidwell Constr. Co. 268n105

TABLE OF CASES

[References are to pages and footnotes.]

Exchange Nat'l Bank v. Beshara 125n47
Executive Bank v. Tighe 185n85

F

Fairfield County Trust Co. v. Steinbrecher 190n127; 191n133
Falls Church Bank v. Wesley Heights Realty, Inc. 125n46
Far West Citrus, Inc. v. Bank of Am. 268n102, n107
Farmers Bank v. Sinwellen Corp. 334n68
Farmers & Merchants State Bank v. Ferguson 336n83
Farmington Nat'l Bank v. Basin Plastics, Inc. 183n76
Farns Assocs., Inc. v. South Side Bank ... 145n175
Fasano/Harriss Pie Co., In re 79n36
Federal Deposit Ins. Corp. v. Blue Rock Shopping Center, Inc. 184n80
Federal Deposit Ins. Corp. v. Culver 149n201; 150n207
Federal Deposit Ins. Corp. v. Kirkland ... 187n100
Federal Deposit Ins. Corp. v. Marine Nat'l Bank 217n94
Federal Deposit Ins. Corp. v. Newton ... 191n133
Federal Deposit Ins. Corp. v. Wood 148n195
Federal Ins. Co. v. Bank of N.Y. .. 265n82
Federal Land Bank v. Taggart .. 183n76
Federal Trade Comm'n v. World Travel Vacation Brokers, Inc. 375n122
Fewox v. Tallahassee Bank & Trust Co. .. 74n6
Fidelity & Cas. Co. v. Constitution Nat'l Bank 252n9
Fidelity & Deposit Co. v. Chemical Bank N. Y. Trust Co. 257n38
Fidelity & Deposit Co. v. First Nat'l Bank 257n37
Fireman's Fund Ins. Co. v. Bank of N.Y. . 257n39
Fireman's Fund Ins. Co. v. Security Pac. Nat'l Bank 234n66; 326n11; 329n29
First Am. Nat'l Bank v. Commerce Union Bank 333n65
First Am. Sav., F.A. v. M & I Bank 320n143
First Arlington Nat'l Bank v. Stathis 106n17
First Bank & Trust Co. v. Post .. 187n110

First Citizens Bank & Trust Co. v. Perry 327n16
First Georgia Bank v. Webster .. 307n73
First National City Bank v. Altman .. 234
First Nat'l Bank v. Blackhurst .. 160n264
First Nat'l Bank v. Continental Bank ... 310n92
First Nat'l Bank v. Fazzari 149n202; 150n212, n213
First Nat'l Bank v. Hobbs 334n68
First Nat'l Bank v. McKay 338n92
First Nat'l Bank v. Montgomery 109n31; 204n38
First Nat'l Bank v. Nunn 210n61
First Nat'l Bank v. Plymouth-Home Nat'l Bank 221n115; 330n35
First Nat'l Bank v. Price 330n40
First Nat'l Bank v. Trust Co. ... 217n93; 220n109
First Nat'l Bank; United States v. 42n186
First Nat'l Bank v. Ward 243n103
First Nat'l Bank of Chicago v. Midamerica Fed. Sav. Bank 216n89; 272n122
First Nat'l City Bank v. Bankers Trust Co. 209n60
First Nat'l City Bank v. Valentine 124n36
First New Haven Nat'l Bank v. Tirkot ... 185n85; 188n112
First Piedmont Bank & Trust Co. v. Doyle 337n88
First Sec. Bank v. Fastwich, Inc. .. 24n81; 74n7
First State Bank v. Clark 20n55
First State Bank v. Dixon 340n110; 341n111
First State Bank v. Perryman .. 283n174
First State Bank v. Raiton 187n104
Firth v. Farmers-Citizens Bank 149n200
Flagship Bank v. Complete Interiors, Inc. 257n39; 265n78
Fleck v. Ragan 87n83
Floor v. Melvin 91n110
Florida Frozen Foods, Inc. v. National Commercial Bank & Trust Co. 201n24
Florida Nat'l Bank v. Citizens Bank 105n14
Ford Motor Credit Co. v. Milhollin 360n15
Ford Motor Credit Co. v. United Serv. Automobile Ass'n 330n36
Foremost Ins. Co. v. First City Sav. & Loan Ass'n 60n84

TABLE OF CASES

TC-5

[References are to pages and footnotes.]

Forest-All Corp. v. New England Merchants Nat'l Bank 186n98
Four Million, Two Hundred Fifty-Five Thousand; United States v. 80n46
Franklin Credit Recovery Fund, XXI, L.P. v. Huber 124n37
Franklin Nat'l Bank v. Chase Manhattan Bank 272n121
Franklin Nat'l Bank v. Shapiro 272n120
Frantz v. First Nat'l Bank 125n47; 133n86
Fred Meyer, Inc. v. Temco Metal Prods. Co. 256n34
Freeport, Town of v. Ring 54n48
Funding Consultants, Inc. v. Aetna Cas. & Sur. Co. 129n68; 162n280
Funds For Business Growth, Inc. v. Woodland Marble & Tile Co. 95n133
Fur Funtastic, Ltd. v. Kearns . . 342n120
Futrelle v. Duke University . . . 196n170

G

G & R Corp. v. American Security & Trust Co. 265n82
Gabalac, State ex rel. v. Firestone Bank . . 268n98
Gabovitch v. Coolidge Bank & Trust Co. . . 160n267
Galaxy Boat Mfg. Co. v. East End State Bank 79n43
Garnac Grain Co., Inc. v. Boatmen's Bank & Trust Co. 211n64; 268n102
Gast v. American Gas. Co. 257n36
General Inv. Corp. v. Angelini . . . 71n146
General Motors Acceptance Corp. v. General Accident Fire & Life Assurance Corp. . . 79n42
Gentner & Co., Inc. v. Wells Fargo Bank 232n57
George Whalley Co. v. Nat'l City Bank . . . 261n58
German Educational Television Network, Ltd. v. Bankers Trust Co. 330n34
G.F.D. Enterprises, Inc. v. Nye . . 330n30
Ghitter v. Edge 77n26
Gill v. Commonwealth Nat'l Bank 89n100
Gill v. Cubitt 128n62; 130n74
Gina Chin & Associates, Inc. v. First Union Bank 278n146
Girard Bank v. Mount Holly State Bank . . 209n58; 220n108; 238n85; 330n35
Godfrey State Bank v. Mundy . . . 186n89

Gonderman v. change Bank, State ex . . . 135n97
Goodman v. Harvey 128n63
Goodman v. Simonds 128n63
Grand Island Prod. Credit Ass'n v. Humphrey 76n16
Grand W. Currency Exchange, Inc. v. A:M Sunrise Constr. Co. 147n183
Granite Equip. Leasing Corp. v. Hempstead Bank 345n140
Grasso v. Crow 221n117
Gray v. American Express Co. . . 376n125; 377n132
Great W. Bank & Trust Co. v. Pima Sav. & Loan Ass'n 122n25; 152n223
Green Hills P.C.A. v. R&M Porter Farms, Inc. 123n29
Greer v. White Oak State Bank 195n162
Grimes v. Grimes 77n25
Grumet v. Bristol 193n150
Guaranty Bank v. Thompson . . . 177n45; 178n46
Guaranty Bank & Trust Co. v. Federal Reserve Bank 205n43
Guaranty Nat'l Bank v. Beaver 285n188
Guardian Life Ins. Co. v. Chemical Bank 257n36
Guardianship of (see name of party)
Guida v. Exchange Nat'l Bank . . 186n88; 187n110
Gulf Coast State Bank v. Emenhiser 301n37

H

H&H Operations, Inc. v. West Ga. Nat'l Bank 188n114
Hadley v. Baxendale 405n113
Halbert v. Horton 121n22
Halla v. Norwest Bank Minnesota, N.A. . . 281n162
Halpin v. Frankenberger 184n77
Hane v. Exten 112n53
Hanover Ins. Co. v. Brotherhood State Bank 189n119; 331n50
Hansman v. Imlay City State Bank 334n69
Hardex-Steubenville Corp. v. Western Pa. Nat'l Bank 268n105
Hartford Life Ins. Co. v. Title Guarantee Co. 84n66
Hathorn v. Loftus 97n147; 130n73
Henkin, Inc. v. Berea Bank & Trust Co. . . 143n162

TABLE OF CASES

[References are to pages and footnotes.]

Hennesy Equip. Sales Co. v. Valley Nat'l Bank 325n9
Henrichs v. Peoples Bank 263n67
Hewett v. Marine Midland Bank .. 60n80
Hibernia Nat'l Bank; United States v. ... 301n41
Himelfarb. v. American Express Co. 376n128
Holcomb State Bank v. Adamson .. 88n86
Holly Hill Acres, Ltd. v. Charter Bank ... 21n58; 70n143
Home Center Supply, Inc. v. Certainteed Corp. 21n56; 86n75
Home Indem. Co. v. First Nat'l Bank 220n106
Hotel Riviera, Inc. v. First Nat'l Bank & Trust Co. 157n248
Household Fin. Co. v. Watson ... 90n104; 172n20
Howard Bank v. Iron Kettle Restaurant of Bolton, Inc. 307n71
Howard L. Jacobs, P.C. v. Citibank, N.A. 329n27
Huey v. Port Gibson Bank 184n80; 185n84
Hughes v. Marine Midland Bank 247n120; 341n115
Hughes v. Talley 189n118
Hughes v. Tyler 36n151
Hunter's Modern Appliance, Inc. v. Bank IV Oklahoma, N.A. 279n154
Hutcheson Hardware Co. v. Planters State Bank 228n33
Hyland v. First USA Bank 379n146

I

IBP, Inc. v. Mercantile Bank of Topeka .. 288n204
Illinois State Bank v. Yates 20n55
Imports, Etc., Ltd. v. ABF Freight System, Inc. 40n174
In re (see name of party)
In re Florida Airlines, Inc. 268n107
Insurance Agency Managers v. Gonzales .. 35n148
Insurance Co. of N. Am. v. Purdue Nat'l Bank 253n16
Interstate Mfg., Inc., In re 132n81

J

J. Gordon Neely Enters., Inc. v. American Nat'l Bank 256n31; 257n39
James Pair, Inc. v. Gentry 146n180
Jenkins; United States v. 98n154
Jensen v. Essexbank 262n62
Joffe v. United Cal. Bank 30n121
Jones v. Phillips 68n129
J.R. Simplot, Inc. v. Knight 31n125
Judd v. Citibank 394n46

K

K & K Mfg., Inc. v. Union Bank .. 262n61
Karmin Door Co. v. BankBoston, N.A. ... 266n84; 267n96
Kasper; United States v. 374n110
Katski v. Boehm 148n191
Kaufman v. Chase Manhattan Bank, N.A. 38n166; 310n95
Kaw Valley State Bank & Trust Co. v. Riddle 129n64; 162n282
Kawac, Inc. v. Cohen 32n130
Kelley v. Carson 69n131; 138n126
Kendall Yacht Corp. v. United Cal. Bank 336n80
Kiernan v. Union Bank 262n62, n64
Kimberly A. Allen Trust v. Firstbank of Lakewood, N.A. 308n80
Kirby v. First & Merchants Nat'l Bank .. 307n70
Knut Co. v. Knutson Const. Co. .. 70n140
Koerner & Lambert v. Allstate Ins. Co. .. 252n9; 257n37
Koger v. East First Nat'l Bank .. 334n68
Kraftsman Container Corp. v. United Counties Trust Co. 268n102
Krajcir v. Egidi 32n133
Kruser v. Bank of America 395n52
Kunkel v. First Nat'l Bank 340n108
Kupersmith v. Manufacturers Hanover Trust Co. 247n121

L

La Junta State Bank v. Travis ... 62n94; 157n249
La Sara Grain Co. v. First Nat'l Bank ... 64n107; 330n33
Lamson v. Commercial Credit Corp. 54n45
Landrum v. Security Nat'l Bank 334n70
Larkin Gen. Hosp., Ltd. v. Bank of Florida 285n186
Laurel Bank & Trust Co. v. Sahadi 75n13; 98n153; 100n162
Leaderbrand v. Central State Bank 38n161
Levy v. Bank of United States ... 227n30

TABLE OF CASES TC–7

[References are to pages and footnotes.]

Lewittes Furniture Enter., Inc. v. Peoples Nat'l Bank 206n47
License of (see name of party)
Lincoln Nat'l Bank & Trust Co. v. Peoples Trust Bank 327n18; 346n143
Lindsey v. Zeller 87n76
Littky & Mallon v. Michigan Nat'l Bank .. 24n84
Logan v. Central Bank 188n115; 189n126
Lombardo v. Mellon Bank, N.A. ... 305n59
Long v. Cuttle Const. Co. 194n158
Lord Mansfield in Miller v. Race 14
Loucks v. Albuquerque Nat'l Bank 334n68; 336n79
Lowenstein v. Barnett Bank of South Florida, N.A. 267n93
Lynnwood Sand & Gravel, Inc. v. Bank of Everett 243n102
Lyons v. Citizens Commercial Bank 187n108

M

Mac v. Bank of Am. 262n63
Maddox v. First Westroads Bank 272n123
Madill Bank & Trust Co. v. Herrmann ... 86n74
Madison Park Bank v. Field ... 269n109
Mandel v. Sedrish 69n135
Manufacturer & Traders Trust Co. v. Murphy 332n59
Manufactures Hanover Trust Co. v. Ava Indus., Inc. 244n109
Marine Midland Bank v. Berry .. 340n106
Marine Midland Bank, N.A. v. Price, Miller, Evans & Flowers 203n35
Marriage of (see name of party)
Martin v. American Express, Inc. 371n93
Marx v. Whitney Nat'l Bank ... 256n33; 265n79
Massey-Ferguson Credit Co. v. Wiley 163n284
Mastercard v. Newport, Town of 372n103
Matter of (see name of party)
McCain v. P.A. Partners, Ltd. ... 68n128
McDonald's Chevrolet, Inc. v. Johnson ... 11n6
McHenry State Bank v. Y&A Trucking ... 186n91
McIntyre v. Harris ... 144n169; 243n98, n103

McLaughlin v. Franklin Soc. Fed. Sav. & Loan Ass'n 338n96
McMickle v. Girard Bank 262n66
Means v. Clardy 26n94
Medford Irrigation Dist. v. Western Bank 239n87
Meng v. Maywood Proviso State Bank ... 275n129
Mercantile Bank & Trust Co. v. Hunter .. 295n17
Mercantile-Safe Deposit & Trust Co. v. Delp & Chapel Concrete & Constr. Co. 326n14
Mercer v. Braziel 283n174
Merchants Nat'l Bank v. Blass .. 190n128
Merchants Nat'l Bank & Trust Co. v. Professional Men's Ass'n, Inc. 69n131; 70n141, n142; 138n126
Merriman v. Sandeen 104n3
Mesnick v. Hempstead Bank ... 267n95; 268n103
Mid-Atlantic Tennis Courts, Inc. v. Citizens Bank & Trust Co. 64n104
Mid-Continent Nat'l Bank v. Bank of Independence 130n71
Migden v. Chase Manhattan Bank 340n109
Mikelberg; United States v. 374n111
Miller v. Race 7n28; 14n21; 128n61
Misemer v. Freda's Restaurant, Inc. 138n121
Mitchell v. Republic Bank & Trust Co. ... 247n122
Mitchell v. Ringston 187n105, n109
Modoc Meat & Cattle Co. v. First State Bank 334n72
Mohr v. State Bank 289n210
Mooney v. GR & Associates 89n92
Moore v. Richmond Hill Sav. Bank 282n167
Morgan v. Depositors Trust Co. ... 132n80
Morgan Guar. Trust Co. v. Chase Manhattan Bank, N.A. 211n64; 286n195
Mortimer Agency, Inc. v. Underwriters Trust Co. 259n47
Motorcity of Jacksonville, Ltd. v. Southeast Bank 144n167
Mourning v. Family Publications Serv., Inc. 359n12
Mowrey v. Walsh 12n9
Mundaca Investment Corp. v. Febba 92n118; 93n120
Murdaugh Volkswagen, Inc. v. First Nat'l Bank 328n23; 334n68; 335n78
Murphy v. Bank of Dahlonega ... 87n81; 90n106

[References are to pages and footnotes.]

Murray Walter, Inc. v. Marine Midland Bank 330n42
Myrick v. National Sav. & Trust Co. 262n65

N

NAB Asset Venture II, L.P. v. Lenertz, Inc. 97n148; 100n161
Nance, In re 44n4
National Acceptance Co. of Am. v. Demes 188n112
National Bank v. Refrigerated Transp. Co. 259n46
National Bank of Commerce v. Seattle Nat'l Bank 201n23
National Bank of N. Am. v. Beinhorn ... 38n164
National Credit Union Admin. v. Michigan Nat'l Bank 330n41
National Park Bank v. Seaboard Bank ... 205n44
National Recovery Sys. v. Ornstein 148n194
National Sav. & Trust Co. v. Park Corp. .. 120n15; 232n57; 235n73
National Shawmut Bank v. International Yarn Corp. 100n162
National State Bank v. Kleinberg 143n161
Nat'l Credit Union Admin. v. Michigan Nat'l Bank 94n126
Nautilus Leasing Serv., Inc. v. Crocker Nat'l Bank 309n89; 310n94
Neo-Tech Sys., Inc. v. Provident Bank ... 268n104
Nesso Surgical Prods., Inc. v. Long Island Trust Co. 301n40
Nester v. O'Donnell 88n87
Nevada State Bank v. Fischer ... 112n54
New Covenant Community Church v. Federal Nat'l Bank & Trust Co. 339n103
New Jersey Lawyers' Fund for Client Protection v. First Fidelity Bank, N.A. 286n194
New Jersey Mortgage & Inv. Corp. v. Berenyi 148n197
New Ulm State Bank v. Brown .. 114n59
New York Credit Men's Adjustment Bureau, Inc. v. Manufacturers Hanover Trust Co. 267n97
New York Flameproofing Co., Inc. v. Chemical Bank 345n139
Newman v. Manufacturers Nat'l Bank ... 332n53
Nichols v. Seale 74n7

Nida v. Michael 151n220
Ninth RMA Partners, L.P. v. Krass 66n113
Norman v. World Wide Distrib., Inc. 165n290
North Valley Bank v. National Bank 25n85
Northside Bldg. & Inv. Co. v. Finance Co. of Am. 53n42; 60n78; 152n221
Northwest Cooperage & Lumber Co. v. Byers 45n6
Northwestern Nat'l Ins. Co. v. Maggio ... 129n70
Norton v. Knapp 75n10
Norwood; People v. 41n183
Nu-Way Serv., Inc. v. Mercantile Trust Co., N.A. 261n59; 266n91

O

Oak Park Currency Exchange, Inc. v. Maropoulos 86n74; 204n39
Ognibene v. Citibank 393n41
O'Hara v. First Nat'l Bank 87n78; 184n79
Olin Corp. v. Cargo Carriers, Inc. ... 11n5
O'Melveny & Myers v. F.D.I.C. 144n167
O.P. Ganjo, Inc. v. Tri-Urban Realty Co., Inc. 122n23
Osborn v. Chicaro Dev. Corp. ... 155n241
Ossip-Harris Ins., Inc. v. Barnett Bank .. 263n67
Overton v. Tyler 20n52
Owensboro Nat'l Bank v. Crisp .. 259n45

P

Pamar Enterprises, Inc. v. Huntington Banks of Michigan 60n84; 288n208
Pan Am. World Airways v. Bankers Trust Co. 302n44
Parent Teacher Ass'n v. Manufacturers Hanover Trust Co. 267n97
Park State Bank v. Arena Auto Auction, Inc. 257n35
Parr v. Security Nat'l Bank ... 340n108; 341n112
Patterson v. First Nat'l Bank ... 120n16
Payne v. Payne 87n79
Payroll Check Cashing v. New Palestine Bank 201n24; 230n44
Peacock v. Rhodes 7n28; 15n22
Pennington County Bank v. First State Bank 228n33
Penny v. Kelley 177n45

TABLE OF CASES

[References are to pages and footnotes.]

People v. (see name of defendant)
People ex (see name of defendant)
People ex rel. (see name of defendant)
Peoples Bank v. Haar 126n53
Peoria Sav. & Loan Ass'n v. Jefferson Trust & Sav. Bank 344n134
Peppers v. Citizens & S. Nat'l Bank 188n115
Perdue v. Crocker National Bank 328n24
Perini Corp. v. First National Bank 236, n75
Perley v. Glastonbury Bank & Trust Co. . . 330n36
Perry v. Cain 70n139
Petersen v. Roylin Enterprises, Inc. 154n228
Peterson v. Holtrachem, Inc. 93n121
Petition of (see name of party)
Phoenix Assurance Co. v. Davis 220n110
Pickard, Estate of 191n131
Pine Bluff Nat'l Bank v. Kesterson 262n61
Pittsburgh Nat'l Bank v. United States . . 310n90
P.J. Panzeca, Inc. v. Llobell 84n62
Planters' Chem. & Oil Co. v. Morris . . . 24n81
Poullier v. Nacua Motors, Inc. . . 340n107
Price v. Neal . . 202n26; 216n92; 226; 227; 228, n37; 229, n43; 230, n44; 231; 236; 237
Professional Sav. Bank v. Galloway Farm Nursery, Inc. 247n121
Prouty v. Roberts 156n242
Provident Sav. Bank v. United Jersey Bank 268n106
Prudential Ins. Co. v. Marine Nat'l Exchange Bank 257n39
Pulaski State Bank v. Kalbe 326n13

Q

Quigley v. Acker 193n150

R

Rakestraw v. Rodrigues 95n135
Ramsey v. First Nat'l Bank & Trust Co. . . 185n86; 186n97; 188n113
Rascar, Inc. v. Bank of Or. 268n106
Ratner v. Chemical Bank of N.Y. Trust Co. 370, nn83, 84
Ravin; State v. 189n121

Ray v. Farmers State Bank 256n31; 331n51; 332n52
Raymer v. Bay State Nat'l Bank 310n94, n96; 334n69
Read v. South Carolina Nat'l Bank 239n88
Reading Trust Co. v. Hutchison 151n214
Reagan v. City Nat'l Bank 189n120
Real Good Food Stores, Inc. v. First Nat'l Bank 325n5
Reed v. Roark 23n76
Rex Smith Propane, Inc. v. National Bank of Commerce 70n138
Reynolds-Wilson Lumber Co. v. People's Nat'l Bank 285n187
Rezapolvi v. First Nat'l Bank . . 147n182; 155n236
Rich v. Franklin Sav. Bank 114n60
Richards v. Arthaloney 94n130
Richardson Co. v. First Nat'l Bank 137n117; 235n68
Riedel v. First Nat'l Bank 221n115
Riegler v. Riegler 89n93
Riggs Nat'l Bank v. Security Bank, N.A. . . 286n195
Rimberg v. Union Trust Co. . . . 341n114
Robbins v. First Fed. Sav. Bank 284n185
Rockland Trust Co. v. South Shore Nat'l Bank 125n45; 343n132
Rose v. United States Nat'l Bank . . 104n2
Rotuba Extruders, Inc. v. Ceppos 93n122
Russell v. First of Am. Bank-Mich., N.A. 395n57

S

Sabin Meyer Regional Sales Corp. v. Citizens Bank 80n46
Salomonsky v. Kelly 21n61
Salsman v. National Community Bank . . . 64n106
Salter v. Vanotti 133n85
Sam Goody, Inc. v. Franklin Nat'l Bank . . 255n23
San Tan Irrigation District v. Wells Fargo Bank 130n75; 252n8; 280n155
Sanden v. Hanson 70n142
Santos v. First Nat'l State Bank 100n160; 342n120
Sawgrass Builders, Inc. v. Realty Coop Inc. 243n100
Sayan v. Riggs Nat'l Bank 327n16

TABLE OF CASES

[References are to pages and footnotes.]

Schaller v. Marine National Bank 327n20
Scheid v. Shields 50n31
Schnitger v. Backus 124n40
Schranz v. I.L. Grossman, Inc. .. 122n25
Scott D. Leibling, P.C. v. Mellon PSFS (NJ) N.A. 345n142
Seattle-First Nat'l Bank v. Kim ... 80n47
Seattle-First Nat'l Bank v. Pacific Nat'l Bank 259n49
Sebastian v. D & S Express, Inc. 288n204
Seigel v. Merrill Lynch, Pierce, Fenner & Smith, Inc. 243n103
Seinfeld v. Commercial Bank & Trust Co. 149n199
Senate Motors, Inc. v. Industrial Bank ... 92n113
Serve v. First Nat'l Bank 107n25
Shaffer v. Brooklyn Park Garden Apartments 134n89
Shaffer v. Rawlins Fin. Co. 185n84
Shanteau, Estate of v. Shanteau 32n131
Shaw v. Union Bank & Trust Co. 336n79
Shepherd Mall State Bank v. Johnson ... 54n49
Siegel v. New England Merchants Nat'l Bank 248n126; 332n59
Silk v. Merrill Lynch, Pierce, Fenner & Smith, Inc. 195n167
Simpson v. Bilderbeck, Inc. 87n77
Simpson v. MBank Dallas, N.A. .. 184n77
Simpson v. Milne 74n9
Skov v. Chase Manhattan Bank .. 335n78
Slaughter v. Jefferson Fed. Sav. & Loan Ass'n 133n86
Smith v. Federated Dep't Stores 377n132
Smith v. Gentilotti 32n135
Smith, In re 325n8
Snethen v. Oklahoma State Union of Farmers Ed. & Co-op. 283n174
Snyder v. Town Hill Motors, Inc. 158n256
Sochaczewski v. Wilmington Sav. Fund Soc'y 39n168
Society Nat'l Bank v. Capital Nat'l Bank 206n46
Society Nat'l Bank v. Kienzle .. 372n104
Southeast First Nat'l Bank v. Atlantic Telec, Inc. 244n107; 248n126
Southern Indus. Banking Corp., In re ... 160n266
Southern Provisions, Inc. v. Harris Trust & Sav. Bank 221n115
Spancom Services, Inc. v. Southtrust Bank, N.A. 267n93
Spears Carpet Mills, Inc. v. Central Nat'l Bank 268n99
Spenser v. Sterling Bank 64n106
Springfield Oil Services, Inc. v. Mermelstein 50n29
St. Cloud Nat'l Bank & Trust Co. v. Sabania Const. Co., Inc. 125n41
St. Francis Hospital v. Vaughn .. 194n151
St. James v. Diversified Commercial Fin. Corp. 141n145
Staff Serv. Associates, Inc. v. Midatlantic Nat'l Bank 341n113
Standard Fin. Co., Ltd. v. Ellis 148n193; 149n200
Stapleton v. First Security Bank 217n93
State v. (see name of defendant)
State Bank v. Omega Electronics, Inc. ... 89n99
State Bank v. Owens 90n105
State ex (see name of state)
State ex rel. (see name of state)
State of (see name of state)
State & Sav. Bank v. Meeker ... 305n61
Stefano v. First Union Nat'l Bank of Virginia 284n184; 287n197
Stone & Webster Engineering Corp. v. First Nat'l Bank & Trust Co. 214n83; 253n16; 288; 325n10
Story v. Lamb 199n7
Strickland v. Kafko Mfg., Inc. 21n60
Suit and Wells Equip. Co. v. Citizens Nat'l Bank 126n53
Sullivan v. United Dealers Corp. 132n80
Sullivan v. Wilton Manors Nat'l Bank ... 172n14
Summerlin v. National Serv. Indus., Inc. 56n64
Sunbelt Savings, FSB v. Cashin Constr. Co. 144n168
Sunshine v. Bankers Trust Co. .. 247n123
Swiss Credit Bank v. Balink ... 244n109

T

Taylor v. Equitable Trust Co. 326n11
Taylor v. Roeder 26n90
Tennessee Farmers Mut. Ins. Co. v. Scott 186n90
Tette v. Marine Midland Bank .. 289n211

TABLE OF CASES

TC–11

[References are to pages and footnotes.]

Texaco, Inc. v. Liberty Nat'l Bank & Trust Co. 339n104
Thiele v. Security State Bank ... 328n21
Third Nat'l Bank v. Hardi-Gardens Supply of Ill., Inc. 124n35
Thomas v. Ford Motor Credit Co. 166n300
Thomas v. Marine Midland Tinkers National Bank 248n124
Thompson Maple Products v. Citizens National Bank 258
Thomton, Sperry & Jensen, Ltd. v. Anderson 146n179
Thrash v. Georgia State Bank ... 334n68
Transamerica Ins. Co. v. Long ... 14n21
Transamerica Ins. Co. v. Standard Oil Co. 372n103
Travelers Indemnity Co. v. Good 258n41; 266n89
Trenton Trust Co. v. Western Sur. Co. ... 147n185
Tri-Power Electronics, In re ... 194n154
Trust Estate of (see name of party)
Tufi; United States v. 55n50
Tusso v. Security Nat'l Bank ... 339n105
Twin City Bank v. Isaacs 336n81

U

Unadilla Nat'l Bank v. McQueer 172n19
Underpinning & Foundation Constructors, Inc. v. Chase Manhattan Bank 64n107
Unico v. Owen 140, n141; 165n292
United Bank & Trust Co. v. Schaeffer ... 149n203; 150n210
United Credit Corp. v. Necamp .. 180n55
United Nat'l Bank v. Airport Plaza Ltd. Partnership 22n65
United Overseas Bank v. Veneers, Inc. ... 53n41
United States v. (see name of defendant)
United States Fidelity & Guar. Co. v. Bank of Bentonville 279n154
United States Fidelity & Guar. Co. v. Federal Reserve Bank 314n109
Universal Acceptance Corp. v. Burks 148n189
Universal C.I.T. Credit Corp. v. Guaranty Bank & Trust Co. ... 125n48; 243n102
Universal C.I.T. Credit Corp. v. Ingel ... 35n149
University Sav. Ass'n v. Intercontinental Consol. Cos., Inc. 156n243

V

Vail Nat'l Bank v. J. Wheeler Constr. Corp. 243n98
Valley Nat'l Bank v. Tang 325n5
Van Balen v. Peoples Bank & Trust Co. ... 187n106, n108
Van Gohren v. Pacific Nat'l Bank 129n67
Van Senus Auto Parts, Inc. v. Michigan Nat'l Bank 303n51
Vaughan v. United States Nat'l Bank ... 372n104
Vending Chattanooga, Inc. v. American National Bank & Trust 266n86
Ventures, Inc. v. Jones . 69n132; 139n127
Virginia Nat'l Bank v. Holt 160n271
Voelker, In re Estate of 185n85

W

Walker v. Texas Commerce Bank 326n11
Walker Bank & Trust Co. v. Jones 372n105
Wallach Sons, Inc. v. Bankers Trust Co. ... 255n23
Warren; State v. 283n174
Weast v. Arnold 151n220
Weaver Landfill, Inc. v. Eastman Envtl. Transp. Services 97n146
Wells Fargo Bank, N.A. v. Hartford Nat'l Bank & Trust Co. 111n48
Werting v. Manufacturers Hanover Trust Co. 301n36
West v. Turchioe 70n142
Western Nat'l Bank v. Rives 97n146
Western State Bank v. First Union Bank & Trust Co. 142n157
Western Union Telegraph Co. v. People's Nat'l Bank 26n93
Westervelt v. Gateway Fin. Serv. 148n192
Westport Bank & Trust Co. v. Lodge 262n65
White v. Household Fin. Corp. .. 188n112
Whiteside v. Douglas County Bank 76n21
Whitmire v. Woodbury .. 337n89; 338n97
Wilder Binding Co. v. Oak Park Trust & Sav. Bank 265n82
Wildman Stores, Inc. v. Carlisle Distrib. Co., Inc. 113n56
Wiley v. Bunker Hill National Bank 336
Williams v. Cooper 32n132

TABLE OF CASES

[References are to pages and footnotes.]

Williams v. Lafayette Prod. Credit Ass'n .. 186n99
Williams v. Montana Nat'l Bank 256n31
Williams v. Stansbury 156n244
Willis v. Willis 89n93
Winkie, Inc. v. Heritage Bank ... 265n79
Winkler v. Commercial Nat'l Bank 265n77
Wippert v. Blackfeet Tribe of the Blackfeet Indian Reservation 199n7
W.J. Miranda Const. Corp., Inc. v. First Union Nat. Bank 267n97; 268n99
Wohlhuter v. St. Charles Lumber & Fuel Co. 185n81
Wolfe v. Eaker 170n5
Wolverton Farmers Elevator v. First Am. Bank 104n2
Worthen Bank & Trust Co., N.A. v. Utley 90n104
Wright v. Bank of Cal., N.A. 53n44; 104n7

X

Xanthopoulos v. Thomas Cook, Inc. 41n180; 160n270

Y

Young v. Adams 227n30
Young v. Grote ... 249, 250, n1; 256, n29
YYY Corp. v. Gazda 97n148

Z

Zatal v. First Nat'l City Bank ... 334n71

TABLE OF STATUTES AND AUTHORITIES

[References are to pages and footnotes.]

Uniform Commercial Code

Section	Page
1-102(2)(b)	24n79
1-103	5n22; 228; 229n38
1-201	23n78; 24n82, n83
1-201(8)	160n266
1-201(9)	12n12
1-201(14)	50n30; 67, n122; 98n149
1-201(15)	2n5
1-201(16)	129n65
1-201(19)	129n64
1-201(20)	31n123; 49n24; 53n40; 99n156; 119n7; 172n18; 296n21
1-201(24)	3n15; 27n95
1-201(25)(b)	134n88
1-201(25)(c)	131n78; 132n82; 133n83
1-201(27)	137n112; 346n146
1-201(28)	334n67
1-201(30)	334n67
1-201(31)	106n20; 160n268; 289n210
1-201(35)	91n111; 285n190
1-201(37)	47n17
1-201(38)	262n64
1-201(39)	24n81; 94n128
1-201(43)	56n63; 94n125; 251n6; 269n108; 330n33
1-201(44)(d)	119n12
1-201(46)	23n75; 388n6
1-203	301n38
1-205(25)	132
1-205(26)	132
1-206(1)	45n8
1-208	34n141
2A-304(1)	10n4
2A-305(1)	10n4; 11n6
2-103(1)(b)	129n67
2-105(1)	1n2
2-208	328n22
2-210	47n14
2-301	96n137
2-312	198n1
2-313	141n150; 198n1
2-314	198n1
2-315	198n1
2-403(1)	10n4; 12n10
2-403(2)	12n11
2-601	141n146
2-602	141n146
2-607(1)	141n148; 244n104

Uniform Commercial Code—Cont.

Section	Page
2-607(5)	247n120
2-714	244n105
3-102	3
3-102(a)	3n11, n14; 14n18
3-103	18n35; 19n49, n51; 130n75; 260n53
3-103(a)(2)	19n48; 37n160
3-103(a)(3)	19n46; 37n159
3-103(a)(4)	252n8; 273n125; 275n130; 280n155
3-103(a)(5)	18n38; 37n156
3-103(a)(6)	18, n41, n42; 23, n72; 388n5
3-103(a)(7)	255n28; 260n52; 266n85; 278n144; 279n151
3-103(a)(9)	18n34, n36; 23, n71; 388n5
3-103(a)(11)	39n169; 69n136; 342n118
3-103(f)	19n45
3-104	23n73; 27n100; 36; 37n158; 40n178, n179; 41n185
3-104(a)	3n8; 17; 18n33; 25n86; 56n56; 70n144; 119n10; 166n299; 388n5
3-104(a)(2)	27n99; 31n127
3-104(a)(3)	35n146, n147; 36n152
3-104(b)	3n12; 119n9
3-104(c)	17n30; 27n100
3-104(e)	3n9; 18n37; 19n43; 36n153; 79n36
3-104(f)	38n161
3-104(g)	38n165
3-104(h)	40n175
3-104(i)	40n177
3-104(j)	18n39, n40; 37n155, n157
3-105	29n115; 67; 68n130
3-105(a)	67n119; 68n125; 69n137; 246n116; 274n128
3-105(b)	68n127; 69n134; 138n123, n125
3-106	18; 20n54; 22n63, n66, n68, n69; 41n182; 166n301
3-106(a)	21n57, n59; 70n145
3-106(a)(ii)	70n143
3-106(b)(i)	22n62
3-106(b)(ii)	22n64
3-106(c)	22n67; 41n181, n182; 139n131
3-106(d)	166n302
3-107	25; 27n97, n98
3-108	31; 34n144, n145
3-108(a)	31n129

[References are to pages and footnotes.]

Uniform Commercial Code—Cont.

Section	Page
3-108(b)	32n137, n138; 33n139
3-108(c)	34n143
3-109	27; 29n114
3-109(a)(1)	28n103, n106
3-109(a)(2)	28n107
3-109(a)(3)	28n101
3-109(b)	28n110; 29n111, n113
3-110	31n124, n126
3-110(a)	29n116, n117
3-110(b)	29n116
3-110(c)	30n118; 31n123
3-110(c)(1)	30n119
3-110(c)(2)	30n120
3-110(c)(2)(iv)	30n122
3-110(d)	60n84
3-112	25, n87
3-112(b)	25n88; 26n91
3-113	32n135
3-114	26n93
3-115	28n108, n109; 252n12
3-115(a)	189n122
3-115(b)	76n19; 189n123; 191n136
3-115(c)	189n121
3-116(a)	76n24; 87n82
3-116(b)	77n25; 87n83
3-117	20n53; 70, n141; 71n146; 139n129, n130
3-118(g)	220n111
3-201	51, n36; 52n38; 157n249; 283n179; 330n36; 364n42
3-201(a)	44n3; 51n35; 58n72; 67
3-201(b)	54n47, n48; 178n51; 282n168; 296n22
3-202	98n152; 157, n250; 158n252, n255
3-203	48, 49n23, n26; 50n32; 60n81, n83, n84; 67n117; 151n220; 153n225, n227; 157n246; 201n23
3-203(a)	49n28; 98n149; 105n12; 202n31; 204n37; 246n116; 283n178
3-203(b)	66n114; 68n124; 143n164; 151, n219; 153n226; 181n57; 207n53; 212n70; 233n62; 330n37
3-203(c)	54n46; 59n77
3-203(d)	60n79, n82
3-204	53; 55n52
3-204(a)	54n49; 55n50, n52, n53; 58n70; 75n10
3-204(d)	58n67, n68
3-205	55, 88n89
3-205(a)	53n43; 56n55, n57, n59

Uniform Commercial Code—Cont.

Section	Page
3-205(b)	54n45; 58n69, n71, n72
3-205(c)	58n73
3-205(d)	88n88; 204n38
3-206	61, n89, n91
3-206(a)	61n90
3-206(b)	62n92
3-206(c)	62n93; 289, n213; 321n151
3-206(c)(1)	61n87; 63n97; 289n217
3-206(c)(2)	61n87; 64n105; 289n215; 290n219
3-206(c)(3)	63n96; 289n216
3-206(c)(4)	289n214
3-206(d)(2)	65n108
3-206(e)	61n86
3-206(f)	139n132
3-207	157n251; 170n1; 179; 180n56
3-301	49n24, n25; 57n66; 65, n110; 66n113; 77n28; 97n144; 171n13; 172n18; 181n57; 207n55; 231n55; 284n180; 296n24; 330n38
3-301(ii)	161n275; 284n181
3-302	14n16; 124n33; 139n135; 142n156, n158; 143n163; 144n165, n168, n169, n170; 170n6
3-302(a)	59n74; 118, n1; 145n174; 166n298; 282n169
3-302(a)(1)	118n2; 142; 167n307
3-302(a)(2)	132n79; 134
3-302(a)(2)(i)	119n3
3-302(a)(2)(ii)	119n4; 167n306
3-302(a)(2)(iii)	134n92, n93; 173n22
3-302(a)(2)(iii)–(vi)	119n5
3-302(a)(2)(iv)	141n153
3-302(a)(2)(v)	162n281
3-302(a)(2)(vi)	141n152; 170n7
3-302(b)	134n91; 139n136; 151n215, n216; 173n25; 178n52
3-302(c)	119n6; 143
3-302(vi)	162n281
3-303	120, n18, n19; 122n26; 123n30, n32; 124n36; 233n63, n64
3-303(a)(1)	120n13; 121n22; 125n42
3-303(a)(2)	123n31; 125n42
3-303(a)(3)	124n35
3-303(a)(4)	122n24
3-303(a)(5)	122n24
3-303(b)	120n16, n17, n18; 139n133; 141n147; 205n40
3-304	134; 135n100; 143n160
3-304(1)(a)	142n159
3-304(a)(1)	135n94

Uniform Commercial Code—Cont.

Section	Page
3-304(a)(2)	135n95
3-304(a)(3)	135n96
3-304(b)(1)	135n98
3-304(b)(2)	135n97; 173n22
3-304(c)	135n99
3-305	14n17; 138n122; 140n137; 141n149, n151; 146n181; 147n185, n186; 148n189, n190, n193, n196; 149n204; 174n32; 177n43
3-305(a)(1)	139n135; 140n138; 146n177; 147; 154n233
3-305(a)(1)(i)	147n184
3-305(a)(1)(ii)	148n188, n192
3-305(a)(1)(iii)	149n198
3-305(a)(1)(iv)	151n218; 213n76
3-305(a)(2)	120n16; 138n119; 153n224; 154n233; 205n40
3-305(b)	120n16; 138n118; 144n171; 146, n178; 154n232; 205n40; 243n99
3-305(c)	99n157; 154; 155n235, n239, n241; 159n260; 174n28, n31; 176n41, n42; 177n43; 344n133, n136
3-305(d)	90n103; 91n107
3-306	14n17; 49n27; 59n75; 136n102, n103; 145, n173; 152n222; 154, n229, 155n240; 158n253, n254; 175n38; 283n170, n175
3-307	65n109; 136n108; 137n111, n115
3-307(b)	136n106
3-307(b)(1)	136n105
3-307(b)(2)	137n109
3-307(b)(2)(iii)	137n110
3-307(b)(3)	136n107
3-307(b)(4)	137n114
3-308	159; 160n264, n270, n271; 161n274, n275, n276; 162n278, n279; 195n168
3-308(a)	159n263; 160n265, n267; 161n272
3-308(b)	161n273, n275
3-309	96, n139; 100n161; 195n166
3-309(a)	97n143, n145; 247n119
3-309(a)(iii)	98n151
3-309(b)	97n142; 98n155
3-310	193; 195n164; 287n201
3-310(a)	194n153, n155, n160; 416n191
3-310(b)	96n138; 193n147; 194n152; 283n172
3-310(b)(1)	193n149; 194n156, n158, n159

Uniform Commercial Code—Cont.

Section	Page
3-310(b)(2)	193n148; 194n156
3-310(b)(3)	195n161, n162, n167
3-310(b)(4)	195n163, n165, n166; 247n119; 287n202
3-311	196, n173, n175
3-311(a)	196n169
3-311(b)	196n169
3-311(c)(1)	196n172
3-311(c)(2)	196n174
3-311(d)	196n171
3-312	100, n163, n164, n165; 170n1
3-312(a)(3)	100n166
3-312(b)	100n166
3-312(b)(1)	100n167
3-312(b)(2)	100n168
3-312(b)(4)	100n169
3-312(c)	101n170
3-401	73, n1; 74n8
3-401(a)	74n2, n3; 75n12; 79n37; 80n45; 94n126; 159n261; 199n8; 223n4; 246n113
3-401(a)(ii)	92n115
3-401(b)	74n7
3-402	56n62; 91; 92n116; 93n123; 159n261; 210n61; 246n113
3-402(a)	91n112; 92n114, n115
3-402(b)(2)	93n119
3-402(c)	93n121
3-403	94, n130
3-403(a)	94n124, n127, n129; 159n261; 210n62; 223n4; 252n7; 330n32; 331n43; 332n55
3-403(c)	94n131
3-404	130n75; 237n80, n82; 270n115; 271; 272n123; 274n127; 275n129, n131; 276n133, n135, n137; 277n138; 278n146, n147, n149
3-404(a)	270n114; 272n120, n124; 277n139; 331n46
3-404(b)	331n47
3-404(c)(i)	278n143
3-404(c)(ii)	277n141
3-404(d)	278n145
3-405	130n75; 271n117; 272n119; 276n134, n136; 278n148; 279; 280n156, n157; 281n163, n165; 331n48
3-405(a)(2)	279n152
3-405(a)(3)	281n159, n162
3-405(b)	279n154
3-405(c)	279n153

[References are to pages and footnotes.]

Uniform Commercial Code—Cont.

Section	Page
3-406	76n18; 130n75; 159n261; 211n66; 236n77; 250; 251n3, n5; 252n9; 256n30, n31, n33; 257n35; 258n41; 259n50; 278n145; 279n154; 331n44; 332n52; 373n106
3-406(a)	246n115; 251n2
3-406(b)	259n44
3-407	76n17, n20; 170n1; 188; 189n126; 190n128; 191n132, n133, n138; 211n63; 253n15
3-407b	191n131
3-407(3)	76n20
3-407(a)(i)	188n117
3-407(a)(ii)	189n121; 211n68
3-407(b)	188n115; 189n124; 190n127; 191n135; 211n65; 253n14
3-407(c)	191n137; 252n11; 253n13
3-407(c)(i)	211n65
3-407(c)(ii)	211n67
3-408	79n37; 80n46; 231n54; 333n64; 337n90; 338n91
3-409	79n38, n41; 110n42
3-409(a)	79n39, n40, n43; 80n44, n45
3-409(c)	110n43
3-409(d)	39n171; 79n38; 111n46; 192n140; 342n121
3-410	75n10; 78n33; 170n1; 192; 193n145, n146
3-410(a)	193n144
3-410(c)	193n146
3-411	343n126, n128
3-411(b)	343n127
3-411(c)	343n129
3-412	39n167; 75; 76n14, n19; 77n27; 109n39; 188n116; 344n135
3-412–3-415	74n4; 99n157
3-413	38n164; 39n172; 78; 342n122
3-413(a)	79n35; 81n56; 188n116; 192n141
3-413(a)(i)	78n30
3-413(a)(ii)	78n33
3-413(b)	78n33, n34
3-414	80, n49; 81n53, n54; 84n63, n65; 192n142
3-414(a)	76n14; 81n50
3-414(b)	81n50, n51; 188n116; 223n3; 338n93
3-414(c)	81n57; 192, n139
3-414(d)	104n1; 107n22
3-414(e)	83, n61; 84n64
3-414(f)	108, n27; 112, n55; 200n11

Uniform Commercial Code—Cont.

Section	Page
3-415	81; 113n57, n58
3-415(a)	82n58; 182n64; 188n116; 206n49; 223n3
3-415(b)	83, n61; 199n9; 200n13
3-415(c)	82n59; 112; 200n11
3-415(d)	192, n143
3-415(e)	108, n28; 112n53; 195n162; 200n11
3-416	74n5; 198n2, n3; 200n14, n15, n17, n18; 204; 205n41; 207n54; 208n56; 213n73, n77
3-416(a)	200n19; 201n21, n22; 207n52
3-416(a)(1)	216n88
3-416(a)(2)	202n28; 209n59; 218n100
3-416(a)(4)	121n21; 212n69
3-416(a)(5)	213n74
3-416(b)	219; 220n112; 221n113
3-416(c)	200n14; 219n105
3-416(d)	200n12; 219n104
3-417	74n5; 105n11; 198n2; 200n14, n15; 214, n81; 216n89, n92; 219n103; 221n117; 229n43; 254n22; 269n113
3-417(a)	200n19; 201n20, n22; 214n78; 219n101
3-417(a)(1)	216n87, n88; 230n50; 321n149
3-417(a)(2)	217n95
3-417(a)(3)	202n29; 216n91; 223n2; 230n48
3-417(b)	219; 221n116, n118
3-417(c)	254n21; 269n112; 279n150; 281n161
3-417(d)	219n102; 230n47; 231n53
3-417(d)(1)	200n19; 201n20, n22; 214n79; 218n98; 230n50
3-417(d)(2)	221n116
3-417(e)	200n14; 219n105
3-417(f)	219n104
3-418	228, 229n39, n40; 238n84; 306n66
3-418(c)	229n41, n42; 230n50; 343n131
3-418(d)	231n55
3-419	85; 88n91; 89n98, n99
3-419(a)	85n69, n70, n71; 182n63
3-419(b)	86n73; 89n97
3-419(c)	88n86, n88, n90
3-419(d)	91n108, n109
3-419(e)	87n79; 181n59; 182n66
3-420	282; 283n177; 287n197, n198; 288n203, n207

TABLE OF STATUTES AND AUTHORITIES

[References are to pages and footnotes.]

Uniform Commercial Code—
Cont.

Section	Page
3-420(a)	172n16; 237n79; 246n118; 255n26; 282n166; 283n173, n176; 284n182, n185
3-420(a)(i)	288n204
3-420(a)(ii)	287n196
3-420(b)	289n209, n212
3-501	81n52; 104, n8
3-501(a)	104n2; 330n39
3-501(b)(1)	105n15; 106n16, n17; 300n32
3-501(b)(2)	104n6; 105n9; 201n23
3-501(b)(2)(iii)	51n33; 173n23, n24
3-501(b)(3)	105n14; 109n31
3-501(b)(4)	110n41
3-502	81n52; 106; 108; 109n40
3-502(a)(1)	109n37
3-502(a)(2)	109n38
3-502(a)(3)	76n22; 109n38
3-502(b)(1)	108n29; 109n32
3-502(b)(2)	109n33; 305n63
3-502(b)(3)(i)	109n35
3-502(b)(3)(ii)	110n45
3-502(b)(4)	110n44
3-502(d)(1)	109n34
3-502(d)(2)	109n36
3-502(e)	96n141; 106n18
3-503	107
3-503(a)	82n59; 104n1; 107n22
3-503(b)	82n59; 107n24, n26
3-503(c)	111, n47, n50, n51; 112n53
3-504	114
3-504(a)	96n141; 114n61
3-504(c)	114n59
3-505	106n19
3-505(b)	106n21
3-601	170n6; 171n9; 180n54
3-601(3)	181n60
3-601(a)	170n4
3-601(b)	105n13; 151n217; 171n10; 173n21; 178n52
3-602	171; 175n34, n35; 199n10; 285n189
3-602(a)	51n37; 99n157; 104n5; 105n10; 155n237; 159n258; 171n12; 173n26; 194n157; 218n99; 283n171; 306n64; 343n125
3-602(b)(1)	175n37
3-602(b)(1)(i)	174n30
3-602(b)(1)(ii)	174n29; 175n33
3-602(b)(2)	176n40
3-603	177
3-603(a)	177n45
3-603(b)	178n46

Uniform Commercial Code—
Cont.

Section	Page
3-603(c)	177n44, n45
3-604	178; 180n54
3-604(a)	170n5
3-604(a)(i)	178n48
3-604(a)(ii)	178n53
3-604(b)	178n50; 182n67
3-604(e)	187n107
3-604(f)	185n82
3-604(g)(i)	185n83
3-604(g)(ii)	186n87
3-604(g)(iii)	186n94
3-605	181; 182n64, n65, n68; 183n70, n71, n76
3-605(b)	178n49; 181n62
3-605(c)	182n69
3-605(d)	183n72, n73; 190n129
3-605(e)	184n77
3-605(g)(iv)	186n93
3-605(h)	88n84
3-605(i)	188n111
3-605(i)(i)	183n74
3-605(i)(ii)	183n75
3-803	247n120
4A-101	407n120
4A-102	407n120, n124
4A-103(a)(1)	408n126; 410n136, n138
4A-103(a)(1)(i)	410n139
4A-103(a)(1)(ii)	410n140
4A-103(a)(1)(iii)	4n16; 407n122
4A-103(a)(2)	409n129
4A-103(a)(3)	409n129, n133
4A-103(a)(4)	408n128
4A-103(a)(5)	408n127
4A-104	407n121; 409n135; 410n139
4A-104(a)	409n130
4A-104(b)	409n134
4A-104(c)	409n131
4A-104(d)	409n132
4A-108	410n137
4A-201	419n217; 421n229
4A-202(a)	421n226
4A-202(b)	422n231
4A-202(c)	421n230
4A-203	421n227, n228, n230; 422n231, n232, n235
4A-203(a)(2)	422n234
4A-205	420n218, n222
4A-205(a)(1)	420n219
4A-205(a)(2)	420n220, n223
4A-205(a)(3)	420n221, n223
4A-205(b)	420n224, n225

[References are to pages and footnotes.]

Uniform Commercial Code—Cont.

Section	Page
4A-209	411n141; 412n157
4A-209(a)	411n142
4A-209(b)(1)	412n155; 416n185
4A-209(b)(2)	412n156; 415n177
4A-209(b)(3)	412n158
4A-210(a)	415n175, n176
4A-210(b)	415n173, n174
4A-212	413n168; 414n169
4A-301(a)	411n143
4A-301(b)	415n173
4A-302	411n146
4A-302(a)	411n144
4A-302(a)(2)	411n147; 412n148
4A-302(b)	411n145, n146
4A-302(c)	411n147
4A-303	418n207; 420n223
4A-303(a)	418n208; 419n210, n211
4A-303(b)	419n212, n213
4A-303(c)	419n214, n215
4A-305	412n150
4A-305(a)	412n149
4A-305(d)	414n170, n171
4A-402(b)	413n163; 415n178; 419n216
4A-402(c)	412n151, n152; 415n178; 418n209; 419n216
4A-402(d)	412n153
4A-403	412n156; 413n167; 417n197, n199; 418n203; 423n239, n241
4A-403(a)(1)	417n196
4A-403(a)(2)	418n201, n202
4A-403(a)(3)	418n204
4A-403(b)	417n198; 423n238
4A-403(c)	417n200; 423n240
4A-404(a)	413n159; 415n179
4A-404(b)	413n160, n161
4A-405	415n182; 416n184, n187
4A-405(a)	412n154
4A-405(a)(i)	415n180
4A-405(a)(ii)	415n181
4A-405(c)	416n183
4A-405(d)	416n186, n188
4A-406	416n189; 417n193
4A-406(a)	416n190
4A-406(b)	416n191; 417n192, n194
4A-506	412n149
4-102(a)	5n20; 203n33
4-103	335n74
4-103(a)	242n96
4-104(a)(4)	300n31
4-104(a)(5)	203n35; 295n13; 324n4; 334n66; 343n130

Uniform Commercial Code—Cont.

Section	Page
4-104(a)(9)	4n18; 203n34; 388n8
4-104(a)(10)	111n48; 302n45; 304n54
4-104(c)	130n72
4-105(1)	38n162
4-105(2)	63n99; 295n14
4-105(3)	63n100; 333n62
4-105(5)	63n100; 295n15
4-106	40n176
4-106(a)	4n19; 40n176
4-106(b)	4n19
4-111	220n111; 268n101
4-201	295n17
4-201(1)	285, n191
4-201(a)	63n98; 124n39; 295n12; 299n26
4-201(b)	63n101; 289n213; 321n151, n152
4-202	301
4-202(2)	302n44
4-202(a)(1)	301n39
4-202(a)(4)	302n42
4-202(b)	302n43
4-202(c)	296n19
4-204	301
4-204(a)	301n35
4-204(b)(1)	299n30
4-205(1)	277n140; 296, n23
4-207	74n5; 198n2; 204
4-207(a)	200n19; 201n21, n22; 203n36; 205n42; 207n52; 219n101
4-207(a)(1)	216n87, n88
4-207(a)(2)	202n28; 209n59; 217n95; 218n100
4-207(a)(3)	202n29; 216n91
4-207(a)(4)	212n69
4-207(a)(5)	213n74
4-207(b)	202n32; 206n48
4-207(c)	220n112; 221n113
4-207(d)	218n98; 219n102, n105
4-207(e)	200n12; 219n104
4-208	74n5; 105n11; 125n41; 198n2; 214
4-208(a)	200n19; 201n20, n22; 214n78; 246n116; 254n18; 306n66
4-208(a)(1)	216n88; 230n50; 254n20; 286n192; 321n149
4-208(a)(2)	254n20
4-208(a)(3)	223n2; 230n48
4-208(b)	221n116, n118
4-208(c)	254n21; 269n112; 279n150; 281n161
4-208(d)	200n19; 201n20, n22; 214n79; 221n116; 230n47, n50; 231n53

TABLE OF STATUTES AND AUTHORITIES TS-7

[References are to pages and footnotes.]

Uniform Commercial Code— Cont.

Section	Page
4-208(e)	219n105
4-208(f)	219n104
4-209	198n2
4-210	124, n38, n40
4-210(a)(1)	125n44
4-210(a)(2)	126n49
4-210(a)(3)	126n54; 214n84
4-210(c)	127n56, n57
4-211	124, n38; 125n42, n43; 127n58
4-212(a)	311n102; 312n103
4-213(1)	313n105
4-213(4)(a)	313n105
4-213(c)	313n105
4-213(d)	313n105
4-214(a)	308n80
4-215(a)	306; 313n105
4-215(a)(1)	307n69
4-215(a)(2)	307n72; 308
4-215(a)(3)	305n62; 308n77
4-215(c)	299n27
4-215(e)	126n50
4-215(e)(1)	313n105
4-216	306n68
4-301	108n29; 302; 304n52, n56
4-301(a)	311n100
4-301(a)(1)	308n79
4-301(a)(2)	109n32
4-301(b)	311n101
4-302	108n29
4-302(a)	311n99
4-302(a)(1)	305n59, n61; 306n65
4-302(b)	305n60
4-303	306n67; 308
4-303(1)(a)	342n123
4-303(a)	310n91; 339n100; 400n86
4-303(a)(1)	310n95
4-303(a)(4)	310n96
4-303(a)(5)	311n98
4-401	232n58; 325; 329n28; 331n49; 332n57; 374n107; 399n82
4-401(a)	99n158; 105n10; 215n86; 216n90; 224n5; 232n59; 288n208; 302n46; 303n49
4-401(b)	327n19
4-401(c)	32n136; 245n111; 332n54, n56, n58
4-401(d)	217n97
4-401(d)(1)	231n52
4-401(d)(2)	252n11
4-402	326n12; 333; 335n75, n76; 336n85; 337n86; 399n81; 400n91

Uniform Commercial Code— Cont.

Section	Page
4-402(a)	333n60; 334n72
4-402(b)	333n61; 335n78; 336n79
4-402(c)	335n73
4-403	95n134; 159n259; 242n96; 243n97; 309n85; 332n54; 337; 338n92, n95; 342n117, n124
4-403(a)	242n95; 338n94, n98
4-403(b)	342n116
4-403(c)	247; 332n58
4-404	344, n137, n138
4-405	309n84, n85; 345; 346n144; 347n148, n149, n150
4-406	130n75; 260; 262n63; 264n76; 331n45; 332n52
4-406(a)	264n72
4-406(b)	261n57; 263n69
4-406(c)	260n55, n56; 261n60; 262n63; 263n71
4-406(d)(1)	264n73
4-406(d)(2)	264n75
4-406(e)	265n80
4-406(f)	266n92; 269n110; 325n6
4-407	105n11; 241; 244n106; 306n66
5-106(a)	123n28
5-108(a)	122n27
7-201(2)	2n5
7-501(4)	128n60
7-504(1)	10n4
8-102(a)(4)	2n7
8-301(1)	10n4
9-102(a)(11)	3n10
9-102(a)(42)	1n3
9-102(a)(44)	1n2
9-102(a)(47)	2n6
9-109	47n18
9-109(a)(3)	47n16
9-207	186n95
9-308(a)	47n19
9-310(a)	47n19
9-310(b)	47n19
9-315(a)(1)	10n4
9-317(a)	309n88
9-317(b)	11n7
9-317(d)	11n7, n8
9-318(1)	10n3
9-320(a)	12n11
9-322(a)	309n88
9-322(a)(1)	47n21
9-334(d)	309n88
9-403	46n11
9-403(b)	167n309

[References are to pages and footnotes.]

Uniform Commercial Code—Cont.

Section	Page
9-403(e)	167n304
9-404(a)	11n8; 46n11; 48n22
9-501	47n20
9-502	47n20

Uniform Consumer Credit Code

Section	Page
Generally	364n37
3.201	364n42
3.307	165n293

Uniform Negotiable Instruments Law

Section	Page
Generally	7
62	228n35
65	228n35
66	228n35
88	173, n27
196	228, n36

Code of Federal Regulations

Title:Section	Page
12:30	319n136
12:35	55n51
12:201	16n28
12:205	364n39; 389n13; 393n42; 394n44, n49; 395n57; 399n79
12:205.2(a)(1)	391n29
12:205.2(a)(2)	391n31
12:205.2(b)	402n105
12:205.2(b)(1)	390n20
12:205.2(h)	396n61
12:205.2(m)	393n39; 394n43
12:205.3(b)	390n22
12:205.3(b)(5)	389n18
12:205.3(c)(2)	390n21
12:205.3(c)(3)	390n23; 402n105
12:205.3(c)(4)	390n24
12:205.3(c)(5)	390n26
12:205.3(c)(6)	391n27
12:205.3(c)(7)	391n28
12:205.5(a)	391n31
12:205.5(b)	391n32
12:205.5(b)(1)	392n33
12:205.5(d)	364n41
12:205.6	398n72
12:205.6(a)	394n46
12:205.6(b)	394n47

Code of Federal Regulations—Cont.

Title:Section	Page
12:205.6(b)(2)	394n48
12:205.6(b)(3)	395n51, n53
12:205.6(b)(5)	396n58
12:205.7	392n34
12:205.7(a)	392n35
12:205.7(b)	392n36
12:205.8(a)	393n38
12:205.8(b)	393n37
12:205.9	396n59
12:205.9(a)	396n60
12:205.9(b)	396n62
12:205.9(c)	397n63
12:205.10(c)	399n78
12:205.10(d)	403n109
12:205.11(a)(1)	397n65
12:205.11(a)(2)	397n66
12:205.11(b)(1)	397n67
12:205.11(b)(1)(ii)	397n69
12:205.11(b)(2)	397n68
12:205.11(c)(1)	397n70; 398n73, n74
12:205.11(c)(2)(i)	398n71, n72
12:205.11(c)(2)(iii)	398n73
12:205.11(c)(2)(iv)	398n74
12:205.11(d)(1)	398n75
12:205.11(d)(2)	398n76
12:205.11(iii)	397n69
12:210	293n2; 402n106; 404n110; 406n119
12:210.25(c)	405n111
12:210.32(a)	405n112
12:210.38(b)	405n113
12:220.38	318n129
12:220.38(a)	318n130
12:226.1(c)(1)	360n16
12:226.1(c)(2)	360n17
12:226.2	361n18, n19, n20, n21, n22
12:226.2(a)(10)	361n25
12:226.2(a)(17)(i)	364n43
12:226.2(a)(17)(ii)	364n44
12:226.2(a)(17)(iii)	362n27
12:226.2(a)(17)(iv)	362n28
12:226.2(a)(20)	361n18
12:226.2(a)(21)	367n66
12:226.5a	365n51
12:226.5a(ii)	367n59
12:226.5a(a)(1)	365n52
12:226.5a(a)(2)	365n54
12:226.5a(b)	365n53; 366n56
12:226.5a(d)(1)	366n57
12:226.5a(d)(2)	366n58
12:226.5a(d)(2)(i)	367n59

Code of Federal Regulations— Cont.

Title:Section	Page
12:226.5a(e)(1)	367n60
12:226.5a(e)(2)	367n61
12:226.5a(e)(3)	367n63
12:226.5a(c)	365n53
12:226.5(b)(1)	365n47; 367n64
12:226.5(b)(2)(i)	365n48
12:226.5(b)(2)(ii)	365n50
12:226.6(a)	367n65
12:226.6(b)	368n69, n71
12:226.6(c)	368n72
12:226.6(d)	368n75
12:226.7	368n78
12:226.7(j)	365n49
12:226.9(b)	365n46
12:226.9(c)(1)	365n46
12:226.10(a)	375n120
12:226.12	371n94; 372n100; 393n40
12:226.12(C)(2)	379n148
12:226.12(a)	371n91
12:226.12(a)(1)-1	371n89
12:226.12(a)(1)-4	371n90
12:226.12(a)(2)	371n91
12:226.12(b)	371n92
12:226.12(b)(1)	371n97
12:226.12(b)(3)	371n98; 372n99
12:226.12(b)(5)	374n109
12:226.12(c)(1)	362n29; 378n140; 379n147
12:226.12(c)(3)(i)	378n144
12:226.12(c)(3)(ii)	379n145
12:226.12(c)(3)(iii)	379n146
12:226.12(d)(1)	379n150
12:226.12(d)(2)	368n74; 380n153
12:226.12(d)(3)	380n153
12:226.12(e)	375n122
12:226.12(e)(2)	376n123
12:226.12(f)(1)	362n30
12:226.13	368n76
12:226.13(a)	376n127
12:226.13(b)(1)	376n128
12:226.13(c)(1)	376n129
12:226.13(c)(2)	376n130
12:226.13(d)(1)	377n131
12:226.13(d)(2)	377n132
12:226.13(e)	377n133
12:226.13(f)	377n134
12:226.13(g)(1)	377n135
12:226.13(g)(3)	377n137
12:226.13(g)(4)	377n138
12:226.13(h)	377n136
12:226.14(b)	366n55

Code of Federal Regulations— Cont.

Title:Section	Page
12:226.28(a)(1)	363n33
12:226.28(a)(2)(i)	363n35
12:226.28(a)(2)(ii)	363n36
12:226.28(a)-5	363n35
12:227.14	90n101
12:229	7n32; 126n51; 293n3
12:229.2	307n74; 317n125
12:229.2(f)	315n111
12:229.2(g)	315n110
12:229.2(r)	315n112
12:229.2(s)	315n112
12:229.2(z)	317n125
12:229.2(bb)	319n142
12:229.2(cc)	307n74
12:229.2(ee)	317n127
12:229.10	316n117
12:229.10(a)	413n162
12:229.10(b)	413n162
12:229.12	316n117
12:229.12(b)	315n113
12:229.12(c)	315n114
12:229.13	315n115
12:229.13(e)	320n146
12:229.13(h)	315n116
12:229.14(a)	316n120
12:229.16(a)	316n118
12:229.16(b)	316n119
12:229.21	316n121
12:229.30	317n124
12:229.30(2)	319n141
12:229.30(a)	317n122
12:229.30(a)(1)	317n126; 318n128
12:229.30(a)(2)	317n126; 318n133; 319n134
12:229.30(c)	308n82; 317n123
12:229.31(a)	317n122
12:229.31(a)(1)	318n128
12:229.31(a)(2)	317n123; 318n133; 319n134
12:229.31(c)	307n75; 319n138
12:229.31(d)	319n135
12:229.31(2)	319n141
12:229.32	319n140
12:229.32(b)	307n75; 319n139
12:229.33	320n144
12:229.33(a)	320n145
12:229.34(a)	322n154
12:229.34(b)	322n156
12:229.35(a)	320n148; 321n150
12:229.35(c)	63n102; 321n152
12:229.36	295n16; 304n58; 308n76, n81

[References are to pages and footnotes.]

Code of Federal Regulations—Cont.

Title:Section	Page
12:229.36(c)	300n32
12:229.36(d)	295n11; 299n28; 304n55; 319n137
12:229.38	320n147
12:229.38(d)	321n153
12:535.3	90n101
16:433	46n9; 141n144; 166n295; 378n142
16:433.2(a)	166n296
16:444.3	90n102
31:100.5(a)	354n29, n30
31:100.5(a)(1)	354n28
31:100.5(a)(2)	354n28
31:100.6	354n31
31:100.7(a)(1)	354n29
31:100.7(a)(2)	354n30
31:100.7(b)(2)	354n30

United States Code

Title:Section	Page
11:542(b)	309n83
12:341	16n28
12:461-466	298n25
12:1823(e)(1)	144n167
12:4001–4010	7n31; 126n51; 293n4
12:4008(a)	293n6
12:4008(b)	293n7
12:4008(c)(1)	293n8
12:4010(f)	293n8
15:45	167n305
15:45(m)(1)(A)	166n297
15:1601	358n6
15:1601–1641	358n5
15:1601(a)	359n9
15:1604(a)	359n12
15:1610(a)(1)	363n32
15:1640(a)	369n79, n81
15:1640(a)(1)	370n86
15:1640(a)(2)(A)(ii)	369n80
15:1640(a)(2)(B)	370n85, n86
15:1640(c)	369n82
15:1640(f)	360n14
15:1642	370n88; 391n30
15:1642-1644	359n7
15:1643	371n92
15:1644(a)	374n110
15:1644(d)	374n111
15:1644(f)	374n112
15:1645	374n108, n109
15:1666	359n8
15:1666f(a)	362n30
15:1666f(b)	362n30

United States Code—Cont.

Title:Section	Page
15:1666h	379n150
15:1666j(a)	363n32
15:1666(b)	376n127
15:1666(e)	369n81; 377n139
15:1681	359n9
15:1691	359n9
15:1692	359n9
15:1693	389n15
15:1693a(1)	391n31
15:1693a(6)	389n16
15:1693a(6)(A)	390n21
15:1693a(6)(B)	402n105
15:1693a(6)(C)	390n24
15:1693a(6)(D)	390n25
15:1693a(6)(E)	391n27
15:1693a(7)	396n61
15:1693a(11)	393n39; 394n43
15:1693c	392n34
15:1693c(a)	392n36
15:1693c(b)	393n38
15:1693d	396n59
15:1693d(a)	396n60
15:1693d(c)	396n62
15:1693e(a)	399n78
15:1693f(a)	397n67, n68, n69
15:1693f(b)	398n73
15:1693f(d)	398n75
15:1693f(e)	398n77
15:1693f(f)	397n65
15:1693f(c)	398n71
15:1693g(a)	394n46, n47, n48; 395n51
15:1693g(a)(2)	396n58
15:1693g(b)	394n46; 395n50
15:1693h(a)	401n98
15:1693h(a)(1)	399n80
15:1693h(a)(1)(A)	399n83
15:1693h(a)(1)(B)	400n85
15:1693h(a)(1)(C)	399n83
15:1693h(a)(1)(D)	400n87
15:1693h(a)(2)	399n84
15:1693h(a)(3)	400n90
15:1693h(b)	400n89
15:1693i(a)	391n31
15:1693i(b)	391n32; 392n33
15:1693j	400n88
15:1693m	400n92
15:1693m(a)(2)(B)	400n94
15:1693m(b)(1)	400n95
15:1693m(b)(2)	400n96
15:1693m(d)	401n99
15:1693m(e)	401n100
15:1693m(f)	400n93

[References are to pages and footnotes.]

United States Code—Cont.

Title:Section	Page
15:1693m(c)	401n97, n98
15:1693n(a)	401n101
15:1693n(b)	401n102
15:1693(a)(6)(B)	390n22
15:1693-1693r	364n38; 389n12
18:47	375n113
18:471	354n32
18:472	354n32
18:473	354n33
18:492	354n34
18:1029	401n103
18:1029(a)	375n117
18:1029(b)(2)	375n118
18:1029(c)	375n119
18:1029(e)(1)	375n114
18:1956	352n22
31:392	27n96
31:5311–5322	352n22

Bankruptcy Reform Act of 1978

Section	Page
542(b)	309n83

Federal Trade Commission Act

Section	Page
5	166

Model Consumer Credit Act

Section	Page
2.603(3)	165n293

Truth in Lending Act

Section	Page
Generally	358

STATE STATUTES

California Civil Code

Section	Page
1747.40	376n124
1747.50	376n124

Minnesota Statutes

Section	Page
540.11	87n80

ANALYTICAL MATERIALS

Restatement of Restitution

Section	Page
1	224n6
15	225n8
18	225n9
23(1)(a)	225n10
23(1)(b)	225n10
29	225n11
30	225n13; 228n34
31	228n34
31(a)	225n15
33	225n14; 231n56
34	226n17, n18; 228n34
34(c)	226n17
34(a)	226n16
34(b)	226n16
35	225n12; 228n34
37	225n12; 228n34
162	241n91, n92; 242n93; 246n117

Restatement (Second) of Agency

Section	Page
7	372n101
7-8	92n113
8	372n102
438	92n117
439	92n117

Restatement (Second) of Contracts

Section	Page
317(1)	45n7
317(2)(a)	45n5
333(1)	199n4
333(1)(a)	46n12
333(4)	199n5
336	11n8
336(2)	10n3

Restatement of Security

Section	Page
82	85n68
104	87n79
108	87n79
112	87n80
122	181n61
141(a)	87n77
141(b)	184n78

[References are to pages and footnotes.]

Restatement of Security—Cont.

Section	Page
149	87n83

INDEX

[References are to page numbers.]

A

ACCEPTANCE
Dishonor, acceptance and time requirements involving . . . 110
Drafts
    Bank, acceptance by . . . 192
    Varying draft . . . 192
Electronic fund transfers (See ELECTRONIC FUND TRANSFERS)

ACCEPTOR
Contract obligations . . . 78
Payor bank . . . 342

ACCOMMODATION
Discharge (See DISCHARGE, subhead: Indorsers and accommodation parties, discharge of)
Signing for . . . 85
Status, establishment of . . . 88

ACCORD AND SATISFACTION
Discharge . . . 196

ACCOUNT
Joint accounts, overdrafts involving 327
Unconditional promise or order, associated with . . . 22

ACTUAL KNOWLEDGE
Defined . . . 132

ALLOCATION OF LOSS
Electronic fund transfers (See ELECTRONIC FUND TRANSFERS)
Payment by cash . . . 352

ALTERATIONS
Implicit contract . . . 331
Material alteration, discharge and (See DISCHARGE)
Negligence contributing to (See NEGLIGENCE, subhead: Forgeries or alterations, contributing to)
Notice of . . . 141
Warranty liability
    Presentment warranty . . . 217
    Transfer warranty . . . 210

ANTECEDENT DEBT
Payment or security for . . . 124

ARTICLE 3
Notice under (See HOLDER IN DUE COURSE, subhead: Notice)

ARTICLE 3—Cont.
Value under (See HOLDER IN DUE COURSE, subhead: Value)
Warranty liability, applicability to . . 202

ARTICLE 4
Check collection and payment
    Generally . . . 292
    Amendments to Article 4 . . . 294
Value under . . . 124
Warranty liability, applicability to . . 202

ARTICLE 4A
Electronic fund transfers (See ELECTRONIC FUND TRANSFERS)

ASSIGNMENT
Transfer by
    Common law . . . 44
    Uniform Commercial Code (UCC) . . . 47
Warranty liability, correlation with . . 199

ATM (AUTOMATED TELLER MACHINE)
Electronic fund transfers . . . 384

AUTHENTICITY
Holder in due course . . . 142

AUTOMATED CLEARING HOUSES
Electronic fund transfers
    Generally . . . 382
    Operating rules and Regulation J . . . 402

AUTOMATED TELLER MACHINE (ATM)
Electronic fund transfers . . . 384

B

BEARER
Payable to (See PAYABLE TO ORDER OR BEARER)

BREACH OF WARRANTY
Cause of action, accrual and termination of . . . 219
Damages . . . 220

BURDEN OF PROOF
Holder-in-due-course rights, burden to prove . . . 161
Subrogation . . . 247

[References are to page numbers.]

C

CASH, PAYMENT BY
Allocation of loss . . . 352
Concept of cash . . . 349
Free transferability of cash . . . 351
Legal tender . . . 351

CASHIER'S CHECKS
Generally . . . 38
Lost, destroyed, or stolen . . . 100

CERTIFIED CHECKS
Generally . . . 39
Lost, destroyed, or stolen . . . 100

CHECK COLLECTION AND PAYMENT
Article 4
    Generally . . . 292
    Amendments to . . . 294
Clearinghouses, collection through . . 300
Collecting banks
    Direct presentment by . . . 299
    Duties of collecting banks in forwarding checks . . . 301
    Holder, collecting bank as . . . 296
    Special agents, rights as . . . 295
Competing claims to drawer's account balance, priority and . . . 308; 310
Deferred posting
    Statutory authorization . . . 302
    Time limits, noncompliance with . . . 304
Federal Reserve, collection through . . 297
Final payment
    Generally . . . 306
    Definition . . . 307
Forward collection
    Agency status of collecting banks
        Holder, collecting bank as . . 296
        Special agents, rights as . . 295
    Duties of collecting banks in forwarding checks . . . 301
    Methods of check collection (See subhead: Methods of check collection)
Indorsements, revised check return and . . . 320
Methods of check collection
    Generally . . . 296
    Clearinghouses . . . 300
    Direct presentment by collecting banks . . . 299
    Federal Reserve, through . . . 297
    Presentment by customer . . . 301
    Transmission of information . . . 300
    Truncation . . . 300
Notice of nonpayment, revised check return and . . . 320

CHECK COLLECTION AND PAYMENT—Cont.
Over-the-counter presentment for cash . . 305
Payor banks
    Competing claims to drawer's account balance, priority and . . . 308; 310
    Deferred posting
        Statutory authorization . . . 302
        Time limits, noncompliance with . . . 304
    Final payment
        Generally . . . 306
        Definition . . . 307
    Over-the-counter presentment for cash . . . 305
Presentment
    Customer, by . . . 301
    Direct presentment by collection banks . . . 299
    Over-the-counter presentment for cash . . . 305
Regulation CC . . . 293
Regulation CC, return under
    Generally . . . 311
    Check-hold practices, regulation of . . . 312
    Inefficient check-return procedures, correction of . . . 311
Return process
    Funds availability . . . 314
    Regulation CC (See subhead: Regulation CC, return under)
    Revised check return (See subhead: Revised check return)
Revised check return
    Generally . . . 317
    Expeditious return . . . 317
    Indorsements . . . 320
    Notice of nonpayment . . . 320
    Warranties . . . 322
Transmission of information, collection through . . . 300
Truncation, collection through . . . 300
Warranties, revised check return and . . . 322

CHECKS
Cashier's checks
    Generally . . . 38
    Lost, destroyed, or stolen . . . 100
Certified checks
    Generally . . . 39
    Lost, destroyed, or stolen . . . 100
Electronic fund transfers, check guarantee and . . . 385
Postdated checks . . . 322

INDEX

[References are to page numbers.]

CHECKS—Cont.
Stale checks . . . 344
Teller's checks
    Generally . . . 40
    Lost, destroyed, or stolen . . . 100
Traveler's checks . . . 40

CLAIMS
Competing claims to drawer's account balance, priority and . . . 308
Credit cards, holders of . . . 378
Holder in due course (See HOLDER IN DUE COURSE)

COLLATERAL
Discharge rights in . . . 183

COLLECTING BANKS
Check collection and payment (See CHECK COLLECTION AND PAYMENT)
Conversion . . . 285

COLLECTION
Check collection and payment (See CHECK COLLECTION AND PAYMENT)
Conversion and . . . 284; 285
Deposit indorsements, collection and . . 62
Words guaranteeing . . . 91

COMMON LAW
Assignment, transfer by . . . 44

COMPARATIVE NEGLIGENCE
Forgeries or alterations, contributing to . . . 258
Imposters and nominal or fictitious payees, involving . . . 278
Statement of account, bank's negligence involving . . . 265

CONDITIONS
Express conditions . . . 20
Implied conditions . . . 20
Satisfaction of contract conditions (See SATISFACTION OF CONTRACT CONDITIONS)
Unconditional promise or order (See UNCONDITIONAL PROMISE OR ORDER)

CONSIDERATION
Value under Article 3 . . . 120
Warranty transfer, for . . . 204

CONSTRUCTIVE NOTICE
Defined . . . 134

CONSUMERS
Holders in due course and
    Federal Trade Commission Rule . . . 166
    Problems involving . . . 163

CONTRACT OBLIGATIONS
Generally . . . 75
Acceptor . . . 78
Conditions, satisfaction of (See SATISFACTION OF CONTRACT CONDITIONS)
Disclaimer of contract liability . . . 83
Drawer . . . 80
Indorser . . . 81
Liability on instrument, fundamentals as to . . . 73
Lost, destroyed, or stolen instruments (See LOST, DESTROYED, OR STOLEN INSTRUMENTS)
Maker . . . 75
Payor bank (See PAYOR BANK AND CUSTOMER, RELATIONSHIP BETWEEN)
Satisfaction of conditions (See SATISFACTION OF CONTRACT CONDITIONS)
Sign, authority to
    Authorized representative . . . 91
    Unauthorized signatures . . . 94
Surety (See SURETY)

CONVERSION
Damages . . . 289
Indorsement
    Indorsees not receiving delivery 287
    Missing indorsements . . . 284
    Restrictive indorsements . . . 289
Proper defendant
    Collecting banks . . . 285
    Collection and payment . . . 284
    Depositary banks . . . 285
    Finders and their transferees . . 282
    Indorsements missing . . . 284
    Payment . . . 284
    Representatives . . . 285
    Thieves . . . 282
Proper plaintiff
    Generally . . . 286
    Acceptors excluded . . . 288
    Indorsees not receiving delivery 287
    Issuers excluded . . . 288
    Payees not receiving delivery . . . 287
Restrictive indorsements . . . 289

COUNTERSIGNATURES
Unconditional promise or order . . . 22

CREDIT CARD, PAYMENT BY
Anti-setoff provision . . . 379
Application, disclosure as to . . . 365
Claims of cardholders . . . 378
Credits, treatment of . . . 375
Defenses of cardholders . . . 378

[References are to page numbers.]

CREDIT CARD, PAYMENT BY—Cont.
Disclosure
    Application . . . 365
    Initial disclosure statement . . . 367
    Periodic statements . . . 368
    Solicitation . . . 365
Federal legislation
    Generally . . . 358
    Disclosure (See subhead: Disclosure)
    Regulation Z . . . 360 et seq.
    Scope . . . 360
Fraud, criminal liability for . . . 374
Issuance of card . . . 370
Participants in credit card system . . 355
Regulation Z . . . 360 et seq.
Sanctions . . . 369
Solicitation and disclosure . . . 365
Unauthorized use . . . 371

D

DAMAGES
Breach of warranty . . . 220
Conversion . . . 289
Wrongful dishonor . . . 335

DEBIT CARDS
Electronic fund transfers . . . 403

DEFINITE TIME
Payable on (See PAYABLE ON DEMAND OR AT DEFINITE TIME)

DEMAND
Payable on (See PAYABLE ON DEMAND OR AT DEFINITE TIME)

DERIVATIVE TITLE RULE
Generally . . . 10

DESTROYED INSTRUMENTS (See LOST, DESTROYED, OR STOLEN INSTRUMENTS)

DISCHARGE
Generally . . . 169
Accommodation parties, discharge of (See subhead: Indorsers and accommodation parties, discharge of)
Alteration (See subhead: Material alteration)
Holder in due course, defense against . . . 151
Indorsers and accommodation parties, discharge of
    Generally . . . 181
    Collateral, rights in . . . 183
    Recourse, rights of . . . 181
Liability on instrument
    Acceptance of draft by bank . . . 192

DISCHARGE—Cont.
Liability on instrument—Cont.
    Acceptance varying draft . . . 192
    Accommodation parties (See subhead: Indorsers and accommodation parties, discharge of)
    Cancellation . . . 178
    Indorsers (See subhead: Indorsers and Accommodation Parties, discharge of)
Liability on underlying transaction
    Accord and satisfaction . . . 196
    Effect of taking an instrument . . 193
Material alteration
    Generally . . . 188
    Effect . . . 190
    Requirements . . . 188
Payment (See subhead: Payment, liability for)
Payment, liability for
    Exceptions
        Generally . . . 173
        Indemnity . . . 174
        Injunction . . . 174
        Stolen instruments . . . 175
    General rule . . . 171
Payment, tender of . . . 177
Reacquisition . . . 179
Renunciation . . . 178

DISCLAIMER
Contract liability . . . 83

DISCLOSURE
Credit cards (See CREDIT CARD, PAYMENT BY)
Electronic fund transfers . . . 392

DISHONOR
Payor bank and customer, relationship between (See PAYOR BANK AND CUSTOMER, RELATIONSHIP BETWEEN)
Satisfaction of contract conditions (See SATISFACTION OF CONTRACT CONDITIONS)
Wrongful dishonor (See PAYOR BANK AND CUSTOMER, RELATIONSHIP BETWEEN, subhead: Wrongful dishonor)

DISHONOR, NOTICE OF
Article 3 specifics . . . 135
Satisfaction of contract conditions (See SATISFACTION OF CONTRACT CONDITIONS)

DRAFTS
Generally . . . 37
Acceptance
    Bank, by . . . 192
    Varying draft . . . 192

DRAFTS—Cont.
Overdrafts (See PAYOR BANK AND CUSTOMER, RELATIONSHIP BETWEEN, subhead: Overdraft, items creating)
Warranty liability
   Instruments other than unaccepted drafts . . . 218
   Unaccepted drafts, presentment warranties as to (See WARRANTY LIABILITY, subhead: Unaccepted drafts, presentment warranties as to)

DRAWER
Contract obligations . . . 80
Failure to satisfy contract conditions, consequences of . . . 112
Payor bank . . . 342

DURESS
Holder in due course, defense against . . . 148

E

ELECTRONIC FUND TRANSFERS
Generally . . . 382
Acceptance
   Generally . . . 410
   By beneficiary's bank . . . 412
   By receiving bank other than beneficiary's bank . . . 411
Allocation of loss
   Generally . . . 418
   Erroneous execution . . . 418
   Erroneous payment orders . . . 419
   Insolvency . . . 422
   Unauthorized transfers . . . 421
Article 4A (UCC)
   Generally . . . 407
   Acceptance (See subhead: Acceptance)
   Allocation of loss (See subhead: Allocation of loss)
Automated clearing houses (ACHs)
   Generally . . . 382
   Operating rules and Regulation J . . . 402
Automated teller machine (ATM) . . . 384
Check guarantee . . . 385
Debit cards . . . 403
Disclosure . . . 392
Documentation . . . 396
EFT card issuance . . . 391
Electronic Fund Transfer Act and Regulation E
   Generally . . . 388
   Disclosure . . . 392
   Documentation . . . 396

ELECTRONIC FUND TRANSFERS—Cont.
Electronic Fund Transfer Act and Regulation E—Cont.
   EFT card issuance . . . 391
   Enforcement . . . 400
   Error resolution . . . 397
   Financial institution liability . . . 399
   Scope . . . 389
   Stop payment . . . 399
   Unauthorized transfers, liability for . . . 393
Enforcement . . . 400
Errors
   Execution . . . 418
   Payment orders . . . 419
   Resolution . . . 397
Financial institution liability . . . 399
Liability
   Financial institution liability . . . 399
   Unauthorized transfers . . . 393
Operating rules and Regulation J
   Generally . . . 401
   Automated clearing houses (ACH) . . . 402
   Debit cards . . . 403
   Wire transfers . . . 404
Payment
   Generally . . . 415
   Erroneous payment orders . . . 419
   Stop payment . . . 399
   Telephone, bill payment by . . . 384
Point-of-sale systems (POS) . . . 385
Regulation E (See subhead: Electronic Fund Transfer Act and Regulation E)
Regulation J (See subhead: Operating rules and Regulation J)
Rejection . . . 414
Smart cards . . . 387
Stop payment . . . 399
Telephone, bill payment by . . . 384
Unauthorized transfers
   Allocation of loss . . . 421
   Liability . . . 393
Wire transfers . . . 386; 404

EMPLOYEES
Fraudulent indorsements by . . . 279

ENFORCEMENT
Electronic fund transfers . . . 400
Lost, destroyed, or stolen instruments . . . 97
Person entitled to enforce instrument
   Presentment warranty . . . 215
   Transfer warranty . . . 207

INDEX

[References are to page numbers.]

ERRORS
Credit card payment error-resolution procedures . . . 376
Electronic fund transfers (See ELECTRONIC FUND TRANSFERS)

EXPRESS CONDITIONS
Generally . . . 20

F

FEDERAL TRADE COMMISSION
Consumer claims and defenses, preservation of . . . 166

FICTITIOUS PAYEES
Strict liability (See STRICT LIABILITY, subhead: Imposters and nominal or fictitious payees)

FIXED AMOUNT OF MONEY
Generally . . . 25
Fixed amount requirement, meaning of . . . 25
Money defined . . . 26

FORGERY
Double forgery, unjust enrichment pertaining to . . . 236
Negligence contributing to (See NEGLIGENCE)

FRAUD
Credit card fraud, criminal liability for . . . 374
Employees, fraudulent indorsements by . . . 279
Holder in due course, defense against . . . 148

FUND
Unconditional promise or order, associated with . . . 22

G

GOOD FAITH
Holder in due course . . . 128

GOODS
Negotiability, relevance of . . . 11
Sales of goods, warranty liability correlated with . . . 198

H

HOLDER
Collecting bank as . . . 296
Status . . . 52

HOLDER IN DUE COURSE
Article 3
  Notice under (See subhead: Notice)
  Value under (See subhead: Value)
Article 4, value under . . . 124
Authenticity, questions of . . . 142
Claims
  Free from claims . . . 145
  Notice . . . 135
  Recoupment, notice any party has defense or claim in . . . 138
  Rights, absence of . . . 154
Consumers, holders in due course and Federal Trade Commission Rule . . . 166
  Problems involving . . . 163
Defenses
  Free from defenses
    Generally . . . 146
    Holder, defenses against . . 146
    Real defenses (See subhead: Real defenses)
  Recoupment, notice any party has defense or claim in . . . 138
  Rights, absence of . . . 154
Exclusions . . . 143
Free from defenses
  Generally . . . 146
  Holder, defenses against . . . 146
  Real defenses (See subhead: Real defenses)
Good faith . . . 128
Notice
  Generally . . . 131
  Article 3 specifics
    Generally . . . 134
    Alteration, notice of . . . 141
    Claim, notice of . . . 135
    Dishonored, notice instrument has been . . . 135
    Overdue, notice instrument is . . . 134
    Recoupment, notice any party has defense or claim in . . . 138
    Unauthorized signature, notice of . . . 141
  Definitions
    Generally . . . 132
    Actual knowledge . . . 132
    Constructive notice . . . 134
    Imputed knowledge . . . 132
Payee as . . . 144
Procedural considerations
  Burden to prove holder-in-due-course rights . . . 161
  Production of the instrument . . . 161
  Signatures, effectiveness of . . . 159

INDEX

[References are to page numbers.]

HOLDER IN DUE COURSE—Cont.
Qualification requirements
    Generally . . . 118
    Value (See subhead: Value)
Real defenses
    Generally . . . 147
    Discharge in insolvency proceedings . . . 151
    Duress . . . 148
    Fraud . . . 149
    Illegality . . . 148
    Incapacity . . . 148
    Infancy . . . 147
Rescission, negotiation subject to
    Effectiveness of negotiation . . . 157
    Remedy of rescission . . . 157
Rights
    Free from claims . . . 145
    Free from defenses (See subhead: Free from defenses)
Rights, absence of
    Claims . . . 154
    Defenses . . . 154
    Jus tertii, assertion of third parties' rights . . . 154
Shelter, rights passed through . . . 151
Value
    Generally . . . 119
    Article 3 definitions
        Generally . . . 120
        Antecedent debt, payment or security for . . . 124
        Consideration performed . . 120
        Executory promise exceptions . . 122
        Lien on instrument . . . 123
        Security interest on instrument . . . 123
    Article 4 definition . . . 124

I

IMPLIED CONDITIONS
Generally . . . 20

IMPOSTERS
Strict liability (See STRICT LIABILITY)

IMPUTED KNOWLEDGE
Defined . . . 132

INCAPACITY
Holder in due course, defense against . . . 148

INDEMNITY
Liability exception . . . 174

INDISPENSABLE PAPER
Negotiability, relevance of . . . 13

INDORSEMENT
Check return procedures and . . . 320
Contract obligations of indorser . . . 81
Conversion (See CONVERSION)
Discharge of indorsers (See DISCHARGE, subhead: Indorsers and accommodation parties, discharge of)
Failure to satisfy contract conditions by indorsers . . . 112
Imposters and nominal or fictitious payees . . . 277
Transfer and negotiation (See TRANSFER AND NEGOTIATION)

INFANCY
Holder in due course, defense against . . . 147

INJUNCTION
Liability exception . . . 174

INSOLVENCY
Allocation of loss . . . 422
Discharge in insolvency proceedings 151
No knowledge of insolvency proceedings, warranty of . . . 213

INSTRUMENTS (GENERALLY)
Historical considerations . . . 5
Liability on (See LIABILITY)
Personal property, distinguishing instruments from . . . 1
Scope . . . 3
Transfer and negotiation (See TRANSFER AND NEGOTIATION)

ISSUANCE
Conversion plaintiff, issuers excluded as . . . 288
Credit card . . . 370
Delivery . . . 67
Electronic fund transfer card . . . 391
Relationship of original parties . . . 70

J

JOINT ACCOUNTS
Overdrafts involving . . . 327

JUS TERTII
Defined . . . 154

K

KNOWLEDGE
Actual knowledge . . . 132

KNOWLEDGE—Cont.
Imputed knowledge . . . 132
Warranty liability
    Insolvency proceedings, transfer warranty as to no knowledge of . . 213
    Signature of drawer is unauthorized, presentment warranty as to no knowledge . . . 216

L

LEGAL TENDER
Generally . . . 351

LIABILITY
Contract liability, disclaimer of . . . 83
Electronic fund transfers
    Financial institution liability . . . 399
    Unauthorized transfers . . . 393
Instrument, on
    Discharge (See DISCHARGE)
    Fundamentals as to . . . 73
    Warranty liability distinguished 199
Underlying transaction, on
    Accord and satisfaction . . . 196
    Effect of taking an instrument . . 193
Warranty (See WARRANTY LIABILITY)
Wrongful dishonor (See PAYOR BANK AND CUSTOMER, RELATIONSHIP BETWEEN, subhead: Wrongful dishonor)

LIEN
Value under Article 3 . . . 123

LOSS, ALLOCATION OF (See ALLOCATION OF LOSS)

LOST, DESTROYED, OR STOLEN INSTRUMENTS
Generally . . . 96
Adequate protection against loss . . . 98
Cashier's checks, special rules on . . . 100
Certified checks, special rules on . . . 100
Enforcing instrument . . . 97
Liability exception . . . 175
Teller's checks, special rules on . . . 100

M

MAKER
Contract obligations . . . 75

MATERIAL ALTERATION
Discharge and (See DISCHARGE)

MONEY
Fixed amount (See FIXED AMOUNT OF MONEY)

MONEY ORDERS
Generally . . . 41

N

NEGLIGENCE
Account statement, customer negligence involving (See subhead: Customer negligence involving statement of account)
Comparative negligence (See COMPARATIVE NEGLIGENCE)
Customer negligence involving statement of account
    Comparative negligence of bank 265
    Duty of customer . . . 260
    Noncompliance of customer, consequences of . . . 264
    Time limits on customer's rights . . . 266
Forgeries or alterations, contributing to
    Comparative negligence . . . 258
    Preclusion
        Application . . . 251
        Rationale . . . 251
    Substantial contribution to negligence . . . 258
    Tort standard for negligence . . . 255
    Young v. Grote . . . 250
Preclusion involving forgeries . . . 251
Statement of account, customer negligence involving (See subhead: Customer negligence involving statement of account)
Substantial contribution . . . 258
Tort standard . . . 255
Young v. Grote . . . 250

NEGOTIABILITY (GENERALLY)
Cashier's checks . . . 38
Certified checks . . . 39
Derivative title rule . . . 10
Drafts . . . 37
Fixed amount of money (See FIXED AMOUNT OF MONEY)
Goods, relevance to . . . 11
Indispensable paper, relevance to . . . 13
Money orders . . . 41
No other undertaking or instruction (See NO OTHER UNDERTAKING OR INSTRUCTION)
Notes . . . 37
Payable on demand or at definite time (See PAYABLE ON DEMAND OR AT DEFINITE TIME)
Relevance of
    Generally . . . 10; 11
    Derivative title rule . . . 10

NEGOTIABILITY (GENERALLY)—Cont.
Relevance of—Cont.
    Goods . . . 11
    Indispensable paper . . . 13
    Shelter principle . . . 16
Requisites of negotiability
    Generally . . . 17
    Fixed amount of money (See FIXED AMOUNT OF MONEY)
    No other undertaking or instruction (See NO OTHER UNDERTAKING OR INSTRUCTION)
    Payable on demand or at definite time (See PAYABLE ON DEMAND OR AT DEFINITE TIME)
    Payable to order or bearer (See PAYABLE TO ORDER OR BEARER)
    Unconditional promise or order (See UNCONDITIONAL PROMISE OR ORDER)
    Writings signed by maker or drawer (See WRITINGS, subhead: Signed by maker or drawer)
Shelter principle, relevance to . . . 16
Teller's checks . . . 40
Transfer and negotiation (See TRANSFER AND NEGOTIATION)
Traveler's checks . . . 40
Types of negotiable instruments
    Generally . . . 36
    Basic categories . . . 36
    Drafts . . . 37
    Notes . . . 37
    Variations (See subhead: Variations of negotiable instruments)
Unconditional promise or order (See UNCONDITIONAL PROMISE OR ORDER)
Variations of negotiable instruments
    Generally . . . 38
    Cashier's checks . . . 38
    Certified checks . . . 39
    Money orders . . . 41
    Traveler's checks . . . 40
Writings signed by maker or drawer (See WRITINGS, subhead: Signed by maker or drawer)

NOMINAL PAYEES
Strict liability (See STRICT LIABILITY, subhead: Imposters and nominal or fictitious payees)

NO OTHER UNDERTAKING OR INSTRUCTION
Generally . . . 34
Exceptions . . . 35
Principle . . . 35

NOTES
Generally . . . 37

NOTICE
Alteration, of . . . 141
Claim, of . . . 135
Constructive notice defined . . . 134
Dishonor, notice of
    Article 3 specifics . . . 135
    Satisfaction of contract conditions (See SATISFACTION OF CONTRACT CONDITIONS)
Holder in due course (See HOLDER IN DUE COURSE)
Nonpayment, of . . . 320
Overdue, instrument is . . . 134
Recoupment, notice any party has defense or claim in . . . 138
Unauthorized signature, of . . . 141

O

ORDERS
Defined . . . 18
Electronic payment orders, errors in 419
Payable to (See PAYABLE TO ORDER OR BEARER)
Stop-payment order . . . 242
Unconditional (See UNCONDITIONAL PROMISE OR ORDER)

OVERDRAFTS
Items creating (See PAYOR BANK AND CUSTOMER, RELATIONSHIP BETWEEN, subhead: Overdraft, items creating)

OVERDUE
Notice instrument is . . . 134

P

PAYABLE ON DEMAND OR AT DEFINITE TIME
Generally . . . 31
Definite time, payable at . . . 31
Demand, payable on . . . 31

PAYABLE TO ORDER OR BEARER
Generally . . . 27
Bearer, payable to . . . 28
Order, payable to . . . 28
Words of negotiability . . . 27

PAYEE
Conversion plaintiff, payees not receiving delivery as . . . 287
Holder in due course, as . . . 144

[References are to page numbers.]

PAYEE—Cont.
Nominal or fictitious payees (See STRICT LIABILITY, subhead: Imposters and nominal or fictitious payees)

PAYMENT
Cash, by (See CASH, PAYMENT BY)
Check collection and payment (See CHECK COLLECTION AND PAYMENT)
Credit card, by (See CREDIT CARD, PAYMENT BY)
Discharge (See DISCHARGE)
Electronic fund transfers (See ELECTRONIC FUND TRANSFERS)
Stop payment (See STOP PAYMENT)

PAYOR BANK
Check collection and payment (See CHECK COLLECTION AND PAYMENT)

PAYOR BANK AND CUSTOMER, RELATIONSHIP BETWEEN
Generally . . . 323
Acceptor, bank as . . . 342
Alterations as implied contract . . . 331
Checks
    Postdated checks . . . 322
    Stale checks . . . 344
Contractual basis of relationship
    Deposit contract . . . 324
    Implicit contract (See subhead: Implicit contract)
Damages for wrongful dishonor . . . 335
Death of customer . . . 345
Dishonor
    Overdraft created by dishonor following pattern of honoring . . . 327
    Wrongful dishonor (See subhead: Wrongful dishonor)
Drawer, bank as . . . 342
Implicit contract
    Generally . . . 325
    Alterations . . . 331
    Overdraft, items creating (See subhead: Overdraft, items creating)
    Postdated checks . . . 322
    Signatures, unauthorized or missing . . . 329
    Stop-payment orders . . . 322
Incompetence of customer . . . 345
Joint accounts, overdrafts involving . . . 327
Overdraft, items creating
    Generally . . . 326
    Dishonor following pattern of honoring . . . 327
    Joint accounts . . . 327
    Service charges . . . 328

PAYOR BANK AND CUSTOMER, RELATIONSHIP BETWEEN—Cont.
Postdated checks . . . 322
Reasonable opportunity to act to stop payment (See subhead: Stop payment, customer's right to)
Service charges involving overdraft . . 328
Signatures, unauthorized or missing 329
Stale checks . . . 344
Stop payment, customer's right to
    Generally . . . 337
    Acceptor, bank as . . . 342
    Drawer, bank as . . . 342
    Orders (See subhead: Stop-payment orders)
    Reasonable opportunity to act
        Generally . . . 338
        Manner . . . 340
        Timeliness . . . 339
Stop-payment orders
    Implicit contract . . . 322
    Oral order . . . 341
    Written order . . . 341
Timeliness involving stop payment . . 339
Wrongful dishonor
    Damages . . . 335
    Liability
        Generally . . . 333
        Customer . . . 333
        Payor bank . . . 333; 334

PERSONAL PROPERTY
Instruments distinguished from . . . 1

PRESENTMENT
Check collection and payment (See CHECK COLLECTION AND PAYMENT)
Satisfaction of contract conditions (See SATISFACTION OF CONTRACT CONDITIONS)

PRIORITY
Competing claims to drawer's account balance . . . 308

PRODUCTION OF THE INSTRUMENT
Holder in due course, procedural consideration as to . . . 161

PROMISE
Defined . . . 18
Executory promise exceptions . . . 122

R

REACQUISITION
Discharge of liability following . . . 179

INDEX

[References are to page numbers.]

RECOUPMENT
Claim in, notice any party has defense or ... 138
Warranty of no defense or claim in .. 212

REGULATION CC
Check collection and payment (See CHECK COLLECTION AND PAYMENT)

REGULATION E
Electronic fund transfers (See ELECTRONIC FUND TRANSFERS, subhead: Electronic Fund Transfer Act and Regulation E)

REGULATION J
Electronic fund transfers (See ELECTRONIC FUND TRANSFERS, subhead: Operating rules and Regulation J)

REGULATION Z
Credit cards ... 360 et seq.

RENUNCIATION
Discharge of liability ... 178

RESCISSION
Effectiveness of negotiation ... 157
Remedy of rescission ... 157

RESTITUTION
Unjust enrichment, prevention of (See UNJUST ENRICHMENT, PREVENTION OF)

S

SALES
Goods, warranty liability correlated with sale of ... 198

SATISFACTION OF CONTRACT CONDITIONS
Generally ... 103
Dishonor
    Generally ... 106
    Time requirements
        Generally ... 108
        Acceptance context ... 110
        Payment context ... 108
Dishonor, notice of
    Generally ... 107
    Excused notice of dishonor
        Complete excuse ... 114
        Delay ... 114
    Time requirements ... 111
Failure to satisfy conditions, consequences of
    Drawers ... 112
    Indorsers ... 112
Presentment
    Generally ... 104

SATISFACTION OF CONTRACT CONDITIONS—Cont.
Presentment—Cont.
    Excused presentment
        Complete excuse ... 114
        Delay ... 114
    Time requirements ... 108
Time requirements
    Dishonor (See subhead: Dishonor)
    Dishonor, notice of ... 111
    Presentment ... 108

SECURITY INTEREST
Value under Article 3 ... 123

SERVICE CHARGES
Overdrafts ... 328

SHELTER PRINCIPLE
Holder in due course rights passed through shelter ... 151
Negotiability, relevance of ... 16

SIGNATURES
Accommodation, signing for ... 85
Authorized representative ... 91
Countersignatures ... 22
Effectiveness of ... 159
Maker or drawer, of (See WRITINGS, subhead: Signed by maker or drawer)
Missing ... 329
Unauthorized
    Generally ... 94
    Notice of ... 141
    Payor bank and customer, relationship between ... 329
Warranty liability
    Presentment warranties ... 216
    Transfer warranty ... 209

SMART CARDS
Electronic fund transfers ... 387

STOLEN INSTRUMENTS (See LOST, DESTROYED, OR STOLEN INSTRUMENTS)

STOP PAYMENT
Electronic fund transfers ... 399
Stop payment, customer's right to (See PAYOR BANK AND CUSTOMER, RELATIONSHIP BETWEEN, subhead: Stop payment, customer's right to)
Unjust enrichment, prevention of ... 242

STRICT LIABILITY
Generally ... 269
Employees, fraudulent indorsements by ... 279
Fictitious payees (See subhead: Imposters and nominal or fictitious payees)

INDEX

[References are to page numbers.]

STRICT LIABILITY—Cont.
Imposters and nominal or fictitious payees
    Comparative negligence . . . 278
    Indorsement . . . 277
    Rules
        Imposter rule . . . 271
        Nominal or fictitious payee rule . . . 273
Nominal payees (See subhead: Imposters and nominal or fictitious payees)

SUBROGATION
Unjust enrichment, prevention of (See UNJUST ENRICHMENT, PREVENTION OF)

SURETY
Accommodation
    Signing for . . . 85
    Status, establishment of . . . 88
Collection, words guaranteeing . . . 91
Defenses . . . 89
Liability . . . 86
Rights . . . 86

T

TELEPHONE
Bill payment by . . . 384

TELLER'S CHECKS
Generally . . . 40
Lost, destroyed, or stolen . . . 100

THIEVES
Conversion defendant . . . 282

THIRD PARTIES
Rights of, assertion of . . . 154

TIME CONSIDERATIONS
Deferred posting . . . 304
Definite time, payable at (See PAYABLE ON DEMAND OR AT DEFINITE TIME)
Satisfaction of contract conditions (See SATISFACTION OF CONTRACT CONDITIONS)
Statement of account, customer's rights pertaining to . . . 266
Stop payment . . . 339

TORT CONCEPTS
Generally . . . 250
Conversion (See CONVERSION)
Negligence (See NEGLIGENCE)
Strict liability (See STRICT LIABILITY)

TRANSFER AND NEGOTIATION
Generally . . . 43
Assignment, transfer by
    Common law . . . 44

TRANSFER AND NEGOTIATION—Cont.
Assignment, transfer by—Cont.
    Uniform Commercial Code (UCC) . . . 47
Electronic fund transfers (See ELECTRONIC FUND TRANSFERS)
Holder status . . . 52
Indorsement
    Generally . . . 53
    Blank indorsements (See subhead: Special and blank indorsements)
    Restrictive and nonrestrictive indorsement (See subhead: Restrictive and nonrestrictive indorsement)
    Special indorsements (See subhead: Special and blank indorsements)
Instrument
    Negotiation of (See subhead: Negotiation of instrument)
    Person entitled to enforce instrument . . . 65
    Transfer . . . 48
Issue
    Delivery . . . 67
    Relationship of original parties . . 70
Negotiation of instrument
    Generally . . . 51
    Holder status . . . 52
    Indorsement (See subhead: Indorsement)
Person entitled to enforce instrument . . . 65
Restrictive and nonrestrictive indorsement
    Generally . . . 61
    Collection and deposit indorsements . . . 62
    Conditional indorsements . . . 62
    Prohibiting further transfer . . . 61
    Trust indorsements . . . 65
Special and blank indorsements
    Generally . . . 56
    Blank . . . 58
    Must convey entire instrument . . 60
    Right to require special indorsement . . . 59
    Special . . . 55
Warranties (See WARRANTY LIABILITY)

TRAVELER'S CHECKS
Generally . . . 40

U

UCC (See UNIFORM COMMERCIAL CODE (UCC))

[References are to page numbers.]

UNCONDITIONAL PROMISE OR ORDER
Generally . . . 19
Account, reference to . . . 22
Countersignatures . . . 22
Express conditions . . . 20
Fund, reference to . . . 22
Implied conditions . . . 20
Negotiable instrument as . . . 18
Order defined . . . 18
Promise defined . . . 18
Writings associated with, reference to . . . 21

UNIFORM COMMERCIAL CODE (UCC)
Article 3 (See ARTICLE 3)
Article 4 (See ARTICLE 4)
Article 4A (See ELECTRONIC FUND TRANSFERS)
Assignment, transfer by . . . 47
Electronic fund transfers (See ELECTRONIC FUND TRANSFERS, subhead: Article 4A (UCC))
Restitution for unjust enrichment (See UNJUST ENRICHMENT, PREVENTION OF, subhead: Restitution)

UNJUST ENRICHMENT, PREVENTION OF
Assertion of rights of others, recovery by (See subhead: Subrogation)
Finality doctrine, restitution and
    Generally . . . 229
    Beneficiaries of finality . . . 233
    Rationales . . . 237
Mistaken payments, recovery of (See subhead: Restitution)
Restitution
    Generally . . . 223
    Finality doctrine (See subhead: Finality doctrine, restitution and)
    Pre-Code law
        Dominant case law . . . 226
        Restatement of Restitution . . . 224
    Uniform Commercial Code (UCC)
        Generally . . . 228
        Customers' accounts, problems with . . . 231
        Double-forgery . . . 236
        Finality doctrine . . . 229; 233
        Warranties . . . 229
Subrogation
    Generally . . . 241
    Burden of proof . . . 247
    Objection by buyers, other grounds for . . . 245
    Stop-payment orders . . . 242

UNJUST ENRICHMENT, PREVENTION OF—Cont.
Uniform Commercial Code (UCC), restitution under (See subhead: Restitution)

V

VALUE
Holder in due course (See HOLDER IN DUE COURSE)

W

WARRANTY LIABILITY
Generally . . . 198
Alterations
    Presentment warranty . . . 217
    Transfer warranty . . . 210
Article 3, applicability of . . . 202
Article 4, applicability of . . . 202
Assignments, correlation with . . . 199
Breach of warranties
    Cause of action, accrual and termination of . . . 219
    Damages . . . 220
Category of warranty, determination of . . . 200
Check return procedures . . . 322
Consideration for transfer of warranty . . . 204
Correlations with other warranty law
    Assignments . . . 199
    Sales of goods . . . 198
Damages for breach . . . 220
Drafts
    Instruments other than unaccepted drafts . . . 218
    Unaccepted drafts, presentment warranties as to (See subhead: Unaccepted drafts, presentment warranties as to)
Knowledge
    Insolvency proceedings, transfer warranty as to no knowledge of . . . 213
    Signature of drawer is unauthorized, presentment warranty as to no knowledge . . . 216
Liability on instrument, distinguished from . . . 199
Organization of warranty provisions
    Generally . . . 200
    Article 3, applicability of . . . 202
    Article 4, applicability of . . . 202
    Category of warranty, determination of . . . 200
Person entitled to enforce instrument
    Presentment warranty . . . 215
    Transfer warranty . . . 207

[References are to page numbers.]

WARRANTY LIABILITY—Cont.
Presentment warranties
    Generally . . . 215
    Instruments other than unaccepted drafts . . . 218
    To whom warranties run . . . 214
    Unaccepted drafts, presentment warranties as to (See subhead: Unaccepted drafts, presentment warranties as to)
Recoupment, warranty of no defense or claim in . . . 212
Sales of goods, correlation with . . . 198
Signatures
    Presentment warranty . . . 216
    Transfer warranty . . . 209
Transfer warranties
    Generally . . . 204; 207
    Alterations, warranty of no . . . 210
    Knowledge of insolvency proceedings, warranty of no . . . 213
    Person entitled to enforce instrument, warrantor as . . . 207
    Recoupment, warranty of no defense or claim in . . . 212
    Signatures, warranty of authentic and authorized . . . 209
    To whom warranties run . . . 205
    Who gives warranties
        Generally . . . 204
        Consideration . . . 204
        Transfer . . . 204

WARRANTY LIABILITY—Cont.
Unaccepted drafts, presentment warranties as to
    Alterations, warranty of no . . . 217
    Person entitled to enforce instrument . . . 215
    Signature of drawer is unauthorized, warranty of no knowledge . . . 216
Unjust enrichment, restitution for . . 229
Who gives warranties
    Presentment warranties . . . 214
    Transfer warranties (See subhead: Transfer warranties)

WIRE TRANSFERS
Electronic fund transfers . . . 404

WRITINGS
Signed by maker or drawer
    Generally . . . 23
    Signed defined . . . 24
    Writing defined . . . 23
Unconditional promise or order, associated with, . . . 21

WRONGFUL DISHONOR
Payor bank and customer, relationship between (See PAYOR BANK AND CUSTOMER, RELATIONSHIP BETWEEN, subhead: Wrongful dishonor)